docQbot
合通机器人

外商投资中国的新时代曙光

THE DAWN OF A NEW ERA FOR FDI IN CHINA

外商投资实务指南

《外商投资法》时代合同模板与适用指引（中英双语）

A Practical Guide to China's New Foreign Investment Law

Fully Annotated Bilingual FIL-Compliant JV and WFOE Templates and Additional Resources for Investors and Legal Professionals

[美]吕立山 (ROBERT LEWIS) 著

法律出版社 LAW PRESS · CHINA

The Foreign Investment Law Will Bring a Second Spring for Foreign Investment in China

Wei Jianguo

Special Expert of the China Going Global Think-tank (CGGT)

Former Vice Minister of the Ministry of Commerce

Vice Chairman of the China Center for International Economic Exchanges (CICEE)

The Foreign Investment Law, which came into effect on January 1, 2020, is the first comprehensive and systematic basic law in the field of foreign investment in China. The domestic and foreign business communities have high expectations for this new law. Executives of the international Chambers of Commerce and multinational companies in China have told me that the original "Three Laws on Foreign Investment" could be summarized in two words: "administration" and "limitation." This reflected the fact that there were more than 400 restricted categories, 300 to 400 permitted categories and more than 1000 categories requiring approval under the old system. I think that the Foreign Investment Law can also be summarized in two words: "promote" and "open." The principal highlights of this new law are the principle of pre-establishment national treatment and the negative list. The purpose of the new law is to encourage foreign investors to invest in China under the rule of law. It is in fact a "protection law" providing "assurance" for foreign investors as they invest in China.

The Foreign Investment Law is formulated to reflect China's actual requirements in respect of the transition to high-quality development. It is centered on the concerns and interests of foreign-invested enterprises, utilizing the implements of the rule of law to resolve many painful and difficult problems that have long plagued foreign-invested enterprises in

《外商投资法》将带来外商来华投资的第二个春天

魏建国

走出去智库（CGGT）特约专家

商务部原副部长

中国国际经济交流中心副理事长

2020 年 1 月 1 日正式生效实施的《外商投资法》，是中国外商投资领域首部全面系统的基本法，国内外工商界对此都抱有很高期待。在华商会及跨国公司高管向我反映，原先的“三资法”可以精简成两个字：“管”与“限”。限制的项目有 400 多种，允许的项目也有三四百种，需要审批的项目有 1000 多种。我认为，《外商投资法》也可以精简成两个字：“促”与“放”。这部法律最大的亮点就是准入前国民待遇加负面清单，目的是以法治鼓励促进外商来华投资，实际上这是一部外商的“保护法”，一颗外商来华投资的“定心丸”。

《外商投资法》基于我国转向高质量发展的现实要求并围绕外商投资企业的关切和诉求而制定，以法治手段解决长期困扰外资企业的痛点难点问题，为进一步扩大对外开放、积极有效利用外资提供了更加有力的制度保障。这部法律的出台，有利于推动中国更高水平开放型新体制，有利于树立中国全球化的国际形象，

China, and providing a stronger institutional guarantee for further expansion of and opening-up to, and more effective utilization of, foreign investment. The promulgation of this law is designed to promote a new and superior system for opening-up, further establishing China's international image as a leader in globalization, promoting a higher standard for development of China's utilization of foreign investment as well as promoting a stable foundation for foreign investor expectations. As a result, I expect that foreign enterprises will usher in a "second spring" for foreign investment in China.

In order to conform to the new legal and regulatory requirements, it will now be necessary for the more than 500,000 existing foreign-invested enterprises to manage their operations in accordance with the corporate governance requirements under the Company Law. This will significantly change the corporate governance model of foreign-invested enterprises, and will also significantly change the nature of their corporate documents. Therefore, legacy foreign investment contracts will no longer be able to be used, and a new set of FDI contract templates will need to be drafted. As a practical matter, the enormous workload involved in respect of the redrafting of such contract documentation will present a major obstacle to foreign-invested enterprises in connection with the modifications to their investment and operation models in accordance with the Foreign Investment Law.

Such professional problems need professional solutions. In the present instance, at the initiative of Robert Lewis, the Chief Expert of the China Going Global Think-tank (CGGT) and docQbot, more than 20 Chinese and foreign experts from institutions such as Bayer, Accenture, Sinopec Group, China Resources, Zhong Lun Law Firm, King & Wood Mallesons, O'Melveny & Myers, Latham & Watkins and Herbert Smith Freehills have come together to form the "Foreign Investment Law Expert Committee," the first expert committee of its kind in China. In order to promote the development of the Chinese business environment and the introduction of foreign investment, the Expert Committee has drafted Chinese-English bilingual templates for a greenfield Joint Venture Agreement/Articles of Association and a greenfield WFOE Articles of Association, which are being made available to the market free of charge, which will be a very valuable reference for Chinese and foreign legal professionals and investors. At the same time, docQbot, originally founded by the CGGT, has combined the work product of the Expert Committee together with docQbot's legal AI technology to provide the market with automated contract templates for WFOE and JV documentation that meet the

还有利于促进我国利用外资高质量发展和稳定预期。我预计，外商来华投资将迎来“第二个春天”。

对于现存的50多万家外商投资企业而言，为适应新的法律监管要求，将需要根据《公司法》规定的公司治理要求运营企业。这将使外商投资企业的公司治理模式发生巨大的变化，也将极大改变外商投资企业公司文件的性质。因而，以前的投资合同不再能用，需要重新起草一套FDI的合同模板。在实际操作中，巨大的合同文件修订工作量将是阻碍外资企业根据《外商投资法》转变投资运营模式的困难因素。

专业的问题，可以使用专业的应对方案。目前，由走出去智库（CGGT）& 合通机器人首席专家吕立山（Robert Lewis）倡议，来自拜耳、埃森哲、中石化、华润、中伦、金杜、美迈斯、瑞生、史密夫·斐尔等机构的20多位中外专家组成了国内第一个推动中国营商环境、引进外商投资的“《外商投资法》专家委员会”，起草了中英双语的新设合资协议/合资企业章程以及新设外商独资企业章程模板样本，并免费向市场提供，这将为中外法律工作者和投资者提供非常有价值的参考。同时，最初由走出去智库（CGGT）主导研发的合通机器人将专家委员会的工作成果与其法律AI功能相结合，向市场提供符合《公司法》要求的外商独资企业和合资企业自动化合同模板，可以帮助外商投资企业高效完成大量的法律文件修订工作，这将大大提高外商投资企业的转化进程。

在发起成立“《外商投资法》专家委员会”的同时，吕立山律师笔耕不辍，撰写了本书，专就《外商投资法》的实际应用进行详细分析，并根据《外商投资法》提出修改投资协议的建议，提供了附有详细注解的新设合资协议/合资企业章程以及新设外商独资企业章程模板样本。这本书的出版在提高外商投资法律文件修改进度的同时，将助力《外商投资法》的尽快落地。

requirements of the Company Law, which can help foreign-invested enterprises produce a large number of unique versions of legal documents very efficiently. This will greatly improve the efficiency of the conversion process for foreign-invested enterprises.

In parallel with the establishment and management of the work of the "Foreign Investment Law Expert Committee," Mr. Lewis also undertook the writing of this book, which sets out a detailed analysis of the practical application of the Foreign Investment Law, and puts forward recommendations on revising investment agreements to conform to the Foreign Investment Law. The book also provides annotated sample templates of the greenfield Joint Venture Agreement/Articles of Association and the greenfield WFOE Articles of Association. The publication of this book thus will improve the progress of the revision of foreign investment legal documentation for China, and will help ensure the timely implementation of the Foreign Investment Law.

Mr. Lewis has accumulated deep experience in the fields of corporate M&A, telecommunications, IT, infrastructure, clean energy, and strategic partnership arrangements, etc. He has been working in China for nearly 30 years. As a foreign legal expert advisor to SASAC, he has made significant contributions to the development of the "general council system" and "corporate legal risk prevention system" for large Chinese state-owned enterprises. In 2017, he published his book entitled "*Why So Many Chinese Outbound Investments Fail*," which provides a methodological approach for solving practical problems in order to improve the success rate of cross-border M&A transactions of Chinese enterprises. We look forward to his continued contribution to the promotion of foreign investment in China.

吕立山律师在公司并购、电信、IT、基础设施、清洁能源、战略伙伴安排等领域积累了丰富的执业经验，近30年来一直在中国工作。作为国资委外国法律专家顾问，吕立山律师对中国大型国企“总法律顾问制度”和“企业法律风险防范体系”的建设作出了重大贡献。2017年，他出版专著《国际并购游戏规则：如何提高中国走出去企业成功率》，为提高中国企业跨境并购交易成功率给出了解决实战问题的方法论。期待吕立山律师继续在推动外商在华投资方面作出更多贡献。

Pioneering Legal Services in the New Age of Foreign Direct Investment in China

Thomas Y. Man

Deputy Dean of Peking University School of Transnational Law

The enactment in March 2019 of the *Foreign Investment Law of the People's Republic of China* (effective January 1, 2020) ushered in a new era of foreign direct investment in China.

Forty years ago, China launched its reform and open-up policy in the foreign direct investment area by promulgating in 1979 the *Law of the People's Republic of China on Chinese-Foreign Equity Joint Ventures*, which, together with the *Law of the People's Republic of China on Wholly Foreign-Owned Enterprises* of 1986 and the *Law of the People's Republic of China on Chinese-Foreign Cooperative Joint Ventures* of 1988, formed the foundation of China's foreign direct investment regulatory regime. These "Three Laws" not only guided thousands of foreign investment projects of various forms and sizes for the past four decades but also, by virtue of the fact that they predated China's national Company Law, introduced legal forms and concepts of modern corporate entity into China and played a pivotal role in the rapid growth of China's market economy.

At the same time, a regulatory regime for foreign direct investment based on these "Three Laws" developed largely in parallel with the legal regime regulating domestic enterprises, resulting in a dual-track regulatory system for business and commercial activities. Upon China's accession to the WTO in 2001, these two largely separate regulatory regimes (one for domestic enterprises and another for foreign-invested enterprises) began to converge under the WTO principle of national treatment. More and more national legislation was made equally

引领中国外商直接投资新时代的法律服务

满运龙

北京大学国际法学院副院长

2019年3月通过的《中华人民共和国外商投资法》（自2020年1月1日起施行），开启了我国外商直接投资的新时代。

40年前，中国开始了外商直接投资领域的改革开放，于1979年颁布了《中华人民共和国中外合资经营企业法》，1986年颁布了《中华人民共和国外资企业法》，1988年颁布了《中华人民共和国中外合作经营企业法》（以下简称“三资法”），奠定了我国外商直接投资管理体制的基础。过去40年来，“三资法”不仅指导了成千上万的各种形式和规模的外商投资项目，而且由于它们先于中国的公司法，将现代公司法人的法律形式和概念引入中国，在中国市场经济的快速发展中起到了举足轻重的作用。

同时，以“三资法”为基础的外商直接投资监管体制与国内企业监管法律体系同步发展，形成了对企业活动和商业活动的双轨监管体制。2001年中国加入世界贸易组织后，这两个基本上不同的监管体制（一个针对内资企业，另一个针对外资企业）在WTO国民待遇原则下开始趋同。越来越多的国家立法对内资企业和外商投资企业一视同仁。《外商投资法》标志着这一趋同的完成。该法于2020年元旦生效后，一个新的统一的内外资企业法律制度

applicable to domestic as well as foreign-invested enterprises. The Foreign Investment Law signifies the completion of this convergence. When it takes effect on the New Year's Day of 2020, a new uniform legal regime governing both domestic and foreign-investment enterprises will be borne.

As the most important change in the legal environment for foreign direct investment in China in almost half a century, the new uniform legal regime brings about new opportunities and challenges to legal service providers. For one thing, most foundation documents for foreign-invested enterprises need to be substantially revised to meet the new requirements under the uniform legal regime. The present book rises to the occasion by addressing these issues looming in the horizon. It provides not only a succinct overview of the historical evolution of the regulatory regime for foreign direct investment in China by highlighting its major features and changes, but also a set of model foundational documents for Chinese-foreign joint venture and wholly foreign-owned enterprises. Prepared in bilingual format of both Chinese and English languages by a group of leading practitioners in the China market from major Chinese and international law firms and companies, these model documents meet the requirements of the uniform legal regime, thus providing valuable reference guide for legal professionals in the new era of foreign direct investment.

As a work of collective efforts, credits should naturally go to all collaborators who have made contributions in different forms and aspects. But I must use this opportunity to highlight the significance of one person's dedication and leadership that have made it possible not only for the publication of the present book but also a series of book-form publications over the last thirty years. He is Robert Lewis, the book's editor-in-chief and the driving force behind all the efforts that let to the successful birth of this book. I have had the good fortune to work in the same foreign law firm's Beijing office with him as fellow partners, and I am not surprised at all that Robert has masterfully engineered yet another pioneering legal product for public use.

Known affectionately to his Chinese lawyer friends by his adopted Chinese name "吕立山" or "老吕," Robert is widely regarded, at least by the Chinese lawyers I have met, the best known foreign lawyer in the China legal market. He has devoted most of his lawyering career to the foreign direct investment practice by working in China for almost 30 years. He is not only an internationally renowned practitioner but also a thought and action leader,

将形成。

作为近半个世纪以来中国外商直接投资法律环境最重要的变化，新的统一法律制度给法律服务提供者带来了新的机遇和挑战。一方面，外商投资企业的大多数基础性文件需要进行实质性修订，以适应统一法律制度下的新要求。本书通过解决这些即将到来的问题而应运而生。本书简要概括了中国外商直接投资管理体制的历史沿革，突出了该管理体制的主要特点和变化，同时也提供了一套适用于中外合资经营企业和外资独资企业的基础性文件范本。这些文件范本由一批扎根中国市场的来自中国及国际顶尖律师事务所和大型公司的领先法律从业者以中英双语起草，符合统一法律制度的要求，为法律专业人士提供了外商直接投资新时代的极具价值的参考指引。

作为一项集体努力的成果，功劳自然应归功于所有以不同形式、在不同方面作出贡献的合作者。但我必须借此机会强调一个人的奉献精神和领导才能的重要性，这不仅使得本书的出版成为可能，还在过去 30 年中使一系列图书出版物得以出版。他就是吕立山（Robert Lewis），也是促成这本书成功诞生的所有努力背后的推动力。我有幸曾和他一起在同一家外国律师事务所的北京办事处工作，对于 Robert 精心设计出又一款供公众使用的开创性法律产品，我丝毫也不感到惊讶。

Robert 被他的中国律师朋友们亲切地称为“吕立山”（他的中文名字）或“老吕”，至少在我遇到的中国律师中，Robert 被广泛认为是中国法律市场上最著名的外国律师。他在中国工作了近 30 年，把他的律师生涯的大部分时间投入到了外商直接投资业务中。他不仅是一位国际知名的律师，也是一位思想和行动的领导者，是中国法律市场的真正开拓者。20 世纪 90 年代，他是第一批为中国企业法务和私人执业律师进行系统培训的外国律师之一。在 21 世纪的前十年里，他构思并牵头组建了由中国领先律师

a true pathfinder in the China legal market. In the 1990s, he was among the first foreign lawyers who conducted systematic training programs for Chinese in-house lawyers and private practitioners. During the first decade of the new century, he conceived and took the lead to organize the first nationwide alliance of leading Chinese law firms with an international law firm (UK's Lovells), the Sino-Global Legal Alliance, which set a model for close cooperation between Chinese and foreign law firms. I worked with him on the alliance and witnessed his vision, charm and dedication.

In addition to busy law practice and firm management, Robert has written and edited numerous books and other publications to provide perceptive observations and invaluable practical knowledge. One common thread of all Robert's publications is that they all invariably deal with in profound depth some burgeoning field of law before the tidal wave has come ashore. Taken together, they form a distinctive formation of lightening houses guiding legal practitioners to navigate the deep waters of cross-border business transactions by or with Chinese companies. A partial list of these nascent fields Robert has fruitfully expounded includes: bilingual contract drafting (*The Art of Legal Drafting,* 2007), law firm management (*Pioneering Modern Management for Chinese Law Firms,* 2009), Chinese outbound investments (*Rules of the Game*, 2011, and *Why So Many Chinese Outbound Investments Fail,* 2017). The present book is the newest addition to this impressive list of titles. It will serve as the standard guide for all legal services relating to not only converting the existing 500,000 foreign-invested enterprises within the five years after January 1, 2020, but also setting up new and managing existing foreign-invested enterprises beyond the five-year transitional period. Any lawyer working this broad field should have a copy as ready reference.

事务所与国际律师事务所（英国路伟律师事务所的）组成的第一个全国性联盟——中世律所联盟，为中外律师事务所之间的紧密合作树立了典范。我曾和他一起在该联盟工作，见证了他的远见、魅力和奉献精神。

除了繁忙的法律业务和事务所管理之外，Robert 还撰写和编辑了大量书籍和其他出版物，为读者提供敏锐的观察和宝贵的实践知识。Robert 的所有出版物都有一个共同点，那就是他们都无一例外地在浪潮上岸之前，深入探讨某个新兴的法律领域。总之，它们形成了一种独特的灯塔形式，引导法律从业人员在中国企业或与中国企业进行跨境商业交易的深海中航行。Robert 对这些新兴领域进行了卓有成效的阐述，其中包括：中英双语合同起草（2007 年出版的《合同与法律咨询文书制作技能》）、律师事务所管理（2009 年出版的《引领中国律所现代管理的探索》）、中国境外投资（2011 年出版的《中国企业"走出去"的游戏规则》和 2017 年出版的《国际并购游戏规则：如何提高中国走出去企业成功率》）。本书是这一令人印象深刻的书目清单上的最新补充。本书将作为所有相关法律服务的标准指南，不仅适用于 2020 年 1 月 1 日后 5 年内现有外商投资企业的转化，也适用于 5 年内和更长时间内外商投资企业的设立和运营。任何在这一领域工作的律师都应该持有一本作为参考。

CONTENTS

目　录

Part Ⅰ The Dawn of a New Era for FDI in China

Part Ⅱ New Sample Templates for the Post-FIL Era

Part Ⅲ Acknowledgments and Contributors Introduction

Mapping Out the Road Ahead

On 28 March 2019, I was speaking to a group of more than 80 in-house legal counsel from major multinational corporations (MNCs) and leading Chinese companies in Beijing on the topic of the new Foreign Investment Law (FIL). When my colleagues and I had signed up to do this workshop earlier in the year, the draft FIL had just been circulated for comment. Like most other observers, we assumed that the FIL would not be formally submitted to the National People's Congress (NPC) until the legislative session in 2020 at the earliest. This was a reasonable assumption since the first draft of the FIL was circulated for comment in early 2015, and had lain dormant for more than four years, and significant new legislation in China usually has to wind its way through various committees and ministries before it can be formally issued. The process typically takes a year or more, not mere weeks.

But the timeline for the adoption of the FIL was accelerated at a pace not previously seen for a major new piece of legislation in China, and on 15 March 2019 the FIL became law. So as we stood before this group of in-house lawyers not quite two weeks later, we were addressing not the draft FIL as we had anticipated, but instead we had to try to explain the potential implications of a significant new law that had just been adopted in record time.

From the content of the abbreviated FIL (in the form as adopted, the FIL was less than a quarter of the length of the original 2015 draft FIL), it was apparent that the FIL was adopted in large part as a negotiating tool in the ongoing trade negotiations between China and the US as several of the provisions of the FIL directly addressed points which were under negotiation at the time, including strengthening of intellectual property rights (IPR) protections, elimination of non-tariff trade barriers, discontinuance of mandatory transfer of technology in exchange for market access, etc. All of these trade negotiation points in the FIL are of significant importance (and many of these points were addressed as part of the phase one trade

规划未来之路

2019 年 3 月 28 日，我在北京与来自大型跨国公司和顶尖中国企业的 80 多位企业法务就《外商投资法》进行了交谈。当我和我的同事在 2019 年早些时候决定参加这个研讨会时，《外商投资法（草案）》刚刚发布。像大多数其他评论人士一样，我们认为《外商投资法》最早要到 2020 年才会被正式提交给全国人民代表大会（以下简称全国人大）审议。这一假设合情合理，因为《外国投资法（草案征求意见稿）》［2015 年《外国投资法（草案）》］已于 2015 年年初发布，并且已经搁置了四年多，而在中国，重要的新立法通常需要先经各部委通过后才能正式发布。这一过程通常要经历一年或数年，而不是仅仅几周。

但《外商投资法》在审议通过的进程中，速度之快前所未有，这种速度在以往中国通过重要的新法时都没有出现过。2019 年 3 月 15 日，《外商投资法》正式审议通过。因此，在《外商投资法》颁布不到两周之后，当我们站在这些企业法务面前时，我们没有像预想的那样讨论《外商投资法（草案）》，而是在试图解释以惊人的速度颁布的这一重要新法的潜在影响。

从《外商投资法》内容上有所删减［新通过的《外商投资法》，其篇幅不及 2015 年《外国投资法（草案）》的 1/4］来看，这可能与持续中的中美贸易谈判有一定关系。我们可以看到，《外商投资法》的若干条款对谈判涉及的一些问题做出了回应，包括加强知识产权保护、消除非关税贸易壁垒、停止强制技术转让以换取市场准入等。《外商投资法》中的所有这些贸易谈判要点都非常重要（且

deal signed by China and US) , but these were not the primary focus of this group of in-house lawyers or our presentation.

From the perspective of lawyers engaged in foreign direct investment (FDI) work in China, the most important legacy of the FIL is that it introduces a fundamental shift in the legal basis for foreign-invested enterprises (FIEs) in China. Up to this point, FDI had been subject to a collection of laws known as the Three FIE Laws—the Sino-Foreign Equity Joint Venture Enterprise Law of the People's Republic of China (EJV Law), the Sino-Foreign Cooperative Joint Venture Enterprise Law of the People's Republic of China (CJV Law) and the Wholly Foreign-Owned Enterprise Law of the People's Republic of China (WFOE Law), together with their respective implementation regulations. The EJV Law had been issued initially in 1979, while the WFOE Law and the CJV Law were adopted in 1986 and 1988, respectively, placing these foundational laws at the earliest stages of the opening up of China to foreign investment. Not surprisingly, the Three FIE Laws had in many respects long since become outdated. More importantly they put FIEs on a different regulatory foundation than their domestic counterparts, which were subject to the generally superior corporate governance requirements under the PRC Company Law which was first adopted in 1993.

With a single stroke of the pen, the FIL signaled an end to the disparate treatment of FIEs and domestic companies. Under the banner of "national treatment" as championed in the FIL, starting 1 January 2020 the Three FIE Laws were to be repealed and all new FIEs were to be subject to the provisions of the Company Law, putting them on equal standing with Chinese domestic companies. But the FIL applies not only to all new FIEs but also to the estimated 500,000-plus existing FIEs, consisting principally of WFOEs (more than 375,000 in number) and Sino-foreign joint ventures (with more than 125,000 in existence, principally EJVs with a smaller number of CJVs). Each of these existing FIEs will be required to convert to a limited liability company (LLC) or other permitted entity form under the Company Law or the Partnership Law and the FIEs which now fall under the Company Law will need to make corresponding updates to the corporate governance provisions of their articles of association to conform to the requirements of the Company Law within five years following the effectiveness of the FIL.

Entering a New Era Without a Roadmap

The in-house counsel attending our presentation at the end of March of 2019 were

很多这些要点作为中美两国签署的第一阶段经贸协议的一部分得到了解决），但并不是这些企业法务或我们的演讲的主要关注点。

从在中国从事外商直接投资业务的律师角度来看，《外商投资法》最重要的影响是它使中国外商投资企业所适用的法律基础发生了根本性的转变。到目前为止，外商直接投资一直受“三资法”——《中华人民共和国中外合资经营企业法》（以下简称《中外合资经营企业法》）、《中华人民共和国中外合作经营企业法》（以下简称《中外合作经营企业法》）和《中华人民共和国外资企业法》（以下简称《外资企业法》）及其各自的实施条例的约束。《中外合资经营企业法》最初于 1979 年颁布，而《外资企业法》和《中外合作经营企业法》分别于 1986 年和 1988 年通过，即在中国对外商投资开放的初期确立了这些基础性法律。因此，“三资法”在很多方面已经过时许久也就不令人奇怪了。更重要的是，外商投资企业与同等内资企业适用了不同的监管体系，内资企业适用 1993 年首次通过的《公司法》项下总体上更为优越的公司治理条款。

笔尖一动，《外商投资法》即标志着对外商投资企业和内资企业区别对待的终结。在《外商投资法》倡导的“国民待遇”的原则下，“三资法”从 2020 年 1 月 1 日起废止，所有新的外商投资企业都将受《中华人民共和国公司法》（以下简称《公司法》）的约束，与中国内资企业处在同等地位。但《外商投资法》不仅适用于所有新的外商投资企业，也适用于现存的 50 多万家外商投资企业，主要包括外商独资企业（现存超过 37.5 万家）和中外合营企业（现存超过 12.5 万家，多数为中外合资企业，少数为中外合作企业）。这些现存外商投资企业须在《外商投资法》生效后五年内转化为有限责任公司或《公司法》或《合伙企业法》项下允许的其他组织形式，并且现在受《公司法》规制的外商投资企业需要对其公司章程的公司治理规定进行相应更新以符合《公司法》的要求。

all keen to know how the Company Law provisions would affect the corporate governance arrangements for their companies in China as a practical matter. This was new ground for them – and for us. This is not surprising since in-house lawyers working for FIEs or law firm lawyers specializing in FDI work in China had little reason to be familiar with the provisions of the Company Law since the Three FIE Laws took precedence over the Company Law for FIEs. As my colleagues and I talked through the practical implications of the Company Law for FIEs going forward, it was apparent to all that this represented a fundamental watershed event in the history of FDI-related legal work in China. We were entering a new era.

Not only would the corporate governance for FIEs change under the Company Law (almost uniformly for the better), but the nature of the corporate documentation for FIEs would also change dramatically, more especially for joint ventures. The joint venture contracts which have been in use since the opening up of China to foreign investment had been drafted to reflect the requirements set out in the EJV Law, many of which reflected government policies, administrative procedures and market conditions which no longer apply. Under the Company Law, domestic LLCs commonly adopt a simpler set of articles of association (AoA) and then separately enter into a shareholders' agreement (SHA) as appropriate. Sino-foreign joint ventures are now expected to follow suit and as such will no longer be required to use the traditional legacy JV contract and will now have greater flexibility to adopt an SHA or a joint venture agreement (JVA) that is more consistent with international practice.

While joint venture contracts take a variety of forms, most are derived from a common base developed by a small group of foreign law firms in the late 1980s and early 1990s. On the other hand, while SHA/JVA forms around the world all share many of the same provisions, a wide variety of SHA/JVA forms have proliferated over the years under the laws of different jurisdictions. Many of such SHA/JVA terms will be suitable for use in China, while others will not be as they will not be compliant with the provisions of the Company Law or consistent with local practice. Conversely, SHA/JVA forms commonly used for domestic companies in China are compliant with the requirements of the Company Law but may not incorporate all of the provisions which MNCs expect to see in an SHA or JVA for a Sino-foreign joint venture.

As we presented this background to the assembled in-house counsel, not only was it apparent that we were entering a new era for FDI in China, it was clear that we were doing so without a roadmap. As noted above, up to this point, the EJV Law had provided a structure

在没有路线图的情况下进入一个新时代

> “在我和我的同事谈到《公司法》对外商投资企业的实际影响时，很明显，这代表了中国外商直接投资相关法律工作历史的一个转折点。我们正在进入一个新时代。”

在 2019 年 3 月底参加我们演讲活动的企业法务都非常希望了解《公司法》规定在实践中将对其在中国的企业的公司治理安排产生何种影响。这对他们和对我们而言都是新的挑战。这也并不奇怪，因为外商投资企业优先适用“三资法”而非《公司法》，中国的外商投资企业的法务或专注外商直接投资业务的律师都没有理由熟悉《公司法》的规定。在我和我的同事谈到《公司法》对外商投资企业的实际影响时，很明显，这代表了中国外商直接投资相关法律工作历史的一个转折点。我们正在进入一个新时代。

在《公司法》项下，不仅外商投资企业的公司治理会发生变化（几乎都是向更好的方向变化），而且外商投资企业的公司文件的性质也会发生巨大变化，特别是对合资企业而言。自中国对外商投资开放以来一直在使用的合资合同反映了《中外合资经营企业法》所载的要求，其中许多反映了已经不再适用的政府政策、行政程序和市场条件。在《公司法》项下，内资有限责任公司通常采用更简洁的公司章程，然后另外签订适当的股东协议。现在中外合资企业预计也将适用同样的标准，因此将不再必须使用传统的合资合同，可以更灵活地采用更符合国际标准的股东协议或合资协议。

虽然中外合资合同有多种形式，但大部分都源自 20 世纪 80 年代末和 90 年代初少数外国律师事务所起草的通用基础模板。另外，尽管世界各地的股东协议 / 合资协议有许多相同的条款，但多年来在不同司法管辖区的法律项下，股东协议 / 合资协议已经发展出了各种各样的形式。此类股东协议 / 合资协议中的许多条款可适用于中国，而有些条款则因与《公司法》规定或中国惯例不符而无法适用。相反，中国内资企业常用的股东协议 / 合资协议模板符合《公司法》要求，但可能不包含跨国公司期望在中外合资企业的股东协议或合资协议中看到的所有条款。

当我们向企业法务介绍这一背景时，很明显的是，我们正在

for Sino-foreign joint venture contracts, and most JV contract forms in the market all derived from a common original base, so there was a common touchstone for the market. However, the Company Law imposes much fewer requirements on the form of an SHA or JVA, and since these foundational documents would no longer be subject to government review and approval, the parties would now have a broad scope to agree both the form and content of these agreements. This threatened to create a vacuum in the market, which likely would be filled with of a proliferation of multiple competing forms. This in turn would engender a battle of the forms each time the parties undertook a new foreign investment project and—perhaps even more daunting—each time an existing Sino-foreign joint venture was to convert to an LLC under the Company Law. This would inevitably result in an excessive misallocation of time and money and, as we will illustrate in this book, place an extraordinary burden on limited market resources to the detriment of all.

Consequently, in our presentation to this group of in-house counsel at the end of March 2019, I suggested that a working group of senior lawyers from leading domestic and international law firms as well as law departments in major Chinese and international corporations be formed to create a new set of FIE templates to reflect the pending legal changes. This proposal received enthusiastic support from the attendees.

Creating the Expert Committee for the FIL Forms Project

The event at which we were speaking was sponsored by the In-House Community™ (IHC), which is a platform comprised of more than 20,000 individual members with responsibility for legal and compliance issues in the Asia-MENA region. I approached IHC shortly after the event to discuss how we might work together on this initiative. Since the objective of the proposed initiative was to produce an authoritative set of high-quality base standard templates for the China legal market, it was critical that we assemble a top-shelf team of legal experts to form the drafting committee. This could not be the product of a single lawyer or even a single law firm—it was imperative that this be a group effort involving experienced lawyers from multiple law firms and corporate law departments in order to produce templates which would set the new standard for the entire China legal market. IHC was keen to support this initiative as they saw that this would make an important contribution to their members with investment activities in China. Accordingly, IHC Co-director Patrick

进入中国外商直接投资的新时代，但我们手中并没有路线图 。如上所述，到目前为止，《中外合资经营企业法》已经为中外合资企业合同提供了一个架构，市场上大多数合资合同都源自通用的基础模板，因此市场上有共同的标准。但是，《公司法》关于股东协议或合资协议的形式的要求少很多，而且由于这些基础文件不再受制于政府审查和批准，因此各当事方现在可以广泛地对这些协议的形式和内容进行约定。这可能会在市场上造成真空，其中充斥着多种互相竞争的协议形式。每次当事方开展新的外国投资项目时，以及——甚至更令人生畏的是——每次现存的中外合资企业要转化为《公司法》项下的有限责任公司时，都会引起合同模板之争。这样会不可避免地造成时间和金钱的过度不合理分配，并且如我们在本书中所述，会给有限的市场资源造成巨大的负担，从而损害所有主体的利益。

因此，在 2019 年 3 月底我们面向这些企业法务的演讲中，我建议成立一个由中国和国际顶尖的律师事务所及国内外大型公司法务部门的资深律师组成的工作组，编写一套新的外商投资企业的模板，以反映即将到来的法律变更。该提议得到了与会者的热烈支持。

为《外商投资法》模板项目组建专家委员会

我们进行演讲的活动由 In-House Community™（IHC）主办。IHC 是一个拥有超过 20,000 名在亚太和中东、北非地区负责公司的法律及合规事宜的个人成员所组成的平台。在活动结束后不久，我即联系 IHC 讨论我们可以就此提议如何合作。由于提议的初衷是为中国法律市场制定一套权威的高质量标准基础模板，集合顶级的法律专家团队组成起草委员会这一点至关重要。这不能由单一律师或单一律师事务所创造——这必须是来自多家律师事务所和公司法务部门的资深律师集体努力的成果，从而制定为整个

> “由于提议的初衷是为中国法律市场制定一套权威的高质量标准基础模板，集合顶级的法律专家团队组成起草委员会这一点至关重要。”

Dransfield, assisted by Development Manager Yvette Tan, agreed to help organize the Expert Committee.

At the March 2019 event in Beijing, I was wearing two hats, one as senior international counsel at Zhong Lun Law Firm, and a second as co-founder of docQbot, an independent platform which produces automated bilingual trade and investment contracts for the China market. For more than 25 years, I have been a practicing lawyer in China in top US, UK and Chinese law firms, and during that time I have conducted numerous multi-day legal skills training programs with the All China Lawyers Association (ACLA), for law firm lawyers across China, and with the State-owned Assets Supervision and Administration Commission (SASAC), for in-house lawyers in state-owned enterprises (SOEs). The new docQbot platform is a natural extension of my work in connection with these prior training programs, and over the preceding two years leading up to the publication of this book the vast majority of my professional time has been devoted to building up this new independent platform. The docQbot platform was a perfect fit for this new FDI templates initiative, as we had already created an entire ecosystem of online customizable bilingual templates for outbound, inbound and domestic transactions, so in my docQbot capacity I was pleased to take the lead on this joint IHC-docQbot project.

Working in conjunction with IHC, we were able to assemble an outstanding group of experts, and we are deeply indebted to them for their invaluable contributions to this project. Each of the members of the Expert Committee are introduced in greater detail in Part Ⅲ of this book, but some of their key contributions bear mention up front. For example:

- Walker Wallace, managing partner of the Shanghai office of O'Melveny & Meyers, suggested that we produce a comprehensive set of annotations to the templates to explain the basis for the drafting decisions made by the group. This provided an important platform for us to present options in addition to those which were ultimately included in the sample base FIE templates set out in Part II below (Sample Templates). Moreover, where divergent views existed among the members of the Expert Committee as to a particular point, we were able to set out the competing rationales in the annotations so that the final package appropriately reflects the broadest possible range of views in the market.
- Dr. Zhang Xi, then Vice President and Head of Law Patents & Compliance for Greater

中国法律市场设定新标准的模板。IHC 支持这一提议，因为他们认为这将为其在中国开展投资活动的成员做出重要贡献。因此，IHC 的主席 Patrick Dransfield，在发展经理 Yvette Tan 的协助下，同意帮助组织专家委员会。

在 2019 年 3 月北京的活动中，我有着双重身份，一个是中伦律师事务所的高级国际顾问，另一个是合通机器人的联合创始人。合通机器人是一个独立平台，生产面向中国市场的自动化双语贸易和投资合同。超过 25 年来，我一直在中国境内的顶级美资、英资和内资律师事务所担任执业律师。在此期间，我分别与中华全国律师协会（以下简称全国律协）、国务院国有资产监督管理委员会（以下简称国资委）合作，为中国各地律师和国有企业的法务开展了许多为期多日的法律技能培训项目。新的合通机器人平台是对我的这些与以往培训项目相关的工作的自然延伸。在本书出版前两年的绝大部分工作时间里，我都致力于建立这个新的独立平台。合通机器人平台与这个新外商直接投资模板的提议非常契合，因为我们已经为出境、入境和境内交易创建了一个完整的在线定制化双语模板的生态系统。因此，我谨代表合通机器人表示很高兴能够在 IHC—合通机器人联合组织的项目中发挥带头作用。

通过与 IHC 合作，我们组建起了一支优秀的专家团队，我们非常感谢他们为这个项目做出的宝贵贡献。本书的第三部分对专家委员会的每个成员做了更详细的介绍，但我们在这里要对他们的一些核心贡献先做出简要介绍。例如：

- 万孝杰（Walker Wallace），美迈斯律师事务所（O’ Melveny & Meyers）上海办事处管理合伙人。Walker Wallace 建议我们为模板编写一套全面的注解说明，以解释专家委员会在模板起草时做出决策的基础。这为我们提供了一个重要的平台，以呈现下文第二部分（模板样本）所载的《外商投资法》基础模板样本中最终包含的选项之外的其他选项。

China, Bayer Group, recommended that we work with other authoritative platforms to ensure the broadest acceptance of the templates as the new market standard. The publication of this book with Law Press China is a direct result of Dr. Zhang's insightful proposal.

- Frank Sun, a partner in the Hong Kong office of Latham & Watkins, evaluated the draft templates in the context of international norms for SHAs and JVAs, while Scott Guan and Aaron Yu of Zhong Lun in Shanghai undertook an extensive review of shareholders agreement for domestic Chinese companies to identify best practices that should be reflected in these FDI templates. Both of these perspectives provided an invaluable context for the work of the Expert Committee.
- Sinopec Group's Li Chi, Legal Counsel in the Contract Management Division, was among the first to sign on to the Expert Committee, noting that having access to FIL-compliant forms filled a critical need for Sinopec in respect of its onshore joint ventures with foreign partners. (Sinopec's participation was particularly gratifying for me as a personal matter since I had conducted a major consulting project for Sinopec more than 15 years ago on the structure and management of corporate law departments and have maintained a continuing friendship with the Sinopec legal team over the years.)
- Xiong Jin, an international partner in the Beijing office of King & Wood Mallesons who is qualified in Australia and came to the merged firm from the Mallesons side, and his colleague Luo Hai, who is a foreign legal consultant qualified in New York, provided scores of thought-provoking comments that challenged us as a working group to think outside the box across the board while still maintaining consistency with best practices in the China market.
- Li Ge, Deputy Group General Counsel for China Resources, had the most unusual backstory in connection with his participation in the FIL forms initiative. Not long after the Expert Committee commenced its work, I was invited to make a presentation to a group of in-house counsel from all of the first-tier subsidiaries of China Resources, and as part of my presentation I mentioned the work we were doing on this FIL forms project. After my presentation Li Ge sought me out to ask how China Resources could join the Expert Committee, explaining that since China Resources is

此外，如果专家委员会成员对某一问题存在观点分歧，我们则在注解说明中列出不同的理由，从而使最终的文件能够反映市场中各种不同的观点。

- 张曦博士，前拜耳大中华区副总裁兼总法律顾问。张曦博士建议我们与其他权威平台合作，确保模板作为新的市场标准能够在最广泛的范围内被接受。本书在法律出版社的出版也是直接得益于张博士富有远见的提议。
- 孙秋宁，瑞生国际律师事务所（Latham & Watkins）香港办事处合伙人。孙律师从股东协议和合资协议的国际规范的角度评估了模板初稿，而中伦律师事务所上海办公室的管云翔和於灵骏律师则对大量的中国内资企业的股东协议进行了审阅，以找出应体现在外商直接投资模板中的最佳实践。这两种视角均为专家委员会的工作提供了非常宝贵的背景。
- 李驰，中国石油化工集团法律部合同项目处主管，是第一批加入专家委员会的成员。他表示，获得符合《外商投资法》规定的文件满足了中石化在其与外国合作伙伴在境内合资方面的迫切需求。（从个人角度而言，我很开心中石化能够加入，因为我在15年前就中石化公司法务部门的架构和管理开展过一次重要的咨询项目，并且多年来一直与中石化法律团队保持着友好关系。）
- 熊进，金杜律师事务所北京办公室的国际合伙人，其在澳大利亚获得律师资格并从万盛国际律师事务所（Mallesons）来到合并后的金杜律师事务所（King & Wood Mallesons）。他的同事罗海，是具有纽约律师资格的外国法律顾问。他们提供了大量启人深思的建议，帮助工作组打破常规、全面思考，同时仍保持与中国市场最佳实践的一致性。
- 李舸，华润集团副总法律顾问，在参与《外商投资法》文件专家委员会这一点上有着最不寻常的背景故事。在专家委员会开始工作后不久，我被邀请面向华润集团所有一级

headquartered in Hong Kong, all of its entities in China are WFOEs or joint ventures. Moreover, he had a personal interest in this initiative since he had previously worked for the Ministry of Commerce and had been responsible in the early days for review and approval of joint venture contracts, so he was keen to participate in the development of the new templates for this new era of FDI in China. Obviously, I was happy to confirm the participation of China Resources on the spot, and Li Ge assigned one of his top lieutenants, Senior Group Legal Counsel, Yvonne Yao, to join him on the Expert Committee. They jointly made very valuable comments on how to address issues involving SOEs in the templates.

- Nanda Lau and Angela Zhao of Herbert Smith Freehills in Shanghai brought a high level of technical rigor to their detailed review of the corporate governance provisions of the templates, as did Scott Yu and Rachel Li of Zhong Lun's Beijing office. In both cases, they were able to provide very astute and sensible analyses of relatively arcane points of the Company Law that filled in important gaps in our original drafts. (Two further asides are warranted here. First, in the course of this process I also learned that HSF is a leader in alternative legal services in China, so our docQbot team looks forward to learning more from them in this regard. Second, I would be remiss if I failed to mention that Scott Yu and Rachel Li were my co-presenters at the IHC event in Beijing where the idea for this FIL forms project was first conceived, so they have been the earliest and most enthusiastic supporters of this project, for which I am extremely grateful.)
- Andy See, then Managing Director for the Accenture Asia-Pacific law department, attended a presentation I made at another IHC event in Shenzhen, and was intrigued not only by the FIL forms project but also by the broader docQbot ecosystem into which the new templates would be integrated. In addition to providing valuable comments on the templates, Andy and his colleagues took a very close look at the overall user experience for the docQbot online platform. (Andy left Accenture at the end of August 2019 after the completion of the work of the Expert Committee, but he continues to cooperate with docQbot on the FIL forms projects and other related initiatives.)
- The docQbot content development team also deserves tremendous credit for the

子公司的法务进行一场演讲，作为演讲的一部分，我提到了我们在《外商投资法》文件项目中所做的工作。在我的演讲结束之后，李舸向我咨询华润集团如何可以加入专家委员会，并解释说，由于华润集团总部设在中国香港，所以其在内地的所有实体都是外商独资企业或合资企业。此外，他之前曾在商务部工作，并在早期负责审查和批准合资合同，因此他个人对此项目颇感兴趣，并热切希望参与开发用于中国外商直接投资新时代的新模板。当然，我很高兴华润集团能够参与进来，李舸带领了其团队中的一名高级职员——资深集团法律顾问姚尔芳与他一起加入专家委员会。他们就如何解决模板中涉及国有企业的问题提出了非常宝贵的意见。

- 史密夫·斐尔律师事务所（Herbert Smith Freehills）上海办事处的刘依兰和赵秋丹，中伦北京办公室的余昕刚和李瑞以高度的技术严谨性对模板的公司治理条款进行了详细的审阅，他们都对《公司法》中相对晦涩的要点进行了非常精确和合理的分析，填补了我们原始初稿中的某些重要空白。（此外，还有两点值得在此提及：首先，在这一过程中我还了解到史密夫·斐尔律师事务所是中国境内替代性法律服务的领导者，因此我们的合通机器人团队期待在这方面更多地向他们学习。其次，余昕刚和李瑞和我同是IHC北京活动中的演讲人，《外商投资法》文件项目的想法也是在此活动中诞生的，所以他们是这个项目最早和最热心的支持者，对此我非常感谢。）
- 时任埃森哲大中华区法务董事总经理的施俊侃（Andy See）参加了我在深圳举办的另一场IHC活动上的演讲，他不仅被《外商投资法》文件项目所吸引，同时还被将涵盖新模板的整个合通机器人生态系统所吸引。除了对模板提供宝贵的建议外，Andy和他的同事们还非常仔细地分析

final work product. Sara Yu and Zimin Zhou provided the foundational analysis of the impact of the FIL on the traditional FDI templates, identifying all of the legacy provisions which would no longer be required following the repeal of the Three FIE Laws and cataloguing the scores of new provisions which would now have to be added under the Company Law, which rippled throughout the base templates. Their outstanding work held up remarkably well under the scrutiny of the members of the Expert Committee, no small achievement given the high-powered nature of the group. Adam Channer had the unenviable task of turning my conceptual drafts into useable base templates, which involved a level of technical skill that goes well beyond the typical contract drafting exercise, as these templates were to form the foundation of the automated versions to be made available on the docQbot online platform. This exercise is akin to three-dimensional chess as the final version to be used on the docQbot platform needs to incorporate all of the alternative clauses that can be assembled automatically into literally trillions of different combinations with the simple click of a button. After the work by these members of the docQbot content development team, the templates were then turned over to Liming Yang to put them into final customizable form. Liming's automation work is nothing short of genius, and he is without peer in the China market. I am fortunate to work with such an outstanding team.

An Ambitious Undertaking—Drafting New Standard FDI Templates for China

All of the members of the Expert Committee learned a great deal in the process of working together on this project. I certainly did. There have been numerous articles written and presentations made on the impact of the FIL, but the objective of our Expert Committee was to progress the analysis from the conceptual to the practical, and as part of this exercise we have had to grapple with a host of issues not just in a theoretical manner but in the context of particular contract clauses and against the backdrop of actual market realities. The goal we set for ourselves was clearly ambitious, and even though there will always be room for different views and for improvement, I am confident that the templates that we have created as a working group set a new standard of quality in the China market and will provide a valuable

了合通机器人在线平台的整体用户体验。（Andy 在完成了专家委员会的工作后，于 2019 年 8 月底离开了埃森哲，但他仍将持续与合通机器人在《外商投资法》模板项目以及其他相关举措中合作。）

- 合通机器人内容开发团队对工作产品的最终呈现也功不可没。余倩倩和周自敏就《外商投资法》对传统外商直接投资模板的影响进行了基础性的分析，找出了在“三资法”废止后不再适用的所有传统条款，并整理了《公司法》项下需要加入的贯穿整个基础模板的一系列新条款。他们的出色工作成功经受住了专家委员会成员的审查，考虑到工作组能力的强大，这是一项不可小觑的成就。陈明盛（Adam Channer）负责将我的概念性初稿转化为便于使用的基础模板，其中涉及的技术能力远远超出了传统的合同起草工作，因为这些模板旨在构建合通机器人在线平台上自动化版本的基础。这一工作类似于三维国际象棋，因为用于合通机器人平台上的最终版本需要包含所有替代条款，这些替代条款通过简单点击按钮便可自动集合成数以万亿计的不同组合。经过合通机器人内容开发团队成员的工作后，模板被转交给杨黎明，从而变为最终可定制化的形式。黎明在自动化工作方面的表现无异于天才，他在中国市场上是独一无二的。我很荣幸能与这样一支优秀的团队一起工作。

“我们专家委员会的目标是将对《外商投资法》影响的分析从概念推进到实践，而作为这项工作的一部分，我们不得不努力克服很多问题，不仅仅是理论上的问题，而且包括在特定合同条款和实际市场现实的背景下的问题。”

一项宏伟的事业——为中国市场起草新的外商投资标准模板

专家委员会的所有成员在共同合作完成这个项目的过程中学到了很多。我当然也是一样。关于《外商投资法》的影响的文章和演讲已经有很多，但我们专家委员会的目标是将对《外商投资法》影响的分析从概念推进到实践，而作为这项工作的一部分，我们不得不努力克服很多问题，不仅仅是理论上的问题，也包括在特定合同条款和实际市场现实的背景下的问题。很显然，我们

starting point for all investors and legal practitioners engaged in FDI projects in China going forward.

But we have done more than produce high-quality annotated bilingual templates, although that alone would still have significant value. In Part Ⅰ of this book we provide an overview of both the historical background of the Three FIE Laws and the FIL to provide further context for the annotated templates. Note that this overview is not intended as an exhaustive legal treatise but takes more the form of a general narrative to tell the backstory for the FIL-compliant Sample Templates in a way that is accessible to as broad range of readers as possible, including Chinese legal professionals with extensive experience with FDI projects, foreign lawyers with limited exposure with WFOEs and joint ventures in China, as well as business managers who are interested more in the practical implications of the FIL rather than technical legal analysis.

In Part Ⅰ we also assess the implications of the FIL for the China legal services market. (spoiler alert—the FIL will be the single biggest driver of work for FDI lawyers in China over the next five years, with a potential total market size of up to RMB 70 billion in legal services fees, making the FIL perhaps the best example of a "lawyers full employment act" anywhere in the world!)

The bilingual Sample Templates are set out in Part Ⅱ together with some additional background information on the drafting process as well as related caveats, limitations and assumptions. The book is formatted with English and Chinese versions of the same content on facing pages so that comparison of the two language versions can be made more easily. It is hoped that this book will thus serve as a useful reference guide for all domestic and foreign legal practitioners involved with FDI projects in China.

However, we recognize that while producing static templates on a printed page has significant reference value, it has limited practical value. Consequently, we have agreed with Law Press China that electronic copies of the Sample Templates in English and Chinese will be made available free of charge to the public on the docQbot website. Access to and use of these Sample Templates will be subject to standard conditions. Please see further information at the end of Chapter 5 in Part Ⅱ. Readers are also welcome to scan the QR code below or go to www.docqbot.com/en/newFIL to access the electronic versions of the templates.

为自己设定的目标是宏大的，尽管仍有不同观点和改进的空间，但我相信，我们作为工作组所创建的模板会在中国市场树立新的标准，未来将为所有在中国从事外商直接投资项目的投资者和法律从业者建立宝贵的起点。

但我们所做的不仅仅是编写高质量的附有注解说明的双语模板，虽然仅仅这一点也具有重要的价值。在本书的第一部分中，我们概述了“三资法”和《外商投资法》的历史背景，为附有注解说明的模板提供了进一步的背景。请注意，这一概述并非详尽的法律论述，而是以一般叙述的形式讲述符合《外商投资法》规定的模板样本的背景故事，让尽可能广泛的读者能够理解，包括具有丰富外商直接投资项目经验的中国法律专业人士、对中国外商独资企业和合资企业经验有限的外国律师，以及对《外商投资法》的实际影响而非技术性法律分析更感兴趣的商业管理人士。

在第一部分中，我们还评估了《外商投资法》对中国法律服务市场的影响。（剧透预警——《外商投资法》将成为未来五年中国外商直接投资业务律师工作的单个最大驱动力，潜在相关法律服务市场的总规模可能高达 700 亿元人民币，从而将使《外商投资法》成为世界上“律师充分就业法案”的最佳范例！）

双语模板样本载于本书第二部分，并附有关于起草过程的一些额外背景资料，以及相关声明、限制和假设。本书采取中英文奇偶页对照排版，从而可以更容易地对照两种语言版本。因此，我们希望本书能够成为所有参与中国外商直接投资项目的国内外法律从业者的实用参考指南。

但是，我们意识到，虽然纸质版的静态模板具有重要的参考价值，但它的实用价值受到限制。因此，我们与法律出版社约定在合通机器人网站上免费向公众提供电子版的中英双语模板样本。获取和使用这些样本模板将受标准条件的限制。请参阅本书第二部分第五章末尾获取更多信息。我们也欢迎读者扫描下面的二维码或访问 www.docqbot.com/cn/newFIL 以获取模板的副本。

Moreover, while the templates and the annotations reflect the input of the Expert Committee as a whole, I alone am responsible for the base drafts. Similarly, while members of the Expert Committee commented on certain sections included in Part Ⅰ, the overview of the FIL reflects my personal analysis of the relevant laws and the related potential market impact, so again I alone am responsible for this content. If there are any errors, I welcome feedback. We need everyone's contribution as we embark on this new era of FDI in China.

Finally, it is the nature of a major change in law such as the FIL and related regulations that it can present a bit of a moving target. The Expert Committee completed its work in August 2019, and the first drafts of this book were prepared the following month. While Part Ⅱ has remained substantially unchanged in the intervening period (since the Sample Templates and annotations reflect the fairly stable provisions of the Company Law), Part Ⅰ has undergone multiple major rewrites in the intervening months as new rules and regulations were issued in the wake of the FIL on a piecemeal basis, with certain critical policy positions shifting from draft to draft. As will be hinted at several points throughout the book, we should anticipate that there will be more changes to come either in terms of official notices, interpretations or practical applications. Consequently, this book may already be out of date by the time it goes to print or by the time you are reading this. But as noted above, that is an unavoidable challenge any author faces in such a situation as this. My only hope is that this book provides a useful reference base against which all such future legal developments can be assessed.

Robert Lewis

docQbot Chief Expert

Email: lvlishan@docQbot.com

17 January 2020

Scan for access to electronic versions of the Sample Templates

此外，虽然模板和注解说明反映了专家委员会的整体意见，但我对基础初稿单独负责。同样，虽然专家委员会的成员对本书第一部分中的某些章节发表了意见，但《外商投资法》概述反映了我对相关法律以及相关潜在市场影响的个人分析，因此我个人对此内容负责。如果本书存在任何错误，欢迎您提供反馈。在我们迈向中国外商直接投资新时代的道路上，我们需要每一位的贡献。

最后，法律的重大变化（例如《外商投资法》及其相关法规）的性质决定了其可能会带来一些不断变化的目标。专家委员会于 2019 年 8 月完成了工作，而本书的初稿于 9 月完成。从本书初稿完成至今，本书的第二部分基本没有变化（因为模板样本和注解说明反映的是《公司法》中比较稳定的规定），但第一部分在这几个月中历经多次重大修改，因为其间零星地出台了一些配套《外商投资法》的新规定，一些重要的政策立场在草案的修订过程中不断变化。正如本书中好几处所暗示的那样，我们应该预料到，无论是在官方通知、解释或实际应用中，还会有更多的变化。因此，在本书付印之时或在您阅读本书时，它可能已经过时了。但是，如上所述，在这种情况下，这是任何作者都无法避免的挑战。我唯一的希望是，本书为所有这些未来的法律发展的评估提供了一个有用的参考基础。

吕立山
合通机器人首席专家
电子邮箱：lvlishan@docQbot.com
2020 年 1 月 17 日

扫描二维码获取模板样本的电子版

Assessing the Impact of the COVID-19 Pandemic on the FIL

As can be seen from the original Introduction above, the drafting of the final manuscript for this book was completed in mid' January of 2020. This was a time of renewed optimism in China as the FIL had taken effect on 1 January 2020 and then shortly thereafter on the 15th of January, China and the US signed the phase one trade agreement, which was hoped would reduce the trade tensions which had suppressed both GDP and trade levels in China over the preceding year or more.

Even with this hopeful start to the year, the trade war clearly had left some scars. As I made presentations on the FIL in San Francisco, Seattle, New York and Washington D.C. over the course of that month,[1] there were still lingering concerns about the direction of Sino-US relations. More than one China law expert in the US questioned whether the title of my presentation, "China's New Foreign Investment Law—the Dawn of a New Golden Age for FDI in China," might not be overly optimistic. I took that as a challenge to justify my generally positive projections for the FIL, drawing on much of the material set out in this book. I think that most attendees at these events in the US found the case I presented to be persuasive, at least in terms of the favorable prospects presented by the FIL for FDI lawyers in China.[2]

But as outlined in Chapter 1 of this book, the base case for continued growth in FDI inflows to China is much stronger than most casual observers recognize—China continues to set

1 I wish to thank my hosts at these events for their kind hospitality and support: Keith Hand at UC Hastings College of the Law, Dongsheng Zang at University of Washington School of Law, Katherine Wilhelm at New York University School of Law, and Thomas Kellogg, Lucille Barale and James Feinerman at Georgetown University Law Center.

2 Donald Clarke. "Robert Lewis on the new Foreign Investment Law: a full employment bill for lawyers." *The China Collection* (blog). https://thechinacollection.org/robert-lewis-new-foreign-investment-law-full-employment-bill-lawyers/.

评估新型冠状病毒肺炎疫情对《外商投资法》造成的影响

从上文的简介中可以看出，这本书终稿的写作工作是在2020年1月中旬完成的。当时正是中国恢复乐观情绪的时期，因为《外商投资法》已于2020年1月1日生效，并且随后中美于1月15日签署了第一阶段经贸协议，大家都希望这将缓解贸易紧张局势，中美之间的贸易紧张局势在过去一年或更长时间里抑制了中国的国内生产总值和贸易水平。

尽管今年的开局充满希望，但贸易冲突显然也留下了一些阴影。我在旧金山、西雅图、纽约和华盛顿特区就《外商投资法》的相关问题发表演讲时，[1]发现人们对中美关系的发展方向仍然存在一些挥之不去的忧虑。不止一位美国的中国法专家质疑我的演讲题目“中国的新《外商投资法》——中国外商直接投资新时代的曙光”是否过于乐观。我将此视为一项挑战，尝试利用本书中所列举的诸多材料来证明我对《外商投资法》总体上的积极预测的合理性。我认为，在美国的演讲活动中的大多数与会者都认为我的论述是具有说服力的，至少就《外商投资法》将为中国外商

“不止一位美国的中国法专家质疑我的演讲题目‘中国的新《外商投资法》——中国外商直接投资新时代的曙光’是否过于乐观。”

1 我希望在此感谢所有这些活动的主办人的盛情款待和支持：加州大学黑斯廷斯法学院(UC Hastings College of the Law)的Keith Hand，华盛顿大学法学院(University of Washington)的Dongsheng Zang，纽约大学法学院(New York University School of Law)的Katherine Wilhelm，以及乔治华盛顿大学法律中心(Georgetown University Law Center)的Thomas Kellogg、Lucille Barale和James Feinerman。

new records for FDI inflows, and even the 2008-2009 global financial crisis caused only a brief and relatively modest dip in inbound FDI, and China then quickly resumed its steady upward advance in terms of FDI levels. In addition, China has also continued to make dramatic leaps up the World Bank Ease of Doing Business rankings as the series of measures adopted by the Chinese government over the last several years have taken effect, creating an ever more favorable investment environment. And as we discuss in more detail in Chapter 1, the fundamental attractiveness of China's market is not low-cost labor but rather a vibrant economy, unparalleled market size, well-developed infrastructure, a strong work force, an improving regulatory system and a stable business environment. The FIL will only accelerate these key trends. So the FIL heralds not just a new era for FDI lawyers (which it certainly does) but also an expansion and extension of existing trends which will create an increasingly attractive investment environment for foreign investment.

That was my view at the time I completed the original manuscript for this book, The question we must now address is whether and to what extent the ensuing COVID-19 pandemic changes this analysis.

As news of the outbreak of the novel coronavirus in China spread around the world in the latter half of January 2020, I, like many others, initially was of the view that this new virus would follow the pattern of the SARS outbreak in 2002-2003, i.e. it would be contained principally within the boundaries of China and after an accompanying sharp decline in economic activity there would be a very strong rebound in the form of a "V-shaped" recovery.[1] Based on those original assumptions, it was also anticipated that the impact on FDI activity in China would be temporary and modest over the medium term. By way of reference, FDI inflows in China remained essentially flat over the 2002-2003 time period affected by SARS, and then FDI levels continued their strong upward trend, as has been the case for almost 30 years with minimal interruption.[2]

As China started to emerge from the depths of the pandemic domestically, COVID-19 had already started to spread to other parts of the world, with parts of Europe and the US particularly seriously affected. Strict mitigation measures were adopted to slow the spread of the virus, but

1 See Ben May. "Coronavirus to deepen the near-term downturn." Oxford Economics. January 31, 2020; Zhao Huanxin. "IMF expects V-shaped recovery from outbreak." China Daily. February 14, 2020. http://www.chinadaily.com.cn/a/202002/14/WS5e46058aa310128217277883.html.

2 See related discussion in Chapter 1 below.

直接投资律师带来的有利前景这一点上来说。[1]

正如本书第一章所概述的那样，流入中国的外商直接投资持续增长，其背后的基础远比大多数观察者所认识到的强大得多——中国不断地创造外商直接投资流入额的新纪录，甚至2008—2009年全球金融危机也只造成中国外商直接投资短暂且相对缓和的下降，随后中国的外商直接投资水平又迅速恢复至稳步上升的趋势。此外，由于中国政府近几年来采取的一系列措施已初见成效，创造了更加良好的投资环境，中国在世界银行《营商环境报告》的排名中亦不断取得大幅跃升。正如我们在第一章中所详细讨论的，中国市场的根本吸引力并非低成本劳动力，而是充满活力的经济，无与伦比的市场规模，发达的基础设施，强大的劳动力，逐步完善的监管体系以及稳定的营商环境。《外商投资法》只是进一步加速了这些核心趋势。因此，《外商投资法》不仅预示着外商直接投资律师进入了一个新的发展时期（事实确实如此），还预示着现有发展趋势的扩展和延伸，这将为外商投资创造更具吸引力的投资环境。

这就是我在完成本书原稿时的观点。如今我们必须面对的问题是，新型冠状病毒肺炎疫情是否以及在多大程度上改变了这一分析。

随着2020年1月下旬中国暴发新型冠状病毒肺炎疫情的消息传遍世界，我和其他大多数人一样，最初认为这种新型病毒将遵循2002—2003年“非典”暴发的模式，也就是说，它将主要被限制在中国境内，伴随经济活动的急剧衰落之后，将出现非常强劲的“V形”反弹。[2] 基于这些最初的假设，还预计中期内疫情对

1 Donald Clarke. “Robert Lewis on the new Foreign Investment Law: a full employment bill for lawyers.” The China Collection (blog). https://thechinacollection.org/robert-lewis-new-foreign-investment-law-full-employment-bill-lawyers/.

2 See Ben May. “Coronavirus to deepen the near-term downturn.” Oxford Economics. January 31, 2020; Zhao Huanxin. “IMF expects V-shaped recovery from outbreak.” China Daily. February 14, 2020. http://www.chinadaily.com.cn/a/202002/14/WS5e46058aa310128217277883.html.

those measures had the effect of substantially closing down economic activity around the world. At this point it became clear that the impact of COVD-19 would not be as limited as was the case with the SARS outbreak. This was both a global pandemic and a global economic crisis, potentially more devastating than either SARS in 2002-2003 or the global financial crisis of 2008-2009.

The preparation of the final manuscript of this book for publication was delayed until mid' March, by which time the global impact of the COVID-19 virus was already expanding exponentially. Consequently, we decided to hold off on publication of this book until some of the broader trends of the pandemic and the resulting financial crisis became a little clearer in order to assess how this may impact the generally optimistic premise of this book. Stated otherwise, we determined that at a minimum it would be inappropriate to publish this book with no reference to the ongoing global economic crisis that was continuing to unfold.

What Shape Will the Recovery Take?

At the time of this writing, the COVID-19 outbreak has been contained in China and is waning internationally, but while China's economy is already showing some encouraging signs of recovery, the economies of many of China's major trading partners have not yet fully reopened or in some cases even started the process of reopening. The unprecedented nature of the closure of all non-essential business activities in so many advanced economies across so many parts of the world, all at the same time, has resulted in a precipitous decline in global economic activity in the short-term. It is impossible to predict with any precision at this juncture what the medium- to long-term impacts will be. Some economists are still predicting a "V-shaped" recovery with a strong rebound in the near term. Other projections call for a "U-shaped" recovery, with an extended recession before the anticipated economic recovery takes place. There are almost as many opinions and forecasts as there are economists.[1]

1 For a collection of predictions by banks, see https://markets.businessinsider.com/news/stocks/us-recession-coronavirus-pandemic-firms-forecasting-economic-distress-predictions-2020-2020-3-1029019597#4-bank-of-america-the-us-economy-has-fallen-into-recession-4; while some experts expect a deep, but short, recession, see https://www.investopedia.com/a-nasty-short-and-bitter-recession-4801893; others predict a long and difficult road to recovery, see https://www.nytimes.com/2020/04/01/business/economy/coronavirus-recession.html.

中国外商直接投资活动的影响将是暂时且有限的。作为参考，在2002—2003年受到“非典”影响的期间，流入中国的外商直接投资基本保持平稳，随后外商直接投资的水平继续保持强劲的增长趋势，近30年来的情况就是如此，几乎少有中断。[1]

当中国开始从国内疫情大流行的深渊走出来时，新型冠状病毒肺炎疫情已开始在世界其他地区蔓延，其中欧洲和美国的部分地区受到的影响尤为严重。各地区采取了严格的控制措施来减缓病毒的传播，但是这些措施实际上导致了全球经济活动的停宕。就这一点而言，新型冠状病毒肺炎将造成的影响显然不会像“非典”那么有限。这既是一场全球性的疫情，亦是全球性的经济危机，可能比2002—2003年的“非典”或2008—2009年的全球金融危机更具破坏性。

本书最终稿的出版准备工作被推迟至3月中旬，而那时新型冠状病毒肺炎在全球造成的影响已经呈指数级扩大。因此，我们决定推迟出版本书，等到这一疫情以及由此导致的金融危机的大的发展趋势变得更清晰，以便评估这可能对本书总体乐观的基调造成怎样的影响。换句话说，我们认为毫不提及仍在持续发展的全球经济危机便出版本书是不恰当的。

经济将以何种形式复苏?

在撰写本补充简介时，新型冠状病毒肺炎疫情在中国已经得到遏制并在全球范围内逐步减弱，然而，尽管中国经济已经显示出一些令人鼓舞的复苏迹象，但是中国许多主要贸易伙伴的经济尚未完全重启，部分甚至尚未处于重启的进程之中。世界范围内如此广泛的地区中如此多的发达经济体同时停止所有不必要的商业活动，这一情况史无前例，并已导致短期内全球经济活动的急剧萎缩。目前尚难以准确预测这一情况在中长期将会造成怎样的

1 参见下文本书第一章中的相关讨论。

The Asian Development Bank (ADB) published their Asian Development Outlook 2020 report (ADO 2020 Report)[1] in early April 2020, which took into account the impact of COVID-19 to the extent it could be assessed as of the time of publication. As a multi-lateral bank sponsored by the US, Japan, China, India, Australia and other countries, the ADB is able to adopt a more neutral position in its analyses and forecasts, adding to its credibility. Nevertheless, the ADB does not have a crystal ball, and so all of its forecasts are appropriately caveated.[2]

The ADB forecast for China for 2020-2021 is surprisingly optimistic, less so for the major industrial economies of the US, the EU and Japan. China GDP growth, which had already been adversely impacted by the Sino-US trade war in 2019, dropping from 6.7% in 2018 to 6.1% in 2019, is now projected to slow to 2.3% GDP growth in 2020 due to the COVID-19 outbreak. However, the ADB forecasts that China GDP growth will then rebound dramatically to 7.3% in 2021, which is based on the assumption that the global outbreak by that time will have been fully brought under control and that there has been a general return to normalcy in economic activity. In many respects, the ADB forecasts a classic "V-shaped" recovery for China's economy, with the bottom coming somewhere in mid' 2020, and with the ensuing strong rebound being driven by fiscal policy responses and strong exports (in large part redirected away from the US to side-step the continuing impacts of the Sino-US trade conflict which has yet to be fully resolved). To underscore the above projections, the ADB forecasts that merchandise exports for China will shrink 8.5% in 2020 but then grow 9.8% in 2021. Similarly, China merchandise imports will fall 7.8% this year and then bounce back to grow by 8.3% next year.

In contrast, the outlook for the major advanced economies is less rosy. The ADB forecasts only 0.4% GDP growth for the US in 2020, with GDP in the EU and Japan shrinking by 1.0% and 1.5%, respectively, in 2020. The ADB forecast for GDP growth for the US, EU and Japan for 2021 is 2.1%, 1.6% and 0.9%, respectively.

---

1 See *Asia Development Outlook 2020: What Drives Innovation in Asia? Special Topic: The Impact of the Coronavirus Outbreak – An Update.* Manila: Asia Development Bank, 2020. Accessed April 17, 2020. https://www.adb.org/sites/default/files/publication/575626/ado2020.pdf.

2 From the Highlights section of the ADO 2020 Report: "Downside risks to the outlook are severe, most notably from coronavirus disease 2019 (COVID-19). No one can say how widely the COVID-19 pandemic may spread, and containment may take longer than currently projected. The possibility of severe financial turmoil and financial crises cannot be discounted. Sharp and protracted declines in commodity prices and tourist arrivals will challenge dependent economies across the region."

影响。部分经济学家仍预计经济将在短期内出现强劲的“V形”反弹。此外也存在不同的预测观点，认为经济将遵循“U形”复苏，即在预期的经济复苏发生之前，经济将进一步衰退。几乎每名经济学家都有不同的观点和预测。[1]

亚洲开发银行于2020年4月上旬发布了《2020年亚洲发展展望报告》，[2]这一报告已将在发布时新型冠状病毒肺炎造成的可评估的影响考虑在内。作为由美国、日本、中国、印度、澳大利亚和其他国家发起的多边银行，亚洲开发银行能够在分析和预测中采取更为中立的立场，因此具有更高的可信度。尽管如此，亚洲开发银行并没有“水晶球”，因此其所作出的所有预测是受适当限制的。[3]

> “亚洲开发银行对中国2020—2021年的预测出人意料的乐观，然而对美国、欧盟和日本等主要工业经济体的预测则不那么乐观。”

亚洲开发银行对中国2020—2021年的预测出人意料的乐观，然而对美国、欧盟和日本等主要工业经济体的预测则不那么乐观。中国GDP的增长已经受到2019年中美贸易冲突的不利影响，从2018年的6.7%下降到2019年的6.1%，由于新型冠状病毒肺炎的暴发，目前预计2020年GDP增速将放缓至2.3%。然而，亚洲开发银行预测，到2021年，中国GDP增速将大幅反弹至7.3%，而这一判断所基于的假设是届时全球疫情将得到完全控制，经济活动总体上恢复正常。在许多方面，亚洲开发银行预测中国经济将以经典的“V形”复苏，在2020年年中触底，而后受到财政政

---

1 有关银行的预测的汇总，参见 https://markets.businessinsider.com/news/stocks/us-recession-coronavirus-pandemic-firms-forecasting-economic-distress-predictions-2020-2020-3-1029019597#4-bank-of-america-the-us-economy-has-fallen-into-recession-4；部分专家预计经济衰退将会短暂而严重，参见 https://www.investopedia.com/a-nasty-short-and-bitter-recession-4801893；其他学者预测经济恢复的道路漫长而艰难，参见 https://www.nytimes.com/2020/04/01/business/economy/coronavirus-recession.html。

2 参见 Asia Development Outlook 2020: What Drives Innovation in Asia? Special Topic: The Impact of the Coronavirus Outbreak – An Update. Manila: Asia Development Bank, 2020. https://www.adb.org/sites/default/files/publication/575626/ado2020.pdf, 2020年4月17日访问。

3 摘自亚洲开发银行2020报告的重点部分：“前景的下行风险很严重，最明显的是从2019年新型冠状病毒肺炎起。没有人能断言新型冠状病毒肺炎疫情可能扩散到何种程度，同时控制工作可能需要的时间比目前预计的更长。出现严重的金融动荡和金融危机的可能性不可小视。商品价格和游客人数的长期急剧下降将对整个区域的依赖型经济体构成挑战。”

Prospects for FDI in a Post–coronavirus World

While this forecast for China may suggest that the most severe impact of the COVID-19 outbreak on FDI will be relatively short-lived (as was the case with the impact of the SARS outbreak), the global pandemic and resulting global financial crisis may bring additional longer-term risks to China's FDI prospects. The mitigation measures adopted by affected countries around the world have in some cases led to the closing of borders and heightened concerns about the national security aspects of pandemic response, which will tend to result in the onshoring of the production of critical medical supplies and pharmaceuticals. Many have expressed concerns that the pandemic may also accelerate existing nationalist and protectionist sentiments in many developed nations, reducing cross-border trade and investment generally. In the US there is also increasing discussion of "decoupling" from China, and senior White House officials have floated the idea that the US government may reimburse the costs of US companies relocating operations out of China,[1] in order to diversify geographic risks to global supply chains and reduce over-reliance on China. Japan has taken similar steps, announcing that it will provide direct loans totaling 220 billion yen (RMB 14.5 billion or USD 2 billion) for Japanese companies to shift production from China back to Japan, plus an additional 23.5 billion yen (RMB 1.5 billion or USD 200 million) to help Japanese companies move out of China to other countries.

How big a threat is this to China's position as the second most popular destination in the world for FDI, trailing only the US? There is no question that the global pandemic and financial crisis will have a major negative impact on FDI in the near term, but there are also important countervailing considerations that should also be taken into account in respect of the medium- to longer-term:

- Even before the global pandemic, there was already some contraction in the total value of global trade, with a 1% drop in 2019 against the record levels achieved in 2018, but at US$19 trillion, global trade for 2019 was still up more than 3.5-fold over 1995 levels (US$5.19 trillion), and a remarkable 63 times higher than 1970 levels (US$302.3 billion). Even looking just at trade between China and the US, trade declined from US$630 billion in 2017 to US$560 billion in 2019, dropping bilateral trade figures to 2013 levels, but this was still five times what it was in 2001. As one commentator has put it, when we assess

1 See Rapoza, Kenneth. "Kudlow: 'Pay The Moving Costs' of American Companies Leaving China." Forbes. April 10, 2020. https://www.forbes.com/sites/kenrapoza/2020/04/10/kudlow-pay-the-moving-costs-of-american-companies-leaving-china/.

策反应和强劲出口（在很大程度上重新导向，以避开尚未完全解决的中美贸易冲突所造成的持续影响）的推动实现强势反弹。为了强调上述预测，亚洲开发银行预测中国的商品出口在2020年将萎缩8.5%，然后在2021年增长9.8%。同样，中国的商品进口今年将下降7.8%，然后在明年反弹至增长8.3%。

相反，主要发达经济体的前景并不乐观。亚洲开发银行预测，2020年美国的GDP增长率仅为0.4%，而2020年欧盟和日本的GDP将分别收缩1.0%和1.5%。亚洲开发银行对2021年美国、欧盟和日本的GDP增长率的预测是分别为2.1%、1.6%和0.9%。

新型冠状病毒疫情过后全球外商直接投资的前景

尽管对中国的这一预测表明，新型冠状病毒肺炎疫情对外商直接投资的最严重影响将是相对短暂的（就如“非典”暴发所产生的影响一样），但全球疫情和由此引发的全球金融危机可能为中国外商直接投资的前景带来额外的长期风险。世界各地受影响的国家所采取的缓解措施在某些情况下导致了边境的关闭，并加剧了人们对疫情应对中的国家安全方面的顾虑，这将导致重要医疗用品和药品的生产本地化。许多人担心，疫情可能还会加剧许多发达国家现有的民族主义和保护主义情绪，导致跨境贸易和投资的普遍减少。在美国，关于与中国“脱钩”的讨论也越来越多，白宫的高级官员也提出了一种想法，即美国政府可以通过补偿美国公司将业务迁出中国所需费用，[1]以使地理风险分散至全球供应链，减少对中国的过度依赖。日本已经采取了类似的措施，其宣布将向日本公司提供总计2200亿日元（约145亿元人民币或20亿美元）的直接贷款，用于将其制造业务从中国转移回日本，外加235亿日元（约15亿元人民币或约2亿美元），以帮助日本公

1 参见 Rapoza, Kenneth. “Kudlow: ‘Pay The Moving Costs’ of American Companies Leaving China.” Forbes. April 10, 2020. https://www.forbes.com/sites/kenrapoza/2020/04/10/kudlow-pay-the-moving-costs-of-american-companies-leaving-china/。

the prospects for global trade going forward in the full historical context, it would appear more plausible that "the post-coronavirus future will see not an end to the globalizing trend of recent decades but a new chapter in that story." [1]

- Even with all the talk in the US of decoupling with China, it would not be that simple or easy. China's comparative advantage is no longer inexpensive labor. In fact, labor costs in China continue to rise. But Chinese producers have substantially upgraded their capabilities, first, by organizing and coordinating complex supplier networks, managing inventory and performing quality control on materials and components, and second, by moving into production of more sophisticated key components which previously were supplied from abroad. For example, in 2009, China performed only assembly work for the Apple iPhone 3G, representing 3.6% of the total bill for materials. By 2018, China was producing many of the more complex components for the iPhone X, including the printed circuit board, battery pack and camera module, increasing its share of the bill of materials to 25% of the total. This is representative of the overall trends for China manufacturing. Based on OECD figures, China's domestic content as part of total exports increased from 74% to 84% from 2005 to 2015. This comprehensive ecosystem of the value-added manufacturing supply chain in China will be difficult to replicate elsewhere, Consequently, even if foreign governments do provide subsidies to cover some of the costs of relocation of certain manufacturing facilities out of China, as a practical matter many MNCs are likely to make a show of moving only some manufacturing from China without fully or even substantially decoupling from China. [2]
- It is also important to recognize that inbound FDI into China is not focused solely or perhaps even primarily on manufacturing for export. The most dynamic part of the China FDI story is focused on access to the massive China market for both goods and

1 See Karabell, Zachary. "Will the Coronavirus Bring the End of Globalization? Don't Count on It." March 20, 2020. https://www.morningstar.com/news/dow-jones/202003209907/will-the-coronavirus-bring-the-end-of-globalization-dont-count-on-it and "Trade, Merchandise exports (current US$)." Data. Accessed April 17, 2020.https://data.worldbank.org/topic/trade.

2 See Van Assche, Ari. "Washington hopes tariffs will force multinationals away from China, but times have changed. Companies use China for far more than cheap assembly now." Policy Options. February 7, 2020. https://policyoptions.irpp.org/magazines/february-2020/decoupling-from-china-is-hard-to-do/ and Kharpal, Arjun. "Apple, Microsoft, Google look to move production away from China. That's not going to be easy." CNBC. March 4, 2020. https://www.cnbc.com/2020/03/05/coronavirus-apple-microsoft-google-look-to-move-production-away-from-china.html.

司从中国迁往其他国家。

这将对中国作为仅次于美国的世界第二大外商直接投资目的地的地位造成多大威胁？毫无疑问，全球疫情的蔓延和金融危机将在短期内对外商直接投资产生重大负面影响，但就中长期来说，还需要考虑重要的抵销因素：

- 即使在全球疫情蔓延之前，全球贸易总值已经出现收缩，与 2018 年的创纪录水平相比，2019 年的贸易总值下降了 1%，但 2019 年的全球贸易额仍达到了 19 万亿美元，相较于 1995 年（5.19 万亿美元）增长了 3.5 倍以上，是 1970 年（3,023 亿美元）的 63 倍。即使仅就中美之间的贸易来看，贸易额从 2017 年的 6300 亿美元下降为 2019 年的 5600 亿美元，双边贸易额降至 2013 年的水平，但仍是 2001 年的 5 倍。正如同一位评论员所说，当我们在整个历史背景下评估全球贸易的前景时，似乎更合乎情理的结论是："在新型冠状病毒疫情过后的未来，近几十年来的全球化趋势并不会终结，而是一个新篇章的开始。"[1]

"当我们在整个历史背景下评估全球贸易的前景时，似乎更合乎情理的结论是：'在新型冠状病毒疫情过后的未来，近几十年来的全球化趋势并不会终结，而是一个新篇章的开始。'"

- 虽然美国一直在谈论与中国脱钩一事，但是脱钩并不是一件那么简单或容易的事。中国的比较优势不再是廉价劳动力。事实上，中国的劳动力成本在持续上升。但中国制造商已经大幅提升了自身的能力，通过组织和协调复杂的供应商网络，管理库存并对材料和部件进行质量控制；通过转向生产以前由国外供应的更复杂的关键部件。例如，2009 年，中国仅完成了苹果 iPhone 3G 手机的组装工作，占材料总费用的 3.6%。到 2018 年，中国为 iPhone X 生产了许多更为复杂的部件，包括制作电路板、电池组和摄像头模块，从而将其在材料费用中的份额增加到 25%。这反

1 参见 Karabell, Zachary. "Will the Coronavirus Bring the End of Globalization? Don't Count on It." March 20, 2020. https://www.morningstar.com/news/dow-jones/202003209907/will-the-coronavirus-bring-the-end-of-globalization-dont-count-on-it and "Trade, Merchandise exports (current US$)." Data. https://data.worldbank.org/topic/trade，2020 年 4 月 17 日访问。

services. For example, China is Apple's third-largest market, accounting for 20% of its global sales, trailing only the US and EU markets. GM sells more than 3 million vehicles in China every year, making China its number one market, eclipsing US sales by more than 200,000 vehicles annually. Cummins sells approximately one-third of its engines in China. KFC now sells more chicken in China than it does in the US. McDonalds opened its 2000th store in China in 2014 and now operates more than 3000 locations across the country. Intel generated more than US$20 billion in sales in China in 2019, while Qualcomm's sales in China and Hong Kong amounted to more than US$11.5 billion, more than quadrupling its US sales.[1] Many foreign SMEs also derive a substantial part of their global sales in China. These companies are not going to walk away from the China market, and most other MNCs and many SMEs will continue to find the China market opportunity too compelling to ignore.

- China is also responding to changing conditions arising out of the COVID-19 pandemic. China has already announced an infrastructure development plan valued at approximately RMB 50 trillion (roughly US$7 trillion) designed to stimulate its economy in order to accelerate the anticipated "V-shaped" recovery.[2] In addition China has indicated that it will open more sectors to foreign investment by reducing the number of categories which are currently subject to restrictions under the Negative List.[3]

Keeping Pace with an Evolving China

This last point is critical—China presents a moving target, and foreign perception of China generally tends to lag behind the reality of actual Chinese market conditions. This can be illustrated by the following story. In late 2017 I was invited to participate in a panel discussion

1 See "How many multinational corporations operate in China?" Investopedia. February 3, 2020. https://www.investopedia.com/ask/answers/021015/how-many-multinational-corporations-operate-china.asp; "General Motors – vehicle sales by country." Data. Accessed April 16, 2020. https://www.statista.com/statistics/304367/vehicle-sales-of-general-motors-by-country/; "Intel's net revenue by country." Data. Accessed April 16, 2020. https://www.statista.com/statistics/263560/net-revenue-of-intel-by-region-since-2006/; "Qualcomm's revenue by region." Data. Accessed April 16. 2020. statista.com/statistics/737844/revenue-of-qualcomm-by-region/.

2 "Traditional Projects to Lead China Infrastructure Investments in 2020." FitchRatings. April 8,2020. https://www.fitchratings.com/research/corporate-finance/traditional-projects-to-lead-china-infrastructure-investments-in-2020-08-04-2020.

3 "'Morale pills' for global firms." English.gov.cn. Accessed April 17, 2020. http://english.www.gov.cn/statecouncil/ministries/202003/18/content_WS5e71821cc6d0c201c2cbe90a.html.

映出中国制造业的总体的发展趋势。根据经合组织（OECD）的数据，从2005年至2015年，中国出口总额中境内产值的比重从74%上升到84%。中国这一增值制造业供应链的综合生态系统很难在其他地方复制，因此，即使外国政府确实提供补贴，用于补偿某些制造工厂迁出中国所需的部分费用，但实际上，许多跨国公司很可能会表现出仅将一部分制造业从中国转移出去，而不会完全或者甚至不会实质上与中国脱钩。[1]

- 同样重要的是要认识到，流入中国的外商直接投资并非仅集中于或主要集中于出口制造业。进入庞大的中国商品和服务市场才是中国外商直接投资中最具活力的部分。例如，中国是苹果公司的第三大市场，占其全球销售额的20%，仅次于美国和欧盟市场。通用汽车每年在中国销售超过300万辆汽车，使中国成为其第一大市场，每年超出美国的销量多过200,000辆。康明斯约1/3的发动机在中国销售。肯德基如今在中国的销售额比在美国多。麦当劳于2014年在中国开设了第2000家门店，目前在全中国经营着3000多个门店。2019年英特尔在中国的销售额超过200亿美元，与此同时高通在中国内地和香港特别行政区的销售额超过115亿美元，是其在美国销售额的4倍多。[2]许多外国中小

1 参见 Van Assche, Ari. "Washington hopes tariffs will force multinationals away from China, but times have changed. Companies use China for far more than cheap assembly now." Policy Options. February 7, 2020. https://policyoptions.irpp.org/magazines/february-2020/decoupling-from-china-is-hard-to-do/ and Kharpal, Arjun. "Apple, Microsoft, Google look to move production away from China. That's not going to be easy." CNBC. March 4, 2020. https://www.cnbc.com/2020/03/05/coronavirus-apple-microsoft-google-look-to-move-production-away-from-china.html。

2 参见"How many multinational corporations operate in China?" Investopedia. February 3, 2020. https://www.investopedia.com/ask/answers/021015/how-many-multinational-corporations-operate-china.asp;"General Motors – vehicle sales by country." Data. https://www.statista.com/statistics/304367/vehicle-sales-of-general-motors-by-country/, 2020年4月16日访问；"Intel's net revenue by country." Data. https://www.statista.com/statistics/263560/net-revenue-of-intel-by-region-since-2006/，2020年4月16日访问；"Qualcomm's revenue by region." Data. statista.com/statistics/737844/revenue-of-qualcomm-by-region/，2020年4月16日访问。

for a small group of senior managers from major Chinese companies. The other panelists included a former senior Chinese government official and a senior trade expert from the US who had participated in all of the trade and investment negotiations between the US and China from the 1980s to the present. In response to pointed criticisms from the US panelist about US-Chinese trade imbalances, the retired Chinese official noted that China was already in the process of evolving from an export-oriented economy to an import-oriented economy. This came as a surprise to me and to the US trade expert. The retired Chinese official explained that with the continuing dramatic expansion of the Chinese domestic economy, it was expected that domestic producers would not be able to meet all of the growing market demand, so China would naturally need to open up more sectors to allow more foreign goods and services to enter into the China market, not only to fill the domestic supply gap but also to provide healthy competition to spur the next stage of development of Chinese producers. By the same logic, the strength of the China market would be impossible for foreign companies to ignore, so it would be a win-win scenario, and at that point the current concerns about trade deficits would no longer apply.

Of course, there will be new issues and concerns at that stage, and some current criticisms and tensions on both sides will still be unresolved. The COVID-19 global pandemic likely will exacerbate many of those tensions given that the immediate health and economic impacts have been so devastating.[1] Mutual trust on both sides had already reached a low ebb during the Sino-

1 Some politicians and pundits in a number of leading industrialized countries have called for reparations from China to compensate for losses caused by the COVID-19 pandemic. Class action lawsuits also have been filed against China for related claims in the US. These actions may be principally political or symbolic in nature, and all of these actions will be subject to significant, likely insurmountable, legal and practical obstacles (see, e.g. Sanklecha, Jay Manoj. "COVID-19 Outbreak: Can China be Legally Made to Pay 'Damages'?" The Quint. April 5, 2020. https://www.thequint.com/voices/opinion/china-covid-19-who-responsibility-international-law and Stockler, Asher, "At least four class-action suits filed against China, seeking trillions over coronavirus outbreak in U.S." Newsweek. April 16, 2020. https://www.newsweek.com/china-class-action-lawsuits-covid-19-1498400). Some lawmakers in the US have also proposed stripping China of the defense of sovereign immunity, but that could prove to be unwise and counter-productive for US interests (see, e.g. McCarhthy, Andrew, "The Foolish GOP Proposal to Open China to American Lawsuits over COVID-19." National Review, April 21, 2020. https://www.nationalreview.com/2020/04/the-foolish-gop-proposal-to-open-china-to-american-lawsuits-over-covid-19/). However, the harshness of the rhetoric employed by many vocal critics does reflect the immediate impact of the pandemic on public sentiment among certain sectors of society and may in some cases ultimately affect bilateral and international relations as well as business opportunities for some Chinese companies. As a related matter, governments around the world may also face claims arising out of their responses to the pandemic. See, e.g., Benedettelli, Massimo. "Could COVID-19 emergency measures give rise to foreign investment claims?" FDIIntelligence. April 14, 2020. www.fdiintelligence.com/article/77393, which discusses possible remedies available to foreign investors under bilateral investment treaties

企业在中国的销售额也占其全球销售总额的很大一部分。这些公司不会离开中国市场，并且其他的大多数跨国公司和中小型企业将继续发现中国市场的机会令人难以忽视。

• 中国也在应对由新型冠状病毒肺炎疫情所引起的形势变化。中国已经宣布了一项价值约 50 万亿元人民币（约合 7 万亿美元）的基础设施发展计划，旨在刺激经济发展，以加速预期的“V 形”复苏。[1] 此外，中国表示，将通过减少目前负面清单项下受限制的类别的数量，向外资开放更多的行业部门。[2]

紧随中国发展的步伐

最后一点很关键——中国始终保持着不断变化，外国对中国的看法通常落后于中国市场的实际情况。下面的这个故事可以说明这一点。2017 年年底，我应邀参加了一个与中国大型公司的高级管理人员共同进行的小组讨论。其他小组成员还包括一名前中国政府高级官员和一名来自美国的资深贸易专家，他们参与了 20 世纪 80 年代至今中美之间所有的贸易和投资谈判。这位退休的中国官员在回应美国讨论组成员对中美贸易不平衡的尖锐批评时指出，中国已经处于从出口导向型经济向进口导向型经济转变的过程中。我和美国贸易专家都对此感到惊讶。这位退休的中国官员解释说，随着中国国内经济的持续快速增长，预计国内生产商将无法满足不断增长的市场需求，因此中国自然需要开放更多的行业部门，以使更多的外国商品和服务进入中国市场，这不仅是为了填补国内供应缺口，也是为了形成良性竞争，以刺激中国生产商下一阶段的发展。按照同样的逻辑，外国公司不可能忽视中国

1 “Traditional Projects to Lead China Infrastructure Investments in 2020.” FitchRatings. April 8,2020. https://www.fitchratings.com/research/corporate-finance/traditional-projects-to-lead-china-infrastructure-investments-in-2020-08-04-2020.

2 “‘Morale pills’ for global firms.” English.gov.cn. http://english.www.gov.cn/statecouncil/ministries/202003/18/content_WS5e71821cc6d0c201c2cbe90a.html，2020 年 4 月 17 日访问。

US trade war, and even with the signing of the phase one trade agreement in January of 2020, only a very tentative and temporary respite had been achieved. The COVID-19 pandemic then abruptly re-scrambled the pieces on the bilateral relationship chess board. These realities cannot be ignored, and rebuilding trust will take time and require frank and transparent dialogue, with both sides seeking to promote legitimate self-interests through the recognition of shared mutual interests.

In the interim, although FDI dipped only 10% year-on-year in Q1 2020,[1] we should expect a significant downturn in FDI into China in Q2 and Q3 2020 due not only to global economic conditions which have been adversely impacted by the COVID-19 panic but also due to the resulting impact on investor sentiments. Some of these factors may linger, impacting the overall growth trajectory of China FDI.

Looking to the future, though, there are still many reasons for optimism. China's economic foundation remains strong, and if the past is any guide, FDI inflows into China will follow the same "V-shaped" recovery as forecast by the ADB for China's overall GDP growth over the second half of 2020 and extending into 2021. The global economy will start to adapt to the new post-coronavirus normal, and China and other major players will adjust accordingly.

Disruption Drives Innovation

The dramatic disruption created by the global pandemic also creates opportunity and demands innovation. Consequently, over the coming years both China and the rest of the world will undergo a continuing transformation as new technologies and business models emerge. The implications for FDI and FDI lawyers in China will be no less dramatic. New sectors will open and new champions, both foreign and domestic, will emerge in the China market. Lawyers will need to retool to keep up and to capture new market opportunities. As described in Chapter 4, the adoption of the FIL standing alone represents a major disruptive event in the China legal services market. The intervening pandemic compounds the impact of that original disruption exponentially.

For example, in Chapter 4 we put forward the proposition that the FIL on its own would further erode the market share of foreign law firms in China in respect of traditional FDI work.

1 "China sees no large-scale foreign investment withdrawal amid coronavirus impact: MOC." *Xinhua*. Accessed April 17, 2020. http://www.xinhuanet.com/english/2020-04/16/c_138982281.htm.

市场的实力，因此这将是一个双赢的局面，到那时，对贸易逆差的担忧将变得多余。

当然，届时将会有新的问题和担忧出现，目前双方的一些批评和紧张局势可能仍无法得到解决。由于新型冠状病毒肺炎对于健康和经济造成的直接影响是灾难性的，因此新型冠状病毒肺炎的全球流行可能会导致多处紧张局势的进一步加剧。[1] 中美贸易冲突期间，双方互信已处于低谷，即使在 2020 年 1 月签订了第一阶段经贸协议，也只是实现了暂时的缓解，新型冠状病毒肺炎疫情突然搅乱了双边关系棋盘上的棋子。这些现实不容忽视，重建信任需要时间，需要坦率和透明的对话，双方应当在承认共同利益的基础上谋求促进自身的正当利益。

在此期间，虽然外商直接投资在 2020 年第一季度仅同比下降 10%，[2] 但我们预计，进入中国的外商直接投资将在 2020 年第二季度和第三季度出现大幅下降，这不仅是因为全球经济形势受到了新型冠状病毒肺炎所致的恐慌的不利影响，还因为投资者情绪同样受到了影响。其中一些因素可能还会持续下去，影响中国

1 一些主要工业化国家的政客和权威人士要求中国承担赔偿责任，以补偿新型冠状病毒肺炎疫情造成的损失。此前中国也因相关索赔主张而在美国被提起集体诉讼。这些行动实质上可能主要是政治性的或象征性的，而且所有这些行动都将面临严重的、可能无法克服的法律和现实障碍。（参见 Sanklecha, Jay Manoj. “COVID-19 Outbreak: Can China be Legally Made to Pay ‘Damages’?” The Quint. April 5, 2020. https://www.thequint.com/voices/opinion/china-covid-19-who-responsibility-international-law and Stockler, Asher. “At least four class-action suits filed against China, seeking trillions over coronavirus outbreak in U.S.” Newsweek. April 16, 2020. https://www.newsweek.com/china-class-action-lawsuits-covid-19-1498400。）美国的一些立法者也提议剥夺中国的主权豁免，但这可能被证明是不明智的，并且会对美国的利益产生不利影响（参见 McCarhthy, Andrew, “The Foolish GOP Proposal to Open China to American Lawsuits over COVID-19.” National Review, April 21, 2020）。然而，许多评论者所使用的严厉措辞，确实反映了这一疫情对社会某些阶层公众情绪的直接影响，在某些情况下可能最终影响双边和国际关系以及部分中国企业的商业机会。与此相关的是，世界各国政府也可能面临因应对这一疫情而引起的索赔。参见 Benedettelli, Massimo. “Could COVID-19 emergency measures give rise to foreign investment claims?” FDIIntelligence. April 14, 2020. www.fdiintelligence.com/article/77393，这一文章就根据双边投资条约项下外国投资者可获得的救济展开讨论。

2 “China sees no large-scale foreign investment withdrawal amid coronavirus impact: MOC.” Xinhua. http://www.xinhuanet.com/english/2020-04/16/c_138982281.htm，2020 年 4 月 17 日访问。

Now in the immediate aftermath of global pandemic and financial crisis, international law firms are suspending partner profit distributions and furloughing staff.[1] This is reminiscent of the cutbacks made by the foreign law firms in China in the wake of the 2008-2009 global financial crisis, when the larger foreign law firms reduced headcount in their China offices by up to a third. Over the following decade, the foreign firms for the most part had only been able to maintain the new status quo in terms of their China headcount, while over the same time period the top local Chinese law firms expanded dramatically.

The current financial crisis will present significant additional challenges for both foreign and domestic law firms in China. This in turn will drive more intense price competition, even on the part of the foreign firms, which was also the case in the period following the 2008-2009 global financial crisis. Profits will follow prices down, adding to budget pressures in the near term. But if we accept the ADB forecasts for a "V-shaped" rebound for the China economy in 2021, and if we accept the core premise of this book that the FIL over the medium term represents the single largest "full employment act" for FDI lawyers in China, then brighter days are ahead. In fact, if our projections are accurate, in the latter half of the five-year transition period under the FIL, the challenge will be too much work, not too little work, for FDI lawyers.

The startling irony is that both the immediate downturn and the projected medium-term upswing will drive the adoption of innovative legal-tech solutions. In the former case legal-tech tools will help backfill for reduced staffing, while in the latter case the same legal-tech tools will help the entire cohort of FDI lawyers across China (who will be stretched to the limit in the peak periods of the FIL roll-out) to scale up to meet excess market demand. The twin disruptions of the FIL and the global pandemic thus will accelerate this emerging migration from the traditional legal services model where everything is done "by hand" to the AI-driven integrated online-offline human-machine interface legal services model, ushering the Chinese legal profession into a brave new world!

As noted at the end of the original Introduction above, this Supplemental Introduction similarly presents a snapshot in time, and many of the observations and projections about the post-coronavirus business environment may already be out of date by the time you are reading this. But as noted above, that is an unavoidable challenge any author faces in such a situation as

1 Simmons, Richard. "Coronavirus: full details of the law firms affected so far." The Lawyer. Accessed April 17, 2020. https://www.thelawyer.com/coronavirus-law-firm-updates/.

外商直接投资的总体增长轨迹。

然而，展望未来，仍然有理由保持乐观。中国的经济基础仍然稳固，从过去的经验来看，流入中国的外商直接投资将遵循"V形"复苏模式，就如亚洲开发银行对中国在2020年下半年至2021年的GDP总体增长所作出的预测一般。全球经济将开始适应新型冠状病毒肺炎过后的新常态，中国和其他主要国家也将做出相应调整。

"此次全球疫情造成的巨大破坏也创造了机会，并驱动了创新。因此，在未来几年，随着新技术和商业模式的出现，中国和世界其他地区都将经历持续的转型。这对中国外商直接投资和从事外商直接投资的律师而言，影响也同样巨大。"

颠覆驱动创新

此次全球疫情造成的巨大破坏也创造了机会，并驱动了创新。因此，在未来几年，随着新技术和商业模式的出现，中国和世界其他地区都将经历持续的转型。这对中国外商直接投资和从事外商直接投资的律师而言，影响也同样巨大。新的行业部门将开放，中国市场将涌现出新的国内外龙头企业。律师将需要重新武装自己，以紧跟市场发展，抓住市场新机会。如本书第四章所述，《外商投资法》的通过是中国法律服务市场的一个重大的颠覆性事件。新型冠状病毒肺炎疫情的介入使原有颠覆的影响呈指数级放大。

例如，我们在本书第四章中提出，就传统的外商直接投资工作而言，仅因《外商投资法》的实施就将导致外国律师事务所在中国的市场份额被进一步削弱。如今，受全球疫情和金融危机的影响，国际律师事务所正暂停合伙人利润分配并进行裁员。[1]这使人想起2008—2009年全球金融危机之后，外国律师事务所在中国进行的裁员事件，当时较大的外国律师事务所将其在华代表处的人员总数减少了1/3。在接下来的十年中，外国律师事务所在中国的人员总数仅能维持在这一现状，而在同一时期，中国顶级的本土律师事务所的规模却在急剧扩大。

当前的金融危机将给在华的中外律师事务所带来更大的挑战。这反过来将推动更为激烈的价格竞争，即使外国律所也是如

1 Simmons, Richard. "Coronavirus: full details of the law firms affected so far." The Lawyer. https://www.thelawyer.com/coronavirus-law-firm-updates/，2020年4月17日访问。

this. One thing that has not changed over the year-long odyssey of working on this book is the fundamental nature of the transition from the Old FIE Laws to the Company Law. Consequently, it is hoped that this foundation will remain stable for at least the duration of the transition period under the FIL, and that lawyers and investors will find this volume to be a useful reference for many years to come.

Robert Lewis

docQbot Chief Expert

Email: lvlishan@docQbot.com

30 April 2020

此。2008—2009年全球金融危机之后的时期，情况也是如此。利润将随着价格下跌，从而导致在短期内预算的压力增加。然而如果我们接受亚洲开发银行关于2021年中国经济将呈现“V形”反弹的预测，并且认可本书的核心前提，即从中期来看，《外商投资法》对于中国外商直接投资律师而言是最大的“充分就业法案”，那么曙光就在前方。事实上，如果我们的预测是准确的，那么在《外商投资法》规定的五年过渡期的后半段，对于外商直接投资律师而言，面临的挑战将是工作量太大，而不是太少。

具有讽刺意味的是，当前的经济衰退和预计的中期回升都将推动创新型法律科技解决方案的采用。在前一种情况下，法律科技工具将有助于填补人力减少的空缺，而在后一种情况下，相同的法律科技工具将帮助中国的整个外商直接投资律师群体（在《外商投资法》实施后的高峰期，对他们的需求将达到顶峰）扩大规模，以满足过剩的市场需求。《外商投资法》和全球疫情的双重破坏将加速从一切由“人工”完成的传统的法律服务模式向AI驱动的线上线下一体化的人机界面法律服务模式的新兴转变，引领中国法律行业进入一个崭新的世界！

如上文原简介结尾处所述，此次补充简介犹如一张即时快照，在您阅读本书时，有关新型冠状病毒肺炎疫情后商业环境的许多观察和预测可能已经过时。但是如上所述，这是任何作者在这一情况下都无法避免的挑战。在本书长达一年的撰写过程中，唯一不变的是“三资法”向《公司法》过渡的本质。因此，希望这一基础至少在《外商投资法》规定的过渡期内将保持稳定，并且律师和投资者在今后许多年中仍能将本书作为有用的参考。

吕立山
合通机器人首席专家
电子邮箱：lvlishan@docQbot.com
2020年4月30日

Part I

The Dawn of a New Era for FDI in China

第一部分

中国外商直接投资新时代的曙光

Chapter 1 The Era of the Three FIE Laws

To understand just how radical a departure the FIL is in terms of the foundational structure of FIEs in China, it is necessary to understand the Three FIE Laws, which it replaces. At the same time, it is not possible to have a full appreciation of the Three FIE Laws without understanding the overall historical context in which they were first adopted together with the evolution of FDI and the Chinese economy in the following decades.

A Brief History of FDI in China

FDI in China can be divided into four stages which roughly correspond to the four decades since the adoption of the EJV Law. We will provide a brief overview of the core elements of the Three FIE Laws in the context of each stage below as a backdrop to our discussion of the FIL in the next chapter.

Stage 1 — Reform and Opening Up (the 1980s)

The EJV Law was adopted on 1 July 1979. Deng Xiaoping is reported to have stated at the time that the EJV Law was more "a statement of political intent, rather than a piece of legislation," which was a fitting description given that the EJV Law in its original form consisted of a mere 16 articles.[1] It is useful to note that this was 12 years prior to Deng's famous "southern tour talks" when he criticized those in China who had expressed doubts about the reform and opening up policies which he was championing as a means to promote economic development. Looking at World Bank figures for 1980, the need for economic reform was apparent, with China posting a GDP of less than $300 billion, putting it at only 6.7% of US GDP at the time. Similarly, Chinese imports and exports were only 4% of US totals in

1 Mahony, Tarrant. "China Passes Landmark New Foreign Investment Law." The Temple 10-Q, May 14, 2019. https://www2.law.temple.edu/10q/china-passes-landmark-new-foreign-investment-law/.

第一章 “三资法”时代

想要理解《外商投资法》对中国外商投资企业基础结构的改变有多么巨大，就有必要了解它所取代的“三资法”。与此同时，如果不了解“三资法”最初获得通过的整体历史背景以及随后的几十年里外商直接投资和中国经济的演变，就不可能完全理解“三资法”。

中国外商直接投资简史

中国的外国直接投资可分为四个阶段，大致对应《中外合资经营企业法》颁布以来的 40 年。下文我们将在每个阶段的背景下简要概述“三资法”的核心要点，作为我们在下一章讨论《外商投资法》的背景知识。

第一阶段——改革开放（20 世纪 80 年代）

《中外合资经营企业法》于 1979 年 7 月 1 日通过。据报道，邓小平当时表示《中外合资经营企业法》在很大程度上“与其说是法，不如说是我们政治意向的声明”，这一描述非常恰当，因为《中外合资经营企业法》的原始版本仅包括 16 个条款。[1] 值得注意的是，此法颁布 12 年后，邓小平发表了著名的南方谈话，邓小平在南方谈话中批评了那些对中国促进经济发展而实施的改革

1 Mahony, Tarrant. “China Passes Landmark New Foreign Investment Law.” The Temple 10-Q, May 14, 2019. https://www2.law.temple.edu/10q/china-passes-landmark-new-foreign-investment-law/.

1980.[1]

Laying the initial groundwork for Deng's reform and opening up policies required persistent coordinated efforts over an extended period of time. Special economic zones were set up starting in 1980. Decentralization of economic policies commenced in 1984, with this process continuing for most of the next decade. The WFOE Law was adopted in 1986, and the CJV Law was passed in 1988.

The three principle foreign investment vehicles corresponded to the Three FIE Laws, namely Sino-Foreign Equity Joint Ventures (EJVs), Sino-Foreign Cooperative Joint Ventures (CJVs) and Wholly Foreign-owned Enterprises (WFOEs). Each were limited liability companies, but each was a separate and distinct legal entity form for registration purposes. Some key distinguishing characteristics of each of these FIE entity forms included:

- The EJV was the default form of joint venture, and the CJV followed the general outlines of the EJV in terms of corporate governance structures. The main distinctions between the EJV and the CJV related to the form of capital contributions and profit sharing. In an EJV the parties were permitted to contribute cash, specified categories of tangible assets and assignments (but not licenses) of intellectual property rights (IPR), and profits were to be distributed strictly in accordance with the parties' respective shareholdings.
- By contrast, in a CJV parties could also provide soft contributions in the form of "cooperative conditions" such as market access, government relations support, exclusive IPR license rights, etc. which could not be capitalized in connection with an EJV. More importantly, in a CJV the parties could agree to disproportionate distributions of profits, affording substantial additional flexibility. Another feature unique to CJVs was that the parties could provide that the foreign party could recover its capital investment on a preferential basis during the course of the term so long as at the end of the term, usually 15 to 20 years, title to all of the assets would automatically vest in the Chinese party in a structure similar to a BOT arrangement.
- For purposes of this high-level discussion, it should be sufficient to note that WFOE was, as the name suggests, a wholly-owned subsidiary of one or more foreign

1 "Data for China, United States" Data. Accessed 29 August 2019. https://data.worldbank.org/?locations=CN-US.

开放政策表示怀疑的人。回看世界银行 1980 年的数据，中国的国内生产总值不到 3000 亿美元，仅相当于当时美国国内生产总值的 6.7%，经济改革的必要性显而易见。同样，1980 年中国的进出口额仅为美国的 4%。[1]

为邓小平的改革开放政策奠定初步基础需要长时间的持续协调努力。经济特区从 1980 年开始建立，1984 年开始实行经济政策的松绑放权，而这一过程在其后十年内的大部分时间持续推进。《外资企业法》于 1986 年通过，而《中外合作经营企业法》于 1988 年通过。

与“三资法”相对应的是三类主要的外商投资实体形式，即中外合资经营企业、中外合作经营企业和外商独资企业。这三类企业均为有限责任公司，但每类企业在注册时被区分为不同的法人实体形式。区分这些外商投资企业实体形式的关键特征包括：

- 合资经营企业是合营企业的默认形式，合作经营企业遵循合资经营企业在公司治理结构方面的总体架构。合资经营企业和合作经营企业之间的主要区别是关于出资和利润分配的方式。在合资经营企业中，各方可以以现金、特定种类的有形资产和知识产权的转让（非许可）出资，并且须严格按照各方的持股比例分配利润。

- 相比之下，在合作经营企业中，各方还可以以“合作条件”的形式提供软出资，例如市场准入、政府关系支持、知识产权独占许可权等，而这些在合资经营企业中不能作为出资。更重要的是，在合作经营企业中，各方可以同意不按持股比例进行利润分配，灵活性较大。合作经营企业另一个独有特点是，各方可以规定，外方可以在合作期限内以优惠的条件收回其资本投资，只要所有资产的所有权将在合作期限（通常为 15 年至 20 年）届满前自动归属于中方，

1　“Data for China, United States”，https://data.worldbank.org/?locations=CN-US，2019 年 8 月 29 日访问。

investors (generally only a single foreign investor, but in certain cases with multiple investors in the offshore holding company). As such, the governance structure for a WFOE could be much simpler; however, the capital structure requirements (to be discussed below) were essentially the same as for EJVs.

Notwithstanding the Three FIE Laws being put in place and all of the additional foundational measures undertaken during this initial decade, China's GDP, which had remained essentially flat from 1960 to 1980, showed only modest improvement prior to Deng's "southern tour" in 1992, which is uniformly credited as the principal inflection point in China's economic resurgence. The data bears this out. Starting almost immediately after Deng's "southern tour" GDP figures showed marked improvement. Not coincidentally, FDI started to increase at the same time, demonstrating that FDI was a key driver for China's early economic development.

The reform and opening up policies have created an undeniable economic miracle the likes of which the world has never seen. When we look at China's economic standing in 1980 compared with corresponding figures for 2018, the contrast could not be more striking. (See Chart 1-A.) China is now the world's second largest economy, closing fast on the US for the top spot, and has amassed the world's largest reserves of foreign currency. All of this can be traced to the reform and opening up policies initiated 40 years ago.

Chart 1–A China vs. USA [1]

Current US$ (billions)	China		U.S.		China/U.S. Percentage	
	1980	2018	1980	2018	1980	2018
GDP	191.149	13,608	2857	20,494	6.7%	66.4%
Exports	11.3	2656	280.772	2500	4%	106%
Imports	12.45	2549	293.828	3121	4%	81.7%
Reserves (Includes gold)	10.091	3168	171.413	449.907	5.9%	704%

Stage 2 — the Growth and Evolution of FDI (the 1990s)

I arrived in the China market in 1993, joining the Baker & McKenzie China Practice

1 "Data for China, United States ." Data. Accessed 29 August 2019. https://data.worldbank.org/?locations=CN-US.

其结构类似于“建设—经营—转让（BOT）”安排。

- 从高度概括的角度来讲，我们只需了解，外商独资企业，顾名思义，是一个或多个外国投资者（通常只有一个外国投资者，但在某些情况下境外控股公司有多个投资者）的全资子公司。正因如此，外商独资企业的治理结构简单得多，而资本结构的要求（将在下文讨论）基本上与合资经营企业相同。

尽管在此最初的十年里，“三资法”和所有其他的基本措施均已得到实施，但在1992年邓小平南方谈话之前国内生产总值仅略有提升（1960年至1980年，中国的国内生产总值处于基本持平状态）。邓小平南方谈话被视为中国经济复苏的转折点，数据也证实了这一点。南方谈话之后，国内生产总值数据几乎立即表现出明显的上升。并非巧合的是，外商直接投资也同时开始增加，表明了外商直接投资是中国早期经济发展的一个关键驱动因素。

毋庸置疑，改革开放政策创造了世界上前所未有的经济奇迹。当我们对比中国1980年的经济地位与其2018年的相应数据时，其结果令人惊叹（见表1-A）。中国现在是世界第二大经济体，紧逼排名第一的美国，并且已经积累了世界上最多的外汇储备。所有这一切都可以追溯到40多年前开启的改革开放政策。

表 1–A　中国 vs. 美国 [1]

（10 亿美元）	中国		美国		中国 / 美国比例	
	1980	2018	1980	2018	1980	2018
国内生产总值	191.149	13,608	2857	20,494	6.7%	66.4%
出口	11.3	2656	280.772	2500	4%	106%
进口	12.45	2549	293.828	3121	4%	81.7%
外汇储备（包括黄金）	10.091	3168	171.413	449.907	5.9%	704%

1　“Data for China, United States”，https://data.worldbank.org/?locations=CN-US，2019年8月29日访问。

Group in Hong Kong and later in Shanghai. Although the Three FIE Laws had been in place for some time, the overall legal framework was generally lacking. There were few published laws and regulations, and even then the interpretation and application of those laws and regulations were often subject to unpublished internal government rules and policies, creating an uncertain and constantly changing investment environment. Overall, China was a difficult place to do business. Consequently, major multinational companies (MNCs) dominated the foreign investment landscape in China because smaller investors lacked the resources to get a deal done.

WFOEs were restricted to export-oriented and high-technology enterprises meeting strict criteria, so in those early days the vast majority of foreign investment projects had to take the form of a joint venture. Through the course of the mid' 1990s foreign investors continued to push the envelope to get approval to set up WFOEs for business operations outside the original limited permitted scope. In time the exceptions became the rule, and the policies regarding the scope of business for WFOEs were relaxed. With the relaxation of these policies, by the latter part of the 1990s the WFOE structure became the investment vehicle of choice for foreign investors, quickly outstripping the number of joint ventures.

Joint ventures proved to be challenging for both Chinese and foreign investors as western business culture encountered Chinese counterparties newly emerging from the centrally planned economy model. As a result, the standard advice for foreign investors during that time was two-fold: first, unless a joint venture was required by law, the default option for foreign investment should be a WFOE; and second, if a WFOE was permitted under law, then the foreign investor should consider entering into a joint venture only where the value proposition for co-investment with a particular domestic partner was so compelling as a business matter that it overrode the above presumption in favor of a WFOE as the default option.

Whether a joint venture was required as a matter of law depended on how investment in the particular industry sector was handled under the Catalogue of Industries for Guidance of Foreign Investment (Foreign Investment Guidance Catalogue) first issued in 1995. Prior to that time government approval authorities could reference related internal guidance that was not publicly available, so approvals had been issued on a case-by-case basis following consultation with relevant authorities with few if any assurances that approvals would be forthcoming.

第二阶段——外商直接投资的增长和演变（20世纪90年代）

我于1993年进入中国市场，先后加入了贝克·麦坚时（Baker & McKenzie）在香港特别行政区和上海的中国业务团队。尽管“三资法”已经实施了一段时间，但总体上缺乏整体法律框架。已颁布的法律法规少之又少，而且当时那些法律法规的解释和适用往往受非公开的政府内部规定和政策的制约，从而造成了投资环境的不确定性和频繁变化。总体上，当时的中国营商环境不佳。因此，规模较小的投资者缺乏达成交易的资源，大型跨国公司便主导了中国的外商投资格局。

外商独资企业被限于符合严格标准的出口导向型和高科技企业，因此早期绝大多数外商投资项目不得不采取合营企业的形式。至20世纪90年代中期，外国投资者一直努力突破，试图就在原有受限制的经营范围之外设立外商独资企业获得批准。随着时间的推移，这些例外成为常规，关于外商独资企业的经营范围的政策得到放宽。随着这些政策的放宽，到20世纪90年代后期，外商独资企业结构成为外国投资者的首选投资方式，迅速超过合营企业的数量。

> “事实证明，当西方商业文化遭遇中央计划经济模式下兴起的中国商业文化，设立合营企业对中国投资者和外国投资者来说都充满了挑战。”

事实证明，当西方商业文化遭遇中央计划经济模式下兴起的中国商业文化，设立合营企业对中国投资者和外国投资者来说都充满了挑战。因此，在那段期间针对外国投资者的标准建议有两个层面：首先，除非法律要求必须设立合营企业，否则外商投资应默认选择外商独资企业；其次，若法律允许设立外商独资企业，则只有当其与特定的内资合作伙伴进行共同投资的价值定位在商业上远超过设立外商独资企业这一默认选项时，外国投资者才应考虑设立合营企业。

从法律的角度，是否必须设立合营企业，取决于特定行业领域的投资在1995年首次发布的《外商投资产业指导目录》项下是如何规定的。在此之前，政府审批机关可以参考非公开的相关内

With the issuance of the Foreign Investment Guidance Catalogue, foreign investors could see which sectors were listed as prohibited, restricted or encouraged, with all other sectors being deemed to be permitted. The Foreign Investment Guidance Catalogue would in certain cases specify that foreign investments in restricted categories could only be made by means of a joint venture, and often in such cases a cap on the shareholding percentage of the foreign investor would be imposed. Foreign investments in the permitted and encouraged categories could be made either in the form of a WFOE or a joint venture with no restrictions on the foreign investors equity stake, but these investments still required approval, originally by the Ministry of Foreign Trade and Economic Cooperation (MOFTEC) and later by the Ministry of Commerce (MOFCOM) or their local counterparts at the provincial or municipal levels.

During the early stages of FDI in China the approval authorities would often impose additional requirements in addition to the terms agreed by the parties as a condition to approval. This meant that the deal often had to be negotiated twice, first by the parties and then with the approval authorities. It was common to engage in creative drafting so as not to draw the attention of the approval authorities to sensitive terms agreed by the parties.

This approval regime affected more than the initial project approvals, extending to a wide range of issues throughout the life of the joint venture. This also expanded minority shareholder protections as a practical matter because as part of the application for government approvals the parties were required to submit related board resolutions and other required party consents. Under the EJV Law, certain fundamental corporate matters (amendment of the joint venture contract and articles of association, increase or decrease in capitalization, mergers and consolidations and dissolution) required unanimous board approvals.

The requirement for unanimous board resolutions for any amendment to the joint venture contract essentially gave the minority shareholder a veto over many matters of a much less fundamental nature because the EJV Law required joint venture contracts to include many points which in international practice would be set out in a shareholder's agreement which would be a private agreement between the parties. However, under the EJV Law the joint venture contract was a core constitutional document which would take effect only upon approval, and any changes to the joint venture contract similarly required government approvals. As a result, the potential for the parties to reach an impasse extended to a broad range of issues, and as a result many legal practitioners expended substantial efforts to

部指南，因此该等审批是在与有关政府机构协商后进行个案分析的结果，进而很少能够甚至无法获得能否获得审批的保证。随着《外商投资产业指导目录》的发布，外国投资者可以知道哪些行业领域被列为禁止类、限制类或鼓励类，其余所有其他领域则被视为允许类。《外商投资产业指导目录》规定在某些情况下限制类的外商投资只能通过设立合营企业的方式进行，通常在这种情况下，外国投资者的持股比例会有上限。允许类和鼓励类的外商投资可以选择以外商独资企业或合营企业的形式进行，并且对外国投资者的股权没有限制，但这些投资仍需要获得对外贸易经济合作部（以下简称外经贸部）的批准，后来由商务部或其省级或市级部门批准。

在中国外商直接投资的早期阶段，除了当事人约定的条款，审批机关通常会提出额外的要求作为审批条件。这意味着一项交易通常需要进行两次谈判，第一次是在合营各方之间，第二次是与审批机关。很常见的情形是，合营各方之间经常创造性地起草条款以避免双方商定的敏感条款引起审批机关的关注。

该审批制度的影响不仅涉及初始的项目审批，还延伸到贯穿合营企业存续期限的一系列问题。这实际上也增强了对少数股东的保护，因为作为政府审批申请的一部分，各方必须提交相关的董事会决议和其他必需的各方批准。在《中外合资经营企业法》项下，某些根本性公司事项（合资合同和公司章程的修订、增资或减资、合并和解散）需要获得董事会的一致批准。

合资合同的修订要求董事会的一致决议本质上使少数股东对许多非根本性事项拥有了否决权，因为《中外合资经营企业法》要求规定在合资合同中的许多事项在国际惯例中是在作为当事方之间私人协议的股东协议中包含的内容。但是，在《中外合资经营企业法》项下，合资合同是一份核心的章程性文件，只有在获得批准后才能生效，对合资合同的任何修订同样需要政府审批。

drafting around these potential roadblocks through deemed approvals and consents together with related undertakings at each juncture in the contract. However, the utility of such arrangements generally was limited as a practical matter, so in many cases the joint venture partners would encounter difficulties with no clear means of resolution.

There were many other aspects of the corporate structuring requirements during this period that many foreign investors found to be unfamiliar and in many cases overly rigid by comparison with international practice. The capital structure for FIEs is a prime example. The Three FIE Laws provided for equity investments to take the form of "registered capital" as opposed to share capital, which foreign investors found to be both less familiar and less flexible. In addition, the Three FIE Laws also introduced a concept of "total investment amount," which is a legacy of the planned economy system, and which has always been challenging for first time foreign investors to understand. Rigid limits were set as to the ratio of registered capital (equity) to the total investment amount (equity plus permitted debt capacity), which effectively limited the amount of debt that the FIE could incur. This resulted in significant constraints on capital funding options even on an interim basis in many cases.

Strict time limits were imposed on injection of the registered capital amounts subscribed to by the parties in the joint venture contract, with a minimum of 15% to be injected within 90 days following the issuance of the business license and the balance within two years. This posed a challenge to both the Chinese and foreign parties as they had to project capital requirements with significant precision—if they over-capitalized the company then they would need to undertake a capital reduction, which required approvals and was not a simple or straightforward exercise, and if they encountered a capital shortfall, this would give rise to potential problems if one party was unwilling or unable to fund its proportionate share of the required capital increase, which also required approvals. Moreover, as noted above, the parties could not always fall back on shareholder loans as a bridging funding mechanism (which in the case of the foreign investor would be subject to foreign exchange controls as well in any event).

Corporate structuring also presented challenges for many foreign investors. Many foreign investors came to China expecting to be able to set up operations using multiple affiliated entities as would be common elsewhere around the world. However, the Three FIE Laws generally contemplated stand-alone entities tied to a fixed location. Establishment of subsidiaries of FIEs was subject to strict requirements and limitations: the subscribed

因此，各方在很多问题上都可能陷入僵局，所以很多法律从业者花费了大量的精力起草合同，试图通过就合同的每个关键问题规定视为批准和同意的情形以及相关承诺，来绕过这些潜在的障碍。然而，实际上这种安排的功效通常都是有限的，因此许多情况下合营各方会遇到很多困难，而没有明确的解决方法。

在这一时期，许多外国投资者发现他们对公司结构要求中的很多其他方面也不够熟悉，而且在许多情况下这些公司结构要求与国际惯例相比都过于严格。外商投资企业的资本结构就是一个很好的例子。“三资法”规定股权投资的形式为“注册资本”而非股本，而外国投资者对于注册资本的概念既不熟悉也感觉不够灵活。此外，“三资法”提出的“投资总额”是计划经济体制下遗留的概念，一直都让初次在中国投资的外国投资者难以理解。注册资本（股权）与投资总额（股权与经批准的债务额度之和）的比例也设有严格的限制，有效限制了外商投资企业可能发生的债务数额。这甚至在许多情况下对临时性的融资选择都造成了极大的限制。

在合资合同中，注册资本实缴期限受到严格的限制，各方须在营业执照颁发后 90 日内至少实缴 15% 的注册资本，并在两年内实缴剩余注册资本。这给中方和外方都带来了挑战，因为他们必须非常精确地预测资本需求——如果注册资本过高，他们就需要减资，减资需要经过审批而不能直接实施；如果发生资本短缺，而一方不愿或无法按其持股比例实缴增资（而增资也需要经过审批），就会产生潜在的问题。此外，如上所述，各方不能总是依赖股东贷款作为过桥融资机制（对于外国投资者而言，这种机制无论如何都受外汇管制的制约）。

公司结构也为许多外国投资者带来了挑战。许多外国投资者期望在中国能够通过多个关联实体开展业务，这一做法在全球其他地区都很常见。但是，“三资法”总体上规定了独立实体须对

registered capital must be fully paid up, the FIE must have started to turn a profit, and the amount of any downstream investment, whether by way of new greenfield investment or acquisition, was capped at 50% of the FIE's total assets. To respond to the need for larger foreign investors to coordinate the operations of multiple FIEs, China permitted the establishment of foreign-invested holding companies starting in 1995, but the qualification and capitalization requirements proved to be too high for all but the biggest MNCs, and even then the benefits of such holding company structures generally were considered to be modest. Overall, corporate structuring options for FIEs have been artificially constrained in China over the years.

Towards the end of the 1990s, there was already a growing sense that, while the base FIE entity structures had proven durable and functional for the most part, many aspects of the Three EJV Laws and the FIE entity structures established thereunder were overly cumbersome. The Company Law had been adopted at the end of 1993, and over the course of the balance of the decade, Chinese companies had begun the process of regularization of their corporate organizational structures. While the corporate governance provisions of the Company Law in its original form were not entirely up to international standard, many elements were clearly superior to what was provided under the Three FIE Laws. However, for FIEs the Three FIE Laws prevailed over the Company Law, with the latter applying to FIEs only where the Three FIE Laws did not set out express requirements. There was some anticipation even at that time that the days may be numbered for the Three FIE Laws and that at some point in the not so distant future FIEs would also be subject to the full requirements of the Company Law. However, it would take another 20 years for this change to take place.

Stage 3 — WTO and Entry onto the World Stage (the 2000s)

China joined the World Trade Organization (WTO) on 11 December 2001, signaling China's entry as a full member of the international economic order. But it did not signal an end to the Three FIE Laws or to the traditional FIE entity structures. Instead, China's market access commitments were all framed in the language and structures of the legacy FDI legislation, with all foreign investment principally to take the form of WFOEs, EJVs or CJVs under the Three FIE Laws rather than entity forms operating under the Company Law.

China's joining the WTO did spur additional foreign investment in many of the newly opened sectors, and gave many new foreign investors confidence to enter the China market for

应固定的经营地点。外商投资企业子公司的设立受制于严格的要求和限制：注册资本必须全额实缴；外商投资企业必须开始盈利；并且，无论是通过新设绿地投资还是收购，任何再投资的金额上限为外商投资企业总资产的50%。为响应大型外国投资者协调多个外商投资企业运营的需要，中国自1995年开始允许设立外商投资性公司。但是事实证明，除了那些最大型的跨国公司，对于其他所有外国投资者来说，相关资质和资本的要求都有些过高，即使是对于最大型的跨国公司来讲，该等投资性公司结构也收效甚微。总体而言，多年来外商投资企业的公司结构选择在中国都受到了人为的限制。

> “接近20世纪90年代末时，人们已经越来越强烈地感觉到，虽然外商投资企业的基础实体结构在多数情况下被证明是持久和实用的，但‘三资法’的许多方面及在其项下建立的外商投资企业实体结构都过于烦琐。”

接近20世纪90年代末时，人们已经越来越强烈地感受到，虽然外商投资企业的基础实体结构在多数情况下被证明是持久和实用的，但“三资法”的许多方面及在其项下建立的外商投资企业实体结构都过于烦琐。《公司法》于1993年年底通过，在其后的10年里，中国公司开始了规范其公司组织结构的进程。虽然最初《公司法》中的公司治理条款并不完全符合国际标准，但许多要素明显优于“三资法”项下的规定。但是，对于外商投资企业而言，“三资法”优先于《公司法》适用，后者仅在“三资法”没有明确规定的情况下适用于外商投资企业。当时甚至有人预言“三资法”的时代可能即将结束，并且在不远的将来，外商投资企业也将完全受《公司法》的约束。但是，这一变化直到20年后才发生。

第三阶段——加入世界贸易组织和进入世界舞台（21世纪前10年）

中国于2001年12月11日加入世界贸易组织（以下简称世贸组织），标志着中国成为国际经济秩序的正式成员，但并不意味着“三资法”或传统外商投资企业实体结构的终结。相反，中国的市场准入承诺全部以传统的外国直接投资立法的规定和结构为框架，所有外国投资主要采取“三资法”项下的外商独资企业、

the first time. While foreign investment in the 1990s had been undertaken primarily by major MNCs, the post-WTO period was characterized by the inflow of foreign investment by small and medium-sized enterprises (SMEs) as smaller foreign suppliers arrived to fill out the supply chain in China for their foreign MNC industrial customers.

During this period the overall FIE establishment process became more regularized and predictable for manufacturing enterprises and increasingly for investors in the services sector outside of highly regulated industries. Approval authorities, particularly in Beijing, Shanghai, Guangzhou and Shenzhen, increasingly adopted a hands-off approach, and over time it became less common to have government departments seek to impose new requirements as a condition for approval. (By contrast, regional authorities who had seen fewer FDI projects would in many cases be somewhat more intrusive in the course of the approval process.) However, many of the structural problems faced by FIEs as outlined above continued to impose constraints on their operational activities.

Overall, FDI conditions had improved, as indicated by the World Bank's ranking China 91st out of 155 countries surveyed in its Doing Business Report in 2006, putting China into the middle of the pack with many of the other economies in transition.[1] Since 2006 was the first year of the World Bank Doing Business Report rankings, it is not possible to compare against rankings for China during the 1990s, but based on an informal comparison from having done deals during both time periods, it would be reasonable to suppose that China in the mid' 1990s would have had a much lower ranking, well into the bottom half of the rankings, so the initial 2006 ranking should reflect significant improvement over prior conditions, but still with much room for improvement.

The early part of this decade also saw the initial inbound M&A deals. Prior to this, foreign investors had been wary of taking on potential undisclosed liabilities of SOE targets, preferring instead to set up joint ventures which were in nature more similar to asset acquisitions, where the new business could start with a clean balance sheet. But with the rise of an emerging class of privately-owned enterprises (POEs) in China with a shorter period of operations and thus more readily ascertainable assets and liabilities, the number of inbound acquisitions started to increase in number and value.

To address related legal issues arising out of such inbound M&A transactions, China

1 See further discussion of the World Bank Doing Business Report methodology at the end of this chapter.

中外合资经营企业或中外合作经营企业的形式，而不是根据《公司法》运营的企业组织形式。

中国加入世贸组织确实刺激了许多新开放的行业领域的外国投资，并给予了许多新的外国投资者首次进入中国市场的信心。虽然20世纪90年代的外国投资主要由大型跨国公司实施，但在后世贸组织时期，小型外国供应商进入了中国市场，为他们的外国跨国公司工业客户填补了在中国的供应链空缺，所以这一时期以中小型企业的外国投资流入为特点。

在此期间，对于制造业企业和高度监管行业之外的服务领域的投资者来说，整体上外商投资企业的设立过程变得更加规范且可预测。审批机关，尤其是北京、上海、广州和深圳地区的审批机关，越来越采取不干涉的态度，而且随着时间的推移，政府部门设置新要求作为审批条件的情况也变得越来越少。（相比之下，在外商直接投资项目较少的地区，地方机关在许多情况下会在审批过程中干涉较多。）然而，上述外商投资企业面临的许多结构性问题依然限制着其经营活动。

总体而言，外商直接投资环境有所改善，在世界银行2006年《营商环境报告》中调查的155个经济体中，中国排名第91位，与许多其他转型经济体一道位列中游。[1] 由于2006年是世界银行发布《营商环境报告》排名的第一年，因此无法与20世纪90年代中国的排名进行比较。但基于两个时期内完成的交易的非正式对比，我们可以合理地推断中国在20世纪90年代中期的排名会低很多，肯定处于在排名的后半部分，所以2006年的首次排名应该反映出中国对以往环境的显著改善，但仍有很大的改善空间。

首批入境并购交易也出现在这一个十年期的初期。在此之前，外国投资者一直担心承担国有企业目标公司潜在的未披露负债，因此更愿意设立合营企业，其本质上比较类似于资产收购，从而以全新的资

1 见本章末尾关于世界银行《营商环境报告》排名方法的进一步讨论。

adopted the Interim Provisions on Mergers and Acquisitions of Domestic Enterprises by Foreign Investors in 2003, followed by the final set of such provisions in 2006. Under these rules, upon acquisition of an equity stake in the domestic target company by the foreign investor, the target company was to be converted into an FIE, either a WFOE in the case of an acquisition of all of the equity of the target, or a joint venture (almost always an EJV), if the foreign investor acquired less than all of the equity interests. In other words, prior to the acquisition, the target company was a domestic enterprise subject to the requirements of the Company Law, but following the acquisition, it was to be converted into an FIE subject to the Three FIE Laws. This involved a simultaneous process of deregistration of the target company's original entity form (usually an LLC under the Company Law) and re-registration of the post-M&A company with its new FIE status. This was another opportunity for officials to commence the long-anticipated transition from a two-track system to a one-track system with all companies in China, whether domestically-owned or foreign-invested, to come under the common banner of the Company Law, but again the status quo was maintained, and FIEs continued to receive separate but not quite equal treatment under Chinese law.

In the early days of FDI into China, foreign investors benefitted from this unequal treatment. As an incentive to lure foreign investment, FIEs had long been afforded special tax breaks in the form of two years tax free status followed by three years of 50% reduction in otherwise applicable corporate taxes. Other special incentives were provided by various categories of special economic zones, industrial development zones, free trade zones, etc., with local governments offering other inducements, some of which were not always sanctioned by the central government. But with the tax reforms undertaken starting in 2008, these incentives for foreign investors were phased out, so in this respect the playing field had been levelled for domestic and foreign-invested companies in China.

Stage 4 — Post Global Financial Crisis (the 2010s)

The global financial crisis brought Stage 3 to an abrupt and somewhat early conclusion. China was comparatively insulated from the worst effects of the financial crisis, and the stimulus measures undertaken by Chinese authorities mitigated other potential problems arising in connection therewith, but foreign investor sentiment was adversely affected during the immediate aftermath of the crisis, although not as dramatically as might have been expected, with FDI inflows dropping 3.62% in 2009. China weathered the storm, and

产负债表开展新业务。但随着经营时间较短的中国民营企业的兴起，企业的资产和负债更容易确定，入境收购的数量和价值开始增加。

为解决此类入境并购交易中出现的相关法律问题，中国于2003年通过了《外国投资者并购境内企业暂行规定》，并于2006年颁布了该规定的最终版本。根据这些规定，一旦外国投资者收购了内资目标公司的股权，目标公司将转化为外商投资企业，如果外国投资者收购了目标公司的所有股权则转化为外商独资企业，如果外国投资者未收购目标公司的所有股权则转化为合营企业（几乎都是合资经营企业）。换句话说，在收购之前，目标公司是一家内资企业，受《公司法》规定的约束，但在收购后，其将转化为受“三资法”约束的外商投资企业。这同时涉及注销目标公司的原有组织形式（通常是《公司法》项下的有限责任公司）以及重新登记并购后的公司，使其获得新的外商投资企业身份。这是政府工作人员开始实施期待已久的从双轨制向单轨制过渡的又一次机会，从而在《公司法》项下管理中国境内的所有公司，无论是内资公司还是外资公司。但是，现状仍然没有改变，外商投资企业继续在中国法项下受到区别化且不完全平等的待遇。

在外商直接投资进入中国的初期，外国投资者受益于这种不平等待遇。作为吸引外商投资的一种激励措施，外商投资企业长期享受着特别的税收减免政策，即在前两年内免税，其后三年企业所得税减免50%。各类经济特区、工业开发区、自由贸易区等提供了其他特殊激励措施，地方政府也提供了其他优惠政策，其中某些政策并不一定得到了中央政府的批准。但2008年开始实施税收改革后，这些针对外国投资者的激励措施被逐步淘汰，因此在这方面，中国的内资公司和外资公司的竞争环境趋于公平。

第四阶段——全球金融危机后（21世纪第二个10年）

全球金融危机的发生使第三阶段提前戛然而止。相对而言中国没有受到金融危机最严重的影响，中国政府采取的激励措施缓解了与此相关的其他潜在问题。但外国投资者受到了危机直接后

FDI inflow rebounded and continued their upward progression, with only a modest further softening in 2012 interrupting the succession of new record highs. [1]

In fact, China set a new record for FDI in 2018, with approximately USD 135 billion in capital inflows, and more than 60,000 new FIEs established, more than double the historical average and a nearly 70% increase over 2017 levels. Figures for 2019 indicate higher levels of investment on average for each FDI project, with USD 138.14 billion in capital inflows, and more than 41,000 new FIEs established. This is even more impressive when it is noted that all of these record highs for inbound FDI have come against the backdrop of the uncertainties arising out of the US-China trade war.

Overall, in the last 40 years, nearly 1 million FIEs have been established, accounting for a cumulative total amount of FDI in excess of USD 2.15 trillion. According to reports, the industrial output of FIEs in China accounts for almost 25% of the national total.[2] Many of the FIEs established over the last 40 years will have come to the end of their terms or will otherwise have been closed down for business reasons, but according to available statistics this will still leave an estimated 500,000-plus FIEs in operation by the time the FIL takes effect, principally comprised of WFOEs and EJVs. (See Chart 1-B.)

Chart 1–B Estimated numbers of FIEs broken down by entity type through November 2019 [3]

Entity Type	Numbers
WFOEs	384,562
EJVs	122,759
CJVs	10,026
Foreign-invested companies limited by shares	6614
Total FIEs	523,961

During the last few years leading up to the adoption of the FIL, a series of measures had been adopted to address some of the long-standing challenges for FIEs. For example:

- In 2014 the Company Law was amended abolishing both the minimum registered capital requirements and capital injection timelines for newly-established enterprises

1 商务数据中心. Accessed 29 August 2019. http://data.mofcom.gov.cn/lywz/inmr.shtml.

2 Yang, Yi. "China Focus: China adopts foreign investment law," 15 March 2019. http://www.xinhuanet.com/english/2019-03/15/c_137897089.htm. See also Eastmoney.com. 国家发改委副主任宁吉喆:将修外商投资负面清单 2018 年清单扩围到全国〔Ning Jizhe, Deputy Director of the NDRC: the 2018 Negative List to be Implemented Nationwide〕, 6 March 2018. http://finance.eastmoney.com/news/1355,20180306839906194.html.

3 Estimates based on the relevant statistics released by MOFCOM and the National Bureau of Statistics.

果的负面影响，尽管影响没有预想的严重，但 2009 年外商直接投资流入量下降了 3.62%。中国经受住了这场风暴的考验，外商直接投资流入量反弹并持续上涨，仅在 2012 年稍显疲软，中断了历史新高的延续。[1]

事实上，中国在 2018 年创下了外商直接投资新纪录，资本流入量约为 1350 亿美元，新设外商投资企业超过 6 万家，是历史平均水平的两倍以上，比 2017 年增长近 70%。2019 年中国吸引外商投资 1381.4 亿美元，新设外商投资企业超过 4.1 万家，表明每个外商直接投资项目的平均投资水平更高。考虑到所有这些入境外商直接投资的创纪录数字都是在中美贸易战引起的不确定性的背景下出现的，因此这一结果更加令人印象深刻。

总体而言，在过去 40 年中，中国累计设立外商投资企业近 100 万家，累计外商直接投资总额超过 2.15 万亿美元。据报道，中国外商投资企业的工业产值几乎占全国总额的 25%。[2] 过去 40 年内设立的许多外商投资企业的期限将届满，或将因业务原因停业，但根据现有统计数据，至《外商投资法》生效时，预计仍将有 50 多万家外商投资企业在运营中，主要由外商独资企业和合资经营企业构成（见表 1-B）。

表 1-B　截至 2019 年 11 月不同类型的外商投资企业的预估数量[3]

单位：家

实体类型	数量
外商独资企业	384,562
中外合资经营企业	122,759
中外合作经营企业	10,026
外商投资股份有限公司	6614
外商投资企业总数	523,961

1　商务数据中心，http://data.mofcom.gov.cn/lywz/inmr.shtml，2019 年 8 月 29 日访问。

2　Yang Yi，“China Focus: China adopts foreign investment law,” 2019 年 3 月 15 日，http://www.xinhuanet.com/english/2019-03/15/c_137897089.htm。另外请参见“国家发改委副主任宁吉喆：将修外商投资负面清单 2018 年清单扩围到全国”，2018 年 3 月 6 日，http://finance.eastmoney.com/news/1355,20180306839906194.html。

3　预估数量基于商务部和国家统计局发布的相关数据。

(including both domestic companies and FIEs). Consequently, as a practical matter registered capital amounts are now required to be injected only prior to the winding up of the company and a capital verification certificate is no longer required. However, the thin capital rules remained in place, continuing to impose constraints on the capital structures of FIEs.

- The Negative List system (to be discussed in more detail in Chapter 2 below) was first piloted in the Shanghai Pilot Free Trade Zone starting in 2013, and in 2015, it was expanded to apply in four free trade zones in China and was also included in the 2015 Draft FIL. The issuance of the 2017 Foreign Investment Guidance Catalogue, under which the restricted and prohibited categories for foreign investment were unified into a Negative List, signaled the implementation of the Negative List system on a national scale.
- In 2015, MOFCOM issued a decision[1] which removed some of the restrictions on downstream investments by FIEs, eliminating the requirement that the FIE's registered capital be fully paid up and restrictions capping the amount of the downstream investment at 50% of the FIE's net assets, but left the requirement in place that the FIE must have started to turn a profit. At about the same time, the State Administration of Foreign Exchange (SAFE) issued what was known as Circular 19,[2] under which FIEs would be permitted to use their foreign exchange capital for downstream equity investments. However, the application of Circular 19 was limited in practice as some local SAFE authorities as well as bank officers took the position that only FIEs with the word "investment" in their business scopes were permitted to use their foreign exchange capital to make equity investments under Circular 19. Even so, there were reports of FIEs being able to use their foreign exchange capital to make downstream investments in certain cases, so Circular 19 still represented a partial step forward in connection with this long-standing challenge for FIEs.[3] And in July of 2019 the Shanghai Free Trade Zone promulgated new rules confirming that FIEs in the zone could make downstream investments pursuant to Circular 19 even if "investment" is

1 Decisions on Revising Certain Regulations and Regulated Documents, Accessed 3 September 2019. http://www.mofcom.gov.cn/article/b/c/201511/20151101152451.shtml.

2 Circular of the State Administration of Foreign Exchange on Reforming the Management Approach regarding the Settlement of Foreign Exchange Capital of Foreign-invested Enterprises, Accessed 3 September 2019. http://www.safe.gov.cn/safe/2015/0408/5549.html.

3 Riemenschneider, Jakob. "Safe Circular 19 - End or Beginning of the 'China Holding'?" Lexology, 9 November 2015. https://www.lexology.com/library/detail.aspx?g=2de96a60-e732-4cd2-987e-ac84054cd632.

在《外商投资法》通过前的最后几年中，中国采取了一系列措施来解决外商投资企业长期以来面临的挑战。例如：

- 2014年修订《公司法》，废除了针对新设企业（包括内资企业和外商投资企业）最低注册资本额以及实缴期限的要求。因此，实际上目前仅要求注册资本在公司清算之前完成实缴，并且不再需要提供验资报告。但是，投注差规则仍然适用并继续对外商投资企业的资本结构构成限制。

- 负面清单制度（详见下文第二章的论述）于2013年开始在上海自由贸易试验区开始试行，在2015年，这一制度扩大适用于中国的四个自贸试验区，并且也被包含在2015年《外国投资法（草案）》中。2017年版《外商投资产业指导目录》将外商投资限制类与禁止类统一编为负面清单，这标志着负面清单制度在全国范围内的实施。

- 2015年，商务部颁布了一项决定[1]，废除了针对外商投资企业再投资的一些限制，取消了关于外商投资企业的注册资本必须全部实缴以及再投资的金额上限为外商投资企业净资产50%的要求，但是关于外商投资企业已经开始盈利这一要求仍存在。与此同时，国家外汇管理局（外管局）发布了19号文[2]，其中规定了外商投资企业可以使用其外汇资本金进行再投资。但是，19号文的实际实施是受限制的，因为一些地方外管部门和银行认为只有经营范围中明确包含“投资”字样的外商投资企业方可使用外汇资本金进行19号文项下的股权投资。即使如此，据报道有外商投资企业在某些情况下成功使用了外汇资本金进行再投资的案例，因此19号文仍然可以看作针对外商投资企业长久

1 《关于修改部分规章和规范性文件的决定》（商务部令2015年第2号），http://www.mofcom.gov.cn/article/b/c/201511/20151101152451.shtml，2019年9月3日访问。

2 《国家外汇管理局关于改革外商投资企业外汇资本金结汇管理方式的通知》（汇发〔2015〕19号），http://www.safe.gov.cn/safe/2015/0408/5549.html，2019年9月3日访问。

not included in the FIE's approved business scope.[1]

- In 2016, the General Office of the State Council released a Notice[2] with a stated aim of integrating the business license, organization code certificate, tax registration certificate, social insurance registration certificate and statistical registration certificate - into "one license, one code," which was one business license affixed with a unified social credit code issued by the Administration of Industry and Commerce. Instead of separately applying for each of these certificates with each competent government authority, this new approach integrated the entire procedure for applying for all five categories of certificates into one simple procedure by applying for a business license so as to establish a new enterprise.
- As a capstone to all of these prior measures, the FIL was adopted in March of 2019, ushering in what will be the next stage of FDI in China, commencing with the effectiveness of the FIL on 1 January 2020. The implications of the FIL will be discussed in detail in the next chapter.
- Thereafter, in late October and late December 2019 several additional major developments occurred. First, SAFE issued a notice (the 2019 SAFE Notice)[3] in late October confirming the abolishment of prior restrictions on conversion of foreign exchange capital injections by non-investment FIEs for downstream investments nationwide, and then, at the end of December, the implementation regulations for the FIL (Implementation Regulations),[4] the Measures for Reporting Foreign Investment Information, and Circular of the State Administration for Market Regulation on Effective Work on Registration of Foreign-invested Enterprises for the Implementation

1 Rules to Facilitate Pilot Reforms of Foreign Exchange Administration in Shanghai Free Trade Zone issued by the State Administration of Foreign Exchange (SAFE) on 10 July 2019 (Shanghai FTZ Pilot Rules).

2 Opinions on Accelerating the Reform of the Enterprise Registration System to "Integrate Three Certificates into One," Accessed 29 August 2019. http://www.gov.cn/zhengce/content/2016-07/05/content_5088351.htm.

3 Circular of the State Administration of Foreign Exchange on Further Promoting the Cross-border Trade and Investment Facilitation, Accessed 25 October 2019. http://www.safe.gov.cn/safe/2019/1025/14469.html.

4 On 1 November 2019, draft Implementation Regulations were issued for comments (Draft Implementation Regulations) and the final Implementation Regulations were issued on 31 December 2019. The Draft Implementation Regulations can be found at http://www.moj.gov.cn/government_public/content/2019-11/01/657_3235067.html, and the final Implementation Regulations can be found at http://www.moj.gov.cn/government_public/content/2019-12/31/593_3239039.html.

以来面对的这一挑战而前进的一小步。[1]而就在2019年7月，上海自由贸易试验区颁布了新规，确认了试验区内的外商投资企业可以根据19号文进行再投资，即使其经批准的经营范围中并不包括“投资”字样。[2]

- 2016年，国务院办公厅发布了一则通知[3]，旨在将营业执照、组织机构代码证、税务登记证、社会保险登记证和统计登记证合并，实行“五证合一、一照一码”，即在营业执照上附上由工商局签发的统一社会信用代码。这一新规将设立一个新企业时分别向各有关政府部门申请五个不同证照的流程整合成仅需申请一份营业执照的简单手续。
- 作为所有这些先前措施的顶点，《外商投资法》于2019年3月通过，从2020年1月1日《外商投资法》生效开始，中国将迎来外商直接投资的下一个阶段。《外商投资法》的影响将在下一章中详细讨论。
- 此后，在2019年10月底和12月底又有几个重大进展。一是国家外汇管理局于10月底发布通知（以下简称《2019年外管局通知》）[4]，确认在全国范围内取消过去存在的非投资性外商投资企业以资本金结汇开展境内股权投资的限制，然后，在12月底，《中华人民共和国外商投资法实

1 Riemenschneider, Jakob. “Safe Circular 19 - End or Beginning of the ‘China Holding’?” Lexology, November 9, 2015. https://www.lexology.com/library/detail.aspx?g=2de96a60-e732-4cd2-987e-ac84054cd632.

2 国家外汇管理局上海分局2019年7月10日发布《进一步推进中国（上海）自由贸易试验区外汇管理改革试点实施细则（4.0版）》（以下简称上海自贸区细则）。

3 《国务院办公厅关于加快推进“五证合一、一照一码”登记制度改革的通知》，政府信息公开专栏，http://www.gov.cn/zhengce/content/2016-07/05/content_5088351.htm，2019年8月29日访问。

4 《国家外汇管理局关于进一步促进跨境贸易投资便利化的通知》，http://www.safe.gov.cn/safe/2019/1025/14469.html，2019年10月25日访问。

of the Foreign Investment Law were issued. These important developments will also be discussed further in the next chapter.

In sum, many of the most persistent problems for FIEs over the past decades had been mitigated to a significant degree through the above measures taken even prior to the adoption of the FIL and now with the passage of the FIL and the issuance of the 2019 SAFE Notice, foreign investment in China should be subject to many fewer obstacles going forward.

The continued improvement in FDI conditions even prior to the passage of the FIL and the issuance of the 2019 SAFE Notice resulted in China attaining a rank of number 46 out of 190 countries surveyed in the 2019 World Bank Doing Business Report, jumping up 32 places from its rank of number 78 in the 2018 report, ahead of countries such as Israel, Italy and India. Following the adoption of the FIL, China jumped up another 15 spots to rank number 31 in the world in the latest World Bank Doing Business Report, an extraordinary improvement of 45 places in a very short two-year period. (See further analysis below.)

The current decade also saw the rapid expansion of Chinese outbound investment, a trend that had its early beginnings in the prior decade, but which accelerated at a remarkable clip throughout the first half of this decade. The amount of outbound direct investment (ODI) surpassed FDI inflows for the first time in 2015 and hit a peak in 2016 before undergoing a much needed rectification in late 2016 and early 2017 to mitigate problems arising from over-heated ODI market conditions.[1] Since that high point in 2016 ODI has fallen dramatically, and in 2018 total ODI capital outflows once again fell below FDI capital inflows, and ODI fell even more in 2019, while at the same time FDI set another new record high (See Figure 1-A).

1 Lewis, Robert. *Why So Many Chinese Outbound Investment Fail*, (Beijing: China Machine Press, 2016), 6.

施条例》（以下简称《外商投资法实施条例》）[1]、《外商投资信息报告办法》、《市场监管总局关于贯彻落实〈外商投资法〉做好外商投资企业登记注册工作的通知》相继发布。这些重要的事态发展也将在下一章进一步讨论。

总而言之，通过上述措施，外商投资企业在过去几十年中遇到的许多最顽固的问题在很大程度上已得到缓解，现在，随着《外商投资法》的通过和《2019年外管局通知》的发布，外国投资在中国应该会遇到更少的障碍。

“总而言之，通过上述措施，外商投资企业在过去几十年中遇到的许多最顽固的问题在很大程度上已得到缓解，现在，随着《外商投资法》的通过和2019年外管局通知的发布，外国投资在中国应该会遇到更少的障碍。”

即使是在《外商投资法》通过和《2019年外管局通知》发布之前，外商直接投资环境的持续改善，已使中国在2019年世界银行《营商环境报告》调查的190个国家中排名第46位，比2018年的第78位上升了32位，领先于以色列、意大利和印度等国家。在《外商投资法》通过后，在最新的世界银行《营商环境报告》中，中国的排名又跃升了15位，居世界第31位。在短短的两年时间里，中国取得了上升45名的惊人进步。（见下文进一步分析。）

当前十年中国对外投资也在迅速扩张，这一趋势从上一个10年开始，在当前十年的前五年内开始以惊人的速度上升。2015年对外直接投资总额首次超过外商直接投资总额，并在2016年达到峰值，然后在2016年年底和2017年年初经历了必要的调整，以缓解对外直接投资市场过热而产生的问题。[2]对外直接投资总额从2016年的顶峰急剧下降后，在2018年再度低于外商直接投资总额，并且在2019年进一步呈下降趋势，而同时外商直接投资又创造了一个新纪录（见图1-A）。

1 2019年11月1日，《中华人民共和国外商投资法实施条例（征求意见稿）》发布征求意见，2019年12月31日《中华人民共和国外商投资法实施条例》正式发布。《司法部关于〈中华人民共和国外商投资法实施条例（征求意见稿）〉公开征求意见的通知》请参见 http://www.moj.gov.cn/government_public/content/2019-11/01/657_3235067.html，《中华人民共和国外商投资法实施条例》请参见 http://www.moj.gov.cn/government_public/content/2019-12/31/593_3239039.html。

2 ［美］吕立山（Robert Lewis）：《国际并购游戏规则：如何提高中国企业走出去成功率》，机械工业出版社2017年版，第6页。

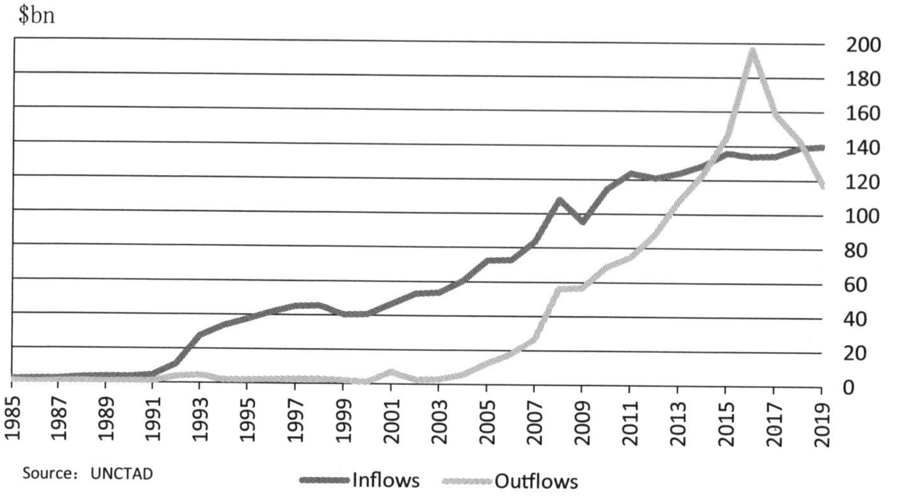

Figure 1–A FDI vs. ODI through 2019[1]

China's ODI story is not over by any means, and as the Chinese economy continues to mature, Chinese companies will naturally continue to look to expand to international markets. At the same time, the growing strength of China's economy will attract, and need, more foreign investment to continue to move up the value chain and improve overall competitive efficiencies.

Projecting Future FDI Trends

Many People may erroneously consider that as production costs continue to rise in China that the golden era of FDI in China has now come to an end. In fact, the opposite is the case: China is in an extremely enviable position in terms of attracting FDI now and going forward.

According to the 2019 World Investment Report published by the United Nations Conference on Trade and Development (UNCTAD), China was ranked the world's second largest FDI recipient after United States and before Hong Kong (although arguably much of the inbound investment into Hong Kong was ultimately destined for China as Hong Kong

1 商务数据中心. Accessed 27 April 2020. http://data.mofcom.gov.cn/lywz/inmr.shtml (FDI data); 商务数据中心. Accessed 27 April 2020. http://data.mofcom.gov.cn/tzhz/fordirinvest.shtml (ODI data). UNCTAD. Accessed 27 April 2020. https://unctadstat.unctad.org/wds/TableViewer/tableView.aspx?ReportId=96740. Xinhua. "China remains second largest FDI recipient in 2019: UNCTAD," January 21, 2020. http://www.china.org.cn/world/Off_the_Wire/2020-01/21/content_75634271.htm. The UNCTAD data on ODI flows for 2019 is not available at the time this book was submitted for publication so it has been supplemented with data available from MOFCOM

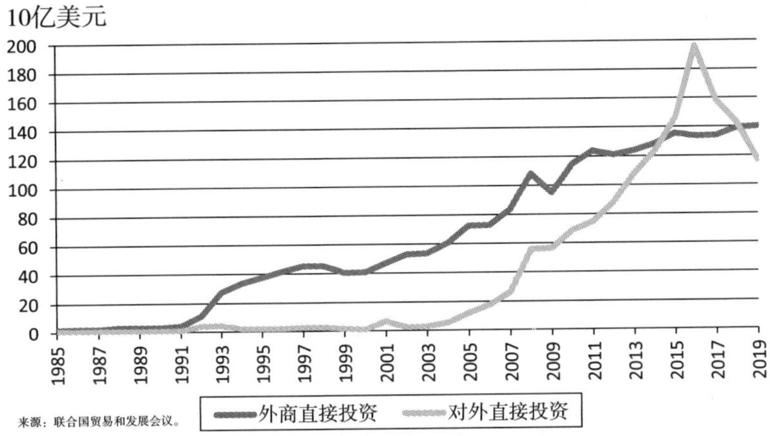

来源：联合国贸易和发展会议。

图 1–A 截至 2019 年外商直接投资 vs. 对外直接投资[1]

无论如何，中国的对外直接投资不会结束，随着中国经济的不断成熟，中国企业会自然而然地希望向国际市场扩张。同时，不断增长的中国经济实力将吸引并需要更多外国投资来继续提升价值链并提高整体竞争效率。

未来外商直接投资趋势的预测

许多人可能会错误地认为，随着中国生产成本的持续上升，中国外商直接投资的黄金时代现在已经结束。事实上，情况正好相反，中国现在和未来都将处于吸引外商直接投资的黄金时代。

根据联合国贸易和发展会议（以下简称“联合国贸发会议”）发布的《2019 年世界投资报告》，中国内地被列为世界第二大外商直接投资接收地，仅次于美国，高于中国香港特别行政区（但是可以说，对香港的入境投资很多都最终投向中国内地，因为香港是中国内地外商直接投资资本流入的最大来源，占所有对华外

1 商务数据中心，http://data.mofcom.gov.cn/lywz/inmr.shtml (FDI data)，2020 年 4 月 27 日访问。商务数据中心，http://data.mofcom.gov.cn/tzhz/fordirinvest.shtml (ODI data)，2020 年 4 月 27 日访问。联合国贸易和发展会议（UNCTAD），https://unctadstat.unctad.org/wds/TableViewer/tableView.aspx?ReportId=96740，2020 年 4 月 27 日访问。新华社，“2019 年中国仍是第二大外资流入国”，2020 年 1 月 21 日，http://www.china.org.cn/world/Off_the_Wire/2020-01/21/content_75634271.htm。由于截至本书送交出版之时，联合国贸发会议 2019 年对外直接投资相关数据尚未公布，本图中 2019 年的对外直接投资数据是基于商务部发布的数据。

is China's single largest source of FDI capital inflows accounting for 83.45% of all FDI into China in 2018). China's economy was ranked the second most attractive to multinational companies for 2017-2019, only behind the U.S.[1]

Perhaps more significantly, FDI into China has been increasing in the last few years at a record pace at a time when FDI into most other leading countries has softened. According to the UNCTAD 2019 World Investment Report:

- Global foreign direct investment (FDI) flows continued their slide in 2018, falling by 13 per cent to $1.3 trillion. (See Figure 1-B.) The decline – the third consecutive year's fall in FDI – was mainly due to large-scale repatriations of accumulated foreign earnings by United States multinational enterprises (MNEs) in the first two quarters of 2018, following tax reforms introduced in that country at the end of 2017.

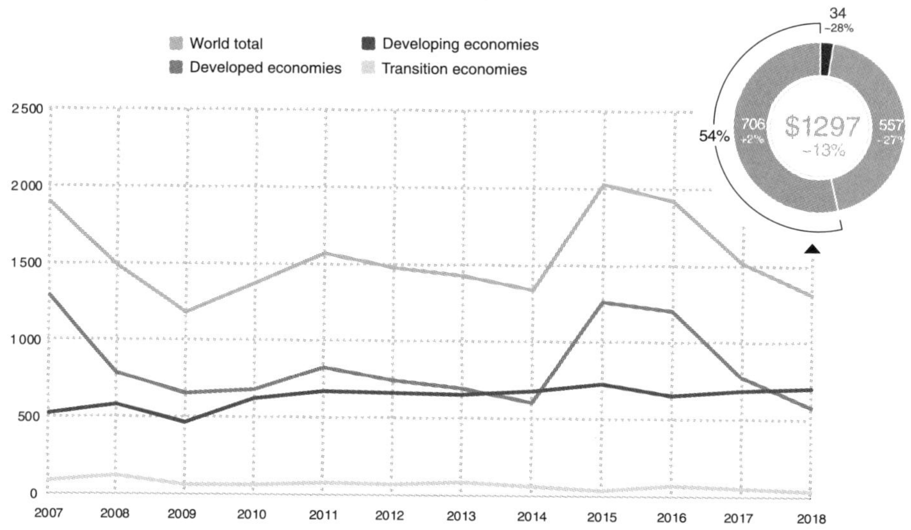

Figure 1–B FDI inflows, global and by economic group, 2007–2018

- FDI flows to developed economies reached their lowest point since 2004, declining by 27 per cent. Inflows to Europe halved to less than $200 billion; a few important host countries of United States MNEs registered negative inflows. (The repatriation of funds by United States MNEs translated into negative inflows in host countries.) FDI flows to Ireland and Switzerland fell to -$66 billion and -$87 billion, respectively.

1 United Nations World Investment Report. https://unctad.org/en/PublicationsLibrary/wir2019_en.pdf (Figure I.3).

商直接投资的 83.45%）。2017—2019 年中国经济对跨国公司的吸引力排名第二，仅次于美国。[1]

可能更显著的是，当其他大多数主要国家的外商直接投资有所疲软时，对中国的外商直接投资在过去几年中以创纪录的速度增长。根据联合国贸发会议的《2019 年世界投资报告》：

- 2018 年，全球外国直接投资流量继续下滑，减少 13%，降至 1.3 万亿美元（见图 1–B）。这是外国直接投资流量连续第三年出现下降，主要原因是，2017 年年底美国实行税制改革后，美国跨国企业在 2018 年前两个季度将累积的国外收益大规模汇回本国……

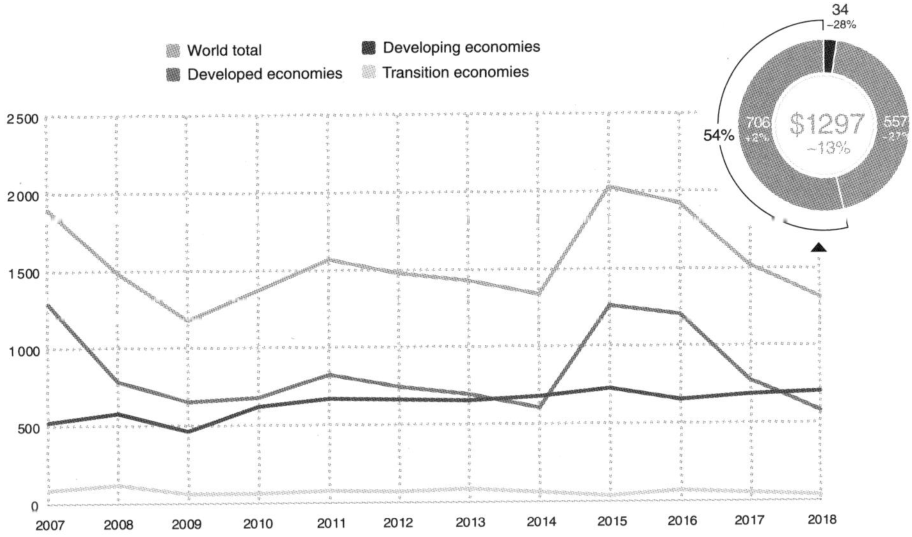

图 1–B　全球及各类经济体的外商直接投资额，2007—2018

- 流入发达经济体的外国直接投资达到 2004 年以来的最低点，减少了 27%。流入欧洲的资金减少了一半，降至低于 2000 亿美元，一些美国跨国企业的重要东道国出现投资负流入（美国跨国企业汇回资金导致东道国出现投资负流入）。流入爱尔兰和瑞士的外国直接投资分别减少至 −660 亿美元和 −870

1　联合国贸发会议《2019 年世界投资报告》，https://unctad.org/en/PublicationsLibrary/wir2019_en.pdf (Figure I.3)。

FDI flows to the United Kingdom also declined, by 36 per cent to $64 billion, as new equity investments halved. FDI into the United States declined as well, by 9 per cent to $252 billion—the average of the last 10 years. That decline was mainly due to a fall by one third in cross-border M&A sales. Australia's FDI inflows reached $60 billion – a record level – as foreign affiliates reinvested a record $25 billion of their profits in the country. FDI flows to developing economies remained stable, rising by 2 per cent to $706 billion. As a result of the increase and the anomalous fall in developed countries, the share of developing economies in global FDI increased to 54 per cent, a record. Their presence among the top 20 host economies remained unchanged (figure 1-B). The United States remained the largest recipient of FDI, followed by China, Hong Kong (China) and Singapore.[1]

One commentator has cited the following factors as being key drivers of FDI into China: (1) China has a well-developed infrastructure and a strong work-force; (2) China's regulatory environment, long a weak point, is improving; (3) China has enjoyed a long period of economic growth and political stability; (4) China boasts a robust business climate with unparalleled market size; and (5) China in general offers export-friendly policies which allow foreign investors to service both the Chinese market as well as foreign markets.[2] Assuming these conditions remain stable or continue to improve, the long term trends for FDI should remain positive for China, and even if there are disruptions (as with the COVID-19 pandemic), the impact should be relatively short-lived, as was the case with the recovery of inbound FDI into China following the global financial crisis.

Many of the elements cited above as key drivers for FDI into China are universal in application, explaining why the US is the top destination for FDI from around the world. The stronger the host country economy, the more foreign investment it will attract. China already has the top economy in the world by the standard of Purchasing Power Parity (PPP), with China leading both the US and the EU.[3]The US still leads China in nominal GDP but China is

1 World Investment Report 2019, World Investment Report 2019 § (n.d.). https://unctad.org/en/PublicationsLibrary/wir2019_en.pdf (page 1).

2 Bloomenthal, Andrew. "Six Factors Driving Investment in China." Investopedia. Investopedia, 29 May 2019. https://www.investopedia.com/articles/economics/09/factors-drive-investment-in-china.asp.

3 "GDP, PPP (Current International $)." Data. Accessed 30 August 2019. https://data.worldbank.org/indicator/NY.GDP.MKTP.PP.CD?locations=CN-US.

> 亿美元。由于新股权投资减半，流入英国的外国直接投资也出现缩减，减少了36%，降至640亿美元。流入美国的外国直接投资也减少了9%，降至2520亿美元——相当于过去10年的平均水平。这种下降主要是因为跨境并购交易减少了1/3。流入澳大利亚的外国直接投资达到创纪录的600亿美元，原因是外国子公司将在该国取得的利润进行了再投资，达250亿美元。流入发展中经济体的外国直接投资保持稳定，增长2%，达到7060亿美元。由于这种增幅以及对发达国家的外国直接投资的异常下降，发展中经济体在全球外国直接投资流入量中所占份额上升到54%，创下历史新高。排名前20的东道国经济体中的发展中经济体保持不变（见图1–B）。美国仍然是外国直接投资的最大接受地，其次是中国内地、中国香港和新加坡。[1]

有评论人士指出，以下因素是外商直接投资进入中国的关键驱动因素：（1）中国基础设施完善，劳动力充足；（2）中国的监管环境——长期以来的薄弱点——正在不断改善；（3）长期以来中国经济增长，政治稳定；（4）中国拥有稳健的商业环境，有着无与伦比的市场规模；（5）中国总体上提供出口友好型政策，允许外国投资者同时为中国市场和国外市场提供服务。[2]假设这些条件保持稳定或继续改善，中国外商直接投资的长期趋势应保持积极态势，即使出现中断（比如新型冠状病毒肺炎疫情的暴发导致的中断），其影响也应该相对短暂，就如全球金融危机之后流入中国的外商直接投资的恢复情况一样。

上述作为中国外商直接投资的关键驱动因素中，很多要素都具有普适性，也解释了为什么美国是世界各地外商直接投资的首

---

1 World Investment Report 2019, World Investment Report 2019 § (n.d.). https://unctad.org/en/PublicationsLibrary/wir2019_en.pdf（第1页）。

2 Bloomenthal, Andrew. “Six Factors Driving Investment in China.” Investopedia. Investopedia, May 29, 2019. https://www.investopedia.com/articles/economics/09/factors-drive-investment-in-china.asp.

projected to pass the US by 2030.[1] However, China still lags behind other developed countries in terms of GDP per capita, with China's per capita revenue still less than one-third of South Korea or Spain and only one-fifth that of Singapore or the US.[2] In sum, by many key measures China is already in a leading position for FDI but still with substantial room to grow. China's projected continued economic growth and strength will naturally attract ever increasing investment from foreign MNCs and SMEs, which will continue to come to participate in the most vibrant economy in the world.

The key will be to continue to improve the overall business environment, removing remaining legacy impediments to investment. An analysis of the World Bank Doing Business Report rankings can shed some light on the progress made in China to date and the opportunities for further improvements in the business environment. The Doing Business Report evaluates countries against a uniform set of standards across ten key categories, including the procedures, time and cost to start a business, investor protections, taxes, import/export procedures, registration procedures for commercial real estate, access to credit, debt collection and contract enforcement generally, etc.

From the inception of the World Bank Doing Business Report rankings in 2006 through 2017, China made only modest improvement in its overall ranking, vacillating between a low of 96th in 2014 to a high of 76th in 2017 and 2018 (which ranking was nearly matched in 2011 when it achieved a ranking of 79th), with an average ranking of roughly 87th, placing it at the back end of the top half, well below most developed countries. But in the 2019 report, China jumped 32 spots up to 46th in the world by this measure. What was the reason for this dramatic improvement? According to the World Bank report, the improvement in China's Doing Business ranking appears to be the result of the cumulative effect of the following changes referenced in the Doing Business report over the last few years (which mirror many of the pre-FIL points referenced above):

- The elimination of minimum capital requirements and the need to obtain a capital verification certificate;

---

1 "China Will Overtake the U.S. in Less Than 15 Years, HSBC Says." Accessed 30 August 2019. https://www.bloomberg.com/news/articles/2018-09-25/hsbc-sees-china-economy-set-to-pass-u-s-as-number-one-by-2030.

2 "GDP per Capita (Current US$)." Data. Accessed 30 August 2019. https://data.worldbank.org/indicator/NY.GDP.PCAP.CD?locations=CN-US-KR-ES-SG.

选目的地。东道国经济越强，吸引的外商投资就越多。按购买力平价标准，中国已经是世界上最大的经济体，领先于美国和欧盟。[1]美国仍然在名义国内生产总值上领先中国，但预计中国将在2030年之前超过美国。[2]然而，从人均GDP来看，中国仍落后于其他发达国家，中国的人均收入仍不到韩国或西班牙的1/3，仅为新加坡或美国的1/5。[3]总之，通过一系列关键举措，中国已经处于外商直接投资的领先地位，但仍有很大的提升空间。中国可预计的持续性经济增长和经济实力自然会吸引越来越多的境外跨国公司和中小企业投资，这些外国跨国公司和中小企业将继续参与到这个全球最具活力的经济体当中。

“总之，通过一系列关键举措，中国已经处于外商直接投资的领先地位，但仍有很大的提升空间。中国可预计的持续性经济增长和经济实力自然会吸引越来越多的境外跨国公司和中小企业投资，这些外国跨国公司和中小企业将继续参与到这个全球最具活力的经济体当中。”

核心要素在于继续改善整体商业环境，消除遗留的投资障碍。对世界银行《营商环境报告》排名的分析可以揭示中国迄今为止取得的进步以及进一步改善商业环境的机会。《营商环境报告》以一套涵盖十个核心类别的统一标准对各国进行评估，包括开展新的商业经营的程序、时间和成本、投资者保护、税收、进出口程序、商业不动产登记程序、信贷获取渠道、债务追收和合同执行等。

从2006年世界银行《营商环境报告》排名开始至2017年，中国的总体排名仅略有提升，最低时为2014年的第96位，最高时为2017年和2018年的第78位（与2011年第79位的排名基本持平），平均排名第87位，位于排名前半段国家的末端，远低于大多数发达国家。但在2019年的报告中，中国在全球范围内的排名上升了32位，到达第46位。这一巨大提升的原因是什么？根据世界银行的报告，中国营商环境排名的提升可能归功于以下各项变化的累计

1 “GDP, PPP (Current International $)”，https://data.worldbank.org/indicator/NY.GDP.MKTP.PP.CD?locations=CN-US，2019年8月30日访问。

2 “China Will Overtake the U.S. in Less Than 15 Years, HSBC Says.”，https://www.bloomberg.com/news/articles/2018-09-25/hsbc-sees-china-economy-set-to-pass-u-s-as-number-one-by-2030，2019年8月30日访问。

3 “GDP per Capita (Current US$)”，https://data.worldbank.org/indicator/NY.GDP.PCAP.CD?locations=CN-US-KR-ES-SG，2019年8月30日访问。

- The introduction of the consolidated registration process combining the business license, organization code certificate, tax registration certificate, social insurance registration certificate and statistical registration certificate;
- The adoption of a streamlined online registration process and the replacement of the MOFCOM approval scheme with the record-filing scheme upon the implementation of the Negative List scheme; and
- The relaxation of restrictions on downstream investments.

Taking into account the last factor listed above was perhaps a bit premature on the part of the World Bank given the continuing practical limitations on FIE downstream investments at that time, but with the issuance of the 2019 SAFE Notice, the anticipated benefits of this long hoped-for development should now be fully realized. Other factors that contributed to the large jump up the rankings in the 2019 report also included the streamlined building permit and property registration process, improved access to electricity, abolition of the business tax and streamlining of payment of stamp taxes and implementation of a single window for import/export clearances.

But while these pre-FIL improvements in China's rankings in the 2019 World Bank Doing Business Report are laudatory, it is clear from Charts 1-C and 1-D that prior to the adoption of the FIL, China still lagged behind not only the world's top economies but also many countries/territories in the Asia-Pacific region. In the Asia-Pacific region, New Zealand, Hong Kong and Singapore have consistently been ranked in the top 5 globally, and South Korea has made remarkable progress from early rankings in the high 20s to be a consistent top 5 finisher in the last five years. By contrast, Japan, which was once in the top 10, in last year's World Bank Doing Business Report saw its ranking slide to 39th, going in the complete opposite direction of China (although it did rebound to take 29th position in the 2020 report). India also made dramatic improvement in the 2019 rankings, but still trailed China (and as will be seen below, after giving effect to the FIL, the gap between China and India increased further in the most recent rankings).

效果，这些变化在过去几年的营商环境报告中有所提及（也与上文提及的《外商投资法》通过之前的许多要点相呼应）：

- 取消最低注册资本额以及获得验资证明的要求；
- 采用统一的登记程序，将营业执照、组织机构代码证、税务登记证、社保登记证和统计登记证进行统一；
- 采用更加简化的在线登记程序，并通过实施负面清单制度以商务部门的备案制代替审批制；
- 放宽对再投资的限制。

世界银行将上述最后一个因素考虑在内，可能有点为时过早，因为当时对外商投资企业再投资的实际限制仍持续存在，但随着《2019 年外管局通知》的发布，这一长期以来所期望的发展的预期利益现在应该得到了充分实现。促进 2019 年排名大幅提升的其他因素还包括简化建筑许可和不动产登记程序、改进电力供应、废除营业税、简化印花税缴付以及实施国际贸易单一窗口。

虽然在《外商投资法》通过前中国在 2019 年世界银行《营商环境报告》中排名的这些进步值得肯定，但从表 1-C 和表 1-D 可以清楚地看出，在《外商投资法》通过前，中国内地不仅仍然落后于世界顶级经济体，还落后于亚太地区的很多国家和地区。在亚太地区，新西兰、中国香港和新加坡一直在全球排名前五，而韩国从早先排名前 20 位上升为过去五年中一直保持的前 5 位，取得了显著的进步。相比之下，曾经位于前 10 名的日本，在 2019 年的世界银行《营商环境报告》中其排名已下滑至第 39 位，与中国的趋势完全相反（尽管其在 2020 年的排名中又回升至第 29 位）。印度也在 2019 年排名中取得了显著的进步，但仍落后于中国（并且在下表中可以看到，在《外商投资法》颁布后，在最新的排名中，中国和印度之间的差距进一步加大）。

Chart 1–C Doing Business Rankings for Asia–Pacific (Pre–FIL)[1]

	2006	2007	2008	2009	2010	2011	2012	2013	2014	2015	2016	2017	2018	2019
New Zealand	1	2	2	2	2	3	3	3	3	2	2	1	1	1
Singapore	2	1	1	1	1	1	1	1	1	1	1	2	2	2
Hong Kong SAR	7	5	4	4	3	2	2	2	2	3	5	4	5	4
South Korea	27	23	30	23	19	16	8	8	7	5	4	5	4	5
Malaysia	21	25	24	20	23	21	18	12	6	18	18	23	24	15
Australia	6	8	9	9	9	10	15	10	11	10	13	15	14	18
Thailand	20	18	15	13	12	19	17	18	18	26	49	46	26	27
Japan	10	11	12	12	15	18	20	24	27	29	34	34	34	39
China	91	93	83	83	89	79	91	91	96	90	84	78	78	46
Vietnam	99	104	91	92	93	78	98	99	99	78	90	82	68	69
Indonesia	115	135	123	129	122	121	129	128	120	114	109	91	72	73
India	116	134	120	122	133	134	132	132	134	142	130	130	100	77
Philippines	113	126	133	140	144	148	136	138	108	95	103	99	113	124
Cambodia	133	143	145	135	145	147	138	133	137	135	127	131	135	138
Laos	147	159	164	165	167	171	165	163	159	148	134	139	141	154
Myanmar	N/A	N/A	N/A	N/A	N/A	N/A	N/A	N/A	182	177	167	170	171	172

Chart 1–D Doing Business Rankings for Other Selected Countries (Pre–FIL)[2]

	2006	2007	2008	2009	2010	2011	2012	2013	2014	2015	2016	2017	2018	2019
USA	3	3	3	3	4	5	4	4	4	7	7	8	6	8
UK	9	6	6	6	5	4	7	7	10	8	6	7	7	9
UAE	69	77	68	46	33	40	33	26	23	22	31	26	21	11
Canada	4	4	7	8	8	7	13	17	19	16	14	22	18	22
Germany	19	21	20	25	25	22	19	20	21	14	15	17	20	24
Russia	79	96	106	120	120	123	120	112	92	62	51	40	35	31

1 "Ease of Doing Business Index (1=Most Business-Friendly Regulations)." Data. Accessed 30 August 2019. https://data.worldbank.org/indicator/IC.BUS.EASE.XQ?name_desc=false.

2 "Ease of Doing Business Index (1=Most Business-Friendly Regulations)." Data. Accessed 30 August 2019.https://data.worldbank.org/indicator/IC.BUS.EASE.XQ?name_desc=false.

表 1–C　亚太地区营商环境排名（《外商投资法》通过前）[1]

	2006	2007	2008	2009	2010	2011	2012	2013	2014	2015	2016	2017	2018	2019
新西兰	1	2	2	2	2	3	3	3	3	2	2	1	1	1
新加坡	2	1	1	1	1	1	1	1	1	1	1	2	2	2
中国香港	7	5	4	4	3	2	2	2	2	3	5	4	5	4
韩国	27	23	30	23	19	16	8	8	7	5	4	5	4	5
马来西亚	21	25	24	20	23	21	18	12	6	18	18	23	24	15
澳大利亚	6	8	9	9	9	10	15	10	11	10	13	15	14	18
泰国	20	18	15	13	12	19	17	18	18	26	49	46	26	27
日本	10	11	12	12	15	18	20	24	27	29	34	34	34	39
中国	91	93	83	83	89	79	91	91	96	90	84	78	78	46
越南	99	104	91	92	93	78	98	99	99	78	90	82	68	69
印度尼西亚	115	135	123	129	122	121	129	128	120	114	109	91	72	73
印度	116	134	120	122	133	134	132	132	134	142	130	130	100	77
菲律宾	113	126	133	140	144	148	136	138	108	95	103	99	113	124
柬埔寨	133	143	145	135	145	147	138	133	137	135	127	131	135	138
老挝	147	159	164	165	167	171	165	163	159	148	134	139	141	154
缅甸	N/A	N/A	N/A	N/A	N/A	N/A	N/A	N/A	182	177	167	170	171	172

表 1–D　其他特定国家营商环境排名（《外商投资法》通过前）[2]

	2006	2007	2008	2009	2010	2011	2012	2013	2014	2015	2016	2017	2018	2019
美国	3	3	3	3	4	5	4	4	4	7	7	8	6	8
英国	9	6	6	6	5	4	7	7	10	8	6	7	7	9
阿联酋	69	77	68	46	33	40	33	26	23	22	31	26	21	11
加拿大	4	4	7	8	8	7	13	17	19	16	14	22	18	22
德国	19	21	20	25	25	22	19	20	21	14	15	17	20	24
俄罗斯	79	96	106	120	120	123	120	112	92	62	51	40	35	31

1　“Ease of Doing Business Index (1=Most Business-Friendly Regulations)”，https://data.worldbank.org/indicator/IC.BUS.EASE.XQ?name_desc=false，2019 年 8 月 30 日访问。

2　“Ease of Doing Business Index (1=Most Business-Friendly Regulations)”，https://data.worldbank.org/indicator/IC.BUS.EASE.XQ?name_desc=false，2019 年 8 月 30 日访问。

Continued

	2006	2007	2008	2009	2010	2011	2012	2013	2014	2015	2016	2017	2018	2019
France	44	35	31	31	31	26	29	34	38	31	27	19	31	32
Poland	54	75	74	76	72	70	62	55	45	32	25	24	27	33
Turkey	93	91	57	59	73	65	71	71	69	55	55	69	60	43
Israel	29	26	29	30	29	29	34	38	35	40	53	52	54	49
Italy	70	82	53	65	78	80	87	73	65	56	45	50	46	51
Mexico	73	43	44	56	51	35	53	48	53	39	38	47	49	54
South Africa	28	29	35	32	34	34	35	39	41	43	73	74	82	82
Saudi Arabia	38	38	23	16	13	11	12	22	26	49	82	94	92	92
Brazil	119	121	122	125	129	127	126	130	116	120	116	123	125	109
Argentina	77	101	109	113	118	115	113	124	126	124	121	116	117	119

When we look at the ranking of other prominent countries in Chart 1-D, we can see that prior to the passage of the FIL China not only still trailed by some margin behind the major economies such as the US, UK, Canada, Germany and France, but also Russia, Poland and Turkey. Russia is a particularly instructive example. In 2012, when it was ranked 120th on the Doing Business Report index, Russia set a goal to be ranked in the top 20 by 2018. While it did not achieve this target, Russia still made dramatic progress, achieving a ranking of 25th in 2018 and 31st in the 2019 report, a much better ranking than China's 2019 pre-FIL ranking after starting from a much lower position. As will be seen below, even after taking into account the FIL, China still trails Russia in the rankings. This demonstrates that active measures can improve the business regulatory environment and make a country more attractive for foreign investors, even where the underlying economic conditions are not as robust, as in the case of Russia.

China's post-FIL ranking in the most recent 2020 Doing Business Report confirms that the improvements in China's FDI regulatory environment are continuing to have a positive impact. A look at the top 50 economies in the survey (see Chart 1-E) shows that the gap between China and the world's other leading economies has closed significantly.

续表

	2006	2007	2008	2009	2010	2011	2012	2013	2014	2015	2016	2017	2018	2019
法国	44	35	31	31	31	26	29	34	38	31	27	19	31	32
波兰	54	75	74	76	72	70	62	55	45	32	25	24	27	33
土耳其	93	91	57	59	73	65	71	71	69	55	55	69	60	43
以色列	29	26	29	30	29	29	34	38	35	40	53	52	54	49
意大利	70	82	53	65	78	80	87	73	65	56	45	50	46	51
墨西哥	73	43	44	56	51	35	53	48	53	39	38	47	49	54
南非	28	29	35	32	34	34	35	39	41	43	73	74	82	82
沙特阿拉伯	38	38	23	16	13	11	12	22	26	49	82	94	92	92
巴西	119	121	122	125	129	127	126	130	116	120	116	123	125	109
阿根廷	77	101	109	113	118	115	113	124	126	124	121	116	117	119

当我们查看表 1-D 中其他主要国家的排名时，可以看到在《外商投资法》通过前中国不仅仅落后于美国、英国、加拿大、德国和法国等主要经济体，也落后于俄罗斯、波兰和土耳其。俄罗斯是一个特别具有启发性的例子。2012 年俄罗斯在《营商环境报告》中排名第 120 位，其设定了 2018 年排名前 20 位的目标。虽然没有实现这一目标，但俄罗斯仍取得了显著的进步，于 2018 年排名第 25 位，2019 年排名第 31 位，其起点相对低很多，但排名已经远远超过中国在《外商投资法》通过前的排名。如表 1-E 所示，即使考虑到《外商投资法》，中国在排名上仍落后于俄罗斯。这表明，即使一个国家的基础经济条件不那么强劲，积极的举措也可以改善商业监管环境，让其对外国投资者更具吸引力，正如我们在俄罗斯的例子中所看到的。

《外商投资法》通过后，中国在最近的 2020 年《营商环境报告》中的排名证实了中国外商直接投资监管环境的改善正在持续产生积极的影响。从调查中前 50 强的经济体（见表 1- E）的排名来看，中国与世界其他主要经济体之间的差距已经显著缩小。

Chart 1–E 2020 Doing Business Rankings for Top 50 Economies (Post–FIL)[1]

Rank	Economy	DB Score	Rank	Economy	DB Score
1	New Zealand	86.8	26	Iceland	79.0
2	Singapore	86.2	27	Austria	78.7
3	Hong Kong SAR, China	85.3	28	Russian Federation	78.2
4	Denmark	85.3	29	Japan	78.0
5	Korea, Rep.	84.0	30	Spain	77.9
6	United States	84.0	31	China	77.9
7	Georgia	83.7	32	France	76.8
8	United Kingdom	83.5	33	Turkey	76.8
9	Norway	82.6	34	Azerbaijan	76.7
10	Sweden	82.0	35	Israel	76.7
11	Lithuania	81.6	36	Switzerland	76.6
12	Malaysia	81.5	37	Slovenia	76.5
13	Mauritius	81.5	38	Rwanda	76.5
14	Australia	81.2	39	Portugal	76.5
15	Taiwan, China	80.9	40	Poland	76.4
16	United Arab Emirates	80.9	41	Czech Republic	76.3
17	North Macedonia	80.7	42	Netherlands	76.1
18	Estonia	80.6	43	Bahrain	76.0
19	Latvia	80.3	44	Serbia	75.7
20	Finland	80.2	45	Slovak Republic	75.6
21	Thailand	80.1	46	Belgium	75.0
22	Germany	79.7	47	Armenia	74.5
23	Canada	79.6	48	Moldova	74.4
24	Ireland	79.6	49	Belarus	74.3
25	Kazakhstan	79.6	50	Montenegro	73.8

1 "Doing Business 2020: Comparing Business Regulations in 190 Economies." Accessed 7 November 2019. Available at https://www.doingbusiness.org/content/dam/doingBusiness/pdf/db2020/Doing-Business-2020_rankings.pdf.

表 1-E　2020 年前 50 强经济体营商环境排名（《外商投资法》通过后）[1]

排名	经济体	《营商环境报告》评分	排名	经济体	《营商环境报告》评分
1	新西兰	86.8	26	冰岛	79.0
2	新加坡	86.2	27	奥地利	78.7
3	中国香港	85.3	28	俄罗斯	78.2
4	丹麦	85.3	29	日本	78.0
5	韩国	84.0	30	西班牙	77.9
6	美国	84.0	31	中国	77.9
7	格鲁吉亚	83.7	32	法国	76.8
8	英国	83.5	33	土耳其	76.8
9	挪威	82.6	34	阿塞拜疆	76.7
10	瑞典	82.0	35	以色列	76.7
11	立陶宛	81.6	36	瑞士	76.6
12	马来西亚	81.5	37	斯洛文尼亚	76.5
13	毛里求斯	81.5	38	卢旺达	76.5
14	澳大利亚	81.2	39	葡萄牙	76.5
15	中国台湾	80.9	40	波兰	76.4
16	阿联酋	80.9	41	捷克	76.3
17	北马其顿共和国	80.7	42	荷兰	76.1
18	爱沙尼亚	80.6	43	巴林岛	76.0
19	拉脱维亚	80.3	44	塞尔维亚	75.7
20	芬兰	80.2	45	斯洛伐克	75.6
21	泰国	80.1	46	比利时	75.0
22	德国	79.7	47	亚美尼亚	74.5
23	加拿大	79.6	48	摩尔多瓦	74.4
24	爱尔兰	79.6	49	白俄罗斯	74.3
25	哈萨克斯坦	79.6	50	黑山共和国	73.8

1　“Doing Business 2020: Comparing Business Regulations in 190 Economies”，https://www.doingbusiness.org/content/dam/doingBusiness/pdf/db2020/Doing-Business-2020 rankings.pdf，2019 年 11 月 7 日访问。

As China's overall FDI conditions improve, China's FDI position, already ranked second in the world, will still have ample room to grow. So China's FDI story is not coming to a close, but is merely opening a new chapter, which will usher in a period of more diverse, more sophisticated and more dynamic inbound FDI. The FIL will both facilitate and accelerate these positive trends.

随着中国的整体外商直接投资条件的改善，中国的外商直接投资地位，尽管已经排名世界第二，仍将有很大的增长空间。因此，中国的外商直接投资并未接近尾声，而只是开启了一个新的篇章，这将开辟一个更多样化、更高级和更有活力的入境外商直接投资的时期。《外商投资法》将促进和加速这些积极的趋势。

Chapter 2 An Overview of the New FIL

A first draft of the FIL was circulated on 19 January 2015 (2015 Draft FIL), but the origins of the FIL can be traced back further all the way to China's entry into the World Trade Organization (WTO) in 2001. The concept of "national treatment" (affording foreign and domestic companies equal treatment), which is a foundational concept under the FIL, is one of the core principles of the WTO which member nations are to implement.

The principle of national treatment again came to the fore in the early part of this decade when the US and China were negotiating a bilateral investment agreement (BIT), which similarly emphasizes the principle of national treatment, not just for foreign companies after they have been established but also prior to establishment, which is known as "pre-establishment national treatment." This concept is also common in other international investment agreements (IITs) not just US standard form BITs. Pre-establishment national treatment means that the host country agrees to limit approval requirements, sectoral caps or ownership caps that apply only to foreign investors, but the host country is permitted to maintain a negative list setting out sectors which are subject to additional approvals.[1] A simple summary of the conceptual approach could be expressed as follows:

Pre-establishment + national treatment = open market access – negative list

Although the US and China have not yet signed the BIT, many of the principles from the BIT negotiations are reflected in the 2015 Draft FIL as well as the subsequent implementation of the Negative List system in 2017 and ultimately in the final FIL. With this backdrop in

1 The US-China Business Council, Bilateral Investment Treaties: What They Are and Why They Matter, https://www.uschina.org/reports/bilateral-investment-treaties-what-they-are-and-why-they-matter; Vinayak, Vrinda. "The Pre-Establishment National Treatment Obligation: How Common Is It?" European Federation for Investment Law and Arbitration, January 14, 2019. https://efilablog.org/2019/01/14/the-pre-establishment-national-treatment-obligation-how-common-is-it/.

第二章 《外商投资法》概述

《外商投资法》的初稿［2015年《外国投资法（草案）》］于2015年1月19日对外征求意见，但《外商投资法》的起源最早可以追溯到2001年中国加入世界贸易组织（以下简称世贸组织）。“国民待遇”（为外资和内资企业提供平等待遇）是《外商投资法》下的基本概念，也是世贸组织成员需要实施的核心原则之一。

中国和美国在21世纪初期进行双边投资协定谈判时，国民待遇原则再次进入视野。双边投资协定同样强调国民待遇原则，不仅适用于外国公司设立后，同时也适用于设立前，即“准入前国民待遇”。这一概念不仅出现在美国的标准形式的双边投资协议中，在其他国际投资协议中也很常见。“准入前国民待遇”意味着东道国同意减少仅适用于外国投资者的审批要求、行业限制或所有权限制，但可以保留负面清单，其中列出受制于额外审批的行业部门。[1]从概念上进行简单概括，即可以通过以下公式表达：

准入前＋国民待遇＝开放市场准入－负面清单

虽然美国和中国尚未签署双边投资协议，但双边投资协议谈判中的许多原则都反映在了2015年《外国投资法（草案）》和随

1 The US-China Business Council, Bilateral Investment Treaties: What They Are and Why They Matter, https://www.uschina.org/reports/bilateral-investment-treaties-what-they-are-and-why-they-matter; Vinayak, Vrinda. “The Pre-Establishment National Treatment Obligation: How Common Is It?” European Federation for Investment Law and Arbitration, January 14, 2019. https://efilablog.org/2019/01/14/the-pre-establishment-national-treatment-obligation-how-common-is-it/.

mind, we will now turn first to look at the 2015 Draft FIL, after which we will take a closer look at the final FIL.

The 2015 Draft FIL

When MOFCOM circulated the 2015 Draft FIL, commentators heralded it as a sea change in the way China was to regulate inbound investment, bringing China much closer to international norms. Whereas the Three FIE Laws had regulated not only the organizational form, capital structure, governance structure, merger and division, liquidation and dissolution of FIEs differently from the way domestic enterprises were governed under the Company Law, the Three FIE Laws also regulated finance, tax and accounting, foreign exchange, labor, technology, purchase and sales and other aspects of an FIE's business that were not covered by the Company Law.

The 2015 Draft FIL contained none of these provisions. Instead, it focused on concepts such as national treatment, market entry, information reporting and national security that are common to the foreign investment regimes of countries with more developed economies and greater experience in attracting and dealing with FDI, and in terms of corporate structuring and governance the 2015 Draft FIL provided that upon enactment the Three FIE Laws would be repealed and all FIEs would be governed by the Company Law, subject to a three-year grandfathering period. As such, the 2015 Draft FIL was the first indication that the entity forms and organizational structures of the traditional EJV, CJV and WFOE would eventually be discarded in favour of the LLC entity form and its governance mechanisms under the Company Law.

The 2015 Draft FIL set out a comprehensive approach to management of FDI in China, collecting a wide range of policies and procedures which in the past may have been set out in different laws, regulations, notices and circulars and publishing them in a single new 2015 Draft FIL. The effect was to elevate the overall management of FDI in a more holistic manner, with more centralized and uniform control.

While it is beyond the scope of this exercise to perform a detailed analysis of all of the varied elements of the 2015 Draft FIL, it is important for us to provide a high-level overview of the key points so we then have a basis to compare and contrast the 2015 Draft FIL against

后于 2017 年实施的负面清单制度以及《外商投资法》最终版中。考虑到这个背景，我们首先分析 2015 年《外国投资法（草案）》，随后我们再进一步分析《外商投资法》最终版。

2015 年《外国投资法（草案）》

当商务部发布 2015 年《外国投资法（草案）》时，有评论人士称这是中国对入境投资管理方式的一次巨大改变，使中国更接近国际规范。“三资法”不仅规定了与《公司法》项下的内资企业不同的外商投资企业的组织形式、资本结构、治理结构、合并和分立、清算和解散，“三资法”还对外商投资企业的财务、税收与会计、外汇、劳动、技术、采购和销售以及《公司法》未涵盖的关于外商投资企业业务的其他方面进行了规定。

2015 年《外国投资法（草案）》未包含这些条款。相反，它侧重于国民待遇、市场准入、信息报告和国家安全等概念，这些概念对于经济较发达以及在吸引和处理外商直接投资方面经验较丰富的国家的外商投资制度来说很常见。在公司结构和治理方面，2015 年《外国投资法（草案）》规定其生效后“三资法”将废止，所有外商投资企业将受《公司法》管辖，但提供了三年的过渡期。因此，2015 年《外国投资法（草案）》首次表明了传统的中外合资经营企业、中外合作经营企业和外商独资企业的组织形式和组织机构最终将被废弃，取而代之的是《公司法》项下的有限责任公司组织形式及其治理机制。

2015 年《外国投资法（草案）》提出了综合管理中国外商直接投资的方式，集合过去在不同法律、法规、通知和公告中所载的各种政策和程序，并统一在新的 2015 年《外国投资法（草案）》中公布，从而以更加全面的方式提升对外商直接投资的整体管理，实现更加集中和统一的控制。

“2015 年《外国投资法（草案）》提出了综合管理中国外商直接投资的方式，集合过去在不同法律、法规、通知和公告中所载的各种政策和程序，并统一在新的 2015 年《外国投资法（草案）》中公布，从而以更加全面的方式提升对外商直接投资的整体管理，实现更加集中和统一的控制。”

虽然对于 2015 年《外国投资法（草案）》的所有不同要点

the final FIL, the Implementation Regulations and other related rules and regulations (see related discussion below). We address some of the key elements of the 2015 Draft FIL below.

National Treatment and the Negative List Approach

Under the legacy FDI regime, foreign investment had been subject to various government approval requirements determined by reference to the Foreign Investment Guidance Catalogue. The Negative List concept, which originated in the context of international investment treaties, was first implemented on a trial basis in 2013 in the Shanghai Pilot Free Trade Zone, and then was proposed to be extended for implementation nationwide in the 2015 Draft FIL. Even though the 2015 Draft FIL was not adopted in the form circulated, the Negative List approach was implemented nationwide separately in 2017 as described in Chapter 1.

The Negative List concept represented an important evolutionary step from the original Foreign Investment Guidance Catalogues, which (as described in Chapter 1) listed prohibited, restricted (i.e. requiring special approvals or imposing certain limitations as to foreign ownership) and encouraged categories of foreign investment by industry sector, with all industry sectors not specifically listed in the Catalogue being permitted. Under the Catalogue and the related foreign investment legal regime, foreign investment projects were still subject to approval by MOFCOM or its local branches, although over time this approval process became more a perfunctory ministerial matter in most cases involving permitted foreign investments. By contrast, foreign investment in sectors which were not restricted or barred under the Negative List would no longer be subject to approval, and foreign investors and their local partners would be permitted to proceed directly to establish such FIEs by simple compliance with related record-filing requirements.

In many respects, the Negative List is the mirror image of the Foreign Investment Guidance Catalogue, the difference being that no MOFCOM approval is required in respect of non-restricted categories of investment under the Negative List approach. While MOFCOM approvals had become perfunctory in nature under the legacy Foreign Investment Guidance Catalogue system, the Negative List approach removes this potential barrier to investment altogether consistent with the principle of pre-establishment national treatment.

Access License Review Procedure

One element that featured prominently in the 2015 Draft FIL which was not put in place

进行详细分析已经超出了本书的范围，但仍有必要在此对其核心要点进行高度概述，以便我们在将2015年《外国投资法（草案）》与《外商投资法》最终版、《外商投资法实施条例》以及其他相关规定进行对比时有一个比较的基础（参见下文相关讨论）。下面我们将讨论2015年《外国投资法》草案中的部分核心要点。

国民待遇和负面清单模式

在传统的外商直接投资制度下，外商投资受制于《外商投资产业指导目录》所指向的各种政府审批要求。负面清单概念起源于国际投资条约的背景下，于2013年首次在上海自由贸易试验区试行，然后2015年《外国投资法（草案）》提议在全国范围内实行。尽管2015年《外国投资法（草案）》未通过，但如第一章所述，负面清单模式于2017年在全国范围内开始单独实行。

负面清单的概念代表中国从原来的《外商投资产业指导目录》向前发展了重要的一步，《外商投资产业指导目录》（如第一章所述）列出了禁止类、限制类（需经特殊审批或对外资股权有特定限制）和鼓励类外商投资的行业领域，《外商投资产业指导目录》中未明确列出的所有行业均为允许类。根据该《外商投资产业指导目录》和相关外商投资法律制度，外国投资项目仍需经商务部或其地方分支机构审批，但在大多数涉及允许类外国投资的项目中，这一批准程序随着时间的推移很大程度上变成了形式性的行政程序。相比之下，在负面清单下，不受限制或禁止的行业的外国投资不再需要经过审批，外国投资者及其当地合作方可以在遵守相关备案要求的前提下直接注册外商投资企业。

负面清单在很多方面与《外商投资产业指导目录》相一致，不同之处在于负面清单模式下非限制类投资无须经过商务部批准。虽然在传统的外商投资产业指导目录制度下，商务部的审批已经趋于形式，但负面清单模式消除了这种潜在的投资障碍，使之与准入前国民待遇原则完全一致。

at the time the Negative List system was implemented (presumably because the Negative List as implemented relied upon a traditional MOFCOM approval process for foreign investment projects in the restricted categories), and which is also not addressed in detail in the final FIL, is the market access license review procedure. If a foreign investment fell within a restricted category under the Negative List, then under the 2015 Draft FIL an application for an access license would be required. Such an access license review as contemplated under the 2015 Draft FIL would assess the project's impact on national security, energy resources, technological innovation, environmental protection, employment and other issues related to the public interest, as well as China's international treaty obligations and the international influence of the project on the development of the relevant industry.

The 2015 Draft FIL provided that, absent the need for separate national security review, an access license decision was to be issued within 30 business days of acceptance of an application, subject to extension for a further 30 business days in more "complicated" cases. The 2015 Draft Law further provided that MOFCOM (or its authorized counterpart) was to issue its decision in writing, which would include the reasons for the decision if the decision included additional conditions or objections to an access license. Additional conditions could include removal of the assets or business of a foreign investment project, restrictions on shareholding ratios, requirements on operating terms, restrictions on investment regions, requirements on the ratios or numbers applicable to the use of local labor, or other conditions stipulated by the State Council.

Where a preliminary approval from an industry regulator was required by law as a condition to issuance of an access license, the 2015 Draft FIL provided that MOFCOM (or its authorized counterpart) was to conduct an inter-departmental inquiry. In addition, the 2015 Draft FIL permitted MOFCOM or its authorized counterpart to solicit opinions from other departments or from the public, conduct feasibility studies, etc., but at the same time the foreign investor was to be afforded the opportunity to consult with the government and present its case before an access license decision was rendered.

Where investment caps applied, the 2015 Draft FIL provided that the foreign investment amount would be calculated based on the total capital and debt financing of the foreign investment project. Hence, where a foreign investor was to provide debt financing, directly or indirectly, for one year or more in a domestic enterprise, such amount was also to be included

准入许可审查程序

2015年《外国投资法（草案）》中一个突出要点是市场准入许可审查程序，这一程序在负面清单制度实施时尚未实行（可能是因为所实施的负面清单就限制类外国投资项目是以商务部审批程序为基础），《外商投资法》最终版中对此也没有进行详细规定。如果一项外商投资属于负面清单下的限制类，则根据2015年《外国投资法（草案）》，需要申请准入许可。2015年《外国投资法（草案）》中包含的该等准入许可审查将评估项目对国家安全、能源资源、技术创新、环境保护、就业和其他与公共利益相关的问题的影响，中国的国际条约义务，以及项目对相关行业发展的实际影响。

2015年《外国投资法（草案）》规定，如果不需要单独进行国家安全审查，则应在受理准入许可申请之日起30个工作日内完成审查，情况复杂的可延长30个工作日。2015年《外国投资法（草案）》进一步规定，外国投资主管部门应对外国投资事项作出批准、附加条件批准或不予批准的书面决定，作出附加条件批准或不予批准决定的，应当说明理由。附加条件可包括外国投资的资产或业务剥离、持股比例限制、经营期限要求、投资区域限制、当地用工比例或数量要求，或国务院规定的其他条件。

2015年《外国投资法（草案）》规定，如果法律要求以相关行业主管部门的前置性行业许可作为签发准入许可的条件，外国投资主管部门应在审查时征求相关行业主管部门意见。此外，2015年《外国投资法（草案）》允许外国投资主管部门征求其他部门或公众的意见，进行可行性研究等，但同时外国投资者有机会向政府提出咨询并在作出准入许可决定前进行申辩。

在适用投资上限的情况下，2015年《外国投资法（草案）》规定，外国投资数额将基于外国投资项目的资本总额和债务融资计算。因此，如果外国投资者向内资企业直接或间接提供一年或

in calculating the investment amount. Similarly, where a foreign investor invested in the same project multiple times within two years and the aggregate amount of the investment exceeds the relevant investment caps, it would also be subject to the access licensing review procedure.

As noted above, none of these detailed provisions have been included in the final FIL, nor were they included in the Implementation Regulations, so we may anticipate that these may be incorporated into separate regulations to be adopted at a future time.

New Definition of Foreign Investor

In a noteworthy improvement over legacy Chinese FDI legislation, the 2015 Draft FIL defined the key terms that drive the analysis of what is regarded as foreign investment and what types of foreign investment will be included in the Negative List and thus excluded from national treatment and subject to an access license review procedure.

Under the 2015 Draft FIL, "foreign investor" was defined to mean investment in China by (1) natural persons who are not Chinese citizens, (2) enterprises established in accordance with the laws of other countries and territories, (3) the governments of other countries and territories, or any department or organization under such governments, (4) international organizations, and (5) domestic enterprises under the "control" of those falling within the first four categories of foreign investors above.

By contrast, "Chinese investor" was defined to mean investment by (1) natural persons who are Chinese citizens, (2) Chinese government and related departments and organizations, and (3) Chinese enterprises under the control of either of the first two categories of Chinese investors defined above.

Similarly, an FIE under the 2015 Draft FIL was defined to mean an enterprise established in China in accordance with Chinese law in which all or part of the investment is by a foreign investor. Hence, a company registered in China with any amount of foreign capital was to be regarded as an FIE. In addition, the final clause in the definition of "foreign investor" meant that any downstream investment in a subsidiary company in China by an FIE that was controlled by a foreign investor would be regarded as a foreign investment under the 2015 Draft FIL.

More generally, under the 2015 Draft FIL, "foreign investment" was defined to mean any investment undertaken by a foreign investor directly or indirectly by means of:

一年以上的融资，则该等金额也应纳入投资数额加以计算。同样，如果外国投资者在两年内针对同一投资事项多次实施投资并且投资数额累计超过相关投资上限，则也应受准入许可审查程序的约束。

如上所述，《外商投资法》最终版和《外商投资法实施条例》中均没有包含这些细节性的规定，因此我们可以预计这些条款可能会纳入单独的条例予以实施。

外国投资者的新定义

与传统的中国外商直接投资立法相比，2015 年《外国投资法（草案）》对认定外商投资的核心术语进行了定义，并确定了负面清单将包含哪些类型的外商投资，这些外商投资将被排除在国民待遇之外并受制于准入许可审查程序。

在 2015 年《外国投资法（草案）》项下，“外国投资者”指在中国境内投资的以下主体：（1）不具有中国国籍的自然人；（2）依据其他国家或者地区法律设立的企业；（3）其他国家或者地区政府及其所属部门或机构；（4）国际组织；（5）受上述四类外国投资者“控制”的境内企业。

相比之下，“中国投资者”指：（1）具有中国国籍的自然人；（2）中国政府及其所属部门或机构；（3）受上述两类中国投资者控制的境内企业。

同样，2015 年《外国投资法（草案）》项下的外国投资企业是指全部或者部分由外国投资者投资、依据中国法律在中国境内设立的企业。因此，外国投资者投资的公司，无论外国投资额有多少，只要是在中国注册，即被视为外国投资企业。此外，“外国投资者”定义中的最后一款意味着由外国投资者控制的外国投资企业在中国的子公司的任何再投资都将被视为 2015 年《外国投资法（草案）》项下的外国投资。

(1) Establishment of an enterprise in China;

(2) Acquisition of shares, equity interests, property interests, decision making authority or other types of rights and interests in a domestic enterprise;

(3) Provision of financing for one year or more to a domestic enterprise with any of the above rights and interests;

(4) Obtaining concession rights to explore or develop natural resources in China or a territory under the administration of China, or the construction or operation of infrastructure;

(5) Obtaining land use rights, real estate rights or other immovable property rights; and

(6) Acquiring control of a domestic enterprise, including possession of the rights and interests of a domestic enterprise by contract or trust arrangement.

In addition, under the 2015 Draft FIL an agreement outside China that would result in the transfer to a foreign investor of the actual control rights to a domestic enterprise was to be regarded as a foreign investor investing in China.

This definition represented a significant expansion of the scope of foreign investment under Chinese law. Under legacy FDI laws, foreign investment had been generally limited to greenfield investment, acquisitions of domestic companies by foreign investors, and concession rights. The inclusion of the acquisition of land use rights, real estate rights or other immovable property rights under the 2015 Draft FIL was regarded as relating to potential concerns regarding national security.

Another key defined term in the 2015 Draft FIL was the term "control," which was defined to mean, in regard to any enterprise, a situation where an investor:

(1) directly or indirectly holds 50 percent of the shares, equity interests, property shares, decision making authority or other types of rights and interests of such enterprise;

(2) directly or indirectly holds less than 50 percent of such rights and interests but fulfils one of the following criteria:

a. the right to directly or indirectly appoint one half or more of the members of the board of directors or similar decision-making organ of such enterprise;

b. the ability to ensure the nomination of personnel who obtain one half or more of the seats on the board of directors or similar decision-making organ of such enterprise;

更宽泛地说，在2015年《外国投资法（草案）》项下，“外国投资”指外国投资者直接或者间接从事的如下投资活动：

（1）设立境内企业；

（2）取得境内企业的股份、股权、财产份额、表决权或者其他类似权益；

（3）向其持有前项所称权益的境内企业提供一年期或一年期以上融资；

（4）取得境内或其他属于中国资源管辖领域自然资源勘探、开发的特许权，或者取得基础设施建设、运营的特许权；

（5）取得境内土地使用权、房屋所有权等不动产权利；

（6）通过合同、信托等方式控制境内企业或者持有境内企业权益。

此外，在2015年《外国投资法（草案）》项下，境外交易导致境内企业的实际控制权向外国投资者转移的，视同外国投资者在中国境内投资。

这一定义意味着在中国法律项下外国投资的范围显著扩大。根据传统的外商直接投资法律，外国投资一般仅限于绿地投资、外国投资者收购内资企业以及特许经营权。2015年《外国投资法（草案）》中关于土地使用权、房屋所有权或其他不动产权的取得的规定被视为是与国家安全相关的潜在顾虑有关。

2015年《外国投资法（草案）》中另一个关键的定义术语是“控制”，就某一企业而言，是指符合以下条件之一的情形：

（1）直接或者间接持有该企业50%以上的股份、股权、财产份额、表决权或者其他类似权益的；

（2）直接或者间接持有该企业的股份、股权、财产份额、表决权或者其他类似权益虽不足50%，但具有以下情形之一的：

c. the authority to resolve or exert a "major impact" over the decision-making organ of such enterprise.

(3) possesses the ability to exert a "decisive influence" over the operations, property, human resources or technology, etc. of such enterprise by contract or trust arrangement.

Similarly, an "actual controller" was defined to mean a natural person or enterprise that directly or indirectly controls a foreign investor or a foreign invested enterprise, but the terms "major impact" and "decisive influence" were not defined in the 2015 Draft FIL.

Moreover, under the 2015 Draft FIL, a Chinese national who obtained foreign nationality was to be regarded as foreign investor, while a Chinese national who obtained foreign permanent residence was to be regarded as a Chinese investor, except where laws and administrative regulations provide otherwise. Taiwanese, Hong and Macau compatriots and overseas Chinese were to continue to be regarded as foreign investors, as they have been under legacy FDI laws.

In contrast, the FIL in its final form only briefly defines "foreign investor" as foreign natural persons, enterprises or other organizations and defined "foreign investment" differently than as set out in the 2015 Draft FIL, providing that "foreign investment" includes all investment activity directly or indirectly conducted by a foreign investor, including the following specific circumstances:

(1) A foreign investor establishes a foreign-invested enterprise within the territory of China, independently or jointly with any other investor;

(2) A foreign investor acquires shares, equity interests, property shares or any other similar rights and interests of an enterprise within the territory of China;

(3) A foreign investor makes investment to initiate a new project within the territory of China, independently or jointly with any other investor; and

(4) A foreign investor makes investment in any other way stipulated by laws, administrative regulations or provisions of the State Council.

The Implementation Regulations further clarified that "other investor" mentioned in the definition of "foreign investment" of the final FIL includes Chinese natural persons, which represents an important clarification by comparison with legacy foreign investment rules, which had not permitted Chinese individuals to be a Chinese investor in a Sino-foreign joint

a. 有权直接或者间接任命该企业董事会或类似决策机构半数以上成员；

b. 有能力确保其提名人员取得该企业董事会或类似决策机构半数以上席位；

c. 所享有的表决权足以对该企业决策机构的决议产生“重大影响”。

（3）通过合同、信托等方式能够对该企业的经营、财务、人事或技术等施加“决定性影响”的。

类似地，“实际控制人”是指直接或者间接控制外国投资者或者外国投资企业的自然人或者企业，但“重大影响”和“决定性影响”两个词组在2015年《外国投资法（草案）》中没有定义。

此外，在2015年《外国投资法（草案）》项下，获得外国国籍的中国籍自然人被视为外国投资者，而获得外国永久居留权的中国籍自然人则被视为中国投资者，除非法律和行政法规另有规定。同传统外商直接投资法律的规定一样，中国台湾地区、香港特别行政区、澳门特别行政区同胞和海外华人继续被视为外国投资者。

而在《外商投资法》最终版中，“外国投资者”被简单地定义为外国的自然人、企业或者其他组织，“外商投资”［也不同于2015年《外国投资法（草案）》］被定义为外国投资者直接或间接在中国境内进行的投资活动，包括下列情形：

（1）外国投资者单独或者与其他投资者共同在中国境内设立外商投资企业；

（2）外国投资者取得中国境内企业的股份、股权、财产份额或者其他类似权益；

（3）外国投资者单独或者与其他投资者共同在中国境内投

venture.

The final FIL does not contain any of the provisions cited above under the 2015 Draft FIL relating to the definition of the term "control."

Potential Impact of the 2015 Draft FIL on the VIE Structure

One of the most widely discussed aspects of the 2015 Draft FIL was its potential impact on "variable interest entities" (VIEs). Legacy foreign investment rules had captured only direct ownership and board control, and had not employed the concept of indirect ownership and control commonly used in the US and elsewhere. This enabled foreign investors that operate in restricted industries such as the internet/value-added telecoms sectors to use the contractual arrangements of a VIE structure to gain *de facto* control of domestic companies or to allow domestic businesses in such restricted industry sectors to attract foreign capital through private equity and capital markets in Hong Kong and abroad. As noted above, the 2015 Draft FIL, however, incorporated the concept of indirect control in defining the terms "foreign investor," "foreign investment" and "control" so as to directly impact the analysis of the legal status of such VIE structures.

The 2015 Draft FIL also permitted a foreign investor that is ultimately controlled by a domestic natural or legal person (or an organ of the Chinese government) to apply for recognition as a *de facto* domestic investor. As noted above, this category of "domestic" foreign investment could be subject to the access license review procedure and restrictive conditions included in the 2015 Draft FIL, but it also could be excluded. In regard to the vast number of VIEs that already exist, the Explanatory Note circulated with the 2015 Draft FIL indicated that MOFCOM was still considering the issue and suggested three possible approaches:

(1)VIE investments that declare themselves to be controlled by a Chinese investor will be permitted to operate;

(2)VIE investments that are certified by MOFCOM to be controlled by a Chinese investor will be permitted to operate; or

(3)VIE investments will be subject to the access license procedure regardless, and MOFCOM will assess each situation, including whether the investment is controlled by a Chinese investor, on a case-by-case basis.

资新建项目；

（4）法律、行政法规或者国务院规定的其他方式的投资。

《外商投资法实施条例》进一步明确了《外商投资法》最终版中对“外商投资”的定义中提到的“其他投资者”包括中国的自然人，与传统的外商投资规则相比，这是一个重要的澄清，传统的外商投资规则不允许中国自然人成为中外合营企业的中国投资者。

《外商投资法》最终版未包括上文中引用的2015年《外国投资法（草案）》项下的与“控制”一词定义有关的任何规定。

2015年《外国投资法（草案）》对VIE结构的潜在影响

2015年《外国投资法（草案）》中最被广泛讨论的是其对“可变利益实体（VIE）”可能产生的影响。传统的外商投资规则只规定了直接所有权和董事会控制，并没有采用美国和其他国家常用的间接所有权和控制的概念。这使得从事互联网/增值电信行业等受限制行业的外国投资者能够利用VIE结构的合同安排获得对内资企业的实际控制，或让境内企业在该等受限制行业通过私募股权和香港及海外的资本市场吸引外国资本。如上所述，2015年《外国投资法（草案）》将间接控制的概念纳入“外国投资者”、“外国投资”和“控制”的定义中，从而直接影响了对该等VIE结构的法律地位的分析。

2015年《外国投资法（草案）》还允许由中国自然人或法人（或中国政府机关）最终控制的外国投资者申请认定为事实上的中国投资者。如上所述，此类“境内”外国投资可能受2015年《外国投资法（草案）》中的准入许可审查程序和限制条件的约束，但也可以排除适用。关于已经存在的大量VIE实体，与2015年《外国投资法（草案）》一同发布的说明表明商务部仍在考虑该问题，并提出了三种可能的应对方法：

Hence, it appears that under any of these scenarios a VIE that operates in a restricted industry, including existing name brand companies like Alibaba, Sohu.com and Sina.com, would be permitted to continue to operate if deemed to be under the control of a *de facto* domestic investor. By contrast, a VIE that operates in a restricted industry and that is under the *de facto* control of a foreign entity or individual, would not be permitted to operate, unless it otherwise met the criteria under the 2015 Draft FIL and the restricted schedule of the Negative List.

However, many commentators have noted that neither the 2015 Draft FIL nor the Explanatory Note satisfactorily addressed how foreign investment in these "domestic" VIEs through offshore capital markets would be handled. And on the other hand, it would seem that further opening up of the internet/value-added telecoms sector, where the VIE structure has been most commonly employed, would need to be done in parallel with any efforts to regularize or "look through" the existing VIE structures as proposed under the 2015 Draft FIL.

The fact that the final FIL does not contain any provisions relating to the VIE structure has been considered by some commentators as a victory for the status quo. Some modest references to the non-foreign status of round-tripped Chinese investment were included in the Draft Implementation Regulations, which were expected to be a possible prelude to the setting of the groundwork for a separate re-assessment of the VIE structure, but such references were deleted in the final version of the Implementation Regulations. In any event, it should be expected that at some point these VIE structures will be addressed so that foreign investment can be funnelled through the front door rather than the side or back door as is currently the case in many instances. The key, it would seem, is to ensure that at the same time these side- or back-door arrangements utilizing the VIE structure are closed down that the front door is in fact opened to legitimate foreign investment.

National Security Review Procedures

The national security review procedures outlined in the 2015 Draft FIL appear to have been designed to preserve and strengthen the government's gatekeeping role for foreign investment in sensitive industry sectors. Under a circular promulgated by the State Council in 2011, an acquisition by a foreign investor was already subject to national security review if the target operates in a sensitive industry sector such as national defense, infrastructure, agriculture, energy or natural resources. The 2015 Draft FIL would have elevated this

（1）申报受中国投资者控制的 VIE 投资可继续开展经营活动；

（2）经外国投资主管部门认定受中国投资者控制的 VIE 投资可继续开展经营活动；

（3）VIE 投资将受准入许可审查程序的限制，外国投资主管部门将综合考虑该投资是否受中国投资者控制等因素，根据具体情况作出决定。

因此，看起来在以上任何情况下，在限制类行业中经营业务的 VIE 实体，包括现有的知名企业，如阿里巴巴、搜狐和新浪，如果被视为受中国投资者的*实际*控制，则将被允许继续开展经营活动。相比之下，除非符合 2015 年《外国投资法（草案）》项下的标准和负面清单的限制条件，否则在限制类行业中经营且受外国实体或个人的*实际*控制的 VIE 实体将不能继续开展经营活动。

然而，许多评论人士都指出，2015 年《外国投资法（草案）》及其说明都没有圆满地解决如何处理通过境外资本市场投资“境内”VIE 实体的外国投资的问题。另外，在如 2015 年《外国投资法（草案）》所提议的调整或“穿透”现有 VIE 架构的同时，还需要进一步开放最广泛应用 VIE 模式的互联网 / 增值电信行业。

一些评论人士认为《外商投资法》最终版不包含任何有关 VIE 结构的条款是现状的胜利。《外商投资法实施条例（征求意见稿）》中提及了中方返程投资可不被视为外商投资，这曾被认为是今后对 VIE 架构进行重新评估奠定基础的可能前奏，但是这一规定在《外商投资法实施条例》最终版中被删除了。无论如何，这些 VIE 架构预计在未来某个时间点将得到规范，进而外国投资可以通过正常途径进入，而非像目前多数情况下需要绕道而行。看起来问题的关键在于确保在关闭 VIE 架构渠道的同时对合法外国投资实际上敞开大门。

“一些评论人士认为《外商投资法》最终版不包含任何有关 VIE 结构的条款是现状的胜利。”

concept to the status of law and expanded the scope of the national security review procedure to include most forms of foreign investment, including acquisitions, greenfield investment, the purchase of land use and exploitation rights, and variable interest entity structures, at the formative and operational stages.

The 2015 Draft FIL set out extensive details on the nature and scope of national security review, which are beyond the scope of this analysis. It may be sufficient for our current purposes to note that the provisions on national security review under the 2015 Draft FIL would have set up an interesting interplay with the provisions on access permit review. If a proposed foreign investment gave rise to potential national security concerns, then the access permit review procedure would be suspended pending clearance under the national security review and the burden would shift to the foreign investor to establish that the potential investment will not harm China's national security. To avoid an adverse decision, a foreign investor would be able to propose restrictive conditions during the national security review stage. For a foreign investment that passes the national security review with conditional approval, MOFCOM would be required to supervise the implementation of the conditions in conjunction with other relevant departments and the foreign investor would be required to include information on the restrictive conditions (and its compliance therewith) in its annual report.

Information Reporting Requirements

The 2015 Draft FIL also imposed significant reporting requirements on foreign investors and FIEs in China. While these requirements would not necessarily have provided the government with a gatekeeping tool like the national security review procedure, they would have represented an important mechanism for monitoring foreign investment that would apply at various stages in the life cycle of a foreign investment project and include establishment reporting, change reporting and periodic reporting obligations. To a significant degree, these reporting obligations, combined with the supervision and inspection provisions discussed below, would have replaced the examination and approval requirements under legacy FDI laws by requiring foreign investors to provide a large volume of potentially sensitive information that could be subject to public disclosure.

The main periodic reporting obligations under the 2015 Draft FIL involved the annual report. FIEs would be required to submit an annual report on or before April 30 of every year

国家安全审查程序

2015年《外国投资法（草案）》中概述的国家安全审查程序似乎旨在维持和加强政府对敏感行业领域内外国投资的把关作用。根据国务院于2011年发布的一项通知，如果目标公司在国防、基础设施、农业、能源或自然资源等敏感行业中经营，外国投资者对其进行收购会受制于国家安全审查。2015年《外国投资法（草案）》将这一概念提升到法律层面，并将国家安全审查程序的适用范围扩大到大多数形式的外国投资，包括收购、绿地投资、购买土地使用权和开采权以及在设立和运营阶段的VIE结构。

2015年《外国投资法（草案）》详细阐述了国家安全审查的性质和范围，这不在本书的分析范围之内。在本书中，我们只需了解2015年《外国投资法（草案）》中的国家安全审查条款与准入许可审查条款之间建立了特定关联。如果一项拟议的外国投资可能会引发国家安全担忧，则在通过国家安全审查之前准入许可审查程序将暂停，并且证明潜在投资不会损害中国国家安全的相关责任将转移至外国投资者。为避免作出对外国投资者不利的决定，外国投资者可在国家安全审查阶段提议附加限制性条件。外国投资获得附加限制性条件通过国家安全审查的，外国投资主管部门应当会同有关部门监督限制性条件的执行情况，外国投资者应在其年度报告中说明限制性条件（及其遵守情况）的有关内容。

信息报告要求

2015年《外国投资法（草案）》还针对外国投资者和中国的外商投资企业施加了重要的信息报告要求。虽然这些要求不一定能像国家安全审查程序一样起到为政府把关的作用，但为监管外国投资提供了一个重要机制，这一机制适用于外国投资项目的各个阶段，包括涉及设立和变更的报告义务以及定期报告义务。在很大程度上，这些报告义务连同下文将讨论的监督检查规定，通过要求外国投资者提供大量可能向公众披露的潜在敏感信息，将

covering the period for the prior calendar year. Foreign investors who purchase publicly listed stock are already required to fulfil their reporting obligations in accordance with the *Securities Law of the People's Republic of China*, and those who purchase 10% or more of a publicly listed company (or purchases of less than 10% but which results in a change in control) would also be required to submit an annual report. Furthermore, FIEs with RMB 10 billion or more in total assets, turnover or revenue and those with 10 or more subsidiaries would be required to submit quarterly reports in addition to the annual report. The reporting requirements are based on aggregated information. Hence, the assets, turnover and revenue of an FIE's subsidiaries would be counted in determining the applicability of these thresholds.

The annual report (and presumably the quarterly reports, if any) were to contain basic information on the foreign investor, foreign investment and FIE, plus the FIE's industry sector, main products or services, imports and exports, labor situation, tax payments, research and development activities, assets, debts, ownership rights and interests, income, costs and profits, its investment development and trade situation, as well as information on the FIE in China and abroad involving important litigation, administrative reviews, administrative or criminal penalties, and complaints, etc.

In addition to the information reporting requirements, the 2015 Draft FIL also provided the government with another key tool for monitoring foreign investment activities: the right of government agencies, led by MOFCOM, to conduct inspections of FIEs and other foreign investment projects as part of their expanded supervisory role. Under the 2015 Draft FIL, MOFCOM would have been empowered to utilize internet monitoring, questionnaires, onsite investigations and other methods to carry out inspections. MOFCOM also could utilize tax, accounting, law and other professionals, as well as the results of inspections conducted by other government departments. Any entity or individual could report violations to MOFCOM or its authorized counterpart as a whistle-blower and request that its report remain confidential. Such a report would be required to contain the identity of the whistle-blower and facts and evidence to support its assertions.

Inspections under the 2015 Draft FIL could take the form of periodic sampling, an inspection following a whistle-blower's report, an inspection following the recommendations of government agencies or courts, and *ex officio* inspections. Periodic sampling could include random sampling of FIEs and other foreign investment projects and targeted sampling

取代传统外商直接投资法律项下的检查和审批要求。

2015 年《外国投资法（草案）》项下的定期报告义务主要涉及年度报告。外国投资者应在每年 4 月 30 日前提交上一年度的信息报告。购买公开发行股票的外国投资者应根据《中华人民共和国证券法》履行报告义务，而购买上市公司 10%或 10%以上股票（或购买股票不足 10%但导致控制权发生变更）的外国投资者也应提交年度报告。此外，资产总额、销售额或营业收入超过 100 亿元人民币，或其子公司数量达到或超过 10 家的外商投资企业，除年度报告外，还需要提交季度报告。报告要求是以合计的信息为基础。因此，在确定这些门槛的适用性时，外商投资企业子公司的资产、销售额或营业收入将被计算在内。

年度报告（以及季度报告，如适用）应包含外国投资者、外国投资和外国投资企业的基本信息，以及外国投资企业的行业领域、主要产品或服务、进出口、用工情况、纳税、研发等，资产、负债、所有者权益、收入、费用、利润、投资发展和贸易情况，以及外国投资企业在境内外涉及的重大诉讼、行政复议、行政或刑事处罚以及投诉等。

除了信息报告要求外，2015 年《外国投资法（草案）》还为政府监管外国投资活动提供了另一个重要工具：由商务部牵头的政府部门对外商投资企业和其他外国投资项目进行监督检查的权利，以作为其扩大的监督职责的一部分。在 2015 年《外国投资法（草案）》项下，商务部将有权采用网络监测、问卷调查、实地核查等方式进行检查。商务部还可以委托税务师事务所、会计师事务所、律师事务所等专业机构提供专业服务，以及采用其他政府部门作出的检查结果。对于涉嫌违法的行为，任何单位和个人均有权向商务部举报。举报人可要求商务部予以保密。举报人应当提供举报人的基本情况以及支持其主张的相关事实和证据。

在 2015 年《外国投资法（草案）》项下，检查的形式包括

of foreign investment within a specific industry sector, geographical region, etc. Where an inspection suggested a violation of the 2015 Draft FIL or other laws and regulations, MOFCOM or its authorized counterpart could conduct an investigation and impose administrative penalties on the relevant FIE or other foreign investment project.

An inspection, and any resulting investigation, could examine various issues, including whether the investment is prohibited or restricted, whether an FIE or other foreign investment project has adhered to any restrictive conditions to issuance of an access permit or clearance under a national security review, whether an FIE or other foreign investment project has met its reporting obligations, whether it has fulfilled its obligations under an administrative penalty, whether it harms national security or the public interest, or whether it has otherwise violated the 2015 Draft FIL or other laws and regulations.

The final FIL makes only general reference to the implementation of a foreign investment information reporting system but does not set out any specific reporting requirements. The Implementation Regulations provide that the content, scope and frequency of reports on foreign investment information reports will be determined by MOFCOM in conjunction with SAMR and other relevant departments. On 31 December 2019, MOFCOM and SAMR jointly issued the "Measures for Reporting Foreign Investment Information" (Reporting Measures), setting out some further specifics on the foreign investment information reporting system. These points will be discussed further below following the general overview of the final FIL.

New Ombudsman Office

The 2015 Draft FIL also provided that China's international investment promotion organ was to establish a national ombudsman center responsible for coordinating and resolving complaints involving foreign investment with a "national influence." All levels above the county level of China's government were also to create a similar body to handle complaints raised by foreign investors and FIEs within their jurisdiction. The national ombudsman center could accept and transfer complaints to the lower level centers, which were to be authorized to investigate the complaints, request documents and explanations from the parties. In addition, the national ombudsman office could suggest solutions to local governments and government agencies. These entities were to report back to the national authorities as to how they have addressed the recommendations of the national center. According to the 2015 Draft FIL, complaints must be resolved in accordance with the principles of fairness, justice and law, and

定期抽样检查，根据举报进行检查，根据有关部门、司法机关的建议和反映的情况进行检查，以及其他依职权启动的检查。定期抽样检查包括对外商投资企业和其他外国投资项目的不定向抽样检查，以及对特定行业、地理区域等条件下的外国投资的定向抽样检查。检查中发现被检查人可能存在违反2015年《外国投资法（草案）》或其他法律法规的行为的，商务部可依法对相关外商投资企业或其他外国投资项目开展调查并予以行政处罚。

检查及其所引起的调查的内容包括：是否在禁止或限制实施目录列明的领域实施投资，是否遵守准入许可决定所附加的条件，是否遵守国家安全审查决定所附加的限制性条件，是否履行信息报告义务，是否履行行政处罚决定，是否存在危害国家安全和社会公共利益的行为，是否存在其他违反2015年《外国投资法（草案）》或其他法律法规的情形。

《外商投资法》最终版仅对外商投资信息报告制度的实施作了一般性规定，未载明任何具体要求。《外商投资法实施条例》规定，外商投资信息报告的内容、范围以及报告的频次将由商务部会同国家市场监督管理总局（以下简称市场监管总局）等有关部门确定。2019年12月31日，商务部和市场监管总局共同发布《外商投资信息报告办法》，对外商投资信息报告制度进行了进一步的规定。这些要点将在下文中对《外商投资法》最终版进行概述后探讨。

新的投诉工作机制

2015年《外国投资法（草案）》同时规定，国际投资促进机构设立全国外国投资投诉协调处理中心，协调处理在“全国范围内影响重大”的外国投资投诉事项。县级以上地方各级人民政府根据需要设立外国投资投诉协调处理机构，在本辖区内受理并协调处理外国投资者和外国投资企业的投诉。全国外国投资投诉协调处理中心可以受理、向地方投诉协调处理机构转送外国投资投

foreign investors and FIEs are required to truthfully make complaints and provide supporting evidence.

The Implementation Regulations address similar points but with some potentially significant variations. In particular, under the final Implementation Regulations, if an FIE complains that any administrative action has violated its lawful rights, then it may submit a complaint through the FIE complaint handling system to be established, and the authorities are to address those issues in a coordinated and timely manner. In addition, the Implementation Regulations expressly provide that no government authority or individual may take action to suppress such complaint or retaliate. Finally, under the Implementation Regulations, foreign investors are not limited to the standard FIE complaint system to be set up, but may also report problems to other relevant government departments through other legal channels. [1]

Even with the substantive provisions included in the Implementation Regulations cited above, there are many elements of this FIE complaint management system that will require further clarification and development.

Greater Openness and Transparency

The 2015 Draft FIL expressly required all relevant government agencies and courts to promptly publish laws and regulations and judicial decisions related to foreign investment. Foreign investors and foreign invested enterprises were to be permitted to participate in the formulation of FDI laws and regulations and to form chambers of commerce and other business associations and use them to lobby the Chinese government. The 2015 Draft FIL also contained express provisions on the expropriation and requisition of foreign investment. These high-level undertakings for the most part have been retained in the final FIL and the Implementation Regulations.

Repeal of the Three FIE Laws and Mandatory FIE conversion

Upon the effectiveness of the 2015 Draft FIL the legacy Three FIE Laws were to be repealed and all FIEs would then be subject to the Company Law or Partnership Law. The final FIL has maintained the same position. As a practical matter this means that from the effective date of the FIL, all new FIEs taking the form of companies (as opposed to partnerships) would be required to comply with the corporate governance requirements under the Company Law and all previously established FIEs taking the form of companies would

1 Implementation Regulations, Articles 29-31.

诉事项，地方投诉协调处理机构经授权调查投诉，并要求相关方提供材料和说明。此外，全国外国投资投诉协调处理中心可以向有关地方、部门提出完善政策和改进工作的建议。有关地方和部门应当予以处理并及时反馈处理情况。根据2015年《外国投资法（草案）》，外国投资投诉协调处理机构遵循公平、公正、合法的原则协调处理投诉，并且外国投资者、外国投资企业投诉时应如实反映情况并提供相应证据。

《外商投资法实施条例》涉及了类似问题，但有一些潜在的重大变化。特别是，根据《外商投资法实施条例》最终版，如果外商投资企业或者其投资者认为行政机关及其工作人员的行政行为侵犯其合法权益，其可以通过待建立的外商投资企业投诉工作机制申请协调解决，有关方面应就投诉的问题进行协调并及时处理。此外，《外商投资法实施条例》明确规定，对于该等投诉，任何单位和个人不得压制或者打击报复。最后，除待建立的标准外商投资企业投诉工作机制外，外商投资企业或者其投资者还可以通过其他合法途径向政府及其有关部门反映问题。[1]

尽管《外商投资法实施条例》中包含了如上文所述的一些实质性的规定，这一外商投资企业投诉工作机制仍有许多方面需要进一步澄清和发展。

更高的开放性和透明度

2015年《外国投资法（草案）》明确规定所有相关政府部门和法院应及时公布与外国投资有关的法律法规和司法判决。外国投资者、外国投资企业可依法参与外商直接投资法律法规制定程序，可依法成立商会、协会，开展相关活动，维护自身权益。2015年《外国投资法(草案)》同时对外国投资的征收和征用作出了明确规定。这些一般性承诺中的大部分都保留在了《外商投资法》最终版和《外商投资法实施条例》中。

1 《外商投资法实施条例》第29~31条。

be required to change their organizational structures which are inconsistent with mandatory provisions under the Company Law within a designated transition period. Under the 2015 Draft FIL, the transition period was three years, while under the final FIL, the transition period was extended two years for a total transition period of five years. Since the general principles on corporate governance under the Company Law and FIE conversion are the same under the final FIL as under the 2015 Draft FIL, except for the length of the transition period, we will discuss related points in more detail when we address the provisions of the final FIL later in this Chapter 2 and the specific provisions of the Sample Templates in Part Ⅱ.

However, there are a few related points arising under the 2015 Draft FIL that merit discussion here since they are not addressed in detail, or are in certain cases presented in a different manner, in the final FIL. One key example is that under the 2015 Draft FIL, an existing FIE must apply for an access license if it amends its articles, or reinvests, within the transition period and if the amendment, or reinvestment, is captured by the Negative List due to restrictions on business scope or total investment. Moreover, under the terms of the 2015 Draft FIL, once it had taken effect, any existing FIE which applied to extend its operating term (which was set to expire within the three-year transition period) would be required to undertake the relevant conversion before its current operating term expired. Where its operating term was set to expire after the 2015 Draft FIL was enacted but before it took effect, however, an FIE would be allowed to wait and amend its operating term after the 2015 Draft FIL took effect. Though existing FIEs were to be subject to the information reporting requirements under the 2015 Draft FIL, it is worth noting that most other amendments would not require government approval, which is also currently the case now that the Negative List scheme has been put in place separately.

Aside from these general provisions, the 2015 Draft FIL did not offer specific guidance on how and to what extent an FIE formed before the 2015 Draft FIL took effect would be required to carry out any required amendments in connection with the conversion process. This is also the case with the final FIL. The Implementation Regulations, Guiding Opinions on Effectively Implementing the Administration of the Registration of Foreign-invested Enterprises in Accordance with the Law (Draft for Comment) issued by SAMR on 6 November 2019 (hereinafter referred to as the "Draft SAMR Guiding Opinions") and Circular of the State Administration for Market Regulation on Effective

“三资法”的废除和外商投资企业强制转化

2015年《外国投资法（草案）》一旦生效，传统的“三资法”将废止，所有的外商投资企业将受《公司法》或《合伙企业法》的约束。《外商投资法》最终版也保留了这一规定。实际上，这意味着从生效之日起，所有新设的公司制（而非合伙制）的外商投资企业都必须遵守《公司法》项下的公司治理要求，并且所有先前已经设立的公司制外商投资企业，如果其组织机构不符合《公司法》项下强制性规定的，都需要在指定的过渡期内进行变更。在2015年《外国投资法（草案）》项下，过渡期为三年，而在《外商投资法》最终版项下，过渡期被延长了两年，变为总共五年。除过渡期的长度不同以外，关于外商投资企业转化和《公司法》项下公司治理的一般原则，《外商投资法》最终版的规定与2015年《外国投资法（草案）》中的规定是一致的，鉴于此，我们将在第二章后段分析《外商投资法》最终版的规定以及第二部分中的模板样本的具体条款时更详细地讨论相关要点。

然而，由于《外商投资法》最终版对2015年《外国投资法（草案）》中出现的某些相关要点没有作出详细规定或（在某些情况下）作出了不同的规定，我们需要在此进行讨论。一个重要例子是，在2015年《外国投资法（草案）》项下，如果现有外商投资企业在过渡期内修订其章程或重新投资，且该等修订或重新投资由于经营范围或投资总额的限制而落入负面清单，则该外商投资企业必须申请准入许可。此外，在2015年《外国投资法（草案）》项下，现有外商投资企业的经营期限如果将在三年过渡期内届满且拟延长经营期限的，应在企业既有经营期限内进行变更。如果外商投资企业经营期限在2015年《外国投资法（草案）》颁布后生效前届满，则需要等到2015年《外国投资法（草案）》生效后再修改其经营期限。虽然现有外商投资企业本应受制于2015年《外国投资法（草案）》项下的信息报告要求，但值得注意的是，大多数其他变更并不需要经过政府审批，这也是目前负面清单模式

Work on Registration of Foreign-invested Enterprises for the Implementation of the Foreign Investment Law issued by SAMR on 31 Dec. 2019 (hereinafter referred to as the "SAMR Circular"),[1] on the other hand, do provide some additional clues in this regard. These points will be discussed further below.

The 2019 Final FIL and Related Rules and Regulations

The original expectation was that the 2015 Draft FIL would progress towards formal adoption by the NPC in 2016 or 2017. However, following the close of the public comment period on the 2015 Draft FIL on 17 February 2015, there were no further public announcements regarding the status of the draft law until the draft of the final FIL was circulated for comment on 26 December 2018.

Comparison of Final FIL vs. 2015 Draft FIL

It is in many respects easier to understand the final FIL by comparing it to the 2015 Draft FIL (as we have already done in part above). The 2015 Draft FIL was much more comprehensive in scope than the final FIL passed in March 2019. To illustrate the differences in scope, it is noteworthy that the 2015 Draft FIL was comprised of 11 chapters and 170 articles, while the final FIL has only six chapters and 42 articles.

As with the 2015 Draft FIL, the final FIL incorporated the principles of "national treatment" and provides for the repeal of the Three FIE Laws, with all FIEs to fall under the Company Law or the Partnership Law upon the effectiveness of the FIL. (In this book, we will focus our discussion on conversion into entity forms under the Company Law rather than partnerships under the Partnership Law as the former vastly outnumber the latter.)

As noted above, the 2015 Draft FIL also covered a variety of issues that either were not covered or were addressed only briefly in the final FIL. See the chart 2-A for a high-level comparison of certain key points.

1 It seems that SAMR Circular is the final version of SAMR Guiding Opinions though the name is different as the content are generally the same.

单独实施后的情况。

除了这些一般规定外，2015 年《外国投资法（草案）》未就其生效前成立的外商投资企业应如何以及在多大程度上进行与转化程序相关的必要变更提供具体指导。《外商投资法》最终版在这一点上也是同样的情况。另外，《外商投资法实施条例》、市场监管总局于 2019 年 11 月 6 日发布的《关于依法做好外商投资企业登记管理工作的指导意见（征求意见稿）》（以下简称《外资企业登记管理指导意见（征求意见稿）》）以及 2019 年 12 月 31 日发布的《市场监管总局关于贯彻落实〈外商投资法〉做好外商投资企业登记注册工作的通知》（以下简称《市场监管总局通知》）[1]就此提供了一些额外的线索。这些问题将在下文中进一步探讨。

2019 年《外商投资法》最终版和相关规定

2015 年《外国投资法（草案）》最初预计将在 2016 年或 2017 年经全国人大正式通过。然而，在 2015 年《外国投资法》草案征求公众意见的期限于 2015 年 2 月 17 日届满后，就没有发布过有关 2015 年《外国投资法（草案）》状态的公告，直至《外商投资法（草案）》于 2018 年 12 月 26 日发布并征求公众意见。

《外商投资法》最终版 vs.2015 年《外国投资法（草案）》

通过与 2015 年《外国投资法（草案）》进行对比（我们已经在上文中进行了一部分），《外商投资法》最终版在很多方面都更容易理解了。2015 年《外国投资法（草案）》在范围上比 2019 年 3 月通过的《外商投资法》最终版更为全面。为了说明两版在范围上的差异，值得注意的是，2015 年《外国投资法（草案）》由 11 章，共计 170 条组成，而 2019 年《外商投资法》最终版仅有 6 章，共计 42 条。

1 《市场监管总局通知》似乎是《外资企业登记管理指导意见（征求意见稿）》的最终版，虽然名称不一致，但内容大体相同。

Chart 2–A Comparison Between 2015 Draft FIL and 2019 Final FIL

2015 Draft FIL	2019 Final FIL
Provided that variable interest entity (VIE) nominee shareholder structures were to be subject to stricter scrutiny	Not addressed (and similarly the Draft Implementation Regulations made only brief reference to round-tripped Chinese investment not being treated as "foreign" investment but even this was deleted in the final version of the Implementation Regulations)
Presented the concept of the Negative List in substantial detail	Addressed only at a high level since the Negative List has been separately implemented
Set out detailed rules on applications for market access permits for foreign investment in restricted industry sectors	Not addressed
Set out extensive provisions on National Security Review	Addressed only at a high level (but note that certain elements of National Security Review in the 2015 Draft FIL had already been implemented and presumably were included in that draft to provide a single central repository for laws and regulations related to foreign investment)
Government procurement (not addressed)	Addressed at a high level—provides that China is to guarantee that FIEs can participate in government procurement activities through fair competition (with additional details set out in the Implementation Regulations).
Set out extensive new rules on reporting and inspection requirements for FIEs	Addressed only at a high level but note that (1) under the Implementation Regulations MOFCOM and SAMR are to prepare and issue such new rules in due course and (2) MOFCOM and SAMR jointly issued the Reporting Measures at the end of 2019, setting out some further specifics on the foreign investment information reporting system as discussed below]
Provided for the establishment of a foreign investment ombudsman office to address complaints of foreign investors	Addressed only at a high level in the final FIL (with additional details set out in the Implementation Regulations as discussed above)
Set out basic details on the timing of FIE conversion, including mandatory early conversion of FIEs into LLCs under the Company Law if an FIE applies to extend its term of operation which was set to expire prior to the expiry of the transition period	General concept of conversion is preserved in the 2019 Final FIL but the transition period was changed from three years to five years, with certain additional details set out in the SAMR Circular (see further discussion below)

表 2-A　2015 年《外国投资法（草案）》与 2019 年《外商投资法》比较

2015 年《外国投资法（草案）》	2019 年《外商投资法》最终版
规定可变利益实体（“VIE”）的名义股东结构将受到更严格的审查	未作规定（类似地，《外商投资法实施条例（征求意见稿）》仅对中方返程投资可不以“外商投资”对待作简要规定，但在《外商投资法实施条例》最终版中这一仅有的规定也被删除了）
充分详细地介绍了负面清单的概念	由于负面清单已另行实施，仅作出概括性规定
对受限制领域的外国投资市场准入许可的申请作出详细规定	未作规定
对国家安全审查作出大量规定	仅作出概括性规定［但须注意，2015 年《外国投资法（草案）》中关于国家安全审查的某些要点已经得到实施，该草案包含这些要点可能是为了给外商投资相关的法律法规提供一个中央资料库］
政府采购（未提及）	高度概括性地提及——规定中国将保证外商投资企业能够通过公平竞争参与政府采购活动（《外商投资法实施条例》中规定了更多细节）
对外商投资企业的报告和检查制度作出大量的新规定	仅作出概括性规定［但请注意：（1）根据《外商投资法实施条例》，商务部和市场监管总局将适时制定和颁布这些新规定；（2）商务部和市场监管总局于 2019 年年底共同颁布了《外商投资信息报告办法》，对外商投资信息报告制度进行了进一步的规定，详见下文讨论］
规定了设立外国投资投诉协调处理机构以解决外国投资者的投诉	《外商投资法》最终版中仅作了概括性规定（《外商投资法实施条例》中有一些额外的细节规定，详见上文讨论）
就外商投资企业转化的时间表提供了基本的细节，包括如果经营期限在宽限期届满前到期且拟延长经营期限，则强制要求该外商投资企业在既有经营期限内转化为《公司法》项下的有限责任公司	2019 年《外商投资法》最终版中保留了转化的一般概念，但过渡期从三年改为五年，《市场监管总局通知》中有一些额外的细节规定（见下文的进一步讨论）

Overall, the final FIL was much more abbreviated than the 2015 Draft FIL, and appeared to be designed primarily as a negotiating document in the context of the US-China trade negotiations as many of the new provisions set out for the first time in the final FIL (which have not been listed above as they are not central to the analysis set out herein) corresponded to points reportedly being discussed as part of those negotiations and subsequently addressed in the phase one trade agreement between China and the US. The timeline of the adoption of the final FIL was also accelerated—after the 2015 Draft FIL had lain dormant for four years, the final FIL was passed after a very brief public comment period of less than three months.

In summary, for legal practitioners engaged in China FDI work, the critical content of the final FIL as adopted relates to the shift from the Three FIE Laws to the Company Law and the FIE conversion requirement. But while the references in the final FIL to these changes are brief, the implications are dramatic and far-reaching. This is a major fundamental transition which will affect not only all new FIEs but all existing FIEs, and yet there is very little guidance provided under the FIL.

FIL Implementation Regulations and the SAMR Circular

Given the speed with which the final FIL was passed and its relative brevity, it was not surprising that it was not slated to take effect until 1 January 2020, which would allow time for the new updated Negative List to be issued (which, as discussed further below, took place in the end of June 2019) and, for the related new implementation regulations to be issued. The draft Implementation Regulations were circulated for comment on 1 November 2019 and the final form of the Implementation Regulations were issued on 31 December 2019.

Prior to the issuance of the Draft Implementation Regulations, it was anticipated that the Implementation Regulations may incorporate many of the provisions from the 2015 Draft FIL which were omitted from the final FIL and which had not otherwise been adopted independently. Once the Draft Implementation Regulations were issued, however, it became apparent that the authorities had again adopted a more minimalist approach in this case and had left most of the key details to separate rules and regulations to be issued in the future. The final Implementation Regulations are also quite brief in scope and generally take the form of a modest supplement to the final FIL, which itself was extraordinarily brief.

The brevity of the Implementation Regulations, thus, leaves many important questions unanswered. Most significantly, as already noted, the Draft Implementation Regulations

与2015年《外国投资法（草案）》一样，《外商投资法》最终版纳入了“国民待遇”原则，并规定废除“三资法”，使所有外商投资企业在《外商投资法》生效后适用《公司法》或《合伙企业法》。（在本书中，我们将着重讨论现有外商投资企业转化为《公司法》项下的实体形式而不是转化为《合伙企业法》项下的合伙企业的情形，因为前者的数量远远超过后者。）

如上所述，2015年《外国投资法（草案）》还涵盖了《外商投资法》最终版中未涵盖或仅简要提及的各种问题。表2-A就某些核心问题进行了高度概括的对比。

从整体上看，《外商投资法》最终版比2015年《外国投资法（草案）》简短得多，这可能与持续中的中美贸易谈判有一定关系，因为许多首次在《外商投资法》最终版中作出的新规定（由于不是本书分析的核心内容，未在上表中列出）与部分谈判要点相对应且后续在中美第一阶段经贸协议中进行了约定。《外商投资法》最终版的通过时间表也加快了——在2015年《外国投资法（草案）》搁置四年之后，2019年《外商投资法》最终版在经过不到三个月的简短的征询公众意见期限后便被通过了。

“从整体上看，《外商投资法》最终版比2015年《外国投资法（草案）》简短得多，这可能与持续中的中美贸易谈判有一定关系。”

总之，对于从事中国外商直接投资工作的法律从业人员而言，《外商投资法》最终版的关键内容涉及“三资法”向《公司法》的转变以及外商投资企业转化要求。虽然《外商投资法》最终版对这些变化仅有简要规定，但其影响是巨大而深远的。这个重大的根本性转变不仅会影响所有新设外商投资企业，而且会影响所有现存的外商投资企业，但《外商投资法》对此提供的规定很有限。

《外商投资法实施条例》和《市场监管总局通知》

考虑到《外商投资法》最终版通过的速度及其相对简洁性，它直到2020年1月1日才生效也就不足为奇了，这样可以为更新版负面清单（如下文所述，于2019年6月底发布）的颁布，以及相应的《外商投资法实施条例》的颁布留出时间。《外商投资法

provided that the specific rules on FIE conversion would be issued separately by SAMR. A draft of the SAMR Guiding Opinions was circulated for comment on 6 November 2019, shortly after the Draft Implementation Regulations were released, and took effect in final form as the SAMR Circular on 1 January 2020. The terms of the Implementation Regulations and SAMR Circular relating to FIE conversion will be discussed below.

Key Practical Implications of the FIL and Related Rules and Regulations

There are four key categories of changes for FIEs under the FIL that are all fundamental in nature, relating to corporate governance, capital structures, corporate structures (in connection with the opening up of downstream investments by FIEs), and FIE conversion. We discuss each of these aspects below.

Changes to Corporate Governance Structures and Systems

The changes in the applicable governance provisions under the Three FIE Laws to the corresponding provisions under the Company Law will have a particularly significant impact on Sino-foreign joint ventures (which, as we have noted above, are principally comprised of EJVs). Governance provisions under the Company Law differ significantly from those under the EJV Law. The Company Law provides that the highest authority in the company is the shareholders meeting, while the EJV Law does not provide for a shareholders meeting and designates the board of directors as the highest authority in the joint venture company. In addition, the Company Law provides super-majority shareholders with a higher level of control than permitted under the EJV Law. For example, certain matters which now require unanimous board approval under the EJV Law, now will only require two-thirds majority approval at the shareholders meeting level. In addition, there are scores of other changes that will need to ripple through the various clauses of the joint venture documentation. This change in governance provisions alone will present significant challenges to both Chinese and foreign investors in joint ventures in China. We address these points in more detail in Chapter 3 as well as in connection with the annotations to the new Sample Templates in Part Ⅱ.

Changes in FIE Capital Structures

Another major change for FIEs under the Company Law will be the elimination of the concept of total investment amount, which had its origins in the planned economy system. As

实施条例（征求意见稿）》于2019年11月1日发布公开征求意见，并于2019年12月31日正式发布。

在《外商投资法实施条例（征求意见稿）》发布前，我们预期实施条例可能包含许多2015年《外国投资法（草案）》中包含的但在《外商投资法》最终版中未包含且不存在另行规定的条款。然而，《外商投资法实施条例（征求意见稿）》发布后，可以看到，很明显有关部门在这个问题上再次采取了一种比较简单的方法，将大部分关键细节留待日后另行发布的法规和规章来规定。《外商投资法实施条例》最终版的范围也比较简单，基本上是《外商投资法》最终版的简要补充，内容极其简练。

《外商投资法实施条例》篇幅简短，造成许多重要的问题没有得到回答。最重要的是，如前所述，《外商投资法实施条例（征求意见稿）》规定有关外商投资企业转化的具体规定将由市场监管总局另行发布。《外资企业登记管理指导意见（征求意见稿）》于2019年11月6日（《外商投资法实施条例（征求意见稿）》发布后不久）发布征求意见，其最终版《市场监管总局通知》与《外商投资法实施条例》均于2020年1月1日起生效。《外商投资企业实施条例》和《市场监管总局通知》的规定将在下文中讨论。

《外商投资法》及其相关规定的主要实际影响

对于外商投资企业来说，《外商投资法》项下有四类关键的根本性变化，分别与公司治理、资本结构、公司架构（与外商投资企业再投资的放开相关）和外商投资企业转化相关。我们将在下文中对这几个方面逐一进行探讨。

公司治理结构和制度的变化

“三资法”项下适用的公司治理规定变更为《公司法》项下

previously noted, the total investment amount was comprised of the registered capital (the parties' equity) and the permitted debt capacity of an FIE, which in turn was subject to specific "thin capital" rules, which limited the amount of debt that FIEs could incur in proportion to the registered capital amount. Current debt-to-equity ratio requirements applicable to FIEs range from required registered capital amounting to no less than one third of total investment amount (i.e. an allowable debt basket of two-thirds of the total investment amount) to minimum registered capital amounting to no less than 70% of total investment amount (i.e. an allowable debt basket of 30% of the total investment amount).

The Company Law does not include the concept of total investment amount for domestic companies, so it is anticipated that consistent with the concept of "national treatment" which is enshrined in the FIL, the "thin capital" rules which historically have constrained the amount of debt that FIEs can incur will also be formally repealed. Note that under the July 2019 Shanghai FTZ Pilot Rules, FIEs in the zone will now be permitted to disregard these legacy debt-to-equity restrictions, which is in line with the pending transition from the Three FIE Laws to the Company Law.

This would mean that shareholder loans may become a more important source of capital funding for FIEs in the future. However, for the foreign investor, FIEs will still be subject to a net assets test, where foreign debt cannot exceed two times total net assets, under applicable foreign exchange rules. The 2019 SAFE Notice also provides that a non-financial enterprise in pilot areas may register foreign debts in line with the applicable foreign debt caps at the local SAFE bureau, and then handle related formalities for inward and outward remittance, foreign exchange settlement and purchase and so on at the bank. There will be challenges in setting foreign debt quotas for newly established (and in many cases under-capitalized) FIEs as well as complications which may arise in the event that the value of the FIE borrower's net assets declines, so these changes in the "thin capital" rules will not resolve all related issues, but they are a step in the right direction.

Restrictions on Downstream Investments Lifted

Similarly, as referenced briefly in Chapter 1 above, many foreign investors have long hoped that the legacy limitations on FIEs converting forex capital contributions into RMB for purposes of downstream equity investments either by way of domestic acquisitions or the establishment of subsidiaries or for repayment of shareholder loans denominated in RMB will

的相关规定对于中外合营企业（如上所述，主要由中外合资企业构成）而言影响尤其重大。《公司法》项下的治理规定与《中外合资经营企业法》项下的治理规定大不相同。《公司法》规定，公司的最高权力机构是股东会，而《中外合资经营企业法》并未规定股东会，而是指定董事会为合资公司的最高权力机构。此外，《公司法》为绝对多数股东提供了比《中外合资经营企业法》所允许的更高水平的控制权。例如，《中外合资经营企业法》项下需要获得董事会一致批准的某些事项现在只需要在股东层面获得2/3表决权的多数批准。此外，还有其他变化会在合资企业文件的各个条款中产生影响。治理规定的变化将给中国境内中外合资企业的中国投资者和外国投资者都带来重大挑战。我们将结合本书第二部分中新模板样本的注解说明详细分析这些要点。

外商投资企业资本结构的变化

对于《公司法》项下的外商投资企业来说，另一项重大变化是取消投资总额的概念，这一概念源于计划经济体制。如上所述，投资总额包括注册资本（双方的股本）和外商投资企业经批准的举债能力，而这反过来又受“投注差”规则的约束，该规则限制了外商投资企业可发生的债务数额与注册资本金额的比例。当前适用于外商投资企业的投注差要求在注册资本应不少于投资总额的1/3（允许举债比例占投资总额的2/3）到注册资本应不少于投资总额的70%（允许举债比例占投资总额的30%）。

《公司法》针对内资公司没有规定投资总额的概念，因此为了符合《外商投资法》中的“国民待遇”原则，预计之前限制外商投资企业可举借的外债总额的“投注差”规则也将被正式废除。在2019年7月发布的上海自贸区细则［《进一步推进中国（上海）自由贸易试验区外汇管理改革试点实施细则（4.0版）》］项下，上海自贸区的外商投资企业现在可以忽略这些遗留的投注差限制，这与“三资法”向《公司法》的转变相一致。

be relaxed as a practical matter (and not just a theoretical matter as had generally been the case previously) as part of the implementation of the general concept of "national treatment" enshrined in the FIL.

The Shanghai FTZ Pilot Rules were another indication that this important change was pending, and the 2019 SAFE Notice confirmed and extended this critical new policy position more broadly. Consequently, so long as these new rules are in fact implemented by commercial banks across China, then this would open up opportunities for existing FIEs to re-engineer their corporate structures in China and would also replace the outdated foreign-invested holding company structures which, according to reports, to date had only been adopted by less than one percent of all foreign investors. At the same time, new foreign investors would be able to set up multiple subsidiaries from the outset, without having to wait until initial operations generated sufficient RMB cash revenues that could be used for downstream investments. Also note that for such downstream investments by FIEs, the foreign debt restrictions described above presumably will not apply, potentially opening up more flexible capital structuring in connection with such second- and third-tier FIEs.

Overall, the elimination of these long-standing restrictions on conversion of foreign exchange capital contributions for use in connection with downstream investments by FIEs will have a dramatic impact on all future foreign investment projects in China, removing a substantial disadvantage for FIEs by comparison to their domestic counterparts, and allowing FIEs to regularize their overall group corporate structures to improve operational efficiencies. There are still many related points which will need to be addressed in connection with such new corporate structuring and restructuring activities, including related tax structuring issues, but this will be a key factor for foreign investors to keep in mind in connection with FIE conversion and corporate governance restructuring activities going forward.

FIE conversion

While there are many procedural details which are yet to be released in connection with the FIE conversion requirement under the FIL, a reasonably complete picture of the overall policy positions can now be pieced together by a careful reading of the various references to this requirement in the FIL, the Implementation Regulations and the SAMR Circular. Two of the key points to be assessed in this regard include (1) what is the status of the corporate governance provisions for existing FIEs after the FIL takes effect (i.e. what is the scope and

这意味着股东贷款可能成为未来外商投资企业更重要的融资来源。但是，对于外国投资者而言，外商投资企业仍然会受制于对其净资产的检验，在适用的外汇规则项下，外债不得超过净资产总额的两倍。《2019年外管局通知》还规定在试点地区非金融企业可按相关外债额度上限到所在地外管局办理外债登记，并在银行办理相关外汇资金汇出入和结购汇等手续。为新成立的外商投资企业（而且在许多情况下资本不足）设定外债额度存在挑战，在外商投资企业借款人的净资产减少时还可能出现并发症，因此“投注差”规则的这些变化不会解决所有相关问题，但这是朝着正确方向迈出的一步。

对外商投资企业再投资的限制解除

同样，如第一章所述，许多外国投资者一直以来都希望可以实际上放宽对外商投资企业以通过境内收购或设立子公司进行再投资为目的，或以偿还以人民币计价的股东贷款为目的，将外汇资本转换为人民币的遗留限制（而不仅仅是像以前一样只是在理论上放宽限制），以作为《外商投资法》中的“国民待遇”原则的实际执行。

上海自贸区细则是这一重要变化即将推行的另一个迹象，而《2019年外管局通知》确认了这一重要的新政策立场，并将其延伸至更广的范围。因此，只要这些新规定由全中国的商业银行实际实施，现存的外商投资企业将有机会重新设计其在中国的公司结构，取代过时的外资控股公司结构（据报道，至今只有不到1%的外国投资者采取这种方式）。与此同时，新的外国投资者将能够从一开始就建立多个子公司，而不必等到最初的运营产生足够的人民币现金收入后再用于再投资。还应注意到，对于外商投资企业的再投资，上述的外债限制可能不适用，这可能会为此类二级、三级外商投资企业带来更为灵活的资本结构。

“因此，只要这些新规定由全中国的商业银行实际实施，现存的外商投资企业将有机会重新设计其在中国的公司结构，取代过时的外资控股公司结构（据报道，至今只有不到1%的外国投资者采取这种方式）。”

总体来说，取消这些长期以来对外商投资企业将外汇资本金

extent of the grandfathering provisions), and (2) whether the timing for conversion is voluntary or whether certain circumstances or events will trigger an earlier mandatory conversion. These two points are interrelated to a substantial degree.

Before we turn to those two questions, some additional background as to what is meant by FIE conversion may be helpful. The relevant legislation, starting from the 2015 Draft FIL through to the final Implementation Regulations and SAMR Circular, uses the terms "organizational forms and organizational structures" which we understand refer to entity forms (for example, an LLC) and corporate governance structures and systems (provisions relating to shareholder meeting and board meeting structures, voting arrangements, etc.), respectively. Although most FIEs have always been enterprises with limited liability, as a legacy matter FIEs were separately registered as WFOEs, EJVs, CJVs, etc. rather than LLCs, so for example in years past when all or part of the equity of a domestic LLC was acquired by a foreign investor, it would need to be deregistered as an LLC and reregistered as a WFOE or EJV (rarely if ever a CJV in such instances). So from a legacy perspective it may have been supposed that FIE conversion under the FIL would entail a similar change in registered entity form, but in fact as a practical matter over the course of the last several years the registered entity form for virtually all FIEs has already been automatically changed in the SAMR company registration files from the legacy FIE entity forms (WFOE, EJV, CJV etc.) to LLC with a further notation of the foreign-invested status. This has been done with no application required on the part of the investors and without any corresponding changes to the corporate governance provisions to conform to the requirements of the Company Law.[1] This is consistent with Article 10 of the SAMR Circular, which provides that FIEs with legal person status (which includes virtually all FIEs) do not have to change their organization forms, the unstated rationale being that it has already been done automatically. As a result, for our purposes, when we refer to FIE conversion herein, we will be referring to making the amendments to the FIE constitutional documents to adopt the corporate governance requirements under the Company Law.

Moreover, it is important to note that the related policy positions on FIE conversion

1 The SAMR Circular treats CJVs and WFOEs with no legal person status as a separate category for these purposes and based on a limited review of SMAR company registration files such CJVs and WFOEs with no legal person status have not been automatically re-registered as LLCs, the presumption under the SAMR Circular being that these will be registered as partnerships under the Partnership Law. Because there are so few of these types of non-legal entity cooperation platforms, we will not deal with them specifically in this book.

结汇用于境内再投资的限制将对未来所有在中国进行的外商投资项目产生重大影响，不仅消除了与内资企业相比针对外商投资企业的重大不利条件，而且允许外商投资企业调整其整体集团公司架构来提高运营效率。在这种新的公司架构和重组活动中，仍有许多相关问题需要解决，包括相关税务筹划问题，但这将是外国投资者将来在进行外商投资企业转化和公司治理重组活动时要牢记的关键问题。

外商投资企业转化

虽然《外商投资法》中关于外商投资企业转化的许多程序细节尚未公布，但通过仔细研读《外商投资法》、《外商投资法实施条例》和《市场监管总局通知》，可以对政策的整体情况有一个比较全面的了解。在这方面需要评估的两个关键点包括：（1）《外商投资法》生效后，现有外商投资企业的公司治理规定的地位如何（原有的“三资法”规定将在多大范围和程度上能够继续沿用）；（2）转化时间是否能够自愿选择，还是在特定情形下或特定事件发生时将触发提前强制转化。这两点在很大程度上相互关联。

在我们讨论这两个问题之前，了解有关外商投资企业转化含义的一些额外的背景情况可能会有所帮助。从2015年《外国投资法（草案）》到《外商投资法实施条例》和《市场监管总局通知》，相关立法使用了“组织形式和组织机构”的表述，我们理解这两个术语分别指的是实体形式（如有限责任公司）以及公司治理结构和制度（与股东会和董事会结构、表决安排相关的规定）。尽管大多数外商投资企业一直是有限责任企业，但作为一个遗留问题，外商投资企业被另行登记为外商独资企业、中外合资企业、中外合作企业等，而不是有限责任公司。例如，在过去，当内资有限责任公司的全部或部分股权被外国投资者收购，则需要将其作为有限责任公司注销，然后重新注册为外商独资企业或中外合

have undergone continuing evolution from the time of the circulation of the 2015 Draft FIL to the time of the passage of the final FIL in March 2019 and continuing even through the issuance of the Draft Implementation Regulations and Draft SAMR Guiding Opinions in early November 2019 to the issuance of the final Implementation Regulations and SAMR Circular in late December 2019. As a result, in some cases these provisions appear to still be a work in progress, and it is possible that we may yet see further clarifications and adjustments to these policies going forward.

With that background and those caveats, we now turn to the two questions posed above. With respect to the first point on the grandfathering of the corporate governance provisions of existing FIEs during the five-year transition period, the FIL provides that existing FIEs "may retain their original organization forms *and other aspects*" for the five-year period following effectiveness of the FIL (the italicized language was added only in the final version of the FIL). This policy statement was generally consistent with the terms of the 2015 Draft FIL, which similarly, and somewhat more helpfully, provided that the original "organizational forms and organizational structures" (i.e. entity forms and corporate governance structures and systems) under the Three FIE Laws would continue to apply prior to formal conversion notwithstanding that such laws will have otherwise been repealed.

The Draft Implementation Regulations additionally provided that existing FIEs may continue to distribute profits and allocate residual assets (presumably upon dissolution and most likely in connection with CJV structures), etc. in accordance with the provisions of the existing joint venture contract entered into by the parties, but in the final version of the Implementation Regulations this was revised to provide further that in addition to provisions on distribution of profits and allocation of residual assets, existing provisions on the transfer of equity interests and other rights (presumably beneficial interests) would also remain valid and effective. In addition, the final Implementation Regulations then added for the first time that all such original provisions could remain effective *after* conversion of the organizational form and organizational structures of the FIE. Overall it appears that the intention is to provide existing FIEs set up prior to the effectiveness of the FIL some additional comfort that the core corporate governance provisions originally agreed by the parties prior to the effectiveness of the FIL as a commercial matter can be grandfathered in for the duration of the five-year transition period *and beyond*. None of these elements would necessarily be inconsistent with

资企业（在这种情况下几乎没有中外合作企业）。因此，从传统的角度来看，可能认为《外商投资法》项下的外商投资企业转化将对注册的实体形式进行类似的更改，但实际上，在过去数年中，几乎所有外商投资企业登记的实体形式已经在企业登记系统中，从传统的外商投资企业实体形式（外商独资企业、中外合资企业、中外合作企业）自动变更为了有限责任公司并加注表明其外商投资的性质。这一过程已完成，投资者无须申请进行该项变更，也无须对公司治理规定进行相应变更，以符合《公司法》的要求。[1] 这与《市场监管总局通知》第 10 条的规定一致，该条规定 2020 年 1 月 1 日前设立的外商投资的公司、外商投资合伙企业无须办理企业组织形式变更登记，其未阐明的理由是该操作已自动完成。因此，在本书中，当我们提及外商投资企业转化时，我们指的是对外商投资企业章程性文件进行修订，以采用《公司法》项下的公司治理要求。

此外，需要注意的是，从 2015 年《外国投资法（草案）》发布到 2019 年 3 月《外商投资法》最终版通过，有关外商投资企业转化的相关政策立场一直在不断变化，甚至在从 2019 年 11 月初发布《外商投资法实施条例（征求意见稿）》和《外资企业登记管理指导意见（征求意见稿）》直到 2019 年 12 月底发布《外商投资法实施条例》最终版和《市场监管总局通知》的过程中，还在持续发生变化。因此，在某些情况下，这些规定似乎仍是一项正在进行的工作，未来我们可能会看到对这些政策的进一步说明和调整。

有了上述背景信息和说明，我们现在来分析一下上文中提到的两个问题。关于第一点，即五年过渡期内现有外商投资企业的

1 《市场监管总局通知》将不具有法人资格的中外合作企业和外商独资企业作为单独的一类对待，基于对有限的企业登记信息的检查，该等不具有法人资格的中外合作企业和外商独资企业并未被自动变更登记为有限责任公司，《市场监管总局通知》的假定是这些企业将登记为符合《合伙企业法》的合伙企业。由于这些不具有法人资格的外商投资企业数量太少，我们在本书中对此不作专门讨论。

the mandatory provisions of the Company Law, which in almost all cases is more flexible than the Three FIE Laws in this regard, so this should have been the result irrespective of this provision of the Implementation Regulations.

This brings us to the question of timing, which in turn may help shed further light on the grandfathering question above. Most FIEs and their advisors looked at the five-year transition period and happily concluded that there was no urgency to take any action in this regard. In addition, as noted above, although the 2015 Draft FIL did suggest a few circumstances under which mandatory conversion may be required, the final FIL itself was silent on this point. Accordingly, all were looking to see whether the Implementation Regulations and the related SAMR rules would impose any new requirements that would give rise to a greater sense of urgency.

Once the Draft Implementation Regulations were issued, the passive position so readily adopted by most FIEs and their advisors appeared to be vindicated as a further 6-month grace period was added to the existing five-year transition period for FIE conversion under the FIL.

On the other hand, the Draft Implementation Regulations also imposed a firm deadline to complete the conversion process, expressly providing that if any existing FIE failed to complete such conversion process "in accordance with law" by the end of the five-year transition period plus the 6-month grace period, then SAMR would not process any other registration applications and would issue public notice of the offending FIE's failure to comply with the conversion requirement. The Draft SAMR Guiding Opinions further confirmed this position.

In addition, the Draft SAMR Guiding Opinions provided that if an existing FIE, during the five-year transition period, proposed to amend to its articles of association to make certain fundamental changes to its corporate governance structures and systems in respect of the FIE's internal highest authority (i.e. shareholders and board meeting structures), directors terms of office, voting mechanisms on major issues, profit distribution arrangements or "other matters" in a manner inconsistent with the requirements of the Company Law, then it was to apply to the registration authority for change of registration or record-filing of its articles of association in accordance with applicable laws. The general consensus of many FDI practitioners was that the catch-all language covering all "other matters" in these provisions under the Draft SAMR Guiding Opinions would allow the local SAMR offices to require an FIE to undertake

公司治理规定沿用的问题，《外商投资法》规定现有外商投资企业在其施行后五年内“可以继续保留原企业组织形式等”（斜体文字仅在《外商投资法》的最终版本中出现）。这一政策声明基本与2015年《外国投资法（草案）》的条款一致，后者作出了类似的（并且在某种程度上来说更有帮助的）规定，即“三资法”项下关于企业组织形式和组织机构（实体形式、公司治理结构和制度）的规定将在正式的转化之前继续适用，尽管“三资法”届时已被废止。

《外商投资法实施条例（征求意见稿）》还规定，现有的外商投资企业可以继续按照双方签订的原合营企业合同的约定分配收益和剩余财产（很可能是在解散后且最有可能是在中外合作经营企业的情况下）等，但在《外商投资法实施条例》最终版中，这一规定有所修订，除了收益分配和剩余财产分配外，还规定了原合营企业合同中的股权或者权益转让办法也可继续沿用。此外，《外商投资法实施条例》最终版首次加上了如下规定，即所有这些原有约定在外商投资企业的组织形式、组织结构转化*后*仍可继续沿用。总的来看，起草者的意图似乎是为《外商投资法》生效前设立的现有外商投资企业开出一粒“定心丸”，即双方在《外商投资法》生效前作为商业事项约定的核心公司治理规定在五年过渡期内和之*后*仍可以继续沿用。所有这些要素均未必与《公司法》的强制性规定不符，而在这方面，《公司法》的规定几乎在所有情况下都比“三资法”更加灵活，因此，无论《外商投资法实施条例》是否有此规定，结果都应当如此。

“总的来看，起草者的意图似乎是为《外商投资法》生效前设立的现有外商投资企业开出一粒‘定心丸’，即双方在《外商投资法》生效前作为商业事项约定的核心公司治理规定在五年过渡期内和之后仍可以继续沿用。”

这就引出了时间问题，而这一问题反过来又可能有助于进一步阐明上述的“沿用”问题。大多数外商投资企业及其顾问研究了五年过渡期，并愉快地得出结论，没有必要急于在这方面采取任何行动。此外，如上所述，尽管2015年《外国投资法（草案）》确实提出了可能需要强制转化的一些情况，但《外商投资法》最终版本身在这一点上保持沉默。因此，所有人都在关注《外商投

a full conversion process to update *all* of the corporate governance provisions in its articles of association to conform to the Company Law requirements in connection with *any* amendment to its existing articles, whether or not such amendment was inconsistent with the Company Law. In other words, this could act as a mandatory trigger event, pulling forward the timing of the FIE conversion process in a significant number of cases.

From a practical perspective, this interpretation of the Draft SAMR Guiding Opinions would be eminently sensible — the conversion of so many FIEs in a relatively limited period of time even on a one-time basis, where all of the relevant amendments to the constitutional documents of a particular FIE are undertaken at the same time, is already an enormous project, which is expected to put great pressure on the workload of the local SAMR offices. If the amendment of major provisions of the articles of association could be broken out into two or more steps in a piecemeal manner, it would increase the workload dramatically. The general view among many FDI professionals was that the addition of the catch-all "other matters" in the Draft SAMR Guiding Opinions was designed to make it so local registration officials were not put in a position of having to decide whether a proposed amendment was so fundamental in nature as to trigger a full conversion process, but would give them ample latitude to trigger full conversion in connection with more technical matters as well even if such amendments strictly speaking were not inconsistent with the Company Law. This arrangement would clearly make their lives easier.

Such a policy would be similar to what happened in prior situations where new rules were implemented, such as in connection with the requirement that WFOEs adopt a shareholders meeting and supervisory committee structure under a notice issued by the State Administration for Industry and Commerce in 2006.[1] Although the notice provided that it was not mandatory for WFOEs that had been established before 1 January 2006 to amend the their articles of association to adopt these governance structure under the Company Law, in practice, when these WFOEs applied for any change of registration, the local enterprise registration authorities still required them to amend their articles of association at the same time to adopt the structure of shareholders meeting and supervisory committee structure.

Such a mandatory early conversion trigger under the above reading of the Draft SAMR

1 Circular of the State Administration for Industry and Commerce on Implementing the Execution Opinions on Several Issues concerning Law Application for the Administration on the Examination, Approval and Registration of Foreign Invested Enterprises.

资法实施条例》和相关的市场监管总局规定是否会提出任何新的要求，从而产生更大的紧迫感。

《外商投资法实施条例（征求意见稿）》一经颁布，大多数外商投资企业及其顾问如此轻易采取的消极立场似乎被证明是正确的，因为在外商投资企业转化的5年过渡期的基础上，另外增加了6个月的宽限期。

另外，《外商投资法实施条例（征求意见稿）》还对完成转化程序设定了最后期限，其明确规定，如果现有外商投资企业在5年过渡期加上6个月的宽限期届满时仍未“依法”完成该等转化，企业登记机关将不予办理该企业的其他登记事项，并可以将相关情形在企业信息公示系统中公示。《外资企业登记管理指导意见（征求意见稿）》也进一步印证了这一点。

此外，《外资企业登记管理指导意见（征求意见稿）》规定如果现有的外商投资企业在5年过渡期内拟修改其公司章程，对公司治理结构和制度作出某些根本性的改变，包括对其最高权力机构（股东会和董事会结构）、董事任期、重大事项表决机制、利润分配“等”与《公司法》强制性规定不符事项的，应当依法向登记机关申请变更登记或章程备案等。许多外商投资业务从业人员的普遍共识是，《外资企业登记管理指导意见（征求意见稿）》中的这些规定中涵盖所有其他事项的“等”这一兜底性表述将使地方市场监管局可以要求外商投资企业，在对其原有章程作出*任何*修订时，无论该等修订是否与《公司法》的强制性规定不符，都需要进行完全的转化，即更新其章程中*所有*的公司治理规定以符合《公司法》的要求。换句话说，这可能会成为一个强制触发事件，将大量的外商投资企业转化的时间点提前。

从实践角度来看，对于《外资企业登记管理指导意见（征求意见稿）》的该等解读也是非常明智的——如此多的外商投资企业在相对有限的时间内一次性完成转化（一家外商投资企业将对

Guiding Opinions could present some significant practical challenges to FIEs. For example, full conversion could be triggered in connection with more technical amendments in respect of a simple change of the FIE's registered address, or the transfer of equity to an affiliate or change in investor name as part of an internal corporate restructuring, as well as in connection with more substantive amendments such as an increase or decrease in the registered capital or a change to the business scope. If any such amendment could trigger full conversion of the corporate governance structures and systems, that could give rise to significant delays which could impede the completion of related corporate transactions or the introduction of new categories of business operations. The challenge would be even greater in the context of a Sino-foreign joint venture, where the corporate governance issues may prove to be more sensitive and time-consuming in many cases.

So by way of interim summary, the Draft Implementation Regulations and the Draft SAMR Guiding Opinions presented a bit of a mixed bag—the addition of a 6-month grace period to the already generous five-year transition period did not appear to be designed to induce any greater sense of urgency with respect to the FIE conversion requirement, but on the other hand the fact that any amendment to the FIE's articles of association could trigger a mandatory early full conversion suggested that a passive approach could prove problematic as a practical matter in certain cases.

However, the final version of the Implementation Regulations and the final SAMR Circular (which replaced the Draft SAMR Guiding Opinions) changed the state of play once again. And once again, the results presented a mixed bag:

- First, the 6-month grace period was omitted in the final Implementation Regulations, so all FIE conversions now must be completed by 31 December 2024, failing which the SAMR window will be closed for all other registration matters for such FIE and public announcement of the FIE's non-compliance will be made, which could give rise to questions as to the validity of corporate actions taken after that time which are not in compliance with the requirements of the Company Law.
- Second, the final SAMR Circular, while retaining the original mandatory early conversion trigger language cited above (now set out in Article 11 of the SAMR Circular), adds a new Article 12 governing the handling of "other registration changes," which provides that other unspecified amendments can be accepted for

章程性文件的所有相关修订同时完成）已经是一项浩大的工程，可能会给各地市场监管局的工作量带来巨大的压力。如果对公司章程大量规定的修订可以拆分成两次或多次零碎地进行，将大大增加工作量。许多外商投资专业人士的普遍看法是，《外资企业登记管理指导意见（征求意见稿）》中的“等”这一兜底性表述旨在使地方市场监管局的工作人员可以不必决定某项修订是否是根本性的从而足以触发全面的转化流程，而是赋予他们足够的自由度，使他们可以要求在对章程进行更加技术性的修订时进行全面转化，即使该等修订严格说来并非与《公司法》的强制性规定不符。这种安排显然会让他们的工作更容易进行 。

这一政策与之前实施新规时的情形类似，比如在 2006 年国家工商总局发布了一则通知，要求外商独资企业采用股东会和监事会结构。[1] 虽然该通知规定对于 2006 年 1 月 1 日以前已经设立的外商独资企业是否修改其章程以采用《公司法》项下的治理结构并不做强制要求，但在实践中，当这些外商独资企业申请进行任何变更登记时，地方企业登记机关仍要求其一并修改章程以采用股东会和监事会结构。

上述对《外资企业登记管理指导意见（征求意见稿）》的解读中的这种强制性提前转化触发情形可能会给外商投资企业带来一些重大的现实挑战。例如，在进行一些更加技术性的修订时，如外商投资企业注册地址的简单变化，或由于企业内部重组导致的向关联方转让股权或变更投资者名称，还有在进行增加 / 减少注册资本或变更经营范围等更加实质性的修订时，都可能触发强制转化。如果任何该等修订都可能触发公司治理结构和制度的全面转化，可能会导致重大延迟，从而妨碍相关公司交易的完成或新业务种类的退出。对于中外合营企业来说，挑战会更大，因为在很多情况下，其公司治理问题可能会更加敏感和耗时。

因此，我们可以暂时这样总结，《外商投资法实施条例（征求

1　国家工商行政管理总局《关于实施〈关于外商投资的公司审批登记管理法律适用若干问题的执行意见〉的通知》。

registration or record-filing even before full conversion is undertaken. This suggests that full conversion may not be triggered by amendments in respect of any and all "other matters" as had been the prior understanding under the Draft SAMR Guiding Opinions.

- Finally, the final Implementation Regulations provide that existing FIEs may at any time during the five-year transition period apply to undertake conversion to adopt the corporate governance structures and systems under the Company Law, but they may also elect to keep their original organizational forms and organizational structures during the transition period.

Overall, the terms of the SAMR Circular appear to be designed to emphasize stability of existing FIE corporate governance structures and systems for the duration of the transition period, requiring early conversion only where the FIE proposes to make certain fundamental changes to its corporate governance provisions which are inconsistent with the Company Law (the scenario captured in Article 11), and downplaying the potential for early mandatory conversion triggers for more technical amendments to the articles of association (the scenario intended to be governed under Article 12). It is probably less likely that an FIE will seek to make amendments to only some and not all of the core corporate governance terms in a manner which would trigger mandatory full conversion under Article 11, while other more technical amendments presumably intended to be covered by Article 12 will be more common although still not frequent as a practical matter.

The challenge will be drawing clear distinctions between Article 11 scenarios and Article 12 scenarios, in part because Article 11 enumerates some specific examples of fundamental changes that may trigger full conversion, while both Articles 11 and 12 make more general reference to "other matters" which may engender some confusion if no further official interpretation is provided by central SAMR authorities, preferably listing some of the more technical amendments that would fall under Article 12, and thus not trigger mandatory full conversion. Unless central SAMR provides a clear set of guidelines on how to interpret these provisions, local SAMR authorities in many cases may find themselves in the uncomfortable position of making fine distinctions between what falls under Article 11 and what falls under Article 12 based solely on their own subjective discretion. This may give rise to several different possible scenarios, including:

意见稿）》和《外资企业登记管理指导意见（征求意见稿）》呈现了一个混合的立场——在已经很长的五年过渡期的基础上增加额外6个月的宽限期，似乎并不旨在对外商投资企业转化要求带来更大的紧迫性，但是，对外商投资企业章程的任何修订都可能触发强制性提前转化的事实表明，在某些情况下，被动的方式可能会出问题。

然而，《外商投资法实施条例》最终版和《市场监管总局通知》［《外资企业登记管理指导意见（征求意见稿）》的最终版］又一次改变了局面。并且又一次，结果是呈现了一个混合立场：

- 首先，《外商投资法实施条例》最终版中删除了6个月的宽限期，所以所有的外商投资企业转化现在必须在2024年12月31日前完成，否则市场监督管理部门不予办理其申请的其他登记事项，并将外商投资企业相关不合规的情形予以公示，这可能会导致对此后采取的不符合《公司法》要求的公司行为的有效性产生疑问。

- 其次，《市场监管总局通知》在保留上文引用的原有强制性提前转化触发情形语言（参见《市场监管总局通知》第11条）的同时，新增了第12条有关处理“其他登记事项变更登记”的内容。第12条规定，即使在完全转化完成之前，外商投资企业申请就其他未指明的修订进行变更登记或备案，登记机关应当予以受理。这表明，对任何和所有“其他事项”的修订可能不会像之前在《外资企业登记管理指导意见（征求意见稿）》项下理解的那样触发全面转化。

- 最后，《外商投资法实施条例》最终版规定现有外商投资企业可以在五年过渡期的任何时候申请转化以采用《公司法》项下的公司治理结构和制度，但他们也可以选择在过渡期内保留其原有组织形式和组织机构。

总的来说，《市场监管总局通知》的规定似乎旨在强调过渡期内现有外商投资企业公司治理结构和制度的稳定性，仅在外商投资企业拟对其与《公司法》强制性规定不符的公司治理规定作

(1) the local registration officials may decline to process any such application pending further clarification from central-level SAMR authorities (a common response in the initial period following adoption of any new set of regulations);

(2) some local registration officials may require full conversion in connection with any amendment (as was the case with the roll-out of the shareholders meeting and supervisory board requirements for WFOEs in 2006 as noted above); or

(3) other local registration officials may ignore the catch-all "other matters" language in Article 11 and take the position that only the expressly enumerated matters set out in Article 11, or "other matters" which are demonstrably inconsistent with the Company Law, trigger mandatory full conversion, while all other amendments can be processed in the usual manner without triggering a requirement for early full conversion.

Overall, it is anticipated that most amendments to FIE articles of association will fall under Article 12, and so we may safely assume that the default position taken by SAMR is that the timing of the full conversion process will for the most part be left to the discretion of the FIE, subject only the hard deadline at the end of the five-year transition period. However, we cannot completely dismiss the possibility that in some scenarios even more technical amendments may trigger mandatory early conversion. This may be particularly true if it becomes apparent early on in the process that as the vast majority of FIE conversions are deferred to the latter part of the transition period that related administrative work loads may prove to be overwhelming. Administrative necessity may increase pressure to adopt a de facto policy of early mandatory conversions for all amendments similar to the scenario that played out in connection with the 2006 roll out of amendments to WFOE articles of association, and in fact a substantial number of leading FDI practitioners fully expect that as a practical matter SAMR ultimately will end up requiring early mandatory conversion in cases where *any* amendment is made to the FIE's article of association, notwithstanding the more accommodating language under the SAMR Circular. This potential uncertainty in terms of interpretation and application of the SAMR Circular thus presents some practical challenges for FIEs, which we will discuss in the next chapter.

Other Related Legal Developments

While the main focus of our analysis has been on the practical implications of the

出某些根本性变更（《市场监管总局通知》第 11 条规定的情形）时才要求提前转化，而削减了对公司章程进行其他更加技术性的修订（《市场监管总局通知》第 12 条规定）时触发强制提前转化的可能性。外商投资企业不太可能只对某些而不是全部核心公司治理条款进行修订，这些修订会触发第 11 条项下的强制全面转化，而预计旨在由第 12 条涵盖的其他更加技术性的修订则会更加常见（尽管在实践中仍不会太常见）。

挑战在于明确区分第 11 条和第 12 条规定的情形，部分原因是第 11 条列举了一些可能触发强制转化的根本性变更的具体情形，而第 11 条和第 12 条都更笼统地提及了“其他事项”（或“等”事项），如果市场监管总局不提供进一步的官方解释（最好是能够列出一些属于第 12 条项下规定的更加技术性的不会触发强制性全面转化的修订），则可能会引起一些混乱。除非市场监管总局就如何解释这些规定提供明确指导，否则地方市场监管局在许多情况下可能会无所适从，他们只能根据其自身的主观判断来对哪些事项属于第 11 条规定的情形而哪些规定属于第 12 条规定的情形进行区分。这可能会导致一些不同的情况出现，包括：

（1）在市场监管总局进行进一步澄清之前，地方市场监管局可能会拒绝处理任何此类申请（在任何新法规实施之后的初期，这是常见的反应）。

（2）一些地方市场监管局工作人员可能会要求在进行任何修订时进行全面转化（就像上文中提到的，在 2006 年推行外商独资企业采用股东会和监事会要求时的情况一样）。

（3）其他地方市场监管局可能会忽略第 11 条中兜底性的“等”的表述，而认为只有第 11 条中明确列举的事项或明显与《公司法》强制性规定不符的“其他事项”将触发强制性全面转化，而所有其他修订则可以照常处理，不会触发提前全面转化的要求。

总体而言，预计外商投资企业章程的大多数修订都将归于第 12 条的范围，因此，我们完全可以假设，市场监管总局的默认立

FIL and related rules and regulations on corporate governance, capital structures, corporate structuring and FIE conversion, there are other points which bear mention in order to provide a more complete picture of the new post-FIL legal environments.[1]

FIE Registration Formalities

For FIEs investing in sectors which do not fall under the Negative List, the SAMR Circular clearly puts FIE registration formalities on par with the registration procedures for domestic enterprises, which represents a significant improvement for FIEs. Specifically, Article 2 of the SAMR Circular provides that:

- Foreign investors or FIEs shall file registration applications through the online enterprise registration system. As part of this process the applicant is to select the industry areas under which the FIEs operations are intended to fall and confirm that the FIE is in compliance with the requirements of the Negative List. The local SAMR will then conduct a formal examination of the application materials. If the FIE is in an industry sector that is not restricted or barred under the Negative List, then registration and record-filing shall proceed on the same basis as permitted for domestic enterprises.
- If the FIE's operations fall within a restricted category under the Negative List, then so long as the FIE complies with applicable requirements on foreign investment caps, the nationality of the legal representative and otherwise comply with all other applicable regulations, then registration is to be permitted, and in the case where relevant industry supervisory departments have already issued approvals for the FIE's operations in the restricted industry sector, the local SAMR officials are not to subject the application to re-examination.

Article 3 of the SAMR Circular appears to provide that record-filing with MOFCOM

1 In addition to the regulatory points discussed in this section, we also note that other various prior FIE regulations were abolished. For example, MOFCOM promulgated Announcement of the Ministry of Commerce on the Abolition of Certain Regulatory Documents on 25 December 2019 (effective as of 1 January 2020), according to which 56 regulatory documents, such as circulars, notices and announcements, shall be abolished. MOFCOM further issued Decision of the Ministry of Commerce on Repealing Some Rules on 28 December 2019 (effective as of 1 January 2020) which provided that 6 rules shall be abolished, including the Interim Provisions concerning the Establishment of Foreign-invested Companies Limited by Shares, the Several Provisions on Changes in Equity Interest of Investors in Foreign-invested Enterprises and the Interim Provisions of the Ministry of Commerce on Capital Contribution in the Form of Equity of Foreign-invested Enterprises. Due to space limitations, these are not discussed in detail in this book.

场是全面转化的时间点将主要由外商投资企业自行决定，而仅仅受限于五年过渡期结束时的硬性最后期限。但是，我们无法完全排除在某些情况下，即使是更加技术性的修订也会触发强制性提前转化的可能。如果在过渡期早期就发现，随着绝大多数外商投资企业将转化工作推迟至过渡期的后半段，相关的行政工作量可能被证明是极其繁重的，那么情况可能尤其会如此。与 2006 年推行对外商独资企业章程进行修订的情形类似，如果有必要在行政上减轻市场监管局的压力，可能会促使采用事实上的政策，要求在对章程进行*任何*修订时强制提前转化。并且，事实上许多领先的外商直接投资从业人员完全相信，实践中，如果对外商投资企业的章程作出任何修改，市场监管总局最终会要求强制提前转化，尽管《市场监管总局通知》的措辞更为宽松。这一对《市场监管总局通知》的解释和应用的潜在不确定性，为外商投资企业带来了一些现实挑战，我们将在下一章中讨论。

“总体而言，预计外商投资企业章程的大多数修订都将归于第 12 条的范围，因此，我们完全可以假设，市场监管总局的默认立场是全面转化的时间点将主要由外商投资企业自行决定，而仅仅受限于五年过渡期结束时的硬性最后期限。但是，我们无法完全排除在某些情况下，即使是更加技术性的修订也会触发强制性提前转化的可能。”

其他相关法律发展

尽管我们的分析重点一直放在《外商投资法》和相关法规对公司治理、资本结构、公司架构和外商投资企业转化的实际影响上，但为了更全面地介绍《外商投资法》实施后的法律环境，还有其他几点值得一提。[1]

外商投资企业登记手续

对于投资负面清单之外行业领域的外商投资企业，《市场监管总局通知》明确规定将按照内外资一致的原则进行登记注册，这对于外商投资企业来说是一项重大的进步。具体来看，《市场

1 除了本节所讨论的监管要点外，我们还注意到一些其他的原有的外商投资企业相关法规被废除了。例如，商务部于 2019 年 12 月 25 日发布了《商务部关于废止部分规范性文件的公告》（2020 年 1 月 1 日生效），根据该公告，56 个规范性文件（如通知、公告等文件）被废止。商务部又于 2019 年 12 月 28 日发布了《商务部关于废止部分规章的决定》（2020 年 1 月 1 日生效），规定 6 部规章予以废止，其中包括《关于设立外商投资股份有限公司若干问题的暂行规定》、《外商投资企业投资者股权变更的若干规定》和《商务部关于涉及外商投资企业股权出资的暂行规定》。由于篇幅限制，本书未详细讨论这些内容。

as previously required will now be replaced by the submission of the foreign investment information report (see below). An official announcement of the Shanghai Commerce Commission confirms this.[1]

From our observations of recent and continuing improvements to the SAMR online registration system, it appears that the entire process for applying for the establishment of a new entity and in connection with any changes to the registration for an existing entity will all be able to be done online, at least for domestic companies. According to our consultations with registration agents, FIEs will still need to sign and submit hard copy originals offline in the traditional manners in addition to the online registration process, at least for the time being. Ultimately, it is expected that all registration applications for both domestic companies and FIEs will be handled online, perhaps with notarizations being supported by blockchain certification at some stage. These improvements in the SAMR online registration system are anticipated to be rolled out nationwide, eliminating the long-standing differences in specific SAMR application submission requirements in different localities across China (and further improving China's position in the World Bank Doing Business Report rankings).

If these improvements are rolled out early in the transition period, then FIE conversions will be able to be further streamlined, but because FIE conversion consists of not just changes in registration but also changes in corporate governance, access to SAMR's online registration system will not appreciably reduce the scope of work to be done as part of the FIE conversion process. The practical implications of these registration issues will be discussed further below as appropriate.

FIE Information Reporting

These new SAMR Circular rules on registration formalities together with the separately issued Reporting Measures bring some good news for FIEs in respect of information reporting requirements in two respects: the reporting channels have been streamlined and the information content to be reported appears to have been minimized to a significant degree.

The 2015 Draft FIL provided that foreign investors and FIEs were to report information to MOFCOM (or its authorized counterpart) through the foreign investment information

---

1 Announcement of the Shanghai Commerce Commission Accessed 3 January 2020. http://www.sh.gov.cn/zxxgk/247485.htm.

监管总局通知》第 2 条规定：

- 外国投资者或外商投资企业应当通过企业登记系统申请外商投资企业登记注册。在这个过程中，申请人应当勾选外商投资企业拟从事经营活动的行业领域，并确认其符合负面清单的要求。登记机关将对申请材料进行形式审查。如果外商投资企业所在的行业领域不属于负面清单项下限制或禁止的行业领域，则应当按照内外资一致的原则进行登记注册和备案。

- 如果外商投资企业投资负面清单规定限制投资的领域，则只要外商投资企业符合对出资比例、法定代表人国籍等准入特别管理措施规定条件的，应准予注册。而当行业主管部门在登记注册前已经依法核准相关涉企经营许可事项的，登记机关无须就是否符合准入特别管理措施规定条件进行重复审查。

《市场监管总局通知》第 3 条的规定似乎表明过去需要在商务部门进行的备案现在将被提交外商投资信息报告替代（见下文讨论）。上海市商务委员会的一份公告证实了这一点。[1]

从我们对市场监管总局在线登记系统的近期和持续改进的观察来看，至少对于内资企业来说，申请设立新实体以及对现有实体进行任何变更登记的整个过程似乎都可以在线完成。基于向注册代理的咨询，至少在目前，在线上登记程序之外，外商投资企业仍需要以传统方式在线下签署和提交纸质原件。但最终，预计内资企业和外商投资企业的所有登记注册申请都将在线处理。也许到一定阶段，公证认证可以得到区块链认证的支持。预计市场监管总局在线登记系统的这些改进将在全国范围内推广，消除中国各地在市场监管局具体申请提交要求方面的长期差异（并进一步提高中国在世界银行《营商环境报告》中的排名）。

如果这些改进在过渡期早期推行，则外商投资企业转化将进

1　上海市商务委员会公告，http://www.sh.gov.cn/zxxxgk/247485.htm，2020 年 1 月 3 日访问。

reporting system. In contrast, the Reporting Measures provide that foreign investors or FIEs should submit investment information to MOFCOM through the SAMR business registration system and the national enterprise credit information disclosure system. Then MOFCOM, through the foreign investment information reporting system, receives and processes the investment information posted by SAMR and other information obtained through an inter-department sharing mechanism, which further reduces the burden on foreign investors or FIEs to report the same information to different supervisory departments on a redundant basis.

At the same time, the types of information reports have been further integrated and simplified. However, the specific content of the report has yet to be released by MOFCOM in the form of department announcements. In general, compared with the 2015 Draft FIL, the Reporting Measures appear to be responsive to earlier criticisms that the reporting requirements under the 2015 Draft FIL were unnecessarily and overly burdensome on foreign investors and FIEs, and the information reporting system under the more recent measures limits the scope of reports to more fundamental and necessary information.

The SAMR Circular further clarified the relationship between the information reports and FIE registration—the submission of a foreign investment information report is not a necessary condition for the registration of an FIE, and SAMR does not review these information reports.

Updated 2019 Negative List

It is also important to see the FIL in the context of the current phase of China's further opening up. The adoption of the Negative List approach in 2013 in the Shanghai Pilot Free Trade Zone, and then as presaged in the 2015 Draft FIL, has been a significant part of this overall process, and further updates to the Negative List have been issued in 2017 and 2018 and most recently in June 2019.

With each successive version of the Negative List, additional new sectors are opened up for foreign investment, and the most recent updated Negative List issued in June 2019 was seen as an important companion step to accompany the FIL as this further demonstrated China's commitment to permit more foreign investment in more parts of the economy as well as provide pre-establishment national treatment.

Chart 2-B illustrates some key themes from China's national version Negative Lists (as

一步简化，但由于外商投资企业转化不仅仅包括登记的变更，还涉及公司治理的变更，通过在线登记系统办理也并不会显著减少外商投资企业转化过程中需要完成的工作范围。这些登记注册问题的实际影响将在下文中进一步讨论。

> “《市场监管总局通知》对登记注册手续的这些规定以及单独发布的《外商投资信息报告办法》在信息报告要求方面给外商投资企业带来了好消息：一方面，精简了报告渠道；另一方面，信息报告内容似乎已被大幅缩减。”

外商投资企业信息报告

《市场监管总局通知》对登记注册手续的这些规定以及单独发布的《外商投资信息报告办法》在信息报告要求方面给外商投资企业带来了好消息：一方面，精简了报告渠道；另一方面，信息报告内容似乎已被大幅缩减。

2015 年《外国投资法（草案）》规定，外国投资者、外国投资企业通过外国投资信息报告系统向外国投资主管部门报告信息。与此不同的是，《外商投资信息报告办法》规定，外国投资者或者外商投资企业应当通过网上企业登记系统以及国家企业信用信息公示系统向商务主管部门报送投资信息。商务主管部门通过外商投资信息报告系统，接收处理市场监管部门推送的投资信息以及部门共享信息等，这进一步减轻了外国投资者或者外商投资企业向不同监管部门重复报告相同信息的负担。

同时，信息报告的种类被进一步整合和简化。但是，针对报告的具体内容，还有待商务部以部门公告形式对外发布。总体上，与 2015 年《外国投资法（草案）》相比，《外商投资信息报告办法》似乎回应了人们对于 2015 年《外国投资法（草案）》规定的报告要求不必要且过度加重外国投资者和外商投资企业负担的批评，这一办法项下的信息报告制度将报告的范围限制在了更为基本和必要的信息。

《市场监管总局通知》进一步明确了信息报告和外商投资企业登记注册的关系——提交外商投资信息报告不是办理外商投资企业登记注册的必要条件，且登记机关不对外商投资信息报告进行审查。

2019 年负面清单

中国当前正处于进一步开放的阶段，以此为背景来分析《外商投资法》也很重要。2013 年上海自由贸易试验区采用负面清单模式以及 2015 年《外国投资法（草案）》提出采用负面清单模式，

opposed to the free trade zone Negative Lists) issued since 2017.

Chart 2–B Key Themes from Negative List Issued Since 2017

Date	Key figures	Newly opened sectors
28 June 2017	In comparison with the 2015 Foreign Investment Guidance Catalogue (which was further revised in 2017), the 28 June 2017 Negative List had 30 fewer industry sectors listed in the prohibited or restricted categories, leaving 35 sectors in the restricted category and 28 sectors in the prohibited category.	Restrictions on foreign investment in certain subsectors in the services, manufacturing, and mining sectors were removed or relaxed.
28 June 2018	The 2018 Negative List further reduced the number of prohibited or restricted sectors from 63 to 48. No new items were added.	Restrictions on foreign investment were removed or relaxed in certain subsectors in the agricultural, mining, manufacturing (with the immediate and planned removal of certain restrictions on foreign investment in the auto sector being a key highlight), infrastructure, transportation, financial services (including removal or gradual removal of restrictions on foreign investment in commercial banks, securities firms and insurance companies) and technology services sectors.
30 June 2019	The 2019 Negative List further reduced the number of prohibited or restricted sectors from 48 to 40. No new items were added.	Highlights of 2019 Negative List include: • Removal of the 50% cap on foreign ownership in multi-party communications, store-and-forward and call center value-added telecoms operations. • Removal of requirements that the Chinese side control the construction and operation of cinemas. • Removal of limitations on the exploration and development of oil and natural gas (excluding coalbed methane, oil shale, oil sands, shale gas, etc.). • Removal of restrictions on foreign participation in the construction and operation of gas and heat supply infrastructure in cities with populations of over 500,000.

The above changes to the Negative List are consistent with the general trends towards further opening up of the services sector. This is also a major point of emphasis in the ongoing US-China trade negotiations, and the phase one deal reached by China and the US on 15

均是这一整套流程的重要组成部分，之后在 2017 年、2018 年以及最近一次的 2019 年 6 月，负面清单又进行了进一步的更新。

随着负面清单的不断更新，更多的新行业为外商投资敞开了大门，2019 年 6 月最新发布的负面清单被视为与《外商投资法》配套的重要一步，因为其进一步表明了中国为外商投资开放更多经济领域并提供准入前国民待遇的承诺。

表 2-B 说明了自 2017 年以来发布的适用于全中国范围的外资负面清单（相对于自贸区负面清单）中的一些核心内容。

表 2-B　2017 年以来负面清单核心内容

日期	重点数据	新开放的行业领域
2017 年 6 月 28 日	与 2015 年《外商投资产业指导目录》（2017 年进一步修订）相比，2017 年 6 月 28 日发布的负面清单中的禁止或限制类行业领域减少了 30 个，剩余 35 个限制类行业，28 个禁止类行业。	取消或放宽了服务业、制造业和采矿业项下某些细分领域的外国投资限制。
2018 年 6 月 28 日	2018 年负面清单进一步将禁止或限制类行业领域的数量从 63 个减少到 48 个。没有增加新的内容。	取消或放宽了农业、采矿业、制造业（计划立即取消对汽车行业外商投资的某些限制是关键亮点）、基础设施、运输、金融服务（包括取消或逐步取消针对商业银行、证券公司和保险公司的外商投资的限制）以及技术服务领域项下某些细分领域的外商投资限制。
2019 年 6 月 30 日	2019 年负面清单进一步将禁止或限制类行业领域的数量从 48 个减少到 40 个。没有增加新内容。	2019 年负面清单的亮点包括： ・取消针对增值电信业务中的多方通信、存储转发类和呼叫中心业务的外资所有权 50% 的上限要求。 ・取消电影院建设和运营须由中方控股的要求。 ・取消对石油和天然气（含煤层气、油页岩、油砂、页岩气等除外）的勘探和开发的限制。 ・取消针对外商参与人口 50 万以上的城市燃气和热力供应基础设施的建设和运营的限制。

January 2020 included additional openings for foreign investment in the financial services sector, many of which had been in planning as indicated in the 2018 Negative List, so it is anticipated that additional areas may be opened in conjunction with the further rounds of negotiations planned in connection with the current trade talks. Related areas which may be ripe for further opening up at some stage include additional aspects of the internet/value-added telecoms sector (which as noted above would be a critical companion step were the VIE nominee shareholder structures so common in the internet sector to be placed under additional scrutiny as proposed under the 2015 Draft FIL) and even legal services. A further update to the Negative List is anticipated to be forthcoming to further open up additional industry sectors, in part as a response to the economic impacts of the coronavirus pandemic.

Overall, these trends reflect the changing FDI environment in China. When China first opened up to foreign investment 40 years ago it was to help develop a nascent market economy that was focused on manufacturing and exports. As China's economy grew, China's FDI policies were designed to selectively open up sectors to foreign investment to give Chinese enterprises sufficient room to grow and develop as the economy gained strength. Now, with China already positioned as the second largest economy in the world behind only the US, and with strong local players which no longer need protection, we can project that related FDI policies will be further liberalized.

Government Procurement

Although government procurement is not directly related to the core issues addressed in this book in respect of FIE corporate governance and conversion, it is so fundamental to the concept of "national treatment" that it merits some discussion here at least at a high level. As noted above, this is a matter which was not addressed in the 2015 Draft FIL but is mentioned, albeit only briefly, in the final FIL, with some modest supplemental provisions in the Implementation Regulations.

As alluded to above, Article 16 of the FIL states that "*The State guarantees that foreign-invested enterprises may fairly and equally compete and participate in government procurement activities in accordance with the law. Government procurement shall ensure equal treatment of domestic products and services provided and produced by foreign-invested enterprises in China in accordance with law.*" By way of background, on multiple occasions

负面清单的上述变化与服务领域进一步开放的总体趋势是一致的。这也是正在进行的中美贸易谈判中的一个重点问题，并且中国和美国于2020年1月15日达成的第一阶段经贸协议包括进一步开放金融服务领域的外商投资，如2018年负面清单所示，其中许多已经在规划中。因此我们预计与当前贸易谈判有关的计划的下几轮谈判可能会开放更多领域。可能已发展成熟以供在某个阶段进一步开放的相关领域包括互联网/增值电信领域的其他方面[如上所述，由于VIE名义股东结构在互联网领域非常普遍，如果如2015年《外国投资法（草案）》中提出的将对其进行额外审查，那么同时进一步开放该行业将非常关键]，甚至包括法律服务行业。预计负面清单将进一步更新，以进一步开放更多的行业领域，部分原因是为了应对新型冠状病毒疫情的经济影响。

总体而言，这些趋势反映了中国不断变化的外商直接投资环境。中国40年前首次对外商投资开放是为了发展以制造业和出口为主的新兴市场经济。随着中国经济的增长，中国的外商直接投资政策旨在有选择地开放外商投资领域，在中国经济发展壮大的同时为中国企业提供足够的增长和发展空间。现在，由于中国已经处于仅次于美国的世界第二大经济体的位置，随着实力强劲的本国企业不再需要保护，我们预计相关的外国直接投资政策将进一步放松。

“现在，由于中国已经处于仅次于美国的世界第二大经济体的位置，随着实力强劲的本国企业不再需要保护，我们预计相关的外国直接投资政策将进一步放松。”

政府采购

虽然政府采购与本书中关于外商投资企业公司治理和实体转化的核心问题没有直接联系，但对于“国民待遇”这一概念来说至关重要，在这里我们至少需要进行概括性地分析。如上所述，这一点在2015年《外国投资法（草案）》中没有提及，但是在《外商投资法》最终版中有规定（虽然仅是简略的规定），并且《外商投资法实施条例》对此有一些补充规定。

如上文所提及，《外商投资法》第16条规定：“国家保障

in 2018, Chinese officials reaffirmed that China would expedite its process of acceding to the WTO Agreement on Government Procurement (GPA). When China joined the WTO in 2001, it only made a general commitment (without a timeline) to accede to the GPA, and it was not until 2007 that China started its accession process and tabled its first market access offer. China tabled its sixth market access offer in 2014 but according to reports that offer still falls short of the expectations of the existing 48 member countries to the GPA.

China remains one of the 33 observer countries to the GPA, with nine of those countries at some stage in the accession process. If China accedes to the GPA, it would open up significant market opportunities for foreign-invested enterprises (likewise and reciprocally for Chinese enterprises for public procurement opportunities in the other member countries of the GPA). For the past decades, as China is not a party to the GPA, its public procurement market (including procurement by government agencies and SOEs) has not been fully opened up to FIEs. It is apparent that when it comes to public procurement, products and services of domestic enterprises have been favored by the government and SOE clients as a practical matter.

Due to the highly publicized cybersecurity breaches around the world over the last several years, the situation has become even more challenging for FIEs as government and SOE buyers routinely cite to reasons of national security, state secrecy, cybersecurity etc., as well as to the broader theme of "indigenous innovation" (that seeks to foster the development and growth of domestic enterprises), to exclude FIEs from certain bids, which message is in many cases communicated verbally on an informal basis.

Notwithstanding the numerous repeated assurances by Chinese officials that FIEs would not be discriminated against when it comes to public procurement and that all SOEs would make purchasing decisions solely based on commercial considerations (e.g., price, quality, marketability and availability), the reality has been that domestic enterprises have continued to be afforded preferential status. Foreign parties hope that the principles set out under Article 16 of the FIL and Articles 15, 16, 17 and 42 of the Implementation Regulations will in fact be implemented fully and promptly through China's accession to the GPA or its own public procurement reform.

外商投资企业依法通过公平竞争参与政府采购活动。政府采购依法对外商投资企业在中国境内生产的产品、提供的服务平等对待。”此外，中国政府曾在2018年多次重申，中国将加快加入世贸组织《政府采购协议》的进程。当中国在2001年加入世贸组织时，只对加入《政府采购协议》作出了一般性承诺（无时间表），直到2007年中国才启动加入的进程，并提交了第一份市场准入提议。中国于2014年提交了第六份市场准入提议，但据报道该提议仍然远低于《政府采购协议》的现有48个成员的预期。

中国仍然是《政府采购协议》的33个观察员之一，其中9个观察员正处于加入进程中。如果中国加入《政府采购协议》，将为外商投资企业开辟重要的市场机会（同样反过来也为内资企业开辟了进入《政府采购协议》其他成员的公共采购机会）。在过去几十年，由于中国不是《政府采购协议》的成员，其公共采购市场（包括政府和国有企业的采购）未向外商投资企业完全开放。在公共采购方面，很明显内资企业的产品和服务实际上一直受到政府和国有企业客户的优待。

过去几年中对外商投资企业来说，形式变得更加严峻，由于网络安全漏洞高度曝光，政府和国有企业客户经常借助国家安全、国家机密和网络安全等原因以及更宽泛的“自主创新”（旨在促进内资企业的发展和增长）概念将外商投资企业排除在某些投标之外，很多情况下这些信息都是以非正式的口头方式传达的。

尽管中国政府多次保证外商投资企业在公共采购方面不会受到歧视，且所有国有企业仅基于商业考量（如价格、质量、适销性和可用性）作出采购决定。但现实情况是内资企业一直享有优势地位。外方希望通过中国加入《政府采购协议》或其自身的公共采购改革使《外商投资法》第16条以及《外商投资法实施条例》第15~17条和第42条项下的原则实际上得到全面和快速的实施。

Responses to the FIL

The FIL attracted a wide range of comments within China and around the world. Many considered that the FIL was in many respects vague and incomplete. It was, as was the case with the EJV Law 40 years ago, more a statement of policy than a comprehensive piece of legislation.[1] This, of course, is a different time, and the FIL by a simple cross-reference to the Company Law was able to incorporate a very substantial body of existing law and apply that to FIEs going forward. The subsequent issuance of the 2019 SAFE Notice, the Implementation Regulations, and the SAMR Circular have further fleshed out the scope of the FIL, although it must be acknowledged that even taking into account all of the related laws and regulations, the overall approach has still remained relatively minimalist in nature and scope, particularly for such a major piece of legislation.

The vast majority of commentators addressing the FIL focused on the points relating to the ongoing US-China trade talks, while those who focused on the corporate governance and FIE conversion issues did so more at a general conceptual level. Overall, commentators had widely divergent views as to the projected overall impact of the FIL, some positive and others more neutral.

Much of the content of Chapters 1 and 2 in this Part I is similar in nature to many of the commentaries that have already been published, although the content included here may be more extensive and detailed in scope, particularly in respect of the corporate governance and FIE conversion points we have selected as our primary focus. However, the mandate we have chosen for ourselves is to apply the conceptual analysis in a more practical context and manner. Having laid a suitable conceptual foundation, we now turn to the practical application.

1 Mahony, Tarrant. "China Passes Landmark New Foreign Investment Law." The Temple 10-Q, 14 May 2019. https://www2.law.temple.edu/10q/china-passes-landmark-new-foreign-investment-law/.

对《外商投资法》的反响

《外商投资法》在中国和世界范围内引起了广泛的评论。许多人认为《外商投资法》在很多方面都是模糊和不完备的。正如40年前的《中外合资经营企业法》一样，《外商投资法》在更大意义上属于政策声明而非一部全面的立法。[1]当然，时代不同了，而且通过对《公司法》进行简单的交叉引用，《外商投资法》能够纳入大量的现有法律，并将其适用于外商投资企业。后续发布的《2019年外管局通知》、《外商投资法实施条例》和《市场监管总局通知》进一步充实了《外商投资法》的范围，但必须看到，即使考虑到所有这些相关法律法规，总体来说仍然是在性质和范围上保持了相对简约，尤其是对于这一项重要的立法来说更是如此。

绝大多数对《外商投资法》的评论文章都着眼于与正在进行的中美贸易谈判有关的问题，而关注公司治理和外商投资企业转化问题的评论则更多地停留于一般概念层面。总体而言，不同评论文章就《外商投资法》总体影响的推断存在广泛的不同看法，其中有些持乐观的态度，而其他的则更偏于中立。

本书第一部分第一章和第二章的大部分内容在本质上与许多已发表的评论文章相似，但本书所涵盖的内容在范围上可能更加广泛和详尽，特别是在我们主要关注的公司治理和外商投资企业转化方面。但是，我们的目的是将概念性分析在更实用的背景和方式下进行应用。在奠定了合适的概念基础后，现在我们将转向实际应用。

1 Mahony, Tarrant. “China Passes Landmark New Foreign Investment Law.” The Temple 10-Q, May 14, 2019. https://www2.law.temple.edu/10q/china-passes-landmark-new-foreign-investment-law/.

Chapter 3 What the New FIL Means for Foreign-invested Enterprises in China

The radical change in the fundamental legal basis for the establishment and governance of FIEs represented by the FIL is not merely a matter of theoretical interest for investors, but rather is a matter of critical practical concern. This is particularly true for both Chinese and foreign investors in joint ventures, as the shift from the legacy Three FIE Laws to the Company Law affects the structure, management and operation of the company as well as the relationship between the co-investors.

This change in law will dramatically alter the way the parties draft, negotiate and implement the terms of the base FIE documentation for greenfield joint venture projects. Investors which have had experience with traditional forms of EJV and CJV entity structures and documentation will now not only need to learn new concepts and terms but will have new options to consider under the Company Law, presenting significant additional flexibility at all levels in the corporate governance framework. Of course, more options also means more issues which may be put on the table to be negotiated.

But while the impact of the changes on investors in new greenfield FDI projects should not be underestimated, the challenge for existing Sino-foreign joint ventures will be even greater—in connection with the mandatory conversion requirement under the FIL prior to the end of the five-year transition period, all existing joint ventures will need to transition mid-stream from the legacy style joint venture documentation to an entirely new corporate governance system under the Company Law, potentially reopening the existing joint venture contract to renegotiation on a broader scale in a significant number of cases.

In the sections below, we will explore some of the principal implications of the FIL on the base documentation for both greenfield FIEs and existing FIEs. Because the impact on

第三章 《外商投资法》对中国外商投资企业意味着什么

以《外商投资法》为代表的关于外商投资企业的设立和治理的基本法律基础的根本性变化，对投资者来说不仅是一个理论问题，也是一个重要的实际问题。对于合营企业的中外投资者来说尤其如此，因为从传统的“三资法”到《公司法》的转变会影响公司的结构、管理和运营以及共同投资者之间的关系。

法律上的这一变化将极大地改变各方就新设合营企业项目中基础外商投资企业文件条款的起草、谈判和实施方式。对传统形式的合资经营企业和合作经营企业的实体结构和文件编制有经验的投资者，现在不仅需要学习新的概念和术语，由于《公司法》在公司治理框架的各个层面都提供了很多额外的灵活性，还将对新的选择进行考虑。当然，更多的选择也意味着可能会有更多的问题需要进行谈判。

虽然该变化对新的绿地外商直接投资项目的投资者的影响不可低估，但对现存中外合营企业来说面临的挑战将更大——关于《外商投资法》项下在五年过渡期内进行强制转化的要求，所有现存合营企业都需要从传统风格的合营企业文件过渡到《公司法》项下的全新公司治理体系，为现有的合营企业合同可能在更大范围内的大量重新谈判重新敞开了大门。

我们将在下文探讨《外商投资法》对新设外商投资企业和现存外商投资企业的基础文件编制的一些原则性影响。由于其对合

joint ventures is significantly more pronounced, we will focus primarily on joint ventures (with a particular emphasis on EJVs, which outnumber CJVs by more than ten-fold), but we will also address the implications for WFOEs in certain cases where appropriate.

Where noted, the points set out below reflect the consensus views of the members of the Expert Committee. Corresponding points will be noted as appropriate in the annotations to the Sample Templates set out in Part II below.

Sino-foreign Joint Venture Documentation in the Post-FIL Era

Transitioning from the legacy form of Sino-foreign joint venture contracts and articles of association under the EJV Law to the new style of FIL-compliant documentation under the Company Law is a matter of both subtraction and addition—certain legacy clauses required under the EJV Law will no longer apply and can be omitted while numerous new governance provisions required under the Company Law need to be inserted. Each category of changes is described briefly below.

Out with the Old—Certain Legacy EJV Contract Terms Omitted

Traditional Sino-foreign joint venture contracts in China include numerous terms which were required under the EJV Law but which are not mandated or even referenced under the FIL or the Company Law and so will no longer apply after the FIL takes effect. In many cases these legacy provisions are not consistent with current best practices and could give rise to confusion and misinterpretation. The Expert Committee accordingly has concluded that certain of these legacy provisions can be omitted from the new post-FIL documentation (or where retained in whole or in part, are to be modified as appropriate), including the following (representative precedent clauses[1] are set out below for each for ease of reference):

1 The sample precedent clauses set out in this section are drawn from the All China Lawyers Association – Lovells Contract Templates published in 2003 (these may be found in various China-related online contract databases). John Jiang, then of Eastbright Law Offices. and I, then managing partner of the Beijing office of Lovells, were the principal drafters of these templates. These precedent clauses were already drafted in such a way so as to ameliorate many of the issues inherent in such clauses

营企业的影响更加显著，我们将主要着眼于合营企业（尤其侧重于合资经营企业，其数量超过合作经营企业十倍之多），但我们在特定情况下也将酌情讨论对外商独资企业的影响。

如本书所说明，下文所载的要点反映了专家委员会成员的一致意见。本书第二部分所载的样本模板的注解说明中适当解释了相应的要点。

《外商投资法》时代的中外合资企业文件编制

从《中外合资经营企业法》项下传统形式的中外合资企业合同和章程转变为《公司法》项下符合《外商投资法》规定的新式文件，是一个减法和加法并存的问题——《中外合资经营企业法》项下要求的某些传统条款将不再适用并可以删除，而《公司法》项下要求的许多新的治理条款则需要添加。下文将简要介绍各类变化。

“从《中外合资经营企业法》项下传统形式的中外合资企业合同和章程转变为《公司法》项下符合《外商投资法》规定的新式文件，是一个减法和加法并存的问题。”

摒弃旧条款——删除某些传统中外合资企业合同条款

中国传统的中外合资企业合同包括《中外合资经营企业法》项下的许多必备条款，但这些条款在《外商投资法》或《公司法》项下都不做强制要求或甚至没有提及，所以在《外商投资法》生效后将不再适用。在很多情况下，这些传统条款不符合当前的最佳实践，可能会引起混淆和误解。因此，专家委员会认为某些传统条款可以从《外商投资法》时代的新文件中删除（或如果全部或部分保留，则须进行适当的修改），其中包含以下条款（表 3-A 列出了每一类条款的代表性先例条款[1]以便参考）：

1 本部分中所载的先例样本来自 2003 年发布的中华全国律师协会－路伟合同模板（可从中国相关的线上合同数据库中获取）。江宪胜（当时任职于北京市东易律师事务所）和吕立山（当时在路伟律师事务所北京办公室担任管理合伙人）是这些模板的主要起草人。这些先例条款的起草方式已经改善了其中的很多固有问题。

Chart 3–A Sample Legacy Clauses

Legacy Clause	Sample Precedent
Purpose, Scope and Scale of Operation	Purpose of Joint Venture The purpose of the joint venture shall be to utilize the combined technological, management, operational and marketing strengths of the Parties within the approved scope of business of the Company to achieve good economic results and a return on investment satisfactory to the Parties. Scope of Business The scope of business of the Company shall be to [design, manufacture and market [JV products] [to provide [•] services.] Business Plan The Business Plan of the Company shall be established by the Board in view of actual market conditions, expected sales volumes, the employees' ability to absorb new technology and any other factors considered important by the Board. Such plan may be expanded or reduced by the Board from time to time in light of market and other relevant conditions. Independent Entity The Company shall conduct its business as an independent economic entity and will operate autonomously.
Responsibilities of the Parties	In addition to its other obligations under this Contract, Party A shall have the following responsibilities: (a)assist in obtaining the relevant Permits, and approvals and registrations required in respect of the Ancillary Documents (if any), and promptly and in any event within [three(3)] Business Days provide to Party B and (following establishment) the Company all documents received by Party A from any government department in respect of any Permits and/or any of the Ancillary Contracts or otherwise in relating to the establishment, operations or business of the Company; (b)assist in obtaining amendments to, or renewals of, any of the Permits as required by the Business from time to time; (c)make its contribution to the registered capital of the Company as provided in Article 5.4 hereof; (d)promptly following the Business License Issuance Date, sign and perform each Ancillary Contract to which it is a party (if any) and cause each of its Affiliates to sign and perform each Ancillary Contract to which such Affiliate is a party (if any); (e)handle other matters entrusted to it pursuant to separate written agreement entered into by the Company and Party A from time to time. Responsibilities of Party B In addition to its other obligations under this Contract, Party B shall have the following responsibilities: (a)make its contribution to the registered capital of the Company as provided herein; (b)promptly following the Business License Issuance Date, sign and perform each Ancillary Contract to which it is a party (if any) and cause each of its Affiliates to sign and perform each Ancillary Contract to which such Affiliate is a party (if any); (c)handle other matters entrusted to it pursuant to separate written agreement entered into by the Company and Party B from time to time.

表 3–A 传统条款样本

传统条款	先例样本
经营目的、范围和规模	合资企业经营目的 合资企业的经营目的是在合资公司经批准的经营范围内利用双方的综合技术、管理、运营和营销优势，以取得良好的经济效益和双方满意的投资回报。 经营范围 合资公司的经营范围应为【设计、制造和营销[合资产品]以[提供(•)服务]】 经营计划 合资公司的经营计划应由董事会根据市场实际情况、预期销售量、员工吸收新技术的能力以及董事会认为重要的任何其他因素确定。董事会可根据市场及其他相关条件不时扩大或缩减该计划。 独立实体 合资公司作为独立经济实体开展业务，并将自主运营。
双方的责任	除本合同项下的其他义务，甲方应承担以下责任： (a) 协助取得有关许可，以及附属文件（如有）所需的批准及注册，并且就任何许可和/或任何附属文件或其他与合资公司设立、运营或经营有关的文件，甲方应在其接收到任何政府部门的所有文件的【三（3）】个工作日内及时向乙方和（设立后的）合资公司提供； (b) 协助获取目标业务不时提出的任何许可的修订或续期要求； (c) 按照本协议第 5.4 条的规定向合资公司出资； (d) 在营业执照颁发日后及时签署并履行其作为一方的附属合同（如有），并促使其各个关联方签署并履行该关联方所属的各个附属合同（如有）； (e) 处理合资公司与甲方不时订立的书面协议所委托的其他事项。 乙方的责任 除本合同项下的其他义务，乙方应承担以下责任： (a) 按照本协议的规定向合资公司出资； (b) 在营业执照颁发日后及时签署并履行其作为一方的附属合同（如有），并促使其各个关联方签署并履行该关联方所属的各个附属合同（如有）； (c) 处理合资公司与乙方不时订立的书面协议所委托的其他事项。

Continued

Legacy Clause	Sample Precedent
Marketing and Sales	Marketing Policy The General Manager shall be responsible for formulating the marketing policy and strategy of the Company for approval by the Board. All marketing activities of the Company shall be conducted in accordance with such approved policy and strategy. Market for [Products][Services][Products and Services] The Company may [sell the Products] [provide the Services to customers] in the PRC domestic market and on the international market. Sales and Distribution [Services] [Products] [Products and Services] may be sold through direct sales by the Company or otherwise as decided by the General Manager in accordance with the sales and distribution guidelines (if any) approved by the Board from time to time. The pricing of [Services] [Products] [Products and Services] shall be decided by the General Manager in accordance with budgetary guidelines approved by the Board [subject to the requirements of Applicable Laws of the PRC concerning the pricing of the [Services] [Products] [Products and Services] (if any).
Equipment and Service Procurement	Procurement Policy The Company shall purchase its required equipment, software, material, means of transportation and articles for office use and other supplies in or outside the PRC on the basis of the competitiveness of the terms and conditions of procurement, quality, quantity, pricing, and delivery terms of the products and in accordance with the procurement policy formulated by the General Manager and approved by the Board from time to time. Preference for Party A and Party B Where Party A or Party B or any of their respective Affiliates is willing to provide services to the Company , the Company shall give preference to Party A or Party B or any of their respective Affiliates (as the case may be) over other service suppliers, provided that the terms, conditions, price and quality offered by Party A, Party B or any of their respective Affiliates (as the case may be) are equal to, or more favourable than those offered by the other service suppliers, and the experience and expertise of Party A, Party B or any of their respective Affiliates (as the case may be) is equal to or better than that of the other service suppliers.
Site of the Company	The Company will conduct operations at the Site and at such other locations as approved by the Board and the relevant government departments. In accordance with the terms of this Contract, promptly following the Business License Issuance Date, the Company will sign the [Land/Building Lease Contract] and submit it to the relevant government departments for registration as required under Applicable Laws.

续表

传统条款	先例样本
市场营销与销售	营销政策 总经理负责制定合资公司的营销政策和战略，并提交董事会批准。合资公司的所有营销活动均应按照该等经批准的政策和策略进行。 【产品】【服务】【产品和服务】的市场 合资公司可在中国国内市场及国际市场中【出售产品】【向客户提供服务】。 销售和分销 【服务】【产品】【产品和服务】可以由合资公司直接销售或以总经理根据董事会不时批准的销售和分销方针（如有）决定的方式出售。【服务】【产品】【产品和服务】的定价应由总经理根据董事会批准的预算方针决定，受制于【中国适用法律关于[服务][产品][产品和服务]的规定（如有）】。
设备和服务采购	采购政策 合资公司应根据采购条款和条件的竞争力、质量、数量、价格和产品的交付情况，并遵守经总经理制定、董事会不时批准的采购政策，在中国境内外购买其所需的设备、软件、材料、运输工具和办公用品及其他用品。 对甲方和乙方的偏好 如果甲方或乙方或其各自关联方愿意向合资公司提供服务，合资公司应优先于其他服务提供者考虑甲方或乙方或其各自关联方（视情况而定），前提是甲方、乙方或其任何关联方（视情况而定）提供的条款、条件、价格和质量等于或优于其他服务提供商，且甲方、乙方或其各自关联方（视情况而定）的经验和专业知识等于或优于其他服务提供商。
合资公司的地址	合资公司将在注册地和董事会及相关政府部门批准的其他地点开展业务。根据本合同的条款，在营业执照颁发日后，合资公司将签署【土地/建筑租赁合同】，并按照适用法律的要求提交相关政府部门进行登记。

Continued

Legacy Clause	Sample Precedent
Labor Management	Company Staff Matters relating to the recruitment, employment, dismissal, resignation, wages and welfare of, and other matters concerning, the staff and workers of the Company shall be determined autonomously by the Company without outside interference, in accordance with Applicable Laws and the policies adopted by the Company from time to time. Labour Union Working Personnel shall have the right to establish a Labour Union in accordance with Applicable Laws. Working Personnel shall be employed by the Company in accordance with the terms of a collective labour contract or individual labour contracts entered into between the Company and the Working Personnel. Labour Protection The Company shall conform to the Applicable Laws of China concerning labour protection and ensure safe and civilized operation. Labour and social insurance for the Working Personnel of the Company shall be handled in accordance with Applicable Laws. General Manager's Discretion The General Manager shall determine the qualification and number of employees in accordance with the operating needs of the Company.
Taxation and Insurance	Income Tax, Customs Duties and Other Taxes (a)The Company shall pay tax under the Applicable Laws of China relating to taxation. (b)Promptly following the Business License Issuance Date, or promptly following the first date the Company is eligible to do so under Applicable Laws, the Company will submit applications to the relevant government authorities for the Tax Concessions in compliance with Applicable Laws. (c)The Chinese and expatriate employees of the Company shall pay tax on their individual income in accordance with the relevant provisions of the Applicable Laws of China relating to taxation. Insurance (a)The Company shall, at its own cost and expense, at all times take out and maintain full and adequate insurance for the Company against loss or damage by fire and such other risks as are customarily insured against by taking out insurance policies with issuers established in the PRC. (b)The property, transportation and other items of insurance of the Company will be denominated in Chinese and foreign currencies, as appropriate. The types, scope and amounts of insurance coverage shall be determined by the General Manager.

By way of further background, the legacy provisions relating to Purpose, Scope and Scale of Operation reflected certain elements of the planned economy system which were still in effect at the time of the adoption of the EJV Law. These provisions (other than the

续表

传统条款	先例样本
劳动管理	合资公司员工 合资公司职工的招聘、聘用、解雇、辞职、工资福利等事项，以及与合资公司职工有关的其他事项，由合资公司根据适用法律和合资公司不时采取的政策自行确定，不受外界干涉。 工会 工作人员有权根据适用法律成立工会。合资公司应根据集体劳动合同的条款或合资公司与工作人员签订的个人劳动合同聘用工作人员。 劳动保护 合资公司应当遵守中国有关劳动保护的适用法律，确保安全文明运营。合资公司工作人员的劳动和社会保障应根据适用法律处理。 总经理的裁量权 总经理应根据合资公司的经营需要确定员工的资格和人数。
税收和保险	所得税、关税和其他税收 (a) 合资公司应根据中国有关税收的适用法律缴纳税款。 (b) 在营业执照颁发日后，或在适用法律项下合资公司有资格提交税收优惠申请的第一天之后，合资公司将及时根据适用法律向相关政府部门提交税收优惠申请。 (c) 合资公司的中国和外籍员工应按照中国有关税收的适用法律的有关规定对其个人收入进行纳税。 保险 (a) 合资公司应自费购买并保持全面和充足的保险，通过向在中国成立的保险公司出具保单以防止因火灾以及通常投保的其他风险而导致的损失或损害。 (b) 合资公司的财产、运输及其他保险项目将以人民币及外币（如适用）计值。保险范围的类型、范围和金额由总经理确定。

作为进一步的背景介绍，有关经营目的、范围和规模的传统条款反映了计划经济体制下的某些要素，其在《中外合资经营企业法》通过时仍然有效。这些条款（仍然适用的经营范围条款除外）在随后的几十年中几乎没有实际意义，因此多年来其范围和效力已在很大程度上减弱。因此，这些传统条款未保留在本书第二部分的模板样本中。

“有关经营目的、范围和规模的传统条款反映了计划经济体制下的某些要素，其在《中外合资经营企业法》通过时仍然有效。”

business scope section, which remains applicable) have had little practical relevance in the ensuing decades, and thus have been substantially diluted in scope and effect over the years. Consequently, these legacy provisions have not been retained in the Sample Templates in Part II.

Similarly, the legacy provisions on the Site of the Company were, at least in part, originally connected to the allocation or grant of land use rights as an extension of some of the same concepts inherited from the planned economy system. These provisions also reflected the fact that when the EJV Law was adopted almost all foreign investment in China was in the manufacturing sector, and in accordance with traditional legal concepts and policies then in effect, productive enterprises were typically viewed as being tied to a particular fixed location. As the scope and nature of foreign investment has evolved over the years, this traditional view has also evolved, and the registration process for registered addresses of both domestic and foreign-invested companies has been streamlined and updated accordingly. Consequently, this legacy clause has now largely become redundant. (However, it should be noted that for a greenfield joint venture, the parties will still need to secure a site for the new company which can be used as its registered address, which is more commonly done by entering into a lease agreement on behalf of the company with the owner/landlord of the commercial office or industrial space, but it can also be done by way of purchase of the facility to be used or by in-kind contribution of the site and facility by the Chinese party.)

The legacy Responsibilities of the Parties section often would include generalized and sometimes ill-defined undertakings that could give rise to disagreements as to the scope and enforceability of the undertakings and whether separate consideration was to be paid for performance thereof. The better practice that has developed over the years now is to address many such more formal undertakings in separate ancillary contracts to be entered into between the company and the relevant party where the relevant terms could be set out in appropriate detail. By so doing, this has rendered this legacy section generally unnecessary in its original form, and so this has not been included in the Sample Templates.

The other legacy clauses relating to Marketing and Sales, Equipment and Service Procurement, Labor Management, Taxation and Insurance are all matters which may best be left to determination by the board of directors or to separate ancillary contracts between the company and the relevant parties, subject in each case to compliance with the relevant provisions of applicable laws and regulations. Accordingly, these also have not been included

同样，关于合资公司地址的传统条款最初也与土地使用权的划拨或出让有关（至少部分有关），土地使用权的划拨或出让是计划经济体制遗留的一些相同概念的延伸。这些条款也反映出，在《中外合资经营企业法》通过时，中国几乎所有外商投资都集中在制造业，且根据当时有效的传统法律概念和政策，制造企业通常被限制在某个固定地点。随着多年来外商投资的范围和性质的不断发展，这种传统观念也有所改变，内资公司和外资公司的注册地址的登记流程也相应得到了简化和更新。因此，这个传统条款现在已经基本上变得多余。（但是，需要说明的是，对于一个新设合资企业，双方仍然需要为新合资公司获取一个可以用于注册的地址，通常是通过代表该合资公司与商业办公场所或工业场所的所有权人/业主签订一份租赁协议来完成的，但也可以通过购买所使用的设施或由中方通过提供场地和设施作为非货币出资来完成。）

传统的双方的责任条款通常包括一般性的（并且有时是模糊的）承诺，这可能引起双方就承诺的范围和可执行性，以及是否应就该等承诺的履行支付额外的对价发生分歧。多年来发展出的相对好的做法是在合资公司与相关方之间另行签订的附属协议中作出正式承诺，其中相关条款可适当地进行详细规定。如此，就使得这一传统条款总体上不再有必要以其原有的形式存在，因此模板样本中没有纳入该部分。

与市场营销和销售、设备和服务采购、劳动管理、税收和保险相关的其他传统条款，最好由董事会决定或在合资公司与相关方之间另行签订的附属合同中约定，但在任何情况下，均须符合适用法律法规的相关规定。因此，这些条款也未包含在模板样本中。

当然，如果双方同意，可以根据具体情况将这些条款或类似事项纳入中外合资企业协议中。例如，由于《外商投资法》特别

in the Sample Templates.

Of course, these or similar matters can be inserted into Sino-foreign joint venture agreements on a case by case basis as appropriate if the parties so agree. For example, parties may wish to include provisions relating to labor management and trade unions in the SHA/JVA since the requirements that FIEs comply with relevant provisions on labor protection and social insurance and establish a trade union are specifically mentioned in the FIL. However, for purposes of the Sample Templates, the Expert Committee has taken the position that it is not necessary in each case to restate all such legal requirements in the SHA/JVA which will apply in accordance with the terms of applicable law whether or not set out in the document. Again, this will be a matter for negotiation and agreement on a case-by-case basis as determined by the parties in the context of each particular transaction.

In addition to the foregoing, interim changes in law or changes in names of administrative bodies have required other updates to legacy provisions (see, for example, some of the changes referenced in Chapter 1 made in the last several years). The Expert Committee has taken these changes into account as well in the Sample Templates.

In with the New—Provisions Required Under the Company Law

At the same time, numerous provisions in the post-FIL era SHA/JVA templates will need to be revised or supplemented to reflect the corporate governance provisions under the Company Law. The most obvious example is the requirement under the Company Law to establish a shareholders meeting and to take some fundamental matters which under the EJV Law required unanimous board approval and provide that these are now to be approved by the vote of more than two-thirds of the voting rights at the shareholders meeting level. However, in addition, there are scores of additional changes which now will need to be incorporated into the post-FIL SHA/JVA templates to reflect other requirements under the Company Law or to reflect additional new flexibility now permitted under the Company Law.

A non-exhaustive list of such changes is set out below for reference:

- The shareholders meeting is the highest authority of the company (whereas under the EJV Law the board of directors was the highest authority of the company).
- Either the general manager or the chairman of the board/executive director may act as the legal representative of the company (whereas under the EJV Law, only the chairman could be the legal representative of the company).

规定外商投资企业应遵守劳动保护和社会保险的相关规定并且建立工会，双方可能希望在股东协议 / 合资协议中加入与劳动管理和工会有关的条款。但是，就模板样本而言，专家委员会认为，没有必要在每种情况下都在股东协议 / 合资协议中重申所有该等法律要求，这些要求无论是否在文件中载明都将根据适用法律的条款而得到适用。同样，这个问题也需要双方在每个特定交易的背景下根据具体情况通过协商一致来决定。

除上述内容外，法律的临时变更或行政机构名称的变更也对传统条款的更新提出了要求（例如，参见第一章中提到的过去几年发生的一些变更）。专家委员会在模板样本中也将这些变化纳入了考虑范围。

纳入新条款——增加《公司法》项下要求的条款

同时，《外商投资法》时代的股东协议 / 合资协议模板中的许多条款都需要进行修订或补充，以反映《公司法》中的公司治理规定。最明显的例子是，《公司法》要求设立股东会，且对于《中外合资经营企业法》中要求董事会一致批准的一些基本事项，《公司法》规定这些事项须经股东会层面超过 2/3 表决权投票通过。但是，《外商投资法》股东协议 / 合资协议模板还需要额外纳入许多其他变化，以反映《公司法》项下的其他要求或其他新的弹性待遇。

> “《外商投资法》时代的股东协议 / 合资协议模板中的许多条款都需要进行修订或补充，以反映《公司法》中的公司治理规定。”

以下清单不完全列举出部分此类变化，以供参考：

- 股东会是合资公司的最高权力机构（而根据《中外合资经营企业法》，董事会是合资公司的最高权力机构）。
- 总经理或董事长可以担任合资公司的法定代表人（而根据《中外合资经营企业法》，只有董事长可以担任合资公司的法定代表人）。
- 不要求董事会席位的分配（如《中外合资经营企业法》所规定的）大体上参照每一方在合资公司注册资本中的比例确定。

- No requirement (as under the EJV Law) that the allocation of board seats be generally in proportion to each party's percentage of the registered capital of the company.
- The method of appointment of the chairman and vice chairman of the board can be agreed by the parties (whereas under the EJV Law where one party appointed one, the other party would appoint the other).
- Under the EJV Law, the parties could directly appoint the members of the board of directors, but under the Company Law the directors are elected at the shareholders meeting.
- Quorum requirements at the shareholders meeting and the board meeting can be set by agreement of the parties (whereas under the EJV Law, a board meeting requires a quorum of more than two-thirds of the directors).
- Certain fundamental matters which under the EJV Law required unanimous board approval [including (a) amendments to the articles of association of the company, (b) increase or reduction in the registered capital of the company and (c) merger or division or dissolution of the company] can now be approved by affirmative vote of more than two-thirds of the voting rights of the company at the shareholders meeting.
- Additional minority shareholder protections are provided for under the Company Law which were not available under the EJV Law (e.g. shareholders representing 10% of the voting rights may call an interim shareholders meeting or, if the company encounters serious difficulties, petition a People's Court to dissolve the company, although such unilateral dissolution right may be toothless as a practical matter).
- The current "thin capital" rules capping the amount of debt an FIE can incur should no longer apply (given that the Company Law has no corresponding concept of total investment amount as exists under the EJV Law) (see further discussion below).
- No minimum contribution requirements on the proportion of a company's capital to be contributed by the foreign party as originally provided under the EJV Law (although as noted above such requirements have been modified over time).
- Elimination of current restrictions on conversion of forex capital injections into RMB for purposes of downstream investments (whereas previously only capital from operations in China was available for downstream investments as a practical matter)

- 董事长和副董事长的产生办法可由双方约定（而根据《中外合资经营企业法》，如果一方指定其中一个职位，另一方将指定另一个职位）。
- 根据《中外合资经营企业法》，双方可以直接任命董事会的成员，而根据《公司法》，董事由股东会选举产生。
- 股东会会议和董事会会议召开的法定人数要求可以由双方约定（而根据《中外合资经营企业法》，董事会会议须经2/3以上董事出席方可举行）。
- 根据《中外合资经营企业法》须获得董事会一致批准的某些基本事项［包括（a）合资公司章程的修订；（b）合资公司增资或减资；（c）合资公司的合并、分立或解散］，现在可以经代表2/3以上表决权的股东投票通过。
- 《公司法》对少数股东提供《中外合资经营企业法》中没有规定的额外保护（例如，代表10%表决权的股东可以召集临时股东会会议，或者，在公司遇到严重困难的情形下，代表10%表决权的股东有权向人民法院申请解散公司，虽然这种单方面解散权可能实际上很难发挥作用）。
- 当前限制外商投资企业举债金额的“投注差”规则不再适用（鉴于《公司法》中没有与《中外合资经营企业法》中规定的投资总额相对应的概念）（详细讨论见下文）。
- 《中外合资经营企业法》原来对外方出资额比例的最低要求不再适用（尽管如上所述，这些要求已经随着时间的推移而经历过修改）。
- 取消目前对用于再投资的外汇资本转换为人民币的限制（过去实际上只有通过在中国经营所得的资金可用于再投资）（参见第一章和第二章中的相关讨论）。
- 双方可以在章程中约定不按照各自的出资比例分配股息，

(see related discussions elsewhere in Chapters 1 and 2).

- The parties may agree in the AoA not to distribute dividends in line with their respective proportions of capital contributions, which may achieve many of the structural objectives of the traditional CJV entity structure.
- The parties may agree in the AoA on the terms to apply in respect of certain transfers of registered capital (whereas under the EJV Law, transfers of registered capital must be agreed by the non-transferring party).
- Under the EJV Law, a party to the JV can object to the transfer of equity, which is sufficient to block the proposed transfer. However, under the Company Law, a party to the JV who objects to the sale must purchase the equity proposed to be transferred, failing which, the party shall be deemed to consent to the transfer.
- Previously, EJVs (and WFOEs) were approved only for a fixed term of operation, usually between 10 and 30 years, although in some cases an operating term of up to 50 years had been approved. Under the Company Law, an indefinite term is permitted.

These and other changes will be noted and discussed further as appropriate in the detailed annotations to the Sample Templates set out in Part II below.

FIE Conversion

While the guidance set out above and in the annotated Sample Templates set out in Part II are designed for use in connection with new greenfield joint ventures to be set up after the effectiveness of the FIL, they are also intended to provide a road map for amendment of the constitutional documents for the 500,000-plus existing FIEs. In this regard, most existing FIEs will need to assess what changes to make and when in response to the new legal scheme that has taken effect from 1 January 2020.

As discussed in more detail in Chapter 2, it is clear that all FIEs must complete the conversion process before the end of the five-year transition period, unless the SAMR Circular is interpreted and implemented in such a manner so as to trigger earlier mandatory conversion in connection with certain other amendments to its articles of association. The question that each FIE will need to deal with is whether there is an advantage to undertaking this conversion process sooner rather than waiting until there is no other option.

从而可以实现传统中外合作企业结构的许多结构性目标。

- 双方可以在章程中就特定的注册资本转让所适用的条款进行约定（而根据《中外合资经营企业法》，注册资本的转让必须经非转让方的同意）。
- 根据《中外合资经营企业法》，合资一方可以反对股权转让，这足以阻止拟议的股权转让。但是根据《公司法》，反对股权出售的一方必须购买拟转让的股权，否则，该方被视为同意转让。
- 过去，中外合资企业（和外商独资企业）只能设定固定的经营期限，通常为 10 年到 30 年，但有时也可长达 50 年。根据《公司法》，允许设定无限期的经营期限。

以上及其他变化将在本书第二部分所载的模板样本的详细注解中进一步说明和讨论。

外商投资企业转化

虽然上述指南和本书第二部分所载的模板样本旨在用于《外商投资法》生效后设立的新绿地合资企业，但它们也将为现存的超过 50 万家外商投资企业修订章程性文件提供路线图。就这一点而言，大多数现存的外商投资企业需要评估自己应作出哪些改变以及何时作出改变，来应对 2020 年 1 月 1 日生效的新法律体系。

如第二章中更详细地讨论的那样，很明显，所有的外商投资企业必须在五年过渡期结束前完成转化程序，除非《市场监管总局通知》被解读为在对章程作出某些其他修订时将触发提前强制转化，并在实践中如此执行。每家外商投资企业都需要面临的问题是，尽早转化相比于等到没有别的选择时再转化是否有一定的优势。

“每家外商投资企业都需要面临的问题是，尽早转化相比于等到没有别的选择时再转化是否有一定的优势。”

这个问题可以更简洁地表述为，外商投资企业在这个问题上应当更加积极还是消极？当然，当问题以这种形式提出时，答案

To frame the question more succinctly, should FIEs be pro-active or passive in this regard? Of course, when the question is presented in this form, the answer becomes patently obvious—the pro-active approach is always the most sensible approach. We examine below some of the related considerations that should be taken into account in formulating a pro-active approach to the issues of the timing and nature of the FIE conversion process.

First point—FIEs probably will not want to proceed with conversion on a voluntary basis immediately following the effectiveness of the FIL

Although the SAMR Circular has been issued, SAMR offices most likely will not be in a position to accept applications for voluntary FIE conversions in the initial period immediately following the effectiveness of the FIL, the Implementation Regulations and the SAMR Circular. Based on past experience, it typically takes up to six months following the effectiveness of new regulations for the local enterprise registration authorities to come up to speed on the practical aspects of the new registration system. Taking into account the impact of the COVID-19 pandemic in Q1 2020,that will centainly be the case in this instance. Therefore, we can expect that many SAMR offices in China may not be fully geared up to accept applications for voluntary FIE conversions until sometime in the latter part of the second quarter of 2020 or even later in some locations.

Moreover, it is likely to take time to obtain clarification as to the actual application process requirements. However, we may infer that, according to relevant provisions of the SAMR Circular, the application process and application materials for FIE conversion generally will be set by reference to the existing process and materials submission requirements for change of registration and record-filing applicable to domestic enterprises, although for the time being it appears that FIEs will need to continue to make submissions offline in most cases while the trend is for domestic enterprises to make most if not all submissions solely online. In addition, the FIE conversion application process will also need to comply with the information reporting requirements applicable to foreign investment projects.

For much of the preceding decades, the relevant registration and filing formalities for domestic enterprises have been much simpler as compared with those for FIEs, so any proposed harmonization of the registration and filing systems can only be good news for FIEs. Moreover, as noted in Chapter 2, authorities are continuing to make improvements to the SAMR online registration system, so we can expect that over time the level of process

是显而易见的——积极主动的做法永远是最明智的做法。我们将在下文中讨论，在就外商投资企业转化程序的时间和性质问题制定积极方法时应考虑的一些相关考虑因素。

第一点——外商投资企业很可能不希望在《外商投资法》生效后立即自愿进行转化

虽然《市场监管总局通知》已经发布，但在《外商投资法》、《外商投资法实施条例》和《市场监管总局通知》生效后的初期阶段，各地市场监管局很有可能无法接受自愿转化的申请。基于过去的经验，自新规生效到地方企业登记机关将新的登记制度付诸实践，这中间通常需要长达 6 个月的时间。考虑到 2020 年第一季度新型冠状病毒肺炎疫情的影响，这一情况肯定如此。因此，我们可以预计，中国的许多地方企业登记机关在 2020 年第二季度或（在某些地区）甚至更晚的时间之前可能无法完全准备好接受自愿转化的申请。

另外，很可能需要时间才能明确实际的申请流程要求。但根据《市场监管总局通知》的相关规定，我们可以推断外商投资企业转化的申请流程和申请材料应主要参考现有内资企业变更登记和备案的流程和材料。对于内资企业来说，趋势是所有申请将完全通过线上提交处理，尽管目前看来似乎外商投资企业在大多数情况下仍需要继续在线下提交材料。此外，外商投资企业转化申请还需要符合适用于外商投资项目的外商投资信息报告的要求。

在过去几十年中，内资企业的相关登记备案手续相对外商投资企业而言要简化得多，因此拟统一登记备案制度对外商投资企业而言只能是利好消息。此外，如第二章中所述，政府在持续改进市场监管局在线登记系统，因此我们可以预计，随着时间推移，相比于过去即使是纯粹的行政性事务（过去在中国传统实践中也一直算是一件麻烦的事），这些行政 / 登记事项在程序上的复杂程度将显著降低。预计在适当的时候全国范围内将采用统一的登

complexity for such administrative/registration matters will be substantially reduced by comparison to the traditionally cumbersome nature of even such purely administrative matters as a practical matter in China historically. We also expect that that uniform registration submission requirements will be adopted nationwide in due course, which will serve to ameliorate the significant regional variations which have historically existed in respect of the particular filing requirements in different localities across China. But this is a work in process that will take some time, so it should be expected that few if any FIEs will voluntarily initiate the conversion process in the first half of 2020. It will be important to track how this is handled early on while at the same time not drawing too many conclusions from inconsistent implementation across different localities as this should be expected in the early stages (and perhaps even beyond).

Point two—FIEs also should not postpone conversion until too late in the transition period

Just as it may not be prudent to initiate voluntary FIE conversion in the first few months of the transition period, it would also be manifestly unwise to put it off until too late in the transition period. One key reason not to wait is to avoid being caught up in the expected last-minute crush of applicants. If the majority of FIEs wait until the last two years of the transition period, the conversion of so many FIEs in such a relatively limited period of time will be a massive undertaking that may threaten to overwhelm the resources of both the relevant government departments as well as the capacity of legal service providers and entity registration service providers in the market. Even if the SAMR Circular is interpreted and implemented so as to impose a mandatory early conversion trigger in connection with all or only some amendments to the FIE's existing articles of association as a practical matter, that will only pull forward a modest percentage of FIE conversions to earlier stages in the transition period, with most FIE conversions still taking place in the latter part of the transition period.

We will examine the likely conversion scenarios in terms of timing and volumes in more detail in the next chapter, but for purposes of this discussion we can simply note that in the more likely scenario in which the timing of conversion is 100% voluntary, the actual volumes of FIE conversions in the latter part of the five-year transition period will be as much as ten times higher than historical norms for new FIE establishment.

In addition, all of this FIE conversion activity will be on top of increasing levels of inbound FDI resulting from the anticipated further opening up of various industry sectors to

记注册要求，这将有助于弥合长期存在的中国不同地区的具体登记注册要求的显著区域性差异。但这是一项正在进行的工作，需要一些时间，因此，预计在2020年上半年，很少有外商投资企业会自愿启动转化程序。尽早跟踪此问题的处理方式非常重要，但同时也不要从不同地方不一致的实施情况中得出太多结论，因为这应该是在早期阶段（也许甚至更长时间内）可预期的情况。

第二点——外商投资企业也不应将转化推迟到过渡期的晚期

正如在过渡期的头几个月启动外商投资企业自愿转化可能不够审慎一样，将其推迟到过渡期过晚的时候显然也是不明智的。不要等待的一个关键原因是避免在最后时刻陷入与预期的大批申请者“千军万马挤独木桥”的境地。如果大多数外商投资企业等到过渡期的最后两年，那么如此多的外商投资企业在相对有限的时间内进行转化将是一项浩大的工程，可能会给相关政府部门的资源以及市场上法律服务提供者和企业登记注册服务机构的工作量带来巨大的压力。即使《市场监管总局通知》被解释为在对外商投资企业章程作出任何或仅有某些修订时将触发强制提前转化，并在实践中如此执行，这也仅会使少部分的外商投资企业转化提前到过渡期较早的阶段进行，大部分的外商投资企业转化仍会发生在过渡期的后期。

“正如在过渡期的头几个月启动外商投资企业自愿转化可能不够审慎一样，将其推迟到过渡期过晚的时候显然也是不明智的。”

我们将在下一章中更详细地从时间和数量两个方面研究可能的转化场景，但为了目前讨论的目的，我们可以简单地指出，在更可能的情况下，转化的时间点是完全自愿决定的，5年过渡期后半程的外商投资企业转化的实际数量将高达新设外商投资企业的历史水平的10倍。

除了所有这些外商投资企业转化活动之外，许多行业领域将对外商投资进一步开放，加上外商投资企业再投资机会的开放，包括外商投资企业集团架构的重组（见第二章相关论述）都将使入境外商直接投资水平不断提高，这都将进一步推动外商直接投

foreign investment and the opening up of FIE downstream investment opportunities, including reorganization of FIE corporate group structures (see related discussion in Chapter 2), all of which will contribute further to increased levels of FDI work going forward, placing even more demands on limited resources.

Also, as noted above in Chapter 2, if the parties fail to complete the conversion process prior to the end of the five-year period, then under the Implementation Regulations the local SAMR will close its window and not process any other registration formalities for the non-complying FIE. In addition, it would appear that at that point the legality of actions undertaken which do not conform to the corporate governance requirements of the Company Law could be subject to challenge, which may have ramifications which cannot be fully anticipated at this time but which may in some cases also have a potential negative impact on operational aspects of the business beyond the inability to complete various registration formalities with SAMR. In some cases, failure to reach agreement on the revised SHA/JVA could also constitute a deadlock, which may also give rise to undesirable and unintended outcomes and changes to the balance of negotiating leverage between the parties, depending on how such deadlock matters are addressed in the existing JV contract.

Point three—the corporate governance provisions under the Company Law are superior to the legacy provisions under the EJV Law

Given the overall superiority of the corporate governance provisions under the Company Law, many joint venture parties will prefer to undertake conversion earlier in the five-year period so as to provide a more stable foundation for the joint venture company at an earlier stage. Further improvements in the Company Law have long been rumored to be in the pipeline, so those FIEs that have already converted will be in a position to take full advantage of such anticipated changes as they occur (but, of course, such further changes and improvements to the Company Law during the five-year transition period may also serve as an inducement for FIEs with legacy corporate governance structures and systems to undertake conversion at that time).

Early voluntary conversion may be more common in cases in which partner relationships are relatively harmonious and it is anticipated that the changes to be incorporated into the new SHA/JVA can be agreed with little or no difficulty as more of a mechanical exercise without reopening the whole of the original JV contract to renegotiation (which we will refer to herein as a "simple JV conversion" process, not because the joint venture arrangement itself is simple

资工作量水平的提高，对有限的资源提出更高的需求。

此外，如我们在第二章中提到的，如果双方未能在五年期限届满前完成转化手续，根据《外商投资法实施条例》的规定，企业登记机关将不予办理不合规的外商投资企业的其他登记事项。此外，届时企业采取不符合《公司法》项下公司治理要求的行为，其合法性就可能会受到质疑，后果目前无法完全预估，但除了不能在企业登记机关办理各类登记事项外，在某些情况下也可能对业务运营方面产生负面影响。在某些情况下，未能就股东协议/合资协议的修订达成一致也可能构成僵局，并可能导致不希望的或意想不到的负面后果，使双方之间谈判筹码的平衡发生变化，这具体取决于现有的合营企业合同是如何解决此类僵局问题的。

第三点——《公司法》项下的公司治理规定优于《中外合资经营企业法》项下的传统规定

鉴于《公司法》项下的公司治理规定整体上更优，许多合营方将倾向于在五年期限内的较早时期进行转化，以便尽早为合营公司提供更稳定的基础。长期以来，一直有传言称《公司法》将有进一步的改进，因此，那些已经转化的公司在这些预期变化发生时将可以充分利用这些变化（当然，在5年过渡期内《公司法》的进一步变化和改进也可能会促使仍采用传统的公司治理结构和制度的外商投资企业在此类变化发生时进行转化）。

“早期自愿转化在合作伙伴关系相对和谐的情况中可能更加常见，预计双方对于在新股东协议/合资协议中纳入的变更将很容易或毫无障碍地达成一致，因为这一过程更多的是技术性处理，而无须对原始的合营企业合同进行整体上的重新谈判。”

早期自愿转化在合作伙伴关系相对和谐的情况中可能更加常见，预计双方对于在新股东协议/合资协议中纳入的变更将很容易或毫无障碍地达成一致，因为这一过程更多的是技术性处理，而无须对原始的合营企业合同进行整体上的重新谈判（我们将在本书中称之为“简单的合营企业转化”，这并非因为合营安排本身简单或规模较小，而是因为合营企业合同的修订过程在性质上更为技术性，因而较为简单）。

此外，对于中外合营企业和外商独资企业，在转化后将可以

or small in scale, but because the joint venture contract amendment process will be more technical in nature and thus simpler to implement).

Moreover, for both Sino-foreign joint ventures and WFOEs, conversion will allow the FIE to adopt an open term, avoiding complications that routinely arise in connection with extensions of a fixed term. Of course, some investors may not wish to extend the existing fixed term of their joint venture, particularly if the partner relationships are difficult. This is a matter for strategic and tactical assessment and planning.

Point four—a one-step process is superior to a multi-step process

Even in the absence of the mandatory conversion triggers under the SAMR Circular, it would still be advisable for the parties to Sino-foreign joint ventures to voluntarily undertake conversion and to fold the new corporate governance requirements under the Company Law into the AoA and the related SHA/JVA in connection with any major corporate action as this will solidify the corporate governance foundation of the joint venture at the same time as these other fundamental revisions are to be made. For example, if a new investor acquires a stake in an existing Sino-foreign JV, or a foreign investor restructures multiple affiliated FIEs under a new onshore FIE group holding structure, it would not only be sensible but perhaps also critical to bring the corporate documentation into alignment with the Company Law requirements at the same time.

The rationale for doing so is compelling whether conversion is undertaken on a voluntary or mandatory basis in connection with such other amendments to the articles of association: Completing all changes at one time will save time and costs in handling related changes of registration and to avoid concerns arising in connection with other corporate actions which will require registrations and filings with SAMR. A multi-step process in respect of Sino-foreign JVs also carries risks that one party or the other may seek to leverage the second-stage process to negotiate additional changes. So the rule should be do it once and be done with it.

Point five—the conversion of Sino-foreign JVs will require additional time and attention

This conversion process will play out differently for WFOEs and for Sino-foreign joint ventures. Existing WFOEs will have to revise their AoA to comply with the Company Law in conjunction with the conversion process, but since WFOEs have only a single investor they can take unilateral action to amend the AoA, which will be more a more straight-forward

设定无限期的经营期限，避免因延长固定期限而经常出现的复杂情况。当然，一些投资者可能不希望延长其合营企业的现有固定期限，特别是在合作伙伴关系不太顺畅的情况下。这是一个战略和战术评估和规划的问题。

第四点——一站式程序优于多步骤的程序

即使在《市场监管总局通知》项下不存在强制转化的触发条件，对于中外合营企业的双方来说，在进行任何重大公司行为时自愿进行转化，并将《公司法》项下新的公司治理要求纳入章程和相关的股东协议 / 合资协议仍然是可取的做法，因为这将使其在作出其他根本性修订的同时巩固合营企业的公司治理基础。例如，如果新投资者收购了现有中外合营企业的股权，或者外国投资者在新的境内外商投资企业集团控股结构下重组多个关联外商投资企业，同时使公司文件符合《公司法》的要求不仅是明智的，也可能是非常关键的。

无论是在自愿基础上进行，还是在与章程的该等其他修订相关的强制性基础上进行转化，这么做的原因都令人信服：一次性完成所有变更也将节约办理相关变更登记事务的时间和成本，同时避免因其他需要在市场监管局进行登记备案的公司行为产生的顾虑。对于中外合营企业而言，采取多步骤的程序还会存在风险，即一方或另一方可能试图利用第二阶段的程序来协商其他变更。所以规则应该是只做一次，并彻底完成。

第五点——中外合营企业的转化需要花费更多的时间和精力

> “对外商独资企业和中外合营企业来说，转化过程将有所不同。”

对外商独资企业和中外合营企业来说，转化过程将有所不同。现存外商独资企业需要在转化过程中修改其章程以符合《公司法》的规定，但由于外商独资企业只有一个投资者，它们可以单方面修订章程，无论如何外商独资企业的章程都是一份较为简单的文件。因此，外商独资企业可以撕毁其原有章程，替换为一份重新起草的符合《公司法》的全新章程，或者它们可以修改其原有章

document in any event. As a result, WFOEs can either rip and replace their old AoA and start with a completely new AoA that complies with the Company Law or they can amend their original AoA to introduce the Company Law corporate governance requirements. We expect that it will be much more common for WFOEs to adopt the former approach rather than the latter since it will be much simpler to replace their legacy AoA than to take the time and expense to make the full range of detailed amendments to the articles on a clause-by-clause basis to fold in the new requirements under the Company Law.[1]

The parties to an existing joint venture, on the other hand, are unlikely to dispose of their original JV contract and AoA and replace them with an entirely new set of base documents. There are too many points in their existing constitutional documents that were the product of extensive negotiations, and they will not want to start over from scratch, so they will for the most part look to make amendments to their existing documentation to introduce terms conforming to the requirements of the Company Law. This may be much more difficult than starting with a clean sheet of paper as will be the case for new joint ventures.

But in many cases this will be just the tip of the iceberg. Investors (particularly those with multiple EJVs and CJVs) will hope to limit the amendments to the SHA/JVA only to the minimum required changes to the corporate governance provisions which may be less controversial while leaving the remaining base contractual terms intact (our so-called simple JV conversion scenario). However, it is inevitable that in a significant number of cases, this amendment process will likely give rise to substantial renegotiation of many previously settled points of corporate governance as one or both of the parties may seek to take advantage of some of the additional flexibility afforded under the Company Law by comparison with what was previously permitted under the EJV Law.

For example, as noted previously, matters previously requiring unanimous board approval under the EJV Law can now be controlled by a more than two-thirds majority vote at the shareholders meeting level, so a 60% majority shareholder may be incentivized to buy down or dilute down the minority shareholder's equity interest to below the one-third threshold. But, of course, even if the minority shareholder agrees to sell down or be diluted

1 Of course, it should also be noted that since the WFOE corporate governance structure is already more closely aligned with the requirements of the Company Law. Even so, the number of detailed amendments required to be made to legacy WFOE articles of association should not be under-estimated. By way of example, a sample mark-up of a legacy WFOE AoA to incorporate the required changes to come into compliance with the Company Law can be downloaded free of charge at www.docqbot.com/en/newFIL.

程以纳入《公司法》的公司治理要求。我们预计，外商独资企业将更普遍采取前一种而不是后一种做法，因为相较于花费时间和费用逐条对章程进行详细修订以纳入《公司法》的新要求，更换其传统的章程要简单得多。[1]

另外，现存合营企业的各方则不太可能丢弃其原有合营企业合同和章程并用一套全新的基础文件代替。他们现有的章程性文件中有很多要点是大量谈判的结果，因此他们不会想要从头开始，所以他们在大多数情况下会选择修改现有文件以纳入符合《公司法》要求的条款。这比新合营企业从零开始起草文件的过程可能要困难得多。

但在许多情况下，这只是冰山一角。投资者（尤其是拥有多家中外合资企业和中外合作企业的投资者）会希望将对股东协议/合资协议的公司治理规定的修订限制在最低必要的范围内，就该等修改发生争议的可能性较小，同时会希望保持其余基本合同条款不变（我们所说的“简单的合营企业转化”情形）。但是，不可避免的是，在许多情况下，这一修订程序可能会导致对许多先前已经解决的公司治理问题进行实质性的重新谈判，因为一方或双方可能会寻求利用《公司法》与《中外合资经营企业法》先前允许的内容相比所提供的某些额外的灵活性。

例如，如前所述，以前在《中外合资经营企业法》项下需要董事会一致批准的事项现在可以由股东会层面的2/3多数票决定，因此持股60%的多数股东可能更愿意对少数股东的股权进行收购或稀释，使其股权比例降至1/3以下。但是，即使少数股东同意出售或稀释股权，也可能不同意放弃对此类事项的否决权。

---

1 当然，还应该指出，外商独资企业的公司治理结构已经更加符合《公司法》的要求。即便如此，需要对传统的外商独资企业章程进行的细节修订的数量也不应被低估。例如，可以在 www.docqbot.com/cn/newFIL 免费下载一份带有修订标记示例的传统外商独资企业章程，看看为符合《公司法》的规定需要对其作出哪些修订。

down, it may not agree to relinquish its veto rights over such matters.

This may then set off other discussions to allow the majority shareholder to take advantage of more flexible quorum requirements under the Company Law to ensure that the directors it has nominated can constitute a quorum to avoid potential blockages at that level at least in part. In exchange for any concessions along these lines, the minority shareholder may seek other accommodations, which could take the form of disproportionate profit distributions or a reshuffling of the management nomination rights. And the list of potential issues under the Company Law goes on and on. In addition, as previously noted, the renegotiation process will give both sides an opportunity to air old grievances and to raise new points to address changed circumstances.

In short, unless the parties can impose strict discipline on the process to limit the changes only to those which are absolutely necessary (as in our "simple JV conversion" scenario), in many cases once the original contract has been reopened for amendments to conform to the requirements of the Company Law, it may not be possible to keep the amendments within that narrow scope. In many such cases it may give rise to a full renegotiation.This will have to be done prior to submission of the filings for conversion as the AoA will be among the documents required to be filed. Under the new system, the JVA will not be subject to separate review and approval, but the JVA will need to be fully renegotiated and signed up front together with the AoA, otherwise this may adversely affect a party's negotiating leverage in ways that may be difficult to predict in advance. This will in many cases be a time-consuming process, so it will be imperative for parties to plan ahead and to leave a sufficient buffer towards the end of the transition period so as not to be under artificial time pressure from the looming final deadline. Similarly, it is important to note from a broader market perspective that internal and external professional support resources will be at a premium in the latter stages of the transition period as the volumes of joint venture renegotiations and conversions threaten to exceed available market capacity by a significant margin. This will be particularly true for foreign investors with multiple joint ventures which may be engaged in renegotiations and conversions on a parallel track.

However, it is the potential mandatory early conversion requirement under the SAMR Circular that presents the greater challenge. If the parties to a Sino-foreign JV fail to plan ahead, then if other routine amendments to the AoA and JV contract end up triggering full conversion in certain circumstances as a practical matter, this will require additional time and potentially complicate the process. For example, a change to the business scope may be critical for operational

这可能进一步引发其他讨论，使多数股东能够利用《公司法》项下更灵活的法定人数要求，确保其提名的董事可构成法定人数，以避免董事层面的部分潜在僵局。作为在以上方面做出让步的交换，少数股东可以寻求其他变通方式，如不按出资比例进行利润分配或重新分配管理层提名权。在《公司法》项下，潜在问题还有很多。此外，如前所述，重新谈判的过程将使双方有机会重提原有问题以及提出新的看法来应对变化的情况。

简言之，除非双方能够对程序施加严格约束，将变更仅限于绝对必要的变更（如我们所说的“简单的合营企业转化”的情形），在许多情况下一旦原有合同被置于为符合《公司法》要求而进行修订的情形下，修订就不太可能被限制在这一狭窄的范围内。在许多情况下，这可能引起全面的重新谈判。因为章程是需要提交的文件之一，修订章程必须在提交转化申请之前完成。在新制度下，合营企业协议无须另经审查和批准，但合营企业协议需要与章程一起进行全面的重新谈判和提前签署，否则可能会以难以提前预测的方式对一方的谈判筹码产生不利影响。在许多情况下，这将是一个耗时的过程，因此各方必须提前计划并在过渡期结束前留下足够的缓冲时间，以免在最后关头承受人为的时间压力。同样，从更广泛的市场角度来看，由于合营企业重新谈判和转化的数量有可能大幅超过可用的市场服务能力，在过渡期后期，内部和外部专业支持资源将是非常昂贵的。对于拥有多家合营企业的外国投资者尤其如此，这些合营企业可以在平行的轨道上进行再谈判和转化。

但是，《市场监管总局通知》潜在的强制提前转化要求带来了更大的挑战。如果中外合营企业的各方未能提前计划，则如果对章程和合营企业合同的其他常规修订在实践中某些情况下触发了全面转化，这将延长这些常规变更程序的时间，并可能使其复杂化。例如，变更经营范围对于经营来说可能至关重要，但在各方协商对公司治理规定进行全面合规性修订（假设进行这些修订

purposes but delayed while the parties negotiate the full range of conforming changes to the corporate governance provisions (assuming for these purposes that this triggers mandatory early conversion as a practical matter). Moreover, if the parties are not able to limit this to a simple JV conversion process, both the parties' relationship and the business may be impacted.

Point six—make a plan now even if action is deferred to later

Given the fundamental nature of the changes to the foreign investment regime in China and the broader market implications, all parties (both foreign and domestic) to existing Sino-foreign JVs should give appropriate consideration at an early stage of what steps should be taken to address the issues and opportunities raised by the FIL together with an assessment of the advantages and disadvantages of the timing for such actions.

The process ideally should roll out as follows:

Step 1	With the assistance of legal counsel, the joint venture party should undertake a unilateral analysis of the implications of the Company Law for the corporate governance of the joint venture. This diagnostic exercise will need to take into account the party's equity share (majority, 50-50, minority) and other indicia of control (veto rights, management appointment/nomination rights, rights under ancillary agreements, etc.) and then evaluate what new options may be available to it under the provisions of the Company Law.
Step 2	The party then should determine (1) its walk-in position and (2) its walk-out position in respect of the changes to be made to the JV contract and AoA to achieve its preferred outcomes in the renegotiation process. This will need to take into account the overall dynamics in the joint venture relationship to assess what outcomes can realistically be achieved. It will also be appropriate to consider what changes the other party may request as part of this process and plan responses and counter-proposals accordingly. Of course, an ideal outcome (but not necessarily an attainable outcome in all cases as a practical matter) would be to undertake only a simple JV conversion and make only the bare minimum of changes.
Step 3	The party should make initial contact with the joint venture partner to exchange views on the proposed timeline for initiating the renegotiations of the JV contract as part of the conversion process. If it turns out that the SAMR Circular as a practical matter is interpreted and implemented in a manner which requires earlier conversion be undertaken in connection with certain other amendments to the articles of association, then it will be important to assess what pending corporate actions may trigger such a conversion, as that may impose timing constraints outside of the control of the parties. It will also be important to establish which side will take the lead on drafting the amendments to the JV contract.
Step 4	Drafts of the amended documents should be prepared and presented to the other party.
Step 5	The parties engage in negotiation of the amendments and finalize and sign the revised JVA and AoA in English and Chinese.
Step 6	The joint venture company will then be in a position to undertake and complete the conversion process.

在实践中将触发强制提前转化）时可能被延迟。此外，如果各方无法将此限制为简单的合营企业转化流程，双方的关系和业务可能都会受到影响。

“鉴于中国的外商投资制度发生的根本性变化及其对市场更为广泛的影响，现有中外合营企业的所有（境外和境内）投资方应在早期适当考虑应采取哪些措施来处理《外商投资法》带来的问题和机遇，并针对实施此类措施的时机进行利弊评估。”

第六点——现在就制订计划，即使行动推迟到以后

鉴于中国的外商投资制度发生的根本性变化及其对市场更为广泛的影响，现有中外合营企业的所有（境外和境内）投资方应在早期适当考虑应采取哪些措施来处理《外商投资法》带来的问题和机遇，并针对实施此类措施的时机进行利弊评估。

理想情况下该过程应以如下步骤展开：

步骤 1	在法律顾问的协助下，合营方应单方面分析《公司法》对合营企业公司治理的影响。这项分析工作需要考虑到该方的股权比例（多数、50-50、少数）和其他控制权的象征（否决权、管理层任命/提名权、附属协议项下的权利等），然后评估《公司法》项下新的可选方案。
步骤 2	该方应确定其（1）初始立场和（2）对于合营企业合同和章程变更的底线，以在重新谈判的过程中达到其希望的结果。这需要考虑合营关系的整体动态，以评估实际可以实现的结果。同时也要考虑对方可能要求进行哪些修订并制定相应的回复和反提议。当然，理想的结果（但实际上并非在所有情况下都可以实现）是进行简单的合营企业转化，只作最小的改动。
步骤 3	该方应与合营伙伴进行初步联系，就拟议的作为转化一部分的合营企业合同的重新谈判时间表交换意见。如果《市场监管总局通知》实际上被解释为要求在对章程进行某些其他修订时提前转化，并在实践中如此执行，则评估哪些待决的公司行为可能触发该等转化非常重要，因为这可能会施加双方无法控制的时间限制。确定哪一方将主导起草合营企业合同的修订也很重要。
步骤 4	应起草修订文件并提交给另一方。
步骤 5	双方对修订案进行谈判并确定最终版本，并签署修订后的中英文合营企业协议和章程。
步骤 6	合营公司实施并完成转化过程。

It will be prudent for each joint venture party to undertake the diagnostic/analysis exercise outlined in Steps 1 and 2 above at as early a time as possible, ideally around the mid's point of 2020, by which time the FIE conversion process should be more settled. Once the scope of the proposed amendments is confirmed, then this will help inform the decision on the timing for the initial approach to the partner in Step 3 and the initiation of the remaining steps as part of the overall renegotiation and conversion process (subject, of course, to the possibility of mandatory triggers under the SAMR Circular). There may be other regulatory considerations under the applicable industry regulatory scheme as well as partner relationship considerations that may impact the proposed timing arrangements.

In addition, the parties may wish to take into account the availability of their preferred outside legal counsel. Under the worst-case scenario outlined above where the vast majority of Sino-foreign joint ventures all defer renegotiation of their JV contracts to the last two years of the transition period, all of the top FDI lawyers may already be at or beyond capacity (even though they will already be charging premium rates). In such a scenario, the parties may have no choice but to seek new legal counsel, who will have to read into the file. This is not something that can be commoditized, so the client will have to pay full rates for the new legal team to come up to speed on the deal background. This will certainly be good news for lawyers at the edges of the market, but clients may end up paying more for a lawyer without the same understanding of the client's objectives, expectations and operating style.

In sum, depending on how SAMR implements the FIE conversion requirement, foreign investors may have no choice as a practical matter when to undertake conversion. If, as many leading FDI practitioners expect, mandatory early conversion will be triggered when any amendment is made to the FIE's articles of association, then many foreign investors may find themselves in a difficult position if they are not prepared to make all of the changes to the corporate governance requirements required under the Company Law at the same time. Consequently, the most sensible approach will be to take care of this earlier in the process in order to take advantage of the superior corporate governance provisions under the Company Law and to avoid any adverse implications that may arise simply because it seemed easier to wait until later.

每个合营方都应尽早开展上述步骤 1 和步骤 2 中所述的诊断 / 分析工作，最好是在 2020 年年中左右，届时外商投资企业转化流程应当会更加明朗。一旦确定了拟议修订的范围，这将有助于决定步骤 3 项下初步联系合营伙伴的时间，以及作为整体重新谈判和转化过程一部分的剩余步骤的启动时间（当然，这受限于《市场监管总局通知》项下潜在的强制转化的要求）。在（适用的行业监管制度项下的）监管以及合营伙伴关系方面，也可能存在可能影响拟议时间安排的其他考量因素。

此外，各方可能要考虑到他们首选的外部法律顾问的可用性。在上文所述的最坏的情形下，大多数合营企业将其合营企业合同的重新谈判推迟到过渡期的最后两年，这就会达到或超过顶尖外商直接投资律师事务所所能提供的总体服务能力（即使他们已经提高费率）。在这种情况下，各方别无选择，只能寻找新的法律顾问，而新法律顾问必须阅读相关文件。这一工作无法商品化，因此客户将不得不支付全额费用，让新的法律团队快速了解交易背景。对于处于市场边缘的律师来说，这肯定是个好消息，但对于客户来说，结果可能是花更多钱聘请了一个不了解客户的目标、期望和经营风格的律师。

总而言之，取决于市场监管总局如何实施外商投资企业转化的要求，外国投资者可能实际上无法选择何时转化。如果像许多领先的外商直接投资从业人员预期的那样，对外商投资企业的章程作出任何变更都会触发强制提前转化，则许多外国投资者可能会发现，如果他们没有准备好同时根据《公司法》所要求的公司治理要求进行所有变更，自己将处于困难的境地。因此，最明智的做法是在这一过程中尽早处理这一问题，以便利用《公司法》项下更优的公司治理规定，并避免仅仅因为似乎更容易等到后期而可能产生的任何不利影响。

Avoiding the Nightmare Scenario

The nightmare scenario in this conversion process would be for all 500,000-plus FIEs to queue up to the window at the local SAMR office in year five of the transition period to undertake this conversion process. If the SAMR Circular is interpreted and implemented so as to provide for an earlier mandatory conversion trigger in connection with certain amendments to the existing articles of association, then it may be possible to escape this highly undesirable fate or at least blunt the full impact of such mass deferred action.

But, of course, even if mandatory early conversion is required as a practical matter under the SAMR Circular, FIEs do not make amendments to their existing AoA on a regular basis. Consequently, under either scenario it is very probable that the vast majority of FIEs will still be left to determine the timing of conversion on their own. Human nature being what it is, it is still likely that the majority will wait until later in the transition period even if that is not the prudent option. Given the magnitude of the numbers, any back-end loading of the volume of conversions will put a significant strain on existing market resources.

No matter how much the authorities may streamline the conversion process, it will not be a simple click of a button or tick of a box as the transition from the Three FIE Laws to the Company Law will involve a series of new options requiring informed decisions on the part of investors. Moreover, whatever the process, we can be confident that it will disclose that most FIEs have many items in their files that will need to be updated, supplemented or otherwise cleaned up. It will not be a tidy straight-forward process—and even if the SAMR Circular is interpreted so as to induce more FIEs to undertake conversion earlier in the transition period, there are still bound to be long lines and short tempers as we approach the end of the five-year transition period.

If not a nightmare scenario, this will still be a cause for significant heartburn. That is the challenge that we address in the next chapter.

避免噩梦般的情形

转化过程中噩梦般的情形是所有 50 多万家外商投资企业全都在过渡期第五年到当地市场监督管理局窗口排队进行转化程序。如果《市场监管总局通知》被解释为在对章程进行某些修订时会触发强制提前转化，且在实践中如此执行，则我们有可能避免这一极不愿意看到的情形，或者至少如此大规模推迟行动的全面影响将有所减弱。

但是，当然，即使根据《市场监管总局通知》在实践中要求强制提前转化，由于外商投资企业并不会经常修改其现有章程，无论在哪种情况下，极有可能的是，绝大多数的外商投资企业仍将自行决定转化的时间。人的本性就是如此，很有可能大多数人还是会等到过渡期的后期，尽管这不是明智的选择。鉴于数量庞大，任何转化量在后期堆积都会给现有市场资源带来巨大压力。

无论政府部门可能在多大程度上简化转化流程，这都不会像点击一下鼠标或勾选一个选项这么简单，因为从“三资法”到《公司法》的转变涉及一系列新的选项，需要投资者作出知情决定。而且我们相信，无论是怎样的程序，都意味着大多数外商投资企业都需要更新、补充或清理其档案中的许多内容。这将不会是一个整齐直接的程序——即使《市场监管总局通知》被解释为促使更多外商投资企业在过渡期的早期实施转化，在临近五年过渡期尾声时，仍会出现“队伍长长、怨声满满”的情景。

即使不是噩梦般的情形，也仍然会引起极大不适。我们将在下一章中对这一挑战提出应对方法。

Chapter 4 What the New FIL Means for the Legal Services Market in China

The FIL promises to be the single largest contributor to the growth of the legal services market over the next five years. This is not necessarily good news for investors as they will be picking up the tab, but the FIL will also open up new opportunities to structure their operations in China in ways that will pay dividends over the longer term. In the shorter term, adjusting to major changes in law always drives demand for legal services, and the FIL will be no exception. This should be good news for lawyers, but the benefits will not be spread evenly across the market, and some of the work generated by the FIL may prove to be unprofitable for many FDI lawyers.

As a result, the FIL should prove to be disruptive on multiple levels. First, because many lawyers at the top end of the market will not be in a position to deliver some of the lower-end work to their legacy clients at the projected market price points, this will create an opening for other lawyers and service provider platforms to race in to try to capture new client relationships. Second, and perhaps more importantly, these market dynamics will in turn drive the adoption of legal-tech solutions to enable legal service providers to meet the unprecedented levels of demand for both high-end and low-end legal services to be generated in the wake of the FIL. Ultimately, these legal-tech solutions should be one of the most important legacies of the FIL, opening up access to legal services to a broader range of businesses in China at more competitive rates while at the same time creating important new revenue streams for lawyers.

Breaking Down the Impact of the FIL

The FIL will impact both new and existing FIEs, but the impact will be different for the two sub-groups, and within each sub-group the impact will be different for WFOEs as

第四章 《外商投资法》对中国法律服务市场意味着什么

《外商投资法》有望成为未来五年法律服务市场增长的最大贡献者。对于投资者来说这不一定是个好消息，因为他们要为此埋单，但《外商投资法》也会为他们构造中国业务提供新的机遇，从更长时间来看将给他们带来红利。在短期内，要适应法律出现的重大变更，必然会推动对法律服务的需求，《外商投资法》也不例外。对于律师而言，这应该是个好消息，但由此产生的利益不会在整个市场中平均分配，《外商投资法》创造的一些工作对许多外商直接投资律师来说可能是无利可图。

因此，《外商投资法》应该在多个层面上具有影响性。由于许多高端市场的律师无法以预计的市场价格向其传统客户提供某些低端服务，这将为其他律师和服务提供商平台创造机会，让他们能够竞相争取新的客户关系。并且也许更重要的是，这些市场动态将反过来推动法律科技解决方案的采用，使法律服务提供者能够满足《外商投资法》之后对高端和低端法律服务的空前需求。归根结底，这些法律科技解决方案应是《外商投资法》最重要的产物之一，其以更具竞争力的价格向更广泛的中国企业提供法律服务，同时为律师创造重要的新的收入来源。

详解《外商投资法》的影响

《外商投资法》将同时影响新的和现存的外商投资企业，但

compared to joint ventures.

Scoping the Post-FIL Legal Services Market—Some Context

Before we dive more deeply into how the FIL will impact these different market sub-sets, we should provide some historical context as well as an overall view of the FDI legal services market. This will provide a baseline for purposes of comparison and projections.

From 2010 to 2016, the number of new FIEs set up in China held steady in a range between a low of 22,773 new FIEs in 2013 to a high of 27,900 in 2016, which was only modestly higher than the levels in 2010 and 2011, when 27,406 and 27,712 new FIEs were set up respectively. The average for this period was 25,867 new FIEs per year.[1] We will use this as our historical average for new FIE entity set up.

Over this same seven-year period, the total FDI inflows increased from USD 108 billion to USD 126 billion, with an average year-on-year rate of increase of 3.1% percent from 2010 through 2015, with the amount of foreign investment remaining essentially flat from 2015 (USD 126.27 billion) to 2016 (USD 126.00 billion).

In 2017 there was a notable uptick in new FIEs to 35,652, and in 2018 this figure jumped to 60,533, while in 2019 China hit just more than 41,000 new FIEs. The overall trend in the value of foreign investment over this most recent period is roughly in line with historical year-on-year averages, posting average growth rates of 3.4% over this more recent period. Total FDI inflows were USD 131.04 billion for 2017, USD 134.97 billion for 2018 and USD 138.14 billion for 2019, setting another new high for FDI in China. Consequently, it appears that the more recent trend is towards an increasing number of smaller-value FIEs, which will also have implications for the market if this trend continues.

Next we will take a closer look at the breakdown of existing FIEs which will also be directly affected by the FIL over this next five-year period. According to available statistics, there are over 500,000 existing FIEs in China, with roughly three times as many WFOEs as joint ventures (EJVs and CJVs combined, with EJVs making up the bulk of the joint ventures). Foreign-invested companies limited by shares are relatively few in number by comparison, so we will focus on WFOEs and joint ventures in this analysis.

1 商务数据中心 , Accessed September 02, 2019. http://data.mofcom.gov.cn/lywz/inmr.shtml。

对这两类企业的影响会有所不同，并且在每类企业中，对外商独资企业的影响与对合营企业的影响也有所不同。

界定《外商投资法》实施后的法律服务市场——一些背景

在我们对《外商投资法》将如何影响这些不同细分市场进行更深入的分析前，我们应当提供一些历史背景以及对整个外商直接投资法律服务市场的整体看法。我们首先分析入境外商直接投资一方，为对比和预测提供基础。

自 2010 年至 2016 年，在中国新设立的外商投资企业的数量稳定在最低 22,773 家（2013 年）至最高 27,900 家（2016 年）之间，仅略高于 2010 年和 2011 年分别设立的 27,406 家和 27,712 家新外商投资企业。这一时期的平均值为每年设立 25,867 家新外商投资企业。[1] 我们将此作为新设外商投资企业实体的历史平均值。

在同一个七年期间，外商直接投资总额从 1080 亿美元增加到 1260 亿美元，2010 年至 2015 年平均每年同比增长率为 3.1%，外商投资额从 2015 年（1262.7 亿美元）到 2016 年（1260 亿美元）基本保持不变。

2017 年，新设外商投资企业小幅增加至 35,652 家，2018 年这一数字跃升至 60,533 家，而在 2019 年，中国新设外商投资企业超过 41,000 家。在最近一段时期内，外商投资额的整体走势持续与历史上每年同比平均水平保持大体一致，在此期间平均增长率为 3.4%。2017 年外商直接投资总额为 1310.4 亿美元，2018 年为 1349.7 亿美元，2019 年为 1381.4 亿美元，再创外商直接投资额新高。因此，最近的趋势似乎是有越来越多的小型外商投资企业设立，如果这种趋势持续下去，也会对市场产生影响。

接下来我们将仔细分析现存的不同类型的外商投资企业，这些外商投资企业也将在未来五年内受到《外商投资法》的直接影

1 商务数据中心，2019 年 9 月 2 日访问，http://data.mofcom.gov.cn/lywz/inmr.shtml。

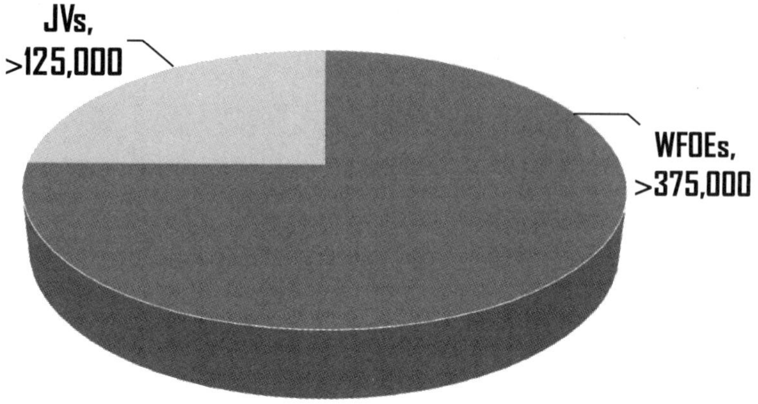

Figure 4–A Breakdown of FIEs

As we have noted, all existing FIEs will need to adjust their organization form, organizational structures, corporate governance, etc. in accordance with the mandatory provisions under the Company Law, which very likely will result in renegotiation of their existing JV contracts in connection with a significant number of joint ventures (those which are not able to limit the changes only to the minimal revisions necessary as in the case of what we referred to in Chapter 3 as a "simple JV conversion"). So while there are many more WFOEs than joint ventures, the projected total costs of FIL-compliance for joint ventures will be much higher than the total costs of FIL compliance for WFOEs. Even a simple JV conversion will be much more time-consuming and costly than a WFOE conversion. We will address related points in more detail below.

The foregoing provides some preliminary context with respect to the demand side of the post-FIL legal services market. Next we turn to the supply side. We can summarize the development of the legal services market in China in the FDI space over the last four decades essentially as follows:

响。根据现有统计数据，中国有超过 50 万家外商投资企业，其中外商独资企业的数量约为合营企业（合资经营企业和合作经营企业的总和，其中大部分为合资经营企业）的 3 倍。相比之下，外商投资的股份有限公司的数量相对较少，因此我们将在本章着重分析外商独资企业和合营企业。

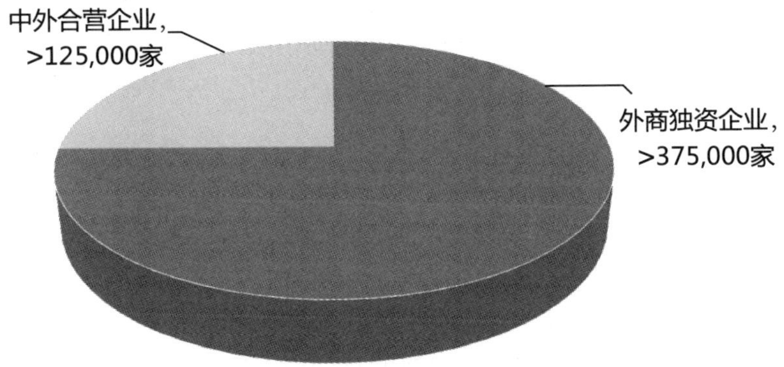

图 4–A　外商投资企业的分类

正如我们所指出的，所有现存外商投资企业将需要根据《公司法》的强制性规定调整其组织形式、组织机构、公司治理等，这将很可能导致大量合营企业（也即是那些不能像我们在第三章中提到的“简单的合营企业转化”情形那样，将其对合营企业合同的修订限制在最小必要范围内的合营企业）对其现有的合营企业合同进行重新谈判。因此，虽然外商独资企业的数量超出合营企业很多，但合营企业就《外商投资法》合规预计支出的总成本将远远高于外商独资企业。即使一个简单的合营企业转化也会比外商独资企业转化更加费时且成本更高。我们将在下文更详细地讨论相关要点。

“因此，虽然外商独资企业的数量超出合营企业很多，但合营企业就《外商投资法》合规预计支出的总成本将远远高于外商独资企业。即使一个简单的合营企业转化也会比外商独资企业转化更加费时且成本更高。”

上述内容提供了一些《外商投资法》实施后法律服务市场的需求方的一些初步情况，接下来我们把目光转向供应方。我们可以将过去 40 年中国在外商直接投资领域法律服务市场的发展基本总结如下：

Chart 4–A Historical Overview of China FDI Legal Services Market

Decade	FDI legal services market conditions	Foreign law firms market position	Chinese law firms market position
1980s	Small FDI market Only major MNC clients No Chinese clients	A handful of firms had monopoly position	Virtually no market presence
1990s	Growing FDI market Still mostly major MNC clients Few Chinese clients	A growing number of firms collectively continued to hold a dominant market position	Chinese firms started to emerge slowly over the decade Primarily played supporting role
2000s	Strong FDI growth in post-WTO era Nature of FDI expanded to include M&A, SMEs, service sectors, etc. More Chinese clients used outside counsel for Sino-foreign JV projects	Market share for traditional FDI (WFOEs and JVs) started to erode Maintained strong position in inbound M&A and highly-regulated services sectors	Became the preferred option for traditional FDI work, particularly for mid-cap projects Continued to climb up the value chain in terms of all other aspects of FDI Emergence of Red Circle firms
2010s	After a brief post-financial crisis dip, FDI inflows rebounded and maintained strong steady growth Growing confidence on the part of Chinese clients with respect to onshore JVs	Retrenched in the aftermath of 2008-2009 finan-cial crisis and thereafter have for the most part maintained status quo in terms of staffing levels, but staff levels may again be reduced in the aftermath of the COVID-19 pandemic Have a good position on ODI while maintaining a continuing flow of FDI work, albeit with a reduced overall market share	Experienced explosive growth Dramatic expansion of practice area expertise Continued to move up the value chain and gain share in both FDI and ODI work Red Circle firms consolidated leading market position

I have personally witnessed the development of the Chinese legal profession over the last three decades. I arrived in Hong Kong to join the China Practice Group of Baker & McKenzie in 1993 just as the first private domestic law firms were being set up in mainland China. At the same time, a few select foreign law firms were able to register a formal office in China for the first time. In those early days, the only clients were major MNCs, and almost every foreign investment had to take the form of a joint venture. It only took a few months to get your arms around the entire corpus of foreign investment laws, and in the absence of a centralized public database of laws and regulations, every scrap of official notice or response was guarded as a closely held trade secret. We never saw Chinese clients being represented by local lawyers,

表 4–A 中国外商直接投资法律服务市场历史概览

时期	外商直接投资法律服务市场状况	外资律师事务所市场地位	内资律师事务所市场地位
1980—1989 年	外商直接投资市场较小 客户仅为大型跨国公司 无中国客户	少数律师事务所拥有垄断地位	市场上几乎没有
1990—1999 年	外商直接投资市场不断扩大 客户仍主要为大型跨国公司 少数中国客户	越来越多律师事务所共同持续地占据市场主要地位	内资律师事务所在此十年中缓慢出现 主要扮演配角
2000—2009 年	外商直接投资在后 WTO 时代快速增长 外商直接投资的性质有所延伸，包括并购、中小企业、服务业等 越来越多中国客户就中外合营项目聘用外部法律顾问	传统外商直接投资（设立外商独资企业和合营企业）市场份额开始下降 入境并购和受高度监管的服务业保持强势地位	成为传统外商直接投资业务（特别是中型项目）的首选 在外商直接投资其他方面的价值链中不断攀升 “红圈所”出现
2010—2019 年	经历金融危机后的短暂下滑后，外商直接投资反弹并保持强劲稳定的增长 中国客户对境内合营企业业务的信心日益增强	2008—2009 年金融危机后实施缩紧开支，此后人员编制水平基本维持现状，但受新型冠状病毒肺炎疫情影响，人员编制水平可能再次减少 在对外直接投资业务上处于有利地位，同时保持外商直接投资工作的流量，尽管总体市场份额有所下降	经历了爆炸式增长 实践领域专业技能的急剧增长 持续向价值链上游攀升，并获得外商直接投资和对外直接投资业务份额 “红圈所”巩固其领先市场地位

我亲眼见证了过去 30 年里中国法律界的发展。1993 年我在香港加入了贝克·麦坚时的中国业务团队，当时中国内地第一批民营内资律师事务所正在设立。与此同时，一些一流外资律师事务所首次在中国注册了正式代表处。在早期，大型跨国公司是唯一的客户，几乎所有的外国投资都不得不采取合营企业的形式。从事外商投资业务的律师只需要几个月的时间就可以完整了解所有外国投资法律规定，并且在没有统一的法律法规公共数据库的情况下，每一份正式通知或回复都被视为需要严格保护的商业秘

and the only time we engaged with local lawyers was when we drafted the Chinese law legal opinions for the Chinese lawyers to sign.

For the second half of the 1990s, I took an in-house counsel position in Hong Kong and later Beijing where I eventually assumed the role of Asia General Counsel of a major MNC. From this position I was able to observe the continued development of the legal profession from the perspective of a client. I also gained an appreciation for the critical role that in-house counsel play in MNCs and domestic companies in China. (Now almost 20 years later, top-flight bilingual Chinese lawyers populate the law departments of MNCs in China, further altering the competitive landscape.)

When China joined the WTO, I returned to private practice to head up the Beijing office of Lovells (now Hogan Lovells). By this time, the Chinese firms had already started to emerge to take more and more traditional FDI work from MNC clients, but the foreign firms maintained a substantial advantage in terms of inbound M&A and higher end FDI work for MNCs. But that advantage has, in my opinion, long since eroded. In the aftermath of the 2008-2009 global financial crisis, the foreign firms retrenched and have for the most part only maintained the status quo in terms of scope and scale over the last decade, while the Chinese firms have experienced explosive growth. In 2010 I voted with my feet and became one of the first senior foreign lawyer to make the move from a major international law firm to join a leading Chinese firm.

Given my professional background, I have a unique perspective on the Chinese legal services market. So what do I see as the market trends in China for the post-FIL era?

In my view, after an initial period of further retrenchment in the immediate aftermath of the COVID-19 pandemic, over the medium term FDI lawyers in the international law firms will still enjoy boom times in the post-FIL era as the amount of high-value FDI work is projected to explode in the latter half of the five-year transition period, but over the longer term, if these international firms continue to adopt a traditional legal service business model, they are likely to face a significant erosion of their market position for FDI work. The same may be true for many of the top FDI lawyers in the Red Circle firms as hungrier FDI lawyers in emerging domestic firms compete aggressively on price for the lower-end FIL-related work in order to capture new client relationships. However, this may turn out to be a pyrrhic victory for these emerging firms as it will be very challenging for even these emerging firms to

密。彼时我们从未见过中国本土律师代理中国客户，我们唯一一次与中国本土律师打交道，是我们撰写中国法律的法律意见需要中国律师的签字。

在20世纪90年代后半期，我在香港从事一份跨国公司法律顾问的工作，随后在北京担任了该跨国公司的亚洲区总法律顾问。在这一职位上，我从客户的角度见证了法律界的持续发展。同时，我也认识到企业法务在跨国公司和中国内资企业中的关键性作用。（现在，差不多20年后，顶级的中国双语律师占据了中国境内的跨国公司法律部门的职位，进一步改变了竞争格局。）

当中国加入世贸组织时，我回归律所并作为管理合伙人任职于路伟（现为霍金路伟）律师事务所北京代表处。到这个阶段为止，内资律师事务所已经开始出现并从跨国公司客户那里获得越来越多的传统外商直接投资业务，但外资律师事务所在跨国公司的入境并购和高端外商直接投资业务方面保持着很大的优势。但在我看来，这种优势早已开始削弱。在2008—2009年全球金融危机之后，外资律师事务所缩减开支并在过去十年中仅在业务范围和规模方面保持了现状，而内资律师事务所则经历了爆炸式增长。2010年，我毅然决定成为首批从大型国际律师事务所加入领先的内资律师事务所的资深外国律师之一。

鉴于我的专业背景，我对中国法律服务市场有独特的看法。那么，我如何看待《外商投资法》时代的中国市场趋势？

我认为，在新型冠状病毒肺炎疫情之后不久的最初一段时间内，中期内国际律师事务所中的外商直接投资律师仍将享受《外商投资法》时代的繁荣时期，因为预计在五年过渡期的后半期，高价值外商直接投资业务将爆炸式增长。但是，从长期看来，如果这些国际律师事务所继续采用传统的法律服务商业模式，其外商直接投资市场地位很可能受到侵蚀。对于“红圈所”的许多顶尖的外商直接投资律师来说也是一样，因为新兴国内律师事务所中更渴望获得工作的外商直接投资律师为了争夺新的客户关系，

perform these low-end services at scale on a profitable basis so long as they continue using the traditional legal services model.

In contrast, the legal services arms of the Big 4 accounting firms as well as certain other alternative legal services (ALS) provider platforms (in certain cases attached to leading international law firms) will be in a position to exploit new market openings created by these changing market dynamics, and they will be able to leverage off of their ability to systematize the delivery of services and scale up on a level which traditional law firms cannot match, capturing more market share and capturing more high-end work as a result. However, because there are only a small number of such platforms, their overall market share will continue to be relatively modest.

The great equalizer may prove to be the emergence and adoption of legal tech tools which will allow top players to retain key client relationships (and access to some of the higher-end work that they otherwise may have missed out on) by delivering lower-end services on a cost-competitive basis (either on an in-sourced or an out-sourced basis), while at the same time allowing the emerging firms to climb up the value chain and achieve somewhat greater scale. Even with all their advantages in the post-FIL era, the legal services arms of the Big 4 and the ALS providers will still not be able to achieve target levels of profitability on the commoditize-able elements of the work to be generated in the post-FIL era without adoption of legal-tech tools to supplement and supercharge their managed legal services systems. So appropriate legal-tech solutions will be a critical element of the overall service offering for all players in the post-FIL legal services market.

Implications for New FDI Projects

The first application of the FIL will be for new FDI projects. The new WFOEs and joint ventures that are set up after 1 January 2020 will all need to comply with the requirements of the Company Law. These new FIEs will start from a clean sheet of paper so can start directly from the base provided by the Sample Templates set out in Part II, subject to revisions to reflect the requirements of each particular deal.

Foreign investors (and Chinese investors in Sino-foreign joint ventures) will need to consult legal counsel to understand the implications of the change from the Three FIE Laws to the corporate governance requirements under the Company Law. Because the Company Law provides so many more options for the parties in terms of structuring and governance, this is likely to add another ten percent in additional advisory fees for WFOE projects but perhaps as much as a 20 to 30 percent bump up over the usual benchmark pricing for legal services for joint ventures because there are

会对低端外商直接投资业务开展激烈的价格竞争。但是，对于这些新兴律师事务所而言，这可能是得不偿失的胜利，因为即使对这些新兴律师事务所而言，如果其继续采用传统法律服务模式，想要在盈利的基础上大规模开展这些低端业务也将是一个巨大的挑战。

相比之下，四大会计师事务所的法律服务部门以及某些其他替代性法律服务提供商平台（在某些情况下属于领先的国际律师事务所）将能够利用这些由不断变化的市场动态创造的新的市场机会，并且它们将能够利用其能力使其服务系统化，并将服务规模扩大到传统律师事务所无法匹敌的水平，从而获得更多的市场份额和更多的高端业务。但是，由于此类平台的数量较少，因此其市场份额总体上仍将相对有限。

法律科技工具的出现和采用可能是最好的均衡器。法律科技工具将使顶尖的市场参与者在具有成本竞争力的基础上（无论是基于内部资源还是外包）提供低端服务，从而维系重要客户关系（并接触到一些它们原本可能错过的高端工作），同时允许新兴律师事务所向价值链上游攀升并实现更大规模。即使四大会计师事务所的法律服务部门和替代性法律服务提供商在《外商投资法》时代具备了种种优势，但如果不借助法律科技工具对其管理的法律服务体系进行补充和赋能，它们仍无法就《外商投资法》时代所产生的工作中可商品化的部分实现目标盈利。因此，合适的法律科技解决方案将成为《外商投资法》时代法律服务市场所有参与者的整体服务供应的关键因素。

对新外商直接投资项目的影响

《外商投资法》将首先适用于新外商直接投资项目。在 2020 年 1 月 1 日之后设立的新外商独资企业和合营企业都需要遵守《公司法》的要求。这些新的外商投资企业没有历史文件，因此可以直接以本书第二部分所载的模板样本为基础进行编制，并根据每项特定交易的要求进行修订。

more options and each has to be negotiated by the joint venture partners.

Investors will need these services but will not be willing to subsidize outside counsel as they ramp up the learning curve on their first post-FIL deals. Clients will rightly expect their legal counsel will have invested sufficient time at their own cost to come up to speed on all aspects of the post-FIL legal requirements and to have already prepared FIE documentation that complies with the requirements of the Company Law. That is another key rationale for the work of the Expert Committee. The high-quality bilingual Sample Templates, together with the accompanying annotations, are designed to level the playing field, to help the top firms compete more effectively on price, and to help the emerging tier of law firms compete more effectively on quality .

As noted above, based on historical levels, more than 25,000 new FIEs are set up each year, and the trend in the last few years is for increasing numbers of new FIEs each year (roughly 45,000 per year in the last three years), with these volumes expected to continue to increase going forward, including not only new greenfield FDI and inbound M&A projects in those industry sectors that are currently open but also FDI projects in all sectors to be newly opened as China continues to reduce the number of sectors subject to restriction under the Negative List. To these expanding traditional categories of FDI projects, we also need to take into account the substantial volumes of FIE group restructuring work that will be undertaken now that downstream investments will be permitted under the 2019 SAFE Notice. In many cases, this will likely include multiple tiers of subsidiaries, all of which will be treated as FIEs. So the combination of the increasing numbers of traditional new FIEs in the last few years leading up to the FIL, plus additional FDI opportunities in sectors still to be opened, plus FIE group restructuring and FIE downstream investments, will continue to push up the number of new FIEs to be set up in the post-FIL era (see Figure 4-B).

As FDI volumes increase, particularly in respect of smaller-value FIEs (which appears to be an important trend) and in many cases in connection with simple FIE downstream investments and group restructurings, demand for efficiencies will increase commensurately. This will further drive adoption of related legal-tech tools for those elements which can be commoditized even in respect of traditional FDI work. At the same time, tax aspects of FIE group restructurings will give the Big 4 a further opening to introduce their expanding legal services arms into the process.

Assessing the Scope and Scale of FIE Conversions

While the anticipated growth in FDI work is expected to be very significant, it will be

外国投资者（以及中外合营企业的中国投资者）需要咨询法律顾问以了解从“三资法”向《公司法》项下的公司治理要求进行转变的影响。由于《公司法》在结构和治理方面为各方提供了更多选择，这很可能会为外商独资企业项目额外增加10%的律师费，而对于合营企业来说，由于更多选择出现，而每个选择都必须由合营各方谈判决定，这可能会使针对合营企业的法律服务的一般基准定价提高20%~30%。

投资者需要这些服务，但由于这是《外商投资法》时代的首批交易，投资者不会愿意为外部法律顾问交学费。客户有理由期望他们的法律顾问自费投入足够的时间来学习《外商投资法》时代的各项法律要求，并且已经准备好符合《公司法》要求的外商投资企业文件。这也是专家委员会工作的另一个关键理由。高质量的双语模板样本，以及附带的注解说明，旨在促进公平竞争，帮助顶级律师事务所在价格上更有效地竞争，并帮助新兴的律师事务所在质量上更有效地竞争。

“高质量的双语模板样本，以及附带的注解说明，旨在促进公平竞争，帮助顶级律师事务所在价格上更有效地竞争，并帮助新兴的律师事务所在质量上更有效地竞争。”

如前所述，根据历史水平，每年有超过25,000家新的外商投资企业设立，并且从过去几年的趋势看来，每年新设外商投资企业数量都在增加（过去三年中每年约增加45,000家），并且预计今后这些数量会继续增加，不仅包括那些目前开放的行业领域内的新设外商直接投资和入境并购项目，还包括随着中国不断减少负面清单中的限制类领域而对外商投资新开放的领域内的外商直接投资项目。对于这些不断扩大的传统类型的外商直接投资项目，我们还需要考虑到将进行的大量外商投资企业集团重组工作，因为根据《2019年外管局通知》，非投资性外商投资企业资本金境内股权投资限制被取消。在许多情况下，这可能包括多级子公司，所有这些子公司都将被视为外商投资企业。因此，在《外商投资法》颁布之前的过去几年中传统的新设外商投资企业数量不断增加，加上待开放领域内外商直接投资机会的增加，加上外商投资企业集团重组和外商投资企业再投资，将持续推动《外商投资法》时代新设外商投资企业数量的增长（见图4-B）。

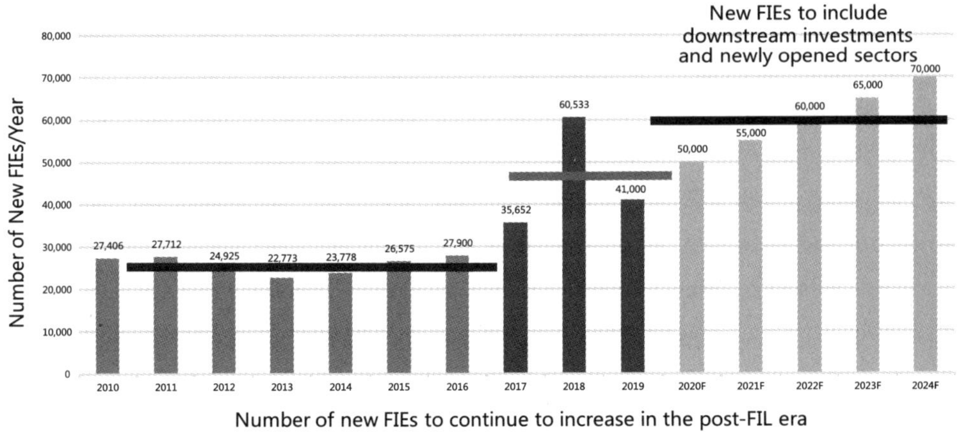

Figure 4–B Historical and Projected Volumes of New FIEs

dwarfed by the volume of FIE conversion work in the five-year transition period following the effectiveness of the FIL. Moreover, the conversion of 500,000-plus existing FIEs will not roll out in a smooth straight-line process over the transition period.

There are several factors that need to be taken into account as we project the timing and volumes of FIE conversion under the FIL. First, as noted in Chapter 3, it is to be expected that the local SAMR offices will not be geared up to handle FIE conversion applications for the first six months or so of 2020, particularly in light of the impact of the COVID-19 pandemic. Second, given that the transition period was extended from three years under the 2015 Draft FIL to five years under the final FIL, it would be expected that the normal tendency for many investors would be to wait until the latter part of the transition period, skewing the volumes heavily to the last few years, which we consider to be unwise for the reasons set out in Chapter 3. However, if the SAMR Circular is interpreted and implemented in a manner so as to trigger mandatory early conversion for a significant number of FIEs, that will counter the tendency to defer the conversion process to later in the transition period and will tend to pull more FIE conversions forward to earlier in the transition period.

Finally, to the extent that investors undertake an early assessment and come up with a strategic and tactical FIE conversion plan, that will likely also result in more unilateral WFOE conversions and non-contentious simple JV conversions earlier in the transition period to avoid the anticipated crush of conversion work, and corresponding constraints on available market resources, in the latter stages. That would leave many of the full JV renegotiations to the latter

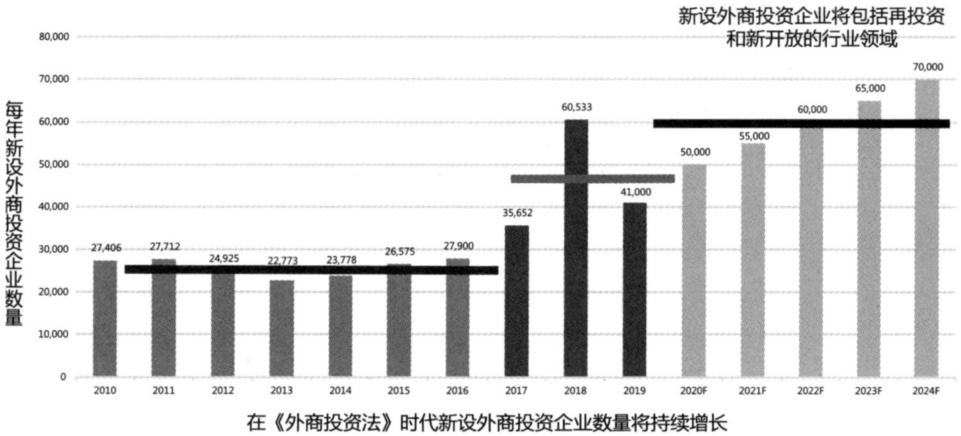

图 4–B　新设外商投资企业的历史和预计数量

随着外商直接投资量的增加，特别是价值较小的外商投资企业（这似乎是一个重要趋势），以及在与简单的外商投资企业再投资和集团重组相关的许多情况下，对效率的要求将相应提高。这将进一步推动对那些即使在传统的外商直接投资工作中也可以商品化的要素采用相关法律科技工具。同时，外商投资企业集团重组的税务方面将为四大会计师事务所提供进一步的机会，以将其不断扩张的法律服务部门引入这一流程。

评估外商投资企业转化的范围和规模

虽然外商直接投资工作的预期增长预计将非常显著，但与《外商投资法》生效后的五年过渡期内的外商投资企业转化工作量相比将相形见绌。此外，现有 50 多万家外商投资企业的转化在过渡期内也不会一帆风顺。

在我们预测《外商投资法》项下的外商投资企业转化的时间和数量时，需要考虑几个因素。如第三章所述，预计在 2020 年前 6 个月左右的时间里，尤其是考虑到新型冠状病毒肺炎疫情的影响地方市场监管局将不会准备好处理外商投资企业转化申请。由于过渡期从 2015 年《外国投资法（草案）》项下的 3 年延长至《外商投资法》最终版项下的 5 年，预计许多投资者的正常倾向是等

half of the period, ideally being kicked off no later than the mid-point of the transition period so as not to artificially constrain the negotiation timeline to the detriment of the negotiating leverage of one or both of the parties.

Given these working assumptions, the possible breakdown of FIE conversions on a year-by-year basis over the transition period may end up generally as shown in Figure 4-C and 4-D below. Figure 4-C reflects the more likely scenario that the timing of the FIE conversion process is left entirely to the discretion of the FIEs, which will likely result in the volumes being pushed more to the latter half of the transition period. Figure 4-D is intended to show the impact of an interpretation of the SAMR Circular which results in more early mandatory conversions, which will tend to pull forward more conversions and flatten out the rate of growth more evenly across the transition period, while still reflecting significant back-end loading. Note that the scale for the two charts is not identical, but in real numbers the second (less likely scenario) results in an approximately 30% decrease in volumes in the last year of the transition period. Again, these are just estimates for reference purposes only.

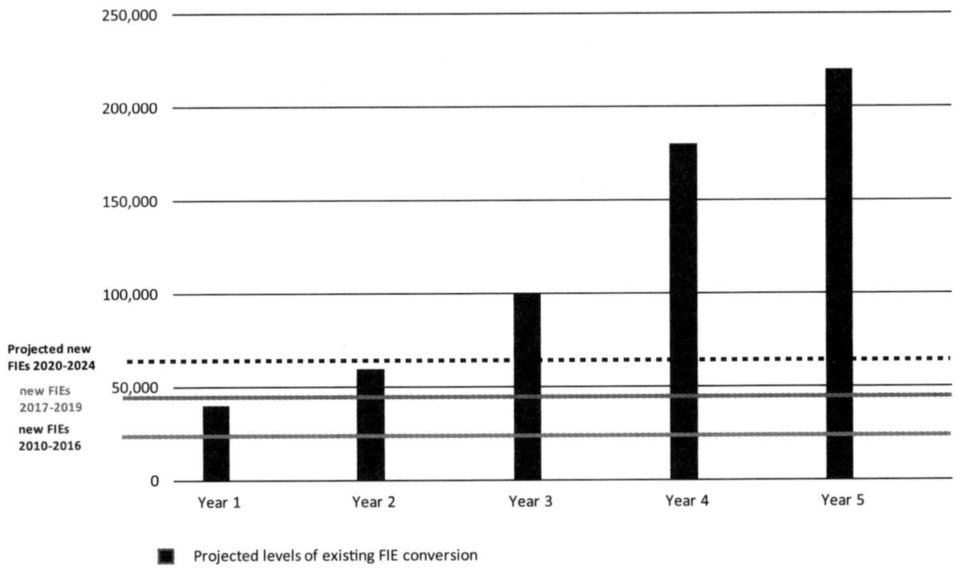

Figure 4–C　Projected breakdown of FIE conversions (with no mandatory early conversion triggers)

到过渡期的后期，从而导致转化量在后几年大规模堆积，而根据第三章中所列的原因，我们认为这是不明智的做法。但是，如果《市场监管总局通知》被解读为将使大量外商投资企业强制提前转化，且在实践中如此执行，则可以应对这种将转化程序推迟到过渡期后期的倾向，使更多的外商投资企业转化提前到过渡期较早期进行。

最后，如果投资者进行早期评估并提出战略性和战术性的外商投资企业转化计划，将很可能导致在过渡期早些时候进行更多的外商独资企业单方面转化和无争议的简单的合营企业转化，从而避免转化工作在后期像预期的那么拥挤，并避免受限于可用的市场资源。这将使许多合营企业在过渡期后半期内进行全面的重新谈判，最好不迟于过渡期的中点开始，以免人为地限制谈判时间表，损害一方或双方的谈判筹码。

基于这些工作假设，过渡期内外商投资企业转化每年的数量分解可能最终大致如图 4-C 和图 4-D 所示。图 4-C 反映了更可能出现的情形，即外商投资企业转化的时间点完全由外商投资企业自行决定，这很可能使大量转化推迟至过渡期的后期。图 4-D 旨在显示将《市场监管总局通知》解读为导致更多强制提前转化所产生的影响，这将使更多转化提前进行，并使过渡期内转化量的增长率更加均衡，同时仍然反映出转化将在后期大量堆积。请注意，两个图表的比例并不相同，但以实际数量表示，第二种情形（可能性较小的情形）将导致过渡期最后一年的转化量减少 30%。同样，本预测仅供参考。

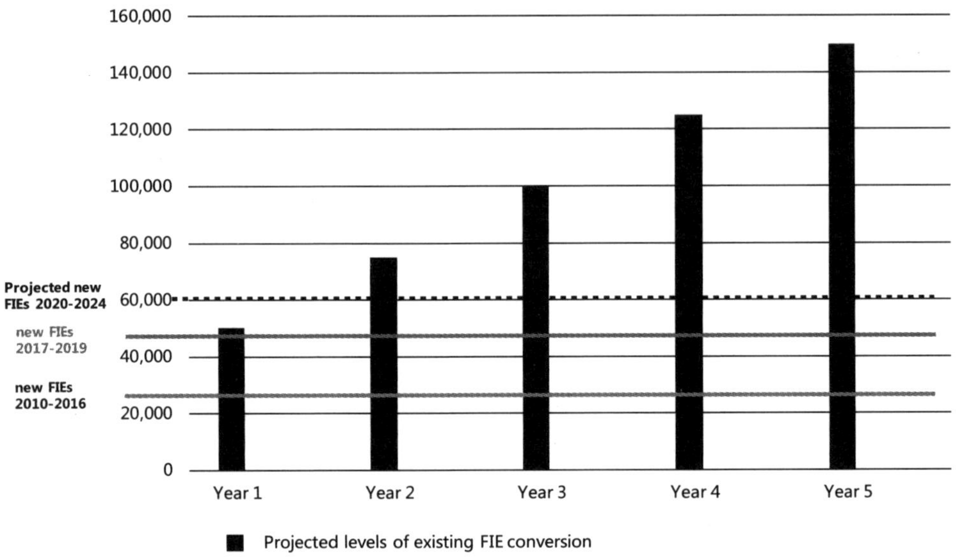

Figure 4–D　Projected breakdown of FIE conversions (with some mandatory early conversion triggers)

In the more likely scenario shown in Figure 4-C, in which the timing is entirely discretionary, the volumes of FIE conversions in the final three years of the transition period will be between four- and almost ten-times higher than historical levels for new FIE entity set up. Even assuming that the implementation of the SAMR Circular is done in a way that requires more early conversions on a mandatory basis, together with pro-active management of the conversion process by a significant number of investors, in fact pull forward the timing for many FIE conversions as shown in Figure 4-D, the numbers are still staggering, with the volumes of FIE conversions still being four- to six-times higher than historical new FIE entity set up levels in the last three years of the transition period. Moreover, all of this comes on top of the projected increased levels of new FDI projects. Combined, over the period from 2022 to 2024 this represents FDI-related work levels of more than six- to almost 12-times historical averages under the more likely scenario reflected in Figure 4-C and between five- to eight-times higher than historical averages for the somewhat less likely scenario as shown in Figure 4-D. Accordingly, under either scenario this may threaten to overwhelm existing market resources for FDI services, distorting long-standing market dynamics.

One additional challenge will be that many investors in Sino-foreign joint ventures may

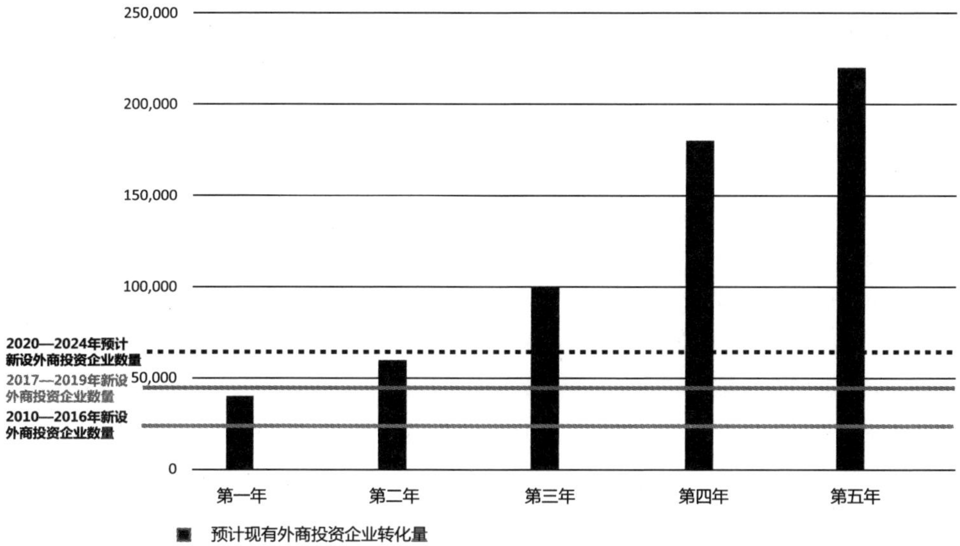

图 4-C　预计外商投资企业转化量分解

（不存在触发强制提前转化的情形）

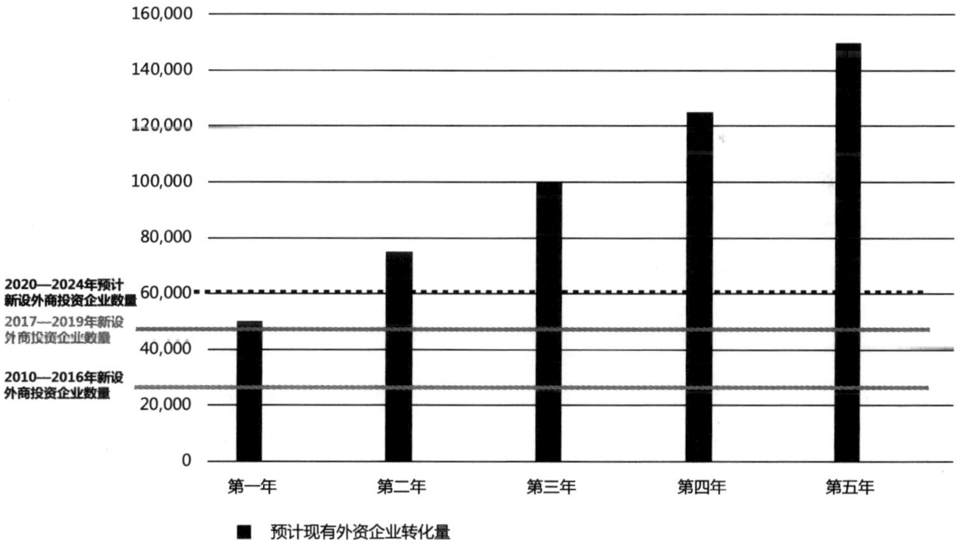

图 4-D　预计外商投资企业转化量分解

（存在某些触发强制提前转化的情形）

图 4-C 显示的情形更可能发生，即转化时间完全由外商投资企业自行决定，这种情况下，过渡期后 3 年的转化量将比新设外

be overly optimistic that they can undertake only a simple JV conversion with little or no negotiation and avoid a full renegotiation scenario in the vast majority of cases. Based on early soundings of investors with multiple JVs, we expect that investors will hope that simple conversion will be all that is required for four out of five JVs with only one in five requiring more extensive renegotiation of the base JV contract as one or both of the parties seek to take advantage of new flexibility under the corporate governance provisions of the Company Law or to address long-standing points of concern or irritation in the original JV contract. The reality is likely to be closer to two out of five JVs will end up in more extensive renegotiations of the original JV contract as part of the conversion process, meaning that one in five (which represents roughly 25,000 JVs) will start out as a simple JV conversion only to end up being more contentious than originally hoped. That risk argues in favor of not postponing even simple JV conversions until the later stages of the transition period as that may leave the parties with insufficient time to iron out all of the issues which will get put on the table so late in the process in such a scenario. The likelihood that a significant number of conversion projects that start out as simple JV conversions in fact will end up requiring more extensive renegotiations may also have significant implications for the service provider side of the equation as well, which we will explore further below.

Projected Value of FIL-related Legal Services

The scale and complexity of the transition to the Company Law will be the key drivers for the post-FIL legal services market. WFOE and simple JV conversion work will more readily lend itself to commoditization, driving per-unit pricing down as investors will not be willing to pay bespoke rates for work that can be systematized. On the other hand, only the initial advisory and initial drafting aspects of full joint venture renegotiation work will be susceptible to being systematized, while the ultimate structuring work and negotiation support will of necessity be bespoke in nature, driving costs up as demand spikes.

The overall value of FIL-related legal services, for these purposes consisting only of WFOE and simple JV conversions and existing JV contract renegotiation and excluding new FIE set up, is conservatively estimated to be nearly RMB 70 billion over five years, and it could be much higher as this figure does not take into account legal fees for FIE group restructuring, which could generate substantial additional legal and tax advisory service fees. Of course, in coming up with such a projection, some assumptions need to be made

商投资企业的历史水平高出 4 倍到近 10 倍。即使假设对《市场监管总局通知》的实施强制要求更多外商投资企业提前转化，并且大量的投资者积极管理其转化流程，实际上使得许多外商投资企业转化的时间如图 4-D 所示提前，数字仍然很惊人，即在过渡期的后 3 年，外商投资企业转化数量仍将比新的外商投资企业实体设立历史水平高出 4 到 6 倍。此外，所有这些都发生在新的外商直接投资项目预计增加的水平之上。综合来看，这意味着在 2022 年到 2024 年，与外商直接投资相关的工作量水平，在图 4-C 反映的更可能发生的情形下，将比历史平均水平高出 6 倍到近 12 倍，在图 4-D 反映的可能性较小的情形下，将比历史平均水平高出 5 到 8 倍。因此，无论是哪种情况都可能会使外商直接投资服务的现有市场资源不堪重负，从而扭曲长期存在的市场动态。

> “综合来看，这意味着在 2022 年到 2024 年，与外商直接投资相关的工作量水平，在图 4-C 反映的更可能发生的情形下，将比历史平均水平高出 6 倍到近 12 倍。”

另一个挑战是，许多中外合营企业的投资者可能过于乐观地认为他们可以仅进行简单的合营企业转化，而无需或只需很少的谈判，并在绝大多数情况下可以避免完全的重新谈判。基于早期与拥有多个合营企业的投资者的探讨，我们预期投资者会希望其 4/5 的合营企业只需进行简单的转化，而只有 1/5 的合营企业需要对其基础合营企业合同进行更广泛的谈判，因为一方或双方希望利用《公司法》项下更灵活的公司治理规定，或解决原有合营企业合同中长期存在的担忧或不满之处。现实很可能是，在转化过程中，接近 2/5 的合营企业将对原有合营企业合同进行更广泛的谈判，这意味着 1/5 的合营企业（大约相当于 25,000 家合营企业）将以简单的合营企业转化开始，而最终的过程却比最初所希望的更具争议性。这一风险表明，即使是简单的合营企业转化，也不应推迟到过渡期的后期，因为在这种情况下，双方可能会没有足够的时间来解决在此过程中过晚才提出的所有问题。从简单的合营企业转化开始的大量转化项目最终可能需要更广泛的重新谈判的可能性，也可能对等式另一端的服务提供商产生重大影响，我们将在下面进一步探讨。

《外商投资法》相关法律服务的预期价值

向《公司法》过渡的规模和复杂性将成为《外商投资法》时

with respect to key variable. We set out below some considerations for the different market segments.

Chart 4–B Projected Value of FIE Conversion Services

Market segment	Projected value of related legal services	Scope of services
WFOE conversion	RMB 13.125 billion 375,000 WFOEs × RMB 35,000 per entity	Includes review of existing AoA and SAMR file, provision of basic legal advice / consultation on Company Law requirements, preparation of new revised AoA, collection and preparation of registration documents in English and Chinese, filing services, provision of bilingual templates and related guidance for conduct of shareholder and board meetings under new governance provisions Excludes other clean-up and updates to SAMR file, etc.
Simple JV conversion	RMB 6 billion 75,000 JVs (of total of 125,000 JVs) × RMB 80,000 per entity	Same scope of services as for WFOE conversion except that review of JV contract and related advice will be much more comprehensive and complicated than for WFOE, and parties will need to make amendments to existing JV contract and AoA rather than replace with completely new SHA/JVA Excludes negotiation services
Full JV contract renegotiation	RMB 50 billion 50,000 JVs (of total of 125,000 total JVs) × 2 parties x RMB 500,000 per entity (estimated 250 hours × RMB 2,000/hour)	Includes legal services fees for simple JV conversion work plus negotiation support and repeated turns of drafts Excludes FIE group restructuring, equity transfers, capital increases or other work outside the scope outlined above

Note that the above figures are not suggested market prices, but rather are indicative estimates solely for illustration purposes to provide a sense of the size of the market. Each client and each deal will be different. Some clients will want a lot of hand-holding, while others will be happy to do most of the work in-house with minimal guidance from outside legal counsel. However, overall it is anticipated that because the WFOE conversion and simple JV conversion work *can* be commoditized, then the market will demand that these matters *must* be systematized so that clients can receive the benefit from related improvements in efficiencies.

On the other hand, JV renegotiation work cannot be commoditized, but in some cases the related negotiations may be relatively limited in scope while in other cases they may be more

代法律服务市场的关键驱动力。外商独资企业和简单的合营企业转化工作将更容易具有普适性，进而推动单位价格的下降，因为投资者不会愿意为可以系统化的工作支付定制化工作的价格。另外，只有全面的合营企业重新谈判的初期咨询和起草工作容易被系统化，而最终的架构工作和谈判支持必然需要定制化，随着需求的激增将推动成本上升。

《外商投资法》相关法律服务在 5 年内的整体价值保守估计为近 700 亿元人民币，这一数字只考虑了外商独资企业和简单的合营企业转化和现有合营企业合同的重新谈判的工作，而不包括新设外商投资企业的业务。这个数字还有可能更高，因为还没有把外商投资企业集团重组的法律费用算在内，这一工作可能产生大量的额外法律和税务咨询服务费用。当然，作出这一预测需要对一些关键变量进行假设。我们针对不同的细分市场列出了一些考量因素，具体如下：

表 4–B　外商投资企业转化服务的预计价值

细分市场	相关法律服务的预期价值	服务范围
外商独资企业转化	131.25 亿元人民币 375,000 家外商独资企业 x 每家 35,000 元人民币	包括审阅现有章程和登记档案，就《公司法》要求提供基本法律建议 / 咨询、准备经修订的章程，收集和准备登记文件的中英文版本、登记服务、提供双语模板以及在新的治理规定项下召开股东会和董事会会议的相关指导 不包含其他对市场监管局登记档案的整理和更新等
简单的合营企业转化	60 亿元人民币 （总计 125,000 家合营企业中的）75,000 家合营企业 x 每家 80,000 元人民币	与外商独资企业转化的服务范围一致，但合营企业合同的审阅和相关建议将比外商独资企业的相关工作广泛和复杂得多，并且双方将需要对现有合营企业合同和章程进行修订，而不是替换为全新的股东协议 / 合营协议 不包括谈判服务
合营企业合同的全面重新谈判	500 亿元人民币 （总计 125,000 家合营企业中的）50,000 家合营企业 x 2 方 x 每家 500,000 元人民币（预计 250 小时 x 2,000 元人民币 / 小时）	包括如下法律服务费：简单的合营企业转化工作、谈判支持以及协议草稿的反复修改 不包括外商投资企业集团重组、股权转让、增资或其他超出上述范围的工作

contentious and extended. Similarly, in some cases, both sides will engage legal counsel on an hourly rate basis (and the number of hours and the rates may be higher than what we have used above for purposes of this estimate), while in other cases one side will rely on in-house legal counsel or insist that outside counsel provide a fixed fee arrangement (which may be more typical for some Chinese clients in smaller deals). Accordingly, the above estimates are intended only to provide an indication of the *potential* total market size without accounting for what will be out-sourced and what will be in-sourced.

Our expectation is that if the WFOE conversion and simple JV conversion services are delivered based on the traditional legal services model, then perhaps only between one-third and one-half of the total potential demand will be out-sourced, while if a high-quality integrated legal-tech/systematized solution is available at a suitable price, then the ratio flips, with between one-half and two-thirds of such conversion matters being out-sourced. Presumably higher percentages of JV contract renegotiation work will be out-sourced or require some level of outside counsel support.

If we compare the volume to the value for each work category using the above indicative figures, it is clear that the volume of WFOE conversions and simple JV conversions is comparatively high while the value of such services is comparatively low, with the JV contract renegotiation work potentially generating much higher levels of fees per project (see Figure 4-E).

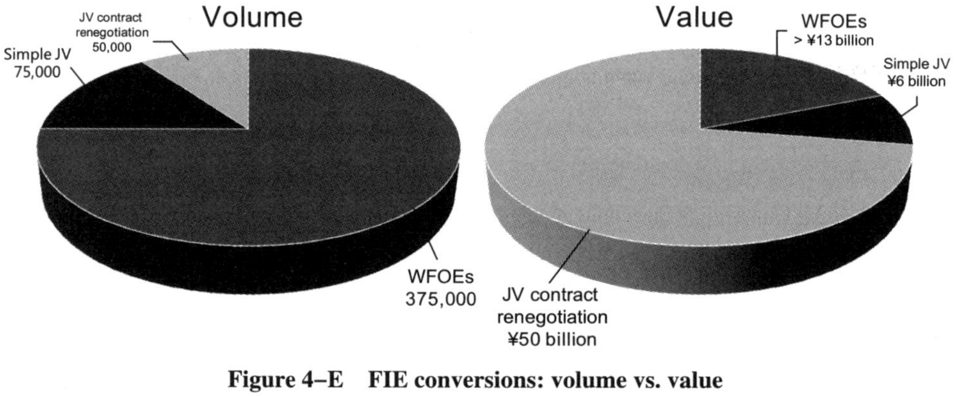

Figure 4–E FIE conversions: volume vs. value

In such a scenario, it is abundantly clear that the top FDI lawyers will all naturally gravitate towards the higher value JV contract renegotiation work. As noted above, we anticipate that investors will identify about one in five JVs up front as likely requiring extensive renegotiation of the JV contract. In such cases, they will likely go back to their original outside

请注意，上述数字并非建议的市场价，而是仅用于说明目的的参考性预估，以描述大概的市场规模。每个客户和每笔交易都会有所不同。某些客户需要大量的外部帮助，而其他客户则愿意在企业内部完成大部分工作，而仅需要最低限度的外部法律顾问的指导。但是，总体来说，由于外商独资企业转化和简单的合营企业转化工作可以商品化，因此市场将要求对这些事项进行系统化，以使客户从相关的效率提升中获益。

另外，合营企业重新谈判的工作不能商品化，但是在某些情况下，相关的谈判范围可能相对有限，而在其他情况下，谈判可能更具争议性且范围更广。同样，在某些情况下，双方将按小时付费（并且小时数和费率可能会高于我们为进行此估算而使用的价格）聘请法律顾问，而在其他情况下，一方将依靠其内部法律顾问，或坚持让外部法律顾问提供固定费用安排（这在由一些中国客户委托的规模较小的交易中可能更为常见）。因此，以上估计只是为了提供一个*潜在*的总市场规模的指标，而没有考虑哪些工作将被外包，哪些工作将在内部解决。

我们的预期是如果外商独资企业转化和简单的合营企业转化服务基于传统法律服务模式提供，则也许仅有潜在总需求的 1/3 到 1/2 将被外包，而如果可以以一个合适的价格获得高质量的、整合的法律科技 / 系统化的解决方案，则这一比例将会翻转，即 1/2 到 2/3 的转化事项将会被外包。合营企业合同重新谈判工作中可能有更高比例的工作将被外包或需要某种程度的外部法律顾问支持。

如果我们使用以上指示性的数字，将每种工作类型的数量与价值进行比较，很明显，外商独资企业转化和简单的合营企业转化工作量相对较大而其服务价值却相对较低，而合营企业合同重新谈判工作的每个项目则可能产生高得多的费用（见图 4-E）。

legal counsel (unless he or she is not available during periods of peak demand in the latter stages of the five-year transition period) or select new outside legal counsel through a traditional beauty contest. But also as indicated above it is expected that there will be another group of JVs where it starts out as a simple JV conversion process and then unexpectedly flips into a more extensive JV contract renegotiation scenario part way through the process.

Let's do a little game-planning to see how outside legal counsel can best position themselves to capture both of these categories of higher-value JV contract renegotiation work, starting first with the latter scenario. The anticipated price point for a simple JV conversion process as used for our calculation purposes is RMB 80,000 per project. As we will discuss further below, if a law firm uses the traditional legal services delivery model, it will lose money on each such simple JV conversion project and based on our projections will have only a one-in-four chance that it will actually flip into a more extensive JV contract renegotiation that will generate more profits. Those are not great odds if you are losing a significant amount of money on each such simple JV conversion project. But if you don't do the simple JV conversion work, you risk losing the potential JV contract renegotiation work to a competitor, which may be a worse outcome since that may disrupt your existing long-term client relationship. This thus presents a significant potential dilemma: lose money or lose clients.

The straight-up JV contract renegotiation scenario carries with it some similar risks. Before you can get to the more lucrative JV contract renegotiation stage, you need to review the existing JV contract and SAMR file and produce a roadmap for the client outlining what changes *must* be made to the JV contract to reflect the mandatory terms of the Company Law corporate governance requirements as well as well as what changes *may* be made pursuant to the greater flexibility permitted under the Company Law (a sample roadmap of such changes to a legacy JV contract is available at www.docqbot.com/en/newFIL at no charge as a companion to the electronic versions of the Sample Templates). All of this will have to take into account the parties' relative shareholdings and negotiating positions. Once you have received the client's instructions on how to proceed, you then need to make the detailed amendments to the base JV contract and articles of association in both English and Chinese, which will be a painstaking exercise. Once that work is completed, you will then be in a position to commence with the JV contract renegotiation work, presumably at full rack rates and perhaps even with a premium if this comes later in the transition period at a time of peak demand.

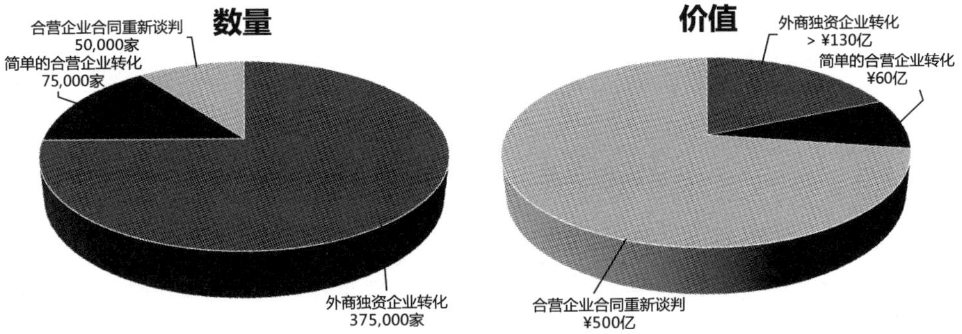

图 4–E　外商投资企业转化：数量 vs. 价值

在这种情况下，很明显，顶级的外商投资律师都会自然地倾向于价值更高的合营企业合同重新谈判工作。如上所述，我们预计投资者会提前确定约 1/5 的合营企业可能需要对其合营企业合同进行广泛的重新谈判。在这种情况下，他们可能会回到原来的外部法律顾问那里（除非在 5 年过渡期后期需求高峰期间该法律顾问没有时间），或通过传统的方式挑选新的外部法律顾问。但如上所述，预计还有另外一部分合营企业以简单的合营企业转化流程开始，但在过程中意外地转变为更广泛的合营企业合同重新谈判的情形。

让我们来做一点游戏规划，看看外部法律顾问是如何最好地定位自己，以获得这两类更高价值的合营企业合同重新谈判工作。我们首先从后一种情形开始分析。根据我们的计算，简单的合营企业转化流程的预期价格是每个项目 80,000 元人民币。正如我们在下文中将进一步讨论的那样，如果一家律师事务所使用传统的法律服务模式提供服务，其将会在每个这样的简单合营企业转化项目中亏损，并且根据我们的预测，这样的项目只有 1/4 的机会转变为更加广泛的合营企业合同重新谈判，从而产生更多的利润。如果您在每一个这样的简单合营企业转化项目中都亏损，仅有这 1/4 的机会也并不能成为您继续做这种工作的理由。但如果您不做简单的合营企业转化工作，您将面临将潜在的合营企业合同重新

The challenge, however, is that everything up to and including the point of completing the preparation of the revised JV contract and AoA in English and Chinese is almost exactly the same work scope as the corresponding part of the simple JV conversion process. That means that this front-end work is also fully commoditize-able and can be done at a reduced fixed fee. In a beauty contest, all other things being equal, a law firm which adopts systems and tools which can achieve greater levels of efficiency and can pass on those savings to the client will have a distinct competitive advantage, while a firm that proposes to provide such services solely in accordance with the traditional legal services model will either have to cut their fees to match or lose the project.

Again, it bears repeating that the sheer volume of FIE conversion matters means that the market will have reasonable expectations that legal services providers will put in place systems to create efficiencies since there will be substantial overlap in how such matters are to be handled. But law firms are not wired to be efficient. The traditional legal services model is built on an hourly rate fee structure which actually rewards inefficiencies in many cases. This model works fine when you have sophisticated clients demanding bespoke solutions for high stakes matters, but it falls apart when it comes to commoditize-able work such as the front end of FIE conversion matters.

Thus, while the big prize in the FIE conversion market is JV contract negotiation work, the gateway to this back-end higher-value work will in many cases be through the front-end commoditize-able work.

Scoping Out the FIE Conversion Process

Let's now turn to an examination of the base FIE conversion process, and see what challenges it presents under the traditional legal services model. If FDI lawyers provide the basic WFOE conversion services on a traditional time-spent basis without adopting expert systems, this could very easily take up to 75 hours or more of professional time per project, between review of existing documentation, drafting of advice memoranda and revised corporate documents, in-person or online consultations, document collection and application preparation, etc.

By comparison, simple JV conversion will be even more time-consuming, requiring somewhere in the range of 125 hours per project, as the document review, advisory memos, corporate document drafting and related consultations will all be more complex and involve

谈判工作让给竞争对手的风险，这可能是更糟糕的结果，因为这可能会破坏您现有的长期客户关系。因此，这带来了一个潜在的巨大困境：要么亏损，要么失去客户。

> “但如果您不做简单的合营企业转化工作，您将面临将潜在的合营企业合同重新谈判工作让给竞争对手的风险，这可能是更糟糕的结果，因为这可能会破坏您现有的长期客户关系。因此，这带来了一个潜在的巨大困境：要么亏损，要么失去客户。”

直接的合营企业合同重新谈判情形也带有一些类似风险。在进入利润更高的合营企业合同重新谈判阶段之前，您需要审阅现有合营企业合同和市场监管局档案，并为客户制定一份路线图，说明*必须*对合营企业合同作出哪些修改，以反映《公司法》对公司治理要求的强制性条款，以及根据《公司法》允许的更大的灵活性*可以*进行哪些修改（对于一份传统合资合同作出这些修改的路线图示例，以及模板样本的电子版，均可在 www.docqbot.com/cn/newFIL 免费获取）。所有这些都必须考虑到双方的相对持股比例和谈判立场。收到客户关于如何开展业务的指示后，您即需要对中英文基础合营企业合同和章程进行详细的修改，这是一项艰巨的工作。一旦完成这项工作，您将可以开始合营企业合同重新谈判的工作，很可能是以全价收费，而如果是在过渡期晚些时候的需求高峰期进行这项工作，甚至可能会产生一些溢价。

然而，挑战在于，直到完成对中英文的合营企业合同和章程的修订工作为止，所有工作几乎都与简单的合营企业转化过程中相应部分的工作范围完全相同。这意味着前期工作也可以完全商品化，并且可以以较低的固定费用完成。在律所竞标时，在所有其他条件相同的情况下，采用系统和工具从而能够实现更高的效率并可以将节省下来的费用回馈给客户的律所将具有明显的竞争优势，而提议仅以传统的法律服务模式提供该等服务的律所要么削减其费用来竞争，要么失去该项目。

此外，值得重申的是，外商投资企业转化事项的数量之多意味着，市场将有合理的预期，即法律服务提供商将建立系统以提高效率，因为处理此类事项的方式将有大量重叠。但是律师事务所并不是为高效而存在的。传统的法律服务模式建立在按小时计

many more corporate governance elements to be assessed in the context of the partner relationship, while WFOE conversion can be done on a unilateral basis. Moreover, as noted above, for a simple JV conversion it will still be necessary to make clause-by-clause revisions to the original JV contract, which will be much more time consuming and complicated than the simple rip-and-replace exercise for a WFOE AoA. So, while the simple JV conversion process by definition will not include negotiations, it will still require careful work which takes much more time under the traditional legal services model.

At the same time, FIE conversion in China will attract the attention of the general counsel, the company secretary or other senior officers of the foreign investor at the headquarters level. They will want to understand what is going on, what is changing, and what the legal and practical implications are. There will be a lot of questions and a lot of hand-holding. There will be a lot of back-and-forth about documentation and filing status. Some of these things a paralegal will be able to handle independently, but in other cases the client will want to talk to a senior lawyer. The team from headquarters will want to communicate in English, while the team on the ground at the FIE level likely will prefer to communicate in Chinese, so the process will in the vast majority of cases need to be run bilingually, both in respect of the documentation and the client communications.

As should be readily apparent from this outline, there are two main problems with running the FIE conversion process on the traditional legal services model. First, it will be much more expensive than what the market will bear. Assuming a blended rate of RMB 2000 per hour, a WFOE conversion exercise would cost RMB 150,000 compared to a projected market price of RMB 35,000, and a simple JV conversion would cost RMB 250,000 compared to a projected market price of RMB 80,000. So clearly this is not competitive pricing and will be a non-starter for the vast majority of clients, who will simply do it on an in-house basis rather than outsource this work at these traditional law firm rates, while if they can leverage off the greater expertise and efficiencies of outside services providers at the lower target market rates, then in the majority of cases they will be more than happy to out-source this work to free up their own internal time and resources and ensure that it is done right. (Note also that the reference rate of RMB 2000 per hour is intended to be conservative, as it is clearly far lower than the rack rates quoted by foreign firms or even the Red Circle firms, but based on 1500 billed hours per fee earner per year, the revenues per lawyer (RPL) generated using this rate

费的收费结构上，这种结构实际上在很多情况下奖励效率低下的人。当您有经验丰富的客户需要针对高风险事务定制解决方案时，此模式很好用，但是在涉及可商品化的工作（如外商投资企业转化事务的前期工作）时，该模式就不适用了。

因此，尽管外商投资企业转化市场的大奖是合营企业合同谈判工作，在许多情况下通往这一后期高价值工作的大门将是前期的可商品化的工作。

界定外商投资企业转化流程

现在，我们来研究一下基本的外商投资企业转化流程，看看在传统法律服务模式下它会带来什么挑战。如果外商直接投资律师不采用专家系统，而是在传统的计时收费的基础上提供基本的外商独资企业转化服务（包括审阅现有文件、起草建议备忘录以及经修改的公司文件、面对面或线上咨询、文件收集和申请准备等），则非常容易在每个项目上花费多达 75 小时或更多的专业时间。

相比较而言，简单的合营企业转化将更加耗时，每个项目需要花费 125 小时左右的时间，因为文件审阅、起草建议备忘录、起草公司文件和相关咨询都将更加复杂，且涉及更多的公司治理要素需要在合营关系的背景下进行评估，而外商独资企业转化则可以单方面进行。此外，如上所述，对于一个简单的合营企业转化，仍有必要逐条修改原有的合营企业合同，这将比外商独资企业合同简单的撕毁和替换操作要耗时和复杂得多。因此，尽管简单的合营企业转化流程本身不包括谈判，但其仍需要细致的工作，而在传统法律服务模式下，这需要花费更多的时间。

同时，在中国的外商投资企业的转化将引起总法律顾问、公司秘书或外国投资者总部层面的其他高级管理人员的关注。他们希望了解正在发生的事情，正在发生的变化以及法律和实践上的影响。届时将会有很多的问题和密集的指示，还将会就文件编制和申请状态进行多次反复沟通。其中一些问题可以由律师助理独

would still reach the pinnacle of the Chinese domestic legal profession (see related discussion below), so this seems to be a fair reference point.)

The second problem is that if outside service providers do this work on the traditional legal services model but have to accept the lower target market price, then this will not be attractive, sustainable or scalable since it will be unprofitable . As things stand at present, it is not clear that any of the traditional legal services providers in China are in a position to meet the requisite service quality expectations at the projected lower price point that the market will require, and none of them are building systems to handle the projected volumes in an efficient, high quality, cost-effective manner. Let's take a brief look at each of the traditional service providers to assess their relative competitive positioning in respect of FIE conversion work under the FIL.

Chart 4–C Assessment of Potential FIE Conversion Service Providers

Service Provider	Pros	Cons	Conclusion
Foreign law firms	High quality Bilingual capability	High price Inconsistent with core business model Cannot scale to meet demand	Will likely cede this market to local Chinese firms almost entirely (although in the im-mediate aftermatch of the coro-navirus pandemic, many foreign firms may move down market to chase lower value work to generate cash flow) Alternatively, will out-source this work to a platform which will provide a satisfactory solution at an accep-table price point but which is not connected to a potential competitor
Red Circle firms	High quality Bilingual capability	Moderately high price No systems in place Uneven quality control Cannot scale to meet demand	Will service certain key clients on a loss-leader basis to retain relationships Limited market share overall in the aggregate

立处理，但在其他情况下客户会希望咨询资深律师。外商投资企业总部的团队会希望用英语沟通，而本地团队可能更愿意用中文进行沟通，因此在绝大多数情况下，无论是在文件编制还是客户沟通方面，这一过程均需要以双语进行。

从以上分析中显而易见的是，在传统法律服务模式下进行的外商投资企业转化流程存在两个主要问题。首先，该工作的收费将比市场能够承受的价格昂贵得多。假设采用 2000 元人民币 / 小时的混合费率，外商独资企业转化将花费 150,000 元人民币，而预期市场价格为 35,000 元人民币；简单的合营企业转化将花费 250,000 元人民币，而预期市场价格为 80,000 元人民币。因此，这显然不是有竞争力的价格，对绝大多数的客户来说这是不可接受的，他们只会以内部资源完成这些事项，而不是以传统律师事务所的费率外包这些事项 ，而如果他们能够以较低的目标市场费率利用外部服务提供商更强的专业知识和更高的效率，那么在大多数情况下，他们将更愿意将这项工作外包，以释放自己内部的时间和资源，并确保正确地完成此工作。［请注意，2000 元人民币 / 小时的参考费率是出于保守考虑，因为这显然远低于外资律师事务所或甚至是“红圈所”的标准费率，但以每个创收人员每年 1500 个计费小时为基础，按此费率计算的律师人均创收仍将达到中国国内律师行业的顶尖水平（见下文中相关讨论），所以这似乎是一个公平的参照点。］

第二个问题是，如果外部服务提供商以传统法律服务模式进行这项工作，但必须接受较低的目标市场价格，那么这将是没有吸引力的、不可持续的且不可规模化的，因为它将无利可图。从目前的情况来看，尚不清楚中国的任何传统法律服务提供商能够以市场所需的预期较低价格满足必要的服务质量期望，并且他们都没有建立系统来以高效率、高质量、高成本效益的方式处理预计数量的工作。让我们简要分析一下每一类传统法律服务提供者，以评估他们在《外商投资法》项下的外商投资企业转化工作中的相对竞争地位。

“如果外部服务提供商以传统法律服务模式进行这项工作，但必须接受较低的目标市场价格，那么这将是没有吸引力的、不可持续的且不可规模化的，因为它将无利可图。”

Continued

Service Provider	Pros	Cons	Conclusion
FDI lawyers in emerging local firms	Reasonably good quality Bilingual capability	Moderate price No systems in place Average to poor quality control Cannot scale to meet demand	Will aggressively chase new clients on price Moderate market share overall in the aggregate
Big 4 accounting firms	High quality Bilingual capability Have the ability to introduce systems to achieve scale at competitive market price but without automated expert systems may still not be able to deliver conversion services at market price points on a profitable basis	May or may not be part of core business model for China Can in most cases provide wide range of related legal services at scale	Not clear that all will enter this market on their own to address short-term opportunity given the up-front costs to build related systems
Alternative Legal Services Providers	Same as for Big 4 but perhaps at slightly smaller scale Currently, only a limited number of ALS platforms in China, typically connected to a leading law firm Stand-alone ALS providers may enter market but will need to start from scratch	For current limited number of ALS providers, this would require an expansion of existing core service offering but this would constitute a natural complement to existing services For ALS platforms connected to leading law firms, they will be able to provide the full range of related legal services, including for top-end matters	If relying only on traditional ALS optimized systems without integration with related legal-tech tools, will still be difficult to achieve target price point on a profitable basis
Domestic registration agents	Low pricing Strong know-how re: SAMR system, but the transition to full online registration will tend to undercut their advantages in this regard This is part of core business	Limited or no bilingual capability Poor quality documentation No systems in place Cannot scale to meet demand	Will be primary beneficiaries of FIE conversion under the FIL but will have challenges meeting increased demand Moderate market share overall in the aggregate

The great irony is that excessive demand in this case will drive down pricing and thus potentially drive out the traditional legal service providers, leaving a service-side gap in the market. Of course, that just creates a new opportunity for different players (or for some of the

表 4–C　潜在外商投资企业转化服务提供者评估

服务提供者	优势	劣势	结论
外资律师事务所	高质量 双语能力	价格昂贵 与其业务模式不一致 无法规模化以满足需求	很可能会把这部分市场几乎全部让给内资律师事务所 （虽然在新型冠状病毒疫情发生后不久，许多外国律所可能会进军低端市场，争取较低价值的工作以产生现金流） 或者，会将此工作外包给能够以可接受的价格提供符合要求的解决方案且与潜在竞争对手无关联的平台
“红圈所”	高质量 双语能力	价格较高 无系统 质量控制不统一 无法规模化以满足需求	将为某些核心客户亏本服务以维护客户关系 总体上市场份额有限
新兴的本土律师事务所中的外商直接投资律师	质量较高 双语能力	价格适中 无系统 质量控制在平均水平与低水平之间 无法规模化以满足需求	将以低价积极追逐新客户 总体上市场份额适中
四大会计师事务所	高质量 双语能力 有能力引入系统以富有竞争力的市场价格大规模提供服务，但如果没有自动化的专家系统，仍然可能无法在盈利的基础上以市场价格点提供转化服务	可能不是其在中国核心业务模式的一部分 在大多数情况下可以大规模提供广泛的相关法律服务	考虑到构建系统的前期成本，尚不清楚是否都会自行进入这个市场以抓住短期机会
替代法律服务提供商	与四大会计师事务所相同，但可能规模稍小 目前，中国的替代法律服务平台的数量非常有限，通常与领先的律师事务所相关联 独立的替代法律服务提供商可能会进入市场，但需要从零开始	对于当前数量有限的替代法律服务提供商来说，其需要扩展其现有的核心服务，但这将是对其现有服务的自然补充 对于与领先律师事务所相关联的替代法律服务平台，他们将能够提供全方位的相关法律服务，包括高端业务	如果仅依靠传统的替代法律服务的优化系统，而不与相关的法律科技工具相整合，仍然很难在盈利的基础上以目标价格点提供服务

same old players) to provide a different, more efficient service offering.

Driving Value Creation in the Post-FIL Market Through Legal-Tech Solutions

For all of the reasons set out above, the FIL is expected to create substantial disruption in the China legal services market. The emergence of legal-tech expert systems and tools will be an important factor in driving value creation in the market by mitigating the down-side risks in connection with high volume/low-value work and maximizing the upside potential in connection with the higher value/bespoke work to be generated by the FIL.

Chinese Law Firm Profitability Benchmarks

In order to understand how legal-tech tools will impact the post-FIL market, it is important to benchmark existing levels of profitability of Chinese law firms. To date there are only 21 of the top 45 domestic law firms in China which achieve more than RMB 1 million per year in RPL,[1] 12 firms with RPL above RMB 2 million,[2] and only five firms with RPL over RMB 3 million.[3] The average RPL for the top 45 Chinese law firms is RMB 1.44 million, which is only one-fourth of the average RPL for the Global 100 law firms,[4] and (perhaps most surprisingly) virtually the same as the median RPL for sole practitioners and small firm lawyers in the U.S.[5]

These comparisons also ignore the fact that RPL figures in Chinese law firms may be

1 Llinks Law Offices, JunHe, Zhong Lun Law Firm, MWE China Law Offices, Jingtian & Gongcheng, Commerce & Finance Law Offices, King & Wood Mallesons, Han Kun Law Offices, FenXun Partners, Fangda Partners, Chen & Co., Haiwen & Partners, Dentons, Tian Yuan Law Firm, Global Law Office, Jia Yuan Law Offices, Grandall Law Firm, Allbright, Anjie Law Firm, JunZeJun Law Offices, Wintell & Co.] "The China 45: Ranked by Revenue, Profits and RPL." The American Lawyer, September 24, 2019. Available at https://www.law.com/americanlawyer/2019/09/24/the-china-45-ranked-by-revenue-profits-and-rpl/.

2 Llinks Law Offices, JunHe, Zhong Lun Law Firm, MWE China Law Offices, Jingtian & Gongcheng, Commerce & Finance Law Offices, King & Wood Mallesons, Han Kun Law Offices, FenXun Partners, Fangda Partners, Chen & Co., Haiwen & Partners.

3 Llinks Law Offices, JunHe, Zhong Lun Law Firm, MWE China Law Offices, Jingtian & Gongcheng.

4 "The China 45 Are Growing Rapidly—and Not Just the Elites," The American Lawyer, September 24, 2019. https://www.law.com/americanlawyer/2019/09/24/the-china-45-are-growing-rapidly-and-not-just-the-elites-405-43715/.

5 "2019 Attorney Compensation Report." Martindale-Avvo, 2019. Available at https://www.martindale-avvo.com/wp-content/uploads/2019-Attorney-Compensation-Report.pdf. It is expected that RPL figures around the world in 2020 likely will be seriously impacted by the COVID-19 pandemic, but we will use these 2019 figures for purposes of our analysis.

续表

服务提供者	优势	劣势	结论
内资注册代理机构	价格低廉 对市场监管局系统非常了解，但向全面在线注册的转变将削弱他们在这方面的优势 核心业务的一部分	不具备双语能力或双语能力有限 文件质量较差 无系统 无法规模化以满足需求	将会是《外商投资法》项下的外商投资企业转化的主要受益者，但在满足不断增长的需求方面面临挑战 总体上市场份额适中

极具讽刺意味的是，在这种情况下，过多的需求将压低价格，因此可能将传统的法律服务提供商挤出市场，从而在市场上留下服务端缺口。当然，这为不同的参与者（或某些相同的原有参与者）创造了一个提供不同的、更有效地服务的新机会。

运用法律科技解决方案推动《外商投资法》时代市场价值创造

基于上述原因，预计《外商投资法》将对中国法律服务市场造成实质性的影响。法律科技专家系统和工具将成为推动市场价值创造的重要因素，其有助于缓解高工作量 / 低价值工作带来的下行风险，并最大化《外商投资法》产生的更高价值 / 定制工作的上升潜力。

中国律师事务所盈利能力基准

为了解法律科技工具对《外商投资法》时代市场的影响，有必要对中国律师事务所现有的盈利水平进行测算。截至目前，中国 45 强律所中只有 21 家内资律师事务所的律师人均收入超过 100 万元人民币，[1]12 家律师事务所律师人均收入超过 200 万元人

1　通力律师事务所、君合律师事务所、中伦律师事务所、元达律师事务所、竞天公诚律师事务所、通商律师事务所、金杜律师事务所、汉坤律师事务所、奋迅律师事务所、方达律师事务所、瑛明律师事务所、海问律师事务所、大成律师事务所、天元律师事务所、环球律师事务所、嘉源律师事务所、国浩律师事务所、锦天城律师事务所、安杰律师事务所、君泽君律师事务所、瀛泰律师事务所。“The China 45: Ranked by Revenue, Profits and RPL.” The American Lawyer, 2019 年 9 月 24 日。参见 https://www.law.com/americanlawyer/2019/09/24/the-china-45-ranked-by-revenue-profits-and-rpl/。

artificially inflated because law graduates who have passed the Chinese bar exam but not yet obtained their practicing license certificate (a process which can take up to two years) are not included in the number of lawyers for purposes of this calculation even though they are actually providing legal services and generating revenues. But even using these more generous calculations of RPL for Chinese law firms, it is clear that even at the top end of the China legal services market, there is substantial room to grow in terms of profitability.

An analysis of the traditional legal service business model helps us better assess these benchmark figures. The basic business model for the legal profession is essentially the same as for all service industries. While this can be expressed in more complex and detailed terms,[1] for our purposes we can describe it simply as revenues less costs equals profits, with revenues being a function of hours worked multiplied by the effective hourly rate. Note that the concept of effective hourly rate can include both the traditional hourly rate fee basis commonly used outside of China and fixed fee arrangements which are more common within China. In the case of fixed or capped fees, the effective hourly rate is simply calculated by dividing total revenues by the number of hours actually worked to produce those revenues. This provides a more effective way to measure the profitability of different firms, practice areas and individual matters against a consistent standard.

In order to achieve an RPL of RMB 1 million, each lawyer would only need to work 1,000 hours per year at an effective rate of RMB 1000 per hour. Both of these metrics are extraordinarily low by international standards, particularly when considering that this represents the top end of the legal profession in China. It would be astonishing if the lawyers in the top 20-plus law firms in China were working only 1000 hours of billable time per year – this would represent a massive under-utilization of the law firm's key resource, namely the time or working capacity of the lawyers in the firm. By contrast, the top law firms around the world would expect their lawyers to be working well in excess of 2000 billable hours per year, in addition to time spent on non-billable matters such as marketing, training, know-how development, administration, etc.

If we reasonably assume that the lawyers in the top 20-plus firms in China with RPL in

1 Common metrics in law firm budgeting include leverage, capacity, utilization, fee rates, realization, costs, etc. While many of these metrics can be used to measure Chinese law firm performance as well, it is more difficult to do so where the firm is structured as a loose confederation of independent profit centers rather than managed on a unified integrated basis across the entire law firm as a whole.

民币，[1] 而仅有 5 家律师事务所律师人均收入收入超过 300 万元人民币。[2] 中国 45 强律师事务所的平均律师人均收入为 144 万元人民币，仅为全球 100 强律师事务所律师人均收入的 1/4，[3] 并且（或许最令人惊讶的是）几乎与美国个体执业律师和小型律师事务所律师人均收入的中位数持平。[4]

这些比较还忽视了一个事实，即中国律师事务所律师人均收入可能被人为地夸大，因为在这一测算中，通过了中国律师资格考试但未取得律师执业证（该过程可能需要长达两年的时间）的法学院毕业生并未计入律师总数中，即使他们实际提供了法律服务并产生了收入。但即便采用这种更加宽松的计算方法计算中国律师事务所律师人均收入，我们也可以清楚地看到，即使在中国法律服务的高端市场，盈利能力也有很大的增长空间。

对传统法律服务业务模式的分析有助于我们更好地评估这些基准数据。律师职业的基本业务模式与所有服务业基本相同。虽然这一点可以用更为复杂和详细的术语来表述[5]，但在这里，我们可以简单地将其描述为收入减去成本等于利润，其中收入等于工作小时数乘以实际小时费率。需要注意的是，实际小时费率的概念既包括中国境外常用的传统计时收费基础，也包括中国境内更为常见的固定收费安排。在固定或封顶收费的情况下，实际小时

1 通力律师事务所、君合律师事务所、中伦律师事务所、元达律师事务所、竞天公诚律师事务所、通商律师事务所、金杜律师事务所、汉坤律师事务所、奋迅律师事务所、方达律师事务所、瑛明律师事务所、海问律师事务所。

2 通力律师事务所、君合律师事务所、中伦律师事务所、元达律师事务所、竞天公诚律师事务所。

3 “The China 45 Are Growing Rapidly—and Not Just the Elites,” The American Lawyer, 2019 年 9 月 24 日。参见 https://www.law.com/americanlawyer/2019/09/24/the-china-45-are-growing-rapidly-and-not-just-the-elites-405-43715/。

4 “2019 Attorney Compensation Report.” Martindale-Avvo, 2019. 下载地址：https://www.martindale-avvo.com/wp-content/uploads/2019-Attorney-Compensation-Report.pdf。预计 2020 年全球律师人均收入数据可能会受到新型冠状病毒肺炎疫情的严重影响，但我们将使用这些 2019 年的数据进行分析。

5 律师事务所预算中常用的指标包括杠杆率、产能、利用率、费率、实现、成本等。虽然许多这些指标也可以用来衡量中国律师事务所的业绩，但如果律所的结构是一个松散的独立利润中心联盟，而不是在整个律师事务所范围内统一管理，则更难做到这一点。

excess of RMB 1 million per year are not sitting on their hands for six months of the year but are working somewhere in the range of 2000 hours per year,[1] then that is very bad news in terms of the effective hourly rate over the course of the year. Again, the math is very simple – if a lawyer works 2000 hours a year but produces only RMB 1 million in revenues, then that results in an effective hourly rate of RMB 500. As you move up the RPL ladder in the group of 20-plus firms, we can safely assume a consistent level of working hours in the range of 2000 hours per year, so that means that to achieve RPL levels of RMB 2 million and 3 million, the effective hourly rates would be RMB 1000 and 1500, respectively. Compare that against the roughly RMB 6 million equivalent in RPL for the top 100 global law firms—if we assume the same 2000 billable hours per year, that would require an effective hourly rate of RMB 3000, double the rates achieved by the very elite Chinese firms.

How Legal-Tech Drives Improved Law Firm Profitability

Of course, there are differences between the rates clients are willing to pay in the international legal services market and what they are willing to pay in the China legal services market, but in the context of the post-FIL market the primary client base will still be foreign investors, so there should not be so great a disparity. What may be more important is the actual and perceived value of legal services provided by the top international law firms and the top Chinese law firms.

This in turn is shaped in no small part by the differences in management philosophies between leading international law firms and traditional Chinese law firms. The traditional Chinese law firm management model focuses primarily if not exclusively on controlling costs, and as a result the top Chinese law firms enjoy exceptionally high pre-tax gross profit margins. By contrast, the cost base for international law firms is higher because their management focus is on driving up the revenue side of the equation through higher value services delivered more efficiently. This results in higher net profits. (See Figure 4-F)

1 As noted earlier in this chapter, we assume that the benchmark for actual working hours per year across the entire legal profession in China is more likely in the range of 1500 hours, but at the top end of the legal market 2000 hours is more representative and provides a more consistent basis for comparison against foreign law firms.

费率可以简单地用总收入除以创造这些收入的实际工作小时数来计算。这提供了一种基于一致标准来测量不同律师事务所、不同执业领域和个别事项盈利能力的更有效的方法。

为了达到 100 万元人民币的律师人均收入，每名律师每年只需以每小时 1000 元人民币的实际费率工作 1000 小时。从国际标准来看，这两个指标都非常低，特别是考虑到这代表了中国法律界的高端水平。如果中国 20 多家顶级律师事务所的律师每年只工作 1000 个可计费小时，那将是令人震惊的——这意味着对律师事务所的关键资源，即律师在事务所的工作时间或工作能力的利用严重不足。相比之下，世界各地的顶级律师事务所会期望其律师除了在市场、培训、知识开发、行政等非计费事项上花费的时间外，每年还将工作超过 2000 个可计费小时。

如果我们合理地假设，中国 20 多家律师人均收入超过 100 万元人民币的律所中的律师并没有在一年的六个月中无所事事，而是每年工作约 2000 小时，[1] 那么就全年的实际小时费率而言，这是一个非常坏的消息。同样，计算非常简单——如果一名律师一年工作 2000 小时，但只产生 100 万元人民币的收入，那么这就意味着实际小时费率仅为 500 元人民币。在 20 多家顶级律师事务所中，随着律师人均收入阶梯的提升，我们可以有把握地假设其律师每年的工作小时均为约 2000 小时，这意味着要实现 200 万元和 300 万元人民币的律师人均收入水平，实际小时费率分别是 1000 元和 1500 元人民币。与全球前 100 强律师事务所约等值于 600 万元人民币的律师人均收入相比——如果我们假设每年的计费小时数都是 2000 小时，那么实际小时费率将是 3000 元人民币，这是顶尖中国律师事务所小时费率的 2 倍。

法律科技如何促进律师事务所盈利能力的提高

当然，客户在国际法律服务市场和中国法律服务市场上愿意

1　正如本章前面所述，我们假设中国整个法律界每年实际工作时间的基准更有可能在 1500 小时左右，但在高端法律市场 2000 小时更具代表性，并为与外国律师事务所进行比较提供了更一致的依据。

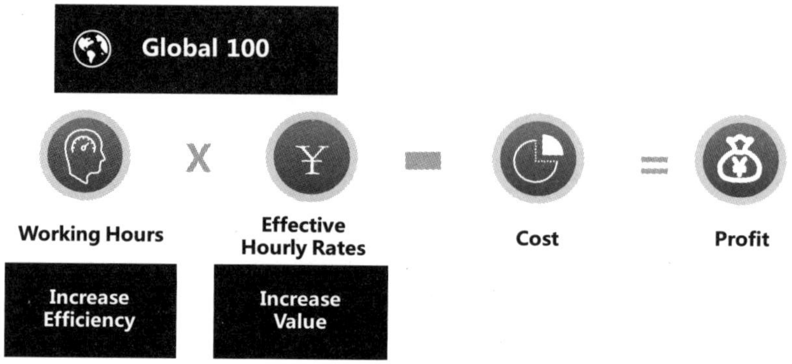

Figure 4–F Global Law Firm Model

This is where legal-tech tools can help Chinese law firms close the gap. It is not possible to create more working hours in a year, but it is possible to increase efficiencies using legal-tech tools to free up more time for additional revenue-generating work. And higher effective hourly rates can be achieved through the use of tech-enabled know-how that helps Chinese law firms move up the value chain. (See Figure 4-G)

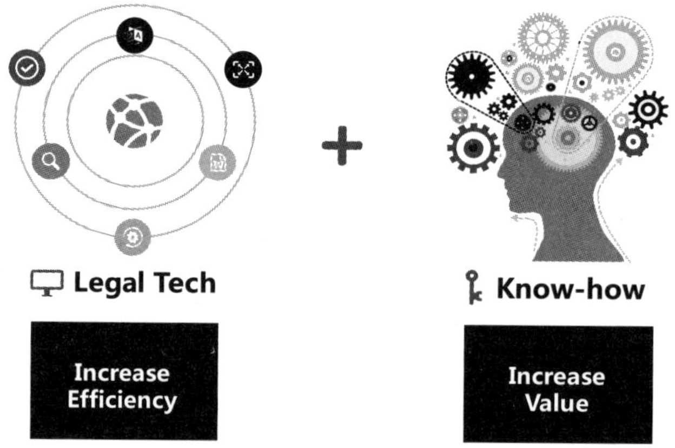

Figure 4–G Tools and Resources to Enhance Profitability

We can illustrate this through a simple example (we will start with a generic example and then will apply these concepts to specific post-FIL business opportunities below). Let's say that a foreign client has engaged your team to draft a set of transaction documents in English and Chinese for an FDI project and that the benchmark price is expected to be RMB 100,000 for the first drafts which will then be sent across to the other side, and that fees for the negotiations stage will be charged on an hourly basis.

Let's further assume that you are an experienced FDI lawyer and have numerous

支付的费率是有差异的，但在《外商投资法》实施后的市场背景下，主要的客户群仍将是外国投资者，因此应该不会有太大的差距，更重要的是顶级国际律师事务所和顶级中国律师事务所提供的法律服务的实际价值和感知价值。

这在很大程度上是由领先的国际律师事务所和传统中国律师事务所管理理念的差异所决定的。中国传统的律师事务所管理模式主要侧重于控制成本。因此，中国顶级律师事务所在税前享有极高的毛利率。相比之下，国际律师事务所的基础成本更高，因为它们的管理侧重于通过更有效地提供更高价值的服务来推动收入的增长。这使其拥有更高的净利润率。（见图 4-F）

图 4–F　国际律师事务所模式

这就是法律科技工具可以帮助中国律师事务所缩小差距的地方。在一年中创造更多的工作时间是不现实的，但利用法律科技工具提高效率，从而腾出更多时间从事额外创收工作则是可能的。并且更高的实际小时费率可以通过使用技术支持的专业知识实现，进而帮助中国律师事务所向价值链上游迈进。（见图 4-G）

precedent forms you can use as a base. These base precedents, of course, will need to be modified to suit the requirements of the particular transaction. You may end up pulling clauses from various precedents and merging them into a new draft contract for this new deal. Since the precedent documents come from different transactions involving different transaction structures and contain different formatting and terminology, and in some cases there will have been intervening changes in law, a significant amount of time will need to be spent harmonizing and updating the various clauses to create a unified new draft. And once you finish the draft in Chinese (assuming your client is the foreign investor), you then have to translate the entire thing into English.

While some of this work inevitably would be done by more junior lawyers on your team, for purposes of this illustration we will assume that you do all of the work yourself. Because you are highly experienced and have a high degree of expertise in this area, for purposes of comparison let's assume that you can complete the work in 25 hours, and that the client is very happy to pay the agreed fee of RMB 100,000 for your work. This results in an effective hourly rate of RMB 4000, which would be generally in line with senior partner rates in many top Chinese firms.

Of course, as a senior partner you do not wish to do all of the drafting work yourself so may choose to assign two junior members of your team to do the work. For the sake of this example we will assume that the associates you assign can produce work of sufficient quality but because their level of expertise is so much lower, it takes them a total of 100 hours to produce the same work product. Assuming the client is still happy to pay the agreed fee of RMB 100,000 for the drafts, then their effective hourly rate is RMB 1000 per hour. (See Figure 4-H)

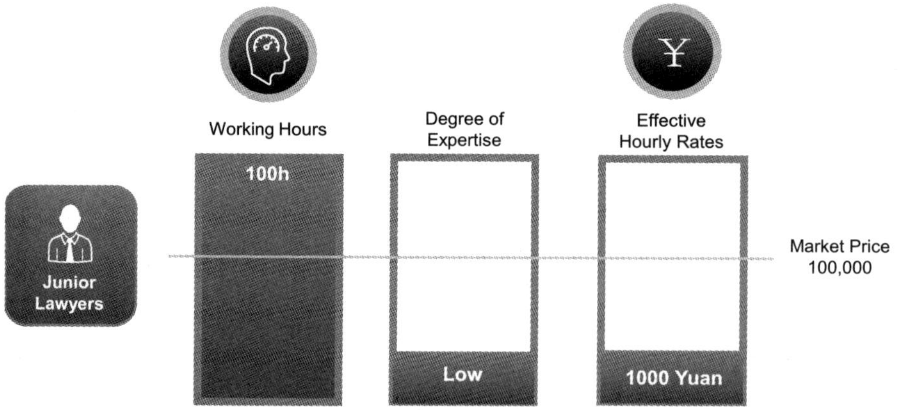

Figure 4–H　Traditional Legal Service Profitability Model

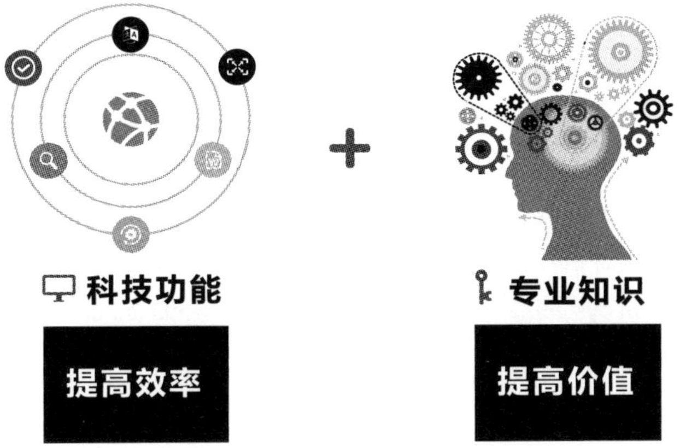

图 4–G　工具和资源提高盈利能力

我们可以通过一个简单的例子说明这一点（下面我们将从一个一般的例子出发，然后将这些概念应用于《外商投资法》实施后具体的商业机会）。假设一个外国客户聘请您的团队为一个外商直接投资项目起草一套中英文的交易文件，并且第一份草稿预计基准价格为 100,000 元人民币，该草稿之后将发送给另一方，谈判阶段的费用按小时收取。

我们进一步假设，您是一位有经验的外商直接投资律师，并且有许多可以作为基础的先例。当然，您需要对这些基础先例进行修改，以适应特定交易的要求。您最终可能会从各种先例中抽取条款，并将其合并为新的合同初稿以用于这一新项目。由于先例文件涉及不同交易结构的不同交易，并且格式和术语不统一，而且在某些情况下新旧交易之间还会发生法律的变化，因此需要花费大量时间来协调和更新各种条款，以形成一个统一的新的文件初稿。并且您完成了中文初稿后（假设您的客户是外国投资者），还需要把整个文件翻译成英文。

虽然这些工作中的一部分将不可避免地由您团队中相对初级的律师完成，但是在这个例子中，我们将假设您自己完成所有的工作。因为您经验丰富且在这方面有丰富的专业知识，为了比较

But now let's compare this against use of tech-enabled know-how and use the docQbot automated contract drafting tools as an example. Users report up to 80% or more improvement in efficiency levels in the bilingual contract drafting process using the docQbot legal-tech tools. For ease of reference in connection with this example, we will assume a 75% improvement in efficiency even though the actual rate of efficiency gains will be much high in practice. (For example, a highly customized bilingual draft agreement can be produced in just 15 minutes using the docQbot system, and then the "last mile" elements are added by the user into the downloaded drafts.)

Because the docQbot automated contract drafting tool incorporates the know-how of very senior China-based international legal experts, when junior lawyers use the system their level of expertise jumps up dramatically. And because the fundamental elements of the drafting process is automated, the time required is dramatically reduced, achieving levels of efficiency equal to or perhaps even better than a very senior lawyer even after taking into account the "last mile" drafting work. (See Figure 4-I)

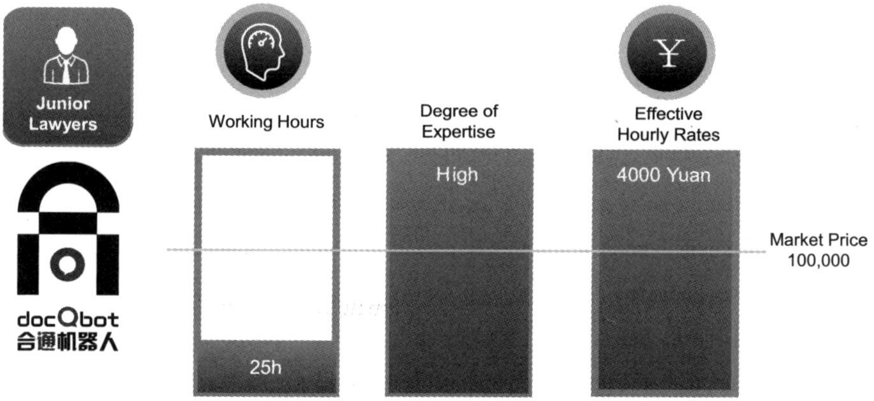

Figure 4–I Tech–Supported Profitability Model

Again, assuming that the client is happy to pay the originally agreed fee of RMB 100,000, this results in a substantial premium of RMB 3000 per hour generated by the use of docQbot's legal-tech tools. We can refer to this as the "know-how dividend" because the know-how embedded into the docQbot system enables the junior lawyers to produce much higher quality work much more efficiently than they could on their own.

But that is only half of the equation. In this example, the team of junior lawyers saved 75 hours of time that they would have otherwise spent doing the drafting in the traditional

的目的，我们假设您可以在 25 小时内完成工作，并且客户很乐意为您的工作支付 100,000 元人民币的约定费用。这意味着实际小时费率为 4000 元人民币，基本上符合许多顶级中国律师事务所的高级合伙人的小时利率。

当然，作为一名高级合伙人，您不希望亲自完成所有的起草工作，所以可能会选择指派团队中的两名初级律师来做这项工作。在这个例子中，我们假设您指派的律师可以高质量地完成工作，但是由于他们的专业知识水平较低，他们总共要花 100 小时来生产相同的工作成果。假设客户仍然乐于为该初稿支付 100,000 元人民币的约定费用，那么他们的实际小时费率是每小时 1000 元人民币。（见图 4-H）

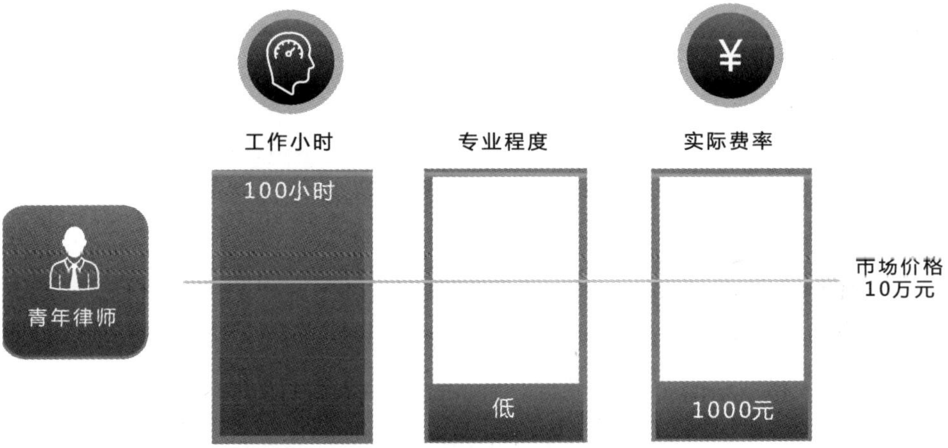

图 4-H　传统法律服务盈利模式

现在让我们将其与使用技术支持的专业知识进行比较，并以合通机器人合同自动生成工具为例。在使用合通机器人法律科技工具后，用户反馈其起草双语合同的效率提高了 80% 或更多。为了在这个例子中更方便地说明，我们将假设效率提高了 75%，尽管实际的效率提升将会高得多。（例如，通过使用合通机器人系统，用户可以在 15 分钟内生成高度定制化的双语协议初稿，然后用户将在下载的初稿中完成“最后一公里”的修改。）

manner. That saved time can be reallocated to other revenue-generating work, creating a second "efficiency dividend." So by utilizing docQbot's legal-tech tools you can reap a "know-how dividend" in the form of a much higher effective hourly rate plus an "efficiency dividend," essentially manufacturing more time to do more revenue-generating work for a double premium. The same principles can also apply to other legal-tech tools, so long as the legal "know-how" content is up to the highest standards and is appropriately powered by leading-edge "tech" elements.

As noted above, one of the characteristics of the China legal services market is that it is less common to charge by the hour and more common to work on a fixed-fee project basis, particularly for Chinese clients (with some exceptions). For FDI work, some foreign clients will agree to hourly rates while others will still require package pricing, but even where the client agrees to hourly rates, it is still common to provide fee estimates for the initial advisory and initial drafting stages. In such cases, the proper use of legal-tech tools can provide an important competitive advantage for FDI lawyers—because you will be able to produce high-quality bespoke work product on a much more efficient basis, you can offer a much more competitive price for these initial up front stages so that you can capture the much higher-value work in the negotiations stage, which would more typically always be billed on a time-spent basis.

More importantly, while legal-tech tools are far superior to humans in performing repetitive technical tasks, legal-tech tools cannot replace human creativity, social interactivity and judgment in the more critical negotiations stage . So by using legal-tech tools such as the docQbot automated contract drafting system for the up-front work segments, you can have a better chance of capturing more higher-value work at the back end, and because you can achieve both the "know-how dividend" and the "efficiency dividend" you will create more time to take on more high-value projects without sacrificing profitability.

因为合通机器人合同自动生成工具包含了在中国工作的资深国际法律专家的专业知识，当初级律师使用该系统时，他们的专业水平将有巨大飞跃。并且由于起草过程的基本要素是自动化的，所需的起草时间大大减少，即使考虑到“最后一公里”的起草工作，也可达到相当于甚至可能优于一名资深律师的效率水平。（见图 4-I）

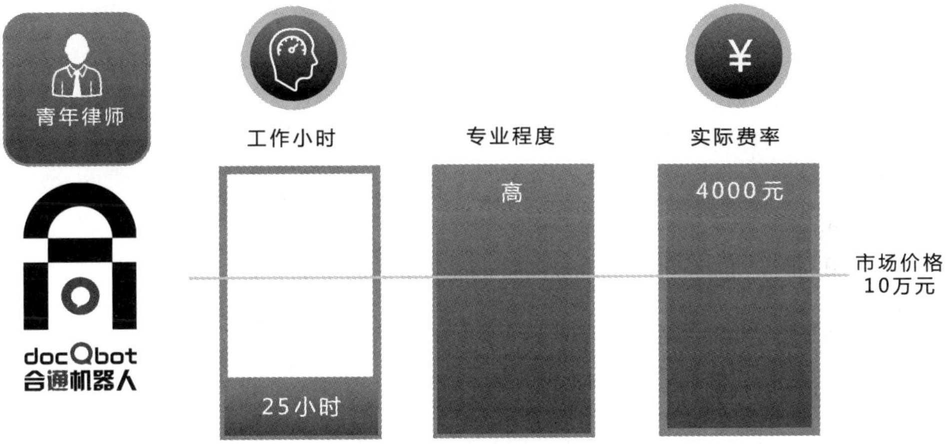

图 4-I　技术支持下的盈利模式

同样，假设客户很乐意支付最初约定的 100,000 元人民币的费用，那么使用合通机器人法律科技工具每小时就会产生 3000 元人民币的额外创收。我们可以将此称为“专业知识红利”，因为嵌入合通机器人系统的专业知识使初级律师能够比他们仅靠自己更高效地完成更高质量的工作。

但这只是等式的一半。在这个例子中，与用传统的方式起草相比，初级律师团队节省了 75 小时。节省下来的时间可以重新分配给其他创收工作，创造第二个“效率红利”。因此，通过利用合通机器人的法律科技工具，您可以获得“专业知识红利”，即更高的实际小时费率加上“效率红利”，实质上就是创造更多的时间来完成更多的创收工作并获得双倍的创收。同样的原则也适用于其他法律科技工具，只要法律“专业知识”内容达到最高标准，并由最先进的“科技”要素提供适当的动力。

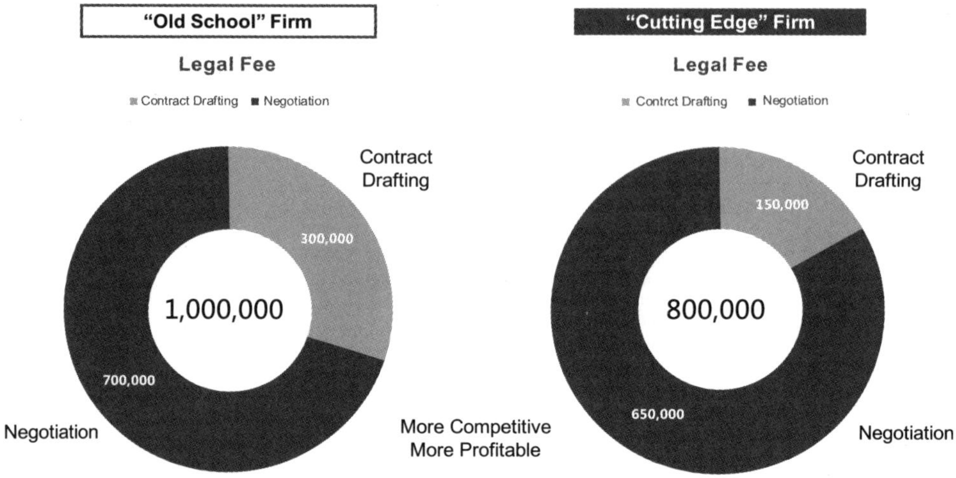

Figure 4–J Improving Competitiveness through Legal–Tech Tools

Figure 4-J helps illustrate this point. This shows two bids from two law firms for the same project. The bid from the "Old School" Firm on the left is based on the traditional legal services model where all of the drafting work is done by hand based on various and sundry precedents of inconsistent quality. The bid from the "Cutting Edge" Firm on the right is 20% lower because it is able to leverage the know-how and efficiency advantages of legal-tech tools such as the docQbot system and pass some of those savings along to the client. Which proposal will the client accept? All other things being equal (which cannot always be assumed), the client will select the less expensive higher-quality bid from the "Cutting Edge" Firm. The winning firm will still make a reasonable and perhaps still very healthy profit on the contract drafting stage, but will capture the full amount of the negotiation stage fees. The losing firm gets nothing. The morale of the story is that proper utilization of legal-tech tools helps you win business.

The Legal-Tech Value Proposition from the Perspective of In-house Counsel

Now let's switch sides and look at this from the perspective of the in-house lawyer. Legal-tech tools have broad application to in-house practice and while the use of these tools will not generate direct monetary benefits to the in-house lawyer personally in the same way as for outside legal counsel, they can still produce similar "efficiency dividends" that will free up time resources that can be applied to more strategic higher-value projects to promote the overall business objectives of the company, resulting in greater job satisfaction and increased

如上所述，中国法律服务市场的特点之一是按小时计费较不常见，而按项目固定收费更为普遍，特别是对中国客户而言（存在部分例外）。对于外商直接投资的工作，一些外国客户会同意按小时计费，而另一些客户仍然要求打包定价，但即使客户同意按小时计费，为最初的咨询和初步起草阶段提供费用预估也很常见。在这种情况下，正确使用法律科技工具可以为外商直接投资律师提供重要的竞争优势——因为您可以在更有效率的基础上生产高质量的定制工作产品，您可以为这些前期阶段的工作提供更具竞争力的价格，这样您就可以获得谈判阶段的价值更高的工作，而谈判阶段的工作通常都是按小时计费的。

更重要的是，虽然法律科技工具在执行重复性技术任务方面比人类优越得多，但在更关键的谈判阶段，法律科技工具无法取代人类的创造力、社会互动和判断。因此，通过在前期工作阶段使用诸如合通机器人合同自动生成系统等法律科技工具，您更有机会在后期获得更高价值的工作，并且因为您既可以实现“专业知识红利”，也可以实现“效率红利”，您将能在不牺牲利润率的情况下创造更多的时间完成更高价值的项目。

“更重要的是，虽然法律科技工具在执行重复性技术任务方面比人类优越得多，但在更关键的谈判阶段，法律科技工具无法取代人类的创造力、社会互动和判断。”

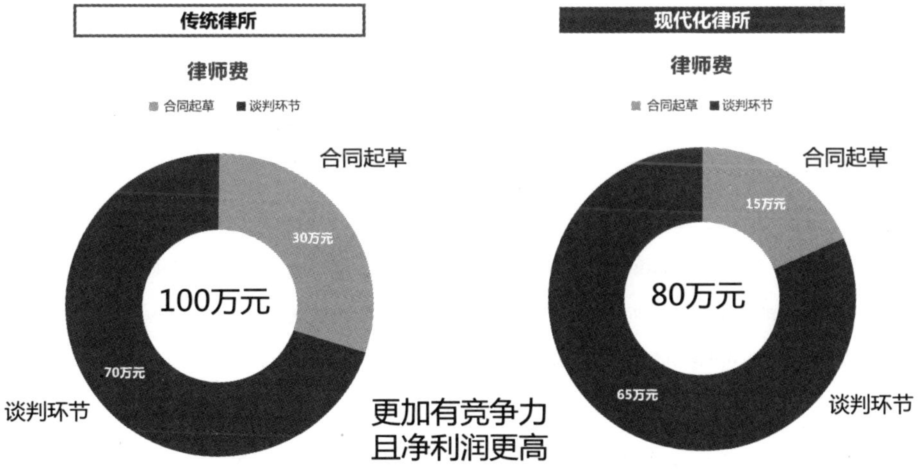

图 4–J　利用法律科技工具提高竞争力

recognition by management of the added value produced by the law department.

In the context of the post-FIL legal market, legal-tech tools can be used effectively by in-house counsel to achieve savings on external legal counsel fees on FDI projects. This can be done in one of two ways: first, the in-house team can use legal-tech tools such as the docQbot system internally to create highly customized bilingual base drafts of the transaction agreements and then have outside counsel prepare a fee proposal for related "last mile" legal services using that draft as the base, or the in-house team can require their external counsel to utilize legal-tech tools such as the docQbot system to produce the initial drafts. In either case, this will save time and reduce external counsel fees. Perhaps more importantly, the "efficiency dividend" will also permit the corporate client to speed up the deal timeline, which in many cases will prove advantageous as a commercial matter, particularly where there may be competitors looking to acquire the same target assets or exclusive business relationship.

Being familiar with the available legal-tech tools empowers in-house counsel to manage external counsel relationships in a much more productive manner and to achieve greater value. For example, if in-house counsel know that outside counsel can produce high-standard bilingual drafts of FDI contracts using docQbot for RMB 50,000, including the "last mile" elements, then in-house counsel will not readily agree to a fixed fee of RMB 150,000 as may have been the case under the traditional legal services model. On the other hand, if in-house counsel is not aware of how legal-tech tools such as docQbot can save both time and money, then outside counsel who adopt such tools may be able to reap arbitrage-like premiums without passing on an appropriate share of such savings to the client.

At the same time, in-house counsel must be aware of what these tools can and cannot do, and be prepared to pay legitimate fees for the actual scope of outside counsel services, and not unreasonably assume that outside counsel can produce all the drafts with a simple push of a button. In the end, knowledge is power, and if in-house counsel know about the efficiencies that can be achieved using these tools, this will drive adoption by outside counsel, resulting in more competitive pricing across the market.

Application of Legal-Tech Solutions to post-FIL Use Cases

As described above, the FIL will directly impact several different FDI work streams, including new FDI projects (greenfield and M&A), existing WFOE and simple JV conversion,

图 4-J 有助于说明这一点。这显示了两家律师事务所对同一项目的两份投标。左侧的传统律师事务所的出价基于传统的法律服务模式，即所有的起草工作都是在各式各样质量不一致的先例基础上完全由人工完成的。右侧的现代化律师事务所的出价要低 20%，因为它能够利用合通机器人系统等法律科技工具的专业知识和效率优势，并将这些节省下来的部分资金回馈给客户。客户会接受哪一项方案？在其他条件相同的情况下（虽然不能总是这样假定），客户将选择现代化律师事务所价格较低、质量较高的方案。胜出的律师事务所在合同起草阶段仍将获得合理而且可能仍然非常可观的利润，但其还将获得谈判阶段全部费用。失败的律师事务所则一无所获。这个故事的启示在于对法律科技工具的恰当利用将帮助您赢得业务。

从企业法务的视角看待法律科技的价值主张

现在让我们换个角度，从企业法务的角度来看待这个问题。法律科技工具在企业内部实践中有广泛的应用，虽然企业法务使用这些工具不会像外部律师使用这些工具那样给企业法务个人带来直接的金钱利益，但他们仍然可以产生类似的“效率红利”，即腾出时间资源用于更具战略性的高价值项目，以促进达成公司的总体经营目标，从而提高工作满意度，并提高管理层对法务部创造的附加价值的认可。

在《外商投资法》时代的市场背景下，企业法务可以有效利用法律科技工具，以节省外商直接投资项目的外部法律顾问费用。这可以通过以下两种方式之一来实现：首先，企业法务团队可以在内部使用合通机器人系统等法律科技工具来创建高度定制化的交易协议的双语草稿，然后让外部律师以该草稿为基础为相关的“最后一公里”的法律服务提供报价；或者企业法务团队可以要求其外部法律顾问利用合通机器人系统等法律科技工具来生成初稿。在任何一种情况下，都将节省时间和减少外部律师费用。也许更重要的是，“效率红利”还将允许企业客户加快交易时间表，

existing JV contract renegotiation, and FIE group restructuring. We will briefly assess how docQbot's legal-tech solutions may be used in connection with the new FDI projects and WFOE/simple JV conversion scenarios by way of illustration of the broader application of legal-tech tools generally. (Note that the structural approach to FIE group restructuring will bear significant resemblance to the new FDI project scenario while the JV contract renegotiation scenario is in most respects a hybrid of the FIE conversion scenario and the new FDI project scenario, so the same principles can be applied to these scenarios on similar terms.)

New FDI Projects

As mentioned in Chapter 3, the first thing which should be noted is that starting from 1 January 2020, all of your legacy FDI templates will need to be tossed in the rubbish bin. The scope of the changes to FIE corporate governance under the Company Law renders all of your old precedents obsolete going forward. That is true for the core documentation for both WFOEs and joint ventures, but it is more particularly true for JVs.

Using the framework outlined above in respect of legal-tech tools, let's evaluate how these principles would work in the context of a greenfield joint venture after the FIL takes effect. Since you will now be bereft of your legacy FDI precedent bank, this book and the Sample Templates and annotations contained in Part II are designed to fill this gap. The Sample Templates and the related annotations reflect more than 1000 hours of professional time invested by the docQbot team and the other members of the Expert Committee. These templates already incorporate all of the corporate governance provisions under the Company Law and conform to both international standards as well as domestic market practices.

It would be very challenging if not impossible for any domestic Chinese law firm to create such know-how on their own—the relatively small number of senior lawyers who have the capability to produce such templates will typically be unwilling to set aside other revenue-generating work to produce such a comprehensive set of know-how without compensation, but given the typical management structures of almost all Chinese law firms, the firm cannot provide such compensation at appropriate levels. Smaller China offices of even major foreign law firms will face similar constraints even if their management model is more accommodating.

The docQbot team and the Expert Committee have provided all of this valuable baseline

这在某些情况下将被证明是有利的商业事项，特别是在可能有竞争者寻求获得相同的目标资产或独家业务关系的情况下。

熟悉现有的法律科技工具，能使企业法务更加富有成效地管理外部律师关系，并实现更大的价值。例如，如果企业法务知道外部律师可以使用合通机器人工具以50,000元人民币起草包括“最后一公里”要素的高标准的外商直接投资合同的双语初稿，那么企业法务不会轻易地同意支付在传统法律服务模式下可能产生的150,000元人民币的固定费用。另外，如果企业法务不知道合通机器人等法律科技工具能够如何节省时间和金钱，那么使用这种工具的外部律师可能能够获得类似套利的额外费用，而无须将节省下来的费用的适当份额回馈给客户。

同时，企业法务必须意识到这些工具可以做什么以及不能做什么，并有准备为外部律师服务的实际范围支付合理费用，而不能不合理地假设外部律师只需按一下按钮就可以完成所有草稿。归根结底，知识就是力量，如果企业法务了解利用这些工具可以实现的效率，这将推动外部律师采用这些工具，从而提高整个市场的价格竞争力。

法律科技解决方案在《外商投资法》时代的应用实例

如上所述，《外商投资法》将直接影响不同的外商直接投资工作的工作量，包括新的外商直接投资项目（新设和并购）、现有外商独资企业和简单的合营企业转化、现有合营企业合同重新谈判以及外商投资企业集团重组。我们将举例说明法律科技工具的更广泛的应用，简要评估合通机器人的法律科技解决方案可以如何应用于新的外商直接投资项目和外商独资企业/简单的合营企业转化。（请注意，外商投资企业集团重组的结构性方法将与新的外商直接投资项目情形有大量相似之处，而合营企业合同重新谈判的情形在大多数方面是外商投资企业转化情形和新的外商

know-how as a public service in hopes that this will convey a significant benefit to the market as a whole and provide a base of templates that can serve as a common reference base. In addition, to make this valuable know-how even more accessible, fully editable electronic versions of the Sample Templates are also being made available without charge at www.docqbot.com/en/newFIL. This thus provides FDI practitioners in the market with a very solid foundation from which to start and constitutes an important basis for FDI practitioners to reap the "know-how dividend" in connection with FDI projects in the post-FIL era.

But even using the Sample Templates in fully editable form is not sufficient to achieve the necessary levels of efficiency to be competitive in the post-FIL legal services market. These Sample Templates only reflect the particular requirements of one scenario as set out in the reference base case for each template. Since each transaction is unique, even if you start with the Sample Templates, you will still need to make all of the necessary revisions in both English and Chinese to reflect the particular requirements of the specific project. And since each deal is unique, you have to repeat this process for each new deal.

This is where docQbot's cutting-edge legal-tech tools come into play. All of the Sample Templates included in Part Ⅱ have been fully automated on the docQbot platform to produce literally trillions of unique customized bilingual versions addressing virtually all of the various scenarios referenced in the annotations. And it takes 15 minutes or less on the docQbot platform compared to up to 50 hours or more to produce the same content using the traditional legal services model, even working off of the same base. This thus helps deliver the critical "efficiency dividend" for FDI practitioners in connection with post-FIL projects.

As an example, the sample JVA template included in Part Ⅱ is designed for a simple two-party joint venture, but on the docQbot platform we can accommodate a joint venture including up to four parties in different combinations, including aligned and unaligned parties. Using the docQbot system it literally takes one click of the mouse to make this change while making the same technical changes "by hand" using the traditional legal services model would take a skilled bilingual practitioner at least 10 or more hours. Similarly, changing from a greenfield joint venture to a post-M&A joint venture is a simple matter of selecting the corresponding template on the docQbot system, again saving more than 10 hours of traditional technical legal work. Further time savings can be achieved for a multitude of other options that are built into the docQbot tool (just the automated formatting tools incorporated into the docQbot platform

直接投资项目情形的结合，因此在这些情形中，在类似地条件下可以适用相同的原则。)

新外商直接投资项目

如第三章中提到的，首先要注意的是，从2020年1月1日开始，所有传统的外商直接投资模板都需要扔进垃圾桶。《公司法》对外商投资企业公司治理规定所做修改的幅度之大，使您过去所有的先例文件都已过时。对于外商独资企业和合营企业的核心文件来说都是如此，但对于合营企业来说更是如此。

“从2020年1月1日开始，所有传统的外商直接投资模板都需要扔进垃圾桶。”

使用上面概述的关于法律科技工具的框架，我们来评估一下这些原则在《外商投资法》生效后将如何在一个新设合营企业中发挥作用。由于您现在将失去您的传统外商直接投资先例文档库，本书以及本书第二部分中包含的模板样本和注解旨在填补这一空白。模板样本和相关注解体现了合通机器人团队和专家委员会的其他成员所投入的1000多个小时的专业时间。这些模板已经纳入了《公司法》项下所有的公司治理规定，并符合国际标准和国内市场惯例。

对于任何一家中国内资律师事务所来说，独立创造这些专业知识即使不是不可能，也是非常具有挑战性的——因为有能力制作此类模板的资深律师数量较少且通常不愿意放弃其他创收工作来无偿地制作这样一套完整的专业知识，但考虑到几乎所有中国律师事务所的典型管理架构，律师事务所不可能给予适当水平的补偿。规模较小的外国大型律师事务所在华办事处，即使具有更加灵活的管理模式也会面临类似的制约。

合通机器人团队和专家委员会提供了所有这些宝贵的专业知识，作为一项公共服务，希望使整个市场大大受益，并提供一个可作为共同参考的模板基础。此外，为了使这一有价值的专业知识更加容易获得，我们还在www.docqbot.com/cn/newFIL上免费提供这些模板样本完全可编辑的电子版本。因此，这为市场上的

can save virtually all of the related document formatting time which for many Chinese lawyers can comprise 20%–30% of the total document drafting time when done "by hand"), and the "efficiency dividend" thus is achieved incrementally for each of scores of options on each separate deal, creating a compound benefit each time you use the tool.

It is critical to understand that the docQbot platform is not a fill-in-the blank tool or a database of static templates—it is a dynamic platform which embeds all of the know-how and options from the annotations in Part Ⅱ of this book into a simple-to-use online interface. It allows even less experienced junior FDI lawyers to create a strong bespoke draft in just minutes, and then the more experienced FDI lawyers on the team can do all of the "last mile" drafting on that solid customized base.

Figure 4–K docQbot Ecosystem for Greenfield JV

Moreover, this "efficiency dividend" extends to all of the most common deal documents for FDI transactions. The docQbot system includes an entire ecosystem of automated templates for inbound M&A and greenfield FDI transactions (see Chart 4-K) as well as FIE post-establishment operations. And as deal volumes ramp up through the combination of new

外商直接投资从业者提供了一个非常坚实的基础，也是外商直接投资从业者在《外商投资法》时代获取外商直接投资项目相关的“专业知识红利”的重要基础。

但是，即便使用完全可编辑的模板样本，也不足以达到在《外商投资法》时代法律服务市场上具有竞争力所需的效率水平。这些模板样本只反映了在每个模板的参考基准案例情形中设置的一个场景的特定需求。由于每个交易都是特殊的，即使以模板样本作为起点，您仍然需要进行所有必要的中英文修订，以反映特定项目的特殊要求。并且由于每笔交易都是独一无二的，您必须为每个新的交易重复这一过程。

这就是合通机器人的尖端法律科技工具发挥作用的地方。第二部分中包含的所有模板样本都已经在合通机器人平台上实现了完全自动化，从而可以生成数万亿个独特的定制化双语版本，这几乎解决了注解中提到的各式各样的场景。而且在合通机器人平台上只需花费 15 分钟或更少的时间，而即便是在相同的基础上工作，使用传统的法律服务模式起草相同的内容则需要 50 小时或更长的时间。因此，这有助于在《外商投资法》实施后的项目中为外商直接投资从业者提供关键的“效率红利”。

例如，本书第二部分中包含的合资协议模板样本是为一个简单的两方合资企业设计的，但是在合通机器人平台上，我们可以支持包括不同组合的最多四方的合资企业，且考虑到了结盟方和非结盟方的情形。使用合通机器人系统，只需单击鼠标就可以进行更改，而使用传统法律服务模式手工完成相同的技术性更改，则需要熟练的双语人员花费至少 10 小时或更长时间。同样，要使新设合资企业转变为并购后的合资企业，只需在合通机器人系统上选择相应的模板，这再次节省了 10 多个小时的传统的技术性法律工作。通过在合通机器人工具中内置大量其他选项，可以节省更多的时间（仅仅是合通机器人平台中内置的格式自动调整

inbound investment, FIE conversion, joint venture contract renegotiations, and FIE group restructuring, the related "know-how dividends" and "efficiency dividends" will be multiplied many times over.

This is critically important in the post-FIL market where, particularly in years three through five following the effectiveness of the FIL, the potential volume of new FDI and FIE conversion projects will threaten to overwhelm existing market resources, so it will be an important competitive advantage to be able to perform the up-front drafting work more efficiently to open up more time to perform higher-value negotiation services for as many deals as possible. Thus, docQbot is a very representative example of how legal-tech advances the value proposition for FDI practitioners in the post-FIL era.

FIE Conversion

With approximately 375,000 existing WFOEs, and a projected 75,000 to 100,000 Sino-foreign joint ventures to undergo simple JV conversion, the FIE conversion requirement under the FIL presents a business opportunity of extraordinary scale, and with a projected total potential value of almost RMB 20 billion for FIE conversion over the next five years, this should be an attractive market opportunity on its own. The fact that these front-end commoditize-able services will act as the gateway to up to half of the much higher-value back-end JV contract renegotiation services, valued at another RMB 25 billion (half of the projected RMB 50 billion total), make this an even more compelling target market.

However, as noted above, given the nature and scope of services required, and the modest projected market price for such services, the WFOE conversion and simple JV conversion process could prove to be a significant money loser for top end law firms under the traditional legal services model. For example, at the projected time and fee rates for WFOE and simple JV conversion matters under the traditional legal services delivery model as set out above, the effective hourly rates will range from under RMB 500 to just over RMB 600 per hour, attractive for most emerging domestic firms as it will achieve more than RMB 1 million per year in RPL so long as working levels remain high, but certainly much too low to be attractive to the Red Circle or international law firms in China, which will be looking to bolster their RPL levels more during the projected post-FIL boom times, not dilute it through devoting too much time to lower value work. But as illustrated above, this lower end work will in many cases be the gateway to capturing more of the higher value work, so leading players in the

工具，可以节省几乎全部调整相关文件格式的时间，而调整格式的时间可能会占到许多中国律师“手动”起草文件所需全部时间的20%~30%），因此，对于每个单独的交易中的每个选项，都可以增量地实现“效率红利”，从而在您每次使用该工具时产生复合效益。

理解合通机器人平台不是填空工具或静态模板数据库非常重要——它是一个动态平台，将本书第二部分的注解说明中的所有专业知识和选项纳入一个易于使用的在线界面中。它让经验更少的外商直接投资业务初级律师在短短几分钟内就能生成一个强大的定制化草稿，然后团队中更有经验的外商直接投资律师可以在这一可靠的定制化初稿上完成所有“最后一公里”的起草工作。

图 4–K　合通机器人生态系统——新设合资企业

此外，这一“效率红利”适用于外商直接投资交易的所有最常见的交易文件。合通机器人系统包括用于入境并购和新设外商直接投资交易（见图 4-K）以及外商投资企业成立后运营的自动化模板的完整生态系统。并且新入境投资、外商投资企业转化、合营企业合同的重新谈判和外商投资企业集团重组共同导致交易

market ignore this front end work at their peril.

In order to achieve suitable levels of profitability for this lower value work, a new legal-tech solution will be required. In fact, this is where legal-tech should excel: large scale, high-volume repetitive workflows on a limited budget. But this cannot work solely as a legal-tech solution but must be a bundled solution to provide for a human interface between the client and the legal-tech solution. The reason is simple—for matters of this type, the client wants to talk to a real person at appropriate stages of the process. Consequently, the integrated legal-tech/human interface bundled services model will be the only practical solution.

As outlined in the market size projections above, it is expected that the related services will include the following, and for each stage of the workflow process, we identify where there are opportunities to leverage off the increased efficiencies of legal-tech tools.

Chart 4–D WFOE Conversion Workflow Stages

Workflow Stage	Legal-Tech Application	Human Interface
Review of existing WFOE AoA	Automated / systematized document review tool	
Review WFOE's SAMR file		Paralegal
Preparation of bespoke advice memorandum	Automated / systematized document drafting tool	
Discussion of findings & options		Senior lawyer
Preparation of bespoke new WFOE AoA	Automated / systematized document drafting tool	
Review of new WFOE AoA with investor		Senior lawyer
Collection of investor documents for conversion application		Paralegal
Preparation of bespoke set of application forms	Automated / systematized document drafting tool	
Submission of conversion application document		Paralegal
Training on new corporate governance tools and processes		Senior lawyer/paralegal
New corporate governance tool kit	Automated / systematized document drafting tool	

量增加，相关“专业知识红利”和“效率红利”将成倍增长。

这在《外商投资法》实施后的市场中至关重要，尤其是在《外商投资法》生效后的第三年到第五年，新的外商直接投资和外商投资企业转化项目的潜在数量可能会超过现有市场资源的容量，因此，能够更有效地开展前期起草工作，从而腾出更多时间为尽可能多的交易提供更高价值的谈判服务，将是非常重要的竞争优势。因此，合通机器人是法律科技如何在《外商投资法》时代提高外商直接投资从业者价值定位的非常有代表性的例子。

外商投资企业转化

由于现有外商独资企业约有375,000家，还有75,000~100,000家中外合营企业预计将进行简单的合营企业转化，《外商投资法》项下的转化要求提供了规模巨大的商业机会，预计未来五年外商投资企业转化的潜在总价值近200亿元人民币，这本身就是一个诱人的市场机会。这些前期可商品化的服务将成为获得多达一半的价值更高的后期合营企业合同重新谈判服务的通道，谈判服务的价值又为250亿元人民币（预计的500亿元人民币总额的一半），使这一目标市场具有更大的吸引力。

但是，如上所述，考虑到所需服务的性质和范围，以及此类服务预计的市场价格不高，外商独资企业转化和简单的合营企业转化工作可能会使以传统法律服务模式提供服务的顶级律师事务所蒙受巨大损失。例如，按照上述传统法律服务模式下的外商独资企业和简单的合营企业转化的预计时间和费率，实际小时费率将在500元人民币以下至略高于600元人民币，这对大多数新兴的国内律师事务所来说很有吸引力，因为只要其工作量保持在较高水平，它每年的律师人均创收就会超过100万元人民币。但是这对于红圈所或在中国的国际律师事务所来说则肯定太低了，因而对他们没有吸引力，因为他们会希望在《外商投资法》实施后的预期繁荣的时代创造更高的律师人均创收，而不是在较低价值

All told, we project that by using appropriate legal-tech tools, the offline professional time required for a WFOE conversion project can be reduced from 75 hours to approximately 15 hours. Similarly, if the integration of online legal-tech tools and offline systematized services is properly implemented, this can reduce the offline professional time required for a simple JV conversion (which as indicated, is not so simple as a practical matter) from roughly 125 hours to only 30 hours. (Note also that the anticipated transition to full online registration does not materially alter these time estimates since so long as offline submissions can be bundled together on a bulk handling basis, the time cost per application becomes fairly negligible as a practical matter.) In each case, these improvements in process efficiencies will increase profitability four-fold or more, making this low end work a solid contributor to the bottom line at RPL levels equivalent to the elite domestic law firms while still preserving market positioning (and time) for the higher value work.

The process for a simple JV conversion will be similar to that for a WFOE conversion but will have the additional following steps as outlined in **bold** below.

Chart 4–E Simple JV Conversion Workflow Stages

Workflow Stage	Legal-Tech Application	Human Interface
Review of **existing JV contracts and AoA**	Automated / systematized document review tool	
Review JV's SAMR file		Paralegal
Preparation of bespoke advice memorandum	Automated / systematized document drafting tool	
Discussion of findings & options		Senior lawyer
Preparation of bespoke riders for mark-up of existing JV contract and AoA	Automated / systematized document drafting tool	
Review of **new JV contracts and AoA** with client		Senior lawyer

的工作上投入太多时间从而减少律师人均创收。但是，如上所述，在许多情况下，这些低端工作将成为获取更多高价值工作的通道，因此市场中的领先参与者忽视这种前期工作是很危险的。

为使此较低价值的工作达到合适的盈利水平，一个新的法律科技解决方案将是必须的，事实上，这就是法律科技应该擅长的领域：在有限的预算下完成大规模的大量重复性工作。但仅仅有法律科技解决方案也不够，这必须是一个整合式的解决方案，提供客户和法律科技解决方案之间的真人服务界面。原因很简单——对于此种类型的事务，客户希望在流程中合适的阶段与真人交谈。因此，集成的法律科技/真人服务界面整合服务模型将是唯一可行的解决方案。

> “为使此较低价值的工作达到合适的盈利水平，一个新的法律科技解决方案将是必须的，事实上，这就是法律科技应该擅长的领域：在有限的预算下完成大规模的大量重复性工作。”

根据上述对市场规模的预测，我们预计相关服务将包括以下内容，并且对于工作流程的每个阶段，我们在下表中列出了有机会利用法律科技工具提高效率的情形。

表 4–D　外商独资企业转化的工作阶段

工作阶段	法律科技应用	真人服务界面
审查现有外商独资企业章程	自动化/系统化文件审查工具	
审查外商独资企业登记档案		律师助理
起草定制化建议备忘录	自动化/系统化文件起草工具	
就审查结果和选项进行讨论		资深律师
起草定制化的新设外商独资企业章程	自动化/系统化文件起草工具	
与投资者一同审阅新的外商独资企业章程		资深律师
向投资者收集转化申请所需文件		律师助理
准备定制化申请表格	自动化/系统化文件起草工具	
提交转化申请文件		律师助理
就新的公司治理工具和流程提供培训		资深律师/律师助理
新的公司治理工具包	自动化/系统化文件起草工具	

总之，我们预计通过使用合适的法律科技工具，外商独资企业转化项目所需的线下专业时间可以从 75 小时减少到大约 15 小

Continued

Workflow Stage	Legal-Tech Application	Human Interface
Collection of investor documents for conversion application		Paralegal
Preparation of bespoke set of application forms	Automated / systematized document drafting tool	
Submission of conversion application document		Paralegal
Training on new corporate governance tools and processes		Senior lawyer/paralegal
New corporate governance tool kit	Automated / systematized document drafting tool	

With a projected market price of RMB 35,000 per WFOE conversion project and RMB 80,000 per simple JV conversion project, it is clear that the traditional legal services model would be much too slow and much too expensive for these matters. In fact, for most leading law firms just the initial advisory memorandum would cost at least RMB 20,000 for a WFOE and RMB 40,000 for a Sino-foreign joint venture on a traditional legal services model. Moreover, the same suite of services provided by different teams in the same firm would vary greatly in terms of quality and efficiency under the traditional model, but by adopting legal-tech tools on an integrated online/offline bundled solution basis, consistency of quality can be maintained and efficiencies of more 80% can be achieved, making this a better than break-even business proposition for the emerging group of Chinese law firms while at the same time providing a superior value for money for clients.

As illustrated by the above, for repetitive commoditize-able work performed on a fixed fee basis, the business case for adoption of legal-tech tools is uncontrovertibly compelling. For example, looking at the value proposition from another angle, assuming an effective hourly rate of approximately RMB 500 per hour under the traditional model for a WFOE conversion, if legal-tech expert systems can reduce the amount of professional time by even just one-third for such matters, then (assuming 1,500 chargeable hours per year per legal professional) the RPL figures will jump from RMB 750,000 (1,500 hours multiplied by RMB 500 per hour)

时。同样，如果线上法律科技工具和线下系统化的服务适当地整合集成，则可以将简单的合营企业转化（这一工作实际上并不是那么简单）所需的线下专业时间从约 125 小时减少至 30 小时（还请注意，预期的向完全在线注册的转变不会实质性地影响这些时间估计，因为只要线下资料提交可以打包批量处理，每项申请的时间成本实际上可以忽略不计）。在每种情况下，流程效率的这些改进将使利润率提高 4 倍或更多，使这一低端工作成为达到与顶级国内律师事务所相当的律师人均收入水平的底线的坚实贡献者，同时，对于更高价值的工作而言，律师们仍保持了其市场定位（并留出了时间）。

一个简单的合营企业转化流程与外商独资企业转化流程类似，但会有一些额外的步骤，如下表中**粗体**部分所示。

表 4–E　简单的合营企业转化的工作阶段

工作阶段	法律科技应用	真人服务界面
审查现有**合营企业合同和章程**	自动化 / 系统化文件审查工具	
审查合营企业登记档案		律师助理
起草定制化建议备忘录	自动化 / 系统化文件起草工具	
就审查结果和选项进行讨论		资深律师
为修订现有合营企业合同和章程起草定制化条款	自动化 / 系统化文件起草工具	
与客户一同审阅**新的合营企业合同和章程**		资深律师
向投资者收集转化申请所需文件		律师助理
准备定制化申请表格	自动化 / 系统化文件起草工具	
提交转化申请文件		律师助理
就新的公司治理工具和流程提供培训		资深律师 / 律师助理
新的公司治理工具包	自动化 / 系统化文件起草工具	

每个外商独资企业转化项目的预计市场价格为 35,000 元人民币，每个简单的合营企业转化项目的预计市场价格为 80,000 元人民币。很明显，以传统的法律服务模式做这些工作将缓慢和昂

to 1,000,000 as the team is able to service more clients. If higher levels of efficiency can be achieved, then the RPL figures will increase proportionately.

It is axiomatic that when outside lawyers work on a fixed fee basis, the benefits of improvements in efficiency all flow to the outside lawyer, but it is still too common in the China market for lawyers to resist adopting legal-tech tools. This merely underscores that too many domestic lawyers in China do not fully understand their own business model and do not properly value their own time. The vast scale of the FIE conversion market in the post-FIL era will help shatter this old-school mistaken paradigm and drive the adoption of legal-tech in China to levels that will exceed even those in more developed markets as the market sees that the early adopters were able to grab the greatest market share.

All of the legal-tech tools described above either currently exist or are in development on the docQbot platform, and are to be rolled out in a systematic manner over the period following the issuance and clarification of detailed guidance on FIE conversion by SAMR. The docQbot team will deploy these tools as part of a docQbot bundled services offering for WFOEs and simple JV conversions (excluding JV contract renegotiations), but at the same time docQbot will bundle these tools and make them available to the full range of law firms, alternative legal services providers, legal services arms of accounting firms and registration agents across China. The scale of the opportunity is simply too great for any single platform to be able to capture significant market share. Accordingly, docQbot intends to provide the back-office engine for all players in the market to create a win-win-win scenario.

The End Game—Capturing New Client Relationships

Law firms will need to adopt a longer-term strategic view of this market opportunity and see each FIE conversion project not only as the gateway to higher-value JV renegotiation work in relevant cases but more importantly also as an opportunity to capture a new long-term client relationship as a source of continuing business for years to come. (See Figure 4-L.)

贵得多。事实上，对于大多数领先的律师事务所来说，以传统法律服务模式提供这些服务，仅最初的建议备忘录就会花费人民币20,000元（针对外商独资企业）或40,000元（针对中外合营企业）。此外，在传统模式下，同一家律师事务所中不同团队提供的同一套服务在质量和效率方面会有很大差异。但是，在集成的线上/线下整合式解决方案基础上采用法律科技工具，可以保持质量的一致性，并实现80%以上的效率增长，使之成为中国新兴律师事务所创收的业务方案，并同时为客户提供具有更高性价比的服务。

如上所述，对于固定费用的重复性商品化工作，采用法律科技工具这一模式毫无疑问是具有说服力的。例如，从另一个角度来看法律科技的价值定位，假设传统模式下提供外商投资企业转化服务的实际小时费率约为每小时500元人民币，如果法律科技专家系统可以将该业务的工作时间减少仅1/3，那么（假设每名法律专业人士每年的计费小时为1500小时）律师人均收入将从人民币750,000元（1500小时乘以500元人民币/小时）增加到1,000,000元，因为团队能够为更多客户提供服务。如果可以达到更高的效率水平，则律师人均收入将成比例地增加。

显然，如果外部律师按固定费用收费，则效率提高所获的收益将全部属于外部律师，但中国市场上律师抗拒采用法律科技工具这一情形仍然很常见。这只是凸显了太多的律师并不完全了解自己的业务模式且并未正确地认识自己时间的价值。《外商投资法》时代大规模的外商投资企业转化，将有助于打破这种保守和错误的模式，推动中国采用法律科技的水平甚至超过较发达市场，因为在市场中较早采用法律科技的主体能够抢占最大的市场份额。

“显然，如果外部律师按固定费用收费，则效率提高所获的收益将全部属于外部律师，但中国市场上律师抗拒采用法律科技工具这一情形仍然很常见。”

上述提到的各类法律科技工具，在合通机器人平台上已存在或正在开发中，待市场监管总局关于外商投资企业转化的办事指南发布和明确后，将逐步系统化地上线运行。这些工具将作为合通机器人为外商独资企业和简单的合营企业转化（不包括合营企业合同谈判）提供的整合服务的一部分，与此同时合通机器人也

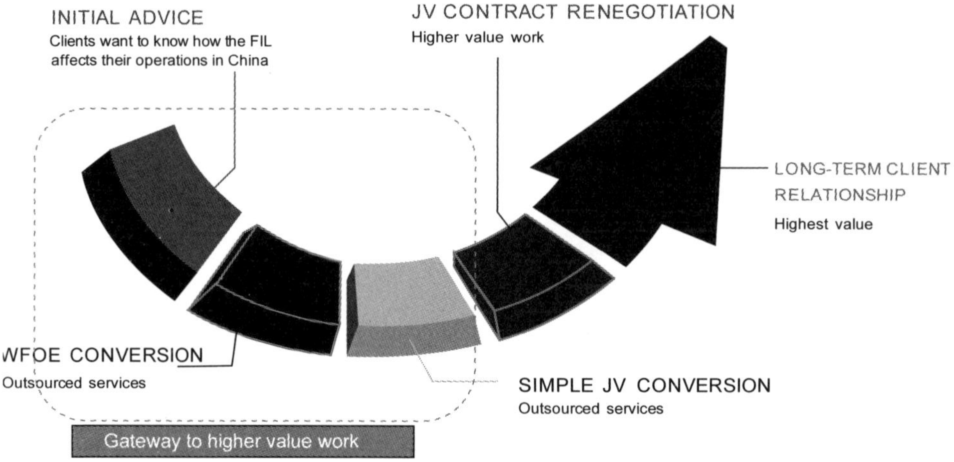

Figure 4–L Multi–stage value chain

The FIL presents outside lawyers with an opportunity to unlock new client relationships first with high-quality low-cost advice on the implications of the transition to the corporate governance provisions under the Company Law. This then leads to the conversion stage for WFOEs and JVs (and the JV contract renegotiation stage for joint ventures in many cases). In most cases, at each of these stages the outside lawyers will have direct communication with the general counsel or senior lawyers at the headquarters level in addition to the people on the ground at the FIE. If the client is happy with the work, then the odds are good that they will come back to you as they have more issues going forward. As with FIE conversion work, the FDI lawyers who can use partially automated expert systems to deliver high-value advisory work product up front will be in a better position to capture these new client relationships in greater numbers, driving longer-term business growth.

Consequently, the FIL presents a major opportunity for disruption of pre-existing client relationships. Because the foreign law firms are generally expected to cede the market for FIE conversion to the Chinese firms and focus primarily on the more profitable joint venture renegotiation and FIE group restructuring work, this presents an opportunity for many Chinese firms to insert themselves into the client relationship and at a minimum become an alternative legal service provider option for the FIE client and the foreign investor client. This is the general trend in the market in any event—foreign clients continue to move more and more of their work to Chinese law firms. The FIL will extend and accelerate this process. The coming

将打包这些工具，并将其提供给中国各地的所有律师事务所、替代法律服务提供商、会计师事务所的法律服务部门和注册代理。这一机遇的规模太大，使任何单一平台都无法占据很大的市场份额。因此，合通机器人希望为市场上的所有参与者提供后台支持，从而创造一个双赢的局面。

终点——获取新的客户关系

律师事务所必须站在长远的战略高度看待这一市场机遇，把每个外商投资企业转化项目不仅视为获得更高价值的合营企业重新谈判工作的通道，更重要的是获取作为未来几年持续性业务来源的新的长期客户关系的契机（见图 4-L）。

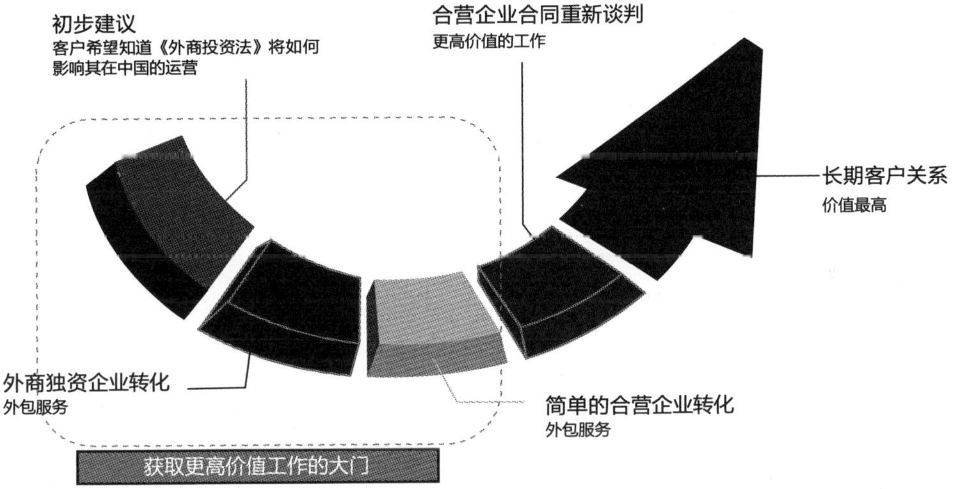

图 4-L　多级价值链

《外商投资法》为外部律师提供了解锁新客户关系的机会，即外部律师首先以低价向客户提供关于向《公司法》项下公司治理规定过渡的影响的高质量法律建议，接下来便是外商独资企业和合营企业的转化阶段（和在许多情况下合营企业合同的重新谈判阶段）。在大多数情况下，在每个阶段，外部律师除了与外商投资企业的本地人员直接沟通外，也将与外商投资企业总部级别

post-FIL era is a period of time in the China legal services market that is akin to a gold rush. The market will reward those who have vision and a strategic and tactical plan to grab market share.

No one needs to be worried about the foreign law firms in China. There will be some immediate pain for them in the aftermath of the COVID-19 pandemic, but as China GDP rebounds, and the FIL more fully starts to drive the demand for legal services for new greenfield FDI projects in newly opened high-end sectors such as financial services and as they capture their proportionate share of JV contract renegotiation work, these will be boom times for them as well. Add to this the continued internationalization of the business operations of Chinese companies, and it is clear that the foreign law firms have a lot of blue skies ahead of them in this market. But at the end of the five-year transition period under the FIL, when the dust has settled, we expect that we will see that the Chinese firms, together with the legal services arms of the Big 4 accounting firms (which are also domestically-registered law firms) and certain ALS platforms, will have taken a major step forward in terms of market share in the FDI/FIE market. The annotated Sample Templates as set out in Part Ⅱ and as automated on the docQbot platform are designed to help promote this continued shift in the China legal services market.

的总法律顾问或高级律师直接沟通。如果客户对律师工作感到满意，那么当他们有更多的问题时很可能会再次找到你。与外商投资企业转化工作一样，外商直接投资律师如果能够使用部分自动化的专家系统在前期提供高价值咨询服务，那么将更有机会获取更多的新客户关系，从而推动长期业务增长。

因此，《外商投资法》为打破现有的客户关系提供了重要机遇。由于普遍认为外资律师事务所可能会将外商投资企业转化的市场让给内资律师事务所，而主要专注于利润更高的合营企业谈判和外商投资企业集团重组的工作，这为许多内资律师事务所提供了发展客户关系的机会，至少会成为外商投资企业客户和外国投资者客户备选的法律服务提供者。无论如何这是市场的总体趋势——外国客户持续将越来越多的工作转移到内资律师事务所。《外商投资法》将扩展并加速这一过程。即将到来的《外商投资法》时代是中国法律服务市场接近于淘金热的一段时期。那些富有远见和有获取市场份额战略战术计划的人将会得到市场的回报。

我们无须担心中国的外资律师事务所。新型冠状病毒肺炎疫情结束后，他们将经历短暂的阵痛，但随着中国 GDP 的反弹，《外商投资法》更加全面地开始推动对新开放的高端行业（如金融服务）中的新绿地外商直接投资项目法律服务的需求，以及随着他们抓住其在合营企业合同重新谈判工作中的份额，这对他们来说也将是一个繁荣的时期。再加上中国企业业务经营的持续国际化，很明显外资律师事务所在这个市场上拥有广阔的天空。但在《外商投资法》规定的五年过渡期结束时，尘埃落定后，我们预期将看到内资律师事务所，以及四大会计师事务所的法律服务部门（同时也是在中国注册的内资律师事务所）以及某些替代法律服务平台，将在外商直接投资 / 外商投资企业市场的市场份额方面向前迈出了一大步。本书第二部分中所列的附有注解说明的模板样本以及合通机器人平台上提供的经过自动化的模板旨在帮助促进中国法律服务市场的持续转变。

Part II

New Sample Templates for the Post-FIL Era

第二部分

《外商投资法》时代的新模板样本

Chapter 5 Overview of the Sample Templates and Annotations

In accordance with the mandate for the Expert Committee, we have undertaken to create a new set of standard templates for FDI projects for the new post-FIL era, incorporating the applicable corporate governance provisions under the Company Law into a base template that more closely conforms to international best practices. This has proved to be an ambitious and challenging exercise, but one which has been rewarding and instructive for all members of the Expert Committee. It is hoped that these Sample Templates will also prove to be beneficial to legal practitioners inside and outside China who work on inbound FDI matters as well as to investors undertaking foreign investment projects in China.

In this Chapter 5 we will provide some background on the drafting objectives, the overall drafting process and our related drafting assumptions. In Chapter 6 we will address some fundamental drafting issues that are so important as to require more extensive discussion than would be appropriate in the comparatively brief annotations to the Sample Templates. The bilingual Sample Templates themselves together with the related annotations are set out in Chapter 7 (Sample JVA Template and Sample JV AoA Template) and Chapter 8 (Sample WFOE AoA Template). All of these Sample Templates are provided for instructional and reference purposes only and are subject to the caveats and limitations set out below in this Chapter 5.

Drafting Objectives

All of the members of the Expert Committee shared a common concern and a common objective in respect of this initiative.

第五章　模板样本及注解说明概述

与专家委员会合作，我们为《外商投资法》时代编写了一套全新的用于外商直接投资项目的标准模板，将《公司法》项下适用的公司治理规定纳入更加贴近国际最佳实践的基础模板。这是一项宏大且具有挑战性的工作，但对专家委员会所有成员来说都是有益的。希望从事外商直接投资法律服务的中国境内外法律从业者以及在中国从事外商投资项目的投资者都能够从这些模板样本中受益。

在第五章中，我们将就起草目标、总体起草过程和相关起草假设提供一些背景信息。在第六章中，我们将讨论一些根本性的起草问题，这些问题非常重要，因此在对模板样本作出相对简短的注解说明的基础上还需要进行更深入的讨论。双语模板样本及其相关注解说明载于第七章（合资协议和合资企业章程模板样本）和第八章（外商独资企业章程模板样本）。所有这些模板样本仅供说明和参考，且受限于本章中下文所载的声明和限制。

起草目标

专家委员会的所有成员都对编写模板样本项目有共同的关注和目标。

共同关注的是，在《外商投资法》项下从传统的“三资法”

The shared concern was that in the transition under the FIL from the legacy Three FIE Laws to the Company Law, there were few if any guideposts for FDI practitioners in the market. This represented a significant change from the pre-FIL period where the EJV Law dictated the form and much of the core content of the JV contract and AoA. But following the repeal of the Three FIE Laws, no such common framework would exist as the Company Law entrusts these drafting points primarily to the discretion of the parties. While that is appropriate and even laudatory, it will also necessarily mean that there will be many different forms that will be created, many of excellent quality and others of lower quality, but with no clear standard which can serve as a common touchstone to the market more broadly.

Since the FIL affects not just all new FIEs but also all existing FIEs, this would mean that in a relatively short period of five years (and mostly in the latter part of that transition period) parties to upwards of 150,000 joint ventures (including both new and existing JVs) would engage in a proverbial "battle of the forms" at both the macro ("your form or mine") level and the micro (clause by clause) level. This would be unproductive and expensive for investors.

This shared concern informed the shared objective of the Expert Committee, which was to create a set of high-quality bilingual base templates for Sino-foreign joint ventures and WFOEs for use in the post-FIL era. We make no claim that the Sample Templates are suitable for all scenarios (in fact, just the opposite), and we have no expectation that even for the base reference case adopted for purposes of this drafting exercise that no improvements or revisions can be made thereto. Our more modest, but yet still very ambitious goal, was to create a set of draft templates that could be used as a shared point of reference, a base upon which individual practitioners could build as appropriate for use in connection with the requirements of each particular transaction.

Lawyers by nature have strong personal preferences when it comes to drafting transaction documents, some of which have critical substantive implications and others which may fall more into the category of stylistic preferences. By creating the Sample Templates the Expert Committee does not expect that entrenched dynamic to change. But what we do hope to achieve is that at a more fundamental level, at the base corporate governance "legal plumbing" level, the Sample Templates provide a valuable baseline which can be used as a standard starting point for the market generally.

向《公司法》的过渡期间，市场上对外商直接投资从业者的指南很少。向《公司法》的过渡代表着巨大的转变，这是因为，在《外商投资法》颁布之前的时代，《中外合资经营企业法》规定了合资合同和公司章程的形式和很多核心内容。但在“三资法”废除后，由于《公司法》将这些起草要点主要留给各方自行决定，因此不再有这样的通用框架。虽然这种做法是合适的甚至是值得称赞的，但也必然意味着市场上将会出现许多不同的文本样式，且质量参差不齐，而对于可以更广泛地适用于市场的通用基准缺乏明确的标准。

由于《外商投资法》不仅影响所有的新外商投资企业，也影响所有现有的外商投资企业，这意味着在相对较短的 5 年期限内（主要在过渡期的后期），超过 150,000 家合营企业（包括新的和现有的合营企业）会在宏观（“你的模板或我的模板”）和微观（每个条款）层面上发生众所周知的“模板之战”。这对于投资者而言不仅徒劳无益而且代价昂贵。

专家委员会基于这一共同关注点确定了共同目标，即为中外合营企业和外商独资企业创建一套高质量的双语基础模板，供其在《外商投资法》时代使用。我们不保证模板样本适用于所有情形（事实上恰恰相反），即使对于为起草模板样本而采用的基础参考情形，我们也不认为该等模板无须改进或修订。我们相对保守但仍然很宏大的目标是，创建一套可作为通用参考的模板初稿，进而每个单独的从业者都可以基于此模板根据每个特定交易的要求进行适当使用。

在起草交易文件方面，律师自然会有强烈的个人偏好，其中一些具有重要的实质性影响，而另一些则可能更多地属于风格偏好。专家委员会并未试图通过创建模板样本改变这一根深蒂固的现状。但我们希望实现的是，在更基础的层面，在基础公司治理的“法律构建”层面，模板样本能够提供一个有价值的基准，这一基准可以被当作市场通用的标准起点。

The Drafting Process

Formation of the Expert Committee

The first step in the drafting process was to form the Expert Committee. This process was described, and the key members of the Expert Committee were introduced, in the Introduction. More information on each of the members of the Expert Committee is provided in Part Ⅳ.

All of the members of the Expert Committee are highly experienced in both FDI and ODI projects. Collectively, we have worked on literally thousands of joint venture and WFOE projects in China over the last three decades. We had good balance between Chinese and foreign lawyers, inhouse lawyers and law firm lawyers.

Preparation of the Base Drafts

This FIL templates project was ambitious in its scope and as such demanded a substantial investment of time over a period of three months. In all, more than 1000 hours of professional time have been invested by the members of the Expert Committee, principally by the docQbot team, which took the laboring oar.

The initial JV template drafts were developed on an international SHA/JVA base incorporating best practices drawn from more than a dozen publicly-available templates from multiple jurisdictions around the world. These initial drafts were prepared on a jurisdiction-neutral basis so as to provide a reference base of the most universal corporate governance provisions which are most commonly used in similar arrangements internationally.

Members of the Expert Committee then compared these international templates against best practices in connection with both legacy JV contracts for Sino-foreign joint ventures as well as representative SHA templates for domestic Chinese companies in order to ensure that these new JV templates are consistent with local market expectations as well. Accordingly, the Sample Templates are intended to reflect the best of both international and domestic best practices.

The group determined that it would not be feasible to create a set of base templates that would be suitable for use in connection with the full range of common FDI transactions. Accordingly, the decision was taken to prepare the Sample Templates to reflect the terms of representative hypothetical base case scenarios (see below for further descriptions).

起草过程

专家委员会的组建

起草过程的第一步是成立专家委员会。本书简介部分已经描述了这一过程并介绍了专家委员会的主要成员。本书第四部分将提供专家委员会成员的更多信息。

专家委员会的所有成员在外商直接投资和境外直接投资项目方面都具有丰富的经验。在过去的30年间，我们处理过的在华合营企业和外商独资企业项目数以千计。专家委员会对中国律师与外国律师的比例、企业法务与律师事务所律师的比例保持适当的平衡。

基础初稿的准备

本《外商投资法》模板项目涉及的范围非常广泛，因此要求在3个月内投入大量时间。专家委员会成员总计投入了超过1000小时的专业时间，其中合通机器人团队的成员承担了主要的工作。

合资企业模板最初的初稿是在国际股东协议/合资协议的基础上开发的，我们借鉴了世界范围内多个司法管辖区的十余个公开模板中的最佳实践，并纳入模板初稿中。这些初稿并没有以在特定司法管辖区适用为基础而编制，从而可以提供国际上类似安排中最常用的最普遍公司治理条款的参考基础。

专家委员会成员将这些国际模板与中外合资企业的传统合资合同以及中国内资公司的代表性股东协议模板的最佳范例进行了比较，以确保这些新合资企业模板同时符合中国市场的预期。因此，这些模板旨在体现国际和国内的最佳实践。

专家委员会认为，创建一套适用于所有常见外商直接投资交易的基本模板是不现实的。因此，专家委员会决定编写可以反映具有代表性的基础预设情形条款的模板样本（请参见下文进一步说明）。

As noted in Chapter 3, we omitted various legacy provisions which were required under the EJV Law but which were no longer required under the Company Law, were not consistent with international best practices and, in the opinion of the Expert Committee, no longer served a legitimate purpose. We then layered in the corporate governance provisions required under the Company Law (again see related discussion in Chapter 3). This was a pains-taking exercise as scores of related changes had to be made throughout the base template. This exercise was central to the overall initiative and is hoped will prove to be a valuable guide for FDI practitioners and investors inside and outside China.

Annotations

The templates then passed through multiple rounds of drafts and comments in order to achieve, where possible, a consensus view of the Expert Committee members. In the early rounds it became apparent that there were divergent views on various key topics. To be able to reflect the range of views of the members of the Expert Committee, it was decided that we also produce annotations to the Sample Templates.

This provided a very valuable and unique platform on which we could present different views of the group as well as alternative approaches that ultimately were not incorporated into the Sample Templates. Moreover, for the corporate governance provisions required under the Company Law, we have provided references to the specific articles of the Company Law for ease of reference. However, the annotations cover not only points of law but also related practical considerations to be taken into account as the templates are used. We are of the view that these annotations, and particularly those which set out the divergent views of the group, form another key part of the overall value proposition of this initiative.

Chinese Versions

Because the base drafts were created from international precedents, the initial drafts were prepared in English and the working language for the group was also English. This also reflects the typical practice for parties to a Sino-foreign joint venture to negotiate first off of the English drafts and then to prepare Chinese versions only once the English version is settled so as to reduce related transaction costs.

Preparation of high-standard Chinese versions was another key objective of the group. Our objective was to ensure that the Chinese version read as though it was drafted originally

如第三章所述，我们删除了《中外合资经营企业法》项下要求但《公司法》不再要求的各种传统条款，这些条款不符合国际最佳实践，并且专家委员会认为这些条款的存在不再具有正当的理由。然后，我们纳入了《公司法》项下要求的公司治理条款（请参见第三章中的相关讨论）。这是一项艰难的工作，因为大量的相关更改须贯穿整个基础模板。这项工作是整个项目的核心，我们希望能为中国境内外外商直接投资从业人员和投资者提供宝贵指南。

注解说明

我们对模板进行了多次修改和征求意见，以便尽可能地在专家委员会中达成一致意见。在前几轮的修改过程中，很明显的是，专家委员会成员对很多核心问题存在不同意见。为了能够反映专家委员会成员的不同意见，我们决定同时编写模板样本的注解说明。

这为我们呈现专家委员会的不同观点以及最终未包含在模板样本中的替代方案提供了一个非常有价值且独特的平台。此外，对于《公司法》项下的公司治理规定，我们指出了《公司法》的具体条款以便于参考。但是，注解说明不仅包括法律要点，还包括在使用模板时要考虑的相关实践问题。我们认为，这些注解说明，特别是那些阐明专家委员会不同意见的说明，构成了这个项目总体价值定位的另一个核心部分。

中文版本

由于基础初稿基于国际先例编写，因此初稿是用英语编写的，并且专家委员会的工作语言也是英语。这也反映了中外合资企业的典型做法，即各方首先对英文初稿进行谈判，待英文版本确定后再准备中文版本，从而减少相关交易成本。

准备高标准的中文版本是专家委员会的另一个核心目标。我们的目标是确保中文版读起来仿佛基础初稿原本即以中文编写，

in Chinese as the base draft and not simply as a translation from the English base. In order to achieve this high standard, we started with a "plain English" drafting style for the base, which in structure and presentation would lend itself more easily to producing a Chinese version which would read more naturally. In addition, the Chinese versions were subjected to intense scrutiny by the group in an effort to achieve the intended standard of quality. While there will never be complete uniformity of opinion on word choices in a Chinese version of a transaction document, the Chinese versions of the Sample Templates do reflect the consensus of the group, which should represent a suitably high standard for the market.

Style and Format

The Sample Templates conform to the docQbot house style. General clauses and common defined terms are consistent with the other bilingual templates in the docQbot online ecosystem to ensure full interoperability.

Base Case Scenarios

As noted above, we have created a separate base case scenario for each of the JVA/JV AoA and the WFOE AoA.

The new Sample JV Templates have been drafted in contemplation of a Sino-foreign joint venture with the following characteristics:

(a) This is a two-party joint venture, with the Chinese party as Party A and the foreign party as Party B.

(b) This is a new mid-cap greenfield joint venture set up as a strategic investment.

(c) Party A holds 60% of the registered capital, and Party B holds 40% of the registered capital. Each party is to make its capital contributions in cash.

(d) The new joint venture company will adopt a standard comprehensive corporate governance system comprised of a board of directors (as opposed to a single executive director) and a board of supervisors (as opposed to a single supervisor).

The new Sample WFOE AoA Template has been drafted in contemplation of a WFOE with the following characteristics:

(a) This is a new small-cap greenfield WFOE set up as a strategic investment.

(b) The investor is to make its capital contributions in cash in a single lump sum.

而不仅仅是英文版的翻译。为了达到这一高标准，我们采用“简明英语”的风格起草初稿，使之在结构和表达方面更容易转换为读起来更自然的中文版本。此外，中文版本接受了专家委员会的严格审查以达到预期的质量标准。虽然一份交易文件中文版中的用词选择永远不会达到完全的意见统一，但模板样本的中文版确实反映了专家委员会的共识，应该代表了市场中的较高标准。

风格与形式

模板样本延续了合通机器人模板的风格。一般条款和通用术语的定义与合通机器人线上生态系统中的其他双语模板是一致的，以确保充分的互通性。

基础案例情形

如上所述，我们为每个合资协议 / 合资企业章程和外商独资企业章程创造了一个单独的基础案例情形。

新合资企业模板样本是针对具有以下特征的中外合资企业起草的：

（a）由中外两方合资，中方为甲方，外方为乙方。

（b）以战略投资的方式设立的新的绿地合资企业。

（c）甲方持有注册资本的 60%，乙方持有注册资本的 40%。双方都以现金出资。

（d）新成立的合资公司将采用标准、全面的公司治理体系，由董事会（而非单唯一执行董事）和监事会（而非唯一监事）组成。

新外商独资企业章程模板样本是针对具有以下特征的外商独资企业起草的：

（a）以战略投资的方式设立新的绿地外商独资企业。

（b）投资者将以现金一次性全额出资。

(c) The new WFOE will adopt a streamlined corporate governance system comprised of a single executive director and a single supervisor.

Accordingly, without applicable substantive modifications, the Sample Templates may not be appropriate for transactions with different characteristics.

Different Templates for Different Use Cases

By way of comparison to the base case scenarios adopted for purposes of drafting of the Sample Templates, we note that there are multiple variations of the SHA/JVA which may be needed in connection with Sino-foreign joint ventures following the effectiveness of the FIL, including:

- Greenfield (strategic investment)
- Post-M&A (strategic investment) (with/without capital increase)
- Existing EJV/CJV conversion
- Greenfield (financial investment) (multiple rounds)
- Post-M&A (financial investment) (multiple rounds, with/without capital increase)
- Simplified SHA/JVA (smaller deals)

As noted above, for purposes of this initiative, we have determined to produce only a greenfield version for strategic investors, but it is anticipated that this set of new JV Templates can also serve as the base upon which the post-M&A and financial investor versions can be drafted and that this template can also provide a roadmap for conversion of existing JV contracts into an SHA/JVA that complies with the Company Law (which the Expert Committee considers may be the preferred option for many existing Sino-foreign joint ventures).

Within each category of joint venture, the drafting options for each project will vary depending on whether it is a 50-50 structure or a majority-minority shareholder structure as well as the relative bargaining power of the parties. Rather than provide a base template designed to cover all of the various options with alternative clauses and language, the Expert Committee has opted to adopt a specific base case and prepare a base template that addresses the specified hypothetical scenario set out above. In this way, the Expert Committee intends that these templates will allow users will be able to focus more readily on the changes required under the Company Law which will be common to a larger group of joint venture companies rather than the variables which are particular to specific transactions.

（c）新外商独资企业将采用精简的公司治理体系，由唯一执行董事和唯一监事组成。

因此，如果未进行适当的实质性修改，模板样本可能不适用于不同特征的交易。

不同模板适用于不同情形

通过对比起草模板样本时使用的基础案例情形，我们注意到，《外商投资法》生效后，中外合资企业可能需要的股东协议 / 合资协议有很多不同的类型，包括：

- 绿地（战略投资）
- 并购后（战略投资）（有 / 无增资）
- 现有中外合资经营企业 / 中外合作经营企业的转化
- 绿地（财务投资）（多轮）
- 并购后（财务投资）（多轮，有 / 无增资）
- 简化版股东协议 / 合资协议（较小交易）

如上所述，在本项目中，我们决定仅制作适用于战略投资者的绿地版本，但预计这套新合资企业模板也可作为起草并购后版本和财务投资者版本的基础。将现有合资合同转换为符合《公司法》的股东协议 / 合资协议时（专家委员会认为这可能是许多现有中外合资企业的首选方案），本模板还可以为需要进行的修订提供指引。

在每一类合资企业中，每个项目起草文本时的选择取决于该企业是 50—50 股权结构还是多数—少数股东结构以及各方相对的谈判地位。专家委员会并没有提供一个涵盖所有情形并包含替代条款的基本模板，而是选择采用特定的基础案例，并对应上述特定的假设情形准备一个基本模板。通过这种方式，专家委员会希望这些模板将使用户能够更容易地关注《公司法》要求的变更，

In addition, there would be a similar range of alternative base templates for WFOEs in the post-FIL era corresponding to the various template categories listed above for Sino-foreign joint ventures. For conversion of existing WFOEs, the foreign investor may choose to create an entirely new FIL-compliant AoA to replace the pre-FIL legacy AoA or it may use the Sample WFOE AoA Template here as a roadmap to making relevant amendments to the existing WFOE AoA (the Expert Committee considers both options to be plausible with the "rip and replace" option perhaps more likely). It is also more likely that WFOEs will adopt a more streamlined corporate governance system since there are no partner considerations, so we have presented that option as part of the Sample Templates.

Equal Treatment of Chinese and Foreign Parties

One final related point is worth noting in this regard – although the base case scenario adopted for these New JV Templates provides that the Chinese investor is the majority shareholder and the foreign investor is minority shareholder, the fundamental principles reflected in these templates would be the same if the roles were reversed. Other than in respect of the questions of governing law and controlling contract language (to be discussed in further detail in Chapter 6), the Expert Committee has taken the view that the positions to be adopted by the investors will be based on their relative shareholdings and bargaining power, irrespective of whether they are the foreign investor or the Chinese investor. Stated otherwise, consistent with the principle of "national treatment" under the new FIL, the Expert Committee has adopted a policy of equal treatment of both the Chinese side and the foreign side in connection with the preparation of this guidance and the new Sino-foreign JV templates.

Caveats and Limitations

Users of the Sample Templates, the annotations and the guidance set out herein are required to exercise independent legal judgment or take independent legal advice in respect of each provision thereof and make any and all revisions or supplements necessary or appropriate to ensure that such provisions (a) are applicable and appropriate to the subject transaction, and (b) comply with relevant requirements of applicable law as then in effect.

This book and the Sample Templates are provided as general guidance only on an "as is" and "as available" basis, and no warranties, assurances and/or representations of any kind, whether express or implied (including, without limitation, implied warranties of fitness for a particular purpose), are made or given in respect hereof. Use of these materials does not create

这些变更将会是大部分合资公司共同的问题，而非针对特定交易的变量。

此外，《外商投资法》时代的外商独资企业将有类似的一系列可选择的基础模板，对应上述各类中外合资企业的模板。对于现有外商独资企业的转化，外国投资者可选择创建全新的符合《外商投资法》规定的公司章程以取代该法生效前传统的公司章程，或者可以使用外商独资企业模板样本作为对现有外商独资企业章程进行相关修订的指引（专家委员会认为两种选择都有其合理性但“撕毁和替换”选项的可能性更大）。由于没有合作伙伴需要考虑，外商独资企业更有可能采用更加精简的公司治理体系，因此我们提供该选项作为模板样本的一部分。

同等对待中方和外方

在这方面值得注意的最后一点——尽管这些新合资企业模板采用的基础案例情形规定中国投资者是多数股东而外国投资者是少数股东，但反过来的话，这些模板中反映的基本原则也是相同的。除了管辖法律和合同语言的效力优先级问题（将在第六章中进一步详细讨论）之外，无论是外国投资者还是中国投资者，专家委员会认为投资者的立场都将以其相应的股权比例和谈判地位为基础。换句话说，根据《外商投资法》的“国民待遇”原则，专家委员会在编写本指南和新中外合资企业模板时采取了同等对待中外双方的政策。

声明与限制

本书所载的模板样本、注解说明和指南的使用者需对其中每个条款进行独立的法律判断或接受独立的法律建议，并进行所有必要或适当的修订或补充，以确保该等条款 (a) 适用于目标交易，且 (b) 符合届时适用法律的相关要求。

本书和模板样本仅以“现状”和“现有”为基础为使用者提

an attorney-client relationship between the user and any law firm which is a member of the Expert Committee.

Online Resources

An electronic bilingual version of the Sample Templates may be downloaded free of charge at www.docqbot.com/en/newFIL. You may also scan the QR code at the end of the Introduction section. Users may use and revise the Sample Templates without restriction for their own internal purposes and in connection with the provision of legal services for their internal or external clients and otherwise subject to the applicable terms of use set out at the above-referenced website. All other rights are reserved.

供一般性指导，其本身不作出或提供任何明示或默示的保证（包括但不限于适用于特定用途的默示保证）。使用这些材料不会在使用者与作为专家委员会成员的任何律师事务所之间建立起律师—客户的代理关系。

线上资源

双语模板样本的电子版可以在 www.docqbot.com/cn/newFIL 免费下载。您也可以扫描简介部分结尾处的二维码获取。使用者可以根据自己的需要，或向内部或外部客户提供法律服务的需要，或在其他符合上述网页所载的适用的使用条款的情况下，不受限制地使用和修改模板样本。合通机器人保留其他所有权利。

Chapter 6 Analysis of Certain Key Fundamental Drafting Issues

The annotations address many (but not all) of the more detailed drafting considerations in respect of specific clauses of the Sample Templates. However, there are a few issues relating to the Sample Templates that are so fundamental in nature that a separate discussion was deemed to be merited to supplement the more abbreviated comments in the annotations. Again, as with other sections of this book, we have approached these points more from a practical perspective and not as a comprehensive legal analysis of the related issues.

Naming Conventions

The question of the title to be used for the new JV template was the subject of considerable discussion among the members of the Expert Committee, and several options were floated for consideration. In the end, it was concluded that in practice this agreement can be called a Shareholders Agreement, a Joint Venture Agreement or other similar name as the parties may agree.

For purposes of this sample greenfield joint venture template, we have opted to use the name "Joint Venture Agreement" as we consider that this aligns generally with market practice for a greenfield joint venture project. On the other hand, for inbound M&A projects, the parties may prefer to style the agreement as a "Shareholders Agreement" given that the company will already be in existence at the time of the acquisition and so in such case the agreement is designed to reflect the agreement of the shareholders on the management and operation of the company on a post-acquisition basis rather than set up a new entity. However, this is a matter left to the discussion and agreement of the parties, as the agreement name will not affect the substantive nature of the agreement.

第六章　对部分核心的根本性起草问题的分析

注解说明针对模板样本中的很多（但不是全部）具体条款都更详细地分析了其在起草时的考虑因素。但是，有些与模板样本相关的根本性问题非常重要，需要提供单独的分析以作为较为简短的注解说明的补充。与本书的其他部分一样，我们更多地从实用性角度分析这些要点，而不是对相关问题进行全面的法律分析。

命名规范

专家委员会成员对新合资企业模板应该用什么名称进行了相当多的讨论，并提出了若干备选方案。最后，专家委员会得出结论，在实践中本协议可称为股东协议、合资协议或双方同意的其他类似名称。

对于本绿地合资协议模板样本，我们选择采用“合资协议”这一名称，因为我们认为这与绿地合资项目的市场惯例基本一致。另外，对于入境并购项目，由于公司在并购时已经存在，因此各方可能更愿意将其称为“股东协议”，因此在此情况下该协议旨在反映股东就收购后而非新设企业时公司的管理和运营达成的协议。但是，这一问题可以留给各方讨论决定，因为协议名称不会影响协议的实质性质。

我们知道，《中外合资经营企业法》中规定了“合资协议”，其形式上更像是加长版的谅解备忘录，而不具有法律约束力，在

We recognize that the EJV Law provided for a "Joint Venture Agreement" which was more in the form of an extended MOU with no legal binding effect, while under the EJV Law only the more formal "Joint Venture Contract" was legally binding. Given that the EJV Law has been repealed effective as of the end of 2019, we are of the view that the title "Joint Venture Agreement" no longer carries the same original connotations as set out under the EJV Law, and referring to this as a "Joint Venture Agreement" is more consistent with international practice for similar agreement forms. In addition, we consider that this title also reflects a modest break from the more rigid JV contract templates in common use prior to the adoption of the new FIL.

One more related comment in respect of the use of the designation "wholly foreign-owned enterprise" or "WFOE" in respect of wholly-owned subsidiaries of foreign investors set up in China. The WFOE name is derived from the WFOE Law, which has been repealed as of 1 January 2020 when the FIL takes effect, and thereafter such wholly-owned subsidiaries of foreign companies will no longer be separately registered as a legal entity designated by the WFOE name but will be established as LLCs or other entity types under the Company Law. As such, there will no longer be a clear legal basis for this entity name, but the name is so well entrenched in the market, that we consider that it is appropriate to continue to employ this designation.

Company as a Party

It is common in international practice for the company to be a party to the SHA or JVA so that it can undertake certain obligations to the parties. This is permissible in China as a matter of law, but not common as a matter of practice, and so we have not included the company as a party in the Sample JVA Template. Accordingly, where appropriate we have provided that the parties will cause the company to take certain actions as specified under the terms set out in the Sample JVA Template.

Note that it may be more common to include the company as a party to the SHA in a post-acquisition context where the company is already in existence. However, it is also possible to include the company as a party in a greenfield JVA even though the company has not yet come into existence. In such case, the agreement can provide that the shareholders will cause the company to sign the agreement promptly following due establishment.

《中外合资经营企业法》项下，只有更正式的“合资合同”具有法律约束力。鉴于《中外合资经营企业法》已于2019年年底废止，我们认为 “合资协议”这一名称与其在《中外合资经营企业法》项下的原本内涵不再相同，将本协议称为“合资协议”更符合类似协议所适用的国际惯例。此外，我们认为此名称还反映了对《外商投资法》出台之前常用的较为刻板的合资合同模板的适度突破。

另一个相关分析是关于外国投资者在中国设立的全资子公司使用“外商独资企业”名称的问题。外商独资企业这一名称源自《外资企业法》，该法已于2020年1月1日《外商投资法》生效时废止，此后外国公司的全资子公司将不再单独注册为以外商独资企业为名称的法人实体，而是设立为《公司法》项下的有限责任公司或其他组织形式。因此，该实体名称将不再具有明确的法律依据，但该名称的使用在市场中根深蒂固，我们认为应当继续使用此名称。

合资公司作为协议一方

在国际惯例中，合资公司通常是股东协议或合资协议的一方，从而承担当事方的某些义务。在中国法项下，这是允许的，但在实践中并不常见，因此我们没有将合资公司列为模板样本的一方，而是在合适的地方规定了双方可促使合资公司采取模板样本条款中规定的特定行动。

需要说明的是，在收购交易情形下，目标公司（在收购前）已经存在，将目标公司作为股东协议的一方可能较为常见。但是，即使合资公司尚未成立，将合资公司列为绿地合资协议的一方也是有可能的。在这种情况下，协议可以规定股东将促使合资公司在其正式成立后立即签署协议。

股东协议 / 合资协议终止的影响

在《公司法》和当前备案制度的体制下，股东协议 / 合资协

Effect of Termination of SHA/JVA

Under the Company Law and the current record filing system, the SHA/JVA is no longer a constitutional document, and as such termination of the SHA/JVA does not affect the existence of the joint venture company. Previously, under the EJV Law if the JV contract was terminated, then either one party had to buy-out the other party, in which case the EJV company was converted into a WFOE or a domestic LLC, or the EJV was dissolved. Given that new Sino-foreign joint venture companies now will be established as LLCs or other permitted entity forms under the Company Law, upon the termination of the SHA/JVA in connection with a buy-out of one party by the other, no conversion will be required, and the company will continue in existence notwithstanding the termination of the SHA/JVA unless the parties agree to dissolve the company in lieu of a buy-out. This is a fundamental change which may affect some of the mechanics under the SHA/JVA. The Expert Committee has made some corresponding changes to the relevant provisions to reflect this key point.

Governing Law

Whereas the EJV Law required that the JV contract be governed by Chinese law, there is no similar requirement under the Company Law. However, the Contract Law provides that Sino-foreign joint venture agreements must be governed by Chinese law. It is anticipated that this requirement under the Contract Law will not be changed by Chinese authorities in connection with the general implementation of the principle of "national treatment" under the FIL. In fact, under the 2015 Draft FIL it was specifically provided that any investment contract signed by a foreign investor in connection with an inbound investment in China is to be governed by Chinese law. The Implementation Regulations to the FIL are silent on this point. However, the Supreme People's Court held a press conference on 27 December 2019, announcing the "Interpretations of the Supreme People's Court on Several Issues Concerning the Application of the Foreign Investment Law of the People's Republic of China" ("SPC Interpretation"), [1]at which in response to reporters' questions, the Supreme People's Court confirmed that Sino-foreign joint venture agreements should still be governed by Chinese law, in line with the corresponding provisions of the Contract Law, at least until such time as such

1 Interpretations of the Supreme People's Court on Several Issues Concerning the Application of the Foreign Investment Law of the People's Republic of China. Accessed 30 December 2019. https://www.chinacourt.org/law/detail/2019/12/id/150011.shtml.

议不再是章程性文件，因此股东协议 / 合资协议的终止不会影响合资公司的存续。此前，根据《中外合资经营企业法》，如果合资合同终止，则须在以下方案中二选一：（1）一方须收购另一方的全部股份，在这种情况下，合资公司被转化为外商独资企业或内资有限责任公司；（2）解散合资公司。鉴于新的中外合资公司将根据《公司法》设立为有限责任公司或其他经许可的组织形式，在一方收购另一方所有股权，股东协议 / 合资协议终止时，组织形式无须变化，且尽管股东协议 / 合资协议终止，公司仍将继续存续，除非双方同意解散公司而非一方收购另一方全部股权。这是一个根本性的变化，可能会影响股东协议 / 合资协议下的一些机制。专家委员会对相关条款作了相应的修改以反映这一关键问题。

适用法律

虽然《中外合资经营企业法》要求合资合同受中国法管辖，但《公司法》没有类似要求。但是《合同法》规定，中外合资经营企业合同必须适用中国法。预计中国政府部门不会为了实施《外商投资法》下的“国民待遇”原则而改变《合同法》项下的这一要求。事实上，2015 年《外国投资法（草案）》中曾特别规定：外国投资者签署的与中国入境投资相关的任何投资合同均受中国法的管辖。《外商投资法实施条例》对此未作规定，但最高人民法院于 2019 年 12 月 27 日召开新闻发布会，发布《最高人民法院关于适用〈中华人民共和国外商投资法〉若干问题的解释》（以下简称《外商投资法司法解释》）[1] 时，在答记者问中确认，在《合同法》的相关规定未作修改前，中外合营企业的协议仍应与《合同法》的

1 《最高人民法院关于适用〈中华人民共和国外商投资法〉若干问题的解释》，参见 https://www.chinacourt.org/law/detail/2019/12/id/150011.shtml，2019 年 12 月 30 日访问。

provisions are revised.[1]

There may be a technical argument that this rule requiring the application of Chinese law to Sino-foreign joint venture agreements does not apply if the agreement is styled as a shareholders agreement as opposed to a joint venture or investment agreement, although this may prove to be a distinction without a practical difference given the views expressed by the Supreme People's Court. If a separate shareholders agreement is entered into between a Chinese party and a foreign party, either in the context of an inbound M&A transaction [in which case the primary transaction document would be the share purchase agreement (SPA) or equity transfer agreement (ETA)] or a greenfield investment (where the principal transaction agreement is an investment agreement), then it may be argued that while the SPA/ETA or the investment agreement would fall within the above-cited provisions requiring that Chinese law apply, the shareholders agreement would not necessarily be subject to the same requirement. If such a separate shareholders agreement can be governed by foreign law as agreed by the parties, then the Expert Committee is of the view that many foreign parties will have a clear preference to select foreign governing law (most commonly Hong Kong law), while Chinese parties will have a strong preference for Chinese governing law since the company is set up in China and this is consistent with traditional practice and market expectations.

Since the new JV templates produced by the Expert Committee incorporate the basic investment terms for the greenfield joint venture consistent with the related base case scenario, which is consistent with traditional market practice, then under the analysis above, these necessarily would be governed by Chinese law, and the Expert Committee accordingly has so provided in the Sample Templates. It will also be important to take into consideration the fact that the AoA will be a Chinese law document, and so if foreign law can be selected to govern the shareholders agreement, there may be issues of conflicts of law in respect of overlapping provisions which are in dispute.

1 Written report of the press conference issuing the Supreme People's Court Press Conference on Interpretations of the Supreme People's Court on Several Issues Concerning the Application of the Foreign Investment Law of the People's Republic of China, Several Opinions on People's Courts Providing Further Judicial Services and Guarantees for Construction of the "Belt and Road" and the Opinion of the Supreme People's Court on Providing Judicial Services and Guarantees for the Construction of the Lingang New Area of the China (Shanghai) Pilot Free Trade Zone), https://www.chinacourt.org/article/subjectdetail/id/MzAwNMixNIABAA.shtml. Accessed 30 December 2019.

相关规定一致，受中国法律管辖。[1]

理论上，可能存在一个争论，即如果协议被设计为股东协议而非合资协议或投资协议，则要求中外合营企业协议适用中国法的规则不适用，但考虑到最高人民法院的观点，这一区别可能实际操作上并无差异。如果在入境并购交易（在此情况下，主要交易文件为股份购买协议或股权转让协议）或绿地投资（在此情况下，主要交易协议是投资协议）的背景下，中方与外方之间签订了单独的股东协议，那么可以认为，虽然股份购买协议 / 股权转让协议或投资协议会落入上文所引用的要求适用中国法的条款的范围，但股东协议不一定受限于同样的要求。如果双方同意该单独的股东协议可以受境外法管辖，专家委员会认为，许多外方会明显倾向于选择适用境外法（最常见的是香港地区法），而中方则会明显倾向于适用中国法，因为合资公司在中国成立且这符合传统惯例和市场预期。

由于专家委员会制定的新合资企业模板与传统市场惯例一致，纳入了符合基础案例情形的针对绿地合资企业的基本投资条款，那么根据上述分析，这些条款必然会受中国法的管辖，专家委员会也因此在模板样本中指出了这一点。还有另一个重要考虑因素是，公司章程将受中国法管辖，因此如果可以选择境外法来管辖股东协议，则就股东协议和公司章程之间重合的条款发生争议时，就可能会存在法律冲突问题。

协议语言的效力优先级

股东协议 / 合资协议的语言是一个不可避免的问题。《中外合资经营企业法》规定合资合同应以中文书写，如果存在外文版

1 《最高人民法院关于适用〈中华人民共和国外商投资法〉若干问题的解释》、《关于人民法院进一步为"一带一路"建设提供司法服务和保障的若干意见》以及《最高人民法院关于为中国（上海）自由贸易试验区临港新片区建设提供司法服务和保障的意见》新闻发布会文字报道，参见 https://www.chinacourt.org/article/subjectdetail/id/MzAwNMixNIABAA.shtml，2019 年 12 月 30 日访问。

Controlling Language

A corollary issue relates to the language of the SHA/JVA. The EJV Law required that the JV contract be in Chinese and that if a foreign-language version was prepared then either the Chinese-language version would prevail in the event of any discrepancy between the two language versions or the two language versions could be equally valid. This was a sensible requirement when the JV contract was subject to review and approval by Chinese authorities – they would naturally rely solely on the Chinese version.

With the repeal of the EJV Law, there will no longer be a statutory requirement on the controlling language of the SHA/JVA, and since the SHA/JVA will not be subject to review and approval by relevant Chinese authorities, it is expected that this point will be re-opened for negotiation, with many foreign parties adopting an initial negotiating position arguing for the English-language version to control in case of discrepancies. It may be useful to note that the 2015 Draft FIL, the final FIL and the Implementation Regulations were all silent on this point.

It remains to be seen how this issue will be resolved over the medium to longer term, but if the foreign party insists on the English version controlling, it is anticipated that this will be the subject of intense negotiations. For purposes of the Sample Templates, the Expert Committee has adopted the position that the English and Chinese versions are to be equally valid, as this is the well-established market standard.

It is recognized that many foreign and Chinese parties have concerns about providing that the two language versions will be equally valid as this is considered by some to introduce additional uncertainty since there may be discrepancies between the language versions, and even the best translations (either from English to Chinese or from Chinese to English) will necessarily present challenges as the translator seeks to balance readability and accuracy. In the end, because the foreign side almost always is unwilling to accept the Chinese version as controlling and the Chinese side similarly may prefer not to agree that the English version be controlling, the compromise position which has been widely adopted is to agree that the two language versions will be equally valid.

This underscores the critical importance of ensuring that both language versions are prepared at a very high standard. Since the contract terms are legally binding, a professional legal translation must be prepared. Informal translations for internal review purposes will not be sufficient for purposes of a legally binding agreement. This further explains the importance

本，则在两种语言版本之间存在任何不一致的情况下，以中文版本为准，或者两种语言版本具有同等效力。当合资合同受中国政府机构的审查和批准时，这一要求是合理的——他们自然会仅依赖于中文版。

随着《中外合资经营企业法》被废除，针对股东协议 / 合资协议的语言版本将不再有法定要求，且由于股东协议 / 合资协议不再受到中国相关政府机构的审查和批准，预计这一要求将被重新放开，供各方谈判决定，而许多外方采取的初步谈判立场将会主张两个版本出现不一致时以英文版本为准。值得注意的是，2015 年《外国投资法（草案）》、《外商投资法》最终版和《外商投资法实施条例》在这一点上均未作规定。

这一问题在中长期内将如何得到解决还有待观察，但如果外方坚持以英文版本为准，预计这将成为各方谈判的焦点问题。就模板样本而言，专家委员会采取的立场是中英文版本具有同等效力，因为这是已经得到认可的市场标准。

一个公认的事实是——许多外方和中方都对中英文版本具有同等效力这一条款感到担忧，一些人认为这一条款会带来额外的不确定性，因为不同语言版本之间可能存在不一致，即便是最好的翻译（英译中或中译英）也必然会带来挑战，因为译者会试图平衡可读性和准确性。最后，由于外方几乎总是不愿接受以中文版本为准，中方同样可能不愿同意以英文版本为准，因此被广泛采用的折中立场是约定中英文版本具有同等效力。

这强调了确保以极高的标准准备两种语言版本的重要性。由于合同条款具有法律约束力，因此必须准备专业的法律翻译。用于内部审阅目的的非正式翻译对于具有法律约束力的协议而言是不够的。这进一步解释了专家委员会对模板样本的中文版本的重视程度，希望这些双语模板样本将为《外商投资法》时代的双语文件提供有价值的参考。

that the Expert Committee has placed on the Chinese versions of the Sample Templates, and it is hoped that these bilingual Sample Templates will provide a valuable reference point for dual-language documentation in the post-FIL era.

One final point in this regard. Even when an agreement is drafted in a single language, or a dual language agreement provides for one version to be controlling, it is still possible, even common, for there to be questions of interpretation which give rise to disputes. In some cases, having a high standard dual-language contract where both language versions are of equal validity may actually provide a basis for clarification of questions of interpretation of points in one language version by making reference to the corresponding clause in the other language version. In other words, having both language versions equally valid may (but does not necessarily) introduce more uncertainty in terms of interpretation, but in some cases this arrangement may provide a further point of reference to clarify points which may not be sufficiently clear in one language, so on balance this market standard approach as to the controlling language presents a workable compromise.

Form of Articles of Association

Under the EJV Law, the JV contract was to include all of the same elements as the AoA in addition to various other terms to be included only in the JV contract, and in the case of any discrepancy between the JV contract and the AoA, the JV contract was to prevail. As a result, in practice it was common to prepare the AoA only after the JV contract was finalized and simply redact the non-overlapping provisions. This meant that the parties needed only to look to the JV contract to confirm the agreed corporate governance terms, and the AoA became an under-utilized appendage in such cases. Under this approach, the provisions of the JV contract that would be redacted related to the private agreements between the parties, leaving only the provisions relating to the establishment and governance of the company. By way of general illustration of which types of clauses would be redacted and which would be retained in the process of creating the AoA from the base JV contract, see the chart below. Note that for purposes of this chart, we have already omitted the legacy JV contract provisions which were required under the EJV Law but which are no longer required under the Company Law.

最后，即使以单一语言起草一份协议，或者一份双语协议中规定以某一语言版本为准，协议解释的问题仍然有可能甚至经常引起争议。在某些情况下，约定两种版本具有同等效力的高标准的双语合同实际上可以通过参考一种语言版本中的相应条款，为另一种语言版本中的相关问题的解释的明确提供基础。换句话说，两种语言版本具有同等效力可能（但不一定）在协议解释方面带来更多的不确定性，而在某些情况下，这种安排也可能为阐明一种语言版本中不够明确的要点提供了进一步的参考，所以总体来说，就语言的效力优先级而言，这一市场标准方法是一个可行的折中方案。

公司章程的样式

根据《中外合资经营企业法》，除了仅适用于合资合同的各种条款外，合资合同中包含的所有其他要素均与公司章程中的要素相同，如果合资合同与公司章程之间存在任何不一致，则以合资合同为准。因此，在实践中，企业通常在合资合同最终确定后再起草章程并且简单地撰写非重叠条款。这意味着双方只需要查看合资合同来确认约定的公司治理条款，而章程在这种情况下则成为未得到充分利用的附属文件。在这种情况下，需要删除有关各方之间的私下协议的合资合同的条款，只留下与合资公司的设立和治理相关的条款。在以合资合同为基础起草公司章程的过程中，哪些类型的条款需要删除，而哪些类型的条款将保留在公司章程中，请参见下表的一般说明。请注意，在本表中，我们已经删除了《中外合资经营企业法》项下要求但是《公司法》不再要求的传统合资合同条款。

Clause type	Status
Establishment of the Company	Retained
Registered Capital	Retained
Transfer of Equity Interests	Redacted
Shareholders Meeting	Retained
Board of Directors	Retained
Board Meetings and Resolutions	Retained
Board of Supervisors	Retained
Operation and Management	Retained
Non-competition and Non-solicitation	Redacted
Financial Affairs and Accounting	Retained
Representations and Warranties	Redacted
Joint Venture Term	Retained
Termination, Dissolution and Liquidation	Retained
Buy-out Upon Termination	Redacted
Breach of Contract	Redacted
Confidentiality	Redacted
Force Majeure	Redacted
Notice	Retained
Settlement of Disputes	Redacted

Now that the Company Law will govern, there are fewer legal requirements on the content of the SHA/JVA, and therefore the relationship between the AoA and the SHA/JVA may no longer need to follow this traditional model.

It should also be noted that the local AMRs will have some standard short-form AoA templates, but these are for reference only, and are not required to be used. The Expert Committee was unanimous in its recommendation that these AMR standard forms not be adopted in the usual case as they were considered to be insufficient to address the typical range of corporate governance arrangements for FIEs. By law, and as a matter of practice, AMRs in the major cities will all accept forms of AoA prepared by the parties so long as the minimum requirements under the Company Law (e.g. party names, registered capital amount, capital

条款类型	状态
公司的设立	保留
注册资本	保留
股权转让	修改
股东会	保留
董事会	保留
董事会会议和决议	保留
监事会	保留
经营与管理	保留
竞业限制和禁止招揽	修改
财务和会计	保留
陈述和保证	修改
合资期限	保留
终止、解散和清算	保留
终止后的全面收购	修改
违约	修改
保密	修改
不可抗力	修改
通知	保留
争议解决	修改

既然《公司法》将得到适用，对股东协议 / 合资协议内容的法律要求将减少，因此公司章程和股东协议 / 合资协议之间的关系可能不再需要遵循这种传统模式。

还应注意，地方市场监督管理局会提供一些标准的简易版公司章程模板，但仅供参考，而并非必须使用。专家委员会一致建议通常情况下不采用这些市场监督管理局的标准模板，因为它们不足以涵盖外商投资企业典型的公司治理安排。根据法律和实践，只要适当纳入了《公司法》项下规定的最低要求（例如，协议各方的名称、注册资本额、出资时间表、股东会和董事会条款等），

contribution schedule, shareholders meeting and board meeting provisions, etc.) are properly incorporated. However, in some regions of China the local AMR may insist that their standard form be used or that other changes be made to the form of AoA produced by the parties.

To address these various potential scenarios, the Expert Committee considered the following alternatives:

- In line with the traditional approach, the parties prepare the AoA from the base JVA by redacting the provisions which relate to the private arrangements between the parties and retaining the provisions relating to the establishment and governance of the company and submit this for registration with the AMR. This approach is designed to give the fullest possible effect to the agreement of the parties on the related governance provisions and to avoid having to renegotiate the base terms when creating the AoA since the terms are all drawn from the final agreed form of the JVA.
- Alternatively, the parties may create a much more simplified form of AoA which largely conforms to the form and structure of the local AMR standard form AoA while still incorporating more suitable governance provisions. This approach is designed to facilitate acceptance by the local AMR without sacrificing the lawful rights and interests of the parties. However, this may entail some additional time and effort to confirm that the provisions of the AoA conform to the provisions agreed in the final JVA, although this should be minimal.
- In some cases where the local AMR adopts a more rigid position as to the form of AoA and requires the parties to adopt its standard form, the parties may prepare both (1) a simplified AoA, which conforms with the AoA form provided by local AMR and which is submitted to the AMR for registration (the "registration form AoA"), and (2) a more robust AoA which contains the full set of AoA provisions as agreed by the parties (the "private form AoA"), where the private form AoA is binding on the parties, the company and the officers and directors of the joint venture and is the controlling version in the event of a discrepancy with the registration form AoA.

All three alternatives had support among different members of the Expert Committee, but the consensus view was to adopt the traditional approach outlined in first option set out above. A plurality also concurred with the third option, but only if the AMR did not accept the AoA prepared as provided in the first option, although some members of the Expert Committee

一些主要城市的市场监督管理局都会接受各方准备的公司章程的样式。但是，在中国的某些地区，当地的市场监督管理局可能会坚持要求使用其标准格式的模板，或者要求对各方准备的公司章程样式进行其他修改。

为解决这些可能发生的情况，专家委员会提出了以下备选方案：

- 根据传统方法，各方可以以合资协议为基础，通过删除与各方之间私下安排有关的条款以及保留与公司的设立和治理有关的条款，来准备公司章程，并将其提交给市场监督管理局进行登记。这种方法旨在使各方之间就相关公司治理条款的约定尽最大可能地发挥效力，并避免在准备公司章程时重新协商基本条款，因为这些条款均来自各方最终同意的合资协议。

- 或者，各方可以准备更加简化的公司章程样式，基本符合当地市场监督管理局的标准公司章程的样式和结构，同时包含更适合的公司治理规定。这种方法旨在在不牺牲各方合法权益的情况下促进当地市场监督管理局对该公司章程的接受。但是，在这种情况下可能需要一些额外的时间和精力来确认公司章程的条款符合最终版合资协议中商定的条款，尽管这应该是最低限度的。

- 在某些情况下，当地市场监督管理局对公司章程的样式采取更严格的态度，并要求各方采用其标准形式，各方可以准备：（1）符合当地市场监督管理局提供的公司章程形式的简易版公司章程，并提交给市场监督管理局进行登记（“登记版公司章程”）；（2）包含双方约定的所有公司章程条款的更全面的公司章程（“私人版公司章程”），其中私人版公司章程对各方、合资企业及其高级管理人员和董事具有约束力，并且如果与登记版公司章程发生不一

expressed reservations about this approach. For purposes of the Sample JV Templates, we have adopted the traditional approach and have prepared the Sample JV AoA Template off the base of the Sample JVA Template. Ultimately, this is a matter left to the discretion of the parties and their legal counsel, and we expect that all of the above options will be adopted to varying degrees in the market. It is also important to note that the AoA will now be the only formal constitutional document which is binding on the Sino-foreign joint venture company, while the SHA/JVA is an agreement between the parties which will no longer constitute a formal constitutional document of the company as was the case under the JV Law. Thus, it will be critical for the AoA to include certain provisions which are intended to be binding on the company and its officers (such as the scope of authority of the officers and directors of the company, who will be subject to the provisions of the AoA but who would not personally be party to, and thus not bound by, the provisions of the SHA/JVA).

Finally, it should be noted that the Sample WFOE AoA Template included in Chapter 8 is based on the Sample JV AoA Template included in Chapter 7 but has been further simplified to reflect the fact that there are no partner issues to be addressed and to reflect the base case scenario adopted in respect of the preparation of that sample form (see related discussion in Chapter 5).

致，以私人版公司章程为准。

三种备选方案都得到了专家委员会不同成员的支持，但成员们的共识是采用上述第一种方案的传统方法。多数人也同意选择第三种方案，但前提是市场监督管理局不接受第一种方案中准备的公司章程，而专家委员会的部分成员对这种方法还存有保留意见。就模板样本而言，我们采用了传统方法，在合资协议的基础上准备了合资企业章程。归根结底，这是一个可以由各方及其法律顾问自行决定的事项，我们预计上述方案将在市场中得到不同程度的适用。同样需要说明的是，公司章程现在将是唯一对中外合资公司具有约束力的正式章程性文件，而股东协议 / 合资协议是双方之间的协议，不再像《中外合资经营企业法》时期那样构成该法项下正式的章程性文件。因此，公司章程中包含对合资公司及其高级管理人员有约束力的特定条款（如合资公司高级管理人员和董事的职权范围，高级管理人员和董事将受到公司章程的约束，但由于其个人不是股东协议 / 合资协议的缔约方，因而不受股东协议 / 合资协议条款的约束）将非常重要。

最后，需要指出的是，第八章中包含的外商独资企业章程样本以第七章中的合资企业章程样本为基础编制，由于无须处理合作伙伴的问题，并且为了反映在编写该样本时所采用的基础案例情形（见第五章的相关讨论），我们对外商独资企业章程样本进行了进一步的简化。

Chapter 7 FIL-Compliant Bilingual Sino-Foreign JV Templates

This Chapter consists of three annexes, as follows:

Annex Ⅰ Sample JVA Template

Annex Ⅱ Sample JV Articles of Association Template

Annex Ⅲ Annotations to Sample JVA and JV Articles of Association Templates

The Sample JV Templates referenced above have been drafted in contemplation of a Sino-foreign joint venture with the following characteristics:

(a) This is a two-party joint venture, with the Chinese party as Party A and the foreign party as Party B.

(b) This is a new mid-cap greenfield joint venture set up as a strategic investment.

(c) Party A holds 60% of the registered capital, and Party B holds 40% of the registered capital. Each party is to make its capital contributions in cash.

(d) The new joint venture company will adopt a standard comprehensive corporate governance system comprised of a board of directors (as opposed to a single executive director) and a board of supervisors (as opposed to a single supervisor).

Accordingly, without applicable substantive modifications, these Sample JV Templates may not be appropriate for transactions with different characteristics.

These Sample JV Templates and the related annotations are provided subject to the caveats and limitations set out in Chapter 5. Electronic bilingual versions of the Sample JV Templates are available free of charge at www.docqbot.com/en/newFIL.

第七章　符合《外商投资法》规定的双语中外合资企业模板

本章包含以下 3 份附件：

附件Ⅰ　合资协议模板样本

附件Ⅱ　合资企业章程模板样本

附件Ⅲ　合资协议和合资企业章程模板样本注解说明

上述合资企业模板样本是针对具有以下特征的中外合资企业起草的：

（a）由中外两方合资，中方为甲方，外方为乙方。

（b）以战略投资的方式设立的新的中型绿地合资企业。

（c）甲方持有注册资本的 60%，乙方持有注册资本的 40%。双方都以现金出资。

（d）新成立的合资公司将采用标准、全面的公司治理体系，由董事会（而非唯一执行董事）和监事会（而非唯一监事）组成。

因此，如果未针对不同特征的交易进行适当的实质性修改，这些模板样本可能不适用于您的特定交易。

这些模板样本和相关注解说明受限于第五章所载的声明和限制。模板样本的电子版可以从 http://www.docqbot.com/cn/newFIL 免费下载。

Annex Ⅰ
Sample JVA Template

Dated [DATE]

JOINT VENTURE AGREEMENT

by and between

[PARTY A NAME]

PARTY A

and

[PARTY B NAME]

PARTY B

in respect of the establishment of

[COMPANY NAME]

COMPANY

附件 I
合资协议模板样本

【填入日期】

合资协议

由

【填入甲方名称】

甲方

与

【填入乙方名称】

乙方

关于设立

【填入合资公司名称】

合资公司

签订

TABLE OF CONTENTS

目录

Annex 1 Definitions and Interpretation

Annex 2 Articles of Association

Annex 3 Capital Contribution Schedule

Annex 4 Funding Conditions

Annex 5 Additional Permits

Annex 6 Ancillary Agreements

Annex 7 Senior Representatives of the Parties

附件一　定义和解释

附件二　公司章程

附件三　出资时间表

附件四　出资条件

附件五　附加许可

附件六　附属协议

附件七　双方高级代表

JOINT VENTURE AGREEMENT

This Joint Venture Agreement ("Agreement") is made on [DATE] (the "Effective Date") by and between:

[PARTY A NAME][(Unified Social Credit Code [NUMBER])], a [PARTY A ENTITY FORM], organized and existing under the laws of China with its registered address at [ADDRESS] (hereinafter referred to as "Party A"), and [PARTY B NAME][([Company Registration Number] [NUMBER])], a [PARTY B ENTITY FORM] organized and existing under the laws of [PARTY B JURISDICTION OF INCORPORATION], with its [registered address][OR][principal place of business] at [ADDRESS] (hereinafter referred to as "Party B").

Each of Party A and Party B shall hereinafter be referred to individually as a "Party" and collectively as the "Parties."

BACKGROUND

Party A and Party B have agreed to establish a joint venture company (the "Company") for the purpose of engaging in the Business.

This Agreement sets out the terms agreed by the Parties with respect to the establishment, governance and management of the Company and the operation of the Business.

Now therefore, after friendly consultations conducted in accordance with the principles of equality and mutual benefit, the Parties hereby agree as follows:

1. DEFINITIONS AND INTERPRETATION

Unless the provisions or context of this Agreement provide otherwise, this Agreement, its Annexes and the terms used herein shall be interpreted in accordance with Annex 1.

合资协议

本合资协议（“本协议”）于【填入日期】（“生效日”）由以下双方签订：

【填入甲方名称】【（统一社会信用代码为【填入号码】）】，一家根据中国法律组建及存续的【填入甲方组织形式】，其注册地址为【填入地址】（以下简称“甲方”），与【填入乙方名称】【（【公司注册号为】【填入号码】）】，一家根据【填入乙方所在地】法律组建及存续的【填入乙方组织形式】，其【注册地址】【或】【主要营业地】为【填入地址】（以下简称“乙方”）。

甲方和乙方以下各称“一方”，合称“双方”。

背景

甲方和乙方同意，为从事目标业务，将设立一家合资公司（“合资公司”）。

本协议载明了双方就合资公司的设立、治理和经营以及目标业务的运营达成的协议条款。

因此，依照平等互利的原则进行友好协商后，双方现协议如下：

1. 定义与解释

除本协议条款另有约定或上下文另有所指，本协议及其附件和本协议中所有相关用语的解释规则见附件一。

2. ESTABLISHMENT OF THE COMPANY

2.1 The Company shall be established in accordance with the terms and provisions of this Agreement.

2.2 The Company particulars shall be as follows:

(a) The name of the Company shall be [COMPANY NAME IN CHINESE] in Chinese and [COMPANY NAME IN ENGLISH] in English.

(b) The Company shall be established as a limited liability company under the laws of China.

(c) The registered address of the Company shall be [ADDRESS].

2.3 The Company's Articles of Association shall be substantially in the form attached as Annex 2.

3. BUSINESS OF THE COMPANY

3.1 The scope of business of the Company shall include [DESCRIPTION OF BUSINESS OF THE COMPANY] (the "Business").

3.2 The Parties shall cause that the Company shall conduct the Business in [China] (the "Territory") and such additional jurisdictions as the Board may approve by Unanimous Board Resolution, subject to compliance with the requirements of Applicable Law.

3.3 Each of the Parties shall use all reasonable endeavors to develop and promote the Business of the Company.

4. CAPITALIZATION OF THE COMPANY

4.1 The registered capital of the Company ("Registered Capital") shall be RMB [AMOUNT].

4.2 The Parties shall hold the following percentages of the Registered Capital:

(a) Party A shall hold [60%] of the Registered Capital (the "Party A Equity Interests"); and

(b) Party B shall hold [40%] of the Registered Capital (the "Party B Equity Interests").

4.3 In consideration of such allocations of the Registered Capital, the Parties shall

2. 合资公司的设立

2.1 合资公司应根据本协议规定的条款设立。

2.2 合资公司的具体信息如下：

（a）合资公司的中文名称为【填入合资公司的中文名称】，英文名称为【填入合资公司的英文名称】。

（b）合资公司为中国法项下的有限责任公司。

（c）合资公司的注册地址为【填入地址】。

2.3 合资公司的公司章程应基本符合附件二的形式。

3. 合资公司的目标业务

3.1 合资公司的经营范围应包括【填入合资公司目标业务的描述】（“目标业务”）。

3.2 双方应促使合资公司，在符合适用法律的规定的情况下，在【中国】（“目标地区”）以及董事会可能通过董事会一致决议批准的其他地区开展目标业务。

3.3 双方应尽一切合理努力发展和推动合资公司的目标业务。

4. 合资公司的资本

4.1 合资公司的注册资本（“注册资本”）应为人民币【填入金额】元。

4.2 双方应持有的注册资本的比例如下：

（a）甲方应持有注册资本的【60%】（“甲方股权”）；且

（b）乙方应持有注册资本的【40%】（“乙方股权”）。

4.3 鉴于上述注册资本的分配情况，双方应按照以下约定向合资公司出资：

make the following capital contributions to the Company:

(a) Party A shall contribute to the Company RMB [AMOUNT] in cash ("Party A Cash Contribution"); and

(b) Party B shall contribute to the Company the [CURRENCY] equivalent of RMB [AMOUNT] in cash ("Party B Cash Contribution").

Subject to the prior satisfaction or waiver of the Funding Conditions, each Party shall make its contribution to the Registered Capital of the Company in accordance with the capital contribution schedule set out in Annex 3.

4.4 When a Party has made all or any part of its contribution to the Registered Capital of the Company, the Parties shall cause that the Company shall issue an Investment Certificate to such Party subject to and in accordance with the requirements of Applicable Law. The failure of the Company to issue any Investment Certificate to either Party shall not affect the rights or interests of either Party with respect to any contributions to the Registered Capital of the Company made by it.

4.5 It is intended by the Parties that the Company shall, as far as practicable, be self-financed through cash flows from the Business and the Parties' capital contributions as provided above. If additional capital is required, then the Company may:

(a) establish credit facilities or obtain loans from commercial banks or other qualified financial institutions, or

(b) obtain additional financing from the Parties in the form of Shareholder Loans in accordance with the terms of Clause 4.7 or a Capital Increase in accordance with Clause 4.8.

4.6 If a bank or other financial institution agrees to lend funds to the Company subject to guarantees being given by the Parties, and if the Parties agree to give such guarantees, then each Party shall issue such a guarantee at the same time, on the same terms and in proportion to its respective percentage share of the Registered Capital of the Company without any joint and several liability. If either Party declines or fails to provide such a guarantee, then the other Party shall have no obligation to provide any such guarantee in any amount on a unilateral basis.

4.7 The Parties may provide Shareholder Loans to the Company as and when required

（a）甲方应以现金向合资公司出资人民币【填入金额】元（“甲方现金出资”）；且

（b）乙方应以现金向合资公司出资等值于人民币【填入金额】元的【填入币种】（“乙方现金出资”）。

受限于对出资条件的事先满足或放弃，每一方应按照附件三所载的出资时间表向合资公司缴纳注册资本。

4.4 当一方已完成其对合资公司注册资本的全部或部分出资时，双方应促使合资公司根据适用法律的要求向该方出具出资证明书。合资公司未能向任何一方出具出资证明书，不影响任何一方就其已完成的对合资公司注册资本的任何出资有关的权利或利益。

4.5 双方希望合资公司能够尽可能地通过目标业务的现金流和上述双方的出资实现财务自给。如果需要额外的资金，合资公司可以：

（a）采取信贷措施或从商业银行或其他具备相关资质的金融机构获得贷款，或

（b）根据本协议第 4.7 条的规定以股东贷款的形式，或根据本协议第 4.8 条的规定以增资的形式，从双方获得额外融资。

4.6 如果银行或其他金融机构同意在双方提供保证的情况下向合资公司提供贷款，并且如果双方同意提供该等保证，则双方应同时以相同的条款签订该等保证合同，按照其各自持有的合资公司注册资本的比例承担保证责任，且双方之间不存在任何连带责任。如果任何一方拒绝或未能提供该等保证，则另一方没有义务单方面提供任何数额的该等保证。

4.7 当合资公司的业务经营需要资金时，双方可以根据合资

for the funding of the Company's business operations. The Parties shall advance the Shareholder Loans at the same time and in the same proportion of their respective percentage shares of the Registered Capital of the Company. The Parties shall cause that the Company shall pay interest on and repay the principal of each Shareholder Loan in accordance with the terms of the relevant Shareholder Loan Agreement, and the tenor and terms of the Shareholder Loan Agreement with each Party shall be the same.

4.8 If the Parties have fully funded their respective capital contributions in accordance with the capital contribution schedule set out in Annex 3, and additional capital is required for the funding of the Company's business operations, the Board may propose an increase of the Registered Capital of the Company ("Capital Increase") for consideration and approval by the Shareholders Meeting. If the Shareholders Meeting approves such Capital Increase, then each Party shall have a pre-emptive right to subscribe to and contribute to such Capital Increase in proportion to its percentage shares of the Registered Capital of the Company.

4.9 If the Shareholders Meeting approves a reduction of the Registered Capital of the Company ("Capital Reduction"), then each Party shall bear its share of such reduction in proportion to its percentage share of the Registered Capital of the Company.

4.10 In respect of any Capital Increase or Capital Reduction, the Parties shall cause the Company to register the same with the AMR[and apply for approval from the Approval and Record-filing Authority].

4.11 If a Party (the "Non-funding Party") fails to make its capital contribution, in whole or in part, in accordance with the capital contribution schedule set out in Annex 3 or to contribute its proportionate share of a Capital Increase in whole or in part in accordance with the provisions of the relevant Supermajority Shareholders Resolution approving such Capital Increase (each a "Funding Default"), then such Party shall be liable to pay simple interest to the Company at a rate equal to [DEFAULT INTEREST RATE] per annum on the unpaid amount from the time due until the time the full outstanding amount including penalty interest is paid to and received by the Company.

公司的需要向其提供股东贷款。双方应按各自所持的合资公司注册资本的比例同时发放股东贷款。双方应促使合资公司按照相关股东贷款协议的条款就每笔股东贷款支付利息并偿还本金，并且与每一方签订的股东贷款协议的期限和条款应相同。

4.8 如果双方已按照附件三所载的出资时间表完成各自的全部出资，而合资公司的业务运营仍需要额外的资金，董事会可以提议增加合资公司的注册资本（“增资”），提请股东会审议并批准。如果股东会批准该等增资，则每一方应拥有按照其所占的合资公司注册资本的比例优先认缴或实缴该等增资的权利。

4.9 如果股东会批准减少合资公司的注册资本（“减资”），则每一方应按其所持的合资公司注册资本中的比例减少其注册资本份额。

4.10 就任何增资或减资，双方应促使合资公司向市场监督管理局进行登记【并申请审批和备案机关的批准】。

4.11 如果一方（“未出资方”）未能按照附件三所载的出资时间表完成其全部或部分出资，或者未能按照批准该等增资的相关绝对多数股东会决议的规定全部或部分缴纳其相应比例的增资（每一种情况均为“出资违约”），则该方有责任自未付金额到期应付之日起至合资公司收到其支付的全部未付金额（包括罚息）止，以【填入违约利息的利率】的年利率就未付金额向合资公司支付单利。

4.12 如果出资违约在【九十天】内仍然未得到补救，则

（a）该等违约应构成未出资方的重大违约，且

（b）只要另一方未违反其任何出资义务，则除了本协

4.12 If a Funding Default remains uncured for a period of [ninety days], then

(a) such failure shall constitute a Material Breach on the part of the Non-funding Party and

(b) so long as the other Party is not in default of any of its Funding Obligations, then in addition to its other rights under this Agreement or Applicable Law:

(i) such other Party (the "Funding Party") shall have the right (but not the obligation) to submit to the Company and the other Party an unconditional and irrevocable Unfunded Capital Subscription Notice in the agreed form confirming that it shall subscribe unilaterally to all or part of the Unfunded Capital Contribution Amount on the terms set out therein;

(ii) the Parties shall amend the Articles of Association and this Agreement to make a corresponding adjustment to the Parties' respective Equity Interests to reflect the disproportionate capital contributions made by the Funding Party (including or not including the Unfunded Capital Contribution Amount, as the case may be), and the Parties shall cause that the Company shall register the change in ownership percentages with the AMR[and apply for approval from the Approval and Record-filing Authority]; and

(iii) if the Funding Party has submitted an Unfunded Capital Subscription Notice in accordance with Clause 4.12(b)(i), then the Funding Party shall contribute such subscribed amounts to the Company within [20] Business Days following completion of the registrations[and approvals] set out in Clause 4.12(b)(ii).

4.13 In connection with the adjustments to be made pursuant to Clause 4.12(b)(ii),

(a) each Party shall exercise all of its Voting Rights to approve the corresponding amendments to the Articles of Association and adjustments to the Parties respective Equity Interests and shall waive any rights under Applicable Law inconsistent with the provisions hereof, and

(b) upon the completion of all related registrations[and approvals] in respect

议或适用法律规定的其他权利外：

（i）该方（“已出资方”）应有权（但没有义务）以约定的形式向合资公司和另一方提交无条件的且不可撤销的未缴纳资本认缴通知，确认其将按照通知所载的条款单方面认缴全部或部分未缴纳资本出资额；

（ii）双方应修订公司章程及本协议，对双方各自的股权做出相应调整，以反映已出资方超出原定比例的出资（根据实际情况，包括或不包括未缴纳资本出资额），双方应促使合资公司向市场监督管理局登记所有权比例的变更【并申请审批和备案机关的批准】；以及

（iii）如果已出资方已根据本协议第 4.12（b）（i）条的规定提交未缴纳资本认缴通知，则已出资方应在根据本协议第 4.12（b）（ii）条的规定在完成登记【和审批】后【20】个工作日内向公司缴纳该等认缴金额。

4.13 关于根据本协议第 4.12（b)（ii）条所作出的调整，

（a）每一方应行使其所有的表决权，以批准对公司章程的相应修订以及对双方各自的股权的调整，并应放弃适用法律项下任何与本协议规定不一致的权利，且

（b）在就上述变更完成所有相关登记【和审批】以反映对双方各自股权的相应调整后，已出资方应被视为已豁免未出资方关于相应的未缴纳资本出资额的重大违约责任。

4.14 一方应自行承担其因根据附件三所载的出资时间表出资、提供股东贷款或保证而产生的，或与认缴增资或

thereof to reflect the corresponding adjustment to the Parties' respective Equity Interests, the Funding Party shall be deemed to have waived the Material Breach on the part of the Non-funding Party in respect of the corresponding Unfunded Capital Contribution Amount.

4.14 All costs and expenses incurred by a Party in connection with making its capital contributions in accordance with the capital contribution schedule set out in Annex 3, the provision of a Shareholder Loan or a guarantee or in connection with the subscription for a Capital Increase or Unfunded Capital Subscription shall be for its own account.

5. CONDITIONS TO FUNDING OF CAPITAL CONTRIBUTIONS

5.1 The obligation of a Party to make its contribution to the Registered Capital of the Company in accordance with the capital contribution schedule set out in Annex 3 shall be subject to prior satisfaction of the conditions to funding set out in Annex 4 ("Funding Conditions").

5.2 Any Funding Condition (other than matters which cannot be waived under Applicable Law) may only be waived by both Parties in writing.

5.3 Primary responsibility for satisfaction of the Funding Conditions shall be allocated as follows:

(a) Party A shall have primary responsibility to produce, obtain or procure the certificates, documents, and other items as set out in Paragraph 1 of Annex 4 (the "Party A Documents");

(b) Party B shall have primary responsibility to produce, obtain or procure the certificates, documents, and other items as set out in Paragraph 2 of Annex 4 (the "Party B Documents"); and

(c) the Parties shall jointly be responsible

(i) to produce, obtain or procure the certificates, documents, and other items as set out in Paragraph 3 of Annex 4 (the "Joint Documents")

(ii) to convene the first meeting of the shareholders and procure the adoption of the First Shareholders Meeting Resolutions in accordance with the provisions of Clause 7.2, and

未缴纳资本认缴相关的所有成本和费用。

5. 实缴出资条件

5.1 一方依照附件三所载的出资时间表对合资公司的注册资本进行实缴出资的义务应以附件四所载的出资条件（“出资条件”）的事先满足为前提。

5.2 任何出资条件只能由双方以书面形式放弃，但适用法律规定不得放弃的事项除外。

5.3 满足出资条件的主要责任的分配如下：

（a）甲方应承担制备、获得或取得附件四第 1 条所载的证明、文件和其他材料（“甲方文件”）的主要责任；

（b）乙方应承担制备、获得或取得附件四第 2 条所载的证明、文件和其他材料（“乙方文件”）的主要责任；以及

（c）双方应共同承担以下责任：

（i）制备、获得或取得附件四第 3 条所载的证明、文件和其他材料（“共同文件”）；

（ii）根据本协议第 7.2 条的规定召开第一次股东会会议并促使通过第一次股东会决议；以及

（iii）根据本协议第 9.1（a）条的规定召开第一次董事会会议并促使通过第一次董事会决议。

每一方应向另一方提供其为完成上述内容所合理需要的所有配合和协助。

5.4 在最后一项出资条件根据本协议得到满足或放弃后：

（a）甲方应立即签署，且双方应立即促使合资公司签署每一份甲方附属协议；

(iii) to convene the first Board meeting and procure the adoption of the First Board Meeting Resolutions in accordance with the provisions of Clause 9.1(a).

In connection with the foregoing, each Party shall provide the other Party with all such cooperation and assistance as may reasonably be required in respect thereof.

5.4 Promptly following the date on which the last of the Funding Conditions has been satisfied or waived in accordance with this Agreement:

(a) Party A shall sign, and the Parties shall procure that the Company shall sign, each of the Party A Ancillary Agreements;

(b) Party B shall sign, and the Parties shall procure that the Company shall sign, each of the Party B Ancillary Agreements; and

(c) the Parties shall procure that the Company shall sign each of the Other Ancillary Agreements.

5.5 Each of the Parties shall use all reasonable endeavors to procure that the Funding Conditions are satisfied as soon as practicable and in any event no later than [5:00 p.m.] in [CITY], China on [DATE] ("Long-stop Date").

5.6 If any of the Funding Conditions have not been satisfied or waived by the Long-stop Date, this Agreement shall automatically and immediately terminate.

5.7 Party A shall bear the costs in respect of producing, obtaining or procuring the Party A Documents. Party B shall bear the costs in respect of producing, obtaining or procuring the Party B Documents. The Parties shall jointly bear the costs in respect of producing, obtaining or procuring the Joint Documents.

5.8 In the event that this Agreement is terminated under Clause 5.6 following the Business License Issuance Date, Party A shall undertake to complete all steps as may be required to deregister the Company, and Party B shall provide all such cooperation and assistance as may reasonably be required in respect thereof.

6. TRANSFER OF EQUITY INTERESTS

6.1 Notwithstanding any other provision of this Agreement, but subject in each case to Clause 6.3, a Transferring Party may Transfer all or part of its Equity Interests to a

（b）乙方应立即签署，且双方应立即促使合资公司签署每一份乙方附属协议；以及

（c）双方应促使合资公司签署每一份其他附属协议。

5.5 每一方均应尽一切合理努力使出资条件尽可能快地得到满足，无论如何不得晚于中国北京时间【填入日期】的【下午5点】（“最终截止日”）。

5.6 如果在最终截止日仍有任何出资条件未得到满足或放弃，则本协议将立即自动终止。

5.7 甲方应承担与制备、获得或取得甲方文件有关的费用。乙方应承担与制备、获得或取得乙方文件有关的费用。双方应共同承担与制备、获得或取得共同文件有关的费用。

5.8 如果本协议在营业执照颁发日后根据本协议第5.6条终止,甲方应承诺完成合资公司注销登记所需的所有步骤,乙方应提供甲方可能合理要求的与之相关的所有配合和协助。

6. 股权转让

6.1 无论本协议有何其他规定，受限于本协议第6.3条的各种情况，转让方均可以不受限制地将其全部或部分股权转让给合格的关联方，但是

（a）转让方应保证该等合格的关联方受让方履行其作为（可能转让给合格的关联方的）本协议、公司章程、转让方为协议一方的任何附属协议的条款项下以及适用法律要求项下的一方的义务，并对该等义务的履行承担连带责任。

（b）如果该等受让方不再是合格的关联方，其应立即（i）将所有该等指定股权再转让给原转让方，或（ii）

Qualified Affiliate without restriction, provided that

(a) The Transferring Party shall guarantee and remain jointly and severally liable for the performance by such Qualified Affiliate transferee of its obligations as a Party under the terms of this Agreement, the Articles of Association, any Ancillary Agreements to which the Transferring Party is a party (as the same may be assigned to the Qualified Affiliate) and the requirements of Applicable Law.

(b) If such transferee ceases to be a Qualified Affiliate, such person shall immediately either (i) re-transfer all such Designated Equity Interests to the original Transferring Party or (ii) transfer all such Designated Equity Interests to another Qualified Affiliate of the original Transferring Party, and pending completion of such re-transfer or transfer, as the case may be, all rights attaching to such Designated Equity Interests shall be suspended.

6.2 If a Transferring Party proposes to Transfer all or part of its Designated Equity Interests to a Proposed Transferee other than a Qualified Affiliate, it must first obtain the prior written consent of the other Party, and the other Party shall have a Right of First Refusal to purchase the Designated Equity Interests, as follows:

(a) As a condition precedent to the Transfer of the Designated Equity Interests by the Transferring Party to the Proposed Transferee, the Transferring Party shall first submit to the other Party a Third-Party Transfer Notice in the agreed form setting out the required details.

(b) Within [10] Business Days following the date of the Third-Party Transfer Notice, the other Party shall submit to the Transferring Party either (i) an unconditional and irrevocable Consent to Transfer in the agreed form or (ii) an unconditional and irrevocable Exercise Notice in the agreed form confirming that it will purchase all of the Designated Equity Interests under the terms specified in the Third-Party Transfer Notice.

(c) If the other Party fails to deliver a qualifying Consent to Transfer or an Exercise Notice within the time specified in Clause 6.2(b), then the other Party shall be deemed to consent to the proposed Transfer to the Proposed Transferee on the terms specified in the Third-Party Transfer Notice.

将所有该等指定股权转让给原转让方的另一个合格的关联方，并且在该等再转让或转让（视情况而定）完成之前，该等指定股权上的所有权利均应中止。

6.2 如果转让方提议将其全部或部分指定股权转让给合格的关联方以外的拟定受让方，则其必须先获得另一方的事先书面同意，且另一方应享有购买指定股权的优先购买权，具体如下：

（a）作为转让方向拟定受让方转让指定股权的先决条件，转让方应首先向另一方提交约定形式的第三方转让通知，通知上载明必要的详细信息。

（b）在第三方转让通知发出后【10】个工作日内，另一方应向转让方提交（i）一份无条件且不可撤销的约定形式的转让同意书，或（ii）一份无条件且不可撤销的约定形式的行权通知，确认其将根据第三方转让通知中的条款购买全部指定股权。

（c）如果另一方未能在第 6.2（b）条规定的时间内交付合格的转让同意书或行权通知，则另一方应被视为同意根据第三方转让通知中的条款向拟定受让方进行的拟议转让。

（d）上述就指定股权向另一方和 / 或拟定受让方的转让，应根据第三方转让通知的规定，在转让方指定的时间和地点完成。

如果另一方根据本协议第 6.2（b）条提交行权通知但未能根据其中的规定购买指定股权，则另一方应被视为同意向拟定受让方进行的拟议转让，转让方可以将该等指定股权转让给拟定受让方，其转让价格不得低于且转让条款不得优于第三方转让通知中所载的价格和条款。

(d) Completion of the Transfer of the Designated Equity Interests to the other Party and/or the Proposed Transferee as provided above shall occur at such time and place as designated by the Transferring Party in accordance with the terms of the Third-Party Transfer Notice.

If the other Party submits an Exercise Notice in accordance with Clause 6.2(b) but fails to purchase the Designated Equity Interests pursuant thereto, then the other Party shall be deemed to consent to the proposed Transfer to the Proposed Transferee, and the Transferring Party may Transfer such Designated Equity Interests to the Proposed Transferee at a price not lower and on terms no more favorable than set out in the Third-Party Transfer Notice.

6.3 In connection with each Transfer of Equity Interests hereunder:

(a) Each Party participating in any such Transfer of Equity Interests, whether as Transferring Party or Purchasing Party, shall take all actions as may reasonably be necessary to consummate such Transfer, including entering into agreements and delivery of such certificates, instruments, consents, waivers and other documents as may be necessary or appropriate, in each case in the agreed form (collectively, the "Transfer Documentation").

(b) Each Party shall exercise all of its Voting Rights to approve the Transfer transactions pursuant to this Clause 6, cause the Company to complete all related registrations in respect thereof, and shall waive any rights under Applicable Law inconsistent with the provisions hereof.

(c) At completion of each such Transfer of Equity Interests between the Parties, upon receipt of confirmation of payment by the Purchasing Party of the purchase price for the Transfer of Equity Interests in the form of confirmed wire transfer of immediately available funds, each of the Transferring Party and the Purchasing Party shall deliver all of the relevant Transfer Documentation in their possession to the designated representative of the Company, who shall be responsible to register the change in ownership with the AMR[and apply for approval from the Approval and Record-filing Authority].

6.4 Notwithstanding any other provision of this Agreement or the Articles of Association, if any person who is not already a Party acquires any Equity Interests, such person shall, as a condition precedent to such acquisition, execute an amended and restated version of this Agreement and the Articles of Association in the agreed form.

6.3 关于本协议项下的每项股权转让：

（a）参与任何该等股权转让的每一方，无论是转让方还是购买方，均应采取一切合理必要的行动来完成该等转让，包括签订约定形式的协议并交付必要或适当的约定形式的证书、文书、同意书、弃权书和其他文件（合称为“转让文件”）。

（b）每一方应根据本协议第6条行使其全部表决权以批准转让交易，促使合资公司完成与此有关的所有相关登记，并应放弃适用法律项下不符合本协议规定的任何权利。

（c）双方间的每项该等股权转让完成后，在收到购买方通过经确认的即时可用资金的电汇完成对股权转让的购买价格的支付的确认后，转让方和购买方应将其拥有的所有相关转让文件交付给合资公司的指定代表，该代表应负责向市场监督管理局登记所有权变更【并向审批和备案机关申请获得批准】。

6.4 无论本协议或公司章程有何其他规定，如果任何尚未成为一方的人获得任何股权，则其应签署一份约定形式的本协议和公司章程的修订和重述版本，作为获得该等股权的前提条件。

6.5 受限于且在遵守适用法律规定的情况下，一方可以对其持有的任何股权设定权利负担。

6.6 一方就股权的转让而产生的所有成本和费用应由其自行承担。

6.7 违反本协议条款的任何声称或试图转让合资公司股权的行为自始至终均为无效，双方应使合资公司不得采取行动向市场监督管理局登记所有权变更【或向审批和备案

6.5 A Party may create an Encumbrance over any Equity Interests held by it subject to and in compliance with Applicable Law.

6.6 All costs and expenses incurred by a Party in connection with a Transfer of Equity Interests shall be for its own account.

6.7 Any purported or attempted Transfer of Equity Interests of the Company in violation of the terms of this Agreement shall be null and void ab initio, the Parties shall cause that the Company shall take no steps to register the change in ownership with the AMR[or apply for approval from the Approval and Record-filing Authority], and the purported transferee pursuant thereto shall have no rights as a holder of Equity Interests of the Company of any nature whatsoever under this Agreement or the Articles of Association.

6.8 [The Parties acknowledge that Party A is a state-owned enterprise and shall comply with relevant SASAC rules when transferring its equity interest . If anything in this Clause 6 is inconsistent with applicable SASAC rules, the SASAC rules shall prevail, and Party B shall provide all reasonable assistance to Party A to fulfil the relevant requirements under the applicable SASAC rules.]

7. SHAREHOLDERS MEETINGS AND RESOLUTIONS

7.1 The Shareholders Meeting is the highest authority of the Company.

7.2 The first meeting of the shareholders shall be held within [five] Business Days following the Business License Issuance Date. The First Shareholders Meeting Resolutions shall be presented for approval at the first meeting of the shareholders, and each Party shall exercise all of its Voting Rights to approve the same.

7.3 The Parties shall cause that the Company shall hold an annual general meeting of the shareholders to conduct the following business:

(a) to elect the Directors and the Supervisors (other than Supervisors representing the employees of the Company);

(b) to approve the annual budget and financial reports of the Company;

(c) to determine the annual allocations to the Company's discretionary accumulation fund and approve the retention of earnings and distribution of Distributable Profits by way of dividends in accordance with the terms of this

机关申请获得批准】，据此所声称的受让方不应享有本协议或公司章程项下作为合资公司股权持有者所享有的任何性质的权利。

6.8 【双方承认甲方是一家国有企业，在转让其股权时应遵守国资委的相关规定。如果本协议第 6 条的任何规定与适用的国资委规定相冲突，应以国资委规定为准，并且乙方应向甲方提供所有合理协助以满足适用的国资委规定项下的相关要求。】

7. 股东会及其决议

7.1 股东会是合资公司的最高权力机构。

7.2 第一次股东会会议应在营业执照颁发日后【五】个工作日内召开。第一次股东会决议应提交第一次股东会会议批准，每一方应行使其全部表决权以使其通过。

7.3 双方应促使合资公司召开年度股东会会议以完成以下事项：

(a) 选举董事及监事（作为合资公司职工代表的监事除外）；

(b) 通过合资公司的年度预算及财务报告；

(c) 确定合资公司任意公积金的年度提取比例，并按照本协议的条款批准留存收益以及以股息的方式对可分配利润的分配；以及

(d) 完成适用法律和公司章程规定的其他事项。

7.4 应 1/3 以上的董事、一方（只要其持有 10% 以上的合资公司注册资本）或监事会的要求，可召开临时股东会会议。在每种情形下，该等请求均应采用书面形式，并以合理的详细程度具体说明拟议事项（该等事项应为本协议、公司章程和适用法律项下在股东会职权范围内的事

Agreement; and

(d) to conduct such other business as provided in the Articles of Association and in accordance with Applicable Law.

7.4 Interim meetings of the shareholders may be held as requested by more than one-third of the Directors of the Board, at the request of a Party (so long as it holds 10% or more of the Registered Capital of the Company), or at the request of the Board of Supervisors. In each case, such request shall be in writing and specify the matters proposed to be discussed in reasonable detail (which shall be matters within the authority of the Shareholders Meeting under this Agreement, the Articles of Association and Applicable Law) and shall be delivered to the Chairman, the Vice Chairman, the Secretary and the Parties (or the other Party as the case may be).

7.5 The Board shall convene and the Chairman of the Board shall preside over the annual general meeting and any interim meetings of the shareholders. If the Chairman is unable or fails to perform his duties, such meetings of the shareholders shall be presided over by the Vice Chairman. If the Vice Chairman is unable or fails to perform his duties, a director nominated by the Board by Simple Majority Board Resolution (the "Responsible Director") shall preside over the meetings of the shareholders.

7.6 The Secretary, under the direction of the Chairman, Vice Chairman or the Responsible Director, shall give each Party at least [20] Business Days written notice in advance of any meeting of the shareholders. Such notice shall specify the date, time and place of such meeting. Such written notice shall be accompanied by a copy of the agenda, the proposed draft resolutions and other related materials. The foregoing notice requirements may be waived in respect of a meeting of the shareholders with the assent of both Parties before, during or after such meeting. If a Party attends a meeting of the shareholders, such Party shall be deemed to have waived notice of such meeting.

7.7 Approval of resolutions in respect of the following matters shall be by shareholders representing more than two-thirds of the Voting Rights of the Company (each a "Supermajority Shareholders Resolution"):

项），且该等书面请求应递交董事长、副董事长、董秘和双方（或另一方，视情况而定）。

7.5 年度股东会会议及临时股东会会议应由董事会召集，董事长主持。如果董事长无法或未能履行其职责，该等股东会会议应由副董事长主持。如果副董事长无法或未能履行其职责，董事会通过简单多数董事会决议选举的董事（“责任董事”）应主持股东会会议。

7.6 董秘在董事长、副董事长或责任董事的指导下，应在股东会会议召开前至少【20】个工作日向每一方发出书面通知。该等通知应载明该等会议的日期、时间和地点。该等书面通知应附有议程、拟议的决议草案和其他有关材料的复印件。在会议之前、期间或之后，经双方同意，可以免除上述有关股东会议的通知要求。一方如果出席股东会议，则视为其已放弃该等会议的通知要求。

7.7 关于以下事项的决议须经代表目标公司 2/3 以上表决权的股东表决通过（“绝对多数股东会决议”）：

（a）对公司章程的修订；

（b）任何增资或减资；

（c）合资公司与任何其他实体或公司的合并或其他形式的联合；

（d）合资公司分立为两个或两个以上独立的法律实体；

（e）合资公司的解散或清算；

（f）合资公司的公司形式的变更；

（g）按照本协议的条款批准留存收益以及以股息的方式对可分配利润的分配；或

（h）本协议或适用法律规定的须经绝对多数股东会决议通过的其他事项。

(a) the amendment of the Articles of Association;

(b) any Capital Increase or Capital Reduction;

(c) the merger, amalgamation or other combination of the Company with any other entity or company;

(d) the division the Company into two or more separate legal entities;

(e) the dissolution, winding up or liquidation of the Company;

(f) the conversion of the corporate form of the Company;

(g) the approval of the retention of earnings and distribution of Distributable Profits by way of dividends in accordance with the terms of this Agreement; or

(h) such other matters which require Supermajority Shareholders Resolution as provided in this Agreement or under Applicable Law.

7.8 The following matters shall be approved by Simple Majority Shareholders Resolution:

(a) the election of the Directors and the Supervisors (other than the Supervisor elected as the workers' representative) and approval of their compensation;

(b) the approval of the company's operation guidelines and investment plans;

(c) the approval of the annual budget and financial reports of the Company;

(d) the determination of the annual allocations to the Company's discretionary accumulation fund;

(e) the review and approval of other reports of the Board of Directors and the Board of Supervisors as required pursuant to Applicable Law;

(f) the approval of the granting by the Company of a financial guaranty on behalf of a shareholder or actual controller of the Company; or

(g) the approval of all other matters which require shareholder approval under Applicable Law other than such matters which require Supermajority Shareholders Resolution as provided in this Agreement or under Applicable Law.

7.9 Meetings of the shareholders may be attended by Party representatives in person, by proxy or by telecommunications.

7.8 以下事项须经简单多数股东会决议通过：

（a）董事及监事（作为职工代表的监事除外）的选举及其报酬的批准；

（b）公司经营方针和投资计划的批准；

（c）合资公司的年度预算及财务报告的批准；

（d）合资公司年度任意公积金提取比例的确定；

（e）审议批准适用法律要求的董事会和监事会的其他报告；

（f）公司为公司股东或者实际控制人提供财务担保的批准；

（g）除本协议或适用法律项下须经绝对多数股东会决议通过的事项以外的须经股东会批准通过的其他所有事项的批准。

7.9 每一方的代表可以亲自、委托他人或通过电信方式出席股东会。

7.10 股东会可以通过书面决议代替任何定期或临时的股东会议，前提是该等决议发送给双方并经双方同意签署和批准。

7.11 股东僵局事件应作如下处理：

（a）如果一项股东僵局事件发生，任一方可在发生股东僵局事件的股东会议后【20】个工作日内，请求召开后续的临时股东会议重新审议股东僵局事件。

（b）在发生股东僵局事件的股东会议至后续临时股东会议召开的期间，双方应就股东僵局事件交换其他信息和观点。除非双方通过临时讨论达成一致，

7.10 In lieu of any regular or interim meeting of the shareholders, a written resolution may be adopted by the Shareholders Meeting if such resolution is sent to both Parties and is affirmatively signed and adopted by both Parties.

7.11 Shareholder Deadlock Matters shall be addressed as provided below:

(a) If a Shareholder Deadlock Matter arises, either Party may, within [20] Business Days after the meeting of the shareholders at which the Shareholder Deadlock Matter arose, request a subsequent interim meeting of the shareholders to reconsider the Shareholder Deadlock Matter.

(b) During the period between the meeting of the shareholders at which the Shareholder Deadlock Matter arose and the subsequent interim meeting of the shareholders, the Parties shall exchange additional information and views with respect to the Shareholder Deadlock Matter. Unless the Parties achieve consensus through interim discussions, the Parties shall meet in-person at such subsequent interim meeting to reconsider and resolve the Shareholder Deadlock Matter.

(c) If the Shareholder Deadlock Matter is not resolved in accordance with Clause 7.11(b), then either Party shall have the right to submit a Termination Notice in accordance with the provisions of Clause 14.3(d).

(d) No Shareholder Deadlock Matter may be referred by a Party for determination by arbitration pursuant to Clause 24.

8. BOARD OF DIRECTORS

8.1 The Parties shall cause that the Company shall establish a Board of Directors to be responsible for the supervision and management of the Company and the Business in accordance with the terms of this Agreement, the Articles of Association and Applicable Law.

8.2 The composition of the Board shall be as follows:

(a) The Board shall consist of [five] Directors.

(b) Party A shall have the right to nominate [three] of the [five] Directors.

(c) Party B shall have the right to nominate [two] of the [five] Directors.

8.3 Directors shall satisfy all qualification requirements under Applicable Law,

双方应亲自出席该等后续临时会议重新审议和解决股东僵局事件。

（c）如果股东僵局事件未根据本协议第 7.11（b）条得到解决，则任一方均有权依据本协议第 14.3（d）条提交终止通知。

（d）任何一方不得根据本协议第 24 条将股东僵局事件提交仲裁解决。

8. 董事会

8.1 双方应促使合资公司根据本协议、公司章程和适用法律的条款设立董事会，负责对合资公司和目标业务的监督和管理。

8.2 董事会的组成如下：

（a）董事会应由【五】名董事组成。

（b）甲方有权提名【五】名董事中的【三】名。

（c）乙方有权提名【五】名董事中的【两】名。

8.3 董事应满足适用法律项下的所有资格要求，包括公司法中的要求。提名董事的一方应将该等提名，连同该等提名的董事的姓名、职位、国籍、任职资格和履历提交另一方以及董事长和董秘。

8.4 董事的选任、罢免和更换应遵守以下规定：

（a）每名董事应由股东会选举产生，任期【三】年，如果经原提名方再次提名并经股东会再次选举通过，可以连任。

（b）受限于股东会的批准，董事应为提名该董事的一方服务并可以由其罢免。如董事席位因任何董事退休、辞职、患病、伤残或死亡，或被提名该董

including those requirements set out in the Company Law. The Party nominating a Director shall submit such nomination to the other Party and the Chairman and the Secretary together with the names, titles, nationalities, qualifications and credentials of the Directors so nominated by it.

8.4 Directors shall be elected, removed and replaced as follows:

(a) Each Director shall be elected by the Shareholders Meeting for a term of [three] years and may serve consecutive terms if re-nominated by the Party originally nominating him and re-elected by the Shareholders Meeting.

(b) A Director shall serve and may be removed at the pleasure of the Party that nominated him subject to the approval of the Shareholders Meeting. If a seat on the Board is vacated by the retirement, resignation, illness, disability or death of a Director or by the removal of such Director by the Party which originally nominated him, the Party which originally nominated such Director shall nominate a successor or replacement for such Director for approval by the Shareholders Meeting.

(c) Each nomination for election or removal of a Director shall be submitted to the Shareholders Meeting for approval at the next regular or interim meeting of the shareholders or by written resolution pursuant to Clause 7.10. The Secretary shall record such election or removal of a Director in the Company's books and register the same with the AMR.

(d) Each Party shall exercise all of its Voting Rights at any regular or interim meeting of the shareholders to elect to the Board each person nominated as a Director by a Party in accordance with this Agreement (including any successor or replacement Director).

8.5 A Director nominated by [Party A] shall serve as Chairman and a Director nominated by [Party B] shall serve as Vice Chairman. The term of appointment of the Chairman and Vice Chairman shall be [three] years and each may serve consecutive terms if re-nominated by the original nominating Party.

8.6 The Chairman shall be the legal representative of the Company (the "Legal Representative"). The Legal Representative shall not perform any act binding on the Company without the prior approval and authorization of the Shareholders

事的一方罢免而空出，则原提名该董事的一方应提名该董事的继任者或替代者，提交股东会批准。

（c）每次提名董事的任免均应在下一次定期或临时股东会议上提交股东会批准，或根据本协议第 7.10 条通过董事会书面决议批准。董秘应在合资公司的名册中记录该等董事的任免，并向市场监督管理局登记。

（d）每一方应根据本协议，在任何定期或临时的股东会会议上行使其全部表决权，以选举一方提名的每位董事（包括任何继任或替代董事）。

8.5 董事长应由【甲方】提名的董事担任，副董事长应由【乙方】提名的董事担任。董事长和副董事长的任期应为【三】年，经原提名方再次提名可连任。

8.6 董事长应为合资公司的法定代表人（“法定代表人”）。未经股东会或董事会（视情况而定）事先批准和授权，法定代表人不得实施任何对合资公司具有法律约束力的行为。

8.7 董事长可以指定一名董秘协助管理董事会事务。董秘应有责任心且成熟，掌握流利的中英文口语和书面写作能力。董秘应在董事长的监督下，按照本协议和公司章程的规定履行其职责。董秘可以是合资公司或一方的职工，但不得担任董事。董秘的任期为【三】年，经董事长再次任命，可以连任。董秘应履行董事长委派的职责。

8.8 董事会可以不时设立一个或多个董事会委员会，其成员及委托权限由董事会一致决议批准。

8.9 董事长、副董事长、董秘和每名董事应依照适用法律或者董事会可能采取的其他道德政策（统称为“适用的道德规则”），对合资公司承担受托责任。

Meeting or the Board, as the case may be.

8.7 The Chairman may appoint a Secretary to assist with the management of the affairs of the Board. The Secretary shall be a responsible and mature individual who is fluent in written and spoken English and Chinese. The Secretary shall perform his duties in accordance with the provisions of this Agreement and the Articles of Association under the supervision of the Chairman. The Secretary may be an employee of the Company or of a Party but shall not be a Director. The term of the Secretary's appointment shall be [three] years and may serve consecutive terms if re-appointed by the Chairman. The Secretary shall have such duties as assigned by the Chairman.

8.8 The Board may from time to time establish one or more Board committees comprised of such Directors and with such delegation of authority as approved by the Board by Unanimous Board Resolution.

8.9 The Chairman, Vice Chairman, Secretary and each Director shall bear fiduciary responsibilities to the Company in accordance with Applicable Law and such additional ethical policies as the Board may adopt (collectively, "applicable ethical rules").

8.10 The Chairman, Vice Chairman, Secretary and each of the Directors shall serve without remuneration, but all reasonable costs incurred by the Chairman, Vice Chairman, Secretary and each Director in connection with the attendance at meetings of the Board and the performance of duties assigned by the Board shall be borne by the Company in accordance with such policies and guidelines as the Board may adopt from time to time by Unanimous Board Resolution.

8.11 None of the Chairman, Vice Chairman, Secretary or the Directors shall bear any personal liability for any acts performed in good faith in such capacity as assigned by the Board, except for willful misconduct, and/or acts in violation of Applicable Law or applicable ethical rules. Subject to the foregoing, the Parties shall cause that the Company shall (a) take out and maintain at all times D&O Insurance at appropriate levels approved by the Board and (b) enter into appropriate indemnity undertakings in favor of the Chairman, Vice Chairman, Secretary and each Director on such terms as the Board may approve from time to time by

8.10 董事长、副董事长、董秘和每名董事不收取报酬，但董事长、副董事长、董秘和每名董事因出席董事会会议和履行董事会职责而产生的所有合理费用应根据董事会一致决议不时通过的政策和准则由合资公司承担。

8.11 董事长、副董事长、董秘和董事均不得因在董事会委派的权限内善意履行的任何行为而承担任何个人责任，但故意不当行为和/或违反适用法律或适用的道德规则的行为除外。受限于上述规定，双方应促使合资公司（a）取得并始终维持董事会批准的适当程度的董事及高级管理人员责任保险，并（b）按照董事会在符合适用法律的情况下可能不时通过董事会一致决议批准的条款，订立以董事长、副董事长、董秘和每名董事为受益人的适当赔偿保证。

9. 董事会会议及其决议

9.1 董事会会议应按照以下规定召开和进行：

（a）第一次董事会会议应在营业执照颁发日后【五】个工作日内召开，并可在第一次股东会会议当日在第一次股东会会议事项（包括第一次股东会决议的正式通过）完成后召开。第一次董事会决议应在第一次董事会会议上提请批准，每一方均应使其提名的董事投票赞成该决议。

（b）定期董事会会议每年至少召开【两】次。会议一般应在合资公司的注册地址或董事会指定的其他地址召开。

（c）经【两名】或【两名】以上董事书面请求，应安排召开临时董事会会议。在请求召开临时董事会会议的情况下，该等请求应采用书面形式，并以合理的详细程度具体说明拟议事项（该等事项应

Unanimous Board Resolution consistent with Applicable Law.

9. BOARD MEETINGS AND RESOLUTIONS

9.1 Meetings of the Board shall be held and conducted in accordance with the following terms:

(a) The first Board meeting shall be held within [five] Business Days following the Business License Issuance Date, and may be held on the same day as the first meeting of the shareholders following the conclusion of the business of the first meeting of the shareholders, including the due adoption of the First Shareholders Meeting Resolutions. The First Board Meeting Resolutions shall be presented for approval at the first Board meeting, and each of the Parties shall cause that the Directors nominated by it shall vote in favor thereof.

(b) Regular Board meetings shall be held at least [two] times per year. Meetings generally shall be held at the registered address of the Company or such other address designated by the Board.

(c) An interim Board meeting shall be scheduled upon the written request of [two] or more of the Directors of the Company. In the case of a request for an interim Board meeting, such request shall be in writing and specify the matters proposed to be discussed in reasonable detail (which shall be matters within the authority of the Board under this Agreement, the Articles of Association and Applicable Law) and shall be delivered to the Chairman, the Vice Chairman, the Secretary and each of the other Directors.

(d) The Chairman of the Board shall convene and preside over all regular and interim Board meetings. If the Chairman is unable or fails to perform his duties, such Board meetings shall be convened and presided over by the Vice Chairman. If the Vice Chairman is unable or fails to perform his duties, a Responsible Director shall convene and preside over the meetings of the Board.

(e) The Secretary, under the direction of the Chairman, Vice Chairman or the Responsible Director, shall give each Director at least [20] Business Days written notice in advance of such each regular or interim Board meeting, specifying the date, time and place thereof. Written notice shall be accompanied

为本协议、公司章程和适用法律项下在董事会职权范围内的事项），且该等书面请求应递交董事长、副董事长、董秘和其他各个董事。

（d）董事长应召集并主持所有定期和临时董事会会议。如果董事长无法或未能履行其职责，该等董事会会议应由副董事长召集并主持。如果副董事长无法或未能履行其职责，责任董事应召集并主持董事会会议。

（e）在董事长、副董事长或责任董事的指导下，董秘应在每一次定期和临时董事会会议召开前至少【20】个工作日向每名董事发出书面通知，载明该等会议的日期、时间和地点。书面通知应附有议程以及董事长、副董事长或责任董事确定的其他相关材料。董事可在收到会议通知后【三】个工作日内提交书面请求，提议在议程中添加议题，董秘应在董事长、副董事长或责任董事的指导下，及时对议程做出相应的修改，并将修改后的会议通知重新分发给每名董事。只有在该等书面通知中提及的事项方可在董事会会议上提交讨论和处理。未经全体董事同意，其他事项不得在该等董事会会议上进行讨论。

（f）在该等董事会会议之前、期间或之后，经全体董事同意，可以免除上述有关董事会会议的通知要求。董事如果出席董事会会议，则视为已放弃该等会议的通知要求。

（g）董事应亲自、委托他人或通过电信方式出席董事会会议。

（h）如果某一董事不能亲自或通过电信方式参加董事

by the agenda and such other materials relating thereto as determined by the Chairman, Vice Chairman or the Responsible Director. A Director may, within [three] Business Days following the receipt of the meeting notice, submit a written request proposing to add items to the agenda, and the Secretary, under the direction of the Chairman, Vice Chairman or the Responsible Director, shall promptly revise the agenda accordingly and re-circulate the revised meeting notice to each Director. Only matters addressed in such written notice may be presented for discussion and action at the Board meeting. Without the consent of all of the Directors, no other business shall be transacted at such Board meeting.

(f) The foregoing notice requirements may be waived in respect of a Board meeting with the assent of all of the Directors before, during or after such Board meeting. If a Director attends a Board meeting, he shall be deemed to have waived notice of such meeting.

(g) Board meetings may be attended by Directors in person, by proxy or by telecommunications.

(h) If a Director is unable to participate in a Board meeting in person or by telecommunications, he may issue a written proxy and entrust a representative to participate in the meeting on his behalf. The representative so entrusted shall have the same rights and powers as the Director.

(i) No fewer than [three] Directors of the Company, including at least one Director nominated by Party B, present in person, by proxy or by telecommunications shall constitute a quorum necessary for the conduct of business at a meeting of the Board. If a quorum is not achieved at any duly called meeting of the Board, such Board meeting may be postponed to a time no earlier than [48] hours after the written notice of such postponement has been given to each of the Directors.

(j) Each Director shall have one vote. The Chairman shall have one vote in his capacity as a Director but shall not have an additional casting vote.

9.2 Approval of the following matters shall be by Unanimous Board Resolution:

会会议，该董事可以出具书面委托书，委托一名代理人代表其参加会议。被委托的代理人应有与董事相同的权利和权力。

（i）不少于【三】名合资公司的董事（包括至少一名由乙方提名的董事）亲自、委托他人或通过电信方式出席，即构成在董事会会议上执行议程所需的法定人数。如果任何经正式召集的董事会会议的出席人数未达到法定人数，则该等董事会会议可推迟至向每名董事发出书面延迟通知后的不少于【48】小时后。

（j）每名董事应有一票表决权。董事长应有其作为董事的一票表决权，但没有额外的决定票表决权。

9.2 以下事项须经董事会一致决议批准：

（a）通过业务计划以及批准（i）业务计划的重大修订和（ii）业务计划批准范围之外的任何重大交易；

（b）根据本协议条款就留存收益以及以股息的方式对可分配利润的分配制定提案，并将其提交股东会批准；

（c）设立子公司；

（d）出售或以其他方式处置全部或实质上全部合资公司的目标业务或资产，或批准就全部或实质上全部合资公司的目标业务或资产设定权利负担；

（e）开始或解决任何担责金额超过人民币【填入金额】元的法律诉讼或协议；

（f）合资公司就（i）重大交易，或（ii）与任何一方、一方关联方或高级管理人员的关联方交易，订立、修改、终止任何协议，或放弃该等协议项下的任

(a) the adoption of the Business Plan and approval of (i) material amendments thereto and (ii) any Material Transactions outside the approved scope of thereof;

(b) formulation of proposals in respect of the retention of earnings and distribution of Distributable Profits by way of dividends in accordance with the terms of this Agreement, and submission of the same to the Shareholders Meeting for approval;

(c) establishment of a Subsidiary;

(d) sale or other disposition of, or granting of an Encumbrance over, all or substantially all of the Business or the assets of the Company;

(e) commencement or settlement of any Legal Action or agreement to assume any liability with a value in excess of RMB [AMOUNT];

(f) the Company's entering into, amending, terminating or waiving any rights under, any Agreement in respect of (i) a Material Transaction, or (ii) a Related Party Transaction with any Party, Party Affiliate or Management Personnel; and

(g) such other matters which require Unanimous Board Resolution as provided in this Agreement or under Applicable Law.

9.3 Approval of the following matters shall be by Simple Majority Board Resolution:

(a) formulation of proposals in respect of the Company's annual budgets and financial reports, and submission of the same to the Shareholders Meeting for reference and/or action as appropriate;

(b) review and approval of the Company's annual production and operation plans;

(c) review and approval of Company policies and procedures regarding management of financial accounts, execution of legal documents, applicable ethical rules and ethical practices and other important matters;

(d) decisions on the appointment, compensation, discipline and dismissal of the Management Personnel;

(e) the establishment of Company bank accounts and the appointment of the Company's Independent Auditor;

何权利；以及

（g）根据本协议和适用法律的规定须经董事会一致决议通过的其他事项。

9.3 以下事项须经简单多数董事会决议批准：

（a）起草合资公司的年度预算及财务报告方案，并将其提交股东会以供参考和/或酌情处理；

（b）审阅并批准合资公司的年度生产和运营计划；

（c）审阅并批准合资公司关于财务账目管理、法律文件签署、适用的道德规则和道德惯例以及其他重要事项的政策和程序；

（d）就高级管理人员的任命、薪酬、纪律和免职做出决定；

（e）开立合资公司银行账户以及任命合资公司的独立审计师；

（f）在单笔交易或一系列相关交易中采取总计价值超过人民币【填入金额】元或等值【美元】【或】【欧元】金额的银行信贷措施或贷款；

（g）在单笔交易或一系列相关交易中购买总计价值超过人民币【填入金额】元或等值【美元】【或】【欧元】金额的固定设备、土地及建筑物或其他资产，根据董事会和股东会（视情况而定）批准的经营预算进行购买的除外；

（h）超出经批准的年度预算或财务计划的任何支出，或严重偏离经批准的年度预算或财务计划的任何交易；

（i）向任何第三方发放任何金额的贷款或信贷（以标准的递延付款条款向客户出售合资公司产品或服务，

(f) the establishment of bank credit facilities or the borrowing of loans having an aggregate value in excess of RMB [AMOUNT] or its equivalent in [USD][OR][EUR] in a single transaction or a series of related transactions;

(g) the purchase of capital equipment, land and buildings or other assets having an aggregate value in excess of RMB [AMOUNT] or its equivalent in [USD][OR][EUR] in a single transaction or a series of related transactions other than such purchases made in accordance with the operating budget approved by the Board and (as appropriate) the Shareholders Meeting;

(h) any expenditure in excess of, or any transaction that materially deviates from the approved annual budget or financial plan;

(i) the granting of loans or credit to any third parties in any amount (other than the sale of the Company's products or services to customers on standard deferred payment terms or the granting of purchase credits to customers in the ordinary course of business);

(j) the giving of any financial guarantee by the Company for the obligations of any third party;

(k) the execution of technology license agreements with third parties other than in the ordinary course of business on customary terms and conditions;

(l) the establishment of branch offices and liaison offices; and

(m) any other matter which, in accordance with the provisions of this Agreement, requires Board approval or which the Board determines shall require Board approval.

9.4 In lieu of any regular or interim meeting of the Board, a written resolution may be adopted by the Board if such resolution is sent to, and affirmatively signed and adopted by, all Directors then holding office.

9.5 Board Deadlock Matters shall be addressed as provided below:

(a) If a Board Deadlock Matter arises, one or more Directors nominated by a Party may, within [20] Business Days after the Board meeting at which the Board Deadlock Matter arose, submit a Deadlock Notice in the agreed form to the Chairman and all other Directors.

或在日常运营过程中向客户授予先发货后收款待遇的除外）；

（j）合资公司就任何第三方的义务提供任何财务担保；

（k）与第三方签署技术许可协议，在日常运营过程中以惯常的条款和条件签订的该等协议除外；

（l）设立分支机构和联络处；以及

（m）根据本协议的条款或根据董事会的决定，须经董事会批准的任何其他事项。

9.4 董事会可以通过书面决议代替任何定期或临时董事会会议，前提是该等决议发送给届时在任的所有董事并经其同意签署和通过。

9.5 董事会僵局事件应按照以下规定处理：

（a）如果一项董事会僵局事件发生，一方提名的一名或多名董事可在发生董事会僵局事件的董事会会议后【20】个工作日内，向董事长和其他所有董事发出约定形式的僵局通知。

（b）在发出僵局通知后【五】个工作日内，董事长应将该等董事会僵局事件提交双方高级代表，该等代表应尽一切合理努力在自该等董事会僵局事件提交之日起【20】个工作日内善意地解决该等董事会僵局事件。由双方高级代表同意的有关该等董事会僵局事件的任何解决方案应为最终决定，对合资公司和双方均具有约束力。

（c）如果未能根据本协议第 9.5（b）条解决董事会僵局事件，则任何一方应有权根据本协议第 14.3（d）条的规定提交终止通知。

（d）任何一方不得根据本协议第 24 条将董事会僵局事

(b) Within [five] Business Days after submission of the Deadlock Notice, the Chairman shall refer such Board Deadlock Matter to the Senior Representatives of the Parties, who shall use all reasonable endeavors in good faith to resolve such Board Deadlock Matter within [20] Business Days from the date of such referral. Any resolution of such Board Deadlock Matter agreed to by the Senior Representatives of the Parties shall be final and binding on the Company and the Parties.

(c) If the Board Deadlock Matter is not resolved in accordance with Clause 9.5(b), then either Party shall have the right to submit a Termination Notice in accordance with the provisions of Clause 14.3(d).

(d) No Board Deadlock Matter may be referred by a Party for determination by arbitration pursuant to Clause 24.

9.6 The corporate governance provisions set out in Clauses 9.1 through 9.4 shall also apply to each Subsidiary, and the Parties shall cause that the Company shall ensure that corresponding provisions are incorporated into the Articles of Association of each such Subsidiary or otherwise adopted by such Subsidiary.

10. BOARD OF SUPERVISORS

10.1 The Parties shall cause that the Company shall have a Board of Supervisors comprised of three Supervisors as follows: one Supervisor nominated by Party A, one Supervisor nominated by Party B, and one Supervisor to be the workers' representative. The Supervisors nominated by Party A and Party B shall be elected by the Shareholders Meeting. The Supervisor who is the workers' representative shall be elected by the workers through the workers' representative congress or other democratic means. The term of office of a Supervisor shall be three years. A Supervisor may serve consecutive terms on expiration of his term if re-elected as provided herein. The position of Supervisor cannot be held concurrently by any Director or other Management Personnel of the Company.

10.2 The Board of Supervisors shall have one chairman, who shall be the Supervisor nominated by [Party A]. The chairman of the Board of Supervisors shall convene and preside over meetings of the Board of Supervisors. If the chairman of the Board of Supervisors is unable or fails to perform his duties, another Supervisor

件提交仲裁解决。

9.6 本协议第 9.1~9.4 条所述的公司治理的规定亦适用于各子公司，且双方应促使合资公司确保相应规定已纳入各子公司的公司章程或以其他方式被该等子公司所采用。

10. 监事会

10.1 双方应促使合资公司设立监事会，监事会由三名监事组成，其中一名监事由甲方提名，一名监事由乙方提名，一名监事为职工代表。甲方和乙方提名的监事应通过股东会选举产生。作为职工代表的监事由职工通过职工代表大会或其他民主方式选举产生。监事的任期为三年。任期届满后，按照本条规定的选举方式可连选连任。监事不得兼任合资公司的任何董事或其他高级管理人员。

10.2 监事会设主席一名，由【甲方】提名的监事担任。监事会主席应召集和主持监事会会议。监事会主席不能或未能履行职责的，由全体监事以简单多数选举一名监事召集和主持监事会会议。

10.3 监事会会议每年应至少召开【一】次。任何监事有权提议召开临时监事会会议。监事会主席应在该等定期和临时监事会会议召开前至少【20】个工作日向每名监事发出书面通知，载明该等会议的日期、时间和地点。该等书面通知应附有议程以及适用法律要求的和监事会主席确定的其他相关材料。监事会决议应经简单多数票通过。每位监事具有一票表决权。监事会主席无决定票表决权。

10.4 如果某一监事退休、辞职、患病或失去法律行为能力，该监事的继任者应以与该监事相同的方式通过提名和选举产生。该等继任监事将完成前任监事的剩余任期。

elected by simple majority vote of all of the Supervisors shall convene and preside over the meeting of the Board of Supervisors.

10.3 Meetings of the Board of Supervisors shall be held at least [once] per year. Any Supervisor is entitled to propose the convening of an interim meeting of the Board of Supervisors. The chairman of the Board of Supervisors shall give each Supervisor at least [20] Business Days written notice in advance of such each regular or interim meeting of the Board of Supervisors, specifying the date, time and place thereof. Such written notice shall be accompanied by the agenda and such other materials relating thereto as required under Applicable Law and as determined by the chairman of the Board of Supervisors. The Board of Supervisors shall take decisions by simple majority vote. Each Supervisor shall have one vote. The chairman of the Board of Supervisors shall not have a casting vote.

10.4 If a Supervisor retires, resigns, falls ill or loses legal capacity, the successor of the Supervisor shall be nominated and elected in the same manner as the Supervisor to be replaced. Such successor Supervisor will serve the remaining term of office of the previous Supervisor. If the re-election of the Supervisor is not conducted in a timely fashion upon the expiration of the term of the Supervisor, or if the Supervisor resigns during his term of office, thereby resulting in the Company temporarily having no successor Supervisor, then during the period prior to the successor Supervisor taking up office, the existing Supervisor(s) shall continue to perform the duties of such Supervisor in accordance with Applicable Law, the provisions of this Agreement and the Articles of Association.

10.5 The Board of Supervisors exercises the following functions and duties:

(a) examining the Company's financial affairs;

(b) supervising the Directors and Management Personnel in the performance of their duties and to propose the removal of Directors or Management Personnel who violate laws, administrative regulations, the Articles of Association or resolutions of the Board;

(c) requiring Directors or Management Personnel to rectify their acts which are

如果在监事任期届满后没有及时重新选举监事，或者监事在任期内辞职，从而导致合资公司暂时没有继任监事，则在继任监事上任之前，现任监事应继续按照适用法律、本协议和公司章程的规定履行监事的职责。

10.5 监事会履行以下职责：

（a）审查合资公司的财务状况；

（b）监督董事及高级管理人员履行职责，并提议罢免违反法律、行政法规、公司章程或董事会决议的董事或高级管理人员；

（c）要求董事或高级管理人员纠正其有损合资公司利益的行为；

（d）向双方提交提案；

（e）应双方的要求，对违反法律、行政法规或公司章程并由此导致合资公司蒙受损失的董事或高级管理人员提起法律诉讼；以及

（f）适用法律和公司章程规定的其他职能和权力。

此外，监事可以作为无表决权的与会者出席董事会会议，并就与董事会决议有关的事项提出问题或建议。

11.管理层

11.1 高级管理人员应由以下人员组成：

（a）总经理，由【乙方】提名；

（b）首席财务官，由【甲方】提名；和

（c）【填入职称】，由【甲方】【或】【乙方】提名。

如果任何高级管理人员被董事会罢免，应由原提名方提名替代者。

detrimental to the Company's interests;

(d) submitting proposals to the Parties;

(e) upon request of the Parties, instituting legal proceedings against Directors or Management Personnel who have violated laws, administrative regulations or the Articles of Association and have thereby caused the Company to incur a loss; and

(f) other functions and powers as provided under Applicable Law and the Articles of Association.

In addition, a Supervisor may attend meetings of the Board of Directors as a non-voting attendee and raise questions or present proposals on matters relating to Board resolutions.

11. MANAGEMENT

11.1 The Management Personnel shall consist of the following:

(a) the General Manager, to be nominated by [Party B];

(b) the CFO, to be nominated by [Party A]; and

(c) the [TITLE], to be nominated by [PARTY A][OR][PARTY B].

If any of the Management Personnel is removed by the Board, the replacement shall be nominated by the original nominating Party.

11.2 If any of the Management Personnel retires, resigns, is unable to perform his duties due to illness, disability or death, or is removed by the Board, the replacement shall be nominated by the original nominating Party.

11.3 Each Party shall cause each of the Directors nominated by it to exercise all of their Voting Rights at any regular or interim Board meeting to appoint the Management Personnel as nominated in accordance with the provisions of this Clause 11 in each case including any successor or replacement nominated by the original nominating Party in accordance with the provisions of this Agreement.

11.4 The Board shall approve the overall operation management structure and system of the Company, and the General Manager shall report to and work under the supervision and direction of the Board. The other Management Personnel shall report to and work under the supervision and direction of the General Manager.

11.2 如果任何高级管理人员退休、辞职，或因患病、残疾或死亡无法履行职责，或被董事会罢免，应由原提名方提名替代者。

11.3 每一方应使其提名的每名董事在任何定期或临时董事会会议上行使其全部表决权，以任命根据本协议第 11 条的规定提名的高级管理人员，包括由原提名方根据本协议的规定提名的任何继任者或替代者。

11.4 董事会应批准合资公司的整体运营管理结构和体系，总经理应向董事会报告，并在其监督和指导下工作。其他高级管理人员应向总经理报告，在其监督和指导下工作。除高级管理人员外，合资公司的全体职工应向高级管理人员和总经理可能决定的其他高级经理报告并在其监督和指导下工作。

11.5 除保留事项外，总经理应负责合资公司的所有日常运营和管理。总经理应对董事会负责，并根据董事会的指示执行所有事项。

12.财务和会计

12.1 双方应促使合资公司始终保持准确完整的会计记录和其他财务记录，并按照企业会计准则——基本准则【和国际财务报告准则】编制所有账目和财务报表。

12.2 双方应促使合资公司采用人民币作为记账本位币，但也可以采用【美元】【或】【欧元】或其他外币作为辅助记账货币。

12.3 合资公司的所有会计记录、凭单、账簿和报表均应以中英文编制和保存。

12.4 合资公司的会计年度应从每年的 1 月 1 日起至同年 12 月 31 日结束，但合资公司的第一个会计年度应从营业

All employees of the Company other than the Management Personnel shall report to and work under the supervision and direction of the Management Personnel and such other senior managers as the General Manager may determine.

11.5 The General Manager shall be responsible for all of the day-to-day operations and management of the Company other than Reserved Matters. He shall be responsible to the Board and shall carry out all matters as directed by the Board.

12. FINANCIAL AFFAIRS AND ACCOUNTING

12.1 The Parties shall cause that the Company shall at all times maintain accurate and complete accounting and other financial records, and shall prepare all accounts and financial statements in accordance with the Accounting Standards for Business Enterprises – Basic Standards [and IFRS].

12.2 The Parties shall cause that the Company shall adopt Renminbi as its bookkeeping base currency, but may also adopt [USD][OR][EUR] or other foreign currencies as supplementary bookkeeping currencies.

12.3 All accounting records, vouchers, books and statements of the Company shall be made and kept in Chinese and English.

12.4 The Company's fiscal year shall begin on January 1 and end on December 31 of each year, except that the first fiscal year of the Company shall commence on the Business License Issuance Date and shall end on December 31 of the same year, and the last fiscal year shall commence on January 1 and end on the termination date in the same year.

12.5 For the purposes of preparing the Company's accounts and financial statements, calculation of declared dividends to be distributed to the Parties, and for any other purposes where it may be necessary to effect a currency conversion, such conversion shall be in accordance with the posted exchange rate, as determined by the median exchange rate for buying and selling Renminbi announced by the People's Bank of China or other legally recognized rate on the date of actual receipt or payment.

12.6 The Parties shall cause that the Company shall prepare its financial statements and reports as directed by the Board, including those set out in Clause 12.7. The

执照颁发日开始，并于同年12月31日结束，最后一个会计年度自1月1日开始，并于同年的终止日期结束。

12.5 为编制合资公司的账目和财务报表，计算要向双方分配的已宣告股息，以及对于影响货币换算可能必要的任何其他目的，货币换算应按照实际收付款之日中国人民银行公布的人民币汇率中间价或其他法定汇率所确定的挂牌汇率计算。

12.6 双方应促使合资公司按照董事会的指示编制财务报表和报告，包括本协议第12.7条规定的内容。合资公司的独立审计师应审查并核实合资公司的年度财务报告。

12.7 双方应促使合资公司向每一方提供以下财务报告：

（a）双方应促使合资公司尽早且无论如何不得迟于每个会计年度结束后【90】【或】【120】个日历日，向每一方提供截至该会计年度末的经审计的合资公司资产负债表和该会计年度的经审计的收益表、现金流量表及股东权益变动表的复印件，以及独立审计师的报告。

（b）双方应促使合资公司尽早且无论如何不得迟于每个财政季度结束后【45】【或】【60】个日历日，向每一方提供截至该财政季度末的合资公司资产负债表和该财政季度的收益表、现金流量表和股东权益变动表，且以上文件均已由首席财务官核实。

（c）双方应促使合资公司根据适用法律的要求或任何协议的条款，不时向每一方提供其他可提供的报告的复印件。

12.8 在不限制每一方在本协议第12.7条项下的权利的情况下，每一方（只要其持有合资公司注册资本的10%或

Company's Independent Auditor shall examine and verify the annual financial report of the Company.

12.7 The Parties shall cause that the Company shall provide the following financial reports to each Party:

(a) As soon as available, and in any event no later than [90][OR][120] calendar days after the end of each fiscal year, the Parties shall cause that the Company shall furnish to each Party copies of the audited balance sheet of the Company as at the end of such fiscal year and the audited statements of income, cash flow and changes in shareholders' equity for such fiscal year together with the report of the Independent Auditor.

(b) As soon as available, and in any event no later than [45][OR][60] calendar days after the end of each fiscal quarter, the Parties shall cause that the Company shall furnish to each Party the balance sheet of the Company as at the end of such fiscal quarter and the statements of income, cash flows and changes in Parties' equity for such fiscal quarter, in each case as certified by the CFO.

(c) The Parties shall cause that the Company shall provide to each Party copies of such other reports prepared from time to time pursuant to the requirements of Applicable Law or the terms of any Agreement as and when available.

12.8 Without limiting its rights under Clause 12.7, each Party (so long as it holds 10% or more of the Registered Capital of the Company) shall have the following inspection and audit rights in respect of the Company:

(a) Such Party shall have the right to have reasonable access to the officers, employees, auditors, properties, offices, plants and other facilities of the Company to inspect the assets, operations and affairs of the Company.

(b) Such Party shall have the right, at its own expense, to appoint either the internal staff of such Party or an independent accountant (which may be either an accountant registered abroad or registered in the Territory) to audit the books, accounts and other financial, commercial and legal records of the Company on behalf of such Party.

The Parties shall cause that the Company shall provide reasonable access to all

以上）应对合资公司享有以下检查和审计权利：

（a）该方应有权就合资公司的高级职员、员工、审计师、财产、办公室、工厂和其他设施拥有合理的权限，以检查合资公司的资产、运营和事务。

（b）该方应有权自费任命该方的内部工作人员或独立会计师（可以是在国外注册或在目标地区注册的会计师）代表该方审计合资公司账簿、账目及其他财务、商业和法律记录。

双方应促使合资公司在得到合理的提前通知的情况下，在正常的工作时间内向该请求方及其授权代表提供对该等人员、设施和记录的合理权限。该方及其授权代表和内部或独立审计师应对所有因此获取的信息和文件保密。

12.9 受限于适用法律的要求，除非股东会就任何特定会计年度通过绝对多数股东会决议另有决定，否则双方应促使合资公司按照以下条款向双方分配股息：

（a）每一方应行使其全部表决权，批准以股息的方式分配每个会计年度的【全部】可分配利润【但在所有的股东贷款全部还清之前，双方应促使合资公司不得宣派、支付或做出任何股息分配或其他分配】。

（b）“可分配利润”指减去以下所有必要、合理和审慎的储备金和准备金后的税后净利润：（i）税款；（ii）偿还合资公司债务；（iii）法定公积金和任意公积金的提取；（iv）其他特殊项目。在每种情况下，均应由股东会根据本协议和公司章程的规定及适用法律的要求确定。

（c）股息应按双方各自所持的注册资本比例分配给双方。

such persons, facilities and records to such requesting Party and its authorized representatives during normal business hours upon reasonable advance notice. Such Party and its authorized representatives and internal or independent auditors shall keep confidential all information and documents so accessed.

12.9 Subject to the requirements of Applicable Law, and unless otherwise determined by the Shareholders Meeting by Supermajority Shareholders Resolution for any particular fiscal year, the Parties shall cause that the Company shall distribute dividends to the Parties in accordance with the following terms:

(a) Each Party shall exercise all of its Voting Rights to approve distribution by way of dividend of [all] of the Distributable Profits of the Company for each fiscal year [provided that the Parties shall cause that the Company shall not declare, pay or make any dividend or other distribution until all Shareholder Loans have been repaid in full].

(b) "Distributable Profits" shall mean After-Tax Net Profits less all necessary, reasonable and prudent provisions and reserves for (i) taxation, (ii) the repayment of debt incurred by the Company, (iii) allocations to Statutory and Discretionary Funds, and (iv) other extraordinary items, in each case as determined by the Shareholders Meeting in accordance with the provisions of this Agreement, the Articles of Association and the requirements of Applicable Law.

(c) Dividends shall be distributed to the Parties in proportion to their respective percentage shares of the Registered Capital.

(d) A distribution under Clause 12.9(a) for any fiscal year shall be made within [three] months following the date of the report of the Independent Auditor in respect of the audited balance sheet and financial statements of the Company for such fiscal year.

13. NON-COMPETITION

13.1 Unless it has obtained the prior written consent from the other Party, a Party must not, either alone or jointly, with, through or on behalf of any person, directly or indirectly:

（d）本协议第 12.9（a）条规定的就任何会计年度的分配应在独立审计师就该会计年度经审计的资产负债表和财务报表提交报告之日起【三】个月内作出。

13.不竞争

13.1 除非得到另一方的事先书面同意，否则一方不得单独或共同，连同、通过或代表任何人，直接或间接地：

（a）在目标地区内经营或从事或关注任何竞争业务；

（b）与合资公司竞争，试图在本协议期限内的任何时间：

（i）从合资公司的任何现有客户或曾经的客户处取得订单；

（ii）与合资公司的任何现有客户或曾经的客户做生意；或

（iii）直接或间接地使其他任何人从合资公司的任何现有客户或曾经的客户处取得订单或与之做生意；

（c）以聘用或雇佣为目的，招揽或联系合资公司的任何人，任何员工、高级职员或经理，或在过去【两年】内曾担任合资公司员工、高级职员或经理的人员，借调给合资公司并在借调期结束后返回其用人单位的员工除外。

13.2 每一方同意促使其每个关联方遵守本协议第 13.1 条的规定，如同该条款直接适用于该等关联方。

13.3 本协议第 13.1 条规定的每项限制都是对每一方及其每个关联方的单独和独立的限制，一项限制的有效性不受其他无效或不可执行的限制的影响。

13.4 每一方认为本协议第 13.1 条中的限制对于保护合资公

(a) carry on or be engaged or concerned or interested in any Competing Business in the Territory;

(b) seek to, in competition with the Company:

(i) procure orders from;

(ii) do business with; or

(iii) procure, directly or indirectly, any other person to procure orders from or do business with, any person who is, or has been, a customer of the Company at any time during the term of this Agreement; or

(c) solicit, or contact with a view to the engagement or employment by any person, any employee, officer or manager of the Company or any person who has been an employee, officer or manager of the Company within the previous [two-year] period, except for an employee who has been seconded to the Company who returns at the end of the secondment period to the Party that previously employed such person.

13.2 Each Party agrees to procure that each of its Affiliates shall comply with the provisions of Clause 13.1 as though it applied directly to the Affiliate.

13.3 Each of the restrictions set out in Clause 13.1 is a separate and independent restriction on each Party and each of its Affiliates and the validity of one restriction shall not be affected by the invalidity or unenforceability of another.

13.4 Each Party considers the restrictions in Clause 13.1 to be reasonable and necessary for the protection of the interests of the Company. If any such restriction shall be held to be void but would be valid if deleted in part or reduced in application, such restriction shall apply with such deletion or modification as may be necessary to make it valid and enforceable.

13.5 The covenants set out in Clause 13.1 shall continue to apply to each Party and each of its Affiliates for a period of [NUMBER] months from the date on which such Party ceases to hold any Equity Interests of the Company. The covenants set out in Clause 13.1 shall be construed during this period by reference to the business, customers, employees, officers or managers or contract counterparties of the Company as at the date on which this

司的利益是合理且必要的。如果任何应被视为无效的限制在部分删除或减少适用后有效，则该等限制应在使之有效和可执行的必要范围内进行删除或修改后适用。

13.5 本协议第 13.1 条所载的约定应在一方停止持有合资公司的任何股权之日起【填入数字】个月内继续适用于该方及其每个关联方。本协议第 13.1 条所载的约定在此期间应适用于本协议终止或该方不再持有合资公司的任何股权之日的合资公司的业务、客户、员工、高级职员或经理或合同相对方。

13.6 每一方同意并承认，尽管存在本协议第 13.1 条的规定，任何一方或其任何关联方可以直接或间接地获得并持有以下股份或可转换为股份的其他股权或权利：（a）总计不超过参与竞争业务的任何第三方在完全稀释的基础上已发行股本总额的【2】%，或总计不得超过参与竞争业务的任何第三方在完全稀释的基础上已发行股本总额的【49】%，只要该等竞争业务对该第三方年营业额的贡献率低于【5】%，或（b）总计不超过参与竞争业务的任何上市公司（在经认可的证券交易所上市的公司）的任何种类的股份或股权的【2】%，且该等股份或股权仅为投资目的而持有。

13.7 如果一方或一方的关联方的高级职员或董事同时也是合资公司的高级职员或董事，其在自己作为合资公司的高级职员或董事的职权范围内获得或获悉明确是针对或代表合资公司提供或介绍的公司机会时，合资公司保留对该等公司机会的所有权利，并且合资公司的该等高级职员或董事应负有将所有与该公司机会有关的信息告知合资公司的受托义务，且不得作为一方或一方的关联方的高级职员或董事代表该方或该方的关

Agreement is terminated or the Party ceases to hold any Equity Interests of the Company.

13.6 Each Party agrees and acknowledges that, notwithstanding Clause 13.1, any Party or any of its Affiliates may acquire and hold, directly or indirectly, shares, or other equity interests or rights convertible into shares, (a) comprising in the aggregate not more than [2]% of the total issued share capital on a fully diluted basis of any third party which is engaged in a Competing Business, or comprising in the aggregate not more than [49]% of the total issued share capital on a fully diluted basis of any third party which is engaged in a Competing Business, so long as such Competing Business contributes less than [5]% of the annual turnover of such third party, or (b) comprising in the aggregate of not more than [2]% of any class of shares or equity interests of any company which is engaged in a Competing Business which is publicly traded on a recognized stock exchange, which shares or equity interests are held for investment purposes only.

13.7 If a Corporate Opportunity is offered or presented to an officer or director of a Party or a Party Affiliate who is also an officer or Director of the Company in such person's capacity as an officer or Director of the Company and is offered or presented expressly for or on behalf of the Company, then the Company reserves all rights in and to such Corporate Opportunity, and such officer or Director of the Company shall have a fiduciary duty to communicate all such information relating to that Corporate Opportunity to the Company and shall not take any action in his separate capacity as an officer or director of a Party or Party Affiliate in respect of such Corporate Opportunity on behalf of such Party or Party Affiliate. Except as expressly provided in the immediately preceding sentence, and subject to the provisions of Clause 13.1, where the information regarding a Corporate Opportunity is obtained independently, no Party, Party Affiliate or their authorized representatives shall have a duty to communicate or present to the Company any Corporate Opportunity or be deemed to have breached any fiduciary or other duty or obligation to the Company as the result of having pursued any such Corporate Opportunity directly or indirectly without communicating information regarding

联方就该等公司机会采取任何行动。除前述明确规定之外，受限于本协议第 13.1 条的规定，如果有关公司机会的信息是独立获得的，则任何一方、一方的关联方或其授权代表均无义务向合资公司告知或呈递任何该等公司机会，也不会因在未向合资公司告知有关该等公司机会的信息的情况下直接或间接地追求任何该等公司机会而被视为违反任何对合资公司的受托义务或其他义务。

13.8 每一方进一步同意，其不会促使或允许合资公司与该方、该方的任何关联方或该方的任何董事或高级管理人员之间进行除公平条款下或董事会根据本协议第 9.2（f）条另行批准以外的任何种类的自我交易。任何对本协议第 13 条的违反均构成本协议所指的重大违约。

14.期限和终止

14.1 本协议自生效日开始生效，并持续有效，直至根据本协议第 14.2 条终止（“期限”）。

14.2 本协议将在以下情形下终止：

（a）双方书面协议终止；

（b）一方获得 100% 股权且已完成所有相关登记程序；或者

（c）出具或正式通过解散或清算合资公司的指令或决议。

14.3 一方（“通知方”）有权向另一方提交终止通知以终止本协议，前提是：

（a）另一方严重违约，且相关补救期（如有）届满；

（b）另一方经历控制权变更；

such Corporate Opportunity to the Company.

13.8 Each Party further agrees that it will not cause or permit the Company to engage in self-dealing transactions of any sort with such Party, any Affiliate of such Party or any Director or Management Personnel nominated by such Party on other than arms-length terms or as otherwise approved by the Board pursuant to Clause 9.2(f). Any breach of this Clause 13 shall constitute a Material Breach for purposes of this Agreement.

14. TERM AND TERMINATION

14.1 This Agreement shall take effect on the Effective Date and shall continue in force for an indefinite term until terminated pursuant to Clause 14.2 (the "Term").

14.2 This Agreement shall terminate:

(a) upon the written agreement of the Parties;

(b) if a Party acquires 100% of the Equity Interests and all registration formalities in respect thereof have been completed; or

(c) if an order is made, or a resolution is duly passed, to dissolve, wind up or liquidate the Company.

14.3 A Party (the "Notifying Party") shall have the right to submit a Termination Notice to the other Party to terminate this Agreement if:

(a) the other Party commits a Material Breach, and the Cure Period (if any) in respect thereof has expired;

(b) the other Party undergoes a Change of Control;

(c) the other Party experiences an Insolvency Event;

(d) a Deadlock Matter arises and cannot be resolved in accordance with the provisions of Clause 7.11(b) or Clause 9.5(b);

(e) the conditions or consequences of Force Majeure have a Material Adverse Effect on the business, assets or operations of the Company and continue for a period in excess of [6] months and the Parties have been unable to find an equitable solution pursuant to Clause 22.1(c); or

(f) a Material Modification is made at any time by any government authority

（c）另一方发生破产事件；

（d）发生僵局事件且该事件无法根据本协议第 7.11（b）条和第 9.5（b）条的规定解决；

（e）不可抗力的条件或后果对合资公司的业务、资产或经营产生重大不利影响，并持续超过【6】个月，且双方未能根据本协议第 22.1（c）条找到公平的解决方案；或者

（f）任何政府机构在任何时候对本协议、公司章程、营业执照、任何附加许可或任何附属协议做出重大修改。

14.4 提交终止通知本身不导致本协议的终止，但应启动以下本协议项下的其他相关程序：

（a）就根据本协议第 14.3（a）-（c）条发出的终止通知而言，本协议第 15 条的规定应适用；且

（b）就根据本协议第 14.3（d）-（f）条发出的终止通知而言，本协议第 16 条的规定应适用。

本协议仅在一方完成对另一方全部股权的收购时，或根据本协议第 15 条或第 16 条的条款终止本协议时终止。

14.5 本协议终止后，本协议项下双方的所有权利和义务应立即灭失，但是：

（a）仅发生本协议的终止，不影响合资公司的存续；并且

（b）一方（i）在终止前根据本协议，（ii）根据任何存续条款，以及（iii）根据适用法律，产生的所有权利和义务，均应根据相关适用条款保持完全有效。

14.6 以下条款（“存续条款”）在本协议终止后继续有效：

to this Agreement, the Articles of Association, the Business License, any Additional Permit or any Ancillary Agreement.

14.4 The submission of a Termination Notice shall not in and of itself result in the termination of this Agreement but shall initiate additional related procedures hereunder as follows:

(a) in respect of a Termination Notice delivered pursuant to Clause 14.3(a)-(c), the provisions under Clause 15 shall apply; and

(b) in respect of a Termination Notice delivered pursuant to Clause 14.3(d)-(f), the provisions of Clause 16 shall apply.

This Agreement shall be terminated only upon completion of the purchase by a Party of all of the Equity Interests of the other Party or the termination of this Agreement in accordance with the terms of Clause 15 or Clause 16.

14.5 Upon the termination of this Agreement, all rights and obligations of the Parties under this Agreement shall forthwith be extinguished, provided that:

(a) termination of this Agreement shall not alone affect the existence of the Company; and

(b) all rights and obligations of a Party arising (i) under this Agreement prior to termination, (ii) under any Surviving Provision, and (iii) under or by operation of Applicable Law, shall remain in full force and effect in accordance with the applicable terms thereof.

14.6 The following provisions ("Surviving Provisions") shall survive the termination of this Agreement: Clause 13, this Clause 14.6, Clause 20, Clause 21 (but only regarding claims arising prior to the termination hereof or regarding other continuing obligations), Clause 23 Clause 24.3, Clause 25.6, Clause 25.13 and Clause 25.15.

15. MANDATORY TRANSFER EVENT CALL OPTION

15.1 If the Notifying Party has submitted a Termination Notice pursuant to Clause 14.3(a)-(c), then the Notifying Party shall have the right to purchase all of the Equity Interests in the Company held by the other Party in accordance with the terms of this Clause 15.

第 13 条、第 14.6 条、第 20 条、第 21 条（但仅适用于本协议终止前产生的索赔或其他存续义务）、第 23 条、第 24.3 条、第 25.6 条、第 25.13 条和第 25.15 条。

15.强制转让事件中的购买选择权

15.1 如果通知方已根据本协议第 14.3（a）-（c）条提交终止通知，则通知方有权根据本协议第 15 条的条款购买另一方持有的合资公司的全部股权。

15.2 双方应根据本协议第 17 条确定另一方的股权的公平市场价值。

15.3 在确定另一方的股权的公平市场价值之日后【10】个工作日内，通知方有权向另一方提交一份无条件且不可撤销的约定形式的购买选择权行权通知，以确认其将以该等参考价格购买另一方的全部股权。该等购买选择权行权通知对通知方和另一方具有约束力。

15.4 如果通知方按照本协议第 15.3 条提交购买选择权行权通知，则另一方向通知方的股权转让应在购买选择权行权通知条款指定的时间和地点完成。完成时，通知方应向另一方全额支付参考价格。

15.5 如果通知方未能在本协议第 15.3 条规定的时间内提交购买选择权行权通知，则应视为已选择不适用本协议第 15 条的规定，在此情况下，应适用本协议第 18.2 条的规定。

15.6 本协议第 6.3 条【和第 6.8 条】的规定应适用于本协议第 15 条项下的股权转让。

16.双向收购

16.1 如果通知方已根据本协议第 14.3（d）-（f）条提交终止通知，则双方应启动本协议第 16 条规定的收购程序。

15.2 The Parties shall determine the Fair Market Value of the other Party's Equity Interests in accordance with Clause 17.

15.3 Within [10] Business Days following the date of determination of the Fair Market Value of the other Party's Equity Interests, the Notifying Party shall have the right to submit to the other Party an unconditional and irrevocable Call Option Exercise Notice in the agreed form confirming that it will purchase all of the other Party's Equity Interests at such Reference Price. Such Call Option Exercise Notice shall be binding on the Notifying Party and the other Party.

15.4 If the Notifying Party submits a Call Option Exercise Notice in accordance with Clause 15.3, then completion of the Transfer of the Equity Interests of the other Party to the Notifying Party shall occur at such time and place as designated in accordance with the terms of the Call Option Exercise Notice. At completion, the Notifying Party shall pay the Reference Price to the other Party in full.

15.5 If the Notifying Party fails to submit a Call Option Exercise Notice within the time specified in Clause 15.3, then it shall be deemed to have opted out of the provisions of this Clause 15, in which case the provisions of Clause 18.2 shall apply.

15.6 The provisions of Clause 6.3 [and 6.8] shall apply to a Transfer of Equity Interests under Clause 15.

16. MUTUAL BUY-OUT

16.1 If the Notifying Party has submitted a Termination Notice pursuant to Clause 14.3(d)-(f), then the Parties shall initiate the buy-out procedures set out in this Clause 16.

16.2 The Parties shall determine the Fair Market Value of the Company in accordance with Clause 17.

16.3 Within [10] Business Days following the date of determination of the Fair Market Value of the Company, each Party shall have the right to submit to the other Party an Indication of Interest to purchase all (but not less than all) of the Equity Interests of the other Party at the applicable Reference Price.

16.4 If neither Party submits an Indication of Interest to the other Party within the time

16.2 双方应根据本协议第17条确定合资公司的公平市场价值。

16.3 在确定合资公司公平市场价值之日后【10】个工作日内，每一方应有权向另一方提交一份收购意向书，表明希望以适用的参考价格购买另一方所持有的全部（而非仅仅部分）股权。

16.4 如果任何一方均未在本协议第16.3条规定的时间内向另一方提交收购意向书，则双方应被视为已选择不适用本协议第16条的条款，在此情况下，应适用本协议第18.2条的规定。

16.5 如果仅有一方（“唯一提交方”）在本协议第16.3条规定的时间内提交了意向函，则该意向函应被视为唯一提交方的无条件且不可撤销的要约，表明其希望以适用的参考价格购买另一方所持有的全部股权，该等意向函对双方均具有约束力。

16.6 如果双方在本协议第16.3条规定的时间内均提交了意向函，则适用本协议第16.6条的规定：

（a）双方应在第二份意向函提交后【10】个工作日内任命一名竞标管理人。竞标管理人应为（i）合资公司的独立审计师，（ii）双方根据本协议第17.3条指定的单一的合格评估机构或根据本协议第17.4条指定的独立的合格评估机构，或（iii）双方可能同意的其他合格的独立专业人士。

（b）在任命竞标管理人后【10】个工作日内（“竞标期间”），每一方应向竞标管理人提交一份密封的竞价文件，载明以不低于适用的参考价格的购买价格（“报价”）购买另一方所持有的全部（而非仅仅部分）股权的无条件且不可撤销的要约。竞标管理人应在第二份密封的竞价文件递交之日

specified in Clause 16.3. then the Parties shall be deemed to have opted out the provisions of this Clause 16, in which case the provisions of Clause 18.2 shall apply.

16.5 If only one Party ("Sole Submitting Party") submits an Indication of Interest within the time specified in Clause 16.3, then such Indication of Interest shall be deemed to be an unconditional and irrevocable offer by the Sole Submitting Party to purchase all of the Equity Interests of the other Party at the applicable Reference Price, which shall be binding on both Parties.

16.6 If both Parties submit an Indication of Interest within the time specified in Clause 16.3, then the provisions of this Clause 16.6 shall apply:

(a) The Parties shall appoint a Bid Manager within [10] Business Days after the submission of the second Indication of Interest. The Bid Manager shall be (i) the Company's Independent Auditor, (ii) the single Qualified Valuation Firm jointly appointed by the Parties under Clause 17.3 or the Independent QVF appointed under Clause 17.4, or (iii) such other qualified independent professional as the Parties may agree.

(b) Within [10] Business Days following the appointment of the Bid Manager (the "Bidding Period"), each Party shall submit to the Bid Manager a sealed bid setting out an unconditional and irrevocable offer to purchase all (but not less than all) of the Equity Interests of the other Party at a purchase price which shall be not less than the applicable Reference Price (the "Offer Price"). The Bid Manager shall open the sealed bids on the [second] Business Day after the earlier of the submission of the second sealed bid or the expiration of the Bidding Period. The Party offering the higher Offer Price shall be the winning bidder. If the Offer Price submitted by both Parties is the same (as calculated on a proportionate basis by reference to the Offer Price divided by the percentage of the Registered Capital to be purchased), then the Notifying Party shall be deemed to be the winning bidder. If at the end of the Bidding Period only one qualifying bid has been submitted, that shall be deemed to be the winning bid. The Bid Manager shall notify the Parties of the results of the bidding no later than the next Business Day following opening of the bids.

或竞标期间届满之日（以较早者为准）后第【二】个工作日开启密封的竞价文件。出价较高的一方为中标人。如果双方提交的报价相同（参考购买价格除以待收购的注册资本比例，按比例计算），则通知方应被视为中标人。如果在竞标期间结束时，只有一份合格竞价文件被提交，则视为其中标。竞标管理人应不迟于开标后的下一个工作日将竞价结果通知双方。

16.7 本协议第 6.3 条【和第 6.8 条】的规定适用于本协议第 16.5 条或第 16.6 条项下的股权转让。双方应在根据本协议第 16.5 条确认唯一提交方或根据第 16.6 条确认中标人之日起【20】个工作日内，就该等转让签订最终的股权转让协议，并应在此之后根据该股权转让协议的条款及时完成该等转让。

17 估值

17.1 为本协议的目的，为了确定合资公司或一方的股权的公平市场价值，双方应根据本协议第 17 条对合资公司进行估值。

17.2 双方应在提交使本协议第 15 条或第 16 条的规定开始适用的相关终止通知之日起【30】日内就合资公司的估值进行协商。如果双方能够就合资公司的估值达成一致，则该协定金额应为本协议目的下的公平市场价值。

17.3 如果双方未能在【30】日期限内或者双方可能书面约定的更长期限内就合资公司的估值达成一致，则双方应共同选择并指定一家在中国注册的、声誉良好的，（a）有权对【国有资产和其他】资产进行评估，并且（b）具有对与合资公司类似的公司进行估值的经验

16.7 The provisions of Clause 6.3 [and 6.8] shall apply to a Transfer of Equity Interests under Clause 16.5 or 16.6. The Parties shall enter into a definitive equity transfer agreement in respect of such Transfer within [20] Business Days from the date of confirmation of the Sole Submitting Party under Clause 16.5 or the confirmation of the winning bidder under Clause 16.6, and shall effect completion of such Transfer promptly thereafter in accordance with the terms of such equity transfer agreement.

17. VALUATION

17.1 In order to determine the Fair Market Value of the Company or of the Equity Interests of a Party for purposes of this Agreement, the Parties shall conduct a valuation of the Company in accordance with this Clause 17.

17.2 The Parties shall conduct negotiations on the valuation of the Company for a period of [30] days from the date of submission of the related Termination Notice triggering the application of the provisions of Clause 15 or Clause 16. If the Parties are able to agree on the valuation of the Company, that agreed amount shall be the Fair Market Value for purposes of this Agreement.

17.3 If the Parties are unable to agree on the valuation of the Company by the end of such [30]-day period, or such longer period as the Parties may agree in writing, the Parties shall jointly select and appoint a reputable independent valuation firm registered in China which (a) is authorized to perform appraisals of[state-owned and other] assets and (b) has experience in determining the value of companies similar to the Company (a "Qualified Valuation Firm") to conduct a valuation of the Company.

17.4 If the Parties are unable to agree on the selection of a Qualified Valuation Firm, then Party A shall select one Qualified Valuation Firm (the "Party A QVF"), Party B shall selection one Qualified Valuation Firm (the "Party B QVF"), and the Qualified Valuation Firms so selected shall select a third (the "Independent QVF"). Each such Qualified Valuation Firm shall determine the Fair Market Value of the Company. If the value determined by either the Party A QVF or by the Party B QVF is not less than 80% or not more than 120% of the value determined by the Independent QVF, then the average of the Independent QVF

的独立评估机构（“合格评估机构”）对合资公司进行估值。

17.4 如果双方未能就选择合格评估机构达成一致，则甲方应选择一家合格评估机构（“甲方合格评估机构”），乙方应选择一家合格评估机构（“乙方合格评估机构”），由此选出的两家合格评估机构应选择第三家合格评估机构（“独立的合格评估机构”）。每家该等合格评估机构应确定合资公司的公平市场价值。如果由甲方合格评估机构和乙方合格评估机构确定的价值不低于独立的合格评估机构确定的价值的 80% 且不超过 120%，则最终的公平市场价值应为独立的合格评估机构、甲方合格评估机构和乙方合格评估机构确定的价值的平均值。如果甲方合格评估机构或乙方合格评估机构确定的价值低于独立的合格评估机构确定的价值的 80% 或超过 120%（“差异过大值”），那么甲方合格评估机构和 / 或乙方合格评估机构确定的该等差异过大值应不予考虑，最终的公平市场价值应为独立的合格评估机构确定的价值和任何非差异过大值的平均值。甲方合格评估机构的费用由甲方承担；乙方合格评估机构的费用由乙方承担；独立的合格评估机构（或双方一致同意的合格评估机构，如适用）的费用应由双方平均分摊。

17.5 合格评估机构应根据适用法律的要求，使用行业评估方法，在持续经营的基础上对合资公司进行估值。每一方应促使合资公司向合格评估机构提供估值所需的所有财务账簿、账目或其他运营文件的访问权限。

17.6 指定股权的“参考价格”不得低于根据本协议第 17 条确定的合资公司的公平市场价值乘以估值时指定股权占合资公司注册资本的百分比。

value, the Party A QVF value and the Party B QVF value shall constitute the final Fair Market Value. If the value determined by either the Party A QVF or by the Party B QVF is less than 80% or more than 120% of the value determined by the Independent QVF (each, a "Widely Varying Value"), then such Widely Varying Value of the Party A QVF and/or Party B QVF shall be disregarded, and the average of the Independent QVF value and any non-Widely Varying Value shall constitute the final Fair Market Value. The costs of the Party A QVF shall be borne by Party A; the costs of the Party B QVF shall be borne by Party B; and the costs of the Independent QVF (or the mutually agreed upon Qualified Valuation Firm, if applicable) shall be shared equally by the Parties.

17.5 The Qualified Valuation Firm(s) shall value the Company on a going concern basis using the Industry Valuation Method subject to and in accordance with the requirements of Applicable Law. Each Party shall cause the Company to provide the Qualified Valuation Firm(s) access to all financial books, accounts or other operational documents that are needed for the valuation.

17.6 The "Reference Price" for the Designated Equity Interests shall be the Fair Market Value of the Company as determined in accordance with this Clause 17 multiplied by the percentage of the Registered Capital of the Company represented by the Designated Equity Interests at the time of valuation.

17.7 The Parties acknowledge that Party A is a state-owned enterprise and shall comply with relevant SASAC rules in connection with the valuation of its interests in the Company. If anything in this Clause 17 is inconsistent with applicable SASAC rules, the SASAC rules shall prevail, and the Party B shall provide all reasonable assistance to Party A to fulfill the relevant requirements under the applicable SASAC rules.

18. DISSOLUTION OF COMPANY

18.1 Voluntary dissolution of the Company shall be undertaken pursuant to a duly passed Supermajority Shareholders Resolution upon the agreement of the Parties or as provided in Clause 18.2.

18.2 If

(a) under Clause 15.5, the Parties are deemed to have opted out of the provisions

17.7 双方承认甲方是国有企业，且其应当遵守与其在合资公司中所持有的利益的评估相关的国资委有关规定。如果本协议第 17 条与适用的国资委规定有任何不一致，以国资委规定为准，且乙方应向甲方提供所有合理协助以满足适用的国资委规定的相关要求。

18.合资公司的解散

18.1 合资公司的自愿解散应在双方协商一致或本协议第 18.2 条规定的情况下，根据正式通过的绝对多数股东会决议进行。

18.2 如果

（a）根据本协议第 15.5 条，双方被视为已选择不适用本协议第 15 条的条款；或

（b）根据本协议第 16.4 条，双方被视为已选择不适用本协议第 16 条的条款，则除非双方另行书面约定，双方应被视为已同意促使合资公司自愿解散，并且每一方应行使其所有表决权以批准合资公司自愿解散。

18.3 合资公司的非自愿解散应根据相关政府机关签发的解散命令和适用法律的要求进行。

18.4 在（a）关于合资公司解散的绝对多数股东会决议得到批准之日；或（b）相关政府机关签发自愿解散命令之日后的【15】个工作日内，双方应任命清算委员会，清算委员会有权代表合资公司处理所有法律事务。

18.5 清算委员会由双方代表组成。甲方应任命清算委员会的【2】名成员，乙方应任命清算委员会的【1】名成员。清算委员会成员应对合资公司承担受托责任，并在履行职责时全面遵守适用法律的要求。清算委员会应以

of Clause 15; or

(b) under Clause 16.4, the Parties are deemed to have opted out of the provisions of Clause 16,then unless otherwise agreed by the Parties in writing, the Parties shall be deemed to have consented to cause the Company to undertake voluntary dissolution, and each Party shall exercise all of its Voting Rights to approve the same.

18.3 Involuntary dissolution of the Company shall be undertaken pursuant to an order for dissolution of the Company issued by the relevant government authority and in accordance with the requirements of Applicable Law.

18.4 Within [15] Business Days following either the date on which (a) the Supermajority Shareholders Resolution for dissolution of the Company was approved; or (b) the order for involuntary dissolution was issued by the relevant government authority, the Parties shall appoint a liquidation committee which shall have the power to represent the Company in all legal matters.

18.5 The liquidation committee shall consist of representatives of the Parties. Party A shall appoint [two] members of the liquidation committee, and Party B shall appoint [one] member of the liquidation committee. The members of the liquidation committee shall bear fiduciary responsibilities to the Company and comply in all respects with the requirements of Applicable Law in the discharge of their duties. The liquidation committee shall act by simple majority vote, and each Party shall chop or sign application or appointment letters approved by the liquidation committee.

18.6 Following such appointment of the liquidation committee, a dissolution application shall be registered with the AMR. If either Party fails to cooperate in such dissolution procedures, then to the extent permitted under Applicable Law, the other Party shall have the unilateral right to register a dissolution application with the AMR.

18.7 Following dissolution registration with the AMR (whether voluntary or otherwise), the Company will cease to carry on business except as necessary to wind up its business and distribute its assets.

简单多数方式进行表决，每一方应在清算委员会通过的申请书或委任书上盖章或签字。

18.6 在指定清算委员会后，解散申请应在市场监督管理局登记。如果任何一方未能配合该等解散程序，则在适用法律允许的范围内，另一方应有权单方面向市场监督管理局登记解散申请。

18.7 在市场监督管理局登记（无论是自愿还是其他情形的）解散后，除为结束其业务和分配其资产而确有必要之外，合资公司将停止经营业务。

18.8 清算委员会应指定一家合格评估机构，根据适用法律要求，按照现时公平市场价值对合资公司的资产进行估值。

18.9 清算委员会有权就合资公司清算适当地采取以下步骤：

（a）仅为结束合资公司事务的目的在必要时继续目标业务的运营；

（b）履行合同并收款、付款，就合资公司的债务以及代表合资公司提起的或针对合资公司提起的索赔达成妥协或和解（包括作为原告或被告参与相关法律诉讼）；

（c）以清算委员会认为合理和适当金额的现金为对价，处置合资公司的全部或部分资产；

（d）以合资公司的名义签订协议并采取清算委员会认为必要或适当的所有其他步骤，以结束合资公司事务；以及

（e）聘请代理人、律师及其他专业顾问协助清算及结束合资公司事务。

18.8 The liquidation committee shall appoint a Qualified Valuation Firm to conduct a valuation of the Company's assets on a current fair market value basis subject to and in compliance with Applicable Law.

18.9 The liquidation committee shall be authorized to undertake the following steps as appropriate in connection with the winding up of the Company:

(a) continue the operation of the Business solely as necessary for purposes of winding up the affairs of the Company;

(b) perform contracts and collect, pay, compromise and settle debts and claims for or against the Company (including participating in Legal Actions, as either plaintiff or defendant, in respect of the same);

(c) Dispose of all or any part of the assets of the Company for cash in such amounts as the liquidation committee shall consider reasonable and appropriate;

(d) enter into agreements and take all such other steps in the name of the Company as the liquidation committee may deem necessary or appropriate in order to wind up the affairs of the Company; and

(e) employ agents, attorneys and other professional consultants and advisors assist with the liquidation and winding up of the affairs of the Company.

18.10 Proceeds from the Disposal of the assets of the Company shall be applied in the following order of priority:

(a) to all debts and liabilities of the Company in accordance with the requirements and priorities as provided under Applicable Law, including wages, insurance premiums, welfare expenses, taxes and the qualified expenses of dissolution and liquidation, but excluding the Shareholder Loans;

(b) to repayment of the outstanding principal owing in respect of all Shareholder Loans together with accrued and unpaid interest thereon;

(c) to undistributed net profits of the Company;

(d) to repayment of the purchase price of the Equity Interests of the Company actually paid by each Party; and

18.10 处置合资公司资产所得的收益应按照以下优先顺序使用：

（a）根据适用法律规定的要求和优先顺序清偿合资公司的所有债务和负债，包括工资、保险费用、福利费用、税款以及合格的解散和清算费用，但不包括股东贷款；

（b）用于偿还所有股东贷款的未偿还的本金及应计的未付利息；

（c）作为合资公司尚未分配的净利润；

（d）用于偿还每一方实际支付的合资公司股权的购买价；以及

（e）按双方各自持有的合资公司股权比例向双方付款。

18.11 根据适用法律完成所有清算程序后，清算委员会应向股东会提交最终报告以供确认。股东应召开紧急会议审核并确认该等报告。而后，清算委员会应根据适用法律开展所有注销登记程序。每一方应有权自费获取合资公司所有会计账簿和其他文件的复印件，但其原件应由【甲方】保管。

19.陈述和保证

19.1 每一方向另一方陈述并保证，在生效日：

（a）该方为一家根据其设立或注册地的法律正式组建、有效存续且声誉良好的独立法人；

（b）该方已经获得全部同意、批准并已实施所有必要的行为以使本协议有效订立及生效，并且其拥有充分的授权以签订本协议并履行本协议项下的义务；

（c）本协议的签字人是其法定代表人或其正式授权代

(e) to the Parties in proportion to the amount of Equity Interests of the Company held by each.

18.11 On completion of all liquidation procedures in accordance with Applicable Law, the liquidation committee shall submit a final report to the Shareholders Meeting for confirmation. The shareholders shall convene an emergency meeting to review and confirm such report. The liquidation committee shall then carry out all de-registration procedures in accordance with Applicable Law. Each Party shall have a right to obtain copies of all of the Company's accounting books and other documents at its own expense but the originals thereof shall be left in the care of [Party A].

19. REPRESENTATIONS AND WARRANTIES

19.1 Each Party represents and warrants to each other Party that on the Effective Date:

(a) it is an independent legal person duly organized, validly existing and in good standing under the laws of the place of its establishment or incorporation;

(b) it has obtained all consents and approvals and taken all actions necessary for it to validly enter into and give effect to this Agreement and it has full authority to enter into this Agreement and to perform its obligations hereunder;

(c) its signatory to this Agreement is either its legal representative or its duly authorized representative and, on signing this Agreement, and from and after the Effective Date, the provisions of this Agreement shall constitute valid, lawful and legally binding obligations of such Party;

(d) no steps have been taken or legal proceedings commenced or threatened against such Party for its winding-up or for it to be declared bankrupt or insolvent or for a liquidation committee or administrator to be nominated in respect of its assets or business;

(e) its execution of this Agreement and its performance of its obligations hereunder: (i) will not violate any provision of its business license, articles of incorporation, articles of association or similar organizational documents; (ii) will not violate any Applicable Law or any governmental authorization or approval; (iii) will not violate or result in a default or breach under any other

表，一旦签署本协议，自生效日开始，本协议的条款应构成该方有效、合法且具有法律约束力的义务；

（d）不存在针对该方所采取的任何措施、提起或威胁提起的任何法律程序申请其解散、申请宣布其破产或资不抵债、或指定清算委员会或管理人管理其资产或业务；

（e）该方签署本协议及履行本协议项下的义务：（i）不会违反其营业执照、成立协议、公司章程或类似组织文件的任何规定；（ii）不会违反任何适用法律或任何政府授权或批准；（iii）不会违反或导致违反其作为当事人一方的任何其他协议，也不会导致其在该等协议项下违约，或违反受之约束的任何单方承诺或保证，或赋予任何第三方对其提起诉讼的权利；并且（iv）将不会违反对其具有约束力的任何判决或仲裁机构仲裁裁决，或对其具有管辖权的任何政府或主管机构的决定或规定；并且

（f）不存在将影响该方履行本协议项下义务能力的未决诉讼、仲裁或其他司法或行政程序，且据其所知无人威胁将采取上述行动。

19.2 如果一方经历控制权变更或破产事件，或者知悉该等控制权变更或破产事件即将发生，应立即以书面形式通知另一方并提供所有相关的支持细节，以便另一方可以根据本协议和适用法律的规定就此采取适当的措施。

20.保密

20.1 在本协议订立前以及在本协议期限内，合资公司或一

Agreement or agreement to which it is a Party or any unilateral commitment or undertaking which binds it or give any third party a right to take action against it; and (iv) will not violate any judgment or arbitration award of any tribunal to which it is subject or the order or ruling of any government or regulatory body to whose jurisdiction it is subject; and

(f) no lawsuit, arbitration or other legal or governmental proceeding is pending or, to its knowledge, threatened against it that would affect its ability to perform its obligations under this Agreement.

19.2 If a Party undergoes a Change of Control or experiences an Insolvency Event, or it is aware that such a Change of Control or Insolvency Event is imminent, it shall promptly so inform the other Party in writing and provide all relevant supporting details so that the other Party may be able to take appropriate steps in respect thereof as provided in this Agreement and under Applicable Law.

20. CONFIDENTIALITY

20.1 From time to time prior to and during the Term the Company or a Party ("Disclosing Party") has disclosed or may disclose Confidential Information to another Party ("Receiving Party"). The Receiving Party shall, during the Term and for [five] years thereafter:

(a) maintain the confidentiality of Confidential Information;

(b) not use Confidential Information for any purposes other than those specifically set out in this Agreement; and

(c) not disclose any such Confidential Information to any person or entity, except to (i) its employees or employees of its Affiliates, its agents, attorneys, accountants and other advisors who need to know such information to perform their responsibilities in connection with this Agreement, (ii) authorized Equity Interests regulators or exchanges in accordance with Applicable Law or the relevant rules of the Equity Interests exchange to which the Receiving Party is subject, and (iii) officials in relevant government departments in accordance with Applicable Law to which the Receiving Party is subject (collectively "Permitted Disclosure Parties").

方（“披露方”）已经或者可能不时向另一方（“接收方”）披露保密信息。在本协议期限内及届满后的【五】年内，接收方应当：

（a）对保密信息予以保密；

（b）不得为除本协议中明确规定的目的之外的其他任何目的使用保密信息；并且

（c）不得向任何人或任何实体披露该等保密信息，下述对象除外：（i）为履行其与本协议相关的职责而确有必要知悉保密信息的接收方雇员或其关联方雇员、接收方的代理、律师、会计师或其他顾问；（ii）根据接收方所受约束的适用法律或相关证券交易所规则授权的证券监管机构或证券交易所；（iii）根据接收方所受约束的适用法律规定的相关政府部门的官员（合称“经允许的披露对象”）。

20.2 本协议上述第 20.1 条的规定不适用于以下信息：

（a）能够通过在披露方向接收方披露前制作的书面记录证明已被接收方掌握的信息；

（b）不重要的或显而易见的信息；

（c）目前或将来非因接收方违反本协议而被公众知悉的信息；或者

（d）接收方从对该信息无保密义务的第三方获得的信息。

20.3 接收方应制定规章制度，告知其董事、高级职员、雇员以及任何其他经允许的披露对象本协议第 20.1 条规定的保密义务。

20.4 如果接收方（或某一经允许的披露对象）的行为导致本协议项下任何保密信息的丢失或未经授权的披露，

20.2 The provisions of Clause 20.1 above shall not apply to information that:

(a) can be shown to be known or independently developed by the Receiving Party by written records made prior to disclosure by the Disclosing Party;

(b) is trivial or obvious;

(c) is or becomes public knowledge otherwise than through the Receiving Party's breach of this Agreement; or

(d) was obtained by the Receiving Party from a third party having no obligation of confidentiality regarding such information.

20.3 The Receiving Party shall formulate rules and regulations to inform its directors, senior staff, employees, and any other Permitted Disclosure Parties of the confidentiality obligations set forth in Clause 20.1.

20.4 If the actions of the Receiving Party (or a Permitted Disclosure Party) result in a loss or an unauthorized disclosure of any of the Confidential Information under the provisions of this Agreement, the Receiving Party will immediately notify the Disclosing Party and use its best endeavors to retrieve the lost or improperly disclosed Confidential Information.

20.5 Upon the Disclosing Party's request at any time, whether before or after the expiration of the Term, the Receiving Party shall:

(a) return to the Disclosing Party, or at the Disclosing Party's direction destroy, all materials (including any copies thereof) embodying the Confidential Information; and

(b) provide written confirmation to the Disclosing Party, within [10] Business Days following the Disclosing Party's request, that all of such materials have been returned or destroyed.

21. BREACH OF AGREEMENT

21.1 In this Agreement "Material Breach" means:

(a) any failure of a Party (the "Breaching Party") to perform an obligation under this Agreement or any Ancillary Agreement to which it is a party which:

(i) is expressly designated as a Material Breach in accordance with the

接收方应立即通知披露方，并且尽其最大努力挽回丢失的或被不当披露的保密信息。

20.5 经披露方随时（无论在协议期限届满之前或之后）提出要求的，接收方应当：

（a）将所有含有保密信息的资料（包括所有复印件）归还于披露方，或根据披露方的指示销毁；以及

（b）在披露方提出请求后【10】日内，书面向披露方确认所有该等资料均已归还或销毁。

21.协议违约

21.1 在本协议中，“重大违约”是指：

（a）一方（“违约方”）未能履行其在本协议或其作为当事人一方的任何附属协议项下的义务，该等不履行义务的行为：

（i）根据本协议或该等附属协议的条款被明确指定为重大违约；或

（ii）已经或随着时间的推移预计会对合资公司或另一方（“非违约方”）的业务、资产或经营产生重大不利影响；或者

（b）违约方的任何陈述或保证在作出时在所有实质方面不真实或不正确。

21.2 在发生重大违约或任何其他违约行为（“其他违约”）后，除了本协议项下的其他权利外，非违约方可以：

（a）以约定的形式向违约方发出书面违约通知，说明违约的性质及范围，并要求违约方在【90】个日历日内（“补救期”）自费予以补救［但是如果一方在本协议第19条项下所做的任何陈述和保证在做出时在所有实质方面不真实、不正确，或者

terms of this Agreement or such Ancillary Agreement; or

(ii) has had or with the passage of time is projected to have a Material Adverse Effect on the business, assets or operations of the Company or the other Party (the "Non-breaching Party"); or

(b) the failure of any representation or warranty of the Breaching Party to be true and correct in all material respects when made.

21.2 Upon the occurrence of a Material Breach or any other breach of contract ("Other Breach"), then in addition to its other rights under this Agreement, the Non-breaching Party may:

(a) give written notice of breach in the agreed form to the Breaching Party describing the nature and scope of the breach and demanding that the Breaching Party cure the breach at its cost within [90] calendar days ("Cure Period") (provided that if any representation and warranty of a Party under Clause 19 is not true and correct in all material respects when made, or if there is a breach of confidentiality undertakings under Clause 20, then there shall be no Cure Period, and provided further that if a Funding Default is deemed to be a Material Breach under Clause 4.12(a) by reason of having remained uncured for a period of [90] calendar days, then there shall be no additional Cure Period); and

(b) if the Breaching Party fails to cure the breach within the Cure Period (or, if there is none, at any time following such breach), then in addition to its other rights hereunder or under Applicable Law, the Non-breaching Party may claim direct and foreseeable damages arising from the breach.

21.3 Notwithstanding any other provision of this Agreement, except for a breach of confidentiality undertakings under Clause 20, neither Party shall be liable to the other Party for damages for loss of revenues or profits, loss of goodwill or any indirect or consequential damages in connection with the performance or non-performance of this Agreement. Except for a breach of confidentiality undertakings under Clause 20, the aggregate liability of a Party for all claims for any loss, damage or indemnity whatsoever resulting from such Party's

违反本协议第 20 条项下的保密承诺，则没有补救期，并且，如果出资违约因在【90】个日历日内仍未得到补救而被视为本协议第 4.12（a）条项下的重大违约，则不应有额外的补救期］；以及

（b）如果违约方未能在补救期（或者如果没有补救期，那么在该等违约后的任何时间）内予以补救，则除了本协议或适用法律规定的其他权利外，非违约方还可就该违约引起的直接和可预见的损失提出索赔。

21.3 无论本协议有任何其他规定，任何一方均不对另一方承担因本协议的履行或不履行而造成的收入或利润损失、商誉损失或任何间接损害的赔偿责任，但违反本协议第 20 条项下的保密承诺的除外。一方对因该方履行或不履行本协议所致的任何损失、损害或赔偿的所有索赔的责任累计总额不得超过【填入货币种类】【填入金额】，但违反本协议第 20 条项下的保密承诺的除外。

22.不可抗力

22.1 如果发生不可抗力事件

（a）一方在本协议项下受不可抗力影响的合同义务在不可抗力造成的延误期间内应中止，并且其履行期限应自动延长与中止期间相等的期间，且该方不应受到惩罚且无须因此承担责任；

（b）提出受不可抗力影响的一方应立即书面通知另一方，并且在随后的【10】个工作日内向另一方提供不可抗力的发生以及持续时间的充分证据；并且

（c）双方应立即进行磋商，寻求一项公正的解决方案。

performance or non-performance of this Agreement shall in no case exceed [CURRENCY] [AMOUNT].

22. FORCE MAJEURE

22.1 If an event of Force Majeure occurs

(a) a Party's contractual obligations affected by such an event under this Agreement shall be suspended during the period of delay caused by the Force Majeure and shall be automatically extended, without penalty or liability, for a period equal to such suspension;

(b) the Party claiming Force Majeure shall promptly inform the other Party in writing and shall furnish within [10] Business Days thereafter sufficient proof of the occurrence and duration of such Force Majeure; and

(c) the Parties shall immediately consult with each other in order to find an equitable solution and the Party claiming Force Majeure shall use its best endeavors to minimize the consequences of such Force Majeure.

23. NOTICE

23.1 Any notice or written communication provided for in this Agreement by either Party to the other, including but not limited to any and all offers, writings, or notices to be given hereunder, shall be made in [LANGUAGE] and delivered:

(a) by hand;

(b) by courier service delivered letter;

(c) by email; or

(d) by facsimile.

23.2 Any notice given by a Party under or in connection with this Agreement shall be delivered to the other Party as follows:

Party A:

Address: [PARTY A MAILING ADDRESS]

Facsimile No: [N/A]

E-mail address: [PARTY A EMAIL ADDRESS]

Attention: [NAME][OR][TITLE]

提出受不可抗力影响的一方要尽其最大努力将不可抗力的影响降至最小。

23.通知

23.1 本协议中规定的一方向另一方发出的通知或书面函件（包括但不限于本协议项下的任何及所有要约、书面文件或通知）均应以【语言】制作，并通过如下方式送达：

（a）当面递交；

（b）专递信函；

（c）电子邮件；或

（d）传真。

23.2 根据本协议或与本协议相关的由一方向另一方发出的任何通知应向如下地址送达：

甲方：

地址：【填入甲方邮寄地址】

传真号码：【不适用】

电子邮件地址：【填入甲方电子邮件地址】

收件人：【填入姓名】【或】【填入头衔】

乙方：

地址：【填入乙方邮寄地址】

传真号码：【不适用】

电子邮件地址：【填入乙方电子邮件地址】

收件人：【填入姓名】【或】【填入头衔】

23.3 在以下时间通知被视为已经送达：

（a）以当面递交方式送达的，送达指定地址并签署回

Party B:

Address: [PARTY B MAILING ADDRESS]

Facsimile No: [N/A]

E-mail address: [PARTY B EMAIL ADDRESS]

Attention: [NAME][OR][TITLE]

23.3 Notices shall be deemed to have been delivered at the following times:

(a) if by hand, on reaching the designated address and subject to return receipt or other proof of delivery;

(b) if by courier, [five] Business Days after the date of dispatch;

(c) if by email, on the date the email is dispatched (so long as written notice of such transmission is sent within [two] Business Days thereafter by another delivery method pursuant to this Clause 23); and

(d) if by fax, upon the next Business Day after the date marked on the confirmation of transmission report by the sender's fax machine, indicating completed uninterrupted transmission to the relevant facsimile number.

23.4 Each Party may change its particulars for receipt of notices at any time by notice given to the other Party pursuant to this Clause 23.

24. SETTLEMENT OF DISPUTES

24.1 In the event of any dispute, controversy or claim arising out of or relating to this Agreement, or the breach, termination or invalidity hereof ("Dispute"), the Parties shall attempt in the first instance to resolve such Dispute through friendly consultations.

24.2 In the event such Dispute is not resolved through consultations within [60] calendar days after the date such consultations were first requested in writing by a Party, then any Party may submit the Dispute for arbitration administered by the Hong Kong International Arbitration Centre ("HKIAC") under the HKIAC Administered Arbitration Rules in force when the notice of arbitration is submitted. The arbitral award is final and binding on both Parties.

(a) The law of this Clause 24 shall be Hong Kong law.

执或其他送达证明时；

（b）以专递信函方式送达的，为递交日后的第【5】个工作日；

（c）以电子邮件方式送达的，为电子邮件发出之日（只要在电子邮件发送后【2】个工作日内根据本协议第23条规定的另一种送达方式发出关于该等传输的书面通知）；以及

（d）以传真方式送达的，为发送传真方的传真机生成的发送确认报告（表明已向相关传真号码发送完整的、未中断的传真）上标记的日期后的下一个工作日。

23.4 一方可随时根据本协议第23条的规定通知另一方变更通知送达地址。

24.争议解决

24.1 如果发生由本协议（或本协议的违反、终止或无效）引起的或与之相关的任何争议、纠纷或者索赔（“争议”），双方应首先争取通过友好协商来解决争议。

24.2 如果该等争议未在一方首次书面提出磋商请求之日后【60】个日历日内通过友好协商解决，则任何一方可将该争议提交香港国际仲裁中心（“香港国际仲裁中心”）按照提交仲裁通知时有效的《香港国际仲裁中心机构仲裁规则》进行仲裁。仲裁裁决具有终局性且对双方均有约束力。

（a）本协议第24条应适用香港法律。

（b）仲裁地为【香港】。

（c）仲裁员的数量为【1名】【或】【3名】。

（d）仲裁程序应以【语言】进行。

(b) The seat of arbitration shall be [Hong Kong].

(c) The number of arbitrators shall be [one][OR][three].

(d) The arbitration proceedings shall be conducted in [LANGUAGE].

24.3 Notwithstanding the foregoing, the Parties agree that each Party has the right to seek for specific performance, injunctions or other similar relief as permitted under Applicable Law in any court of competent jurisdiction for any claims of breach of confidentiality or IPR infringement.

24.4 When any Dispute occurs and is the subject of friendly consultations or arbitration, the Parties shall continue to exercise their remaining respective rights and fulfil their remaining respective obligations under this Agreement, except for those matters under Dispute.

25. GENERAL PROVISIONS

25.1 Nothing in this Agreement shall be construed or implied as:

(a) establishing between the Parties hereto any partnership or any other form of relationship entailing joint liability other than in respect of the joint investment in the Company as contemplated hereunder;

(b) constituting either of the Parties as the agent of the other Party (except with prior written consent from the other Party);

(c) authorizing either Party to make any representation or warranty on behalf of the other Party (except with prior written consent from the other Party); or

(d) authorizing either Party to incur any expenses or any other form of obligation on behalf of the other Party (except with prior written consent from the other Party).

25.2 This Agreement is made for the benefit of the Parties hereto and their respective lawful successors and assignees and is legally binding on them.

25.3 This Agreement shall not be deemed to grant to any third party any interest in or right to enforce the Agreement.

25.4 This Agreement shall not be changed verbally, but only by a written agreement signed by the Parties[and, where required under Applicable Law, on approval by

24.3 无论本协议前述条款有何规定，双方同意每一方均有权就任何违反保密义务或知识产权侵权的主张，向任何一个有管辖权的法院寻求适用法律项下允许的实际履行、禁令或其他类似的救济措施。

24.4 当任何争议发生并且正在通过友好协商或仲裁解决时，双方应继续行使和履行其各自在本协议项下的其他权利和义务，但与争议事项有关的权利和义务除外。

25. 一般规定

25.1 本协议任何条款均不得被解释为：

（a）在双方之间形成任何合伙关系或除本协议下对合资公司的共同投资以外的任何其他导致连带责任的关系；

（b）使一方成为另一方的代理人（另一方事先书面同意的除外）；

（c）授权一方代表另一方作出任何陈述或保证（另一方事先书面同意的除外）；或

（d）授权一方代表另一方产生任何费用或其他任何形式的义务（另一方事先书面同意的除外）。

25.2 本协议为了双方以及各自的合法继受者和受让人的利益而订立且对其有法律约束力。

25.3 本协议不得视为授予任何第三方在本协议项下的任何利益或执行本协议的权利。

25.4 本协议不得以口头方式修改，而须经双方签署书面协议，【且当适用法律要求时，经相关审批和备案机关批准】后方可修改。

25.5 如果一方未行使或延迟行使其根据本协议被授予的任何权利、权力或特权，不构成该方对该等权利、权力

the relevant Approval and Record-filing Authority].

25.5 Either Party's failure to exercise or delay in exercising any right, power or privilege granted pursuant to this Agreement shall not operate as a waiver thereof, and any single or partial exercise of any right, power or privilege shall not preclude any subsequent or further exercise of that or any other right, power or privilege.

25.6 The rights and remedies granted pursuant to this Agreement shall be in addition to, not instead of, any right or remedy available to a Party under Applicable Law.

25.7 The invalidity of any provision of this Agreement shall not affect the validity of any other provision of this Agreement.

25.8 This Agreement and the Annexes hereto constitute the entire agreement between the Parties hereto with respect to the subject matter of this Agreement and supersede all prior discussions, negotiations and agreements between them.

25.9 A Party shall, at any time, upon the request of the other Party, execute or procure the execution of such documents, agreements or deeds and do or procure the doing of such acts and things as may be reasonably necessary (a) to give full effect to the provisions of this Agreement or (b) in connection with any and all registrations and filings to be completed by or on behalf of the Company as provided under Applicable Law.

25.10 Save as otherwise provided in this Agreement, each Party shall bear its own legal and other professional costs in relation to its negotiation, execution and performance of this Agreement.

25.11 In case of any inconsistency between the Articles of Association and this Agreement, this Agreement shall prevail. If any such inconsistency is identified then the Parties shall do all things and execute all documents, including where necessary making amendments to the Articles of Association, as may be necessary to remove the inconsistency and ensure that terms of the Articles of Association conform to the terms of this Agreement.

25.12 The Annexes hereto are made an integral part of this Agreement and are equally binding with the main body of the Agreement. In the event of any conflict

或特权的放弃，并且单独或者部分行使任何权利、权力或特权，并不妨碍其随后或将来行使该等或任何其他权利、权力或特权。

25.6 根据本协议授予的权利和救济应作为一方在适用法律项下可获得的权利或救济的补充，而非代替。

25.7 本协议的任何条款的无效不影响本协议任何其他条款的效力。

25.8 本协议及其附件构成双方就本协议标的事项达成的全部协议，并且取代双方之间此前就该标的进行的所有磋商、谈判以及达成的协议。

25.9 在（a）使本协议条款具有完全的效力，或（b）使合资公司完成或代表合资公司完成适用法律规定的任何和所有登记和备案的合理必要范围内，经一方随时要求，另一方应签署（或促使第三方签署）有关文件、协议或契约并采取（或促使第三方采取）相关行动和事项。

25.10 除非本协议另有规定，每一方应承担其自身与本协议的谈判、签署及履行相关的律师费或其他专业顾问费用。

25.11 如果公司章程与本协议之间存在任何不一致，以本协议为准。如果发现任何该等不一致，则协议双方应实施所有行为并签署所有文件，包括对公司章程进行必要的修订，以消除不一致并确保公司章程的条款符合本协议条款。

25.12 本协议的附件为本协议不可分割的部分，并且与本协议正文的条款具有同等约束力。如果本协议正文的条款与附件的条款有冲突，以本协议正文条款为准。

25.13 本协议及其解释适用中华人民共和国法律。

between the terms and provisions of the main body of the Agreement and the Annexes, the provisions of the main body of this Agreement shall prevail.

25.13 This Agreement is governed by and will be construed in accordance with the laws of the People's Republic of China.

25.14 This Agreement may be executed in counterparts where each counterpart constitutes an original and all counterparts together constitute the same Agreement. A Party may execute this Agreement by signing and sending (including by facsimile or email) a counterpart copy to the other Party.

25.15 This Agreement is executed in both Chinese and English. Both language versions shall be equally valid.

IN WITNESS WHEREOF, each of the Parties hereto has caused this Agreement to be executed by its duly authorized representative on the date first set forth above in [CITY, PROVINCE], People's Republic of China.

[PARTY A NAME]	[PARTY B NAME]
By:________________________	By:________________________
Name:______________________ (NAME IN CHINESE)	Name:______________________
Position:____________________	Position:____________________
Nationality:__________________	Nationality:__________________

25.14　本协议可以签署副本，每一副本构成一份协议原件，且所有副本共同构成同一份协议。一方可以通过签字并向另一方发送（包括通过传真或电子邮件）一份副本的方式签署本协议。

25.15　本协议以中文和英文签署。两种文本具有同等效力。

双方已于本协议首页所载日期在中华人民共和国【填入省市】通过其正式授权的代表签署本协议，以资证明。

【填入甲方名称】	【填入乙方名称】
签署：______________	签署：______________
姓名：______________	姓名：______________
（填入中文姓名）	
职务：______________	职务：
国籍：______________	国籍：______________

Annex 1 Definitions and Interpretation

Part A Definitions

Unless the terms or context of this Agreement otherwise provide, the following terms shall have the meanings set out below:

"Accounting Standards for Business Enterprises – Basic Standards" means the specific accounting standards and other relevant regulations as amended by the Ministry of Finance of China in 2014.

"Additional Permits" means all the government approvals, consents, registrations and licenses listed in Annex 5 hereto in respect of the operation of the Company or the effectiveness or performance of any Ancillary Agreement (other than [the Approval Certificate and] the Business License).

"Affiliate" means any company which, directly or indirectly, is Controlled by, under common Control with, or in Control of, a Party.

"After-tax Net Profits" means revenue plus all other income, minus all costs, including applicable taxes, that may be payable or accruable during an accounting period.

"Agreement" shall have the meaning set out in the preamble.

"AMR" means the State Administration for Market Regulation of China or its relevant local Administration for Market Regulation.

"Ancillary Agreements" means the agreements listed in Annex 6 hereto.

"applicable ethical rules" shall have the meaning set out in Clause 8.9.

"Applicable Law" means the laws, regulations, rules, notices, and other legislative, executive or judicial decisions or pronouncements binding on either Party, the Company or in relation to the subject matter of this Agreement.

["Approval and Record-filing Authority" means the Ministry of Commerce of China or other authority entrusted by it (a) to approve and/or accept the filing of this Agreement in respect of the establishment of the Company, and (b) to approve and/or accept the filing of any amendments hereto or other submissions in compliance with Applicable Law.]

附件一 定义和解释

第一部分 定义

除非本协议条款另有约定或上下文另有所指，下列用语的含义如下：

“企业会计准则——基本准则”指中国财政部于2014年发布及后续修订的具体会计准则和其他有关规定。

“附加许可”指附录五所载的、与合资公司运营或任何附属协议生效或履行有关的政府批准、同意、登记和许可（不包括【批准证书】和营业执照）。

“关联方”指被一方直接或间接控制、与该方共同受控制或者控制该方的任何公司。

“税后净利润”指收入加所有其他收益，减去一个会计期间内可能应付或应计的所有成本，包括适用的税费。

“本协议”具有前言中所给出的含义。

“市场监督管理局”指中国国家市场监督管理总局或相关的地方市场监督管理局。

“附属协议”指本协议附件六所列协议。

“适用的道德规则”应具有本协议第8.9条中所给出的含义。

“适用法律”指对本协议一方或合资公司有约束力的或者与本协议标的有关的法律、法规、规章、通知以及其他立法、行政或司法判决或声明。

【“审批和备案机关”指中国商务部，或由其委托（a）就合资公司的成立批准本协议和/或接受本协议备案，以及（b）批准符合适用法律的任何相关变更或其他申请的提交和/或受理前述事项备案的其他机关。】

["Approval Certificate" means the certificate issued by the Approval and Record-filing Authority approving the establishment of the Company and this Agreement and the Articles of Association.]

"Articles of Association" means the Articles of Association of the Company executed by the Parties in [CITY AND PROVINCE], China on the date hereof.

"Bid Manager" means an independent and qualified third party conforming to the requirements and performing the duties set out in Clause 16.6.

"Bidding Period" shall have the meaning set out in Clause 16.6(b).

"Board" means the board of Directors of the Company, as constituted from time to time.

["Board Deadlock Matter" means any matter required to be decided by the Board in accordance with Clause 9.2 which the Board fails to reach an agreement on so as to enable it to pass the relevant resolution in the manner required under Clause 9 (as the case may be) within [20] Business Days after the date of the Board meeting at which the matter is first tabled for discussion or the date on which a written resolution in relation to the matter is first circulated to the Directors.]

"Board of Supervisors" means the board of Supervisors of the Company, as constituted from time to time.

"Breaching Party" shall have the meaning set out in Clause 21.1(a).

"Business" means the business undertaken by the Company from time to time in accordance with the Business Plan.

"Business Day" means a day (other than a Saturday, Sunday or public holiday) on which banks generally are open for business in the PRC and [PARTY B HOME COUNTRY].

"Business License" means the first business license of the Company issued by the AMR.

"Business License Issuance Date" means the date the Business License is issued to the Company by the AMR.

"Business Plan" means the business plan for the Company as approved by the Board from time to time.

【“批准证书”指由审批和备案机关签发的，批准成立合资公司、本协议以及公司章程的证书。】

“公司章程”指由双方在本协议签署日在中国【填入省市】签订的合资公司的章程。

“竞标管理人”指根据本协议第16.6条的规定遵守要求和履行职责的独立且合格的第三方。

“竞标期间”应具有本协议第16.6（b）条中所给出的含义。

“董事会”指合资公司的董事会，其人员构成可能不时发生变化。

【“董事会僵局事件”指任何需要董事会根据本协议第9.2条决定的事项发生以下任何情形：在董事会将此事项列入董事会议事日程之日或在就此事项做出的书面决议第一次在董事间传阅之日后的【20】个工作日内，董事会因未达成一致而未能就该事项根据本协议第9条要求的方式通过相关决议（视情况而定）。】

“监事会”指合资公司的监事会，其人员构成可能不时发生变化。

“违约方”应具有本协议第21.1（a）条中所给出的含义。

“目标业务”指合资公司根据业务计划不时开展的业务。

“工作日”指中国和【外方本国】的银行通常对外营业的一天（周六、周日或公共假日除外）。

“营业执照”指由市场监督管理局颁发的合资公司的第一份营业执照。

“营业执照颁发日”指由市场监督管理局向合资公司颁发营业执照的日期。

“业务计划”指董事会不时批准的合资公司的业务计划。

"Call Option Exercise Notice" means an irrevocable written notice from the Notifying Party to the other Party claiming the Notifying Party's rights to cause the other Party to sell all of the other Party's Equity Interests to the Notifying Party which shall include the following terms: (a) the Reference Price, (b) the Designated Equity Interests (and the corresponding percentage of Registered Capital) to be purchased, and (c) the anticipated date of completion of the Transfer of the Designated Equity Interests.

"Capital Increase" shall have the meaning set out in Clause 4.8.

"Capital Reduction" shall have the meaning set out in Clause 4.9.

"Chairman" means the Chairman of the Board.

"Change of Control" means a person who Controls a company as at the date of this Agreement ceases to do so or another person acquires Control of it after the date of this Agreement.

"Chief Financial Officer" or "CFO" means the chief financial officer or chief accountant of the Company.

"China" and "PRC" means the People's Republic of China, for the purpose of this Agreement, excluding the Hong Kong and Macao Special Administrative Regions and Taiwan.

"Company" means the Company to be established by the Parties pursuant to this Agreement and the Articles of Association.

"Company Law" means the Company Law of the People's Republic of China.

"Company Registration Documents" means the each of (a) this Agreement, (b) the Articles of Association, (c) the [Lease Agreement] and (d) the Business License (and its duplicate) issued by AMR.

"Company Registration Number" means the unique alphanumeric code associated with a company as provided on its business license or similar document, or on file with the relevant company registration authority.

"Competing Business" means any business which competes with the Business.

“购买选择权行权通知”指通知方向另一方发出的不可撤销的书面通知，主张行使通知方促使另一方将另一方的全部股权出售给通知方的权利，其中应包括以下条款：（a）参考价格；（b）拟购买的指定股权（以及相应的注册资本比例）；和（c）指定股权转让的预计完成日期。

“增资”应具有本协议第4.8条中所给出的含义。

“减资”应具有本协议第4.9条中所给出的含义。

“董事长”指董事会董事长。

“控制权变更”是指在本协议签署日控制公司的人在本协议签署日后不再享有控制权或其他人取得对公司的控制权。

“首席财务官”指合资公司的首席财务官或总会计师。

“中国”和“中华人民共和国”指中华人民共和国，为本协议目的，不包括中国香港特别行政区、中国澳门特别行政区和中国台湾地区。

“合资公司”指双方根据本协议和公司章程设立的合资公司。

“公司法”指《中华人民共和国公司法》。

“公司注册文件”指（a）本协议，（b）公司章程，（c）【租赁协议】和（d）市场监督管理局颁发的营业执照（及其副本）。

“公司注册号”指与公司相关联的，其营业执照或类似文件所载的，或相关公司注册机构档案所载的唯一字母数字代码。

“竞争业务”指与目标业务相竞争的任何业务。

"Confidential Information" means any and all information whether commercial, marketing, technical, scientific or other information relating to the business of the Parties, including without limitation, know-how, data, processes, designs, photographs, drawings, specifications, software programs, and samples, which is marked with an indicator such as "Confidential" or "Proprietary," is disclosed in circumstances of confidence, or would be understood by the Parties, exercising reasonable business judgement, to be confidential. For the avoidance of doubt, the existence and contents of this Agreement shall also be considered Confidential Information, and Confidential Information disclosed by an agent, attorney, accountant or other advisor of a Party shall be deemed to be disclosed by such Party.

"Consent to Transfer" means an irrevocable written waiver of a Party's Right of First Refusal and consent to the proposed Transfer of the Designated Equity Interests from the Transferring Party to a Proposed Transferee.

"Control" means (whether directly or indirectly) the right to exercise more than 50% of the votes exercisable at any meeting of a company, to elect or appoint a majority of directors or to direct the management of a company.

"Corporate Opportunity" means investment or business opportunity or other arrangement of prospective economic advantage to the Company in which the Company may have an interest or expectancy.

"Cure Period" shall have the meaning set out in Clause 21.2(a).

"D&O Insurance" means the liability insurance which the Company may purchase on behalf of its Directors and officers against liability alleged against or incurred by a Director or officer of the Company in connection with claims arising from an act or omission of a Director or officer in his capacity as a director, officer, employee, agent fiduciary or consultant of the Company.

"Deadlock Matter" means either a Shareholder Deadlock Matter or a Board Deadlock Matter.

"Deadlock Notice" means written notice from the Directors of either Party to the Chairman and other Directors of the existence of a Board Deadlock Matter.

"Designated Equity Interests" means the Equity Interests proposed by either Party to be Transferred pursuant to this Agreement.

“保密信息”指标明为“保密”或“……所有”的、在保密情况下披露的、或双方根据合理的商业判断应理解为保密信息的与双方业务相关的任何和所有商业、营销、技术、科学或其他信息，包括但不限于专有技术、数据、工艺、设计、照片、图纸、技术参数、软件程序和样品。为避免疑义，本协议的存在及其内容也应视为保密信息，并且由一方的代理、律师、会计师或其他顾问披露的保密信息也应视为该方披露的保密信息。

“转让同意书”是指一方对优先购买权不可撤销的书面放弃，并同意转让方将指定股权转让给拟定受让方的拟议转让。

“控制”是指（无论直接或间接）行使超过50%在公司任何会议上可行使的表决权，选举或任命大多数董事或指导公司管理的权利。

“公司机会”是指合资公司可能有利益或期望的投资或商业机会或其他对合资公司有预期经济利益的安排。

“补救期”应具有本协议第21.2（a）条中所给出的含义。

“董事及高级管理人员责任保险”指公司可代表其董事和高级管理人员购买的责任保险，以承保与董事或高级管理人员作为合资公司的董事、高级管理人员、雇员、受托代理或顾问行使职权时的作为或不作为而引起的索赔相关的，董事或高级管理人员被指控的或其引起的责任。

“僵局事件”指股东僵局事件或董事会僵局事件。

“僵局通知”指任何一方的董事向董事长及其他董事发出的董事会僵局事件存在的书面通知。

“指定股权”指任何一方根据本协议拟转让的股权。

"Director" means a director of the Board.

"Disclosing Party" shall have the meaning set out in Clause 20.1.

"Dispose" means sell at public or private sale, exchange, convey or otherwise dispose, and "Disposal" shall be construed accordingly.

"Dispute" shall have the meaning set out in Clause 24.1.

"Distributable Profits" shall have the meaning set out in Clause 12.9(b).

"Effective Date" means the effective date of this Agreement, being the date on which this Agreement has been executed by the duly authorized representatives of both Parties.

"Encumbrance" means any claim, deposit, charge, mortgage, security, lien, option, equity, power of sale or hypothecation or other third party right, retention of title arrangement, right of pre-emption, right of first refusal or security interest of any kind.

"Equity Interests" means the Party A Equity Interests and/or the Party B Equity Interests, as the case may be.

["Euro" or "EUR" means the lawful currency of the European Union.]

"Exercise Notice" means an irrevocable written notice from the other Party to the Transferring Party claiming the other Party's Right of First Refusal.

"Fair Market Value" shall have the meaning set out in Clause 17.5.

"First Board Meeting Resolutions" means the resolutions passed at the first meeting of the Board, held in accordance with the provisions of Clause 9.1(a).

"First Shareholders Meeting Resolutions" means the resolutions passed at the first meeting of the shareholders, held in accordance with the provisions of Clause 7.2.

"Force Majeure" means all events which are beyond the control of the Parties to this Agreement, and which are unforeseen, unavoidable or insurmountable, and which prevent total or partial performance by either Party. Such events shall include earthquakes, typhoons, flood, fire, war, strikes, riots, acts of governments, changes in law or the application thereof or any other instances which cannot be foreseen, prevented or controlled, including instances which are accepted as Force Majeure in general international commercial practice.

"Funding Conditions" shall have the meaning set out in Clause 5.1.

"Funding Default" shall have the meaning set out in Clause 4.11.

“董事”指董事会董事。

“披露方”应具有本协议第20.1条中所给出的含义。

“处置”是指公开或私下出售、交换、转让或以其他方式处置。

“争议”应具有本协议第24.1条中所给出的含义。

“可分配利润”应具有本协议第12.9（b）条中所给出的含义。

“生效日”指本协议的生效日，即双方正式授权的代表签署本协议的日期。

“权利负担”指任何索赔、押金、押记、抵押、担保、留置权、期权、股权、出售权或抵押权或其他第三方权利、所有权保留、优先认购权、优先购买权或任何形式的担保权益。

“股权”指甲方股权和/或乙方股权，视情况而定。

【“欧元”指欧盟的法定货币。】

“行权通知”指另一方向转让方发出的主张该另一方有优先购买权的不可撤销的书面通知。

“公平市场价值”应具有本协议第17.5条中所给出的含义。

“第一次董事会决议”指在根据第9.1（a）条的规定举行的第一次董事会会议上通过的决议。

“第一次股东会决议”指在根据本协议第7.2条的规定举行的第一次股东会会议上通过的决议。

“不可抗力”指超出本协议双方控制范围、无法预见、无法避免或无法克服的、妨碍本协议一方全部或部分履行本协议的任何事件。该等事件包括地震、台风、洪水、火灾、战争、罢工、暴动、政府行为、法律或法律适用的变更或任何其他无法预见、无法避免或无法控制的情形，包括在国际商务实践中通常被认定为不可抗力的事件。

“出资条件”应具有本协议第5.1条中给出的含义。

“出资违约”应具有本协议第4.11条中所给出的含义。

"Funding Obligations" means the capital contributions to be made by a Party both (a) in accordance with the capital contribution schedule set out in Annex 3; and (b) in accordance with the terms of any Capital Increase which has been approved by the Shareholders Meeting.

"Funding Party" shall have the meaning set out in Clause 4.12.

"General Manager" means the General Manager of the Company.

"HKIAC" shall have the meaning set out in Clause 24.2.

"HKIAC Administered Arbitration Rules" means the rules of the Hong Kong International Arbitration Centre.

["IFRS" means International Financial Reporting Standards as issued by the International Accounting Standards Board.]

"Independent Auditor" means an internationally recognized independent and competent accountant registered in China.

"Independent QVF" shall have the meaning set out in Clause 17.4.

"Indication of Interest" means written notice from either Party confirming its intent to purchase all of the Equity Interests of the other Party at the applicable Reference Price.

"Industry Valuation Method" means the valuation method selected by the Qualified Valuation Firm(s) in consultation with the Parties, which shall be a valuation method commonly used in international practice in valuing enterprises in the Company's industry on a going concern basis[and which complies with, and satisfies the requirements of Applicable Law relating to the valuation of State-owned assets].

"Insolvency Event" means circumstances under which a Party (i) has an administrator or similar officer appointed over all or a material part of its assets or undertaking; (ii) passes a resolution for winding-up (other than a winding-up for the purpose of, or in connection with, any solvent reorganization) or a court makes an order to that effect or a court makes an order for administration (or any equivalent order in any jurisdiction); (iii) enters into any composition or arrangement with its creditors (other than relating to a solvent restructuring); (iv) ceases to carry on business; (v) is unable to pay its debts as they become due in the ordinary course of business.

“出资义务”指一方（a）根据附件三所载的出资时间表；以及（b）股东会批准的任何增资条款应缴纳的出资。

“已出资方”应具有本协议第 4.12 条中所给出的含义。

“总经理”指合资公司的总经理。

“香港国际仲裁中心”应具有本协议第 24.2 条中所给出的含义。

“香港国际仲裁中心机构仲裁规则”指香港国际仲裁中心的仲裁规则。

【“国际财务报告准则”指国际会计准则理事会发布的国际财务报告准则。】

“独立审计师”指在中国注册的国际认可的独立且胜任的会计师。

“独立的合格评估机构”应具有本协议第 17.4 条中所给出的含义。

“意向函”是指任何一方发出的，确认其有意向以适用的参考价格购买另一方全部股权的书面通知。

“行业评估方法”指合格评估机构在与本协议双方协商后选定的评估方法，该评估方法应为在持续经营的基础上、对合资公司所在行业的企业进行评估的国际实践中常用的评估方法【且符合和满足适用法律有关国有资产估值要求】。

“破产事件”是指一方（i）就其资产或业务的全部或重要部分指定了管理人或类似官员；（ii）通过一项清算决议（以任何重整为目的或与之相关的清算除外），或法院作出清算或管理的命令（或任何司法辖区内的任何同等命令）；（iii）与债权人达成任何（重整相关之外的）和解或安排；（iv）停止营业；（v）无法偿还其在日常经营过程中到期的债务。

"Intellectual Property Rights" or "IPR" means any and all rights in any invention, discovery, improvement, utility model, design patent, copyrightable work, industrial design or mask work, algorithm, data structure, trade secrets or know-how, Confidential Information, or any idea having commercial value. IPR shall include any trademark, trade dress, trade name, domain name, or other marks that serve to identify and distinguish goods or services as coming from, or falling under the control of, a single source. IPR shall include all rights of whatsoever nature in computer software and data, all intangible rights or privileges of a nature similar to any of the foregoing in every case in any part of the world and whether or not registered, and all rights in any applications and granted registrations for any of the foregoing rights.

"Investment Certificate" means a certificate issued by the Company to any Party in accordance with the provisions of Clause 4.4, in respect of any capital contribution made by that Party to the Company.

"Joint Documents" shall have the meaning set out in Clause 5.3(c)(i).

["Lease Agreement" means the rental agreement entered into by the Company for the lease of its registered address.]

"Legal Action" means an action, suit, investigation, inquiry, proceeding or arbitration at law or in equity or before or by any foreign or domestic court, arbitrator or other governmental authority.

"Legal Representative" shall have the meaning set out in Clause 8.6.

"License Agreements" means the license agreements entered into from time to time between the Company and either Party (or its Affiliate).

"Long-stop Date" shall have the meaning set out in Clause 5.3.

"Management Personnel" means the Company's General Manager, Chief Financial Officer and [TITLES OF OTHER MANAGEMENT PERSONNEL].

"Material" means events or circumstances which involve or are likely to involve aggregate amounts payable by or to the Company in excess of RMB [AMOUNT] (or its equivalent in another currency), or involve an item in excess of RMB [AMOUNT] in value, or information which could influence the decisions that the Company makes in respect of the Business if omitted or misstated, as the context may require.

“知识产权”指针对以下任何一项所拥有的权利：发明、发现、改进、实用新型、外观设计、有著作权的作品、工业设计或腌模、算法、数据结构、商业秘密或专有技术、保密信息、或具有商业价值的想法。知识产权还包括商标、装潢、商号、域名，以及识别或区分某一货物或服务来自某一实体或受某一实体控制的其他标记。知识产权包括所有针对计算机软件及数据的任何性质的权利、在任何情况下在世界任何地区与上述权利性质类似的所有已登记或未登记的无形权利或特权，还包括上述权利的申请权以及登记权。

“出资证明书”指合资公司根据本协议第 4.4 条的规定向任何主体出具的证明文件，证明该主体对合资公司的出资。

“共同文件”应具有本协议第 5.3（c）（i）条中所给出的含义。

【“租赁协议”指合资公司就其注册地址的租赁而签订的租赁协议。】

“法律诉讼”指根据法律或衡平法或在任何外国或国内法院、仲裁员或其他政府机构前进行的或由其受理的诉讼、案件、调查、查询、程序或仲裁。

“法定代表人”应具有本协议第 8.6 条中所给出的含义。

“许可协议”指合资公司与任何一方（或其关联方）之间不时签订的许可协议。

“最终截止日”应具有本协议第 5.3 条中所给出的含义。

“高级管理人员”指合资公司的总经理、首席财务官以及【填入其他高级管理人员名称】。

“重大”指涉及或很有可能涉及合资公司应付或应收金额合计超过人民币【填入金额】（或等值的另一种货币），或涉及价值超过人民币【填入金额】的单个项目的事件或情形，或如果发生遗漏或虚假陈述，则会影响合资公司就业务作出的决策的信息，具体视上下文而定。

"Material Adverse Effect" means events or circumstances which are Material in amount and which have a material adverse effect on the assets, liabilities, results of operations, condition (financial or otherwise), business, or prospects of the Company taken as a whole.

"Material Breach" shall have the meaning set out in Clause 21.1.

"Material Modification" means a modification (whether by means of the imposition of additional terms and conditions or otherwise) by the relevant government departments to, as the case may be, this Agreement, the Articles of Association, or the Business License of the Company or the scope and nature of any of the Ancillary Agreements, or the Additional Permits as agreed or anticipated by the Parties, which in the opinion of either Party, will have a material adverse effect on the ability of Parties to achieve through the Company, their respective economic and operational objectives.

"Material Transactions" means any transaction to be entered into by the Company which involves or is likely to involve aggregate amounts payable by or to the Company in excess of RMB [AMOUNT] (or its equivalent in another currency), or involve an item in excess of RMB [AMOUNT] in value.

"Non-breaching Party" shall have the meaning set out in Clause 21.1(a)(ii).

"Non-funding Party" shall have the meaning set out in Clause 4.11.

"Notifying Party" shall have the meaning set out in Clause 14.3.

"Offer Price" shall have the meaning set out In Clause 16.6(b).

"Other Ancillary Agreements" means the agreements listed in Part 3 of Annex 6.

"Other Breach" shall have the meaning set out in Clause 21.2.

"Parties" shall have the meaning set out in the preamble.

"Party" shall have the meaning set out in the preamble.

"Party A" shall have the meaning set out in the preamble.

"Party A Ancillary Agreements" means the agreements listed in Part 1 of Annex 6.

"Party A Cash Contribution" shall have the meaning set out in Clause 4.3(a).

"Party A Documents" shall have the meaning set out in Clause 5.3(a).

"Party A Equity Interests" shall have the meaning set out in Clause 4.2(a).

"Party A QVF" shall have the meaning set out in Clause 17.4.

“重大不利影响”指所涉金额重大，并且对整个合资公司的资产、负债、经营业绩、（财务或其他方面的）状况、业务或前景具有重大不利影响的事件或情形。

“重大违约”应具有本协议第21.1条中所给出的含义。

“重大修改”指由有关政府部门对本协议、公司章程或合资公司营业执照或双方同意或拟定的附属协议或附加许可的范围或性质进行的修改（无论通过附加其他条款和条件或其他方式），而任何一方认为该等修改会对双方通过合资公司实现各自的经济和运营目标的能力产生重大不利影响。

“重大交易”指合资公司将签署的任何交易，该交易涉及或可能涉及合资公司应付或应收金额合计超过人民币【填入金额】（或等值的另一种货币），或涉及价值超过人民币【填入金额】的单个项目。

“非违约方”应具有本协议第21.1（a）（ii）条中所给出的含义。

“未出资方”应具有本协议第4.11条中所给出的含义。

“通知方”应具有本协议第14.3条中所给出的含义。

“报价”应具有本协议第16.6（b）条中所给出的含义。

“其他附属协议”指附件六第3部分所列的协议。

“其他违约”应具有本协议第21.2条中所给出的含义。

“双方”应具有前言中所给出的含义。

“一方”应具有前言中所给出的含义。

“甲方”应具有前言中所给出的含义。

“甲方附属协议”指附件六第1部分所列的协议。

“甲方现金出资”应具有本协议第4.3（a）条中所给出的含义。

“甲方文件”具有本协议第5.3（a）条中所给出的含义。

“甲方股权”具有本协议第4.2（a）条中所给出的含义。

“甲方合格评估机构”应具有本协议第17.4条中所给出的含义。

"Party B" shall have the meaning set out in the preamble.

"Party B Ancillary Agreements" means the agreements listed in Part 2 of Annex 6.

"Party B Cash Contribution" shall have the meaning set out in Clause 4.3(b).

"Party B Documents" shall have the meaning set out in Clause 5.3(b).

"Party B Equity Interests" shall have the meaning set out in Clause 4.2(b).

"Party B QVF" shall have the meaning set out in Clause 17.4.

"Permitted Disclosure Parties" shall have the meaning set out in Clause 20.1(c).

"Proposed Transferee" means a third-party transferee of Designated Equity Interests proposed to be Transferred by the Transferring Party.

"Purchasing Party" means a shareholder purchaser of Designated Equity Interests proposed to be Transferred by the Transferring Party pursuant to Clause 6.

"Qualified Affiliate" means a wholly-owned or majority-owned subsidiary of a Party, or a wholly-owned or majority-owned subsidiary of the (direct or indirect) parent company of such subsidiary (where the Party is the wholly-owned or majority-owned subsidiary of such parent company).

"Qualified Valuation Firm" shall have the meaning set out in Clause 17.3.

"Receiving Party" shall have the meaning set out in Clause 20.1.

"Reference Price" shall have the meaning set out in Clause 17.6.

"Registered Capital" shall have the meaning set out in Clause 4.1.

"Related Party Transaction" means any agreement, arrangement or understanding entered into between the Company and any Party or any Affiliate of a Party or any Director, officer or employee of the Company.

"Renminbi" or "RMB" means the lawful currency of China.

"Reserved Matters" means matters reserved for decision by the Shareholders Meeting (pursuant to Clause 7) or the Board (pursuant to Clause 9).

"Responsible Director" shall have the meaning set out in Clause 7.5.

“乙方”应具有本协议前言中所给出的含义。

“乙方附属协议”指附件六第2部分所列的协议。

“乙方现金出资”应具有本协议第4.3（b）条中所给出的含义。

“乙方文件”具有本协议第5.3（b）条中所给出的含义。

“乙方股权”具有本协议第4.2（b）条中所给出的含义。

“乙方合格评估机构”应具有本协议第17.4条中所给出的含义。

“经允许的披露对象”应具有本协议第20.1（c）条中所给出的含义。

“拟定受让方”指转让方拟向其转让指定股权的第三方受让人。

“购买方”指转让方根据本协议第6条拟转让的指定股权的股东购买方。

“合格的关联方”指一方的全资或控股子公司，或该等子公司（直接或间接）母公司的全资或控股子公司（而该方为该等母公司的全资或控股子公司）。

“合格评估机构”应具有本协议第17.3条中所给出的含义。

“接收方”应具有本协议第20.1条中所给出的含义。

“参考价格”应具有本协议第17.6条中所给出的含义。

“注册资本”应具有本协议第4.1条中所给出的含义。

“关联方交易”指合资公司与任何一方或一方任何的关联方或任何董事、高级职员或合资公司员工之间达成的任何协议、安排或谅解。

“人民币”指中国的法定货币。

“保留事项”指保留由股东会（根据本协议第7条）或董事会（根据本协议第9条）决定的事项。

“责任董事”应具有本协议第7.5条中所给出的含义。

"Right of First Refusal" means, in the event of a proposed Transfer by a Transferring Party to a Proposed Transferee other than a Qualified Affiliate, the right to purchase the Transferring Party's Designated Equity Interest on the same terms, granted to the other Party pursuant to the Company Law and in accordance with this Agreement.

["SASAC" means the State-owned Assets Supervision and Administration Commission of the State Council of the People's Republic of China.]

"Secretary" means the secretary of the Board.

"Senior Representatives of the Parties" means the officer or director from each of Party A and Party B listed in Annex 7, as the same may be revised from time to time by such Party, who are authorized to negotiate, agree and resolve a Board Deadlock Matter on behalf of Party A or Party B, as the case may be.

"Shareholder Deadlock Matter" means any Material matter required to be decided by the Shareholders Meeting in accordance with Clause 7 which the Shareholders Meeting fails to reach an agreement on so as to enable it to pass the relevant resolution in the manner required under Clause 7 (as the case may be) within [20] Business Days after the date of the meeting of the shareholders at which the matter is first tabled for discussion or the date on which a written resolution in relation to the matter is first circulated to the Parties.

"Shareholder Loan" means any advance of funds made by a Party to the Company under a Shareholder Loan Agreement.

"Shareholder Loan Agreement" means an agreement entered into between a Party and the Company binding such Party to advance funds to the Company.

"Shareholders Meeting" means the shareholders meeting of the Company which is the highest authority of the Company in accordance with the provisions of the Company Law, this Agreement and the Articles of Association.

"Simple Majority Board Resolution" means a resolution by the Board requiring the affirmative vote of more than half of all Directors present in person, by proxy or by telecommunications at a duly convened meeting of the Board.

"Simple Majority Shareholders Resolution" means a resolution by the Shareholders Meeting requiring the affirmative vote of shareholders representing more than half of all Voting Rights present in person, by proxy or by telecommunications at a duly convened meeting of the shareholders.

“优先购买权”指在转让方提议对合格的关联方以外的拟定受让方进行转让时，另一方根据公司法和本协议被授予的基于同等条件优先购买转让方指定股权的权利。

【“国资委”指中华人民共和国国务院国有资产监督管理委员会。】

“董秘”指董事会秘书。

“双方高级代表”指该方可对其不时进行修订的附件七中所列的甲方和乙方各自的高级职员或董事，其有权代表甲方或乙方（视情况而定）进行谈判、协议和解决董事会僵局事件。

“股东僵局事件”指任何需要股东会根据本协议第7条决定的重大事项发生以下情形：在股东会将此事项列入股东会议事日程之日或在就此事项做出的书面决议第一次在双方之间传阅之日后的【20】个工作日内，股东会因未达成一致而未能就该事项根据本协议第7条要求的方式通过相关决议（视情况而定）。

“股东贷款”指一方根据股东贷款协议向合资公司提供的资金。

“股东贷款协议”指一方与合资公司之间签订的约束该方向合资公司贷款的协议。

“股东会”指依据公司法、本协议和公司章程的规定，作为合资公司最高权力机构的股东会。

“简单多数董事会决议”指要求亲自参加、通过代理人或电信方式参加正式召开的董事会会议的所有董事半数以上投赞成票的董事会决议。

“简单多数股东会决议”是指股东会通过的决议，要求代表亲自参加、通过代理人或电信方式参加正式召开的股东会会议的所有股东所持表决权的过半数的股东投赞成票。

"Sole Submitting Party" shall have the meaning set out in Clause 16.5.

"Statutory and Discretionary Funds" means the statutory accumulation fund and the discretionary accumulation fund of the Company.

"Subsidiary" means a wholly-owned or majority-owned subsidiary of the Company.

"Supermajority Shareholders Resolution" shall have the meaning set out in Clause 7.7.

"Supervisor" means a supervisor of the Company from time to time.

"Surviving Provisions" shall have the meaning set out in Clause 14.6.

"Term" means the joint venture term of the Company as set out in Clause 14.1.

"Termination Notice" means an irrevocable written notice from the Notifying Party confirming its intent to terminate this Agreement pursuant to Clause 14.3.

"Territory" means [China].

"Third-Party Transfer Notice" means written notice from the Transferring Party to the other Party with regard to the Transfer of Designated Equity Interests to the Proposed Transferee which shall include the following terms: (a) the percentage of Designated Equity Interests it proposes to Transfer, (b) the name of the Proposed Transferee, (c) the proposed transfer price (if any), and (d) the key terms of any offer from the Proposed Transferee or agreement between the Transferring Party and the Proposed Transferee concerning the Designated Equity Interests.

"Transfer" means the assignment, conveyance, sale, transfer, mortgage, grant of a security interest or other disposition, either directly or indirectly, by operation of law or otherwise of Equity Interests.

"Transfer Documentation" shall have the meaning set out in Clause 6.3(a).

"Transferring Party" means a Party which proposes the Transfer all or part of its Equity Interests, pursuant to Clause 6.

"Unanimous Board Resolution" means a resolution by the Board requiring the affirmative vote of all Directors present in person, by proxy or by telecommunications at a duly convened meeting of the Board.

“唯一提交方”应具有本协议第 16.5 条中所给出的含义。

“法定公积金和任意公积金”指合资公司的法定公积金和任意公积金。

“子公司”指合资公司的全资或控股子公司。

“绝对多数股东会决议”应具有本协议第 7.7 条中所给出的含义。

“监事”指合资公司的监事。

“存续条款”应具有本协议第 14.6 条中所给出的含义。

“期限”指本协议第 14.1 条规定的合资公司期限。

“终止通知”指通知方发出的不可撤销的书面通知，确认其有意根据本协议第 14.3 条解除本协议。

“目标地区”指【中国】。

“第三方转让通知”指转让方向另一方发出的有关向拟定受让方转让指定股权的书面通知，其中应包括以下条款：（a）转让方拟转让的指定股权的比例，（b）拟定受让方的名称，（c）拟议转让价格（如有），以及（d）拟定受让方发出的任何要约或转让方与拟定受让方之间关于指定股权的协议的关键条款。

“转让”指通过法律或其他方式，直接或间接转让、让与、出售、转移、抵押，授予担保权益或以其他方式处置股权。

“转让文件”应具有本协议第 6.3（a）条中所给出的含义。

“转让方”指根据本协议第 6 条提议转让其全部或部分股权的一方。

“董事会一致决议”指须经亲自、委托他人或通过电信方式出席经正式召集的董事会的全体董事投票赞成的董事会决议。

"Unfunded Capital Contribution Amount" means the difference between the amount of the capital contributions to be made by a Party in accordance with its Funding Obligations and the amount of such capital contributions actually contributed.

"Unfunded Capital Subscription" means a Funding Party's unilateral subscription to all or part of the Unfunded Capital Contribution Amount resulting from a Funding Default by a Non-funding Party, pursuant to Clause 4.12.

"Unfunded Capital Subscription Notice" means an irrevocable written notice from the Funding Party to the Non-funding Party, confirming the Funding Party's intent to undertake an Unfunded Capital Subscription pursuant to Clause 4.12 and waiving its right to claim for Material Breach in respect of the Funding Default pursuant to Clause 4.13.

["United States Dollars" or "USD" means the lawful currency of the United States of America.]

"Vice Chairman" means the Vice Chairman of the Board of the Company.

"Voting Rights" means the rights to vote the Equity Interests over which the Party has voting control and all other rights within the Party's control, including in its capacity as shareholder (or as the employer or nominating Party in respect of any Director, member of a Board committee or officer of the Company), and whether in connection with a regular or special meeting of the shareholders or the Board or by unanimous written consent.

"Widely Varying Value" shall have the meaning set out in Clause 17.4.

Part B Interpretation

1. A reference to any Applicable Law or to any legislation, or to any provision of Applicable Law or of any legislation includes a reference to such Applicable Law or legislation as amended or modified from time to time.

2. A reference to a person includes any individual or entity (including any company, business or other enterprise or entity, joint venture, institution, state or government department), as the context permits.

3. References in this Agreement to the Agreement, agreements or other documents, shall mean the same as amended from time to time.

4. A reference to any PRC government authority or department includes such authority or department at the State, provincial, municipal and other levels.

“未缴纳资本出资额”指一方根据其出资义务应缴纳的出资金额与其实际缴纳的出资金额之间的差额。

“未缴纳资本认缴”指已出资方单方认缴由未出资方因在本协议第 4.12 条项下的出资违约导致的未缴纳资本出资额的全部或部分。

“未缴纳资本认缴通知”指已出资方向未出资方出具的不可撤销的书面通知，确认已出资方有意根据本协议第 4.12 条进行未缴纳出资认缴，并且放弃其就本协议第 4.13 条项下的出资违约主张重大违约的权利。

【“美元”指美利坚合众国的法定货币。】

“副董事长”指合资公司董事会副董事长。

“表决权”指一方对股权享有的投票控制权以及其控制范围内的所有其他权利，包括其作为股东（或作为合资公司任何董事、董事会成员或高级管理人员的雇主或提名方）所享有的权利，且无论是有关股东会或董事会的定期或特别会议，还是一致的书面同意。

“差异过大值”应具有本协议第 17.4 条中所给出的含义。

第二部分　解释

1. 本协议中提及任何适用法律或任何立法，或任何适用法律或立法的条款包括其不时修订后的版本。

2. 本协议中提及的“人”包括任何个人或实体（包括任何公司、营业或其他企业或实体、合营企业、机构、国家或政府部门），结合上下文语境具体确定其含义。

3. 本协议中提及的本协议、协议或其他文件包括其不时修订后的版本。

4. 本协议中提及的任何中国政府机关或部门包括国家、省、市和其他层级的该等机关或部门。

5. References in this Agreement to government ministries, bureaux, departments, commissions, agencies, etc. shall include all successor entities thereto.

6. In this Agreement, the masculine form includes the feminine form and the singular form includes the plural form, and vice versa.

7. Headings are for convenience of reference only and shall not affect the construction or interpretation of this Agreement.

8. A reference to any Party to this Agreement or to any other party to any agreement or document includes a reference to that party's successors and permitted assigns.

9. A reference to a Director, the Chairman, the Vice Chairman, the General Manager, the Chief Operating Officer or the Chief Financial Officer or similar positions means a person nominated in accordance with this Agreement holding such position in the Company from time to time.

10. A reference to an agreement or document in the agreed form shall refer to such agreement or document in the form so acknowledged and confirmed by the Parties in writing.

11. The words includes or including mean includes without limitation and including without limitation respectively.

5. 本协议中提及的政府部、局、部门、委员会、署等，也指这些机构的继受机构。

6. 在本协议中所使用的男性称谓也包括女性，单数也包括复数，反之亦然。

7. 本协议中各条款标题仅为方便查阅而设，对本协议的理解或解释无影响。

8. 本协议中提及的本协议的任何一方或任何其他协议或文件的一方包括该方的继受者及其允许的受让人。

9. 本协议中提及的董事、董事长、副董事长、总经理、首席运营官或首席财务官或类似职位，指根据本协议不时被提名在合资公司担任该等职位的人。

10. 本协议中提及的约定形式的协议或文件，指形式得到双方书面认可和确认的该等协议或文件。

11. 在本协议中，“包括”指“包括但不限于”。

Annex 2 Articles of Association

[TO INSERT]

附件二　公司章程

【待提供】

Annex 3 Capital Contribution Schedule

Subject to the prior satisfaction or waiver of the Funding Conditions, Party A and Party B shall make their respective contributions to the Company in [NUMBER] installments on the schedule as set out below.

Installment	Party A Amount	Party B Amount	On or before
First	RMB [AMOUNT]	[CURRENCY] equivalent of RMB [AMOUNT]	[DATE]
Second	RMB [AMOUNT]	[CURRENCY] equivalent of RMB [AMOUNT]	[DATE]
Final	RMB [AMOUNT]	[CURRENCY] equivalent of RMB [AMOUNT]	[DATE]

The Parties may, by separate signed agreement in writing, adjust the above capital contribution schedule as may be necessary or appropriate in accordance with the operational requirements of the Company, provided that in any event each Party shall fund the full amount of its share of the Registered Capital of the Company no later than [DATE] or such other date as may be required under Applicable Law.

附件三　出资时间表

出资条件得到满足或被放弃后，甲方和乙方应按照下列时间表分【填入数字】期缴纳其各自的出资。

分期	甲方出资金额	乙方出资金额	在如下日期或之前缴纳
第一期	人民币【填入金额】	人民币【填入金额】的等值【币种】	【填入日期】
第二期	人民币【填入金额】	人民币【填入金额】的等值【币种】	【填入日期】
最后一期	人民币【填入金额】	人民币【填入金额】的等值【币种】	【填入日期】

双方可以，通过另行签署的书面协议，根据合资公司的经营需要在必要时或酌情调整上述出资时间表，但在任何情况下，每一方都不得迟于【填入日期】或适用法律可能要求的其他日期足额缴纳其占合资公司注册资本份额的金额。

Annex 4 Funding Conditions

Neither Party shall have any obligation to make its contribution to the Company's Registered Capital until after the last of the following Funding Conditions has been satisfied or waived in accordance with this Agreement:

1. Party A has obtained or procured each of the following Party A Documents substantially in the agreed form:
   (a) final execution versions of the each of the Party A Ancillary Agreements;
   (b) a copy of the Company Registration Documents without Material Modification as follows:
      (i) final execution version of this Agreement;
      (ii) final execution version of the Articles of Association;
      (iii)final execution version of the [Lease Agreement];
      (iv)Business License (and its duplicate);
   (c) a copy of all of the Additional Permits issued by the relevant government departments without Material Modification; and
   (d) [INSERT OTHER PARTY A DOCUMENTS HERE].
2. Party B has obtained or procured each of the following Party B Documents substantially in the agreed form:
   (a) final execution versions of the each of the Party B Ancillary Agreements; and
   (b) [INSERT OTHER PARTY B DOCUMENTS HERE].
3. The Parties have
   (a) obtained or procured each of the following Joint Documents substantially in the agreed form:
      (i) final execution versions of each of the Other Ancillary Agreements;
      (ii) [INSERT OTHER JOINT DOCUMENTS HERE];

附件四　出资条件

在如下出资条件根据本协议全部得到满足或被放弃之前，任何一方均无义务向合资公司的注册资本出资：

1. 甲方已获得基本符合约定形式的下列每一份甲方文件：

（a）每一份甲方附属协议的最终签署版；

（b）未经重大修改的下列公司注册文件的复印件：

（i）本协议的最终签署版；

（ii）公司章程的最终签署版；

（iii）【租赁协议】的最终签署版；

（iv）营业执照（及其副本）。

（c）相关政府部门颁发的未经重大修改的所有附加许可的复印件；以及

（d）【在此填入其他甲方文件】。

2. 乙方已获得基本符合约定形式的下列每一份乙方文件：

（a）每一份乙方附属协议的最终签署版；和

（b）【在此填入其他乙方文件】。

3. 双方已经

（a）获得基本符合约定形式的下列每一份共同文件：

（i）每一份其他附属协议的最终签署版；

（ii）【在此填入其他共同文件】；

(b) convened the first meeting of the shareholders and procured the adoption of the First Shareholders Meeting Resolutions in accordance with the provisions of Clause 7.2; and

(c) convened the first Board meeting and procured the adoption of the First Board Meeting Resolutions in accordance with the provisions of Clause 9.1.

（b）根据第 7.2 条的规定召集第一次股东会会议并促使通过第一次股东会决议；以及

（c）根据第 9.1 条的规定召集第一次董事会会议并促使通过第一次董事会决议。

Annex 5 Additional Permits

[TO INSERT]

附件五　附加许可

【待提供】

Annex 6 Ancillary Agreements

Part 1 Party A Ancillary Agreements

Party A and the Company shall enter into the following agreements in the agreed form in accordance with the provisions of Clause 5.4(a):

[NAME OF AGREEMENT]
[NAME OF AGREEMENT]
[NAME OF AGREEMENT]

Part 2 Party B Ancillary Agreements

Party B and the Company shall enter into the following agreements in the agreed form in accordance with the provisions of Clause 5.4(b):

[NAME OF AGREEMENT]
[NAME OF AGREEMENT]
[NAME OF AGREEMENT]

Part 3 Other Ancillary Agreements

The Parties shall cause the Company to enter into the following agreements with the designated counterparties in the agreed form in accordance with the provisions of Clause 5.4(c):

Agreement	Counterparty/ies
[Lease Agreement]	[NAME OF LANDLORD]
[NAME OF AGREEMENT]	

附件六　附属协议

第 1 部分　甲方附属协议

甲方和合资公司应根据第 5.4（a）条的规定签署约定形式的如下协议：

【协议名称】
【协议名称】
【协议名称】

第 2 部分　乙方附属协议

乙方和合资公司应根据第 5.4（b）条的规定签署约定形式的如下协议：

【协议名称】
【协议名称】
【协议名称】

第 3 部分　其他附属协议

双方应促使合资公司根据第 5.4（c）条的规定与指定对方签署约定形式的如下协议：

协议	对方
【租赁协议】	【房东名称】
【协议名称】	

Annex 7 Senior Representatives of the Parties

For Purposes of this Agreement, the Senior Representatives of the Parties shall be as follows:

1	[NAME OF PARTY A SENIOR REPRESENTATIVE], a citizen of [NATION OF CITIZENSHIP] with [ID Number][OR][Passport Number] [NUMBER]
2	[NAME OF PARTY A SENIOR REPRESENTATIVE], a citizen of [NATION OF CITIZENSHIP] with [ID Number][OR][Passport Number] [NUMBER]

A Party may change its designated Senior Representative at any time upon written notice to the other Party.

附件七　双方高级代表

为本协议的目的，双方高级代表如下所示：

1	【甲方高级代表的姓名】，【填入国籍国】公民，【身份证号码】或【护照号码】为【填入号码】
2	【乙方高级代表的姓名】，【填入国籍国】公民，【身份证号码】或【护照号码】为【填入号码】

一方可随时书面通知另一方变更其指定高级代表。

Annex Ⅱ
Sample JV Articles of Association Template

Dated [DATE]

ARTICLES OF ASSOCIATION

of

[COMPANY NAME]

COMPANY

by and between

[PARTY A NAME]

PARTY A

and

[PARTY B NAME]

PARTY B

附件Ⅱ

合资企业章程模板样本

【填入日期】

【填入公司名称】

章程

由

【填入甲方名称】

甲方

与

【填入乙方名称】

乙方

签订

TABLE OF CONTENTS

目录

ARTICLES OF ASSOCIATION

These Joint Venture Articles of Association ("Articles of Association") are made on [DATE] (the "Effective Date") by and between:

[PARTY A NAME][(Unified Social Credit Code [NUMBER])], a [PARTY A ENTITY FORM], organized and existing under the laws of China with its registered address at [ADDRESS] (hereinafter referred to as Party A), and

[PARTY B NAME][(Company Registration Number [NUMBER])], a [PARTY B ENTITY FORM] organized and existing under the laws of [PARTY B JURISDICTION OF INCORPORATION], with its [registered address][OR][principal place of business] at [ADDRESS] (hereinafter referred to as Party B).

Each of Party A and Party B shall hereinafter be referred to individually as a "Party" and collectively as the "Parties."

BACKGROUND

Party A and Party B have agreed to establish a joint venture company (the "Company") for the purpose of engaging in the Business in accordance with Applicable Law, the provisions of the Joint Venture Agreement of even date herewith entered into by the Parties ("Joint Venture Agreement") and the provisions of these Articles of Association.

Now therefore, after friendly consultations conducted in accordance with the principles of equality and mutual benefit, the Parties hereby agree as follows:

1. DEFINITIONS AND INTERPRETATION

Unless the provisions or context of these Articles of Association provide otherwise, these Articles of Association, the Annexes and the terms used herein shall be interpreted in accordance with Annex 1.

章　　程

本合资企业章程（“本章程”）于【填入日期】（生效日）由以下双方签订：

【填入甲方名称】【（统一社会信用代码为【填入号码】）】，一家根据中国法律组建及存续的【填入甲方组织形式】，其注册地址为【填入地址】（以下简称甲方），与

【填入乙方名称】【（公司注册号码为【填入号码】）】，一家根据【填入乙方组建地】法律组建及存续的【填入乙方组织形式】，其【注册地址】【或】【主要营业地】为【填入地址】（以下简称乙方）。

甲方和乙方以下各称“一方”，合称“双方”。

背景

甲方和乙方同意，将根据适用法律、双方与此同时签订的合资协议（“合资协议”）的条款以及本章程的条款，设立一家合资公司（“合资公司”）以从事目标业务。

因此，依照平等互利的原则进行友好协商后，双方现协议如下：

1. 定义与解释

除本章程条款另有约定或上下文另有所指，本章程及其附件和本章程中所有相关用语的解释规则见附件一。

2. ESTABLISHMENT OF THE COMPANY

2.1 The Company shall be established in accordance with the terms and provisions of the Joint Venture Agreement and the provisions of these Articles of Association.

2.2 The Company particulars shall be as follows:

(a) The name of the Company shall be [COMPANY NAME IN CHINESE] in Chinese and [COMPANY NAME IN ENGLISH] in English.

(b) The Company shall be established as a limited liability company under the laws of China.

(c) The registered address of the Company shall be [ADDRESS].

3. BUSINESS OF THE COMPANY

3.1 The scope of business of the Company shall include [DESCRIPTION OF BUSINESS OF THE COMPANY] (the "Business").

3.2 The Company shall conduct the Business in [China] (the "Territory") and such additional jurisdictions as the Board may approve by Unanimous Board Resolution, subject to compliance with the requirements of Applicable Law.

3.3 Each of the Parties shall use all reasonable endeavors to develop and promote the Business of the Company.

4. CAPITALIZATION OF THE COMPANY

4.1 The registered capital of the Company ("Registered Capital") shall be RMB [AMOUNT].

4.2 The Parties shall hold the following percentages of the Registered Capital:

(a) Party A shall hold [60%] of the Registered Capital (the "Party A Equity Interests"); and

(b) Party B shall hold [40%] of the Registered Capital (the "Party B Equity Interests").

4.3 In consideration of such allocations of the Registered Capital, the Parties shall make the following capital contributions to the Company:

(a) Party A shall contribute to the Company RMB [AMOUNT] in cash ("Party A Cash Contribution"); and

2. 合资公司的设立

2.1 合资公司应根据合资协议及本章程规定的条款设立。

2.2 合资公司的具体信息如下：

（a）合资公司的中文名称为【填入合资公司的中文名称】，英文名称为【填入合资公司的英文名称】。

（b）合资公司为中国法项下的有限责任公司。

（c）合资公司的注册地址为【填入地址】。

3. 合资公司的目标业务

3.1 合资公司的经营范围应包括【填入合资公司目标业务的描述】（“目标业务”）。

3.2 受限于适用法律的规定，合资公司应在【中国】（“目标地区”）以及董事会可能通过董事会一致决议批准的其他地区开展目标业务。

3.3 双方应尽一切合理努力发展和推动合资公司的目标业务。

4. 合资公司的资本

4.1 合资公司的注册资本（“注册资本”）应为人民币【填入金额】。

4.2 双方应持有的注册资本的比例如下：

（a）甲方应持有注册资本的【60%】（“甲方股权”）；且

（b）乙方应持有注册资本的【40%】（“乙方股权”）。

4.3 鉴于上述注册资本的分配情况，双方应按照以下约定向合资公司出资：

（a）甲方应以现金向合资公司出资人民币【填入金额】（“甲方现金出资”）；且

(b) Party B shall contribute to the Company the [CURRENCY] equivalent of RMB [AMOUNT] in cash ("Party B Cash Contribution").

Subject to the prior satisfaction or waiver of the Funding Conditions, each Party shall make its contribution to the Registered Capital of the Company in accordance with the capital contribution schedule set out in Annex 2.

5. TRANSFER OF EQUITY INTERESTS

Transfer of Equity Interests to any person who is not a Party hereunder, shall be conducted as separately agreed by the parties in writing and in accordance with Applicable Law.

6. SHAREHOLDERS MEETINGS AND RESOLUTIONS

6.1 The Shareholders Meeting is the highest authority of the Company.

6.2 The Company shall hold an annual general meeting of the shareholders to conduct the following business:

(a) to elect the Directors and the Supervisors (other than Supervisors representing the employees of the Company);

(b) to approve the annual budget and financial reports of the Company;

(c) to determine the annual allocations to the Company's discretionary accumulation fund and approve the retention of earnings and distribution of Distributable Profits by way of dividends in accordance with the terms of these Articles of Association; and

(d) to conduct such other business as provided in these Articles of Association and in accordance with Applicable Law.

6.3 Interim meetings of the shareholders may be held as requested by more than one-third of the Directors of the Board, at the request of a Party (so long as it holds 10% or more of the Registered Capital of the Company), or at the request of the Board of Supervisors. In each case, such request shall be in writing and specify the matters proposed to be discussed in reasonable detail (which shall be matters within the authority of the Shareholders Meeting under these Articles of Association and Applicable Law) and shall be delivered to the Chairman, the Vice Chairman, the Secretary and the Parties (or the other Party as the case may be).

（b）乙方应以现金向合资公司出资等值于人民币【填入金额】的【填入币种】（“乙方现金出资”）。

受限于对出资条件的事先满足或放弃，每一方应按照附件二 所载的出资时间表向合资公司缴纳注册资本。

5. 股权转让

向非本章程当事方的任何人转让股权，应按照各方的另行书面约定并按照适用法律的规定进行。

6. 股东会及其决议

6.1 股东会是合资公司的最高权力机构。

6.2 合资公司应召开年度股东会会议以完成以下事项：

（a）选举董事及监事（作为合资公司职工代表的监事除外）；

（b）通过合资公司的年度预算及财务报告；

（c）确定合资公司任意公积金的年度提取比例，并按照本章程的条款批准留存收益以及以股息的方式对可分配利润的分配；以及

（d）完成适用法律和本章程规定的其他事项。

6.3 应 1/3 以上的董事、一方（只要其持有 10% 以上的合资公司注册资本）或监事会的要求，可召开临时股东会会议。在每种情形下，该等请求均应采用书面形式，并以合理的详细程度具体说明拟议事项（该等事项应为本章程和适用法律项下在股东会职权范围内的事项），且该等书面请求应递交董事长、副董事长、董秘和双方（或另一方，视情况而定）。

6.4 The Board shall convene and the Chairman of the Board shall preside over the annual general meeting and any interim meetings of the shareholders. If the Chairman is unable or fails to perform his duties, such meetings of the shareholders shall be presided over by the Vice Chairman. If the Vice Chairman is unable or fails to perform his duties, a director nominated by the Board by Simple Majority Board Resolution (the "Responsible Director") shall preside over the meetings of the shareholders.

6.5 The Secretary, under the direction of the Chairman, Vice Chairman or the Responsible Director, shall give each Party at least [20] Business Days written notice in advance of any meeting of the shareholders. Such notice shall specify the date, time and place of such meeting. Such written notice shall be accompanied by a copy of the agenda, the proposed draft resolutions and other related materials. The foregoing notice requirements may be waived in respect of a meeting of the shareholders with the assent of both Parties before, during or after such meeting. If a Party attends a meeting of the shareholders, it shall be deemed to have waived notice of such meeting.

6.6 Approval of resolutions in respect of the following matters shall be by shareholders representing more than two-thirds of the Voting Rights of the Company (each a "Supermajority Shareholders Resolution"):

(a) the amendment of these Articles of Association;

(b) any Capital Increase or Capital Reduction;

(c) the merger, amalgamation or other combination of the Company with any other entity or company;

(d) the division the Company into two or more separate legal entities;

(e) the dissolution, winding up or liquidation of the Company;

(f) the conversion of the corporate form of the Company;

(g) the approval of the retention of earnings and distribution of Distributable Profits by way of dividends in accordance with the terms of these Articles of Association; or

(h) such other matters which require Supermajority Shareholders Resolution as

6.4 年度股东会会议及临时股东会会议应由董事会召集，董事长主持。如果董事长无法或未能履行其职责，该等股东会会议应由副董事长主持。如果副董事长无法或未能履行其职责，董事会通过简单多数董事会决议选举的董事（“责任董事”）应主持股东会会议。

6.5 董秘在董事长、副董事长或责任董事的指导下，应在股东会会议召开前至少【20】个工作日向每一方发出书面通知。该等通知应载明该等会议的日期、时间和地点。该等书面通知应附有议程、拟议的决议草案和其他有关材料的复印件。在会议之前、期间或之后，经双方同意，可以免除上述有关股东会会议的通知要求。一方如果出席股东会会议，则视为其已放弃该等会议的通知要求。

6.6 关于以下事项的决议须经代表目标公司 2/3 以上表决权的股东表决通过（“绝对多数股东会决议”）：

（a）对本章程的修订；

（b）任何增资或减资；

（c）合资公司与任何其他实体或公司的合并或其他形式的联合；

（d）合资公司分立为两个或两个以上独立的法律实体；

（e）合资公司的解散或清算；

（f）合资公司的公司形式的变更；

（g）按照本章程的条款批准留存收益以及以股息的方式对可分配利润的分配；

（h）适用法律项下规定须经绝对多数股东会决议的其他事项。

provided under Applicable Law.

6.7 The following matters shall be approved by Simple Majority Shareholders Resolution:

(a) the election of the Directors and the Supervisors (other than the Supervisor elected as the workers' representative) and approval of their compensation;

(b) the approval of the Company's operation guidelines and investment plans;

(c) the approval of the annual budget and financial reports of the Company;

(d) the determination of the annual allocations to the Company's discretionary accumulation fund;

(e) the review and approval of other reports of the Board of Directors and the Board of Supervisors as required pursuant to Applicable Law;

(f) the approval of the granting by the Company of a financial guaranty on behalf of a shareholder or actual controller of the Company; or

(g) the approval of all other matters which require shareholder approval under Applicable Law other than such matters which require Supermajority Shareholders Resolution as provided in these Articles of Association or under Applicable Law.

6.8 Meetings of the shareholders may be attended by Party representatives in person, by proxy or by telecommunications.

6.9 In lieu of any regular or interim meeting of the shareholders, a written resolution may be adopted by the Shareholders Meeting if such resolution is sent to both Parties and is affirmatively signed and adopted by both Parties.

6.10 Shareholder Deadlock Matters shall be addressed as provided below:

(a) If a Shareholder Deadlock Matter arises, either Party may, within [20] Business Days after the meeting of the shareholders at which the Shareholder Deadlock Matter arose, request a subsequent interim meeting of the shareholders to reconsider the Shareholder Deadlock Matter.

(b) During the period between the meeting of the shareholders at which the Shareholder Deadlock Matter arose and the subsequent interim meeting of

6.7 以下事项须经简单多数股东会决议通过：

（a）董事及监事（作为合资公司职工代表的监事除外）的选举及其报酬的批准；

（b）公司经营方针和投资计划的批准；

（c）合资公司的年度预算及财务报告的批准；

（d）合资公司年度任意公积金提取比例的确定；

（e）审议批准适用法律要求的董事会和监事会的其他报告；

（f）公司为公司股东或者实际控制人提供财务担保的批准；

（g）除本章程或适用法律项下须经绝对多数股东会决议通过的事项外，须经股东会批准通过的其他所有事项的批准。

6.8 每一方的代表可以亲自、委托他人或通过电信方式出席股东会。

6.9 股东会可以通过书面决议代替任何定期或临时的股东会会议，前提是该等决议发送给双方并经双方同意签署和批准。

6.10 股东僵局事件应作如下处理：

（a）如果一项股东僵局事件发生，任一方可在发生股东僵局事件的股东会会议后【20】个工作日内，请求召开后续的临时股东会会议重新审议股东僵局事件。

（b）在发生股东僵局事件的股东会会议至后续临时股东会会议召开期间，双方应就股东僵局事件交换其他信息和观点。除非双方通过临时讨论达成一

the shareholders, the Parties shall exchange additional information and views with respect to the Shareholder Deadlock Matter. Unless the Parties achieve consensus through interim discussions, the Parties shall meet in-person at such subsequent interim meeting to reconsider and resolve the Shareholder Deadlock Matter.

(c) If the Shareholder Deadlock Matter is not resolved in accordance with Article 6.10(b), then either Party shall have the right to submit a Termination Notice in accordance with the provisions of Article 12.3(d).

(d) No Shareholder Deadlock Matter may be referred by a Party for determination by arbitration.

7. BOARD OF DIRECTORS

7.1 The Company shall establish a Board of Directors to be responsible for the supervision and management of the Company and the Business in accordance with the terms of these Articles of Association and Applicable Law.

7.2 The composition of the Board shall be as follows:

(a) The Board shall consist of [five] Directors.

(b) Party A shall have the right to nominate [three] of the [five] Directors.

(c) Party B shall have the right to nominate [two] of the [five] Directors.

7.3 Directors shall satisfy all qualification requirements under Applicable Law, including those requirements set out in the Company Law. The Party nominating a Director shall submit such nomination to the other Party and the Chairman and the Secretary together with the names, titles, nationalities, qualifications and credentials of the Director so nominated by it.

7.4 Directors shall be elected, removed and replaced as follows:

(a) Each Director shall be elected by the Shareholders Meeting for a term of [three] years and may serve consecutive terms if re-nominated by the Party originally nominating him and re-elected by the Shareholders Meeting.

(b) A Director shall serve and may be removed at the pleasure of the Party that nominated him subject to the approval of the Shareholders Meeting. If a seat on the Board is vacated by the retirement, resignation, illness, disability or

致，双方应亲自出席该等后续临时会议重新审议和解决股东僵局事件。

（c）如果股东僵局事件未根据本章程第 6.10(b) 条得到解决，则任一方均有权依据本章程第 12.3(d) 条提交终止通知。

（d）任何一方不得将股东僵局事件提交仲裁解决。

7. 董事会

7.1 合资公司应根据本章程和适用法律的条款设立董事会，负责对合资公司和目标业务的监督和管理。

7.2 董事会的组成如下：

（a）董事会应由【五】名董事组成。

（b）甲方有权提名【五】名董事中的【三】名。

（c）乙方有权提名【五】名董事中的【两】名。

7.3 董事应满足适用法律项下的所有资格要求，包括公司法中的要求。提名董事的一方应将该等提名提交至另一方以及董事长和董秘，该等被提名的董事的姓名、职位、国籍、任职资格和履历应一并提交。

7.4 董事的选任、罢免和更换应遵守以下规定：

（a）每名董事应由股东会选举产生，任期【三】年，如果经原提名方再次提名并经股东会再次选举通过，可以连任。

（b）受限于股东会的批准，董事应为提名该董事的一方服务并可以由其任意罢免。如董事席位因任何董事退休、辞职、患病、伤残或死亡，或被提名该董事的一方罢免而空出，则原提名该董事的一方应提名该董事的继任者或替代者，提交股东会

death of a Director or by the removal of such Director by the Party which originally nominated him, the Party which originally nominated such Director shall nominate a successor or replacement for such Director for approval by the Shareholders Meeting.

(c) Each nomination for election or removal of a Director shall be submitted to the Shareholders Meeting for approval at the next regular or interim meeting of the shareholders or by written resolution pursuant to Article 6.9. The Secretary shall record such election or removal of a Director in the Company's books and register the same with the AMR.

(d) Each Party shall exercise all of its Voting Rights at any regular or interim meeting of the shareholders to elect to the Board each person nominated as a Director by a Party in accordance with these Articles of Association (including any successor or replacement Director).

7.5 A Director nominated by [Party A] shall serve as Chairman and a Director nominated by [Party B] shall serve as Vice Chairman. The term of appointment of the Chairman and Vice Chairman shall be [three] years and each may serve consecutive terms if re-nominated by the original nominating Party.

7.6 The Chairman shall be the legal representative of the Company (the "Legal Representative"). The Legal Representative shall not perform any act binding on the Company without the prior approval and authorization of the Shareholders Meeting or the Board, as the case may be.

7.7 The Chairman may appoint a Secretary to assist with the management of the affairs of the Board. The Secretary shall be a responsible and mature individual who is fluent in written and spoken English and Chinese. The Secretary shall perform his duties in accordance with the provisions of these Articles of Association under the supervision of the Chairman. The Secretary may be an employee of the Company or of a Party but shall not be a Director. The term of the Secretary's appointment shall be [three] years and may serve consecutive terms if re-appointed by the Chairman. The Secretary shall have such duties as assigned by the Chairman.

7.8 The Board may from time to time establish one or more Board committees

批准。

（c）每次提名董事的任免均应在下一次定期或临时股东会会议上提交股东会批准，或根据本章程第 6.9 条通过董事会书面决议批准。董秘应在合资公司的名册中记录该等董事的任免，并向市场监督管理局登记。

（d）每一方应根据本章程，在任何定期或临时的股东会会议上行使其全部表决权，以选举一方提名的每位董事（包括任何继任或替代董事）。

7.5 董事长应由【甲方】提名的董事担任，副董事长应由【乙方】提名的董事担任。董事长和副董事长的任期应为【三】年，经原提名方再次提名可连任。

7.6 董事长应为合资公司的法定代表人（“法定代表人”）。未经股东会或董事会（视情况而定）事先批准和授权，法定代表人不得实施任何对合资公司具有法律约束力的行为。

7.7 董事长可以指定一名董秘协助管理董事会事务。董秘应有责任心且成熟，掌握流利的中英文口语和书面写作能力。董秘应在董事长的监督下，按照本章程的规定履行其职责。董秘可以是合资公司或一方的职工，但不得担任董事。董秘的任期为【三】年，经董事长再次任命，可以连任。董秘应履行董事长委派的职责。

7.8 董事会可以不时设立一个或多个董事会委员会，其成员及委托权限由董事会一致决议批准。

7.9 董事长、副董事长、董秘和每名董事应依照适用法律和董事会可能通过的其他道德政策（统称为“适用的道德规则”），对合资公司承担受托责任。

comprised of such Directors and with such delegation of authority as approved by the Board by Unanimous Board Resolution.

7.9 The Chairman, Vice Chairman, Secretary and each Director shall bear fiduciary responsibilities to the Company in accordance with Applicable Law and such additional ethical policies as the Board may adopt (collectively, "applicable ethical rules").

7.10 The Chairman, Vice Chairman, Secretary and each of the Directors shall serve without remuneration, but all reasonable costs incurred by the Chairman, Vice Chairman, Secretary and each Director in connection with the attendance at meetings of the Board and the performance of duties assigned by the Board shall be borne by the Company in accordance with such policies and guidelines as the Board may adopt from time to time by Unanimous Board Resolution.

7.11 None of the Chairman, Vice Chairman, Secretary or the Directors shall bear any personal liability for any acts performed in good faith in such capacity as assigned by the Board, except for willful misconduct, and/or acts in violation of Applicable Law or applicable ethical rules. Subject to the foregoing, the Company shall (a) take out and maintain at all times D&O Insurance at appropriate levels approved by the Board and (b) enter into appropriate indemnity undertakings in favor of the Chairman, Vice Chairman, Secretary and each Director on such terms as the Board may approve from time to time by Unanimous Board Resolution consistent with Applicable Law.

8. BOARD MEETINGS AND RESOLUTIONS

8.1 Meetings of the Board shall be held and conducted in accordance with the following terms:

(a) Regular Board meetings shall be held at least [two] times per year. Meetings generally shall be held at the registered address of the Company or such other address designated by the Board.

(b) An interim Board meeting shall be scheduled upon the written request of [two] or more of the Directors of the Company. In the case of a request for an interim Board meeting, such request shall be in writing and specify the matters

7.10 董事长、副董事长、董秘和每名董事不收取报酬，但董事长、副董事长、董秘和每名董事因出席董事会会议和履行董事会职责而产生的所有合理费用应根据董事会可能不时通过董事会一致决议所采纳的政策和准则由合资公司承担。

7.11 董事长、副董事长、董秘和董事均不得因在董事会委派的权限内善意履行的任何行为而承担任何个人责任，但故意不当行为和/或违反适用法律或适用的道德规则的行为除外。受限于上述规定，合资公司应(a)取得并始终维持董事会批准的适当程度的董事及高级管理人员责任保险，并(b)按照董事会在符合适用法律的情况下可能不时通过董事会一致决议批准的条款，订立以董事长、副董事长、董秘和每名董事为受益人的适当赔偿保证。

8. 董事会会议及其决议

8.1 董事会会议应按照以下规定召开和进行：

（a）定期董事会会议每年至少召开【两】次。会议一般应在合资公司的注册地址或董事会指定的其他地址召开。

（b）经【两】名或【两】名以上董事书面请求，应安排召开临时董事会会议。在请求召开临时董事会会议的情况下，该等请求应采用书面形式，并以合理的详细程度具体说明拟议事项（该等事项应为本章程和适用法律项下在董事会职权范围内的事项），且该等书面请求应递交董事长、副董事长、董秘和其他各个董事。

（c）董事长应召集并主持所有定期和临时董事会会议。如果董事长无法或未能履行其职责，该等董事会

proposed to be discussed in reasonable detail (which shall be matters within the authority of the Board under these Articles of Association and Applicable Law) and shall be delivered to the Chairman, the Vice Chairman, the Secretary and each of the other Directors.

(c) The Chairman of the Board shall convene and preside over all regular and interim Board meetings. If the Chairman is unable or fails to perform his duties, such Board meetings shall be convened and presided over by the Vice Chairman. If the Vice Chairman is unable or fails to perform his duties, a Responsible Director shall convene and preside over the meetings of the Board.

(d) The Secretary, under the direction of the Chairman, Vice Chairman or the Responsible Director, shall give each Director at least [20] Business Days written notice in advance of such each regular or interim Board meeting, specifying the date, time and place thereof. Written notice shall be accompanied by the agenda and such other materials relating thereto as determined by the Chairman, Vice Chairman or the Responsible Director. A Director may, within [three] Business Days following the receipt of the meeting notice, submit a written request proposing to add items to the agenda, and the Secretary, under the direction of the Chairman, Vice Chairman or the Responsible Director, shall promptly revise the agenda accordingly and re-circulate the revised meeting notice to each Director. Only matters addressed in such written notice may be presented for discussion and action at the Board meeting. Without the consent of all of the Directors, no other business shall be transacted at such Board meeting.

(e) The foregoing notice requirements may be waived in respect of a Board meeting with the assent of all of the Directors before, during or after such Board meeting. If a Director attends a Board meeting, he shall be deemed to have waived notice of such meeting.

(f) Board meetings may be attended by Directors in person, by proxy or by telecommunications.

(g) If a Director is unable to participate in a Board meeting in person or by telecommunications, he may issue a written proxy and entrust a representative

会议应由副董事长召集并主持。如果副董事长无法或未能履行其职责，责任董事应召集并主持董事会会议。

（d）在董事长、副董事长或责任董事的指导下，董秘应在每一次定期和临时董事会会议召开前至少【20】个工作日向每名董事发出书面通知，载明该等会议的日期、时间和地点。书面通知应附有议程以及董事长、副董事长或责任董事确定的其他相关材料。董事可在收到会议通知后【三】个工作日内提交书面请求，提议在议程中添加议题，董秘应在董事长、副董事长或责任董事的指导下，应及时对议程做出相应的修改，并将修改后的会议通知重新分发给每名董事。只有在该等书面通知中提及的事项方可在董事会会议上提交讨论和处理。未经全体董事同意，其他事项不得在该等董事会会议上进行讨论。

（e）在该等董事会会议之前、期间或之后，经全体董事同意，可以免除上述有关董事会会议的通知要求。董事如果出席董事会会议，则视为已放弃该等会议的通知要求。

（f）董事应亲自、委托他人或通过电信方式出席董事会会议。

（g）如果某一董事不能亲自或通过电信方式参加董事会会议，该董事可以出具书面委托书，委托一名代理人代表其参加会议。被委托的代理人应有与董事相同的权利和权力。

（h）不少于【三】名合资公司的董事（包括至少一名由乙方提名的董事）亲自、委托他人或通过电信

to participate in the meeting on his behalf. The representative so entrusted shall have the same rights and powers as the Director.

(h) No fewer than [three] Directors of the Company, including at least one Director nominated by Party B, present in person, by proxy or by telecommunications shall constitute a quorum necessary for the conduct of business at a meeting of the Board. If a quorum is not achieved at any duly called meeting of the Board, such Board meeting may be postponed to a time no earlier than [48] hours after the written notice of such postponement has been given to each of the Directors.

(i) Each Director shall have one vote. The Chairman shall have one vote in his capacity as a Director but shall not have an additional casting vote.

8.2 Approval of the following matters shall be by Unanimous Board Resolution:

(a) the adoption of the Business Plan and approval of (i) material amendments thereto and (ii) any Material Transactions outside the approved scope of thereof;

(b) formulation of proposals in respect of the retention of earnings and distribution of Distributable Profits by way of dividends in accordance with the terms of these Articles of Association, and submission of the same to the Shareholders Meeting for approval;

(c) establishment of a Subsidiary;

(d) sale or other disposition of, or granting of an Encumbrance over, all or substantially all of the Business or the assets of the Company;

(e) commencement or settlement of any Legal Action or agreement to assume any liability with a value in excess of RMB [AMOUNT];

(f) the Company's entering into, amending, terminating or waiving any rights under, any Agreement in respect of (i) a Material Transaction, or (ii) a Related Party Transaction with any Party, Party Affiliate or Management Personnel; and

(g) such other matters which require Unanimous Board Resolution as provided in these Articles of Association or under Applicable Law.

8.3 Approval of the following matters shall be by Simple Majority Board Resolution:

方式出席，即构成在董事会会议上执行议程所需的法定人数。如果任何经正式召集的董事会会议的出席人数未达到法定人数，则该等董事会会议可推迟至向每名董事发出书面延迟通知后的不少于【48】小时后。

(i) 每名董事应有一票表决权。董事长应有其作为董事的一票表决权，但没有额外的决定票表决权。

8.2 以下事项须经董事会一致决议批准：

(a) 通过经营计划以及批准（i）经营计划的重大修订和（ii）经营计划批准范围之外的任何重大交易；

(b) 根据本章程条款就留存收益以及以股息的方式对可分配利润的分配制订提案，并将其提交股东会批准；

(c) 设立子公司；

(d) 出售或以其他方式处置全部或实质上全部合资公司的目标业务或资产，或批准就全部或实质上全部合资公司的目标业务或资产设定权利负担；

(e) 开始或解决任何责任金额超过人民币【填入金额】元的法律诉讼或协议；

(f) 合资公司就（i）重大交易，或（ii）与任何一方、一方关联方或高级管理人员的关联方交易，订立、修改、终止任何协议，或放弃该等协议项下的任何权利；以及

(g) 根据本章程或适用法律的规定须经董事会一致决议通过的其他事项。

8.3 以下事项须经简单多数董事会决议批准：

(a) 制定合资公司的年度预算及财务报告方案，并将

(a) formulation of proposals in respect of the Company's annual budgets and financial reports, and submission of the same to the Shareholders Meeting for reference and/or action as appropriate;

(b) review and approval of the Company's annual production and operation plans;

(c) review and approval of Company policies and procedures regarding management of financial accounts, execution of legal documents, applicable ethical rules and ethical practices and other important matters;

(d) decisions on the appointment, compensation, discipline and dismissal of the Management Personnel;

(e) the establishment of Company bank accounts and the appointment of the Company's Independent Auditor;

(f) the establishment of bank credit facilities or the borrowing of loans having an aggregate value in excess of RMB [AMOUNT] or its equivalent in [USD][OR][EUR] in a single transaction or a series of related transactions;

(g) the purchase of capital equipment, land and buildings or other assets having an aggregate value in excess of RMB [AMOUNT] or its equivalent in [USD][OR][EUR] in a single transaction or a series of related transactions other than such purchases made in accordance with the operating budget approved by the Board and (as appropriate) the Shareholders Meeting;

(h) any expenditure in excess of, or any transaction that materially deviates from the approved annual budget or financial plan;

(i) the granting of loans or credit to any third parties in any amount (other than the sale of the Company's products or services to customers on standard deferred payment terms or the granting of purchase credits to customers in the ordinary course of business);

(j) the giving of any financial guarantee by the Company for the obligations of any third party;

(k) the execution of technology license agreements with third parties other than in the ordinary course of business on customary terms and conditions;

(l) the establishment of branch offices and liaison offices; and

其提交股东会以供参考和 / 或酌情处理；

（b）审阅并批准合资公司的年度生产和经营计划；

（c）审阅并批准合资公司关于财务账目管理、法律文件签署、适用的道德规则和道德惯例以及其他重要事项的政策和程序；

（d）决定高级管理人员的任命、薪酬、惩戒和免职；

（e）开立合资公司银行账户以及任命合资公司的独立审计师；

（f）在单笔交易或一系列相关交易中采取总计价值超过人民币【填入金额】元或等值【美元】【或】【欧元】金额的银行信贷措施或贷款；

（g）在单笔交易或一系列相关交易中购买总计价值超过人民币【填入金额】元或等值【美元】【或】【欧元】金额的固定设备、土地及建筑物或其他资产，根据董事会和股东会（视情况而定）批准的经营预算进行购买的除外；

（h）超出经批准的年度预算或财务计划的任何支出，或严重偏离经批准的年度预算或财务计划的任何交易；

（i）向任何第三方发放任何金额的贷款或信贷（以标准的递延付款条款向客户出售合资公司产品或服务，或在日常运营过程中向客户授予先发货后收款待遇的除外）；

（j）合资公司就任何第三方的义务提供任何财务担保；

（k）与第三方签署技术许可协议，在日常运营过程中以惯常的条款和条件签订的该等协议除外；

（l）设立分支机构和联络处；以及

(m) any other matter which, in accordance with the provisions of these Articles of Association, requires Board approval or which the Board determines shall require Board approval.

8.4 In lieu of any regular or interim meeting of the Board, a written resolution may be adopted by the Board if such resolution is sent to, and affirmatively signed and adopted by, all Directors then holding office.

8.5 Board Deadlock Matters shall be addressed as provided below:

(a) If a Board Deadlock Matter arises, one or more Directors nominated by a Party may, within [20] Business Days after the Board meeting at which the Board Deadlock Matter arose, submit a Deadlock Notice in the agreed form to the Chairman and all other Directors.

(b) Within [five] Business Days after submission of the Deadlock Notice, the Chairman shall refer such Board Deadlock Matter to the Senior Representatives of the Parties, who shall use all reasonable endeavors in good faith to resolve such Board Deadlock Matter within [20] Business Days from the date of such referral. Any resolution of such Board Deadlock Matter agreed to by the Senior Representatives of the Parties shall be final and binding on the Company and the Parties.

(c) If the Board Deadlock Matter is not resolved in accordance with Article 8.5(b), then either Party shall have the right to submit a Termination Notice in accordance with the provisions of Article 12.3(d).

(d) No Board Deadlock Matter may be referred by a Party for determination by arbitration.

8.6 The corporate governance provisions set out in Articles 8.1 through 8.4 shall also apply to each Subsidiary, and the Company shall ensure that corresponding provisions are incorporated into the articles of association of each such Subsidiary or otherwise adopted by such Subsidiary.

9. BOARD OF SUPERVISORS

9.1 The Company shall have a Board of Supervisors comprised of three Supervisors as follows: one Supervisor nominated by Party A, one Supervisor nominated by

（m）根据本章程的条款或根据董事会的决定，须经董事会批准的任何其他事项。

8.4 董事会可以通过书面决议代替任何定期或临董事会会议，前提是该等决议发送给届时在任的所有董事并经其同意签署和通过。

8.5 董事会僵局事件应按照以下规定处理：

（a）如果一项董事会僵局事件发生，一方提名的一名或多名董事可在发生董事会僵局事件的董事会会议后【20】个工作日内，向董事长和其他所有董事发出约定形式的僵局通知。

（b）在发出僵局通知后【五】个工作日内，董事长应将该等董事会僵局事件提交双方高级代表，该等代表应尽一切合理努力在自该等董事会僵局事件提交之日起【20】个工作日内善意地解决该等董事会僵局事件。由双方高级代表同意的有关该等董事会僵局事件的任何解决方案应为最终决定，对合资公司和双方均具有约束力。

（c）如果未能根据本章程第 8.5（b）条解决董事会僵局事件，则任何一方应有权根据本章程第 12.3（d）条的规定提交终止通知。

（d）任何一方不得将董事会僵局事件提交仲裁解决。

8.6 本章程第 8.1 条至第 8.4 条所述的公司治理的规定亦适用于各子公司，且合资公司应确保相应规定已纳入各子公司的章程或以其他方式被该等子公司所采用。

9. 监事会

9.1 合资公司应设立监事会，监事会由三名监事组成，其中一名监事由甲方提名，一名监事由乙方提名，一名监事

Party B, and one Supervisor to be the workers' representative. The Supervisors nominated by Party A and Party B shall be elected by the Shareholders Meeting. The Supervisor who is the workers' representative shall be elected by the workers through the workers' representative congress or other democratic means. The term of office of a Supervisor shall be three years. A Supervisor may serve consecutive terms on expiration of his term if re-elected as provided herein. The position of Supervisor cannot be held concurrently by any Director or other Management Personnel of the Company.

9.2 The Board of Supervisors shall have one chairman, who shall be the Supervisor nominated by [Party A]. The chairman of the Board of Supervisors shall convene and preside over meetings of the Board of Supervisors. If the chairman of the Board of Supervisors is unable or fails to perform his duties, another Supervisor elected by simple majority vote of all of the Supervisors shall convene and preside over the meeting of the Board of Supervisors.

9.3 Meetings of the Board of Supervisors shall be held at least [once] per year. Any Supervisor is entitled to propose the convening of an interim meeting of the Board of Supervisors. The chairman of the Board of Supervisors shall give each Supervisor at least [20] Business Days written notice in advance of such each regular or interim meeting of the Board of Supervisors, specifying the date, time and place thereof. Such written notice shall be accompanied by the agenda and such other materials relating thereto as required under Applicable Law and as determined by the chairman of the Board of Supervisors. The Board of Supervisors shall take decisions by simple majority vote. Each Supervisor shall have one vote. The chairman of the Board of Supervisors shall not have a casting vote.

9.4 If a Supervisor retires, resigns, falls ill or loses legal capacity, the successor of the Supervisor shall be nominated and elected in the same manner as the Supervisor to be replaced. Such successor Supervisor will serve the remaining term of office of the previous Supervisor. If the re-election of the Supervisor is not conducted in a timely fashion upon the expiration of the term of the Supervisor, or if the Supervisor resigns during his term of office, thereby resulting in the Company temporarily having no successor Supervisor, then during the period prior to the

为职工代表。甲方和乙方提名的监事应通过股东会选举产生。作为职工代表的监事由职工通过职工代表大会或其他民主方式选举产生。监事的任期为三年。任期届满后，按照本条规定的选举方式可连选连任。监事不得兼任合资公司的任何董事或其他高级管理人员。

9.2 监事会设主席一名，由【甲方】提名的监事担任。监事会主席应召集和主持监事会会议。监事会主席不能或未能履行职责的，由全体监事以简单多数选举一名监事召集和主持监事会会议。

9.3 监事会会议每年应至少召开【一】次。任何监事有权提议召开临时监事会会议。监事会主席应在该等定期和临时监事会会议召开前至少【20】个工作日向每名监事发出书面通知，载明该等会议的日期、时间和地点。该等书面通知应附有议程以及适用法律要求的和监事会主席确定的其他相关材料。监事会决议应经简单多数票通过。每位监事具有一票表决权。监事会主席无决定票表决权。

9.4 如果某一监事退休、辞职、患病或失去法律行为能力，该监事的继任者应以与该监事相同的方式通过提名和选举产生。该等继任监事将完成前任监事的剩余任期。如果在监事任期届满后没有及时重新选举监事，或者监事在任期内辞职，从而导致合资公司暂时没有继任监事，则在继任监事上任之前，现任监事应继续按照适用法律和本章程的规定履行监事的职责。

9.5 监事会履行以下职责：

（a）审查合资公司的财务状况；

（b）监督董事及高级管理人员履行职责，并提议罢免违反法律、行政法规、本章程或董事会决议的董事或高级管理人员；

successor Supervisor taking up office, the existing Supervisor(s) shall continue to perform the duties of such Supervisor in accordance with Applicable Law and the provisions of these Articles of Association.

9.5 The Board of Supervisors exercises the following functions and duties:

(a) examining the Company's financial affairs;

(b) supervising the Directors and Management Personnel in the performance of their duties and to propose the removal of Directors or Management Personnel who violate laws, administrative regulations, these Articles of Association or resolutions of the Board;

(c) requiring Directors or Management Personnel to rectify their acts which are detrimental to the Company's interests;

(d) submitting proposals to the Parties;

(e) upon request of the Parties, instituting legal proceedings against Directors or Management Personnel who have violated laws, administrative regulations or these Articles of Association and have thereby caused the Company to incur a loss; and

(f) other functions and powers as provided under Applicable Law and these Articles of Association.

In addition, a Supervisor may attend meetings of the Board of Directors as a non-voting attendee and raise questions or present proposals on matters relating to Board resolutions.

10. MANAGEMENT

10.1 The Management Personnel shall consist of the following:

(a) the General Manager, to be nominated by [Party B];

(b) the CFO, to be nominated by [Party A]; and

(c) the [TITLE], to be nominated by [PARTY A][OR][PARTY B].

If any of the Management Personnel is removed by the Board, the replacement shall be nominated by the original nominating Party.

10.2 If any of the Management Personnel retires, resigns, is unable to perform

（c）要求董事或高级管理人员纠正其有损合资公司利益的行为；

（d）向双方提交提案；

（e）应双方的要求，对违反法律、行政法规或本章程并由此导致合资公司蒙受损失的董事或高级管理人员提起法律诉讼；以及

（f）适用法律和本章程规定的其他职能和权力。

此外，监事可以作为无表决权的与会者出席董事会会议，并就与董事会决议有关的事项提出问题或建议。

10. 管理层

10.1 高级管理人员应由以下人员组成：

（a）总经理，由【乙方】提名；

（b）首席财务官，由【甲方】提名；和

（c）【填入职称】，由【甲方】【或】【乙方】提名。

如果任何高级管理人员被董事会罢免，应由原提名方提名替代者。

10.2 如果任何高级管理人员退休、辞职，或因患病、残疾或死亡无法履行职责，或被董事会罢免，应由原提名方提名替代者。

10.3 每一方应使其提名的每名董事在任何定期或临时董事会会议上行使其全部表决权，以任命根据本章程第10条的规定提名的高级管理人员，包括由原提名方根据本章程的规定提名的任何继任者或替代者。

10.4 董事会应批准合资公司的整体运营管理结构和体系，总经理应向董事会报告，并在其监督和指导下工作。其他高级管理人员应向总经理报告，在其监督和指导

his duties due to illness, disability or death, or is removed by the Board, the replacement shall be nominated by the original nominating Party.

10.3 Each Party shall cause each of the Directors nominated by it to exercise all of their Voting Rights at any regular or interim Board meeting to appoint the Management Personnel as nominated in accordance with the provisions of this Article 10 in each case including any successor or replacement nominated by the original nominating Party in accordance with the provisions of these Articles of Association.

10.4 The Board shall approve the overall operation management structure and system of the Company, and the General Manager shall report to and work under the supervision and direction of the Board. The other Management Personnel shall report to and work under the supervision and direction of the General Manager. All employees of the Company other than the Management Personnel shall report to and work under the supervision and direction of the Management Personnel and such other senior managers as the General Manager may determine.

10.5 The General Manager shall be responsible for all of the day-to-day operations and management of the Company other than Reserved Matters. He shall be responsible to the Board and shall carry out all matters as directed by the Board.

11. FINANCIAL AFFAIRS AND ACCOUNTING

11.1 The Company shall at all times maintain accurate and complete accounting and other financial records, and shall prepare all accounts and financial statements in accordance with the Accounting Standards for Business Enterprises—Basic Standards [and IFRS].

11.2 The Company shall adopt Renminbi as its bookkeeping base currency, but may also adopt [USD][OR][EUR] or other foreign currencies as supplementary bookkeeping currencies.

11.3 All accounting records, vouchers, books and statements of the Company shall be made and kept in Chinese and English.

11.4 The Company's fiscal year shall begin on January 1 and end on December 31 of each year, except that the first fiscal year of the Company shall commence on the

下工作。除高级管理人员外，合资公司的全体职工应向高级管理人员和总经理可能决定的其他高级经理报告并在其监督和指导下工作。

10.5 除保留事项外，总经理应负责合资公司的所有日常运营和管理。总经理应对董事会负责，并根据董事会的指示执行所有事项。

11.财务和会计

11.1 合资公司应始终保持准确完整的会计记录和其他财务记录，并按照企业会计准则——基本准则和国际财务报告准则编制所有账目和财务报表。

11.2 合资公司应采用人民币作为记账本位币，但也可以采用【美元】【或】【欧元】或其他外币作为辅助记账货币。

11.3 合资公司的所有会计记录、凭单、账簿和报表均应以中英文编制和保存。

11.4 合资公司的会计年度应从每年的1月1日起至同年12月31日结束，但合资公司的第一个会计年度应从营业执照颁发日开始，并于同年12月31日结束，最后一个会计年度自1月1日开始，并于同年的终止日期结束。

11.5 为编制合资公司的账目和财务报表，计算要向双方分配的已宣告股息，以及对于影响货币换算可能必要的任何其他目的，货币换算应按照实际收付款之日中国人民银行公布的人民币汇率中间价或其他法定汇率所确定的挂牌汇率计算。

11.6 合资公司应按照董事会的指示编制财务报表和报告，包括本章程第11.7条规定的内容。合资公司的独立审计师应审查并核实合资公司的年度财务报告。

Business License Issuance Date and shall end on December 31 of the same year, and the last fiscal year shall commence on January 1 and end on the termination date in the same year.

11.5 For the purposes of preparing the Company's accounts and financial statements, calculation of declared dividends to be distributed to the Parties, and for any other purposes where it may be necessary to effect a currency conversion, such conversion shall be in accordance with the posted exchange rate, as determined by the median exchange rate for buying and selling Renminbi announced by the People's Bank of China or other legally recognized rate on the date of actual receipt or payment.

11.6 The Company shall prepare its financial statements and reports as directed by the Board, including those set out in Article 11.7. The Company's Independent Auditor shall examine and verify the annual financial report of the Company.

11.7 The Company shall provide the following financial reports to each Party:

(a) As soon as available, and in any event no later than [90] calendar days after the end of each fiscal year, the Company shall furnish to each Party copies of the audited balance sheet of the Company as at the end of such fiscal year and the audited statements of income, cash flow and changes in shareholders' equity for such fiscal year together with the report of the Independent Auditor.

(b) As soon as available, and in any event no later than [45] calendar days after the end of each fiscal quarter, the Company shall furnish to each Party the balance sheet of the Company as at the end of such fiscal quarter and the statements of income, cash flows and changes in Parties' equity for such fiscal quarter, in each case as certified by the CFO.

(c) The Company shall provide to each Party copies of such other reports prepared from time to time pursuant to the requirements of Applicable Law or the terms of any Agreement as and when available.

11.8 Without limiting its rights under Article 11.7, each Party (so long as it holds 10% or more of the Registered Capital of the Company) shall have the following inspection and audit rights in respect of the Company:

11.7 合资公司应向每一方提供以下财务报告：

（a）合资公司应尽早且无论如何不得迟于每个会计年度结束后【90】个日历日，向每一方提供截至该会计年度末的经审计的合资公司资产负债表和该会计年度的经审计的收益表、现金流量表及股东权益变动表的复印件，以及独立审计师的报告。

（b）合资公司应尽早且无论如何不得迟于每个财政季度结束后【45】个日历日，向每一方提供截至该财政季度末的合资公司资产负债表和该财政季度的收益表、现金流量表和股东权益变动表，且以上文件均已由首席财务官核实。

（c）合资公司应根据适用法律的要求或任何协议的条款，不时向每一方提供其他可提供的报告的复印件。

11.8 在不限制每一方在本章程第 11.7 条项下的权利的情况下，每一方（只要其持有合资公司注册资本的 10% 或以上）应对合资公司享有以下检查和审计权利：

（a）该方应有权就合资公司的高级职员、员工、审计师、财产、办公室、工厂和其他设施拥有合理的权限，以检查合资公司的资产、运营和事务。

（b）该方应有权自费任命该方的内部工作人员或独立会计师（可以是在国外注册或在目标地区注册的会计师）代表该方审计合资公司账簿、账目及其他财务、商业和法律记录。

合资公司应在得到合理的提前通知的情况下，在正常的工作时间内向该请求方及其授权代表提供对该等人员、设施和记录的合理权限。该方及其授权代表和内部或独立审计师应对所有因此获取的信息和文件保密。

(a) Such Party shall have the right to have reasonable access to the officers, employees, auditors, properties, offices, plants and other facilities of the Company to inspect the assets, operations and affairs of the Company.

(b) Such Party shall have the right, at its own expense, to appoint either the internal staff of such Party or an independent accountant (which may be either an accountant registered abroad or registered in the Territory) to audit the books, accounts and other financial, commercial and legal records of the Company on behalf of such Party.

The Company shall provide reasonable access to all such persons, facilities and records to such requesting Party and its authorized representatives during normal business hours upon reasonable advance notice. Such Party and its authorized representatives and internal or independent auditors shall keep confidential all information and documents so accessed.

11.9 Subject to the requirements of Applicable Law, and unless otherwise determined by the Shareholders Meeting by Supermajority Shareholders Resolution for any particular fiscal year, the Company shall distribute dividends to the Parties in accordance with the following terms:

(a) Each Party shall exercise all of its Voting Rights to approve distribution by way of dividend of [all] of the Distributable Profits of the Company for each fiscal year, [provided that the Company shall not declare, pay or make any dividend or other distribution until all Shareholder Loans have been repaid in full].

(b) "Distributable Profits" shall mean After-Tax Net Profits less all necessary, reasonable and prudent provisions and reserves for (i) taxation, (ii) the repayment of debt incurred by the Company, (iii) allocations to Statutory and Discretionary Funds, and (iv) other extraordinary items, in each case as determined by the Shareholders Meeting in accordance with the provisions of these Articles of Association and the requirements of Applicable Law.

(c) Dividends shall be distributed to the Parties in proportion to their respective percentage shares of the Registered Capital.

11.9 受限于适用法律的要求，除非股东会就任何特定会计年度通过绝对多数股东会决议另有决定，否则合资公司应按照以下条款向双方分配股息：

（a）每一方应行使其全部表决权，批准以股息的方式分配每个会计年度的【全部】可分配利润，【但在所有的股东贷款全部还清之前，合资公司不得宣派、支付或做出任何股息分配或其他分配】。

（b）“可分配利润”指减去以下所有必要、合理和审慎的储备金和准备金后的税后净利润：（i）税款；（ii）偿还合资公司债务；（iii）法定公积金和任意公积金的提取；（iv）其他特殊项目。在每种情况下，均应由股东会根据本章程的规定及适用法律的要求确定。

（c）股息应按双方各自所持的注册资本比例分配给双方。

（d）本章程第 11.9（a）条规定的就任何会计年度的分配应在独立审计师就该会计年度经审计的资产负债表和财务报表提交报告之日起【三】个月内作出。

12.期限和终止

12.1 本章程自生效日开始生效并持续有效，直至根据本章程第 12.2 条终止（“期限”）。

12.2 本章程将在以下情形下终止：

（a）双方书面协议终止；

（b）一方获得 100% 股权且已完成所有相关登记程序；或者

(d) A distribution under Article 11.9(a) for any fiscal year shall be made within [three] months following the date of the report of the Independent Auditor in respect of the audited balance sheet and financial statements of the Company for such fiscal year.

12. TERM AND TERMINATION

12.1 These Articles of Association shall take effect on the Effective Date and shall continue in force for an indefinite term until terminated pursuant to Article 12.2 (the "Term").

12.2 These Articles of Association shall terminate

(a) upon the written agreement of the Parties;

(b) if a Party acquires 100% of the Equity Interests and all registration formalities in respect thereof have been completed; or

(c) if an order is made, or a resolution is duly passed, to dissolve, wind up or liquidate the Company.

12.3 A Party (the "Notifying Party") shall have the right to submit a Termination Notice to the other Party to terminate these Articles of Association if:

(a) the other Party commits a Material Breach, and the Cure Period in respect thereof has expired;

(b) the other Party undergoes a Change of Control;

(c) the other Party experiences an Insolvency Event;

(d) a Deadlock Matter arises and cannot be resolved in accordance with the provisions of Article 6.10(b) or Article 8.5(b);

(e) the conditions or consequences of Force Majeure have a Material Adverse Effect on the business, assets or operations of the Company and continue for a period in excess of [6] months and the Parties have been unable to find an equitable solution after mutual consultation; or

(f) a Material Modification is made at any time by any government authority to the Joint Venture Agreement, these Articles of Association, the Business License, any Additional Permit or any Ancillary Agreement.

（c）出具或正式通过解散或清算合资公司的指令或决议。

12.3 如果发生下列情况，一方（“通知方”）有权向另一方提交终止通知以终止本章程：

（a）另一方重大违约，且相关补救期届满；

（b）另一方经历控制权变更；

（c）另一方发生破产事件；

（d）发生董事会僵局事件且该事件无法根据本章程第6.10（b）条或第8.5（b）条的规定解决；

（e）不可抗力的条件或后果对合资公司的业务、资产或经营产生重大不利影响，并持续超过【6】个月，且双方未能在共同协商后找到公平的解决方案；或者

（f）任何政府机构在任何时候对合资协议、本章程、营业执照、任何附加许可或任何附属协议作出重大修改。

12.4 提交终止通知本身不导致本章程的终止，但应启动以下本章程项下的其他相关程序：

（a）就根据本章程第12.3（a）—（c）条发出的终止通知而言，经双方另行书面约定，通知方有权收购该另一方持有的合资公司的全部股权，且

（b）就根据本章程第12.3（d）—（f）条发出的终止通知而言，经双方另行书面约定，双方应启动估值收购程序。

本章程仅在一方完成对另一方全部股权的收购时，或根据适用法律规定经双方另行书面约定终止。

12.4 The submission of a Termination Notice shall not in and of itself result in the termination of these Articles of Association but shall initiate additional related procedures hereunder as follows:

(a) in respect of a Termination Notice delivered pursuant to Article 12.3(a)-(c), the Notifying Party shall have the right to purchase all of the Equity Interests in the Company held by the other Party as separately agreed by the Parties in writing, and

(b) in respect of a Termination Notice delivered pursuant to Article 12.3(d)-(f), the Parties shall initiate valuation buy-out procedures as separately agreed by the Parties in writing.

These Articles of Association shall be terminated only upon completion of the purchase by a Party of all of the Equity Interests of the other Party or as separately agreed by the Parties in writing and in accordance with Applicable Law.

12.5 Upon the termination of these Articles of Association, all rights and obligations of the Parties under these Articles of Association shall forthwith be extinguished, provided that all rights and obligations of a Party arising (i) under these Articles of Association prior to termination, (ii) under any Surviving Provision, and (iii) under or by operation of Applicable Law, shall remain in full force and effect in accordance with the applicable terms thereof.

12.6 The following provisions ("Surviving Provisions") shall survive the termination of these Articles of Association: this Article 12.6, Article 15.4 and Article 15.6.

13. DISSOLUTION OF COMPANY

13.1 Voluntary dissolution of the Company shall be undertaken pursuant to a duly passed Supermajority Shareholders Resolution upon the agreement of the Parties.

13.2 Involuntary dissolution of the Company shall be undertaken pursuant to an order for dissolution of the Company issued by the relevant government authority and in accordance with the requirements of Applicable Law.

14. NOTICE

14.1 Any notice or written communication provided for in these Articles of Association by either Party to the other, including but not limited to any and all offers,

12.5 本章程终止后，本章程项下双方的所有权利和义务应立即灭失，但一方（i）在终止前根据本章程，（ii）根据任何存续条款，以及（iii）根据适用法律，产生的所有权利和义务，均应根据相关适用条款保持完全有效。

12.6 以下条款（“存续条款”）在本章程终止后继续有效：第12.6条、第15.4条和第15.6条。

13.合资公司的解散

13.1 合资公司的自愿解散应在双方协商一致的情况下，根据正式通过的绝对多数股东会决议进行。

13.2 合资公司的非自愿解散应根据相关政府机关签发的解散命令和适用法律的要求进行。

14. 通知

14.1 本章程中规定的一方向另一方发出的通知或书面函件（包括但不限于本章程项下的任何及所有要约、书面文件或通知）均应以【填入语言】制作，并通过如下方式送达：

（a）当面递交；

（b）专递信函；

（c）电子邮件；或

（d）传真。

14.2 根据本章程或与本章程相关的由一方向另一方发出的任何通知应向如下地址送达：

甲方：

地址：【填入甲方邮寄地址】

传真号码：【不适用】

writings, or notices to be given hereunder, shall be made in [LANGUAGE] and delivered:

(a) by hand;

(b) by courier service delivered letter;

(c) by email; or

(d) by facsimile.

14.2 Any notice given by a Party under or in connection with these Articles of Association shall be delivered to the other Party as follows:

Party A:

Address: [PARTY A MAILING ADDRESS]

Facsimile No: [N/A]

E-mail address: [PARTY A EMAIL ADDRESS]

Attention: [NAME][OR][TITLE]

Party B:

Address: [PARTY B MAILING ADDRESS]

Facsimile No: [N/A]

E-mail address: [PARTY B EMAIL ADDRESS]

Attention: [NAME][OR][TITLE]

14.3 Notices shall be deemed to have been delivered at the following times:

(a) if by hand, on reaching the designated address and subject to return receipt or other proof of delivery;

(b) if by courier, [five] Business Days after the date of dispatch;

(c) if by email, on the date the email is dispatched (so long as written notice of such transmission is sent within [two] Business Days thereafter by another delivery method pursuant to this Article 14); and

(d) if by fax, upon the next Business Day after the date marked on the confirmation of transmission report by the sender's fax machine, indicating completed uninterrupted transmission to the relevant facsimile number.

电子邮件地址：【填入甲方电子邮件地址】

收件人：【填入姓名】【或】【填入头衔】

乙方：

地址：【填入乙方邮寄地址】

传真号码：【不适用】

电子邮件地址：【填入乙方电子邮件地址】

收件人：【填入姓名】【或】【填入头衔】

14.3 在以下时间通知被视为已经送达：

（a）以当面递交方式送达的，送达指定地址并签署回执或其他送达证明时；

（b）以专递信函方式送达的，为递交日后的第【五】个工作日；

（c）以电子邮件方式送达的，为电子邮件发出之日（只要在电子邮件发送后【两】个工作日内根据本章程第 14 条规定的另一种送达方式发出关于该等传输的书面通知）；及

（d）以传真方式送达的，为发送传真方的传真机生成的发送确认报告（表明已向相关传真号码发送完整的、未中断的传真）上标记的日期后的下一个工作日。

14.4 一方可随时根据本章程第 14 条的规定通知另一方变更通知送达地址。

15.一般规定

15.1 本章程任何条款均不得被解释为：

（a）在双方之间形成任何合伙关系或除本章程下对合资公司的共同投资以外的任何其他导致连带责任

14.4 Each Party may change its particulars for receipt of notices at any time by notice given to the other Party pursuant to this Article 14.

15. GENERAL PROVISIONS

15.1 Nothing in these Articles of Association shall be construed or implied as:

(a) establishing between the Parties hereto any partnership or any other form of relationship entailing joint liability other than in respect of the joint investment in the Company as contemplated hereunder;

(b) constituting either of the Parties as the agent of the other Party (except with prior written consent from the other Party);

(c) authorizing either Party to make any representation or warranty on behalf of the other Party (except with prior written consent from the other Party); or

(d) authorizing either Party to incur any expenses or any other form of obligation on behalf of the other Party (except with prior written consent from the other Party).

15.2 These Articles of Association shall not be changed verbally, but only by a written agreement signed by the Parties, [and, where required under Applicable Law, on approval by the relevant Approval and Record-filing Authority].

15.3 In case of any inconsistency between these Articles of Association and the Joint Venture Agreement, the Joint Venture Agreement shall prevail. If any such inconsistency is identified then the Parties shall do all things and execute all documents, including where necessary making amendments to these Articles of Association, as may be necessary to remove the inconsistency and ensure that terms of these Articles of Association conform to the terms of the Joint Venture Agreement.

15.4 These Articles of Association are governed by and will be construed in accordance with the laws of the People's Republic of China.

15.5 These Articles of Association may be executed in counterparts where each counterpart constitutes an original and all counterparts together constitute the same Articles of Association. A Party may execute these Articles of Association by signing and sending (including by facsimile or email) a counterpart copy to the

的关系；

（b）使一方成为另一方的代理人（另一方事先书面同意的除外）；

（c）授权一方代表另一方做出任何陈述或保证（另一方事先书面同意的除外）；或

（d）授权一方代表另一方产生任何费用或其他任何形式的义务（另一方事先书面同意的除外）。

15.2 本章程不得以口头方式修改，而须经双方签署书面协议，【且当适用法律要求时，经相关审批和备案机关批准】后方可修改。

15.3 如果本章程与合资协议之间存在任何不一致，以合资协议为准。如果发现任何该等不一致，则协议双方应实施所有行为并签署所有文件，包括对本章程进行必要的修订，以消除不一致并确保章程的条款符合合资协议条款。

15.4 本章程及其解释适用中华人民共和国法律。

15.5 本章程可以签署副本，每一副本构成一份章程原件，且所有副本共同构成同一份章程。一方可以通过签字并向另一方发送（包括通过传真或电子邮件）一份副本的方式签署本章程。

15.6 本章程以中文和英文签署。两种文本具有同等效力。

双方已于本章程首页所载日期在中华人民共和国【填入省市】通过其正式授权的代表签署本章程，以资证明。

other Party.

15.6 These Articles of Association are executed in both Chinese and English. Both language versions shall be equally valid.

IN WITNESS WHEREOF, each of the Parties hereto has caused these Articles of Association to be executed by its duly authorized representative on the date first set forth above in [CITY, PROVINCE], People's Republic of China.

[PARTY A NAME]	[PARTY B NAME]
By:____________________	By:____________________
Name:____________________ [in Chinese (NAME IN CHINESE)]	Name:____________________
Position:____________________	Position:____________________
Nationality:____________________	Nationality:____________________

【填入甲方名称】　　　　　　　　【填入乙方名称】

签署：__________________　　　　签署：______________

姓名：__________________　　　　姓名：_________

【中文名（填入中文姓名）】

职务：__________________　　　　职务：______________

国籍：__________________　　　　国籍：______________

Annex 1 Definitions and Interpretation

Part A Definitions

Unless the terms or context of these Articles of Association otherwise provide, the following terms shall have the meanings set out below:

"Accounting Standards for Business Enterprises—Basic Standards" means the specific accounting standards and other relevant regulations as amended by the Ministry of Finance of China in 2014.

"Additional Permits" means as any approval, registration, license or permit necessary for the Company to engage in the Business as the Parties may so designate separately in writing.

"Affiliate" means any company which, directly or indirectly, is Controlled by, under common Control with, or in Control of, a Party.

"After-tax Net Profits" means revenue plus all other income, minus all costs, including applicable taxes, that may be payable or accruable during an accounting period.

"AMR" means the State Administration for Market Regulation of China or its relevant local Administration for Market Regulation.

"Ancillary Agreements" means agreements to be entered into by the Company with a Party or any third party as so designated by the Parties separately in writing.

"applicable ethical rules" shall have the meaning set out in Article 7.9.

"Applicable Law" means the laws, regulations, rules, notices, and other legislative, executive or judicial decisions or pronouncements binding on either Party, the Company or in relation to the subject matter of these Articles of Association.

["Approval and Record-filing Authority" means the Ministry of Commerce of China or other authority entrusted by it (a) to approve and/or accept the filing of these Articles of Association in respect of the establishment of the Company, and (b) to approve and/or accept the filing of any amendments hereto or other submissions in compliance with Applicable Law.]

["Approval Certificate" means the certificate issued by the Approval and Record-filing Authority approving the establishment of the Company and these Articles of Association.]

附件一　定义和解释

第一部分　定义

除非本章程条款另有约定或上下文另有所指，下列用语的含义如下：

“企业会计准则——基本准则”指中国财政部于 2014 年发布及后续修订的具体会计准则和其他有关规定。

“附加许可”指经双方另行书面指定的，合资公司开展目标业务所需的任何批准、登记或许可。

“关联方”指被一方直接或间接控制、与该方共同受控制、或者控制该方的任何公司。

“税后净利润”指收入加所有其他收益，减去一个会计期间内可能应付或应计的所有成本，包括适用的税费。

“市场监督管理局”指中国国家市场监督管理总局或相关的地方市场监督管理局。

“附属协议”指经双方另行书面指定的，合资公司将与一方或任何第三方签署的协议。

“适用的道德规则”应具有本章程第 7.9 条中所给出的含义。

“适用法律”指对本章程任何一方或合资公司有约束力的或者与本章程标的有关的法律、法规、规章、通知以及其他立法、行政或司法判决或声明。

【“审批和备案机关”指中国商务部，或由其委托（a）就合资公司的成立批准本章程和 / 或接受本章程备案，以及（b）批准符合适用法律的任何相关变更或其他申请的提交和 / 或受理前述事项备案的其他机关。】

【“批准证书”指由审批和备案机关签发的，批准成立合资公司及本章程的证书。】

"Articles of Association" shall have the meaning set out in the preamble.

"Board" means the board of Directors of the Company, as constituted from time to time.

"Board Deadlock Matter" means any matter required to be decided by the Board in accordance with Article 8 which the Board fails to reach an agreement on so as to enable it to pass the relevant resolution in the manner required under Article 8 (as the case may be) within [20] Business Days after the date of the Board meeting at which the matter is first tabled for discussion or the date on which a written resolution in relation to the matter is first circulated to the Directors.

"Board of Supervisors" means the board of Supervisors of the Company, as constituted from time to time.

"Business" means the business undertaken by the Company from time to time in accordance with the Business Plan.

"Business Day" means a day (other than a Saturday, Sunday or public holiday) on which banks generally are open for business in the PRC and [PARTY B JURISDICTION OF INCORPORATION].

"Business License" means the first business license of the Company issued by the AMR.

"Business License Issuance Date" means the date the Business License is issued to the Company by the AMR.

"Business Plan" means the business plan for the Company as approved by the Board from time to time.

"Capital Increase" means an increase of the Registered Capital of the Company.

"Capital Reduction" means a reduction of the Registered Capital of the Company.

"Chairman" means the Chairman of the Board.

"Change of Control" means a person who Controls a company as at the date of these Articles of Association ceases to do so or another person acquires Control of it after the date of these Articles of Association.

"Chief Financial Officer" or "CFO" means the chief financial officer or chief accountant of the Company.

“章程”应具有本章程前言所给出的含义。

“董事会”指合资公司的董事会，其人员构成可能不时发生变化。

“董事会僵局事件”指任何需要董事会根据本章程第 8 条决定的事项发生以下任何情形：在董事会将此事项列入董事会议事日程之日或在就此事项做出的书面决议第一次在董事间传阅之日后的【20】个工作日内，董事会因未达成一致而未能就该事项根据本章程第 8 条要求的方式通过相关决议（视情况而定）。

“监事会”指合资公司的监事会，其人员构成可能不时发生变化。

“目标业务”指合资公司根据经营计划不时开展的业务。

“工作日”指中国和【乙方组建地】的银行通常对外营业的一天（周六、周日或公共假日除外）。

“营业执照”指由市场监督管理局颁发的合资公司的第一份营业执照。

“营业执照颁发日”指由市场监督管理局向合资公司颁发营业执照的日期。

“经营计划”指董事会不时批准的合资公司的经营计划。

“增资”指合资公司注册资本的增加。

“减资”指合资公司注册资本的减少。

“董事长”指董事会董事长。

“控制权变更”是指在本章程签署日控制公司的人在本章程签署日后不再享有控制权或其他人取得对公司的控制权。

“首席财务官”或“CFO”指合资公司的首席财务官或总会计师。

"China" and "PRC" means the People's Republic of China, for the purpose of these Articles of Association, excluding the Hong Kong and Macao Special Administrative Regions and Taiwan.

"Company" shall have the meaning set out in the background statement.

"Company Law" means the Company Law of the People's Republic of China.

"Company Registration Number" means the unique alphanumeric code associated with a company as provided on its business license or similar document, or on file with the relevant company registration authority.

"Control" means (whether directly or indirectly) the right to exercise more than 50% of the votes exercisable at any meeting of a company, to elect or appoint a majority of directors or to direct the management of a company.

"Cure Period" means [90] calendar days from delivery of written notice of Material Breach from one Party to the other Party.

"D&O Insurance" means the liability insurance which the Company may purchase on behalf of its Directors and officers against liability alleged against or incurred by a Director or officer of the Company in connection with claims arising from an act or omission of a Director or officer in his capacity as a director, officer, employee, agent fiduciary or consultant of the Company.

"Deadlock Matter" means either a Shareholder Deadlock Matter or a Board Deadlock Matter.

"Deadlock Notice" means written notice from the Directors of either Party to the Chairman and other Directors of the existence of a Board Deadlock Matter.

"Director" means a director of the Board.

"Distributable Profits" shall have the meaning set out in Article 11.9(b).

"Effective Date" means the effective date of these Articles of Association, being the date on which these Articles of Association have been executed by the duly authorized representatives of both Parties.

"Encumbrance" means any claim, deposit, charge, mortgage, security, lien, option, equity, power of sale or hypothecation or other third-party right, retention of title arrangement, right of pre-emption, right of first refusal or security interest of any kind.

“中国”和“中华人民共和国”指中华人民共和国，为本章程目的，不包括中国香港特别行政区、中国澳门特别行政区和中国台湾地区。

“合资公司”应具有本章程背景声明中给出的含义。

“公司法”指《中华人民共和国公司法》。

“公司注册号”指与公司相关联的，其营业执照或类似文件所载的，或相关公司注册机构档案所载的唯一字母数字代码。

“控制”是指（无论直接或间接）行使超过50%在公司任何会议上可行使的表决权，选举或任命大多数董事或指导公司管理的权利。

“补救期”指一方向另一方发出重大违约的书面通知之日起的【90】个日历日。

“董事及高级管理人员责任保险”指公司可代表其董事和高级管理人员购买的责任保险，以承保与董事或高级管理人员作为合资公司的董事、高级管理人员、雇员、受托代理或顾问行使职权时的作为或不作为而引起的索赔相关的，董事或高级管理人员被指控的或其引起的责任。

“僵局事件”指股东会僵局事件或董事会僵局事件。

“僵局通知”指任何一方的董事向董事长及其他董事发出的董事会僵局事件存在的书面通知。

“董事”指董事会董事。

“可分配利润”应具有本章程第11.9（b）条中所给出的含义。

“生效日”指本章程的生效日，即双方正式授权的代表签署本章程的日期。

“权利负担”指任何索赔、押金、押记、抵押、担保、留置权、期权、股权、出售权或抵押权或其他第三方权利、所有权保留、优先认购权、优先购买权或任何形式的担保权益。

"Equity Interests" means the Party A Equity Interests and/or the Party B Equity Interests, as the case may be.

["Euro" or "EUR" means the lawful currency of the European Union.]

"Force Majeure" means all events which are beyond the control of the Parties to these Articles of Association, and which are unforeseen, unavoidable or insurmountable, and which prevent total or partial performance by either Party. Such events shall include earthquakes, typhoons, flood, fire, war, strikes, riots, acts of governments, changes in law or the application thereof or any other instances which cannot be foreseen, prevented or controlled, including instances which are accepted as Force Majeure in general international commercial practice.

"Funding Conditions" means all requirements for the establishment of the Company together with all other conditions to funding as separately agreed by the Parties in writing.

"General Manager" means the General Manager of the Company.

["IFRS" means International Financial Reporting Standards as issued by the International Accounting Standards Board.]

"Independent Auditor" means an internationally recognized independent and competent accountant registered in China.

"Insolvency Event" means circumstances under which a Party (i) has an administrator or similar officer appointed over all or a material part of its assets or undertaking; (ii) passes a resolution for winding-up (other than a winding-up for the purpose of, or in connection with, any solvent reorganization) or a court makes an order to that effect or a court makes an order for administration (or any equivalent order in any jurisdiction); (iii) enters into any composition or arrangement with its creditors (other than relating to a solvent restructuring); (iv) ceases to carry on business; (v) is unable to pay its debts as they become due in the ordinary course of business.

"Joint Venture Agreement" shall have the meaning set out in the background statement.

"Legal Action" means an action, suit, investigation, inquiry, proceeding or arbitration at law or in equity or before or by any foreign or domestic court, arbitrator or other governmental authority.

"Legal Representative" shall have the meaning set out in Article 7.6.

“股权”指甲方股权和 / 或乙方股权，视情况而定。

【“欧元”指欧盟的法定货币。】

“不可抗力”指超出本章程双方控制范围、无法预见、无法避免或无法克服的、妨碍本章程一方全部或部分履行本章程的任何事件。该等事件包括地震、台风、洪水、火灾、战争、罢工、暴动、政府行为、法律或法律适用的变更或任何其他无法预见、无法避免或无法控制的情形，包括在国际商务实践中通常被认定为不可抗力的事件。

“出资条件”指经双方另行书面约定的，设立合资公司的所有要求和所有其他出资条件。

“总经理”指合资公司的总经理。

【“国际财务报告准则”指国际会计准则理事会发布的国际财务报告准则。】

“独立审计师”指在中国注册的国际认可的独立且胜任的会计师。

“破产事件”是指一方（i）就其资产或业务的全部或重要部分指定了管理人或类似官员；（ii）通过一项清算决议（以任何重整为目的或与之相关的清算除外），或法院作出清算或管理的命令（或任何司法辖区内的任何同等命令）；（iii）与债权人达成任何（重整相关之外的）和解或安排；（iv）停止营业；（v）无法偿还其在日常经营过程中到期的债务。

“合资协议”应具有本章程背景声明中所给出的含义。

“法律诉讼”指根据法律或衡平法或在任何外国或国内法院、仲裁员或其他政府机构前进行的或由其受理的诉讼、案件、调查、查询、程序或仲裁。

“法定代表人”应具有本章程第 7.6 条中所给出的含义。

"Management Personnel" means the Company's General Manager, Chief Financial Officer and [TITLES OF OTHER MANAGEMENT PERSONNEL].

"Material" means events or circumstances which involve or are likely to involve aggregate amounts payable by or to the Company in excess of RMB [AMOUNT] (or its equivalent in another currency), or involve an item in excess of RMB [AMOUNT] in value, or information which could influence the decisions that the Company makes in respect of the Business if omitted or misstated, as the context may require.

"Material Adverse Effect" means events or circumstances which are Material in amount and which have a material adverse effect on the assets, liabilities, results of operations, condition (financial or otherwise), business, or prospects of the Company taken as a whole.

"Material Breach" means any failure of a Party to perform an obligation under these Articles of Association, the Joint Venture Agreement or any Ancillary Agreement which has had or with the passage of time is projected to have a Material Adverse Effect on the business, assets or operations of the Company or the other Party.

"Material Modification" means a modification (whether by means of the imposition of additional terms and conditions or otherwise) by the relevant government departments to, as the case may be, these Articles of Association, the Joint Venture Agreement, the Business License of the Company or the scope and nature of any of the Ancillary Agreements, or the Additional Permits as agreed or anticipated by the Parties, which in the opinion of either Party, will have a material adverse effect on the ability of Parties to achieve through the Company, their respective economic and operational objectives.

"Material Transactions" means any transaction to be entered into by the Company which involves or is likely to involve aggregate amounts payable by or to the Company in excess of RMB [AMOUNT] (or its equivalent in another currency), or involve an item in excess of RMB [AMOUNT] in value.

"Notifying Party" shall have the meaning set out in Article 12.3.

"Parties" shall have the meaning set out in the preamble.

"Party" shall have the meaning set out in the preamble.

"Party A" shall have the meaning set out in the preamble.

"Party A Cash Contribution" shall have the meaning set out in Article 4.3(a).

“高级管理人员”指合资公司的总经理、首席财务官以及【填入其他高级管理人员名称】。

“重大”指涉及或很有可能涉及合资公司应付或应收金额合计超过人民币【填入金额】（或等值的另一种货币），或涉及价值超过人民币【填入金额】的单个项目的事件或情形，或如果发生遗漏或虚假陈述，则会影响合资公司就业务做出的决策的信息，具体视上下文而定。

“重大不利影响”指所涉金额重大，并且对整个合资公司的资产、负债、经营业绩、（财务或其他方面的）状况、业务或前景具有重大不利影响的事件或情形。

“重大违约”指一方未能履行其在本章程、合资协议或任何附属协议项下的义务，已经或随着时间的推移预计会对合资公司或另一方的业务、资产或经营产生重大不利影响。

“重大修改”指由有关政府部门对本章程、合资协议、合资公司的营业执照或双方同意或拟定的附属协议或附加许可的范围或性质进行的修改（无论通过附加其他条款和条件或其他方式），而任何一方认为该等修改会对双方通过合资公司实现各自的经济和运营目标的能力产生重大不利影响。

“重大交易”指合资公司将签署的任何交易，该交易涉及或可能涉及合资公司应付或应收金额合计超过人民币【填入金额】（或等值的另一种货币），或涉及价值超过人民币【填入金额】的单个项目。

“通知方”应具有本章程第 12.3 条中所给出的含义。

“双方”应具有前言中所给出的含义。

“一方”应具有前言中所给出的含义。

“甲方”应具有前言中所给出的含义。

“甲方现金出资”应具有本章程第 4.3（a）条中所给出的含义。

"Party A Equity Interests" shall have the meaning set out in Article 4.2(a).

"Party B" shall have the meaning set out in the preamble.

"Party B Cash Contribution" shall have the meaning set out in Article 4.3(b).

"Party B Equity Interests" shall have the meaning set out in Article 4.2(b).

"Registered Capital" shall have the meaning set out in Article 4.1.

"Related Party Transaction" means any agreement, arrangement or understanding entered into between the Company and any Party or any Affiliate of a Party or any Director, officer or employee of the Company.

"Renminbi" or "RMB" means the lawful currency of China.

"Reserved Matters" means matters reserved for decision by the Shareholders Meeting (pursuant to Article 6) or the Board (pursuant to Article 8).

"Responsible Director" shall have the meaning set out in Article 6.4.

"Secretary" means the secretary of the Board.

"Senior Representatives of the Parties" means the officer or director from each of Party A and Party B as separately notified to the other Party in writing, as the same may be changed from time to time by such Party, who are authorized to negotiate, agree and resolve a Board Deadlock Matter on behalf of Party A or Party B, as the case may be.

"Shareholder Deadlock Matter" means any Material matter required to be decided by the Shareholders Meeting in accordance with Article 6 which the Shareholders Meeting fails to reach an agreement on so as to enable it to pass the relevant resolution in the manner required under Article 6 (as the case may be) within [20] Business Days after the date of the meeting of the shareholders at which the matter is first tabled for discussion or the date on which a written resolution in relation to the matter is first circulated to the Parties.

"Shareholder Loan" means any advance of funds made by a Party to the Company under a Shareholder Loan Agreement.

"Shareholder Loan Agreement" means an agreement entered into between a Party and the Company binding such Party to advance funds to the Company.

“甲方股权”具有本章程第 4.2（a）条中所给出的含义。

“乙方”应具有本章程前言中所给出的含义。

“乙方现金出资”应具有本章程第 4.3（b）条中所给出的含义。

“乙方股权”具有本章程第 4.2（b）条中所给出的含义。

“注册资本”应具有本章程第 4.1 条中所给出的含义。

“关联方交易”指合资公司与任何一方或一方任何的关联方或任何董事、高级职员或合资公司员工之间达成的任何协议、安排或谅解。

“人民币”指中国的法定货币。

“保留事项”指保留由股东会（根据本章程第 6 条）或董事会（根据本章程第 8 条）决定的事项。

“责任董事”应具有本章程第 6.4 条中所给出的含义。

“董秘”指董事会秘书。

“双方高级代表”指各方可对其不时进行变更的，甲方和乙方另行书面通知另一方的其各自的高级职员或董事，该等高级职员或董事可有权代表甲方或乙方（视情况而定）进行谈判、协议和解决董事会僵局事件。

“股东僵局事件”指任何需要股东会根据本章程第 6 条决定的重大事项发生以下情形：在股东会将此事项列入股东会会议事日程之日或在就此事项做出的书面决议第一次在双方之间传阅之日后的【20】个工作日内，股东会因未达成一致而未能就该事项根据本章程第 6 条要求的方式通过相关决议（视情况而定）。

“股东贷款”指一方根据股东贷款协议向合资公司提供的资金。

“股东贷款协议”指一方与合资公司之间签订的约束该方向合资公司贷款的协议。

"Shareholders Meeting" means the shareholders meeting of the Company which is the highest authority of the Company in accordance with the provisions of the Company Law and these Articles of Association.

"Simple Majority Board Resolution" means a resolution by the Board requiring the affirmative vote of more than half of all Directors present in person, by proxy or by telecommunications at a duly convened meeting of the Board.

"Simple Majority Shareholders Resolution" means a resolution by the Shareholders Meeting requiring the affirmative vote of shareholders representing more than half of all Voting Rights present in person, by proxy or by telecommunications at a duly convened meeting of the shareholders.

"Statutory and Discretionary Funds" means the statutory accumulation fund and the discretionary accumulation fund of the Company.

"Subsidiary" means a wholly-owned or majority-owned subsidiary of the Company.

"Supermajority Shareholders Resolution" shall have the meaning set out in Article 6.6.

"Supervisor" means a supervisor of the Company from time to time.

"Surviving Provisions" shall have the meaning set out in Article 12.6.

"Term" means the joint venture term of the Company as set out in Article 12.1.

"Termination Notice" means an irrevocable written notice from the Notifying Party confirming its intent to terminate these Articles of Association pursuant to Article 12.3.

"Territory" means [China].

"Transfer" means the assignment, conveyance, sale, transfer, mortgage, grant of a security interest or other disposition, either directly or indirectly, by operation of law or otherwise of Equity Interests.

"Unanimous Board Resolution" means a resolution by the Board requiring the affirmative vote of all Directors present in person, by proxy or by telecommunications at a duly convened meeting of the Board.

["United States Dollars" or "USD" means the lawful currency of the United States of America.]

"Vice Chairman" means the Vice Chairman of the Board of the Company.

“股东会”指合资公司的股东会，根据《公司法》和本章程的规定，是合资公司的最高权力机构。

“简单多数董事会决议”指要求亲自参加、通过代理人或电信方式参加正式召开的董事会会议的所有董事半数以上投赞成票的董事会决议。

“简单多数股东会决议”是指股东会通过的决议，要求代表亲自参加、通过代理人或电信方式参加正式召开的股东会会议的所有股东所持表决权的过半数的股东投赞成票。

“法定公积金和任意公积金”指合资公司的法定公积金和任意公积金。

“子公司”指合资公司的全资或控股子公司。

“绝对多数股东会决议”应具有本章程第 6.6 条中所给出的含义。

“监事”指合资公司的监事。

“存续条款”应具有本章程第 12.6 条中所给出的含义。

“期限”指本章程第 12.1 条规定的合资公司期限。

“终止通知”指通知方发出的不可撤销的书面通知，确认其有意根据本章程第 12.3 条解除本章程。

“目标地区”指【中国】。

“转让”指通过法律或其他方式，直接或间接转让、让与、出售、转移、抵押，授予担保权益或以其他方式处置股权。

“董事会一致决议”指须经亲自、委托他人或通过电信方式出席经正式召集的董事会的全体董事投票赞成的董事会决议。

【“美元”指美利坚合众国的法定货币。】

“副董事长”指合资公司董事会副董事长。

"Voting Rights" means the rights to vote the Equity Interests over which the Party has voting control and all other rights within the Party's control, including in its capacity as shareholder (or as the employer or nominating Party in respect of any Director, member of a Board committee or officer of the Company), and whether in connection with a regular or special meeting of the shareholders or the Board or by unanimous written consent.

Part B Interpretation

1. A reference to any Applicable Law or to any legislation, or to any provision of Applicable Law or of any legislation includes a reference to such Applicable Law or legislation as amended or modified from time to time.

2. A reference to a person includes any individual or entity (including any company, business or other enterprise or entity, joint venture, institution, state or government department), as the context permits.

3. References in these Articles of Association to these Articles of Association, agreements or other documents, shall mean the same as amended from time to time.

4. A reference to any PRC government authority or department includes such authority or department at the State, provincial, municipal and other levels.

5. References in these Articles of Association to government ministries, bureaux, departments, commissions, agencies, etc. shall include all successor entities thereto.

6. In these Articles of Association, the masculine form includes the feminine form and the singular form includes the plural form, and vice versa.

7. Headings are for convenience of reference only and shall not affect the construction or interpretation of these Articles of Association.

8. A reference to any Party to these Articles of Association or to any other party to any agreement or document includes a reference to that party's successors and permitted assigns.

9. A reference to a Director, the Chairman, the Vice Chairman, the General Manager, the Chief Operating Officer or the Chief Financial Officer or similar positions means a person nominated in accordance with these Articles of Association holding such position in the Company from time to time.

“表决权”指一方对股权享有的投票控制权以及其控制范围内的所有其他权利，包括其作为股东（或作为合资公司任何董事、董事会成员或高级管理人员的雇主或提名方）所享有的权利，且无论是有关股东会或董事会的定期或特别会议，还是一致的书面同意。

第二部分　解释

1. 本章程中提及任何适用法律或任何立法，或任何适用法律或立法的条款包括其不时修订后的版本。

2. 本章程中提及的“人”包括任何个人或实体（包括任何公司、营业或其他企业或实体、合营企业、机构、国家或政府部门），结合上下文语境具体确定其含义。

3. 本章程中提及的本章程、协议或其他文件包括其不时修订后的版本。

4. 本章程中提及的任何中国政府机关或部门包括国家、省、市和其他层级的该等机关或部门。

5. 本章程中提及的政府的部、局、部门、委员会、署等，也指这些机构的继受机构。

6. 在本章程中所使用的男性称谓也包括女性，单数也包括复数，反之亦然。

7. 本章程中各条款标题仅为方便查阅而设，对本章程的理解或解释无影响。

8. 本章程中提及的本章程的任何一方或任何其他协议或文件的一方包括该方的继受者及其允许的受让人。

9. 本章程中提及的董事、董事长、副董事长、总经理、首席运营官或首席财务官或类似职位，指根据本章程不时被提名在合资公司担任该等职位的人。

10. A reference to an agreement or document in the agreed form shall refer to such agreement or document in the form so acknowledged and confirmed by the Parties in writing.

11. The words includes or including mean includes without limitation and including without limitation respectively.

10. 本章程中提及的约定形式的协议或文件，指形式得到双方书面认可和确认的该等协议或文件。

11. 在本章程中，“包括”指“包括但不限于”。

Annex 2 Capital Contribution Schedule

Subject to the prior satisfaction or waiver of the Funding Conditions, Party A and Party B shall make their respective contributions to the Company in [NUMBER] installments on the schedule as set out below.

Installment	Party A Amount	Party B Amount	On or before
First	RMB [AMOUNT]	[CURRENCY] equivalent of RMB [AMOUNT]	[DATE]
Second	RMB [AMOUNT]	[CURRENCY] equivalent of RMB [AMOUNT]	[DATE]
Final	RMB [AMOUNT]	[CURRENCY] equivalent of RMB [AMOUNT]	[DATE]

The Parties may, by separate signed agreement in writing, adjust the above capital contribution schedule as may be necessary or appropriate in accordance with the operational requirements of the Company, provided that in any event each Party shall fund the full amount of its share of the Registered Capital of the Company no later than [DATE] or such other date as may be required under Applicable Law.

附件二　出资时间表

出资条件得到满足或被放弃后，甲方和乙方应按照下列时间表分【填入数字】期缴纳其各自的出资。

分期	甲方出资金额	乙方出资金额	在如下日期或之前缴纳
第一期	人民币【填入金额】	人民币【填入金额】的等值【填入货币】	【填入日期】
第二期	人民币【填入金额】	人民币【填入金额】的等值【填入货币】	【填入日期】
最后一期	人民币【填入金额】	人民币【填入金额】的等值【填入货币】	【填入日期】

双方可以，通过另行签署的书面协议，根据合资公司的经营需要在必要时或酌情调整上述出资时间表，但在任何情况下，每一方都不得迟于【填入日期】或适用法律可能要求的其他日期足额缴纳其占合资公司注册资本份额的金额。

Annex Ⅲ
Annotations to Sample JVA and JV Articles of Association Templates

We set out below drafting notes to certain provisions of the Sample JV Templates set out in Annexes 1 and 2. These annotations are not intended to be exhaustive and are provided for reference only and are otherwise subject to the caveats and limitations set out in Chapter 5. Other points applicable to the Sample JV Templates are set out in Chapter 6.

We have endeavored to draft these guidance notes in a manner which will be suitable for a wide range of users, including Chinese legal professionals with limited experience with international SHA/JVA provisions, international legal professionals with limited experience with Sino-foreign joint ventures, as well as for Chinese and foreign business managers with limited understanding of technical legal points. Regardless of the background of the user, these drafting notes are not intended as a substitute for legal advice from qualified legal counsel, and are intended only to highlight issues which will need to be addressed separately in the context of particular transactions.

For convenience, references are made to clause numbers of the templates as appropriate. Terms not otherwise defined in the annotations below shall have the meanings ascribed thereto elsewhere in this book.

附件Ⅲ
合资协议和合资企业章程模板样本注解说明

我们在下文列出了附件一和附件二所载的合资协议模板样本以及合资企业章程模板样本的部分条款的起草说明。这些起草说明并非详尽无遗，仅供参考，并受限于第五章所载的声明和限制。其他适用于模板样本的要点载于第六章。

我们希望这份起草说明能适用于广泛的用户群体，包括在国际股东协议 / 合资协议条款方面经验有限的中国法律专业人士、在中外合资企业方面经验有限的国际法律专业人士，以及对专业性的法律要点了解有限的中外企业管理者。无论用户的背景如何，本起草说明并非旨在替代合格法律顾问提供的法律建议，只是希望强调一些需要在特定交易中单独讨论的问题。

为方便起见，本起草说明适当引用了模板中的条款序号。下文中未另行定义的术语应具有本书其他部分中所给出的含义。

AoA	JVA	Subject	Comments
		Number of parties	These Sample JV Templates are designed for a two-party Sino-foreign joint venture, with the Chinese investor as Party A and the foreign investor as Party B. If there are to be additional parties, significant additional modifications will need to be made to these Sample JV Templates. For example, in a three-party JV, if the interests of two parties are substantially aligned, then you may wish to provide for joint nomination rights, as well as joint exercise of other rights under the agreement, etc. If the joint venture has more than three or four parties, the related contractual and governance mechanics can become very unwieldy. Based on practical experience, joint ventures with only two or three parties tend to be easier to manage.
		Background statements	We have set out a very simple background statement suitable for use in connection with a greenfield joint venture. It is common also to include introductions of the backgrounds of the parties in these preliminary statements, but this is not essential and so we have opted not to include those in the Sample JV Templates. The background statements for an SHA/JVA in the context of an M&A deal, a financial investment involving multiple rounds of capital raising, or in connection with the conversion of an existing FIE into an LLC or other entity form under the Company Law would require substantial modification. This section can also be further modified or supplemented to suit the purposes of the particular transaction. Note that in accordance with international practice, the background statements are considered to be non-binding, so care should be taken to avoid including substantive undertakings in this background section.
1	1	Definitions	We have opted to set out the defined terms in an annex, but it is also common to put the definitions up front in this clause.
2.1	2.1	Company establishment	This clause as drafted applies only to a greenfield joint venture.
2.2	2.2	Company particulars	2.2(a): Only the Chinese name will be registered but the parties are free to select an English name for internal and external use. If the company name is to incorporate the trade name of one or both of the parties, appropriate license terms should be entered into either in the JVA or in an ancillary agreement. 2.2(b): We have assumed that the majority of Sino-foreign joint ventures will take the form of an LLC under the Company Law which can accommodate up to 50 shareholders. If another entity form is selected, such as a company limited by shares or a partnership, the Sample JV Templates may not be appropriate. 2.2(c): The registered address of the company can only be changed by undertaking relevant amendments to the company registrations with the relevant Administration for Market Regulation ("AMR"), and in accordance with Chinese law and practice only the registered address and not a principle place of business is used for identification purposes (as in the party names in the preamble to the Sample JV Templates).

公司章程	合资协议	主题	注解说明
		协议主体的数量	这些合资企业模板样本是为协议主体为两方的中外合资企业设计的，中国投资方为甲方，外国投资方为乙方。如果还有其他当事方，则需要对模板样本进行重大修改。例如，在三方合资中，如果其中两方的利益基本一致，那么您可能希望在协议中规定共同提名权，以及其他权利的共同行使等。如果合资企业有三个或四个以上的当事方，相关的合同和治理机制可能会很难处理。根据实践经验，仅有两个或三个当事方的合资企业更易于管理。
		背景说明	我们提供了非常简单的适用于绿地合资企业的背景说明。这些初步说明中通常也包括对当事方的背景介绍，但这不是必不可少的，因此我们没有在模板样本中包含这些内容。如果是并购交易、涉及多轮融资的财务投资，或关于现有外商投资企业转化为《公司法》项下的有限责任公司或其他组织形式背景下的股东协议／合资协议的背景说明，则将需要进行实质性修改。您也可以对本章节进一步修改或补充以适应特定交易的目的。需要说明的是，根据国际惯例，背景说明不具有法律约束力，因此应注意避免在背景说明部分中规定实质性承诺。
1	1	定义	我们选择在附件中载明术语的定义，但提前在本条中载明定义也很常见。
2.1	2.1	合资公司的设立	本条款仅适用于绿地合资企业。
2.2	2.2	合资公司的详细信息	2.2(a): 合资公司仅登记中文名称，但双方可以自由选择一个英文名称以供内部和外部使用。如果合资公司名称将包含一方或双方的商号，则应在合资协议或附属协议中规定适当的许可条款。 2.2(b): 我们假设大多数中外合资企业将采用《公司法》项下的有限责任公司形式，最多可拥有50名股东。如果选择其他组织形式，例如股份有限公司或合伙企业，则模板样本可能不适用。 2.2(c): 合资公司的注册地址只能通过在相关市场监督管理局（“市场监管局”）进行相关变更登记来变更，并且根据中国法律和惯例，只有注册地址（而非主要营业地）能够用来识别公司（如模板样本前言中双方名称的部分）。

Continued

AoA	JVA	Subject	Comments
3.1	3.1	Scope of business	Chinese companies in practice are not granted a general scope of business permitting the company to engage in any business activities other than those which are subject to special licensing requirements. Instead, the actual permitted scope of business of a company in China will be limited to the specific categories of business activities as set out in the company's business license issued by the AMR. Such business scope categories must conform to the fixed categories in the approved catalogue maintained by the AMR. If there is any discrepancy between the description of the scope of business set out in this clause and as set out in the company's approved business license, the latter will prevail for all purposes. For business categories where foreign investment is restricted to access under the Negative List, FIEs will need to obtain special approvals from the relevant government departments.
4.1	4.1	Registered capital	Registered capital comprises the equity of the company subscribed to by the parties. The concepts of authorized shares and issued and outstanding shares are not used in respect of the equity capital of LLCs under the Company Law in China (which was also the case for FIEs under the Three FIE Laws). The registered capital amount is typically stated in RMB, although it is also possible to set out the registered capital in foreign currency, which would alter the currency conversion risks of the parties should exchange rates change in the interim between signing of the JVA and funding. For purposes of the Sample JV Templates we have denominated the registered capital amount in RMB. Former rules regarding statutory minimum registered capital levels and timelines for injection of registered capital have been abolished, and as a regulatory matter such registered capital amounts are required to be injected only prior to expiry of the term or winding up of the company. Because the concept of "total investment amount" is no longer required under the Company Law, related "thin capital" rules should also no longer apply. See related further discussion in Chapter 2 above.
4.2	4.2	Equity interests	The parties' equity interests in LLCs in China are expressed in terms of percentages of the total registered capital of the company rather than shares or other units (which was also the case for FIEs under the Three FIE Laws).

续表

公司章程	合资协议	主题	注解说明
3.1	3.1	经营范围	中国公司在实践中不会拥有一个广泛的经营范围，允许其从事受限于特殊许可要求之外的任何商业活动。相反，中国公司实际上经允许的经营范围仅限于市场监管局颁发的公司营业执照中规定的特定业务活动类别。该等经营范围类别必须符合市场监管局使用的经批准的目录中的固定类别。如果本条款所载的经营范围与合资公司经批准的营业执照中的经营范围有任何差异，在任何情形下，均以后者为准。对于负面清单中限制外国投资的业务类别，外商投资企业需要获得相关政府部门的特别审批。
4.1	4.1	注册资本	注册资本由双方认购的公司的股本构成。在中国《公司法》项下，额定股份、已发行股份和未发行股份的概念就有限责任公司的股本而言并不适用（对于在“三资法”项下的外商投资企业也同样不适用）。 注册资本通常以人民币表示，也可以以外国货币表示，如果在合资协议签署至注册资本实缴期间发生汇率变化，则会改变双方的货币兑换风险。在模板样本中，我们以人民币计价注册资本。 关于法定最低注册资本和实缴时限的原有规则已经废除，从监管的角度来看，只要求注册资本在公司营业期限届满或公司清算之前缴纳。 由于“投资总额”的概念在《公司法》项下不再适用，因此相关的“投注差”规则也不再适用。参见本书第二章的详细讨论。
4.2	4.2	股权	在中国，双方在有限责任公司中持有的股权以其所占的公司注册资本总额的百分比表示，而非以股份或其他单位表示（这同样适用于“三资法”项下的外商投资企业）。

Continued

AoA	JVA	Subject	Comments
4.3	4.3	Capital contributions	Consistent with the base case scenario for the Sample JV Templates, we have provided that the parties to this joint venture are to make their capital contributions only in cash. Where, as in the Sample JV Templates, registered capital amounts are stated in RMB, foreign parties can inject the equivalent amount in foreign currency at prevailing exchange rates. In-kind contributions are also permitted. Under the Three FIE Laws, only the following categories of assets could be used for capital contributions in FIEs: buildings, factory premises, machinery, equipment or other materials, industrial property, proprietary technology, or site use rights. Similarly, under the Company Law, parties may make in-kind capital contributions using any of the following: material objects, intellectual property rights, land use rights or other non-monetary assets the value of which can be assessed in currency and the ownership of which can be transferred in accordance with the law. In-kind contributions from foreign investors are subject to independent valuation. In the event that the independent valuation is lower than the value assigned by the parties in the JVA, then the contributing party will need to make an additional cash contribution in the amount of the difference. Potential valuation differences for in-kind contributions can also be circumvented by round-tripping cash, i.e. injecting cash contributions which are then earmarked to purchase the assets from the party at the agreed value. While this avoids potential valuation problems, this arrangement may give rise to unfavorable tax consequences. Under the CJV Law, parties were able to provide "cooperative conditions" in lieu of or in addition to capital contributions in the form of cash or permitted in-kind contributions. There is no equivalent concept under the Company Law. Note that only assignments of intellectual property rights are permitted to be used as in-kind capital contributions (subject to independent valuation as above), but not a license of intellectual property rights. Such license rights can be capitalized by round-tripping cash as described above, but again subject to potential unfavorable tax consequences.

续表

公司章程	合资协议	主题	注解说明
4.3	4.3	出资	与模板样本的基础情形一致，我们规定合资企业的双方仅以现金方式出资。如果，如模板样本中所规定，注册资本以人民币表示，外方可依照现行汇率以等值的外币出资。 双方也可以非货币的形式出资。根据“三资法”，只有以下类别的资产可用于外商投资企业的出资：建筑物、厂房、机器设备或其他物料、工业产权、专有技术或场地使用权。 同样，根据《公司法》，当事方可以使用以下资产进行非货币出资：实物、知识产权、土地使用权或其他可以用货币估价并可以依法转让的非货币财产。 外国投资者的非货币出资需要进行独立估值。如果独立估值低于双方在合资协议中指定的金额，则出资方应以现金出资补足差额。 非货币出资的潜在估值差额也可以通过往返现金来避免，即投入现金出资，然后指定该等现金用于以约定价值从该方购买资产。虽然这避免了潜在的估值问题，但这种安排可能会产生不利的税务影响。 根据《中外合作经营企业法》，双方能够以现金或经允许的非货币出资方式提供“合作条件”，以代替或补充出资。《公司法》项下没有相对应的概念。 需要说明的是，只有知识产权的转让可以作为非货币出资（受限于上述独立估值），而知识产权的许可不能作为非货币出资。如上所述，这种许可权利可以通过往返现金来实现出资，但同样会有潜在的不利税收影响。

Continued

AoA	JVA	Subject	Comments
			An alternative approach may be to recognize the value of an exclusive license or other similar arrangement in the form of a "share premium" or "capital surplus" in addition to formal registered capital contributions. In the absence of different classes of shares under the Company Law, the contractual concepts of "share premium" or "capital surplus" have been developed in practice in China and are recognized under Chinese accounting principles. Such a "share premium" or "capital surplus" arrangement is perhaps more common in an M&A scenario in which the acquiror is to inject additional capital into the target as "capital surplus" in order to provide the necessary funds required for the operations of the target company while still achieving the agreed shareholding percentages in the company. Such an arrangement can also be coupled with other preference rights under the provisions of the agreement similar to those typically afforded to preferred shares in international practice. Such an arrangement can also be reflected in the related provisions on dividend distributions. Whereas under the EJV Law, profit distributions were to be made strictly in proportion to the parties' respective percentage shares of the registered capital, under the Company Law the parties may agree to disproportionate profit distributions (similar to what was permitted under the CJV Law). See related comments in respect of clause 12.9(c) of the Sample JVA Template below.
	4.4	Capital verification certificates and investment certificates	Under Article 29 of the 2004 Company Law, capital contributions were required to be independently verified by a qualified registered accountant in all cases. Under the 2014 Company Law, Article 29 was removed, and mandatory capital verification has been abolished for companies operating in most industries except where otherwise provided by law. Consequently, capital verification certificates issued by an accountant are no longer required in most cases as a matter of law, but companies may still procure them for record-keeping or other purposes. On the other hand, investment certificates issued by the company, rather than its accountant are still required under the Company Law. These also confirm that capital contributions have been made, but such certificates are not share certificates and are not transferrable. Thus, the Sample Templates refer to investment certificates but not capital verification certificates.

续表

公司章程	合资协议	主题	注解说明
			除正式的注册资本出资外，双方还可以以“股本溢价”或“资本公积”的方式确认独占许可或其他类似安排的价值。由于《公司法》没有区分不同类别的股份，“股本溢价”或“资本公积”作为合同概念已经在中国实践中得到发展，并在中国会计准则中得到认可。 这种“股本溢价”或“资本公积”安排在并购交易中可能更为常见，收购方向目标公司注入额外资本作为“资本公积”，以提供目标公司运营所需的必要资金，同时达到在目标公司拥有约定的持股比例。 这种安排还可以与协议条款项下的其他优先权相结合，类似于国际惯例中为优先股提供的权利。 这种安排也可以反映在股息分配的相关约条款中。根据《中外合资经营企业法》，应严格按照合营双方各自所占的注册资本比例进行利润分配，根据《公司法》，双方可以同意不按比例进行利润分配（类似《中外合作经营企业法》项下允许的分配方式）。见下文合资协议模板样本第 12.9 (c) 条的相关说明。
	4.4	验资证明和出资证明书	根据 2005 年《公司法》第 29 条的规定，在任何情况下，注册资本的出资必须经合格的注册会计师独立验资。在 2014 年《公司法》中，第 29 条被删除，除法律另有规定外，在大多数行业中，已取消强制验资。因此，在大多数情况下，在法律层面，已不再需要会计师出具的验资证明，但公司仍可以取得验资证明书以用于存档或其他目的。 另外，《公司法》仍要求公司（而不是其会计师）出具出资证明书。出资证明书也证实出资已经缴付，但这类证书不是股票，不能转让。因此，模板样本提及了出资证明书，而未提及验资证明。

Continued

AoA	JVA	Subject	Comments
N/A	4.6	Shareholder guarantees	The Sample JVA Template provides that if shareholder guarantees are required to support commercial loans to the company, then the parties will provide proportionate guarantees on the same terms. This is the most common position, but this is a commercial matter that is subject to discussion and negotiation. Alternatively, the parties may agree to omit this section on shareholder guarantees and handle this concept outside of the JVA and AoA.
N/A	4.7	Shareholder loans	As noted in Chapter 2, with the anticipated repeal of current "thin capital" rules, it is expected that use of shareholder loans as a source of funding may increase. However, shareholder loans from foreign investors will still be subject to foreign exchange controls which currently limit foreign debt of a company (whether domestic or foreign-invested) to two times current assets. Since foreign exchange controls may be subject to change, the related requirements should be confirmed on a case-by-case basis. As with shareholder guarantees above, the Sample JVA Template provides for pro rata shareholder loans, but it is also possible to agree to disproportionate shareholder loan funding. In such cases the parties may also consider adjustments to the profit distribution allocations [see related comments in respect of clause 12.9(c) of the Sample JVA Template below]. The parties may also agree to omit this section on shareholder loans and handle this concept outside of the JVA and AoA.
N/A	4.8	Capital increases	Capital increases are subject to more than two-thirds supermajority approval at the shareholders meeting level. See Company Law, Article 43. For minority shareholders with less than one-third of the voting rights, it will be important to consider whether the majority investor can unilaterally approve a capital increase. In such a scenario, the minority shareholder may not have the capital to invest and thus the majority shareholder can effectively dilute the minority shareholder further if it cannot fund its pro rata share of the capital increase. Consequently, minority shareholders may wish to retain veto rights over such capital increases. As additional protection, we have inserted language providing that the parties are to have pre-emptive rights to subscribe to and contribute additional capital as part of the capital increase on a pro rata basis in order to permit the minority shareholder to preserve its proportionate share of the registered capital in such scenario.

续表

公司章程	合资协议	主题	注解说明
N/A	4.6	股东保证	合资协议模板样本规定，如果需要股东保证来支持公司获得商业贷款，双方将以相同的条件按比例提供保证。这是最常见的做法，但这是一个商业问题，取决于双方的讨论和谈判。或者，双方可以同意删去此章节关于股东保证的规定，并在合资协议和公司章程之外处理这一问题。
N/A	4.7	股东贷款	如第二章所述，由于目前的“投注差”规则即将废除，预计以股东贷款作为融资来源的做法可能会增加。但是，外国投资者的股东贷款仍将受到外汇管制，外汇管制目前限制公司（无论是内资公司还是外资公司）的外债不得超过其净资产的 2 倍。由于外汇管制政策可能会有所变化，因此应根据具体情况确认相关要求。 与上述股东保证一样，合资协议模板样本规定了双方按比例提供股东贷款，但双方可同意不按比例提供股东贷款。在这种情况下，双方也可以考虑调整利润分配比例［见下文合资协议模板样本第 12.9 (c) 条的相关注解说明］。 双方也可以同意删去此章节关于股东贷款的规定，并在合资协议和公司章程之外处理这一问题。
N/A	4.8	增资	增资须经代表 2/3 以上绝对多数表决权的股东通过。见《公司法》第 43 条。 对于拥有不到 1/3 表决权的少数股东来说，考虑多数股东是否可以单方面批准增资这一问题很重要。在这种情况中，少数股东可能没有资金用于投资，如果少数股东不能按比例缴纳增资份额，多数股东可以进一步有效地稀释少数股东的股权。因此，少数股东可能希望保留对此类增资的否决权。作为额外的保护措施，我们加入了相关条款规定双方将就增资部分的资本的认缴和实缴按比例享有优先权，以允许少数股东在该情形下保持其在注册资本中的比例份额。

Continued

AoA	JVA	Subject	Comments
			Note that in the current base case scenario in which Party B as minority shareholder holds 40% of the registered capital, it has veto rights over capital increases. Consequently, in this scenario it would also be appropriate to provided that both parties will be obligated to subscribe to their proportionate shares of such capital increase since both will have approved it. The parties may in the alternative agree to omit this section on capital increase and handle this concept outside of the JVA and AoA as well.
N/A	4.9	Capital reduction	Capital reductions are, similar to capital increases, subject to more than two-thirds supermajority approval at the shareholders meeting level. See Company Law, Article 43. Likewise, we have provided in the Sample JVA Template that both parties are obligated to bear their proportionate shares of such capital reduction since both will have to have approved it in the base case scenario here (60-40 joint venture). Again, the parties may agree to omit this section on capital reduction and handle this concept outside of the JVA and AoA as well.
N/A	4.11–4.12	Funding defaults	Note that these clauses apply both to the original capital funding schedule as well as capital increases. If the clause on capital increases is omitted then this clause should be amended accordingly.
N/A	5.1	Funding conditions	Under the Sample JVA Template, capital funding is subject to the prior satisfaction or waiver of the conditions to funding (see clause 4.3 of the Sample JVA Template). These conditions are designed to encompass all of the basic elements contemplated by the parties in connection with the new entity set up.
N/A	5.2	Waiver of conditions	The Sample JVA Template contemplates joint waivers of conditions. However, in some cases it may be preferable to provide that the party which is the beneficiary of a particular matter have the sole right to waive the corresponding condition.
N/A	5.3	Responsibility for conditions	Chinese registration authorities will want to see that responsibilities for fulfilment of certain company registration matters has been allocated to a specific party. The Sample JVA Template provides a sample allocation of responsibilities. This will need to be modified to reflect the specific requirements of each particular transaction. Note that in many respects this section replaces the legacy Responsibilities of the Parties section of the traditional JV contract. See related discussion in Chapter 5 above.

续表

公司章程	合资协议	主题	注解说明
			需要说明的是，在本基础案例情形下，乙方作为少数股东持有 40% 的注册资本，对增资拥有否决权。因此，在这种情形下，规定双方都有义务按比例认购增资份额也是合适的，因为增资将需要双方的批准。 或者，双方也可以同意删去此章节关于增资的规定，并在合资协议和公司章程之外处理这一问题。
N/A	4.9	减资	与增资类似，减资须经代表 2/3 以上绝对多数表决权的股东通过。见《公司法》第 43 条。 同样，我们在合资协议模板样本中规定，双方都有义务按比例承担减资份额，因为在本模板的基础情形中（60–40 合资），减资将需要双方的批准。 双方也可以同意删去此章节关于减资的规定，并在合资协议和公司章程之外处理这一问题。
N/A	4.11—4.12	出资违约	需要说明的是，这些条款对于首次出资安排和增资均适用。如果增资条款被删除，则本条款应进行相应的修改。
N/A	5.1	出资条件	在合资协议模板样本中，出资受限于出资条件的事先满足或放弃（见合资协议模板样本第 4.3 条）。这些条件旨在涵盖双方在设立新实体时考虑的所有基本要素。
N/A	5.2	出资条件的放弃	合资协议模板样本规定了出资条件的共同放弃。但是，在某些情况下，规定仅作为特定事项受益人的一方有权放弃相应的出资条件可能更为合适。
N/A	5.3	关于出资条件的责任	中国的登记机关希望看到某些公司登记事务的履行责任已分配给特定的一方。合资协议模板样本提供了责任分配的示例，需要根据特定交易的具体要求进行修改。 需要说明的是，本章节在很多方面取代了传统合资合同中关于双方责任的部分。请参见本书第五章的相关讨论。

Continued

AoA	JVA	Subject	Comments
			Note also that the conditions also include holding of the first shareholders meeting and board meeting so that relevant actions can be undertaken in proper sequence. As a practical matter, the first shareholders meeting and first board meeting can be held on the same day following the satisfaction of all other relevant conditions, with the first board meeting to follow the first shareholders meeting at which the initial slate of directors is elected. Then following the conclusion of the first board meeting, the parties can cause the company to enter into the various ancillary agreements with the parties in the approved form, as approved as part of the first board meeting resolutions.
N/A	6.2	Transfer of equity interests	This clause complies with Article 71 of the Company Law. Under the EJV Law, a party to the JV can object to the transfer of equity, which is sufficient to block the proposed transfer. However, under the Company Law, a party to the JV who objects to the sale must purchase the equity proposed to be transferred, failing which, the party shall be deemed to consent to the transfer. We have not included restrictions on indirect transfers as this generally would not be acceptable to financial investors or many MNCs, but may be negotiated and agreed by the parties in other circumstances as appropriate.
N/A	6.5	Encumbrances	This Sample JVA Template permits either party to pledge their equity interests subject to compliance with relevant provisions of applicable law, which would include registration of the pledge with the AMR. Since this arrangement may be the means to effect a backdoor transfer to a third party, in some cases the parties will require prior consent to such an arrangement.
N/A	6.8	State-owned assets	In the event that the Chinese party is a state-owned company, then the valuation and transfer of its interests in the JV company will be subject to compliance with relevant SASAC rules. Corresponding provisions or cross-references are included in clause 15.6 (mandatory transfer), clause 16.7 (mutual buy-out) the definition of Qualified Valuation Firm in clause 17.3, in clause 17.7 (valuation) and in the definition of Industry Valuation Method in the definitions section in Annex 1 of the Sample JVA Template. Accordingly, if the Chinese party is not a state-owned company, the bracketed language may need to be deleted or revised as appropriate.
6	7	Shareholders meeting	This clause is newly added to the Sample JV Templates in compliance with Articles 36, 37, 39, 40 and 43 of the Company Law.

续表

公司章程	合资协议	主题	注解说明
			另外需要说明的是，出资条件还包括召开第一次股东会会议和第一次董事会会议，以便能够按照适当顺序采取相关行动。实际上，第一次股东会会议和第一次董事会会议可以在所有其他相关条件得到满足后的同一天举行，第一次董事会会议将在第一次股东会会议之后举行。然后，在第一次董事会结束后，双方可以促使合资公司与双方签订各种经批准的形式的附属协议，如第一次董事会决议所批准。
N/A	6.2	股权转让	本条款与《公司法》第 71 条的规定相一致。根据《中外合资经营企业法》，合资一方可以反对股权转让，这足以阻止拟议的股权转让。但是根据《公司法》，反对股权出售的一方必须购买拟转让的股权，否则，该方被视为同意转让。 我们未包含针对间接转让的限制，因为这通常是不被财务投资者或许多跨国公司所接受的，但是在其他情况下双方可以就此酌情讨论并达成一致。
N/A	6.5	权利负担	在遵守适用法律相关规定的前提下，合资协议模板样本允许任何一方抵押其股权，其中包括向市场监管局做抵押登记。由于这种安排可能是向第三方秘密转让股权的手段，因此在某些情况下需要双方事先同意该等安排。
N/A	6.8	国有资产	如果中方是一家国有企业，那么其在合资公司中的股权的估值和转让须遵守国资委的相关规则。相应的条款或交叉引用包含在第 15.6 条（强制转让），第 16.7 条（双向收购），第 17.3 条中的合格评估机构的定义，第 17.7 条（估值）和合资协议模板样本附件一定义部分中行业评估方法的定义中。因此，如果中方不是国有企业，则可能需要删除或修改中括号内的内容。
6	7	股东会	根据《公司法》第 36 条、第 37 条、第 39 条、第 40 条和第 43 条，模板样本新增此条款。

Continued

AoA	JVA	Subject	Comments
N/A	7.2	First Shareholder Meeting Resolutions	It is recommended that the parties pre-approve a set of resolutions to be adopted at the first shareholders meeting to elect the initial slate of directors and supervisor(s). The adoption of the pre-agreed shareholder resolutions is included in the conditions to funding.
6.2	7.3	Annual meetings	This clause complies with Article 37 of the Company Law.
6.3	7.4	Interim meetings	This clause incorporates the provisions of Article 39 of the Company Law permitting shareholders which hold at least 10% of the registered capital to request an interim meeting of the shareholders. While in the base case scenario adopted for the Sample JV Templates, the minority shareholder holds a 40% equity interest, we have mentioned the 10% standard as a reminder for possible future reference in the event of the addition of a third smaller shareholder or other changes in the shareholder percentage shares of the registered capital. We have also added other procedural details for convenience.
6.4	7.5	Presiding authority (shareholder meeting)	This clause mirrors the provisions of Article 40 of the Company Law.
6.6	7.7	Supermajority shareholder resolutions	This clause largely mirrors the provisions of Article 43 of the Company Law. As noted above in various chapters of the book, most of these matters previously required unanimous board approval under the EJV Law, so under the Company Law shareholders with more than two-thirds ownership of the registered capital may now be able to unilaterally control approval of these items. However, it may also be common for minority shareholders to insist on retaining veto rights in respect of these matters, which in a two-party joint venture would usually be achieved by changing the voting requirements for these items from super-majority to unanimous, in effect retaining the traditional standard as under the EJV Law. This will be a matter for negotiation on a case-by-case basis. On the other hand, under Article 42 of the Company Law, the parties may agree to changes in their respective voting rights. Consequently, it is possible, at least theoretically, for parties to agree to a voting rights arrangement permitting a party which holds less than two-third of the equity interests to control the decisions on these or other points. This type of arrangement is expected to be rare, but this may still be possible under special circumstances.

续表

公司章程	合资协议	主题	注解说明
N/A	7.2	第一次股东会决议	建议双方预先批准在第一次股东会会议上将要通过的一系列决议，以选举出首任董事和监事。通过预先商定的股东会决议是出资条件的一部分。
6.2	7.3	年度股东会会议	本条款与《公司法》第 37 条的规定相一致。
6.3	7.4	临时股东会会议	本条款体现了《公司法》第 39 条的规定，允许持有至少 10% 注册资本的股东请求召开临时股东会会议。虽然在模板样本采用的基础情形下，少数股东持有 40% 的股权，但我们规定了 10% 的标准，以作为未来增加第三方小股东或股东持有注册资本的比例发生变更时的参考提示。为方便起见，我们还增加了其他程序性细节。
6.4	7.5	主持权限（股东会会议）	本条款反映了《公司法》第 40 条的规定。
6.6	7.7	绝对多数股东会决议	本条款主要反映了《公司法》第 43 条的规定。如本书以上各章节所述，在《中外合资经营企业法》项下，这些事项中的大部分需经董事会一致批准，因而现在根据《公司法》，拥有超过 2/3 股权的股东可能可以单方面控制对这些事项的批准。但是，少数股东在这些事项上坚持保留否决权也可能较为常见，这对于一个两方的合资企业来说，通常可以通过将这些事项的表决要求由绝对多数变为一致同意来实现，实际上保留了《中外合资经营企业法》项下的传统标准。这是一个需要个案谈判的问题。 另外，根据《公司法》第 42 条的规定，当事方可以同意更改其各自的表决权。因此，至少在理论上，当事方可以对表决权安排自由约定，允许持有少于 2/3 股权的一方控制关于这些事项或其他事项的决策。这一类的安排预计较为罕见，但在特殊情况下仍有可能发生。

Continued

AoA	JVA	Subject	Comments
			Note that item (g) in this Clause in respect of the retention of earnings and distribution of profits does not require super-majority approval at the shareholders meeting under the Company Law, but we have included this here as we consider this appropriately reflects the preferred approach in respect of such matters.
6.7	7.8	Simple majority shareholder resolutions	These items require shareholders approval but are not designated as requiring a minimum two-thirds approval (see Article 37 of the Company Law). In the base case scenario adopted for the Sample JVA Template, the minority shareholder holds enough voting rights to block any of the items requiring supermajority approval under clause 7.7 but not the simple majority approval items in this clause 7.8. Consequently, in practice a minority shareholder in this situation may wish to consider requiring supermajority (or unanimous) approval for some or all of the items listed in this clause 7.8 as we have already done in respect of the approvals for retained earnings and distribution of profits as noted above.
6.8	7.9	Written shareholder meeting resolutions	It is anticipated that with rare exceptions, the business of shareholder meetings for Sino-foreign joint ventures will be conducted by written resolution without a formal meeting. Written shareholder resolutions are permitted under Article 37 of the Company Law.
6.10	7.11	Shareholder deadlock	Since under the Company Law certain matters require supermajority shareholder approval, so long as the minority shareholder holds not less than one-third of the total equity interests in the company or has otherwise secured veto rights in respect of such matters, the potential for deadlock exists. The Sample JV Templates provide for the parties to reconvene a second shareholders meeting and exchange additional information in the interim. Since this is already at the shareholder level, we have not provided for escalation as an interim solution (as is the case with board deadlocks), and then if the shareholder deadlock persists a party may trigger buy-out or termination provisions under clause 14.3 of the Sample JVA Template. The shareholder deadlock provision here is presented as an alternative to the board deadlock resolution mechanism in clause 9.5 of the JVA, but it may also be possible to have a deadlock resolution process for deadlocks at both levels using the board deadlock resolution mechanism, in which case the deadlock clause would be broken out as a separate clause and apply to both scenarios.

续表

公司章程	合资协议	主题	注解说明
			需要说明的是，本条款 (g) 项中关于留存收益和利润分配的事项，在《公司法》项下，不要求经绝对多数股东会决议的批准，但我们已将此事项包括在本条中，因为我们认为这适当地反映了处理此类事项的首选方式。
6.7	7.8	简单多数股东会决议	这些事项需经股东会批准，但无须经至少 2/3 表决权的批准（请见《公司法》第 37 条）。在合资协议模板样本采用的基础情形下，少数股东拥有足够的表决权来否决第 7.7 条项下须经绝对多数表决权批准的事项，但不能否决第 7.8 项下须经简单多数表决权批准的事项。因此，在实践中，在这种情况下，少数股东可能考虑对第 7.8 条中列出的部分或全部事项要求经绝对多数（或全体一致）表决权批准，而如上所述，我们已经针对留存收益和利润分配的批准做出了该等设计。
6.8	7.9	股东会书面决议	预计除少数例外情况外，中外合资企业股东会审议的事项将通过书面决议完成，而非召开正式会议。根据《公司法》第 37 条，股东会书面决议是被允许的。
6.10	7.11	股东僵局	由于根据《公司法》，某些事项需要绝对多数股东的批准，因此只要少数股东持有不少于公司总股权的 1/3 或者通过其他方式就此类事项享有否决权，就存在发生僵局的可能性 。模板样本规定双方重新召开第二次股东会会议并在此期间交换额外信息。由于这已经是股东会层面，我们没有规定将提交上级决定作为临时解决方案（在董事会僵局的情形下适用）。如果股东僵局持续存在，一方可以启用合资协议模板样本第 14.3 条规定的收购或终止条款。 此处的股东僵局条款是合资协议第 9.5 条中董事会僵局解决机制的替代方案，但在股东会和董事会两个层面的僵局中都使用董事会僵局解决机制也是可能的。在这种情况下，僵局条款将作为单独条款并适用于这两种情况。

Continued

AoA	JVA	Subject	Comments
			It should be noted that deadlock resolution clauses at both the shareholders meeting level and the board level are not appropriate in all cases and even where appropriate are typically subject to intense negotiation. In order to be effective, a deadlock resolution clause must as a practical matter provide, as we have done in the Sample JV Templates, that if the parties are unable to resolve the dispute through escalation or reconvening of a second meeting, then a party may trigger the termination and mutual buy-out provisions. This may be seen as too drastic a measure by some parties, but the threat of termination can in many instances provide the parties with additional incentive to reach a resolution in order to avoid such an outcome. Even so, for a deadlock resolution clause to work effectively, the parties should have generally equal bargaining power, where the threat of termination induces both parties equally to work together to find a resolution, knowing that each party has the ability to buy out the other. Where the parties' bargaining power is not roughly equal, a highly-capitalized majority shareholder may be able to effectively coerce a minority shareholder with modest capital resources to give up its veto rights, knowing that the minority shareholder does not have sufficient capital to buy out the majority party's share of the registered capital if a deadlock is triggered and so may be at risk of being bought out. For similar reasons, as a rule private equity investors which take a minority position in a company will rarely if ever agree to deadlock resolution clauses which trigger termination and buy out provisions as this would potentially dilute their veto powers and require them to sell under conditions which may not be as favorable. However, even a majority shareholder may be well advised to exercise caution in connection with the triggering a termination event as the result of a deadlock since the majority shareholder as sole owner may not be able to achieve all of the synergies contemplated in connection with the original decision to partner with the minority shareholder. In the end, the parties must assess the practical implications of whether to include such a deadlock resolution clause in a particular transaction, but we have included such provisions in the Sample JV Templates as this is consistent with the approach adopted in connection with many (but not all) greenfield joint ventures undertaken by strategic investors (as opposed to financial investors) in situations similar to the base case scenario adopted for purposes of the Sample JV Templates.

续表

公司章程	合资协议	主题	注解说明
			应当指出的是，股东会级别和董事会层面的僵局解决条款并不适合所有情形，即使在适合的情况下也通常取决于激烈的谈判。为了产生效用，僵局解决条款必须，如我们在模板样本中所设定的，实际上规定如果当事方无法通过提交上级或重新召开第二次会议来解决争议，那么一方可以启用终止条款和双向收购条款。这可能被某些当事方视为过激的措施，但终止条款的威胁在许多情况下可以为当事方提供额外的动力以达成解决方案进而避免这种结果。 即便如此，要使僵局解决条款真正产生效果，双方应具有大体上相等的谈判地位，终止的威胁会促使双方平等地共同努力寻求解决方案，并清楚每一方都有能力收购另一方所持的股权。如果当事人的谈判地位并非大体相当，则资金实力强的多数股东可能能够实际上迫使资本财力相对弱的少数股东放弃否决权，因为他们知道如果触发僵局，少数股东没有足够的资本收购多数股东所持的股权，因此少数股东可能面临被收购股权的风险。 出于类似的原因，通常在公司中占有少数股权的私募股权投资者几乎不会或很少会同意触发终止和收购条款的僵局解决条款，因为这可能会削弱他们的否决权并要求他们在可能不是很有利的条件下出售。 但是，建议即使是多数股东也应就僵局导致的触发终止事件持谨慎态度，因为作为唯一所有人的多数股东可能无法实现最初决定与少数股东合作时所设想的所有协同效应。 最后，双方必须评估是否在特定交易中包含此类僵局解决条款的实际影响，但我们已在模板样本中包含该等条款，因为这与许多（但不是全部）战略投资者（而非财务投资者）在与模板样本所采用的基础案例情形类似的情况下投资绿地合资企业时采用的方法一致。

Continued

AoA	JVA	Subject	Comments
7	8	Board of Directors	Under the Company Law, the parties may establish either a board of directors or appoint a single executive director (see Article 50 of the Company Law). We expect that parties will consider appointing a single executive director only in connection with smaller scale joint ventures where one party is more of a silent partner and is willing to delegate full management authority to the other party. For purposes of these Sample JV Templates, we have adopted the traditional board of directors structure and so will not discuss the executive director structure here.
7.2	8.2	Composition of the board	Under the Company Law the parties are free to agree the total number of board directors (but in any event no fewer than three and no more than 13) as well as the allocation of board seats (see Article 44 of the Company Law). Under the EJV Law, the allocation of board seats was to be roughly proportionate to the parties' respective shares of the registered capital, but in recent years many local authorities have been much more flexible and have in most cases been willing to defer to the agreement of the parties in this regard. The Company Law reinforces this more liberal trend, so it should be possible for parties to agree to disproportionate representation on the board, even permitting minority shareholders to have a majority on the board. However, as a matter of practice, it is expected that in most cases board representation will closely mirror the parties' ownership percentages. The Sample JV Templates follow this more common approach. Note that in a 50-50 joint venture the parties naturally will almost always prefer to have an equal number of board seats, which will obviously tend towards a greater potential for deadlocks. It has also been observed that some local registration authorities may take the position that the board must have an odd number of directors, although this is not required under the Company Law. We also note that, while not required under Chinese law in respect of non-listed companies, in some cases the parties may wish to provide for the election of an independent director. This clause would need to be modified accordingly.

续表

公司章程	合资协议	主题	注解说明
7	8	董事会	根据《公司法》，双方可以设立董事会或任命一名执行董事（见《公司法》第 50 条）。我们预计，只有在合资企业规模较小，且其中一方不负责经营并愿意将全部管理权委托给另一方的情况下，双方会考虑仅任命一名执行董事。在模板样本中，我们采用了传统的董事会结构，因此不会在此处讨论执行董事的结构。
7.2	8.2	董事会组成	根据《公司法》，当事方可自由约定董事会的成员总数（但在任何情况下应在 3~13 人）以及董事会席位的分配（见《公司法》第 44 条）。 根据《中外合资经营企业法》，董事会席位的分配大致与双方各自所占注册资本的份额成比例，但近年来，许多地方政府机构提高了灵活性，并在大多数情况下同意以双方的约定为准。《公司法》强化了这种更为宽松的趋势，因此当事方可以约定不按比例分配董事会席位，甚至允许少数股东在董事会中占多数席位。但是，作为惯例，在大多数情况下，董事会席位仍会密切反映当事方所持有的股权比例。模板样本采用了这一相对常见的方式。 请注意，在双方各出资 50% 的合资企业中，双方自然会更希望董事会席位各占一半，这显然更有可能导致僵局。据了解，尽管《公司法》没有规定，一些地方登记机关可能会要求董事会成员数量必须为奇数。 我们还注意到，虽然中国法律对非上市公司没有要求，但在某些情况下，双方可能希望选举独立董事，在此情况下，本条款则需要相应地修改。

Continued

AoA	JVA	Subject	Comments
7.3	8.3	Director qualifications	The qualifications for directors are set out in Article 146 of the Company Law in the form of disqualifying criteria. By way of illustration, persons who are ineligible for appointment as directors include individuals who are lacking or have limited civil capacity or have a large amount of unpaid debt. These same provisions applied to directors previously since the EJV Law was silent on this point, so this does not represent a new requirement. Note that the names of and other relevant information on the directors will need to be registered with the AMR. This will need to be updated as directors are removed and replaced.
7.4	8.4	Election, removal and replacement of directors	Under the EJV Law, the parties could directly appoint the members of the board of directors, but under the Company Law the directors are elected at the shareholders meeting. This clause is intended to ensure that the directors and supervisors nominated by the parties are in fact so elected at the shareholders meeting level so as to achieve the same result as under the EJV Law.
7.5	8.5	Chairman and Vice Chairman	Under the EJV Law, the chairman was to be appointed by one party and the vice chairman appointed by the other party. This is no longer required under the Company Law, which provides that the method of appointment of the chairman and vice chairman shall be specified by the articles of association (see Article 44 of the Company Law). However, in practice, it likely will still be common for one party to appoint the chairman and the other party to appoint the vice chairman as a matter of courtesy, and we have adopted this traditional arrangement in the Sample JV Templates. Note also that these positions can be appointed from among the elected directors as agreed by the parties and need not be elected by vote of the shareholders or the board. It is also possible to rotate appointment rights for these positions. This would require additional provisions be added to this clause to effect this arrangement. It has also be customary that if one party appoints the general manager then the other party would be given the right to appoint the chairman, but this traditional arrangement was not based on any legal requirement but more out of a sense of respect for the party which did not have the right to appoint the general manager as the position of chairman is given significant respect in China. But see related comments on the legal representative below. We have adopted the more traditional allocation of roles of chairman and vice chairman in the Sample JV Templates.

续表

公司章程	合资协议	主题	注解说明
7.3	8.3	董事资格	《公司法》第146条通过列举不合格情形的方式对董事资格作出了规定。例如，有下列情形之一的不得担任董事：无民事行为能力或限制民事行为能力，或个人所负数额较大的债务到期未清偿。这些规定以前同样适用于董事，因为《中外合资经营企业法》在这一点上未作规定，所以这并不是新的要求。 请注意，董事的姓名和其他相关信息需要在市场监督管理局备案。若董事被免职或更换，则需要进行变更备案。
7.4	8.4	董事的选任、罢免和更换	根据《中外合资经营企业法》，双方可以直接任命董事会的成员，而根据《公司法》，董事由股东会选举产生。本条款旨在确保双方提名的董事和监事事实上由股东会层面选举产生，以达到与在《中外合资经营企业法》项下相同的结果。
7.5	8.5	董事长与副董事长	根据《中外合资经营企业法》，董事长由一方任命，副董事长由另一方任命。《公司法》对此不再作要求，其规定董事长与副董事长的产生方式应由公司章程规定（见《公司法》第44条）。而在实践中，一方任命董事长，另一方任命副董事长可能仍然是较为常见的情形，我们在模板样本中采用了这种传统的安排。另外请注意，这些职位可经双方约定从当选的董事中任命，而无须通过股东或董事会选举产生。 双方也可以轮流行使这些职位的任命权，这需要在本条款中增加额外的规定以实现这种安排。 通常，如果一方任命总经理，另一方则有权任命董事长，但这种传统安排不是基于任何法律要求，而是出于对无权任命总经理一方的尊重，因为董事长职务在中国较受重视。但请参阅下文关于法定代表人的说明。 我们在模板样本中就董事长和副董事长的职责分配采用了相对传统的方式。

Continued

AoA	JVA	Subject	Comments
7.6	8.6	Legal Representative	Under the EJV Law, the chairman was the legal representative of the joint venture company, but under the Company Law either the chairman (or executive director) or the general manager can be designated as the legal representative. This position is formally registered with the AMR and the name of the legal representative appears on the company's business license. In the Sample JV Templates we have maintained the traditional practice of designating the chairman as the legal representative, so we will discuss some of the relevant considerations first from that perspective. The legal representative of the company has actual and apparent authority under Chinese Law to bind the company, so it is common to provide in the AoA and the JVA that the legal representative has no authority to bind the company except as authorized by board or shareholders resolution. This limited the authority of the chairman to the more figurehead role of convening and presiding over meetings of the board and perhaps to other ceremonial roles. The legal representative of the company also is exposed to potential legal liability under Chinese Law. For example, if the company conducts illegal operations beyond the range approved and registered by the registration authority, conceals facts from the registration and tax authorities and practices fraud, or engages in other activities prohibited by law, damages the interests of the state or the public interest, in addition to the company, the legal representative of such company may also be subject to administrative sanctions and penalties and even criminal liability where the conduct violates criminal statutes. Although as a practical matter the legal representative usually bears personal liability only for egregious acts of misconduct, many directors may be unwilling to accept the role of legal representative without an indemnity and coverage by appropriate D&O insurance (see discussion regarding clause 8.11 of the Sample JVA Template below). If the general manager is designated as legal representative, it will be appropriate for the board to adopt a resolution specifying the scope of his authority in order to be consistent with the limiting provisions of this clause.

续表

公司章程	合资协议	主题	注解说明
7.6	8.6	法定代表人	根据《中外合资经营企业法》，董事长是合资公司的法定代表人，但根据《公司法》，董事长（或执行董事）或总经理均可担任法定代表人。此职位在市场监管局正式登记，且法定代表人的姓名会出现在公司的营业执照上。 在模板样本中，我们保留了将董事长指定为法定代表人的传统惯例，因此我们将首先从这个角度讨论一些相关的注意事项。 根据中国法，公司的法定代表人代表公司作出的行为有实际和显著地约束公司的效力，因此公司章程和合资协议中通常规定除非经董事会或股东决议授权，法定代表人无权代表公司作出对公司具有约束力的行为。这使董事长的权限被限制在召集和主持董事会会议的名义性角色以及其他仪式性角色以内。 根据中国法，公司的法定代表人也可能需要承担法律责任。例如，如果公司在登记机关批准和登记的范围之外进行违法经营、向登记机关和税务机关隐瞒事实并实施欺诈行为，或从事法律禁止的其他活动，损害国家或公众利益，除该公司外，该公司的法定代表人也可能受到行政制裁和处罚，若违反刑事法规则须承担刑事责任。虽然实际上法定代表人通常只对严重的不当行为承担个人责任，但很多董事在没有补偿和适当的董事及高级管理人员责任保险承保的情况下，可能不愿意接受法定代表人的职责（见下文关于合资协议模板样本第 8.11 条的讨论）。 如果总经理被指定为法定代表人，董事会应通过决议明确其职权范围，以符合本条款的限制性规定。

Continued

AoA	JVA	Subject	Comments
			Moreover, given the traditional more expansive rights and liabilities of the legal representative under Chinese law and traditional practice, designating the general manager as the legal representative may create some potential conflicts between the chairman and the board of directors on the one hand and the general manager/legal representative on the other hand, undercutting the rights of the board to supervise and direct the work of the general manager. For similar reasons, many companies choose not to permit the general manager simultaneously to serve on the board. However, there is no legal restriction in this regard. It is a matter of internal corporate governance and policy to be decided by the parties. One final point should be noted: since the JVA is not binding on the legal representative, who is not a party to the JVA in his or her personal capacity, it is critical that this provision be retained in the AoA, which is binding on the company and thus also its officers and directors.
7.7	8.7	Board secretary	The board secretary is a required position for listed companies, but is not a required position for unlisted companies. However, it is common for many non-listed Chinese companies to have a board secretary, although it is less common for FIEs. As a practical matter, having a well-qualified individual fill this position can prove very helpful in terms of administration of the business of the board, so we have included such a position here for reference purposes, which can be adopted as appropriate. We have provided in the Sample JV Templates that the secretary is appointed by and reports to the chairman, but these arrangements can be modified as best suits the needs of the parties.
7.8	8.8	Board committees	There are no requirements on what board committees non-listed companies in China may or must establish. In the Sample JV Templates we have moved this to an item to be decided by the board outside of the AoA and JVA in order to provide sufficient flexibility, but where a party wishes to provide for a more rigid structure up front, it is also possible to include relevant provisions here. To ensure that the minority shareholder has a voice in the structure, composition and role of these committees we have provided in the Sample JV Templates for unanimous board approval in respect of such matters.

续表

公司章程	合资协议	主题	注解说明
			此外，鉴于在中国法和传统惯例下法定代表人传统上拥有相对广泛的权责，指定总经理作为法定代表人可能导致董事长和董事会这一方与总经理/法定代表人这一方产生潜在的冲突，削弱董事会监督和指导总经理工作的权利。出于类似的原因，许多公司不允许总经理同时在董事会任职。但是，法律在这方面并没有限制。这类内部公司治理和政策问题需要由双方决定。 最后需要注意的一点：由于法定代表人不以其个人身份作为合资协议的一方，合资协议对法定代表人并没有约束力，因此在对公司及高级管理人员和董事有约束力的公司章程中保留这一条款至关重要。
7.7	8.7	董事会秘书	董事会秘书是上市公司必须设立的职位，法律对非上市公司是否设立董事会秘书并无要求，但是，许多中国非上市公司设立董事会秘书职位的情形很常见，但在外商投资企业中较少见。从实用的角度，选择一个合格的人选担任董事会秘书，对于管理董事会的业务会很有帮助。因此我们在本模板中加入了董事会秘书这一职位以供参考，双方可酌情采用。我们在模板样本中规定，董事会秘书由董事长任命并向董事长报告，但这些安排可以根据双方的需求进行修改。
7.8	8.8	董事会委员会	法律对于中国的非上市公司可以或必须设立何种董事会委员会没有要求。在模板样本中，我们将其作为公司章程和合资协议以外由董事会决定的事项，以提供足够的灵活性，但如果一方希望在初始阶段即建立相对严格的公司治理结构，则也可以在此纳入相关条款。为了确保少数股东可以对相关董事会委员会的结构、组成和职责方面发表意见，我们在模板样本中规定此类事项需要董事会一致批准通过。

Continued

AoA	JVA	Subject	Comments
7.9	8.9	Ethical rules	Articles 147 and 148 of the Company Law provide that directors of a company shall bear fiduciary obligations to the company, for example, a director shall not take any bribe or other illegal gain by taking advantage of his position or misappropriate company assets for personal use, or loan company funds or provide any guaranty to any other person by using company property in violation of the articles of association without first obtaining the consent of the shareholders meeting or the board of directors. These same provisions applied to directors previously since the EJV Law was silent on this point, so this is a continuation of an existing requirement. Either or both of the parties may have certain minimum ethical rules that may be required to be applied to the new joint venture. These can be adopted as part of the first board meeting resolutions, although many foreign parties may also wish to include compliance/ethics clauses directly in the JVA in compliance with applicable laws in their home jurisdiction. This is another provision which should be included in the AoA in order to ensure that it is binding on the directors who are not party to the JVA.
7.10	8.10	Compensation of directors	The Sample JV Templates provide that directors will not be compensated but related costs and expenses will be reimbursed. This assumes that the directors are all senior employees of the parties and thus do not require separate compensation. In some cases the parties may wish to provide that the directors receive additional remuneration. This would be the case for independent directors and also possibly in the case of a single executive director. In such cases, this clause would need to be modified accordingly. As above, this should be included in the AoA as well to be binding on the directors.
7.11	8.11	Director indemnity	The liability exposure of the chairman was discussed above in connection with clause 9.6 of the Sample JVA Template. The potential liability of directors is described in connection with the discussion of clause 8.9 in respect of the directors' fiduciary duties under law. It is increasingly common for the company to provide separate indemnities in favor of the directors in addition to D&O insurance coverage, and so this practice is reflected in the Sample JV Templates.

续表

公司章程	合资协议	主题	注解说明
7.9	8.9	道德规则	《公司法》第 147 条和第 148 条规定，公司董事应对公司承担信托义务，例如，董事不得利用职权收受贿赂或其他非法收入，不得侵占公司的财产，不得违反公司章程的规定，未经股东会或董事会同意，将公司资金借贷给他人或以公司财产为他人提供担保。由于《中外合资经营企业法》对此未作规定，上述《公司法》规定在以前同样适用于合资企业的董事，因此在这并不是一个新的要求。 任何一方或双方都可能有某些最低程度的道德规则需要适用于新合资企业。这些可以作为第一次董事会决议的一部分予以采用，但是许多外方可能还希望依照其所在地区适用法律的规定，将相关的合规 / 道德条款直接加入合资协议中。 这是公司章程中应包含的另一项规定，以确保其对非合资协议缔约方的董事具有约束力。
7.10	8.10	董事的报酬	模板样本规定董事不会获得报酬，但其相关费用和开支将获得报销。该规定假设董事都是双方的高级雇员，因此不需要单独的报酬。在某些情况下，双方可能希望规定董事可以获得额外报酬，如独立董事或唯一执行董事的情形。在这种情况下，本条款需要进行相应的修改。 如上所述，公司章程同样应当纳入此规定以对董事具有约束力。
7.11	8.11	对董事的赔偿	上文有关合资协议模板样本第 9.6 条的说明讨论了董事长的责任风险。第 8.9 条关于董事的法定信托义务的讨论描述了董事的潜在责任。 除了董事及高级管理人员责任保险范围外，公司为董事提供单独的赔偿这一现象越来越普遍，因此模板样本反映了这一惯例。

Continued

AoA	JVA	Subject	Comments
N/A	9.1(a)	First board meeting	It is recommended that the parties pre-approve a set of resolutions to be adopted at the first board meeting, to be held immediately following the election of the first slate of directors as part of the first shareholders meeting, to adopt a series of foundational resolutions regarding matters such as appointment of the general manager and other management personnel, delegation of powers to management personnel, approval of initial business plan and budgets, adoption of various company policies and procedures (including ethical policies, contract signing policies, company chop management policies and where appropriate IP management policies, etc.), approval of entry into ancillary agreements, appointment of the company's independent auditor, etc. The adoption of the pre-agreed board resolutions is included in the conditions to funding.
8.1(a)	9.1(b)	Regular board meetings	The Company Law does not specify how frequently a limited liability company shall hold board meetings. In the Sample JV Templates, we provided at least two times per year by referring to the relevant requirement for joint stock limited companies (see Article 110 of the Company Law) and common practice.
8.1(b)	9.1(c)	Interim board meetings	The Company Law is silent on interim board meetings of a limited liability company, which leaves this to the agreement of the shareholders as set out in the articles of association. In the Sample JV Templates, we provided that an interim board meeting shall be scheduled upon the written request of two or more of the directors by referring to the relevant requirement for joint stock limited companies (see Article 110 of the Company Law).
8.1(e)	9.1(d)	Presiding authority (board meeting)	This clause mirrors the provisions of Article 47 of the Company Law.
8.1(d)	9.1(e)	Notice	The procedures for convening board meetings can be freely agreed in the AoA. In the Sample JV Templates we have provided a relatively generous notice period of 20 business days for reference purposes.
8.1(h)	9.1(i)	Quorum	Whereas the EJV Law provided that a quorum required attendance (in person or by proxy or telecommunications) by more than two-thirds of the directors, the Company Law establishes no minimum number of directors for purposes of comprising a quorum for board meetings of a limited liability company, leaving quorum requirements to the agreement of the parties. In the Sample JV Templates we have provided that attendance by at least one Party B director is required for a quorum as an additional minority shareholder protection.

续表

公司章程	合资协议	主题	注解说明
N/A	9.1（a）	第一次董事会会议	建议双方预先批准在第一次董事会会议上需要通过的一系列决议，第一次董事会会议将在第一次股东会会议选举出第一届董事后立即召开，其将通过一系列根本性决议，涉及总经理和其他高级管理人员的任命、高级管理人员的授权、初始经营计划和预算的批准、各种公司政策和程序（包括道德政策、合同签署政策、公章管理政策和适当的知识产权管理政策等）的采用、订立附属协议的批准、公司独立审计师的任命等事项。对预先商定的董事会决议的批准是合资协议出资条件的一部分。
8.1（a）	9.1（b）	定期董事会会议	《公司法》没有规定有限责任公司召开董事会会议的频率。在模板样本中，我们参考股份有限公司的相关要求（见《公司法》第 110 条）和惯例，规定每年至少召开两次董事会会议。
8.1（b）	9.1（c）	临时董事会会议	《公司法》对有限责任公司的临时董事会会议未作规定，而是以股东在公司章程中的约定为准。在模板样本中，我们参照股份有限公司的相关规定（见《公司法》第 110 条），规定经两名或两名以上董事的书面请求，应安排召开临时董事会会议。
8.1（e）	9.1（d）	（董事会会议的）召集	本条款反映了《公司法》第 47 条的规定。
8.1（d）	9.1（e）	通知	董事会会议的召集程序可以在公司章程中自由约定。在模板样本中，我们提供了相对宽松的 20 个工作日作为通知期限，以供参考。
8.1（h）	9.1（i）	法定人数	虽然《中外合资经营企业法》规定超过 2/3 的董事（亲自、委托他人或通过电信方式）出席方可构成董事会召开的法定人数，但《公司法》没有规定有限责任公司董事会会议召开的最低法定人数，而是将法定人数的要求留给双方约定。在模板样本中，我们规定，至少需要一名乙方董事出席才能达到法定人数，作为对少数股东的额外保护。

Continued

AoA	JVA	Subject	Comments
			A majority shareholder, on the other hand, may wish to have its nominated directors be sufficient to comprise a quorum. If the minority shareholder can block board action by failing to attend meetings such that the board is inquorate, the majority shareholder may choose to include language providing that a smaller number of directors (equal to the directors nominated by the majority shareholder) can constitute a quorum at a rescheduled meeting. Under the EJV Law, the legality of board action taken at a meeting attended by fewer than the minimum number specified in the law was subject to potential legal challenge, but under the additional flexibility offered under the Company Law, the parties will have more freedom to craft appropriate provisions.
8.1(i)	9.1(j)	Casting vote	The legality of a casting or tie-breaking vote has been subject to question given the general principle of "one person one vote" under Article 48 of the Company Law. Even so, in some cases such provisions have previously been included in the AoA and JV contract for Sino-foreign joint ventures and accepted by relevant Chinese authorities. In the base case scenario adopted for the Sample JV Templates, there is an odd number of directors so there is less likelihood of a tie vote unless a director fails to attend. Consequently, we have not provided for the chairman to have a casting vote, which is in line with the more common practice.
8.2/ 8.3	9.2/ 9.3	Board resolutions	For illustration purposes only, in the Sample JV Templates we have included a common set of board resolutions divided into matters in respect of which the minority shareholder retains veto rights with the balance being subject to approval by simple majority vote controlled by the majority shareholder. For additional protection, the minority shareholder may wish to move more items from the simple majority approval category to the unanimous approval category, but this is a matter which is left to the agreement of the parties. The Company Law provides no guidance and imposes no restrictions in this regard. Minority shareholder protections in respect of board voting can be accomplished by requiring unanimous approval, supermajority approval or special majority approval (including at least one director nominated by the minority shareholder). In the context of a 60-40 JV with proportionate board representation, all of these methods achieve the same result, and give the minority shareholder effective veto rights. It is also useful to note that the list of board approval items comprises the matters reserved for board approval (the matters requiring shareholders meeting approval being prescribed by law), and accordingly limit the scope of authority of the general manager.

续表

公司章程	合资协议	主题	注解说明
			另外，多数股东可能希望该方指定的董事就足以构成法定人数。如果少数股东可以通过不参加会议使其未达到法定人数来阻止董事会行动，则多数股东可能会选择规定，较少人数的董事（相当于多数股东提名的董事数量）在重新安排的会议上可构成法定人数。 根据《中外合资经营企业法》，出席人数少于法定最低人数的董事会会议采取的行动的合法性可能会受到质疑，但《公司法》给予了额外的灵活性，使双方有更大的自由制定合适的条款。
8.1（i）	9.1（j）	决定票	鉴于《公司法》第48条规定的“一人一票”的一般原则，决定票的合法性受到质疑。即便如此，在某些情况下，此类规定之前已被纳入中外合资企业的公司章程和合资合同中，并为中国有关部门所认可。 在模板样本采用的基础案例情形下，董事人数为奇数，因此除非有一位董事未能出席，否则投票平局的可能性较小。因此，我们未规定董事长享有决定票投票权，这与常见的做法一致。
8.2/ 8.3	9.2/ 9.3	董事会决议	仅出于说明目的，在模板样本中，我们已经将常见董事会决议分为少数股东保留否决权的事项，和须经多数股东控制的简单多数投票批准的事项。 为了获得额外的保护，少数股东可能希望将更多事项从简单多数批准变为一致决议批准，但这取决于双方的协商一致。《公司法》在这方面没有提供指导或限制。 在董事会投票方面对少数股东的保护可以通过规定一致决议批准、绝对多数批准或特别多数批准（包括至少一名少数股东提名的董事的批准）事项来实现。在合资企业出资比例为60-40且董事席位按双方所持注册资本比例分配的情况下，上述所有方式均会取得相同的结果，并赋予少数股东有效的否决权。 值得注意的是，董事会批准事项清单包含须由董事会批准的保留事项（需要股东会批准的事项由法律规定），因此也限制了总经理的权限范围。

Continued

AoA	JVA	Subject	Comments
			Lastly, the parties may, in the alternative, prefer that the board have authority to decide all matters other than those reserved for the shareholders meeting, without a specific enumeration of the board's scope of authority. This approach vests greater power at the board level, and in such case, the board should grant a specific scope of authority to the general manager, which tends to restrict the scope of authority of the general manager. See related discussion in respect of the scope of authority of the general manager in connection with clause 11.5 of the Sample JVA Template below.
8.4	9.4	Written board resolutions	The Company Law does not require written resolutions of the board to be unanimous, and so it is possible to provide in the AoA and JVA that written resolutions may be approved if circulated to all directors and signed by that number of directors required to pass the resolution at a duly convened meeting of the board. However, in the Sample JV Templates we have provided that written board resolutions require unanimous approval, which has been the more common arrangement in Sino-foreign joint ventures over the years. The rationale for this rule, which is consistent with the requirements of the corporate laws in leading jurisdictions, is to encourage meetings of the board to foster discussion and informed decision making and to limit the potential for abuse of written resolutions by a majority shareholder.
8.5	9.5	Board deadlock	So long as any board approval item requires the affirmative vote of directors from both parties, the potential for deadlock exists. The Sample JV Templates provide for escalation and then if the board deadlock persists then a party may trigger buy-out or termination provisions under clause 15.5 of the Sample JVA Template. In the Sample JV Templates we assume that if a matter is important enough to merit inclusion on the list of unanimous board approval items, then it is material enough (if there is a failure to reach agreement on such matter) to trigger the deadlock resolution provisions. However, it is also possible for the parties to indicate that disagreement on certain matters which require unanimous (or super-majority) approval will not trigger the deadlock resolution procedures. One example could be failure to agree on the annual budgets, in which case the company is to continue operations based on the last approved budget with any agreed adjustments for inflation while the parties continue to discuss the new budget, all without triggering the deadlock resolution provisions. Any such alternative arrangement would need to be drafted into the JVA in both the main body of the agreement as well as in the definition of Board Deadlock Matter in the definitions section.

续表

公司章程	合资协议	主题	注解说明
			最后，当事方可以选择，董事会有权决定除须由股东会决定之外的所有事项，而无须具体列举董事会的职权范围。这种方式使董事会层面拥有更大的权力，在这种情况下，董事会应该向总经理授予特定的权限范围，以此限制总经理的权限。有关总经理权限范围的讨论请参考以下就合资协议模板样本第 11.5 条的讨论。
8.4	9.4	董事会书面决议	《公司法》并未要求董事会书面决议需要全体董事一致同意，因此可以在公司章程和合资协议中规定，如果书面决议经所有董事传阅并由经正式召集的董事会会议通过决议所需数量相同的董事签署，则可以批准该书面决议。 但是，我们在模板样本中已经规定，董事会书面决议需要得到全体董事一致批准，这是多年来中外合资企业相对常见的做法。该规则与世界上主要地区的《公司法》要求相一致，其原理在于鼓励召开董事会会议，促进讨论和明智的决策，并限制多数股东滥用书面决议的可能性。
8.5	9.5	董事会僵局	只要董事会批准事项需要双方董事都投赞成票，就存在陷入僵局的可能。模板样本规定可将僵局事项提交上级，若董事会僵局持续存在，那么一方可能会启用合资协议模板样本第 15.5 条规定的收购或终止条款。 在模板样本中，我们假设如果一个问题非常重要，值得列入董事会一致批准事项清单，则该事项足够重要，（如果就该等问题不能达成一致）可以触发僵局解决条款。但是，双方也可以表明，对需要获得全体一致（或绝对多数）批准的某些事项无法达成一致不会触发僵局解决条款。例如，双方未能就年度预算达成一致意见，在这种情况下，公司将基于最近批准的预算（以及就通货膨胀进行任何商定的调整）继续运营，同时双方继续讨论新预算，而所有这些行为都不会触发僵局解决条款。任何此类替代性安排都需要在合资协议的主体以及定义部分中董事会僵局事件的定义中体现。

Continued

AoA	JVA	Subject	Comments
			See also the notes to clause 7.11 of the Sample JVA Template above setting out considerations to be taken into account in respect of deadlock resolution provisions generally.
9	10	Supervisors	Under the Company Law, a limited liability company shall have a board of supervisors composed of no fewer than three members. Limited liability companies with a smaller number of shareholders or those of a smaller scale may have one to two supervisors without setting up a board of supervisors. The board of supervisors shall include shareholders' representatives and an appropriate proportion of employee representatives which shall not be less than one third of the members of the board of supervisors, the specific proportion of which shall be prescribed by the articles of association. The EJV Law predates the adoption of the supervisor requirement, but under related circulars issued in 2006, this requirement was applied to all FIEs, so these requirements under the Company Law have applied to EJVs since that time. In a two-party joint venture, the primary options may be as follows: 1) a board of supervisors consisting of two members with each nominated by one party respectively; or 2) three members with an additional member jointly agreed by the parties; or 3) a single supervisor nominated by one party or jointly agreed by two parties. In any event, the supervisor(s) nominated shall be elected by the shareholders meeting. Supervisors have the power of inspecting the financial issues of the company, supervising the performance of directors and senior management personnel, etc. In general, a supervisor's role is advisory. Supervisors have no ability to direct the affairs of the company. In the Sample JV Templates we have adopted the more comprehensive three-member board of supervisors structure.
10.1	11.1	Management Personnel	While the EJV Law implementing regulations provided that the board appoint the general manager and deputy general manager, the common practice was to have the parties set out direct appointment rights in the JV contract. Under the Company Law, the more formal nomination and election process will now be followed more strictly. Under Articles 46 and 49 of the Company Law, the board is to appoint the senior management personnel of the company and define the scope of their authority.

续表

公司章程	合资协议	主题	注解说明
			见上述合资协议模板样本第 7.11 条的注解说明中所载的关于僵局解决条款通常应考虑的因素。
9	10	监事	根据《公司法》，有限责任公司应设立监事会，成员不得少于三名。股东数量较少或规模较小的有限责任公司可以设一名到两名监事，不设监事会。监事会应当包括股东代表和适当比例的公司职工代表，职工代表比例不得低于 1/3，具体比例由公司章程规定。 《中外合资经营企业法》的颁布早于设置监事的要求，但根据 2006 年发布的相关通知，此要求开始适用于所有外商投资企业，因此，《公司法》的这些要求自那时起开始适用于合资经营企业。 在一个两方的合资企业中，主要选择如下：（1）设监事会，由三名成员组成，每一方分别提名一名，第三名成员由双方共同商定；或（2）设两名监事，每名成员分别由一方提名；（3）设唯一监事，由一方提名或由双方共同商定。在任何情况下，提名的监事应由股东会选举产生。 监事的职权包括检查公司财务，对董事和高级管理人员执行公司职务的行为进行监督等。一般来说，监事的职权是顾问性质的，无权对公司事务进行指导。 在模板样本中，我们采用了更广泛的三名成员的监事会结构。
10.1	11.1	高级管理人员	虽然《中外合资经营企业法》实施条例规定董事会任命总经理和副总经理，但通常的做法是各方在合资合同中规定直接任命权。在《公司法》项下，则需要更加严格地遵循正式的提名和任命程序。根据《公司法》第 46 条和第 49 条，董事会将任命高级管理人员并界定其职权范围。

Continued

AoA	JVA	Subject	Comments
			The Sample JV Templates provide that the parties now have nomination rights in respect of specific management positions and then under the voting arrangements under clause 11.3 of the Sample JVA Template, the parties agree to cause the directors nominated by them to vote in favor of the appointment of the nominated officers. This achieves the same results as the previous mechanisms and is consistent with international practice. In the Sample JV Templates we have not provided for one party to nominate the general manager and the other party to nominate a deputy general manager as contemplated under the EJV Law. With the repeal of the EJV Law this requirement will no longer apply, but this arrangement had long since fallen out of favor in any event as this had the potential of creating competing power bases in the joint venture management which often proved to be unworkable in practice. Consequently, it has been increasingly common to eliminate the deputy general manager position, and the Sample JV Templates align with this more common market practice. It is also possible to set out in the JVA a more extensive slate of senior management personnel to be nominated by the different parties, in some cases on a rotating basis. This may provide minority shareholders more voice in key aspects of the company's operations and can be coordinated with corresponding rights under related ancillary agreements between a party and the company to maximize a minority shareholder's influence. However, setting out in the JVA a large slate of senior management personnel can prove to be cumbersome as an operational matter, and changes to these arrangements will require a formal amendment to the JVA. If corresponding terms are set out in the AoA, as would be common, then amendments to the AoA would also require more than two-thirds affirmative vote at the shareholders meeting level. In many cases, it will be simpler to have only a shorter list of senior management personnel in the AoA/JVA and then leave other management arrangements to the separate approval by the board or the general manager within the scope of authority granted under the JVA or by the board. This is contemplated in clause 11.4 of the Sample JVA Template. It is also becoming increasingly common for parties to agree that the company will hire some or all of the senior management personnel from outside of the parties on the open market rather than give either party specific nomination rights. This would require corresponding amendments to this clause.

续表

公司章程	合资协议	主题	注解说明
			模板样本规定双方对特定管理人员职位有提名权，并且根据合资协议模板样本第 11.3 条项下的投票安排，双方同意促使由其提名的董事就被提名的高级职员的任命投赞成票。这样就可以达到与先前的机制相同的结果，并且符合国际惯例。 在模板样本中，我们没有参照《中外合资经营企业法》规定由一方提名总经理而另一方提名副总经理。随着《中外合资经营企业法》被废止，这一要求将不再适用，但其实这一安排早已为人所诟病，因为这有可能在合资企业管理中造成权力的竞争，在实践中往往行不通。因此，取消副总经理职位的做法越来越普遍，模板样本与这种更常见的市场惯例相一致。 也可以在合资协议中列出需要由不同当事方提名的更广泛的高级管理人员，在某些情况下可以由双方轮流提名。这可以为少数股东在合资公司运营的关键方面提供更多发言权，并且可以与一方与合资公司之间签署的相关附属协议项下的相应权利进行协调以最大化少数股东的影响力。但是，在合资协议中列出更大范围的高级管理人员名单可能在操作上较为烦琐，并且修改这些安排将需要对合资协议进行正式的修订。如果公司章程中规定了相应的条款，那么修订公司章程也需要在股东会上经代表 2/3 以上表决权的股东投赞成票通过。 在许多情况下，更简单的做法是仅仅在公司章程 / 合资协议中列出较短的高级管理人员的名单，将其他管理层安排交由董事会另行批准，或交由总经理在合资协议或董事会授予的职权范围内另行批准。合资协议模板样本第 11.4 条对此作了规定。 双方同意合资公司将在双方以外的公开市场上雇用部分或全部高级管理人员而不是给予任何一方特定的提名权的做法也越来越普遍。这需要对本条款作出相应的修订。

Continued

AoA	JVA	Subject	Comments
			Finally, there is a trend towards allowing greater flexibility in respect of the titles of the senior management personnel in a Sino-foreign joint venture, but in the Sample JV Templates we have adopted the more traditional title of general manager.
10.5	11.5	Scope of authority of general manager	As drafted, this clause provides the general manager with a broad scope of authority limited only by those reserved matters as enumerated in the AoA/JVA. This arrangement is preferred if the minority shareholder has nomination rights for the general manager. In such a scenario, the minority shareholder will also wish to raise the thresholds for board approvals so as to effect a corresponding expansion of the authority of the general manager. In other situations, the parties may prefer to provide in the AoA/JVA that the general manager shall have only such authority as may be specifically granted by the board. This would be of particular importance where the scope of authority of the board is not specifically enumerated, an approach which we have not adopted for purposes of the Sample JV Templates (see related discussion in comments to clause 9.2/9.3 of the Sample JVA Template above). It may be advisable for the board to adopt a resolution enumerating the powers of the general manger in any event, usually as part of the first board meeting resolutions, so that the board can exercise appropriate supervisory authority over the general manager. This is another provision which should be included in the AoA so as to be binding on the company and the management personnel since they are not a party to the JVA.
11.1 – 12.5	12.1 – 12.5	Financial management	These provisions reflect the requirements of applicable law as supplemented by standard market practice.
11.6 – 11.7	12.6 – 12.7	Financial reports	Pursuant to Articles 164 and 165 of the Company Law, it is required that the company shall, at the end of each financial year, prepare a financial report and have it audited by an accounting firm, and submit its financial report to each shareholder within the time limit prescribed in the articles of association. Such requirements have been supplemented in the Sample JV Templates in line with international practice. Subject to compliance with the basic financial reporting requirements under applicable law, this is a matter for the agreement of the parties.

续表

公司章程	合资协议	主题	注解说明
			最后，中外合资企业高级管理人员的头衔有越来越灵活的趋势，但在模板样本中我们采用了更传统的总经理头衔。
10.5	11.5	总经理职权范围	本条款规定总经理享有广泛的职权，仅受限于公司章程 / 合资协议中列举的保留事项。如果少数股东拥有总经理的提名权，则这种安排是首选。在这种情况下，少数股东还会希望提高董事会批准的门槛，以实现总经理职权相应的扩大。 在其他情况下，双方可能更愿意在公司章程 / 合资协议中规定总经理应仅享有董事会明确授予的权力。在董事会的职权范围未明确列举时，这一规定尤为重要，就模板样本而言，我们未采取此做法（参见上述对合资协议模板样本第 9.2/9.3 条的说明中的相关讨论）。董事会通过一项列举总经理权力的决议也是可取的，这通常作为第一次董事会决议的一部分，以便董事会对总经理适当行使监督权。 这是公司章程中应包含的另一项规定，以便对非合资协议当事方的合资公司和高级管理人员产生约束力。
11.1—12.5	12.1—12.5	财务管理	这些规定反映了适用法律的要求，并按照标准市场实践进行了补充。
11.6—11.7	12.6—12.7	财务报告	根据《公司法》第 164 条和第 165 条，公司应在每个会计年度结束时编制财务报告并由会计师事务所审计，并在公司章程规定的期限内将财务报告送交各股东。模板样本根据国际惯例对这些要求进行了补充。在遵守适用法律规定的基本财务报告要求的前提下，该事项需要双方协商一致。

Continued

AoA	JVA	Subject	Comments
11.8	12.8	Party audit rights	Shareholders are entitled to inspect and copy the articles of association, minutes of shareholders meetings, resolutions of board meetings, resolutions of meetings of the board of supervisors, financial reports and accounting books of the company (see Articles 33 and 169 of the Company Law). Again, the Sample JV Templates supplement these requirements with related provisions to ensure proper coordination and access. The minimum 10% shareholding threshold set out in the Sample JV Templates is not required under law but aligns with the minimum 10% shareholding requirement to call an interim meeting of the shareholders (see clause 7.4 of the Sample JVA Template above) or to present a unilateral petition to wind up the company (see Article 182 of the Company Law). This threshold is proposed for consideration in order to minimize potential disruption to the operations of the company, but in a two- to three-party joint venture, it would generally be expected that all parties would have such audit rights, and minority financial investors, even with shareholdings at or below the proposed 10% threshold, would commonly insist on such audit rights.
11.9 (c)	12.9(c)	Proportionate distributions	It is important to highlight this sub-clause for separate discussion as the Company Law provides substantial additional flexibility to the parties in this regard. Under the EJV Law profits could be distributed only in strict accordance with the parties' respective shareholding percentages. This was in contrast to the CJV Law, which allowed the parties to agree in the AoA/JV contract to disproportionate profit distribution arrangements. This flexibility for CJVs effectively permitted parties to capitalize soft contributions of what were termed "cooperative conditions" that were not otherwise susceptible to independent valuation and which were not permitted to be used as in-kind capital contributions under the EJV Law. Article 34 of the Company Law provides that shareholders shall draw dividends in proportion to their actual capital contributions, unless otherwise agreed by the shareholders. Thus, under the Company Law, parties to Sino-foreign joint ventures will now have substantially broader scope to agree on disproportionate profit distribution if circumstances so warrant. (See related discussion above in respect of clause 4.3 of the Sample JVA Template relating to the form of capital contributions.)

续表

公司章程	合资协议	主题	注解说明
11.8	12.8	双方的审计权利	股东有权查阅和复制公司章程、股东会会议记录、董事会会议决议、监事会会议决议、财务会计报告（见《公司法》第 33 条和第 169 条）。同样，模板样本还对这些要求进行了补充，加入了相关条款以确保能够就上述文件的查阅和复制进行适当地协调和提供访问权限。 模板样本中规定的最低 10% 的表决权的门槛不是法定要求，但与召集临时股东会会议（见上述合资协议模板样本第 7.4 条）或单方提出解散公司申请（见《公司法》第 182 条）的最低 10% 的表决权要求一致。我们在此加入此门槛供考虑，旨在尽量减少对合资公司运营的潜在干扰，但在两到三方的合资企业中，通常各方都预期享有此审计权，即使持有股权小于或等于该拟议的 10% 门槛的少数财务投资者，通常也会坚持享有该审计权。
11.9(c)	12.9(c)	按比例分配	由于《公司法》在按比例分配利润这一问题上为双方提供了极大的灵活性，因此非常有必要强调并单独探讨该子条款。 根据《中外合资经营企业法》，只能严格按照合营各方的持股比例分配利润。这与《中外合作经营企业法》形成鲜明对比，后者允许合作各方在公司章程 / 合资合同中约定不按比例进行利润分配。中外合作经营企业的这种灵活性实际上允许双方将无法独立估值且在《中外合资经营企业法》项下不得用作非现金出资的所谓的“合作条件”的软出资资本化。 《公司法》第 34 条规定，除非股东另有约定，否则股东应按其实缴的出资比例分红。因此，根据《公司法》，如果情况需要，中外合资企业的双方现在可以在更大范围内就不按比例的利润分配达成一致。（参见上文有关合资协议模板样本第 4.3 条有关出资形式的相关说明。）

Continued

AoA	JVA	Subject	Comments
			Notwithstanding this additional flexibility under the Company Law, it is expected that in the vast majority of cases the parties will still provide for proportionate distributions of profits in line with their respective ownership percentages. The Sample JV Templates adopt this more common approach.
N/A	13.5	Non-compete	This clause can be very contentious and may not be appropriate in all circumstances. Financial investors in particular will not agree to be bound by such obligations. Nonetheless, this clause is commonly (but not universally) included in JVAs entered into by strategic investors, and so is included in this Sample JVA Template for reference.
N/A	13.6	Carveouts to non-compete	In addition to these customary carveouts to the non-compete undertakings, if a party already has or expects to have investments which may run afoul of the non-compete undertakings, additional carveouts can be included referencing the specific projects or categories of projects so as to bring these outside the scope of the non-compete.
N/A	13.7	Corporate opportunity	Officers and directors of a company have fiduciary duties in such capacities to take all actions in a manner which is in the best interests of the company. Given that in many cases, the officers and directors of a Sino-foreign joint venture will be senior employees of the respective parties to the joint venture, there is potential for conflicts of interest. This clause sets out the rights and obligations of the parties in respect of opportunities that are presented to the officers and directors of the company in their various capacities and reflects international best practices in this regard.
N/A	13.8	Self-dealing	In addition to requiring that all related party transactions be subject to super-majority board approval, it is also advisable to include a separate undertaking by the parties not to cause the company to enter into any self-dealing transactions with any party to the JV.
12.1	14.1	Term	Historically, the term of a Sino-foreign joint venture has been limited to a fixed period, usually ranging from 10 to 30 years, but sometimes as long as 50 years. Now under Article 74 of the Company Law, the parties can agree on the term of the company which, consistent with current practice for domestic companies, should permit the establishment of Sino-foreign joint ventures with an open-ended indefinite term.

续表

公司章程	合资协议	主题	注解说明
			尽管《公司法》赋予了额外的灵活性，但预计在绝大多数情况下，双方仍将根据各自的股权比例进行相应的利润分配。模板样本采用了这种更常见的做法。
N/A	13.5	不竞争	这一条很可能会引起争议，且可能并不适用于所有情形。财务投资者尤其会拒绝受到该等义务的约束。然而，这一条在由战略投资者签署的合资协议中很常见（但也并非普遍适用），所以本合资协议模板样本中加入了此条款供参考。
N/A	13.6	不竞争的除外规定	除了本条中规定的这些不竞争承诺的常见除外情形，如果一方已经或预期进行与不竞争承诺相违背的投资，也可以在协议中加入其他除外情形，反应具体项目或项目类型以便将这些排除在不竞争条款的适用范围之外。
N/A	13.7	公司机会	公司的高级职员和董事具有信托责任，需要以符合公司最佳利益的方式采取一切行动。考虑到在许多情况下，中外合资企业的高级职员和董事为双方各自的高级员工，可能会存在利益冲突。本条规定了双方就合资公司高级职员和董事在其职权范围内获悉的机会而言的权利和义务，且反映了这方面的国际最佳实践。
N/A	13.8	自我交易	除了要求所有关联方交易须经绝对多数董事会决议批准外，还建议单独加入双方不得促使合资公司与合资企业任何一方进行任何自我交易的承诺。
12.1	14.1	期限	过去，中外合资企业只能设定固定的经营期限，通常为10~30年，但有时也可长达50年。而现在，根据《公司法》第74条的规定，当事方可以就公司的经营期限进行约定，与内资公司的现行做法相一致，应允许设立无限期的中外合资企业。

Continued

AoA	JVA	Subject	Comments
			We note that there were divergent views among the members of the Expert Committee on how to handle the issue of the term. The majority view is that an indefinite term will be preferred as this is consistent with international practice and avoids the challenges relating to renewals and extensions upon expiry of the original term. On the other hand, the Expert Committee recognizes that it is now well-settled practice for FIEs to adopt a fixed term and there is some uncertainty whether AMRs in all localities will agree to register an FIE with an open term. In the Sample JV Templates, we have opted to provide for an indefinite term as the default position, but this will be a matter for negotiation between the parties on a case-by-case basis.
12.2	14.2	Automatic termination	This clause reflects the fact that the JVA is no longer a constitutional document of the joint venture company (as was the case under the EJV Law) but is an agreement between the parties, and thus as set out in clause 14.5(a) of the Sample JVA Template the termination of the JVA does not affect the continuing legal status of the company. As such, if one party buys out the other, then there is no longer any need for this JVA, since it would then be a solely-owned company rather than a jointly-invested company, but the entity form remains unchanged. (See related discussion in Chapter 6.) Similarly, if the parties for any reason voluntarily terminate the JVA or if a court orders the liquidation of the company, the JVA will also terminate.
12.3 – 12.4	14.3 – 14.4	Termination events	The Sample JV Templates adopt the traditional termination event structure commonly found in Sino-foreign joint venture contracts and, as has typically been the case, such termination notices trigger either a put/call, mutual buy-out or liquidation/dissolution process.
N/A	15	Mandatory transfer events	The termination events under 14.3(a) – (c) of the Sample JVA Template may be classified as events of default on the part of a party, giving the other party the right to initiate a mandatory transfer in the form of a put or call. In the Sample JV Templates we have provided only for a call option for purposes of illustration, but it would also be possible to provide for both a put and a call option (although a put option would not be appropriate in the context of the other party's insolvency). The key point is that the non-defaulting party be in a position to drive the process.

续表

公司章程	合资协议	主题	注解说明
			我们注意到专家委员会成员之间就如何处理合资期限这一问题存在分歧。大多数人更倾向于无限期，因为这与国际实践相一致且避免了在原始期限到期时延长期限的种种挑战。另外，专家委员会也意识到，鉴于外商投资企业采用固定经营期限的做法已是惯例，各地的市场监管局是否会同意注册无限期的外商投资企业存在一些不确定性。 在模板样本中，我们选择默认为无限期，但具体也取决于个案中双方之间的谈判。
12.2	14.2	自动终止	该条款反映了合资协议不再是合资公司的章程性文件（《中外合资经营企业法》将其规定为章程性文件），而是双方之间的协议，因此如合资协议模板样本第 14.5（a）条所述终止合资协议不会影响合资公司的法律地位的存续。 因此，如果一方收购了另一方，则不再需要合资协议，因为合资公司将变为独资公司而非共同投资公司，但其组织形式保持不变。（参见第六章相关讨论。） 同样，如果双方因任何原因自愿终止合资协议或法院命令公司清算，合资协议也将终止。
12.3—12.4	14.3—14.4	终止事件	模板样本采用中外合资企业合同中常见的传统终止事件结构，并且通常情况下，此类终止通知会触发出售 / 购买选择权、双向收购或清算 / 解散程序。
N/A	15	强制转让事件	合资协议模板样本第 14.3（a）—（c）条项下的终止事件可被归类为一方的违约事件，使另一方有权以出售或购买选择权的形式发起强制转让。在模板样本中，我们仅规定了购买选择权以供说明，但也可以同时规定出售和购买选择权（尽管出售选择权不适用于另一方破产的情形）。关键点在于非违约方能够推动这一程序。

Continued

AoA	JVA	Subject	Comments
			Also, in a default situation, the non-faulting party may wish to have the right to a discount regarding the buy-out price (e.g. some percent discount off the fair market value). We have not provided for this option in the Sample JVA Template. This is a matter for negotiation between the parties on a case-by-case basis.
N/A	16	Mutual buy-out	The remaining termination events under clause 14.3(d) – (f) of the Sample JVA Template may be considered to be more neutral in nature rather than a default of one party or the other (except in respect of cases in which a deadlock arises because of efforts of a party to block related corporate action). As such, in these cases the Sample JVA Template provides for a modified Texas shoot-out process to provide the parties an equal chance to buy-out the other party. This could be replaced with a modified Russian roulette clause or a put/call option in favor of one party. This is a matter for commercial negotiations between the parties, subject in all cases with compliance with the requirements of applicable law.
N/A	17	Valuation	For purposes of a put/call option or a mutual buy-out, consistent with Chinese law and practice the parties will need to undertake a valuation. This clause provides that the company be valued on a going concern basis, with the value being set by agreement of the parties, by a single valuer jointly appointed by the parties, or by a panel of three valuers, one appointed by each party and the third appointed by the two valuers. Equity transfers in any joint venture to which an SOE is a party will need to comply with relevant legal requirements on valuation of state-owned assets. This is reflected in the definitions of Qualified Valuation Firm and Industry Valuation Method. Subject to compliance with such applicable legal requirements, other valuation principles may be agreed in advance or left to the determination of the valuers. Also see the comments to clause 6.8 of the Sample JVA Template above in respect of the valuation of state-owned assets.
13.1	18.1 – 18.2	Voluntary dissolution/ deemed consent to dissolution	Under Article 43 of the Company Law, dissolution of the company requires a more than two-thirds vote at the shareholders meeting level. The Sample JVA Template also provides for dissolution as the ultimate default option in the case of a termination event where the parties opt out of the put/call option or mutual buy-out provisions.

续表

公司章程	合资协议	主题	注解说明
			同样地，在违约的情况下，非违约方可能希望就收购价获得一定折扣（例如，基于公平市场价值的一定百分比的折扣）。在合资协议模板样本中我们没有提供此选项。这取决于个案中双方之间的谈判。
N/A	16	双向收购	合资协议模板样本第 14.3（d）—（f）条规定的其余终止事件在性质上更为中立，而不是某一方的违约（一方试图阻止相关公司行为而造成僵局的情况除外）。因此，在这些情况下，合资协议模板样本规定了经修改的得克萨斯枪战（Texas shoot-out）程序，为双方提供了平等的收购另一方的机会。 这一条也可以替换为经修改的俄罗斯轮盘赌（Russian roulette）条款或偏向某一方的出售 / 购买选择权。此项取决于双方的商业谈判，但无论如何都应符合适用法律的规定。
N/A	17	估值	就出售 / 购买选择权或双向收购而言，根据中国法律和惯例，双方需要对合资公司进行评估。本条款规定，应在持续经营的基础上对合资公司进行评估，其价值由双方协议确定，或由双方共同指定的一家评估公司或由三家评估公司（双方各指定一家并由这两家评估公司指定第三家）组成的评估小组确定。 国有企业作为一方的任何合资企业的股权转让都需要遵守国有资产评估的相关法律要求。这一点在“合格评估机构”和“行业评估方法”的定义中进行了体现。 在遵守此类适用法律要求的前提下，其他估值原则可以事先商定或由评估公司确定。同时也可参阅上文中对合资协议模板样本第 6.8 条有关国有资产评估的说明。
13.1	18.1—18.2	自愿解散 / 视为同意解散	根据《公司法》第 43 条，公司解散需要在股东会层面经代表 2/3 以上表决权的股东投票通过。若双方在终止事件中选择放弃出售 / 购买选择权或双向收购条款，合资协议模板样本规定解散作为最终默认选项。

Continued

AoA	JVA	Subject	Comments
18.2	18.3	Unilateral petition for dissolution	Article 182 of the Company Law provides that a minority shareholder holding not less than 10% of the equity interests in the company can submit a unilateral petition to the court to dissolve the company if the company encounters serious difficulties in its operations or management that will lead to significant shareholder losses if it persists and the situation cannot be resolved by any other means. Currently, Chinese courts are unlikely to act on such a petition so this provision appears to be toothless. However, we refer to this in the Sample JV Templates as a placeholder in the event that such unilateral petitions may become a more effective tool in the future.
N/A	18.5—18.10	Liquidation procedures	These provisions generally reflect the requirements under Articles 183 through 188 of the Company Law, which provide that a liquidation committee shall be appointed when the circumstances leading to the dissolution of the company have occurred, and that the members of which shall consist of shareholders of the company. Such liquidation committee shall exercise such functions and powers during the course of the liquidation as necessary or related to wind up its business and distribute its assets. In addition, the dissolution application shall be registered with the registration authority. In the Sample JVA Template we have supplemented these provisions with other terms consistent with international practice.
N/A	24	Arbitration	Under Chinese law the parties are free to agree to domestic or international arbitration to resolve disputes under the JVA. International arbitration awards are enforceable in China under the New York Convention. Hong Kong or Singapore are the most common venues for arbitration of disputes under a JVA.
15.3	25.11	JVA controls over AoA	Under traditional law and practice in China, in the event of discrepancies between the AoA and the JVA, the latter prevails. The Company Law is silent on this point, but we have incorporated a provision here that conforms to the traditional practice.
15.4	25.13	Governing law	Please see discussion on the governing law for the JVA in Chapter 6. As noted therein, we have provided for the JVA and the AoA to be governed by Chinese law consistent with prevailing legal requirements.
15.6	25.15	Language	Please see discussion on language of the JVA in Chapter 6. As noted therein, we have opted to provide that the English and Chinese versions are to be equally valid, in line with the traditional practice. It is proposed that the language provisions in the AoA follow suit.

续表

公司章程	合资协议	主题	注解说明
18.2	18.3	单方申请解散	《公司法》第 182 条规定，如果公司经营管理发生严重困难，继续存续会使股东利益受到重大损失，通过其他途径不能解决的，持有公司全部股东表决权 10% 以上的少数股东可以单方面请求法院解散公司。目前，中国法院不太可能根据此类请求采取行动，因此这项规定似乎起不到实际作用。但是，我们在模板样本中作此规定以防该单方请求未来变为更有效的工具。
N/A	18.5—18.10	清算程序	这些规定总体上反映了《公司法》第 183 条至第 188 条的要求，规定在导致公司解散的情况发生时，应当任命清算委员会，其成员应由公司股东组成。清算委员会应当在清算过程中行使其必要的或与结束其业务和分配资产有关的职权。此外，解散申请应在注册机关进行登记。在合资协议模板样本中，我们用符合国际惯例的其他条款对这些规定进行了补充。
N/A	24	仲裁	根据中国法，双方可自由协商通过国内或国际仲裁以解决合资协议下的争议。根据《纽约公约》，国际仲裁裁决可在中国执行。香港或新加坡是合资协议项下的最常见的争议仲裁地。
15.3	25.11	合资协议效力优先于公司章程	根据中国的传统法律和惯例，如果公司章程和合资协议之间存在差异，则以后者为准。《公司法》对此未作规定，但我们在此处纳入了符合该传统惯例的规定。
15.4	25.13	适用法律	请参见第六章中关于合资协议适用法律的讨论。如其所述，我们规定合资协议和公司章程受中国法律管辖，这也是符合现行法律要求的。
15.6	25.15	语言	请参见第六章中关于合资协议语言的讨论。如其所述，我们选择规定中英文版本同等有效，这也是与传统惯例相符的。建议公司章程对语言作出相同的规定。

Continued

AoA	JVA	Subject	Comments
Annex 2	Annex 3	Capital Contribution Schedule	Former rules regarding statutory minimum registered capital levels and timelines for injection of registered capital have been abolished, and as a practical matter registered capital amounts are required to be injected only prior to winding up of the company. In practice, some AMRs may expect to see, and the Parties may in any event find it useful to set out, a specific capital contribution schedule. Consistent with the relevant elements of the base case scenario for the Sample JVA Template, Annex 3 has been drafted to reflect only cash contributions. For additional comments on in-kind contributions, please refer to the annotations to clause 4.3 of the Sample JVA Template above. If capital contributions other than in the form of cash are contemplated, then Annex 3 would need to be modified accordingly.
N/A	Annex 4	Funding Conditions	Please see comments to clause 5.1 of the Sample JVA Template on conditions to funding above. Annex 4 should be coordinated with the provisions of clause 5.1. Note that consistent with the related comments set out in Chapter 5, Annex 4 provides that the parties will enter into a lease agreement with a third-party landlord on behalf of the new joint venture company, which will be among the documents to be presented as part of the company registration process.
N/A	Annex 5	Additional Permits	Additional governmental licenses and permits which are required for the intended operations of the company can be set out in this annex. Obtaining such permits will be a condition to funding.
N/A	Annex 6	Ancillary Agreements	The various ancillary agreements to be entered into by the Company upon establishment and following approval as part of the first board meeting resolutions are listed here. It is recommended that these be negotiated and agreed prior to signing of the JVA and AoA. These ancillary agreements should be listed by name in each of the categories set out in Annex 6. As discussed in connection with Annex 4 above, the Lease Agreement will be one of the Other Ancillary Agreements in Part 3 of Annex 6. Rather than attach the agreed forms of these ancillary agreements as annexes, we have provided for these to be signed in the "agreed form," which as set out in the interpretations section of Annex 1 means "such agreement or document in the form so acknowledged and confirmed by the Parties in writing." The recommended practice is for the parties to sign a separate protocol agreement attaching the ancillary agreements in the agreed form as evidence that these are the forms of the agreements to be signed as part of the conditions to funding so as to avoid disagreements at a later stage.

续表

公司章程	合资协议	主题	注解说明
附件二	附件三	出资时间表	过去关于法定最低注册资本和出资时间的规定已经废除。实践中，只需在公司清算之前缴足注册资本即可。在实践中，一些市场监管局可能期待看到，且合资双方也可能发现实际上规定一个明确的出资时间表是有益的。与合资协议模板样本所假定的基础案例情形的相关要素相一致，附件三仅体现了现金出资的情形。关于非货币出资的其他说明，请参见上文对合资协议模板样本第 4.3 条的注解说明。如果拟进行非货币出资，则附件三也需要相应修改。
N/A	附件四	出资条件	请参见上述对合资协议模板样本第 5.1 条有关出资条件的说明。附件四应与第 5.1 条的规定相协调。需要说明的是，与第五章所载的相关注解说明相一致，附件四规定双方将代表新的合资公司与第三方出租方签署一份租赁协议，该租赁协议将作为合资公司注册程序中待提交的文件之一。
N/A	附件五	附加许可	合资公司进行拟议的经营所需的其他政府许可和批准可在本附件中列出。获得此类许可是出资的条件之一。
N/A	附件六	附属协议	合资公司成立后，经第一次董事会决议批准后，合资公司将签署的各附属协议在此列出。建议在签署合资协议和公司章程之前就此进行谈判并达成一致。这些附属协议的名称应在本附件六中的相应类别下列出。如上文中有关附件四的讨论，租赁协议将作为其他附属协议之一列于本附件六的第 3 部分中。 相比于将这些协商一致的附属协议的样式作为合资协议的附件，我们规定这些附属协议将以“约定形式”签署，即如附件一的解释部分所载，指“形式得到双方书面认可和确认的该等协议或文件”。推荐的做法是双方另行签署一份协议书，将约定形式的附属协议附上，作为证据证明是作为出资条件的一部分将由双方签署的协议的形式，以避免在后期出现分歧。

Note that drafting comments on defined terms or the other annexes have been incorporated into the comments to the provisions of the main body of the Sample JV Templates above.

Conclusion

For more information on the Sample JV Templates and access to many of the alternative clauses and forms of ancillary agreements and documents referenced in the Sample JV Templates and the annotations above but not included in the Sample JV Templates, please go to www.docqbot.com/en/newFIL.

请注意，关于经定义的术语或其他附件的起草说明已纳入上述对公司章程和合资协议正文条款的说明中。

结论

如您希望了解模板样本的更多信息，以及使用更多可选条款、附属协议以及合资协议和上述注解说明中提及的但并未包括在模板样本中的附其他文件，请访问 www.docqbot.com/cn/newFIL。

Chapter 8 FIL-Compliant Bilingual WFOE Template

This Chapter consists of two annexes, as follows:

Annex 1 Sample WFOE Articles of Association Template

Annex 2 Annotations to Sample WFOE Articles of Association Template

The Sample WFOE Articles of Association Template referenced above has been drafted in contemplation of a WFOE with the following characteristics:

(a) This is a new small-cap greenfield WFOE set up as a strategic investment.

(b) The investor is to make its capital contributions in cash in a single lump sum.

(c) The new WFOE will adopt a streamlined corporate governance system comprised of a single executive director and a single supervisor.

Accordingly, without applicable substantive modifications, the Sample WFOE Articles of Association Template may not be appropriate for transactions with different characteristics.

The WFOE Articles of Association Sample Template and the related annotations are provided subject to the caveats and limitations, set out in Chapter 5. Electronic bilingual versions of the Sample Templates are available free of charge at www.docqbot.com/en/newFIL.

第八章　符合《外商投资法》规定的双语外商独资企业模板

本章包含如下两个附件：

附件一　外商独资企业章程模板样本

附件二　外商独资企业章程模板样本注解说明

上述外商独资企业章程模板样本是针对具有以下特征的外商独资企业起草的：

（a）以战略投资的方式设立的新的绿地外商独资企业。

（b）投资者将一次性以现金出资。

（c）新外商独资企业将采用精简的公司治理体系，由一位执行董事和一位监事组成。

因此，如果未进行适当的实质性修改，外商独资企业章程模板样本可能不适用于具有不同特征的交易。

外商独资企业章程模板样本和相关注解受限于第五章所载的声明和限制。模板样本的电子版可以从 www.docqbot.com/cn/newFIL 免费下载。

Annex 1
Sample WFOE Articles of Association Template

Dated [DATE]

ARTICLES OF ASSOCIATION

of

[COMPANY NAME]

附件一

外商独资企业章程模板样本

【填入日期】

【填入公司名称】

章程

TABLE OF CONTENTS

目录

ARTICLES OF ASSOCIATION

THESE ARTICLES OF ASSOCIATION ("Articles of Association") are made on [DATE] by [INVESTOR NAME][([Company Registration Number] [NUMBER])], a [INVESTOR ENTITY FORM] organized and existing under the laws of [INVESTOR JURISDICTION OF INCORPORATION], with its [registered address][OR][principal place of business] at [ADDRESS] (the "Investor") in respect of the establishment of [COMPANY NAME] Co., Ltd., (the "Company").

BACKGROUND

These Articles of Association are prepared in respect of the establishment, governance and management of the Company.

1. DEFINITIONS AND INTERPRETATION

Unless the provisions or context of these Articles of Association provide otherwise, these Articles of Association, the Annex and the terms used herein shall be interpreted in accordance with Annex 1.

2. ESTABLISHMENT OF THE COMPANY

2.1 The Company shall be established in accordance with the terms and provisions of the Company Law, other Applicable Laws and the provisions of these Articles of Association.

2.2 The Company particulars shall be as follows:

(a) The name of the Company shall be [COMPANY NAME IN CHINESE] in Chinese and [COMPANY NAME IN ENGLISH] in English.

(b) The Company shall be established as a limited liability company under the laws of China.

章　　程

本章程（“本章程”）于【填入日期】由【填入投资者名称】，【（【公司注册号】【填入号码】）】，一家根据【填入投资者所在地】法律组建及存续的【填入投资者组织形式】，其【注册地址】【或】【主要营业地】为【填入地址】（“投资者”），就【填入公司名称】（“公司”）的设立而制定。

背景

本章程就公司的设立、治理和管理而制定。

1. 定义与解释

除本章程条款另有约定或上下文另有所指，本章程及其附件和本章程中所有相关用语的解释规则见附件一。

2. 公司的设立

2.1　公司应根据公司法和其他适用法律的条款和规定以及本章程的规定设立。

2.2　公司的具体信息如下：

（a）公司的中文名称为【填入公司的中文名称】，英文名称为【填入公司的英文名称】。

（b）公司为中国法项下的有限责任公司。

（c）公司的注册地址为【填入地址】。

(c) The registered address of the Company shall be [ADDRESS].

3. BUSINESS OF THE COMPANY

3.1 The scope of business of the Company shall include [DESCRIPTION OF BUSINESS OF THE COMPANY] (the "Business").

3.2 The Company shall conduct the Business in China and such additional jurisdictions as the Executive Director may approve by Executive Director Decision, subject to compliance with the requirements of Applicable Law.

4. CAPITALIZATION OF THE COMPANY

4.1 The registered capital of the Company ("Registered Capital") shall be [CURRENCY] [AMOUNT].

4.2 The Investor shall contribute the Registered Capital in [one lump sum] within [NUMBER] [months] after the Business License Issuance Date.

5. SHAREHOLDER DECISIONS

5.1 The Investor, as the sole shareholder, shall approve the following matters by written Shareholder Decision in accordance with the requirements of Applicable Law:

(a) the approval of the Company's operation guidelines and investment plans;

(b) the appointment of the Executive Director and the Supervisor and approval of their compensation;

(c) the review and approval of other reports of the Executive Director and the Supervisor as required pursuant to Applicable Law;

(d) the approval of the annual budget and financial reports of the Company;

(e) the determination of the annual allocations to the Company's discretionary accumulation fund;

(f) amendment of these Articles of Association;

(g) any Capital Increase or Capital Reduction;

(h) merger, amalgamation or other combination of the Company with any other entity or company;

(i) division the Company into two or more separate legal entities;

(j) dissolution, winding up or liquidation of the Company;

3. 公司的目标业务

3.1 公司的经营范围应包括【填入对公司目标业务的描述】（“目标业务”）。

3.2 在符合适用法律规定的情况下，公司应在中国以及执行董事可能通过执行董事决定批准的其他地区开展目标业务。

4. 公司的资本

4.1 公司的注册资本（“注册资本”）应为【填入币种】【填入金额】。

4.2 投资者应在营业执照颁发日后【填入数字】【月】内【一次性全额】缴纳注册资本。

5. 股东决定

5.1 投资者作为唯一股东，应根据适用法律的规定，通过书面股东决定批准以下事项：

（a）决定公司的经营方针和投资计划；

（b）任命执行董事和监事以及决定其报酬事项；

（c）审阅批准适用法律要求的执行董事和监事的其他报告；

（d）通过公司的年度预算及财务报告；

（e）确定公司任意公积金的年度提取比例；

（f）对本章程的修订；

（g）任何增资或减资；

（h）公司与任何其他实体或公司的合并或其他形式的联合；

（i）公司分立为两个或两个以上独立的法律实体；

(k) conversion of the corporate form of the Company;

(l) the approval of the retention of earnings and payment of Distributable Profits by way of dividends in accordance with the terms of these Articles of Association; and

(m) the approval of all other matters which require shareholder approval under Applicable Law.

6. EXECUTIVE DIRECTOR

6.1 The Investor shall appoint an Executive Director to be responsible for the supervision and management of the Company and the Business.

6.2 The Executive Director shall have full authority to take Executive Director Decisions in respect of all matters relating to the operation and management of the Company and the Business in accordance with Applicable Law other than the Reserved Matters.

6.3 The Executive Director shall be the legal representative of the Company.

6.4 The Executive Director shall not bear any personal liability for any acts performed in good faith in such capacity as assigned by the Investor, except for willful misconduct, and/or acts in violation of Applicable Law or applicable ethical rules.

6.5 The term of office of the Executive Director shall be [three] years. The Executive Director may serve consecutive terms on expiration of his term if re-appointed. The Executive Director shall serve and may be removed at the pleasure of the Investor. If the Executive Director retires, resigns, falls ill, loses legal capacity or is removed from office by the Investor, then the Investor shall appoint a successor Executive Director, who shall serve for the remaining term of office of the previous Executive Director.

7. SUPERVISOR

7.1 The Investor shall appoint the Supervisor of the Company. The Supervisor shall have such rights, responsibilities and authority as provided in accordance with Applicable Law.

7.2 The term of office of the Supervisor shall be [three] years. The Supervisor may serve consecutive terms on expiration of his term if re-appointed. The Supervisor

（j）公司的解散或清算；

（k）公司的公司形式的变更；

（l）按照本章程的条款批准留存收益以及以股息的方式支付可分配利润；和

（m）适用法律项下须经股东批准的任何其他事项。

6. 执行董事

6.1 投资者应任命一名执行董事，以负责对公司和目标业务的监督和管理。

6.2 除保留事项外，根据适用法律，执行董事应就公司和目标业务的运营和管理全权作出执行董事决定。

6.3 执行董事应为公司的法定代表人。

6.4 执行董事不应就在投资者委派的权限内善意履行的任何行为而承担任何个人责任，但故意不当行为和/或违反适用法律或适用的道德规则的行为除外。

6.5 执行董事的任期为【二】年，任期届满后经再次任命可以连任。执行董事应为投资者服务并可以由其罢免。如执行董事退休、辞职、患病、失去法律行为能力或被投资者罢免，则投资者应任命执行董事的继任者，该等继任者应履行前任执行董事的剩余任期。

7. 监事

7.1 投资者应任命公司的监事。监事享有适用法律规定的职权和责任。

7.2 监事的任期为【三】年，任期届满后经再次任命可以连任。监事应为投资者服务并可以由其罢免。监事不得兼任公司的执行董事、总经理或首席财务官。如果监事退休、辞职、患病或失去法律行为能力或被投资者罢免，

shall serve and may be removed at the pleasure of the Investor. The position of Supervisor cannot be held concurrently by the Executive Director, General Manager or Chief Financial Officer of the Company. If the Supervisor retires, resigns, falls ill, loses legal capacity or is removed from office by the Investor, then the Investor shall appoint a successor Supervisor, who shall serve for the remaining term of office of the previous Supervisor.

8. MANAGEMENT

8.1 The Executive Director shall appoint the General Manager and the Chief Financial Officer and shall approve the overall operation management structure and system of the Company.

8.2 The General Manager shall be responsible for all of the day-to-day operations and management of the Company as may be delegated to him by the Executive Director. He shall report to and work under the supervision and direction of the Executive Director.

8.3 The Chief Financial Officer shall report to and work under the supervision and direction of the General Manager. All other employees of the Company shall report to and work under the supervision and direction of the General Manager or such other senior managers as the General Manager may determine, subject to the approval of the Executive Director.

9. FINANCIAL AFFAIRS AND ACCOUNTING

9.1 The Company shall at all times maintain accurate and complete accounting and other financial records, and shall prepare all accounts and financial statements in accordance with the Accounting Standards for Business Enterprises—Basic Standards [and IFRS].

9.2 The Company shall adopt Renminbi as its bookkeeping base currency, but may also adopt [USD][OR][EUR] or other foreign currencies as supplementary bookkeeping currencies.

9.3 All accounting records, vouchers, books and statements of the Company shall be made and kept in Chinese and English.

9.4 The Company's fiscal year shall begin on January 1 and end on December 31 of

则投资者应任命监事的继任者，该等继任者应履行前任监事的剩余任期。

8. 管理层

8.1 执行董事应任命总经理和首席财务官，且应批准公司的整体运营管理结构和体系。

8.2 总经理应在执行董事授权下，负责公司的所有日常运营和管理。总经理应向执行董事报告，并在其监督和指导下工作。

8.3 首席财务官应向总经理报告，并在其监督和指导下工作。公司的所有其他职工应向总经理和总经理可能决定的，受限于执行董事批准的其他高级经理报告并在其监督和指导下工作。

9. 财务和会计

9.1 公司应始终保持准确完整的会计记录和其他财务记录，并按照企业会计准则——基本准则【和国际财务报告准则】编制所有账目和财务报表。

9.2 公司应采用人民币作为记账本位币，但也可以采用【美元】【或】【欧元】或其他外币作为辅助记账货币。

9.3 公司的所有会计记录、凭单、账簿和报表均应以中英文编制和保存。

9.4 公司的会计年度应从每年的 1 月 1 日起至同年 12 月 31 日结束，但公司的第一个会计年度应从营业执照颁发日开始，并于同年 12 月 31 日结束，最后一个会计年度自 1 月 1 日开始，并于同年的终止日期结束。

9.5 为编制公司的账目和财务报表，计算要向投资者支付的已宣告股息，以及对于影响货币换算可能必要的任何其他目的，货币换算应按照实际收付款之日中国人民银行

each year, except that the first fiscal year of the Company shall commence on the Business License Issuance Date and shall end on December 31 of the same year, and the last fiscal year shall commence on January 1 and end on the termination date in the same year.

9.5 For the purposes of preparing the Company's accounts and financial statements, calculation of declared dividends to be paid to the Investor, and for any other purposes where it may be necessary to effect a currency conversion, such conversion shall be in accordance with the posted exchange rate, as determined by the median exchange rate for buying and selling Renminbi announced by the People's Bank of China or other legally recognized rate on the date of actual receipt or payment.

9.6 The Company shall prepare its financial statements and reports as directed by the Executive Director. The Company's Independent Auditor shall examine and verify the annual financial report of the Company.

9.7 Subject to the requirements of Applicable Law, the Company shall for each fiscal year pay dividends to the Investor within a year from the date such payment is approved by written Shareholder Decision.

10. TERM

These Articles of Association shall take effect on the Effective Date and shall continue in force for an indefinite term until terminated pursuant to Article 11 (the "Term").

11. TERMINATION, DISSOLUTION AND LIQUIDATION

These Articles of Association shall terminate and the Company shall initiate dissolution and liquidation procedures in accordance with Applicable Law upon:

(a) the adoption by the Investor of a written Shareholder Decision approving the dissolution, winding up or liquidation of the Company; or

(b) issuance by the relevant government authority to dissolve, wind up or liquidate the Company in accordance with the requirements of Applicable Law.

12. GENERAL PROVISIONS

12.1 These Articles of Association are governed by and will be construed in accordance with the laws of the People's Republic of China.

公布的人民币汇率中间价或其他法定汇率所确定的挂牌汇率计算。

9.6 公司应按照执行董事的指示编制财务报表和报告。公司的独立审计师应审查并核实公司的年度财务报告。

9.7 受限于适用法律的要求，在每一会计年度，公司应在书面股东决定批准支付股息之日起 1 年内向投资者支付股息。

10.期限

本章程自生效日开始生效，并持续有效，直至根据本章程第 11 条终止（“期限”）。

11.终止、解散和清算

在以下情况下，本章程终止且公司应根据适用法律提起解散和清算程序：

（a）投资者通过书面股东决定批准公司的解散和清算；或

（b）相关政府机关根据适用法律的要求发出公司解散或清算的命令。

12. 一般规定

12.1 本章程及其解释适用中华人民共和国法律。

12.2 本章程以中文和英文签署。两种文本具有同等效力。

本章程已于本章程首页所载日期在中华人民共和国【填入省市】签署，以资证明。

12.2 These Articles of Association are executed in both Chinese and English. Both language versions shall be equally valid.

IN WITNESS WHEREOF, these Articles of Association have been entered into on the date first set forth above in [CITY, PROVINCE], People's Republic of China.

[INVESTOR NAME]

By:____________________________

Name:__________________________

Position: [Authorized Representative]

Nationality: ____________________

【填入投资者名称】

签署：________________________

姓名：________________________

职务：______【授权代表】______

国籍：________________________

Annex 1 Definitions and Interpretation

Definitions

Unless the terms or context of these Articles of Association otherwise provide, the following terms shall have the meanings set out below:

"Accounting Standards for Business Enterprises—Basic Standards" means the specific accounting standards and other relevant regulations as amended by the Ministry of Finance of China in 2014.

"AMR" means the State Administration for Market Regulation of China or relevant local Administration for Market Regulation.

"Applicable Law" means the laws, regulations, rules, notices, and other legislative, executive or judicial decisions or pronouncements binding on the Investor, the Company or in relation to the subject matter of these Articles of Association.

"Articles of Association" shall have the meaning set out in the preamble.

"Business" means the business undertaken by the Company from time to time.

"Business License" means the first business license of the Company issued by the AMR.

"Business License Issuance Date" means the date the Business License is issued to the Company by the AMR.

"Capital Increase" means an increase of the Registered Capital of the Company.

"Capital Reduction" means a reduction of the Registered Capital of the Company.

"Chief Financial Officer" means the Chief Financial Officer or Chief Accountant of the Company.

"China" and "PRC" means the People's Republic of China, for the purpose of these Articles of Association, excluding the Hong Kong and Macao Special Administrative Regions and Taiwan.

"Company" shall have the meaning set out in the preamble.

"Company Law" means the Company Law of the People's Republic of China.

附件一　定义和解释

定义

除非本章程条款另有约定或上下文另有所指，下列用语的含义如下：

“企业会计准则——基本准则”指中国财政部于 2014 年发布及后续修订的具体会计准则和其他有关规定。

“市场监督管理局”指中国国家市场监督管理总局或相关的地方市场监督管理局。

“适用法律”指对投资者、公司有约束力的或者与本章程标的有关的法律、法规、规章、通知以及其他立法、行政或司法判决或声明。

“章程”应具有前言中所载的含义。

“目标业务”指公司不时开展的业务。

“营业执照”指由市场监督管理局颁发的公司的第一份营业执照。

“营业执照颁发日”指由市场监督管理局向公司颁发营业执照的日期。

“增资”指公司注册资本的增加。

“减资”指公司注册资本的减少。

“首席财务官”指公司的首席财务官或总会计师。

“中国”和“中华人民共和国”指中华人民共和国，为本章程目的，不包括中国香港特别行政区、中国澳门特别行政区以及中国台湾地区。

“公司”应具有前言中所载的含义。

"Company Registration Number" means the unique alphanumeric code associated with a company as provided on its business license or similar document, or on file with the relevant company registration authority.

"Effective Date" means the effective date of these Articles of Association, being the date on which these Articles of Association have been executed by the authorized representative of the Investor.

["Euro" or "EUR" means the lawful currency of the European Union.]

"Executive Director" means the Executive Director of the Company.

"Executive Director Decision" means written decisions of the Executive Director taken in respect of the Company.

"General Manager" means the General Manager of the Company.

["IFRS" means International Financial Reporting Standards as issued by the International Accounting Standards Board.]

"Independent Auditor" means an internationally recognized independent and competent accountant registered in China appointed by Executive Director Decision.

"Investor" shall have the meaning set out in the preamble.

"Registered Capital" shall have the meaning set out in Article 4.1.

"Renminbi" or "RMB" means the lawful currency of China.

"Reserved Matters" means matters reserved for decision by the Investor (pursuant to Article 5).

"Shareholder Decisions" means decisions duly adopted by the Investor in respect of matters which require the approval of the shareholder of the Company pursuant to Applicable Law and the provisions of these Articles of Association.

"Supervisor" means the supervisor of the Company.

"Term" means the term of the Company as set out in Article 10.

["United States Dollars" or "USD" means the lawful currency of the United States of America.]

“公司法”指《中华人民共和国公司法》。

“公司注册号”指与公司相关联的，其营业执照或类似文件中规定的，或相关公司注册机构档案所载的唯一字母数字代码。

“生效日”指本章程的生效日，即投资者的授权代表签署本章程的日期。

【“欧元”指欧盟的法定货币。】

“执行董事”指公司的执行董事。

“执行董事决定”指执行董事就公司所作出的书面决定。

“总经理”指公司的总经理。

【“国际财务报告准则”指国际会计准则理事会发布的国际财务报告准则。】

“独立审计师”指经执行董事决定任命的，在中国注册的国际认可的独立且胜任的会计师。

“投资者”应具有前言中所载的含义。

“注册资本”应具有本章程第 4.1 条中所给出的含义。

“人民币”指中国的法定货币。

“保留事项”指根据本章程第 5 条,保留由投资者决定的事项。

“股东决定”指根据适用法律和本章程的决定，投资者就需要公司股东批准的事项正式通过的决定。

“监事”指公司的监事。

“期限”指本章程第 10 条规定的公司的期限。

【“美元”指美利坚合众国的法定货币。】

Annex 2
Annotations to Sample WFOE Articles of Association Template

We set out below drafting notes to certain provisions of the Sample WFOE AoA Template set out in Annex 4. These annotations are not intended to be exhaustive and are provided for reference only and are otherwise subject to the caveats and limitations set out in Chapter 5. Other points applicable to the Sample Templates are set out in Chapter 6.

The Sample WFOE AoA Template was drafted using the Sample JV AoA Template as a base for reference and then modified to reflect the characteristics set out in the relevant base case scenario. Accordingly, these guidance notes may make reference as appropriate to the annotations to the corresponding provisions set out in Annex 3.

Note that since a WFOE has only a single investor, many provisions which are typically included in a JVA are not necessary or appropriate in the AoA for a WFOE as these matters can be managed unilaterally by the sole investor outside of the AoA. Accordingly, the Sample WFOE Articles of Association Template omits these unnecessary provisions. In addition, consistent with the characteristics of the relevant base case scenario for this template, we have adopted a very streamlined corporate governance system for the Sample WFOE Articles of Association Template, additional related comments will be included in the annotations below as appropriate.

These annotations were also drafted in a manner which will be suitable for a wide range of users, including Chinese legal professionals with extensive experience with WFOEs, international legal professionals with limited experience with WFOEs, as well as for Chinese and foreign business managers with limited understanding of technical legal points. Regardless of the background of the user, these drafting notes are not intended as a substitute for legal advice from qualified legal counsel, and are intended only to highlight issues which will need to be addressed separately in the context of particular transactions.

附件二
外商独资企业章程模板样本注解说明

我们在下文列出了附件四所载的外商独资企业章程模板样本部分条款的起草说明。这些起草说明并非详尽无遗，仅供参考，并受限于第五章所载的声明和限制。适用于模板样本的其他要点载于第六章。

外商独资企业章程模板样本以合资企业章程模板样本为参考基础起草，然后做出修改以反映相关基础案例情形中的特征。因此，这些指导性说明会酌情参考附件三所载的相应条款的注解说明。

需要说明的是，由于外商独资企业只有一个投资者，许多通常包含在合资协议中的条款对于外商独资企业章程而言并非必要的或合适的，因为这些事项可由唯一的投资者在公司章程范畴外进行单方面管理。因此，外商独资企业章程模板样本删除了这些不必要的条款。此外，与本模板样本的相关基础案例情形的特征一致，我们在外商独资企业章程模板样本中采用了非常精简的公司治理体系。其他相关说明将酌情包含在下文的注解说明中。

这些注解说明也旨在适用于广泛的用户群体，包括在外商独资企业方面经验丰富的中国法律专业人士、在外商独资企业方面经验有限的国际法律专业人士，以及对专业性的法律要点了解有限的中外企业管理者。无论用户的背景如何，这些起草说明并非旨在替代合格法律顾问提供的法律建议，仅用来强调需要在特定交易中单独讨论的问题。

For convenience, references are made to clause numbers of the Sample WFOE Articles of Association Template as appropriate. Terms not otherwise defined in the annotations below shall have the meanings ascribed thereto elsewhere in this book.

WFOE AoA	Subject	Comments
	Background statements	We have set out a very simple background statement suitable for use in connection with a new greenfield WFOE. The background statements for a WFOE AoA in the context of an inbound M&A deal or in connection with the conversion of an existing WFOE into an LLC or other entity form under the Company Law would require substantial modification.
1	Definitions	We have opted to set out the defined terms in an annex, but it is also common to put the definitions up front in this article.
2	Company establishment	This article as drafted applies only to a greenfield WFOE.
2.2	Company particulars	2.2(a): Only the Chinese name will be registered but the investor is free to select an English name for internal and external use. 2.2(b): We have assumed that WFOEs will take the form of an LLC under the Company Law. 2.2(c): The registered address of the company can only be changed by undertaking relevant amendments to the company registrations with the relevant Administration for Market Regulation (AMR), and in accordance with Chinese law and practice only the registered address and not a principle place of business is used for identification purposes.
3.1	Scope of business	See corresponding guidance notes to clause 3.1 of the Sample JVA Template.
4	Capitalization of the Company	The Company Law requires that the AoA specify the method, amount and date for capital contributions, which have been reflected in Clause 4 of the Sample WFOE Articles of Association Template here. Often, the AoA templates provided by local AMR in several cities specify these items in a table, which is alternative format for you to consider when setting out these items.
4.1	Registered capital	See corresponding guidance notes to clause 4.1 of the Sample JVA Template. Since this is a WFOE, we have not assumed that the registered capital will be denominated in RMB, so we have left it to the user to select the currency to be used.

为方便起见，这些起草说明适当引用了外商独资企业章程模板样本中的条款序号。下文中未另行定义的术语应具有本书其他部分中所给出的含义。

外商独资企业章程	主题	注解说明
	背景说明	我们提供了适用于新设绿地外商独资企业的非常简单的背景说明。如果是在入境并购交易或现有外商独资企业转化为《公司法》项下的有限责任公司或其他组织形式的背景下起草外商独资企业章程，则需要对这里的背景说明进行实质性修改。
1	定义	我们选择在附件中载明术语的定义，但提前在本条中载明定义也很常见。
2	公司的设立	本条款仅适用于绿地外商独资企业。
2.2	公司的详细信息	2.2(a): 公司仅登记中文名称，但投资者可以自由选择一个英文名称以供内部和外部使用。 2.2(b): 我们假设外商独资企业将采用《公司法》项下的有限责任公司形式。 2.2(c). 公司的注册地址只能通过在相关市场监督管理局（“市场监管局”）进行相关变更登记来变更，并且根据中国法律和惯例，只有注册地址（而非主要营业地）能够用来识别公司。
3.1	经营范围	见合资协议模板样本第 3.1 条的相应注解说明。
4	公司的资本	《公司法》规定，公司章程应载明出资方式、出资额和出资时间，这一点已体现在外商独资企业章程模板样本第 4 条中。有些地区的当地市场监管局提供的公司章程模板会以表格的形式载明这些内容，您也可以考虑以这种形式起草这些内容。
4.1	注册资本	见合资协议模板样本第 4.1 条的相应注解说明。由于这是一个外商独资企业，我们没有假设注册资本以人民币表示，所以我们留给用户选择所使用的货币。

Continued

WFOE AoA	Subject	Comments
	Equity interests	By definition, the investor in a WFOE holds 100% of the registered capital, so this is not separately specified in the Sample WFOE Articles of Association Template.
4.2	Capital contributions	See related comments to Clause 4 above. Consistent with the base case scenario for this Sample Template, we have provided that the investor is to make its capital contributions only in cash in a single lump sum. Also see corresponding guidance notes to clause 4.3 of the Sample JVA Template for further comments.
5	Shareholder Decisions	Since there is only a single investor, we have provided that all matters which require shareholders meeting approval under the Company Law are to be approved by the investor by means of written shareholder decision and have not divided these matters into supermajority or simple majority approval items. The other related governance provisions have similarly been streamlined or eliminated given that there is only one investor in a WFOE.
6	Executive Director	Consistent with the base case scenario for this Sample WFOE Articles of Association Template, we have provided for a single executive director rather than a board of directors. However, in many cases (e.g. for internal corporate governance or "check and balance" reasons) the investor may prefer to have a board of directors instead of a sole executive director. Either option is permissible under the Company Law. We have also provided that the executive director is to have full authority to take all decisions relating to the operation and management of the WFOE other than the matters which by law are reserved for decision by the investor. In turn we have provided that the general manager is to have only such scope of authority as delegated by the executive director. If other arrangements are contemplated, these provisions will need to be amended accordingly.
6.2	Executive Director Decisions	We have provided that all decisions of the executive director (the equivalent of board resolutions) are to be made in writing. See definition of "Executive Director Decisions" in Annex 1 of the Sample WFOE Articles of Association Template. This complies with the requirements of the Company Law which expressly permits action by written resolution.

续表

外商独资企业章程	主题	注解说明
	股权	很显然，外商独资企业的投资者持有 100% 的注册资本，所以外商独资企业章程模板样本没有另外规定这一点。
4.2	出资	请参见上文对第 4 条的相关说明。与本模板样本的基础案例情形一致，我们规定投资者一次性以现金方式全额出资。更多注解说明请参见合资协议模板样本第 4.3 条的相应说明。
5	股东决定	由于只有一个投资者，我们规定所有《公司法》项下要求股东会批准的事项均由投资者以书面股东决议的方式批准，而没有将这些事项分为绝对多数或简单多数决议事项。同理，其他相关治理条款也已经简化或删除。
6	执行董事	与此外商独资企业章程模板样本的基础案例情形一致，我们规定设置一名执行董事而非董事会。但是，在很多情况下（如为了公司内部治理或“制衡”的目的）投资者更偏向于设置董事会而非唯一的执行董事。《公司法》项下两种选择均是允许的。 我们还规定，除根据法律保留给投资者决定的事项外，执行董事全权负责有关外商独资企业经营和管理的所有决定。我们同时规定，总经理的职权范围由执行董事授权。如果考虑作出其他安排，则需要对这些条款进行相应的修改。
6.2	执行董事决定	我们规定执行董事的所有决定（等同于董事会决议）均以书面形式作出。见外商独资企业章程模板样本附件一“执行董事决定”的定义。这与《公司法》项下明确允许书面决议的规定相符。

Continued

WFOE AoA	Subject	Comments
6.3	Legal Representative	We have provided in the Sample WFOE Articles of Association Template that the executive director is to be the legal representative of the WFOE. Under the Company Law the general manager can also be designated as the legal representative. As in the case of all FIEs, this position is formally registered with the AMR and the name of the legal representative appears on the company's business license. In a WFOE it should not be necessary to include restrictions on the authority of the legal representative in the AoA as this is a matter for internal governance on the part of the investor. For more information on the potential legal liability of the legal representative, see corresponding guidance notes to clause 8.6 of the Sample JVA Template.
7	Supervisor	Consistent with the base case scenario for this Sample WFOE Articles of Association Template, we have provided for a single supervisor rather than a board of supervisors. Either option is permissible under the Company Law. The supervisor is to be appointed by the investor. In the Sample WFOE Articles of Association Template we have simply cross-referenced to the provisions of applicable law and have not spelled out the responsibilities of the supervisor in detail. For more information on the role of the supervisor, see corresponding guidance notes to clause 10 of the Sample JVA Template.
8	Management Personnel	For purposes of this Sample WFOE Articles of Association Template we have provided only for a general manager and a CFO. Titles of the management personnel may be changed to suit the preferences of the investor. Other positions in the WFOE are to be set by the general manager under the supervision of the executive director, which can be handled outside of the AoA. As noted above, we have provided that the general manager's scope of authority shall be as delegated by the executive director.
9	Financial management	These provisions reflect the requirements of applicable law as supplemented by standard market practice for WFOEs.
10 – 11	Term and termination	Historically, the term of an FIE has been limited to a fixed period, usually ranging from 10 to 30 years, but sometimes as long as 50 years. Now under Article 74 of the Company Law, the investor can set an open-ended indefinite term. Consistent with (and subject to) the discussion in respect of clause 14.1 of the Sample JVA Template in Annex 3, we have adopted an indefinite term for purposes of this Sample WFOE Articles of Association Template. We have provided only for voluntary termination by the investor or involuntary termination by operation of law by legal proceedings. Dissolution and liquidation would be handled as provided in accordance with applicable law and so related provisions are not set out in this template.

续表

外商独资企业章程	主题	注解说明
6.3	法定代表人	我们在外商独资企业章程模板样本中规定，执行董事是外商独资企业的法定代表人。根据《公司法》的规定，总经理也可以被指定为法定代表人。就所有外商投资企业而言，此职位在市场监管局正式登记，且法定代表人的姓名会出现在公司的营业执照上。在外商独资企业中，没有必要在公司章程中对法定代表人的职权进行限制，因为这是一个投资者的内部治理问题。有关法定代表人可能承担的法律责任的更多信息，参见合资协议模板样本第 8.6 条的相应注解说明。
7	监事	与此外商独资企业章程模板样本的基础案例情形一致，我们规定设置一名监事而非监事会。《公司法》项下两种选择均是允许的。监事将由投资者任命。在外商独资企业章程模板样本中，我们简单地对适用法律的规定进行了交叉引用，并未详细说明监事的责任。有关监事职责的更多信息，参见合资协议模板样本第 10 条的相应注解说明。
8	高级管理人员	就本外商独资企业章程模板样本而言，我们仅规定了设置总经理和首席财务官。高级管理人员的头衔可根据投资者的偏好进行修改。外商独资企业内的其他职位由总经理在执行董事的监督下设置，这可以在公司章程规定之外进行处理。如上所述，我们规定总经理的职权范围应由执行董事授权。
9	财务管理	这些规定反映了适用法律的要求，并按照外商独资企业的标准市场惯例进行了补充。
10—11	期限和终止	过去，外商投资企业只能设定固定的经营期限，通常为 10~30 年，但有时也可长达 50 年。而现在，根据《公司法》第 74 条的规定，投资者可以设立无限期经营的外商独资企业。与附件三中合资协议模板样本第 14.1 条的注解说明相一致（并且受其限制），我们在外商独资企业章程模板样本中采用了无限期的经营期限。 我们仅规定了投资者自愿终止或根据法律要求终止的情形。解散和清算将根据适用法律进行处理，所以本模板未作出相关规定。

Continued

WFOE AoA	Subject	Comments
12.1	Governing law	The AoA is to be governed by Chinese law consistent with prevailing legal requirements.
12.2	Language	We have provided that both the English and Chinese versions of the WFOE AoA are to be equally valid. See related discussion in Chapter 6.

Conclusion

For more information on the Sample Templates and access to many of the alternative clauses and forms of ancillary agreements and documents referenced in the Sample WFOE Articles of Association Template and the annotations above but not included in the Sample Templates, please go to www.docqbot.com/en/newFIL.

续表

外商独资企业章程	主题	注解说明
12.1	适用法律	公司章程受中国法律管辖，符合现行法律要求。
12.2	语言	我们规定外商独资企业章程的中英文版本同等有效。见第六章的相关讨论。

结论

如您希望了解模板样本的更多信息，以及获得更多可选条款、附属协议以及外商独资企业章程模板样本和上述说明中提及的但并未包括在模板样本中的其他文件，请访问 www.docqbot.com/cn/newFIL。

Part III

Acknowledgments and Contributors Introduction

第三部分

致谢和贡献者介绍

docQbot Introduction

docQbot is China's first online/offline cross-border bilingual cloud-based AI contract service platform.

docQbot's mission is to help corporations and professionals by providing legal forms and content that comply with international standards and domestic practices, as well as business and legal support in domestic and international transactions, and doing it all more efficiently and at a lower cost.

Using docQbot's automated contract drafting tool (powered by HotDocs), just by answering a few commercially-focused questions, both non-lawyers and lawyers alike can draft a highly-customized contract in English and/or Chinese, usually in just 15 minutes or less! In addition, docQbot's automated contract review tool uses LegalSifter's leading natural language processing and machine learning AI technology to help both non-lawyers and lawyers to review China-related English-language international trade contracts. And if you need offline legal assistance, docQbot can refer you to a qualified lawyer in more than 100 countries around the world and across all key regions of China.

Contact info: enquiries@docqbot.com

Official website: www.docqbot.com

In-House Community™ Introduction

In-House Community™ (IHC) is a mutual aid community consisted of corporate legal affairs and compliance professionals, where members help each other to fulfill the ethical, legal and business goals and obligations within the organization. IHC has more than 20,000 members responsible of corporate legal and compliance affairs around Asia-Pacific, Middle East and North Africa. 17 forums are organized around 13 jurisdictions annually, with an attendance over 3000. In addition, members will receive magazines published by IHC, and electronic update information from IHC and organizations that offering service to its members. The online community also offers abundant papers, update information, news and online seminars.

The mission of IHC is to energize corporate legal affairs, help them fulfill the ethical, legal, compliance and business obligations more easily. To achieve the goal, IHC offers

合通机器人介绍

合通机器人是中国首个线上线下跨境双语AI智能合同服务云平台。

合通机器人的使命是，通过提供符合国际标准和国内惯例的法律文本和内容，以及跨境交易和境内交易中的商业和法律支持，帮助企业和专业人士以更高效的方式和更低的成本完成交易。

使用合通机器人双语合同定制机器人（由HotDocs提供技术支持），只需回答一系列简单的商务性问题，律师和非律师人士都可以起草高度定制化的英文和/或中文合同，通常只需不到15分钟！并且，合通机器人英文合同审核机器人使用LegalSifter领先的自然语言处理和机器学习AI技术，帮助律师和非律师人士审核与中国相关的英文国际合同。此外，如果您需要线下法律支持，合通机器人可以在全球100多个国家/地区以及中国所有重点地区推荐优质的律师。

联系方式：enquiries@docqbot.com

官网：www.docqbot.com

In–House Community™ 介绍

In-House Community™（IHC）是一个由企业法务和合规专业人士组成的互助型组织，成员间互相帮助，以在自己组织内部实现自身道德、法律与商业目标和职责。IHC拥有超过20,000名在亚太和中东北非地区负责公司的法律及合规事宜的个人成员，每年在13个司法辖区组织17场次论坛活动，每年有超过3000人参加。此外，成员们还会获得IHC出版的杂志和来自IHC和为其成员提供服务的组织提供的电子更新信息。其线上社区还提供大量的文章、更新信息、新闻以及网络研讨会。

IHC的使命是为企业法务赋能，帮助他们更轻松地履行其道

many platforms that exchange professional opinions, build support relationships and share knowledge to anyone who performs corporate legal and compliance duties.

Contact info: patrick.dransfield@inhousecommunity.com

Official website: www.inhousecommunity.com

docQbot & In-House Community™ Foreign Investment Law Expert Committee Members Introduction

docQbot

Name/Title	Bio
Robert Lewis Co-Founder & Chief Expert	Robert was admitted to the California bar in 1985 and practiced in Los Angeles with Sidley & Austin before coming to join the China Practice Group of Baker & McKenzie in Hong Kong and Shanghai in 1993. Following a stint as Asia General Counsel for Nortel, he headed up the Beijing office of Lovells (now Hogan Lovells) for nine years, before becoming one of the first senior lawyers to move from a leading international law firm to a top Chinese law firm, joining Zhong Lun Law Firm in Beijing as Senior International Counsel in 2010. He is fluent in spoken Mandarin and written Chinese. As Chief Expert of docQbot, Robert is directly responsible for development of all content on the docQbot platform, drawing on his experience as a practicing lawyer for a period of more than 30 years. In addition to taking the lead in respect of the drafting of the base templates, he has designed the entire docQbot interface, including the structure and logical sequencing of the online question tree as well as the related guidance notes for the docQbot online automated contract drafting tool. Similarly, he has designed the commercial risk report and drafted all of the guidance notes for the docQbot automated contract review tools. All of the docQbot tools are designed personally by Robert to ensure the best possible user experience. E-mail： lvlishan@docqbot.com
Adam Channer VP Product Development	At docQbot Adam is responsible for multiple aspects of the development of the international templates on the docQbot platform. Adam has worked as a Foreign-Admitted Attorney at Zhong Lun Law Firm, where he mainly worked on cross-border mergers and acquisitions, as well as technology, media and telecommunications (TMT) matters. Prior to working at Zhong Lun Law Firm, Adam worked in Hong Kong with Paul Hastings LLP in their capital markets practice. He is fluent in spoken Mandarin and Cantonese and written Chinese. E-mail: adamchanner@docqbot.com

德、法律、合规和商业职责。为实现这一目标，IHC 为任何履行企业内部法律与合规职能的人，提供众多交流专业意见、建立支持关系和分享知识的平台。

联系方式：patrick.dransfield@inhousecommunity.com

官网：www.inhousecommunity.com

合通机器人 & In-House Community™《外商投资法》专家委员会成员简介

合通机器人

姓名 / 职务	简介
吕立山（Robert Lewis） 联合创始人 & 首席专家	吕立山律师于 1985 年获得美国加利福尼亚州律师资格，并在洛杉矶就职于盛德国际律师事务所（Sidley & Austin），之后于 1993 年加入贝克·麦坚时律师事务所（Baker & McKenzie）香港和上海办公室中国业务组。 吕立山律师是第一个加入中国顶尖律师事务所的资深外国律师。在 2010 年加入中伦律师事务所之前，吕立山律师在路伟国际律师事务所（现霍金路伟国际律师事务所）北京代表处工作了 9 年，担任管理合伙人；在加入路伟之前，吕立山律师任加拿大北电网络公司亚洲区公司总法律顾问。吕立山律师的中文口语及书面表达均十分流利。 作为合通机器人的首席专家，吕立山律师直接负责合通机器人平台上所有内容的开发，其中吸收了其 30 余年的执业经验。除了牵头起草基础模板，他还设计了合通机器人的全部界面，包括合通 – 合同定制机器人线上问题树的结构和逻辑顺序以及相关指南信息。同样地，他也设计了合通 – 合同审核机器人中的交易风险分析报告，并起草了所有的指南。合通机器人的所有工具均由吕律师亲自设计，保证了合通机器人服务的专业性和最佳用户体验。 邮箱：lvlishan@docqbot.com
陈明盛（Adam Channer） 产品开发副总裁	作为合通机器人产品开发副总裁，陈明盛律师负责合通机器人平台上所有国际模板的各方面开发工作。陈律师作为外国执业律师在中伦律师事务所工作数年，期间他的主要执业领域为跨境并购、科技、媒体与电信（TMT）等。 在加入中伦律师事务所之前，他在普衡律师事务所（Paul Hastings LLP）香港办公室从事资本市场业务，普通话和粤语读写流利。 邮箱：adamchanner@docqbot.com

Continued

Name/Title	Bio
Sara Yu VP Product Development & Strategic Partnerships	Sara is responsible for overall coordination of the template development process at docQbot, ensuring the complete integration of the domestic and international elements of the know-how elements as well as integration of the professional content and the technology platform. She has worked as a senior associate in the corporate department of Zhong Lun in Beijing and is a licensed lawyer in China. She is specialized in domestic and cross-border mergers and acquisitions, foreign direct investment and general corporate. E-mail: yuqianqian@docqbot.com
Zhou Zimin Senior Manager Product Development	Zimin is responsible for multiple aspects of the development of the domestic templates on the docQbot platform. She has worked as an associate at Zhong Lun Law Firm and has obtained her bar qualification in China. Zimin is specialized in domestic and cross-border mergers and acquisitions, inbound investment and general corporate. E-mail: zhouzimin@docqbot.com

In-House Community™

Name/Title	Bio
Patrick Dransfield Co-director	Patrick Dransfield is presently a Director of the In-House Community™, wholly owned by Pacific Business Press. Patrick has twenty-two years of experience working in the legal industry: firstly as a Publisher and later Asia Managing Director of Euromoney Institutional Investor, and then as Marketing and Business Development Director for Asia for Shearman & Sterling and White & Case respectively. Patrick joined Pacific Business Press as Publishing Director of the Magazine Asian-MENA Counsel in 2008. His publishing career began with Haymarket Publishing in 1987. Patrick is in frequent demand as a writer and commentator on the business of law and has been published by the Financial Times, Asia Law Portal and Asian-MENA Counsel, among others. Patrick is a graduate of Leeds University (B.A. Joint Hons. in English and History of Art) and also holds a Master's Degree in Far East Area Studies (specializing in Chinese History, Anthropology and Politics) from London University's School of Oriental & African Studies (SOAS). Tel: +852 2542-1113 E-mail: patrick.dransfield@inhousecommunity.com

续表

姓名 / 职务	简介
余倩倩 产品开发和战略合作副总裁	余倩倩律师负责合通机器人模板开发过程的统筹协调，确保专有知识的国内要素和国际要素，以及专业内容和技术平台的完全整合。余律师在中伦律师事务所工作数年，期间作为公司部资深律师，执业领域为境内和跨境并购、外商直接投资和一般公司事务。余律师是中国执业律师。 邮箱：yuqianqian@docqbot.com
周自敏 产品开发高级经理	周自敏律师负责合通机器人平台境内模板的各方面开发工作，在中伦律师事务所工作数年，执业领域为境内和跨境并购、入境投资和一般公司事务，拥有中国法律职业资格证书。 邮箱：zhouzimin@docqbot.com

In-House Community™

姓名 / 职务	简介
Patrick Dransfield 联席董事	Patrick Dransfield，现为 In–House Community™［由太平洋商务出版社（Pacific Business Press）全资所有］的联席董事。 Patrick 拥有 22 年法律从业经验，最初在欧洲货币机构投资者集团（Euromoney Institutional Investor）担任发行人，后来成为该机构亚洲区董事总经理。之后分别在谢尔曼·思特灵律师事务所（Shearman & Sterling ）以及伟凯律师事务所（White & Case）亚洲分部担任市场和业务发展总监。 2008 年，Patrick 作为杂志《亚洲法律顾问》（Asian–Mena Counsel）的出版总监加入太平洋商务出版社。他的出版职业生涯于 1987 年从 Haymarket Publishing 开始。作为著名的法律撰稿人以及评论家，Patrick 的文章常发表在《金融时报》（Financial Times）、《亚洲法律门户》（Asia Law Portal）、《亚洲法律顾问》等知名杂志上。 Patrick 本科毕业于英国利兹大学（英语及艺术史双荣誉学位），并拥有伦敦大学亚非学院远东地区研究方向（主攻中国历史、人类学及政治）的硕士学位。 电话：+852 2542–1113 邮箱：patrick.dransfield@inhousecommunity.com

Accenture

Name/Title	Bio
Andy See Former Managing Director, Asia Pacific	Andy has twenty-five years of cross-border and regional legal experience across high-tech and telecom industries, of which eighteen years have been with two Fortune 500 companies, and seven years with a top international law firm. In leadership roles since 2004, first as China Legal Lead for eight years, and since 2012 as Managing Director for Managing Director for APAC Geographic Legal. Distinguished for his mission, vision, passion, agility and execution in moving legal functions from back-office to the forefront of business and contributing to the accelerated growth of business in China and APAC. Expert proficiency in JV's mergers and acquisitions, IT, cybersecurity and digital laws, complex commercial transactions and compliance, applying multi-dimensional insights on laws, policies, practices and politics to solve for business. Tel: +86 0755 8280 4677 E-mail: shijk@bcisz.org
Yan Zhiyong Senior Counsel, Greater China	Mr. Yan is a Senior Legal Counsel of Accenture and oversees corporate, compliance, regulatory and ethics matters of the company in Greater China. Before joining Accenture in 2017, Mr. Yan spent over twelve years working with international law firms in both Hong Kong and Beijing, during which he advised clients in a broad array of legal matters in connection with market entrance, anti-trust and competition, compliance and enforcement, as well as joint ventures, mergers and acquisitions, and foreign direct investment in China. Mr. Yan graduated from China University of Politics and Law with a Bachelor of Laws degree and also received two Master of Laws degrees from Peking University and New York University respectively. Mr. Yan holds a PRC bar qualification and is also qualified to practice law in New York State. Tel: +86 10-5870-5727 E-mail: zhiyong.yan@accenture.com

Bayer

Name/Title	Bio
Zhang Xi Head of LPC (VP)	Ph. D. in law of University Tuebingen Law School; Vice President & General Counsel of Bayer Greater China, responsible for Legal, IP, Compliance & Data Privacy; listed panel arbitrator at the Beijing Arbitration Commission and Shanghai Arbitration Commission; more than 25 years legal practice experience in law firm and MNCs. Tel: +86 21-6146-8234 E-mail: xi.zhang1@bayer.com
Max Zhang Head of Law Corporate	Master of Law of Potsdam University; General Counsel of Bayer (China) Ltd., responsible for Corporate Governance, M&A and Post-merger Integration and Data Privacy Compliance in China; more than 15 years legal practice experience in law firm and MNCs. Tel: +86 21-6159-3261 E-mail: max.zhang@bayer.com

埃森哲 Accenture

姓名 / 职务	简介
施俊侃 前亚太区区域法律服务董事总经理兼大中华区域法律总监董事总经理	施俊侃先生在高科技和电信行业拥有 25 年跨境和区域法律从业经验。在这 25 年的职业生涯中，其中在两家《财富》500 强公司任职 18 年，在一家顶级国际律师事务所工作 7 年。施先生自 2004 年起担任公司领导职务，先是担任中国法律部主任长达 8 年，自 2012 年起担任亚太区区域法律部董事总经理。 他拥有出众的使命感、远见、激情、敏锐度和执行力，致力于推动法律职能从企业后台走向业务前沿，促进中国和亚太地区业务的加速增长；精通合资企业并购、信息技术、网络安全和数字法律、复杂的商业交易和合规，能够运用法律、政策、实践和政治的多维视角解决商业问题。 电话：+86 0755 8280 4677 邮箱：shijk@bcisz.org
闫致勇 大中华区高级顾问	闫先生是埃森哲高级法律顾问，负责公司在大中华区的公司、合规、监管和道德事务。在 2017 年加入埃森哲以前，闫先生在香港和北京的国际律师事务所工作了 12 年多，为客户提供涉及市场准入、反垄断和竞争、合规执法以及在中国境内的合资、并购和外商直接投资等一系列法律事务的法律意见。闫先生拥有中国政法大学法学学士学位，并拥有北京大学以及纽约大学的硕士学位，并同时拥有中国以及美国纽约州律师资格。 电话：+86 10-5070-5727 邮箱：zhiyong.yan@accenture.com

拜耳

姓名 / 职务	简介
张曦 前大中华区副总裁兼总法律顾问	张曦，德国图宾根大学法学院法学博士，前拜耳大中华区副总裁以及总法律顾问，负责法律、知识产权、合规和数据隐私保护事务。北京仲裁委员会、上海仲裁委员会上市仲裁员；拥有 25 年以上在律所和跨国公司的法律执业经验。 电话：+86 21-6146-8234 邮箱：xi.zhang1@bayer.com
张鹰峰 拜耳（中国）法律总顾问	张鹰峰，德国波茨坦大学硕士；拜耳（中国）有限公司法律总顾问，负责中国公司治理、并购、重组和数据隐私保护方面的工作；拥有 15 年以上律所和跨国公司法律从业经验。 电话：+86 21-6159-3261 邮箱：max.zhang@bayer.com

China Resources

Name/Title	Bio
Li Ge Deputy Group General Counsel	Mr. Li is the Deputy Group Legal Counsel of China Resources Group and has advised on various matters involving mergers and acquisitions, corporate restructuring and industry policing for associated companies within the Group since 2010. Prior to this role, as a Senior Consultant at Vinson & Elkins LLP Beijing Representative Office, Mr. Li advised on foreign direct investments, acquisitions and PRC Company Law and Anti-Monopoly Law advisory for multinational companies. Earlier in his career, Mr. Li held leadership roles for more than ten years at the Consulate General of China in New York as Vice Consul General of Commercial Affairs and at the Department of Foreign Investment Administration in the Ministry of Commerce of China as Deputy Director. Mr. Li obtained his Bachelor of Economics from the University of International Business and Economics and holds a Master of Laws degree from Peking University and a Master of Laws in International Economic Law from the University of Warwick. Tel: +852 2593-8841 E-mail: lige@crc.com.hk
Yvonne Yao Senior Group Legal Counsel	Yvonne is a Senior Group Legal Counsel of China Resources Group and has been a member of the Mergers and Acquisitions team in the Group Legal Department since 2014, providing corporate and commercial advisory with a focus on M&A transactions (cross-border and domestic) and greenfield investments. Before joining China Resources in 2014, Yvonne spent six years working in the Hong Kong office of a leading Chinese law firm (King & Wood Mallesons), where she provided legal advisory in M&A transactions and direct investments in China for multinational corporations, outbound investments for PRC companies and general advisory in PRC corporate and commercial matters. Yvonne obtained her Bachelor of Laws degree from the China University of Political Science and Law in 2006 and a Juris Doctor degree from the Chinese University of Hong Kong in 2008. Tel: +86 755-8266-8888 (3265) E-mail: yaoerfang@crc.com.hk

Sinopec Group

Name/Title	Bio
Li Chi Legal Counsel, Contract Management Division	Li Chi is Legal Counsel for the Contract Management Division of the legal department for Sinopec. He graduated with a masters of law degree from Tsinghua University, and acts as company counsel and is a certified public accountant. He has a great deal of experience in Sinopec's domestic and cross-border joint ventures, investment and M&A contract negotiations and contract management, and has served as overseas legal consultant in connection with projects in South America and South Africa, among others. Tel: +86 10-5996-8064 E-mail: lichi@sinopec.com

华润集团

姓名 / 职务	简介
李舸 华润集团副总法律顾问	李先生现为华润集团副总法律顾问，自 2010 年以来为华润集团内关联公司的并购、企业重组和行业监管等提供法律意见。在担任该职务之前，作为文森艾尔斯律师事务所（Vinson & Elkins LLP）北京代表处的高级顾问，李先生为跨国公司提供外商直接投资、并购以及中国公司法和反垄断法方面的咨询。李先生早年任中国驻纽约总领事馆经济商务处副总领事以及商务部外国投资管理司副司长达 10 余年。李先生拥有对外经贸大学经济学学士学位、北京大学法学硕士学位以及华威大学国际经济法硕士学位。 电话：+852 2593-8841 邮箱：lige@crc.com.hk
姚尔芳 资深集团法律顾问	姚尔芳为华润集团高级法律顾问，并自 2014 年起作为集团法律部并购团队成员，主要为跨境和境内并购交易和绿地投资事项提供公司和商业咨询。在 2014 年加入华润集团之前，姚尔芳曾在金杜律师事务所香港办公室工作了 6 年，为跨国企业在华的并购交易和直接投资、中国企业境外投资提供法律咨询，以及为中国公司和商业事务提供一般咨询。姚尔芳于 2006 年取得中国政法大学法学学士学位，2008 年取得香港中文大学法学博士学位。 电话：+86 755-8266-8888 (3265) 邮箱：yaoerfang@crc.com.hk

中国石油化工集团

姓名 / 职务	简介
李驰 法律部合同项目处主管	中国石化集团法律部合同项目处主管。毕业于清华大学法律硕士专业，公司律师、注册会计师，长期从事中国石化境内外重大合资合作、投资并购项目合同谈判、合同管理，曾作为境外法律顾问常驻南美、南非等海外项目。 电话：+86 10-5996-8064 邮箱：lichi@sinopec.com

Herbert Smith Freehills

Name/Title	Bio
Nanda Lau Partner	Nanda is the head of HSF Shanghai office. Her practice covers a wide range of corporate and commercial work including M&A, foreign direct investment, private equity, joint ventures, corporate restructuring and regulatory compliance matters in China. Her clients include multi-national corporations and Chinese companies in a broad range of sectors, including aerospace, consumer goods, financial services, life sciences, industrial, real estate and TMT. Tel: +86 21-2322-2117 E-mail: Nanda.Lau@hsf.com
Angela Zhao Senior Associate	Angela has extensive experience in advising multinationals and domestic companies on cross-border M&A transactions, restructurings, divestitures, joint ventures and foreign direct investment. Angela also regularly advises Chinese companies on their outbound investments. She advises clients across a broad range of sectors including pharmaceutical, manufacturing, automobiles, consumer goods, chemical and logistics. Tel: +86 21-2322-2167 E-mail: angela.zhao@hsf.com
Alizee Zheng Senior Associate	Alizee specializes in foreign direct investment, cross-border M&A and corporate restructurings in China. She also advises clients on employment law issues and general corporate and commercial matters. She routinely advises and works closely with multi-national corporations and domestic companies in a broad range of sectors, including consumer goods, food and beverages, agriculture, automobile, chemical, manufacturing and TMT. Tel: +86 21-2322-2163 E-mail: alizee.zheng@hsf.com

King & Wood Mallesons

Name/Title	Bio
Xiong Jin International Partner	Jin has a particular focus on cross-border M&As and project investment, with vast experience in representing Chinese investors for their cross-border investment and representing Chinese sellers for their sale of assets to foreign investors. He also advised many multinational companies on their investments and joint ventures in China. Jin has represented a wide range of well-known state-owned enterprises, public and private Chinese companies, M&A funds for their cross-border acquisitions and investments in numerous countries. Drawing on his extensive experience of cross-border transaction management, managing English-Chinese documentation and assisting clients on bilingual negotiations in complex legal and commercial context, Jin acts as lead counsel and successfully assisted clients in complex large transactions across countries and sectors. Tel: +86 10 5878-5158 E-mail: xiongjin@cn.kwm.com

史密夫斐尔律师事务所

姓名 / 职务	简介
刘依兰 合伙人	刘依兰是史密夫斐尔律师事务所上海办公室管理合伙人。她的执业范围涵盖公司法的各个方面，包括并购交易、外商直接投资、私募股权、合资公司、企业重组以及合规等事宜。她的客户包括航天、快消、金融服务、生命科学、工业、房地产及科技新媒体等不同行业的跨国企业和本地公司。 电话：+86 21-2322-2117 邮箱：Nanda.Lau@hsf.com
赵秋丹 资深律师	赵律师在处理跨国企业及本地公司的跨境并购、重组、资产剥离、合资公司及外商在华直接投资方面经验丰富。她还常就中国企业的海外投资提供法律咨询意见，提供法律服务的客户包括生命科学、制造业、汽车、快消、化工以及物流等行业。 电话：+86 21-2322-2167 邮箱：angela.zhao@hsf.com
郑晓夏 资深律师	郑律师擅长外商直接投资、跨境并购以及公司重组事宜。此外，她还就劳动法问题及一般的公司和商业事宜向客户提供法律意见，客户包括快消、食品饮料行业、农业、汽车、化工、制造及科技新媒体等行业的跨国企业和本地公司。 电话：+86 21-2322-2163 邮箱：alizee.zheng@hsf.com

金杜律师事务所

姓名 / 职务	简介
熊进 国际合伙人	熊进律师的主要执业领域为跨境并购与项目投资，在代表中国企业在境外投资方面具有极为丰富的经验。熊律师曾为多家跨国公司的对外投资，以及合资公司的设立提供法律服务。 熊律师曾经为众多知名中国公司在世界多个国家的海外投资提供法律服务，涵盖对私人公司的收购、收购上市公司、项目投资（合资公司）、咨询服务和常见的商业安排（包括长期承销协议、供应和分销安排、联合体协议等）。 熊律师对管理跨境交易、处理中英文双语文件以及协助客户在双语环境中就复杂的法律和商业事务进行谈判具有丰富经验，曾在众多项目中作为牵头法律顾问成功协助客户完成跨国家及地域的各类大型收购交易。 电话：+86 10 5878-5158 邮箱：xiongjin@cn.kwm.com

Continued

Name/Title	Bio
Luo Hai Foreign Legal Consultant	Luo has his practice specialized in cross-boarder M&As (incl. foreign direct investments in the PRC), private equity investments and corporates etc. Luo has represented numerous of clients, covering conglomerate SOEs, private enterprises, listed companies, private equity funds and financial agencies, carrying out a wide range of types of investments and transactions, including, overseas direct investment, cross board corporate M&As, private equity financings, and provided bilingual (Chinese and English) legal service as their lead counsel. Luo has successful track records in assisting foreign investments in the PRC and advising, as Sell-side's advisor, both foreign and domestic companies on their assets sales. Tel: +86 10 5878 5701 E-mail: luohai@cn.kwm.com

Latham & Watkins

Name/Title	Bio
Frank Sun Partner	Frank Sun, a partner in the Hong Kong office of Latham & Watkins and a member of the Corporate Department, specializes in private equity investment and public and private M&A transactions. Mr. Sun regularly advises private equity funds and corporate clients in private equity investments, cross-border acquisitions, PIPEs, privatizations, and a wide range of other complex M&A transactions. A native Mandarin speaker focusing on multijurisdictional work, Mr. Sun has practiced law in London, Beijing, New York, and Hong Kong. Prior to joining Latham, he had been a Hong Kong-based partner of another major international law firm since 2012. He was recognized by Chambers Asia-Pacific 2019 as " Leading Lawyer in China Private Equity: Buyouts & Venture Capital Investment and China." Tel: +852 2912-2512 E-mail: frank.sun@lw.com

续表

姓名 / 职务	简介
罗海 外国法律顾问	罗海律师的主要执业领域专注于跨境并购（包括中国境内外商直接投资）、私募股权投资以及公司业务等。 罗律师曾参与多项跨境并购交易，为众多大型国有企业、民营企业、上市公司、基金和金融机构等客户，在其境外直接投资、跨境公司收购与兼并、私募股权融资等不同类型的投资与合作项目中，作为牵头法律顾问为交易提供双语（中英文）法律服务。同时，罗律师对于代表境外公司在中国进行直接投资以及作为卖方顾问协助境内外公司出售资产也有较为丰富的经验。 电话：+86 10 5878 5701 邮箱：luohai@cn.kwm.com

瑞生国际律师事务所

姓名 / 职务	简介
孙秋宁 合伙人	孙秋宁律师是瑞生国际律师事务所（Latham & Watkins）香港办事处公司部合伙人，专事私募股权投资以及公众及私人并购交易。 孙律师经常代表私募股权基金及企业客户处理私募股权投资、跨境收购、私人投资上市公司股份、私有化及其他各种复杂的并购交易项目。孙律师的母语为普通话，专事跨辖区法律工作，曾经在伦敦、北京、纽约及香港执业。自 2012 年起至加入瑞生之前，他一直是某大国际律师事务所香港办事处的合伙人。他被《钱伯斯亚太 2019》评选为“中国私募股权：收购及风险投资业务及中国企业 / 并购业务顶尖律师”。 电话：+852 2912-2512 邮箱：frank.sun@lw.com

O' Melveny& Myers

Name/Title	Bio
Walker Wallace Managing Partner	Walker J. Wallace is managing partner of O' Melveny's Shanghai office and a leader of the firm's China practice. He has extensive experience in international transactions and has worked with clients in a wide range of projects across Asia, from multi-nationals seeking to invest in China, to private equity funds pursuing investment strategies in Southeast Asia. In China, Walker has helped clients negotiate the complexities of investing and structuring business operations in numerous industries, including consumer products, healthcare, real estate, software, media and entertainment, retail and education. Before moving to Shanghai in 1997, Walker practiced in New York for several years. He is the former Chairman of the Legal Committee for the Shanghai American Chamber of Commerce, and is the co-author of "Acquisitions of Companies with Chinese Assets", "Foreign Private Equity Investment in China: Which Way to the Exit?", "Onshore Financial Investing in China", and "Enforcement on Defaulted Loans and Mortgage on Real Property under Chinese Law." Tel: +86 21-2307-7000 E-mail: wwallace@omm.com

Zhong Lun Law Firm

Name/Title	Bio
Scott Yu Partner	Scott Yu's practice focuses on corporate matters for multinationals and compliance counseling. He has been acting as the leading corporate and/or compliance counsel in a number of global acquisitions and joint venture transactions, as well as antitrust litigations and government investigations. His clients include those global industry leaders, such as Air Products, Alstom, Areva, Avon, Beijing Tourism Group, Beiqi Foton Motors, Cummins, Qualcomm, Schneider Electrics, Volkswagen, and Warburg Pincus, and the start-ups/boutique businesses. He also assisted a number of Hi-Tech multinationals, including Qualcomm, Synopsys and Arm, in their development of new businesses in China. Scott Yu has experiences of working in prominent Chinese, Hong Kong and US law firms, and studied law in China, Europe and the US, which enabled him to develop knowledge and skills in working for clients with different cultural backgrounds. Tel: +86 10-5957-2078 E-mail: scottyu@zhonglun.com

美迈斯律师事务所

姓名 / 职务	简介
万孝杰（Walker J. Wallace） 上海办事处管理合伙人	万孝杰（Walker J. Wallace）是美迈斯律师事务所中国业务部合伙人，已在上海代表处工作近20年。万律师有丰富的国际交易经验，曾在亚洲各地的各种项目中为客户提供服务，包括跨国公司在华投资项目、私募基金在东南亚寻求投资策略等。在中国，万律师曾帮助客户就他们在各行各业的投资和业务结构进行复杂的谈判，包括消费品、保健、房地产、软件、媒体和娱乐业、零售业和教育。 在1997年来上海工作以前，万律师在纽约执业。他还曾担任上海美国商会法律委员会主席。万律师与他人合著了《收购中资公司》、《海外私募资金在中国投资：如何选择退出战略？》以及《中国法律针对房地产领域拖欠贷款和按揭的强制执行》。 电话：+86 21-2307-7000 邮箱：wwallace@omm.com

中伦律师事务所

姓名 / 职务	简介
余昕刚 合伙人	余昕刚律师的业务专注于跨国公司的公司事务和合规咨询领域。 他曾在多个全球并购和合资项目、反垄断诉讼和政府调查项目中担任首席顾问。他的客户包括各行业的世界领先企业，如空气产品公司、阿尔斯通、阿海珐、雅芳、北京首旅集团、北汽福田汽车、康明斯、高通、施耐德电气、大众汽车、美国华平基金以及其他初创/精品企业。他还协助高通、新思科技、英国ARM等一批高科技跨国公司在中国拓展新业务。 余律师具有在中国、香港和美国知名律师事务所工作的经历，并先后在中国、欧洲和美国学习法律，使其具备了为不同文化背景的客户服务的法律知识和技能。 电话：+86 10-5957-2078 邮箱：scottyu@zhonglun.com

Continued

Name/Title	Bio
Scott Guan Partner	Dr Scott Guan is a partner at the Shanghai office of Zhong Lun Law Firm. Dr Guan has extensive experience in mergers and acquisitions, cross border transactions, private equity investments and corporate and commercial matters. Dr Guan is well-recognized and recommended by the Legal 500 and Chambers in the Asia-Pacific region and has been recommended as a leading Chinese lawyer by professional journals for many years. He has worked at prestigious Chinese, Canadian and British law firms in Shanghai, Toronto and Hong Kong. Tel: +86 21 6061 3068 E-mail: scottguan@zhonglun.com
Rachel Li Partner	Rachel Li's practice focuses on the China related cross-border M&A transactions, anti-trust, cybersecurity and other corporate and compliance matters. She has over 10 years of experiences in advising clients across various industries and sectors on Chinese corporate law and compliance issues. She has been serving different types of clients from China State-owned enterprises to large multinationals, which enabled her to develop legal knowledge and expertise as well as the skills of working for clients with different cultural backgrounds. Rachel Li has participated in a number of mega sized acquisitions and joint venture projects, and also participated in a number of transactions from anti-trust perspective and represent a number of clients in China antitrust investigations and litigations. In recent years, she has also participated in transactions from cybersecurity perspective and advised clients on Chinese related cybersecurity law matters. Tel: +86-10-5957 2143 E-mail: lirui@zhonglun.com
Aaron Yu Partner	Aaron Yu is a non-equity partner of Zhong Lun Law Firm Shanghai Office. He has substantial experiences in mergers and acquisitions, private equity investments as well as general corporate and business law. Aaron advices clients in various sectors including manufacturing, distribution and retail, chemical products, technology, automobile, telecom, construction, real estate, food and beverage, private equity investment, and professional service. Aaron also handles dozens of dispute resolution cases every year including Chinese court proceedings, CIETAC, SHIAC and other local arbitration proceedings, and assists clients in various business negotiations and handling government proceedings. Tel: +86-21-6061 3114 E-mail: aaronyu@zhonglun.com

续表

姓名 / 职务	简介
管云翔 合伙人	管云翔博士是中伦律师事务所上海办公室合伙人，在并购、跨境交易、私募股权投资和公司与商业事务方面拥有丰富的经验。 管云翔博士是 Legal 500 以及 Chambers（钱伯斯）在亚太地区重点推荐的知名律师，并常年被各专业杂志推荐为中国领先律师。他曾就职于顶尖中国、加拿大和英国律师事务所的上海办公室、多伦多办公室和香港办公室。 电话：+86 21 6061 3068 邮箱：scottguan@zhonglun.com
李瑞 合伙人	李瑞律师的执业领域为中国跨境并购交易、反垄断、网络安全等企业和合规事务，拥有 10 年以上为不同行业和领域客户提供中国公司法及合规方面的咨询服务的经验。她曾为中国国有企业以及大型跨国公司等各类客户提供服务，积累了丰富的法律知识和专业知识，并掌握了为不同文化背景客户工作的技能。 李瑞律师曾参与多个大型并购和合资项目，并从反垄断角度参与了多项交易，在中国反垄断调查和诉讼中代表多名客户。近年来，她还从网络安全角度参与交易，为客户提供中国网络安全相关法律事务的咨询。 电话：+86-10-5957 2143 邮箱：lirui@zhonglun.com
於灵骏 合伙人	於灵骏律师是中伦律师事务所上海办公室的非权益合伙人。他在并购、私募股权投资以及公司法和商法领域拥有丰富的经验。於律师为客户提供多个行业的专业服务，包括制造业、分销和零售、化工产品、科技、汽车、电信、建筑业、房地产、餐饮、私募股权投资和专业服务等领域。他每年还处理数十件争议解决案件，涉及中国法院诉讼、中国国际经济贸易仲裁委员会、上海国际仲裁中心以及其他仲裁机构的仲裁，并且帮助客户处理各类商务谈判和政府程序。 电话：+86-21-6061 3114 邮箱：aaronyu@zhonglun.com

Acknowledgements

I owe special thanks to a few individuals whose support and assistance have helped realize the potential of this book. I'd like to thank Andy See for proofing the entire manuscript and in particular for his helpful insights regarding the historical relationship and future possibilities in respect of foreign investment and government procurement in China. Thanks to Scott Yu and Rachel Li for their valuable input on sections covering national security review of foreign investments. I'd also like to thank Tim Stratford for high-level guidance on the World Trade Organization and Bilateral Investment Treaty background to the negative list concepts included in this book. Certain parts of the analysis of the 2015 Draft FIL were drawn from a series of special reports published by Zhong Lun Law Firm which I coordinated for the firm. Special acknowledgement should be given to Scott Yu and Ren Qing (currently with Global Law Firm).

Finally, I want to thank the others who provided dedicated assistance with research and translation for the book, its templates and related annotations, including in particular the following individuals: Carl Peterson IV, Michelle Huang, Nannan Li, Qianwen Lu, Spencer Hafen and Xinyi Gu. I also want to thank Ms. Wang Qin, a senior editor with more than 20 years' experience, for editing the Chinese version of the book to make it more readable. Sara Yu's contributions deserve particular mention. She took the labouring oar in the overall editing process for the both the Chinese and English versions of this book and coordinated the efforts of all of the other contributors. Without her expert assistance, this book could not have come to fruition.

致　谢

我要特别感谢一些人，他们的支持和帮助使这本书的面世成为可能。感谢施俊侃（Andy See）先生对整份手稿的校对，特别是他对中国外商投资和政府采购的历史关系和未来可能性的有益洞察。感谢余昕刚和李瑞律师对外国投资国家安全审查有关章节的宝贵意见。我还要感谢夏尊恩（Tim Stratford）对本书中所包含的负面清单概念所提供的关于世界贸易组织和双边投资条约背景的高屋建瓴的指导。本书中对2015年《外国投资法（草案）》的部分分析来自由中伦律师事务所刊发的在吕立山（Robert Lewis）的指导下完成的系列报告。该系列报告的问世特别要感谢中伦律师事务所的余昕刚律师和任清律师（现任环球律师事务所合伙人）。

最后，感谢为本书及其模板和相关注解说明的研究与翻译提供帮助的其他人，特别是以下人员：庞立坤（Carl Peterson IV）、黄秀琰（ Michelle Huang）、李南南、陆倩雯、Spencer Hafen和顾欣怡。感谢有着20多年经验的资深编辑汪沁女士对本书中文版的编辑，使其更具易读性。余倩倩的贡献尤其值得一提，她承担了本书中英文版本的整体编辑过程中最繁重的工作，还协调了所有其他贡献者的工作。没有她的专业协助，这本书不可能完成。

图书在版编目(CIP)数据

外商投资实务指南 :《外商投资法》时代合同模板与适用指引 : 汉英对照 / (美) 吕立山 (Robert Lewis) 著. -- 北京 : 法律出版社, 2020
ISBN 978-7-5197-4030-6

Ⅰ. ①外… Ⅱ. ①吕… Ⅲ. ①外商投资-涉外经济法-基本知识-中国-汉、英 Ⅳ. ①D922.295

中国版本图书馆 CIP 数据核字(2019)第 245504 号

外商投资实务指南:《外商投资法》时代合同模板与适用指引(中英双语)
WAISHANG TOUZI SHIWU ZHINAN: 《WAISHANG TOUZIFA》SHIDAI HETONG MUBAN YU SHIYONG ZHIYIN(ZHONG YING SHUANGYU)

[美] 吕立山 (Robert Lewis) 著

责任编辑 李 群 陈 熙
装帧设计 汪奇峰

出版 法律出版社
总发行 中国法律图书有限公司
经销 新华书店
印刷 中煤(北京)印务有限公司
责任印制 张建伟

编辑统筹 法规出版分社
开本 710 毫米×1000 毫米 1/16
印张 40
字数 608 千
版本 2020 年 8 月第 1 版
印次 2020 年 8 月第 1 次印刷

法律出版社/北京市丰台区莲花池西里 7 号(100073)
网址/www.lawpress.com.cn
投稿邮箱/info@lawpress.com.cn
举报维权邮箱/jbwq@lawpress.com.cn
销售热线/400-660-8393
咨询电话/010-63939796

中国法律图书有限公司/北京市丰台区莲花池西里 7 号(100073)
全国各地中法图分、子公司销售电话:
统一销售客服/400-660-8393/6393
第一法律书店/010-83938432/8433　西安分公司/029-85330678　重庆分公司/023-67453036
上海分公司/021-62071639/1636　深圳分公司/0755-83072995

书号: ISBN 978-7-5197-4030-6　**定价:** 118.00 元